OUR HELLENIC HERITAGE

MACMILLAN AND CO., Limited
LONDON · BOMBAY · CALCUTTA · MADRAS
MELBOURNE

THE MACMILLAN COMPANY
NEW YORK   BOSTON   CHICAGO
DALLAS · SAN FRANCISCO

THE MACMILLAN CO. OF CANADA, Ltd.
TORONTO

THE GOLDEN MASK FOUND IN TOMB V.

within the Double Circle of Stone Slabs in the Citadel of Mycenae.
(See p. 123.) Schliemann himself believed it to be the Death Mask
of Agamemnon, King of Men.

From Schuchhardt's *Schliemann's Excavations.*

OUR HELLENIC HERITAGE

BY

H. R. JAMES, M.A.

SOMETIME PRINCIPAL, PRESIDENCY COLLEGE, CALCUTTA

TWO VOLUMES IN ONE

VOL. I

PART I. THE GREAT EPICS
PART II. THE STRUGGLE WITH PERSIA

VOL. II

PART III. ATHENS—HER SPLENDOUR AND HER FALL
PART IV. THE ABIDING SPLENDOUR

WITH MAPS AND ILLUSTRATIONS

New York

THE MACMILLAN COMPANY

1927

OUR HELLENIC HERITAGE

BY

H. R. JAMES, M.A.

SOMETIME PRINCIPAL, PRESIDENCY COLLEGE, CALCUTTA

VOL. I

PART I.   THE GREAT EPICS
PART II.   THE STRUGGLE WITH PERSIA

WITH MAPS AND ILLUSTRATIONS

New York

THE MACMILLAN COMPANY

1927

TO FRIENDS OF MINE IN GREEK SET 2 AT
SEDBERGH SCHOOL, IN THE YEAR 1918, WHO
ENCOURAGED ME TO RETURN TO A STUDY
OF GREEK HISTORY.

PREFACE

THE aim of this book is to bring together just so much of the elements of Greek legend and history as should be the possession of everyone born into the civilization which we call European. This is taken to be, firstly, the substance of the immortal stories of Troy, the Wrath of Achilles, and the Homecoming of Odysseus, together with what help is lent to the enjoyment of these by Greek mythology and Greek archaeology ; and, secondly, the Greek story of the Great Deliverance (with its stirring analogies to the great deliverance of our own time), the preservation of the Hellenic polity or city-state, and its ideals of personal freedom and dignity and of constitutional government, against the menace of subjugation by an oriental despotism. A second volume will deal, as part of a common plan, with the art and literature of Greece, which attained their full grandeur in the half century following the Persian Wars. It was then that for a brief time it appeared possible that Hellas might be permanently united into an Hellenic nation under the hegemony of Athens. Athens herself, therefore, will here be the main theme—her history and constitution, her rise to imperial greatness, her short-lived splendour, and her political overthrow ; to be followed by chapters on Greek architecture and sculpture, the Attic drama, the Greek historians, the Greek orators, and the great Greek thinkers. The two volumes together are intended to form a course of Hellenic studies for schools which shall be relatively complete, and may, it is hoped, to some extent make good what is lost through the decline of the first-hand study of Greek.

The considerations which prompt the undertaking of this task are not far to seek. The long debate over Greek as a school subject is ended, and the verdict has definitely gone against Greek. However strong our belief in the educational value of Greek language and literature, we cannot hope that Greek will ever recover its old place in the school curriculum. Already comparatively few boys learn Greek at all : the boys who acquire a measure of competent Greek scholarship will soon be very exceptional. Regarding the balance of gain and loss on the linguistic side, two opinions are possible : but at all events the change is inevitable. Regarding the value of what has been conveyed through Greek, difference of opinion is hardly possible. If the influences of Greek literature and Greek life on the formation of mind and character, which by common consent are the more valuable side of classical studies, pass out of our Public School education, the loss is indeed irreparable. It is beyond dispute that European civilization draws from Hellenic sources principles that move and work within it to-day, and without some acquaintance with these sources the spiritual continuity is broken. It is worth while, therefore, to ask whether this more valuable side of Greek as a school subject cannot in some way be kept when the actual study of Greek is, of necessity, greatly restricted. Is it possible without the medium of the Greek language to communicate through general education something, and that the best, of the works of the Greek spirit ? No doubt there is much of the riches of Greek life and thought, as presented in Greek history and expressed in Greek literature, which can only be reached through the original Greek. Surely there is also much which can be apprehended as readily in English as in Greek ; can, perhaps, be more readily apprehended in English. The attempt made in the two volumes of which this book is the first is to gather in convenient form as much as possible of what has been most permanently valuable in the discipline of Hellenic studies. The method is purposely selective : to include what is best and most interesting, to leave out what is less admirable, or not admirable at all. It is not claimed that such a course of study will produce the same effects

as the intensive study of Greek as a part of classical
education, but its reach will be wider in two ways.   Even
for the student of Greek it covers much of the ground
more rapidly.   To the many who read no Greek it may
be a means of communicating some of the best influences
of Greek literature—and this is its main purpose.

The plan was sketched among the woods near Symond's
Yat, the English Vale of Tempe, and it is again in the
valley of the Wye that the first half of my pleasant task
draws to an end.   My plan in its inception and throughout has owed very much to the sympathetic advice,
suggestion and assistance of my brother, Lionel James,
Headmaster of Monmouth, and for many years Sixth
Form Master at Radley.   My debt to scholars of eminence
in the several branches of a complex subject is necessarily
great ; and in a special degree to Dr. Farnell, Dr. Walter
Leaf and Professor Gilbert Murray for the first six
chapters ; to Dr. Macan, Dr. Grundy and Professor Bury
for the history of the Persian Wars ; and all through
to Frazer's " Pausanias," most acceptable companion of
Greek travel, actual or ideal.   I desire also to acknowledge my indebtedness (beyond the ordinary obligations
of writer to publisher) to Mr. G. A. Macmillan, whose
life-long services to the humanities are well known, for
his personal interest in this work, and for practical help
in the choice of illustrations.   It has further been my
good fortune to be added to the long list of bookmen
who owe thanks for courteous assistance to Mr. John
Penoyre, Secretary to the Society for the Promotion of
Hellenic Studies.

If my book at all fulfils its purpose, it will prompt
readers to go direct to the scholars whose work has
advanced our knowledge in these fields.   I shall not be
satisfied unless one here and there is led on to win the
power to read Greek for himself.   For it is to the original
Greek masterpieces that all students of ' Hellenics,' the
least as well as the greatest, in the last resort are debtors.

H. R. JAMES.

The School House,
Monmouth, *May* 30*th*, 1921.

CONTENTS

LIST OF ILLUSTRATIONS

LIST OF MAPS AND PLANS

NOTE ON TRANSLATIONS USED.

For the *Iliad* and *Odyssey*, Lang, Leaf and Myers (1913), and Butcher and Lang (1919).[1]

For the *Homeric Hymns*, *Hesiod*, *Thucydides* and *Plutarch*, the following volumes of the Loeb Classical Library :

> *Homeric Hymns* and *Hesiod*, by Hugh G. Evlyn-White ;
> *Thucydides*, by C. Foster Smith ;
> *Plutarch*, by Bernadotte Perrin.

Most of the passages from Herodotus have been specially translated, but a few are taken from Rawlinson's attractive pages.

[1] **By** kind permission of Mr. C. W. Crawley.

PART I

THE GREAT EPICS

" It is indeed difficult to overrate the amount and the variety of the many hidden threads that unite our modern culture to that of ancient Greece. . . ."

MAHAFFY, *Problems in Greek History*, p. 207.

I   A

CHAPTER I

THE GIFTS OF HELLAS

" But Greece and her foundations are
Built below the tide of war,
Based on the crystalline sea
Of thought and its eternity ;
Her citizens, imperial spirits,
Rule the present from the past ;
On all this world of men inherits
  Their seal is set."

SHELLEY, *Hellas.*

ONE of the ends of life, and therefore one of the ends of education, is to understand our place in the universe, our relation to our surroundings, human and physical ; and so the relation of our civilization to the factors that have made it what it is. For everything about us has a history, and if we know something of the history, we understand the thing better. He is but ill-educated who cannot read with intelligence the literature of his country, understand broadly how it comes to be clothed in the shapes in which it is expressed, respond to the appeals it makes to ideas and emotions through words which store up literary energy and give it forth, as radium stores and gives out physical energy : who cannot apprehend the terms in which the sciences indispensable for the conduct of his everyday life name their elements and processes : who has no vision of the background of his religious worship, his standards of conduct and taste, and the social and political institutions of the nation to which he belongs. Modern civilization is a complex thing ; but in England our civilization is mainly traceable to three sources for its elements, Anglo-Saxon, Hebrew,

Hellenic. To the Anglo-Saxon element we owe the framework of our social and political institutions and our language. The basis of the English language is, as the name English imports, Anglo-Saxon ; so are our main social and political institutions (kings, lords, earls, shires and townships), though these have been deeply modified by Norman-French influences through the Norman Conquest (as words like ' Court,' ' county,' ' manor,' ' jury,' ' Parliament.' show). Our religion comes to us from the Hebrews ; its moral energy from the Hebrew prophets, although it is at the same time necessary to recognize that Christian theology and the Christian church were shaped under powerful Greek influences. To Greek sources we must ascribe the impulses that have given us our science, our literature, our drama, our art, our criticism. The foundations of all European speculation in history, philosophy, politics, in ethics and aesthetics, were laid by Greek thinkers. Our ideas on all these subjects are derived from theirs.

Greek Words in English.—Language is here extraordinarily illuminating. We cannot speak of a modern science without using Greek words : biology, meteorology, psychology, seismology, aeronautics, all carry a plain meaning to any one who knows Greek. Physician and surgeon are both Greek words (the latter much disguised). So are astronomy and astrology, geometry, geography, and geology. Even ' cinema ' is Greek monstrously mispronounced, not to speak of biograph and gramophone ; we use Greek to dignify a base product of the time when a ' jazz band ' becomes a ' syncopated orchestra.' The branches into which we divide poetry are called by Greek names, epic, lyric, elegiac, didactic ; and ' poetry ' itself is Greek : a ' poet ' is in plain English a ' maker,' and that is what old English called him. Drama is a Greek word ; so are tragedy, comedy, critic. Idea and theory and practice are Greek words ; ' cosmic energy ' is a Greek phrase. History is a Greek invention ; so is philosophy : ethical is Greek for moral. The list may be enlarged indefinitely ; but very brief consideration is enough to suggest what and how much we owe to the Greeks.

The World of Homer.—In this way, it is true, we get only a very crude idea of the debt of our civilization to Greece. Our chief debt is different, something subtler and deeper. It is the Greek spirit. What that is, is difficult to put into words, as air is, as light and life are. A sense of it comes of itself as the slow result of familiarity with the works of Greek genius in poetry, in art, in prose literature ; with Greek life as expressed in institutions and history ; but its effluences interpenetrate our own life and literature and affect our modes of thought, feeling and action, when least we are aware of them. It is Greek life itself, social, political, imaginative, speculative— or rather certain aspects of Greek life and thought revealed in the literature of different epochs, which have so much that is valuable to communicate. There is first the vivid picture of the life of a far-off heroic age portrayed for us in the *Iliad* and *Odyssey*, with its code of chivalry, and its domestic manners so like our own at many points and yet so different. It matters little whether the manners are those of some by-gone age which the poet recalls and idealizes, or those of his own age which he throws back into the past and sees through an imaginative glamour. It is the picture itself, whether portraiture or artistic creation—so complete, so intimate ; it is the simplicity, the naïveté, the charm of the domestic relations, the vivid fulness of the public life in peace and war, that have value ; a value that is as fresh to-day and as real, as when the poems were chanted by bards at festivals in Ionia. We can be as thoroughly at home in Homer's world as in our own ; we can know it as well, or better, because we see what in essentials are our own code and our own standard finding play in a simpler and franker medium. It is a world appreciably nearer to us than the social world of historic Greece and Rome. Who would not, if he could, have shared in the morning freshness of that feigned Greek world, as it lives in the sounding music of the *Iliad* and *Odyssey* ; have watched from the heights where the gods sat the battles in the plain of Troy ; have journeyed in a chariot with Telemachus to the court of Helen's Sparta, or followed with Odysseus Nausicaa's waggon into the city of the Phaeacians ? The Tale of Troy has delighted successive generations of men, not only among the Greeks, but among all nations. If we read the *Iliad* and *Odyssey*, this delight will be ours, too.

The Persian Wars.—The *Iliad* and *Odyssey*, though in all probability founded in incidents which really happened before the record of history begins, and dealing with persons some of whom were real, are works in which the imagination of the poet has created large part of his material out of his artistic purpose : they are poetry, not history. Centuries later the Greeks were victorious in a great conflict, the results of which affect our lives deeply to-day. In Greece through the intervening centuries the idea of political liberty, much as we understand it now, had grown up in a number of small self-governing states, in which free institutions had developed with wonderful richness and variety. In Asia political developments had uniformly taken shape in widely extended military empires under monarchical rule. In the fifth century B.C. the vigorous life of the small Hellenic city-states was threatened with extinction by the last and most widely extended of these empires, the Persian, which had rapidly built up a vast dominion stretching from India to the Aegean Sea, and then begun to overspread Europe. The Greeks resisted the attempts of Persia to conquer them and so saved for Europe the idea of constitutional government. The history of the conflict and the fame of Marathon, Thermopylae and Salamis, have been an inspiration to the defenders of free institutions through all succeeding ages.

The Great Age and its Bequest to Europe.—It was in the centuries of quiet growth before this struggle, when the Greeks had been left to shape their mode of life and their institutions free from outside interference, that they developed gradually a distinctive form of civilization,

contrasting both with the rude customs of northern
barbarians and with the highly organized civilizations
of eastern nations. The Greeks themselves had become
conscious of this difference : they called themselves
Hellenes, and the aggregate of Hellenic communities,
Hellas. For Hellas and for Hellenic civilization they
fought against Persia ; and when the victory was won,
the energy generated in the struggle carried Greek genius
on to its supreme achievements in art and literature.
Hellas emerged with new spiritual strength from the
fight for freedom ; but the city-states of Hellas failed
ever to unite into one great and free national state.
Within a century and a half of their great deliverance,
through want of capacity for this permanent combination,
the Hellenic city-states lost the separate political independence, which they had prized overmuch ; but their
work for the civilization of Europe and the world was
already accomplished. The great age of Hellas bequeathed
to Europe ideas in every department of action and
thought which have been living forces through the ages
and are living forces to-day. For what most of all
distinguished the Greeks from all other races before or
since was their power of thought. They reasoned about
everything and sought to make the universe and human
society intelligible. Where other races lost themselves
in bewildered wonderment and in vague awe of the
infinite, or remained at the stage of helpless superstition
with minds stolidly inert, the Greeks boldly asked questions and set their minds to understand and judge. If
we summed up our debt to Hellas in the briefest possible
way, we might say that the Greeks gave us ' ideas.'
They gave us ideas—clear ideas, about education, about
art, about government ; about life and conduct and the
relation of man to the divine. The Greeks invented
philosophy and history ; they invented the theatre and
dramatic criticism : above all, they laid the foundations
of what we know as science. It is worth while to say
something briefly about each of these gifts.

Education.—Not only did the Greeks establish in their

several polities a system of education which in some respects curiously resembles that of our Public Schools, but they thought out its theory. Their ideas, whether we recognize it or not, profoundly affect our education to-day. They conceived of education as inseparably connected with the duties of civic life and they concerned themselves primarily with the formation of character. ' Character ' we are told to-day is the chief end of education. Education the Greeks held should be equally of body and mind : the doctrine of the ' mens sana in corpore sano ' was originally theirs. They carried it out practically in their educational schemes in the different states : the health of the mind must be grounded first in the health of the body. Hence the importance they attached to physical education, the training of the body. " To be a good citizen and to be a good thinker a man must be in good physical condition." [1] Education therefore for the Greeks consisted of ' Music ' and ' Gymnastic ' : gymnastic, to exercise and train the body ; music to discipline the mind : while music and gymnastic together moulded the character. Gymnastic was to give courage and endurance and the robuster virtues ; music, which includes literary studies, humanizes, purifies and uplifts. The reasoned theory of this education is found in Plato's *Republic*, but Plato drew his theory from the best of contemporary practice ; and the elements of that practice, especially on the physical side, had come down from the heroic past. In Homer we find established the custom of holding athletic contests ; for instance there are games held at Patroclus' funeral ; and out of this custom grew the great national athletic meetings at Olympia, Delphi and the Isthmus of Corinth. The custom of holding meetings for athletic sports we certainly learnt from Greek example, however much cricket, football and lawn tennis are English games. The Olympic Games, held at Antwerp in 1920, are avowedly an imitation of the Olympic Games held by the Greeks once every four years at Olympia in Elis.

[1] Freeman, *Schools of Hellas*, p. 119.

Art.—Of all nations in the world the Greeks had the most discriminating sense of the beautiful. They were keenly sensitive to beauty, and they made trained judgment of what is beautiful and ugly a main part of education. As a consequence of this they carried certain of the arts to a perfection unattained either before or since. Greek masterpieces to this day remain the standard of perfection. The rules the Greeks thought out are accepted as the canons of critical judgment. This is particularly true of sculpture. To appreciate what we owe to the Greeks in sculpture we need only go to the British Museum and compare the sculptures in the Egyptian and Assyrian galleries with what we find in the Greek Rooms, above all with the Elgin Marbles. The best of the Assyrian and Egyptian sculptures are life-like up to a certain point —the kings in their chariots shooting at lions, the captives abasing themselves before their conquerors ; but it is in Greek sculpture only that the marble moves and breathes.[1] In the battered fragments of Greek sculpture from the Parthenon at Athens, in the Hermes of Praxiteles at Olympia, we discern a mysterious perfection which is nothing less than a revelation. The more we look upon it, the more marvellous it seems.

Measure and symmetry are the central principles of Greek art. A perfect work of art is one you cannot alter by a stroke, either added or taken away, without spoiling it. Greek art idealizes, yet takes reality always as the ultimate standard. It rules out the grotesque and the merely conventional. The Greeks thought out the principles of artistic representation more clearly than other men, and therefore the standards recognized by the Greeks remain the universal standards by which the art of other times and other races may be tested. We cannot go beyond or beside the standards of Greek art.

---

[1] Of Greek sculpture Mr. Shuckburgh writes in his history of *Greece to A.D. 14* (Story of the Nations Series), p. 33, " The men and horses on the frieze of the Parthenon live and move, their faces express life-like emotions and their eyes see."

Architecture.—Measure, proportion and symmetry are similarly the guiding principles of Greek architecture. The vast temples, tombs and palaces of Egypt and Babylonia, the noblest of our Gothic cathedrals, the Taj Mahal or the Pearl Mosque at Agra, or the Golden Temple at Rangoon, may in various ways rival or excel the temples of the Greeks ; but the Greek temple in its austere simplicity has a dignity and perfection of its own. In their building the Greeks understood and used secrets of proportion and laws of symmetry, and a subtle management of curved lines, which they made into a science, the rudiments of which have only recently been re-discovered by study of their surviving works.

Drama.—Though play-acting is natural to man, as we see in children's delight in make-believe, only three races have originated the drama independently as a form of art, the Chinese, the Hindus and the Greeks. Europe owes its drama entirely to the Greeks. Our modern theatres and plays, in spite of differences which in the course of two thousand years have disguised the connection, are derived from the drama perfected in Attica in the fifth century B.C. The Greeks passed on their theatrical practice to the Romans, who modified it in various ways. Then with the break-up of the ancient world, the rise of Christianity, and the coming of the barbarians, the drama perished for a time. It revived in a religious form about the tenth century A.D., when representations of Bible stories and of scenes from the lives of the Saints began to be used by the mediaeval Church to instruct the body of the people. These dramatized religious stories were known as Miracle Plays and Mysteries. With the recovery of Greek literature at the epoch known as the Renaissance—the re-birth of letters and science in Europe—direct imitation of Graeco-Roman drama came in. In England this began in Edward the VI.'s reign ; on the continent, in France and Italy, it was earlier. A play in one of our theatres to-day is very unlike a Greek play of the time of Pericles or Plato : more unlike still is a musical comedy, a revue, or a picture-play. For all that the derivation of all forms of modern plays from the Attic drama is undoubted. The history of this development in England is traced in comedy to Udall's *Ralph Roister-Doister* [1] (about 1550) ; in serious drama to Sackville and Norton's *Gorboduc* (1562). The connection of the modern theatre with the Greek is attested, as we have partly noticed already, by the many terms proper to the drama which are Greek. ' Theatre ' itself is one of them, and so is ' scene.' ' Episode,' ' catastrophe,' ' pathos,' ' chorus,' are all Greek words, as well as prologue and epilogue, tragedy and comedy.

Ethics.—In the sphere of morals we owe the first speculations on the theory of conduct to Greek thinkers. The Greeks not only recognized distinctions of right and wrong as obligatory on men and supported by divine approval, but asked why things were right and wrong, just and unjust, good and bad. One leading principle by which they sought explanation was the doctrine that virtue lies in a mean between two opposite vices : as courage is a mean between rashness and cowardice, liberality a mean between extravagance and meanness. This has an obvious resemblance to the doctrine of measure and proportion in art. The Greeks had a strong sense also of God's disapproval of the inordinate pride which leads men to abuse success and prosperity. The lawless state of mind that believes that might is right and abuses power, they called *Hubris* (insolence). They were profoundly convinced that this insolent trampling on the rights of others brings down upon it the divine displeasure, which they called *Nemesis*. They even thought there was danger in the very fulness of good fortune, as provoking correction from the hand of destiny, a sort of divine jealousy. This they called *Phthonos*. Their favourite virtue was *Sophrosunê*, a word for which

---

[1] This comedy of Udall's was recently (January the 8th, 1921) reproduced in the Abbot's Hall at Westminster (now the Dining-Hall of the King's Scholars, St. Peter's College, Westminster, and known as College Hall) by the O.U.D.S. in aid of the restoration of the Abbey.

there is no exact English equivalent. Its literal meaning
is 'sound-mindedness.' It implies good sense and self-
restraint. It covers our use of temperance (in a general
sense) and self-control, but is wider as including intellectual
as well as moral balance. There is *sophrosuné* in politics,
in scholarly pursuits, in religious practices ; and the idea
is a very valuable one for our times.

Political Theory.—Conduct appeared to the Greeks to
be first and foremost a question of a man's duty to the
state. No one could be a good man unless he were
first a good citizen. It was not lawful to stand aside
from politics and attend strictly to one's own private
affairs : a man who did this was called in Greek an
idiotes, and the modern meaning of the word in its English
form reflects the reproach which the Greeks attached to
such a character. A man's life was not his own to do
what he liked with. He was bound in all he did to put
first his public duties. Children were educated for the
state.

Europe owes much to the Greek conception of civic
rights and duties. The Greeks were the first people
who developed fully self-governing institutions and who
left a record of the forms of the constitutions under
which they lived. They are the first free people known
to history : they developed the autonomous city-state
in contrast with the nations subject to some form of
autocracy. They worked out the ideal of constitutional
government, government in which loyalty, or respect for
law, takes the place of submission to the will of a personal
sovereign. The very conception of political liberty,
which they called *Eleutheria*, begins with them. For this
' idea ' of civic and personal liberty they fought and
conquered in the Persian wars. To them we owe the
words ' polity ' and ' political,' as well as words for
various forms of government, monarchy, aristocracy,
oligarchy, democracy, plutocracy, and the word ' autonomy ' itself. But for the victories of the Greeks at
Salamis and Plataea the course of European history would
have been altogether different. Our free ' institutions '

differ in important respects from theirs, but without
their eager political life and their great fight for freedom
these might never have taken their present forms. The
Greeks theorized about the state, its origin and constitution and laws ; their speculations have been absorbed
into the political science which influences our thoughts.
We even reflect their prejudices in the ideas we associate
with the words ' tyrant ' and ' despotism,' which embody
the self-respecting Hellene's detestation of arbitrary
power unchecked by legal restraints.

Science.—The greatest of all our debts to the Hellenes
is in the sphere of thought. Every form of modern
speculation goes back to them, every branch of physical
research owes to their thinkers its beginnings ; for all
depend on scientific method. Not only are the names
of all the sciences Greek, but the first advances in the
older and more fundamental sciences were the work of
Greek minds. This is true of psychology and physiology,
of zoology and meteorology, as well as of physics and
mathematics. Mathematics, and with mathematics astronomy, owed their systematic development to the Greeks.
Philosophy was a general term covering all kinds of
abstruse speculation. Even theology is a Greek conception. Other nations have given rein to their imaginations in the attempt to find words to cope with the
unfathomable mystery of the universe. The Greeks
alone sought to question nature patiently and unravel
the wonder, thread by thread. The Greeks were the
only people who were not content merely to look upon
natural phenomena with a religious awe, but sought to
understand their working. The Greeks asked how and
why things were, and so came to the conception of natural
law in a rationally ordered universe. To them the world
was the *Cosmos*, or *Order*. It is no accident, or convention
merely, that the names of the sciences are Greek, but is
witness to the historical fact that scientific investigation
owes to them its beginnings and much of its method.
Not only are the names of the sciences Greek, but so are
many of the terms we use for intellectual processes in the

pursuit of truth, such as *hypothesis*, *axiom* and *theory*. *Logic*, which is the theory of the mind's processes in thinking, was put into scientific form by a Greek. Consequently the whole fabric of modern science, though its greatest wonders were the work of the nineteenth century A.D., has been made possible for us through the mental activities of Hellenic thinkers in the fifth and fourth centuries before Christ. The ideas and principles of that earlier time began to take effect in the field of practical invention at Alexandria in the third century B.C. But the gains of that earlier scientific era were all lost in the decay and overthrow of the Roman empire six hundred years later. Western Europe returned to barbarism, and it was not till the era of the Renaissance that there was such a recovery as made new advances possible. With the seventeenth century of our era man's mind begins once more to attempt the conquest of the world by orderly method. The Royal Society was founded in England in 1660. Newton's *Principia* was published in 1687. Bacon, Galileo, Kepler and Descartes belong to the seventeenth century, Copernicus to the sixteenth. Then for great names in science before theirs we must go back some 1800 years to Hipparchus, Archimedes, and Euclid. It was the advances which these great thinkers made in exact scientific method in the third and second centuries B.C. that Copernicus and Newton continued, and so led on to the marvellous extension of man's knowledge and power in the nineteenth century and to the latest triumphs of the twentieth. It was the Greek thinkers who showed the way. " The scientific spirit of the Greeks," says Marvin in *The Living Past*, " shall stand first in their account."

Greek Humanism.—Mr. Marvin adds one other point of indebtedness so apposite to the purpose of this book that I conclude this chapter by quoting it in full :

" And there are throughout the Greek story traits of character, not strictly intellectual, which yet have many links with the same movement of the mind. They failed to build lasting political unions, they fought violently and sometimes treacherously among themselves, yet in their literature, as in their life, there may be traced a growing sense of human fellowship, a respect for others, a delicacy of feeling and a care for immaterial things to which neither the theocracies before nor the Romans after could claim. These were considerable elements to be infused into the coming world. They are not the least of our debts to Greece." [1]

[1] F. S. Marvin, *The Living Past*, 4. p. 90.

CHAPTER II

THE LAND AND THE PEOPLE

" A shepherd's crook, a coat of fleece,
A grazing flock ;—the sense of peace,
The long, sweet silence,—this is Greece ! "

GREECE has not only played a very great part in the history of the world, but is now, as it has always been, a land of exquisite natural beauty. The charm for the traveller who wanders freely to-day in Attica or the Peloponnese is touched off with wonderful felicity by Sir Rennell Rodd in the three lines [1] taken for a heading to this chapter. It is a land to be sought for its physical loveliness no less than for the poetry and history associated with it. Mountains, sea and sky are the elements on which the beauty of the scenery in Greece mainly depends, and these change little with the passing of the centuries.

" Yet are thy skies as blue, thy crags as wild ;
Sweet are thy groves, and verdant are thy fields,
Thine olive ripe as when Minerva smiled,
And still his honied wealth Hymettus yields.

.   .   .   .   .

Art, Glory, Freedom fail, but Nature still is fair."

wrote Byron early in the nineteenth century, and what he says is just as true to-day. The peculiarities of the physical structure of this Greek land are also very marked. The most important of these are at once apparent if we look attentively at a map of Greece, and they are worth noticing because they afford valuable clues to the understanding of Greek history and Greek life. Further,

[1] *Myrtle and Oak*, p. 72.

for a right understanding we must look at the map of Greece not only in itself, but also in relation to those parts of Asia which face the Greek homeland across the Aegean, and are linked with it by the islands scattered over the sea like gigantic stepping-stones.

Physical Conformation.—The peculiarity which first catches the eye is the shape of the Peloponnese, the odd way in which it is joined to the Balkan peninsula by the Isthmus of Corinth : the Corinthian Gulf runs in deeply from the west to meet the Saronic Gulf on the east, but is just stopped by the barrier of the isthmus, a neck of land so narrow that you can walk leisurely across it in less than an hour and a half. There you see how on the one side the isthmus leads through the rocks of the Megarid to Attica and Northern Greece, while on the other the Peloponnese opens out into Achaia and Elis, Argolis, Laconia and Messenia, with the mass of the Arcadian highlands occupying the centre. In the extreme south Laconia branches into the long promontories of Taenarum (Cape Matapan) and Malea (Cape Malia), with two shorter projections on either side—like a three-fingered hand and thumb. Attica you see as an isosceles triangle based on the mountains which separate it from Boeotia, running in a direction parallel with the coast of Argolis, and reaching out through Sunium (Cape Colonna) to the Aegean and the islands beyond. You see at a glance the great extent of sea-board relatively to area, the deep bays and winding inlets, especially on the eastern side. You see the length of Euboea, lying like a huge protecting sea-mole a hundred miles long, outside the coasts of Attica and Boeotia. You see the Peloponnese as a great natural fortress, with Arcadia to form the central keep, and the Isthmus, a veritable drawbridge, easily closed. The Peloponnese was, in fact, as its name implies, practically an island in ancient times ; it is actually an island now since the opening of the Corinth Canal in 1893. Simple things like these are readily intelligible from any map, and a good deal more from a good physical atlas, which shows contours of land elevation. For then it appears at once to what an extent Greece is a land of mountains with narrow stretches of plain let in between blocks and ridges, and with fringes of lower ground along the sea-board. Rivers of any size are very few; for the most part there are only short stony river-beds down which rush violent torrents during the winter season. The Alpheus in the plain of Elis, and "the fair-flowing Eurotas," which made green the Spartan meadows, are exceptional. Thessaly, away to the North, was quite different; a circuit of lofty mountains enclosing a great plain shaped like a basin,[1] down the sides of which flow numerous rivers, which all unite in the Peneus and make their way to the sea through a single outlet, the defile of Tempe. It is important to notice how the mountains of Northern Greece are laid out in successive lines of ramparts, which stretch right across from a wilderness of interlacing ridges and summits on the west (Albania) to the sea on the east. North of Thessaly are the Cambunian Mountains, culminating near the Gulf of Saloniki in Mount Olympus; and between Mount Olympus and the sea, through the Pass of Tempe, winds the highway into Thessaly. South of the Thessalian basin is the second barrier, Mount Othrys, through which there are several passes of no great difficulty. The third and most formidable barrier is Mount Oeta, closing the way to the south like a great wall, which in the fifth century B.C. left only a narrow passage, at certain points no broader than a roadway, flanked by the sea. This formed the famous Pass of Thermopylae. Beyond Thermopylae again there was the barrier of Mount Cithaeron and Mount Parnes between Boeotia and Attica. These formed a series of natural defences. Finally there was the gate of the Peloponnese through the Isthmus of Corinth. The land of Hellas was thus elaborately fortified by nature against invasion from the north.

Political Life in Ancient Greece.—This homeland of the Greeks corresponded approximately with the modern

[1] It is really a double basin, the plain of Larissa and the plain of Pharsalus.

Hellenic kingdom as it was before the Balkan wars of 1912 ; but its boundaries were not clearly defined, and varied at different times. The Greeks were never in the days of their political independence a people united under one government. They were not really unified politically till they came under foreign dominion. This inability to form one united people was the weakness of the Greeks. But this weakness was the other side of qualities which made the strength of Greece, the extraordinary vitality and diversity of a number of small independent states, the names of many of which are familiar as household words. What these Greek communities prized more than anything else on earth was their ' autonomy,' the sovereign independence of their ' polis,' or city-state,[1] with its customs, institutions and traditions, peculiar and individual for each. Their narrow and intense political life prevented effective and lasting union, but it quickened character and intellect, so that more men of genius were produced in Greece between the fifth and third centuries B.C. than in any population of approximately equal number in a like space of time.

Influence of the Mountains.—The character of the mountains helps us to understand the way in which political life developed among the Greeks. For the mountains are rocky limestone ridges which rise steeply from flat plains and divide like walls of partition one level area from another. The areas so separated readily become distinct political units. Thus Corinth and Megara were separate states. So were Sicyon, Epidaurus, Troezen and Hermione in Argolis. Even in Attica, though Attica in historical times was politically the same as Athens, we can see how the plain of Eleusis is separated from the plain of Athens and the townships of Aphidna and Marathon[2] are isolated among hills. These towns, Eleusis, Aphidna, Marathon and others to the number of twelve, tradition said, had been independent

---

[1] The same Greek word, *polis*, means both city and state.

[2] Marathon was anciently one member of a tetrapolis, or league of four cities.

states, till united under one government by the national hero, Theseus. This characteristic of Greek mountains was not the cause why the Greek city-state came into existence, but it was one of the conditions that made it possible.

Influence of the Sea.—The sea, the other fundamental element in Greek scenery, is no less necessary to the understanding of Greek history. If we now take a map which shows not only the Hellenic peninsula—that is the Peloponnese, Northern Greece and Thessaly—but the whole of the Aegean Sea and all its shores, together with the islands as far south as Crete, we can frame an idea of the Aegean not as separating, but as joining, its opposite coasts ; and as in some sort forming a whole consisting of all the Aegean seaboard and the islands. The Isles of Greece have become proverbial for their calm beauty, and the Aegean in summer is the yachtsman's paradise. It is obvious that, as soon as navigation had advanced but a little way, it was easy and tempting to pass from island to island across from Asia Minor to Greece or from Greece to Asia Minor. Accordingly history shows, as we might expect, that the opposite shores of the Aegean, the Hellenic and the Levantine, have always been intimately connected and have usually been occupied by peoples of the same race. If we mark with a distinctive colour on our map of the Aegean all the places known to have been occupied in ancient times by the Greeks, we shall find the Aegean enclosed by an almost continuous band of this colour.[1] It is further remarkable that a modern ethnographic map of the Aegean shows a similar band of colour for the Greek race, and that we shall find it practically identical with that for classical times. But we must add that in classical times Greek settlements were carried much further north, through the Dardanelles and all round the shores of the Black Sea, and westward to Italy and Sicily and even to Marseilles.

Two Meanings of Hellas.—In one sense we may say the land of Greece extended wherever communities of

[1] See also pp. 206-207 and the map of *Greater Hellas*.

GREECE and the AEGEAN
Fifth Century B.C.

English Miles

0 10 20   40   60   80   100

Greek cities and settlements shown thus:- • **Athens**

Longitude East 22° of Greenwich

BF 176.5 F5513 4

BL 820 J 8 P3 5

PA 3612 A 5 62

B 1180 PL3 3

BL 782 5

BL 820 B 5

PR 5130 F10 76

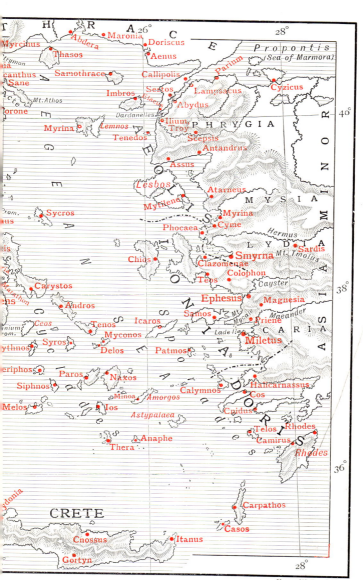

H R A 26° C

28°

Maronia
Myrcinus
Abdera
Doriscus
E
Propontis
(Sea of Marmora)
erymon
Thasos
Aenus
canthus
Sane
Samothrace
Callipolis
Parium
Cyzicus
Acte
Mt.Athos
Imbros
Sestos
Lampsacus
orone
Elaeus
Abydus
Dardanelles
R 40°
Myrina
Lemnos
Ilium
Troy
PHRYGIA
O
Tenedos
Scepsis
G
Antandrus
N
Assus
Lesbos
Atarneus
MYSIA
Prom.
aus
Sycros
Mytilene
Myrina
Cyme
Phocaea
Hermus
LYDIA
Sardis
Mt. Tmolus
is
Chios
Smyrna
Clazomenae
Colophon
Carystos
Teos
Cayster
38°
ns
Andros
Ephesus
Magnesia
Ceos
nium
om.
Tenos
Icaros
Samos
Mt.
Mycale
Priene
Maeander
CARIA
ythnos
Syros
Myconos
Ladelie
Delos
Patmos
Miletus
eriphos
Paros
Naxos
Halicarnassus
Siphnos
Calymnos
Cos
Minoa
Amorgos
Melos
Ios
Cnidus
Astypalaea
Telos
Rhodes
Anaphe
Camirus
Thera
Rhodes
36°

Carpathos

CRETE
Casos
Cnossus
Itanus
Gortyn
28°

Hellenic type, that is city-states and confederations of city-states, were established by men who spoke Greek. In this sense Greece would include the whole of the western coast of Asia Minor, known collectively as Ionia, scores of cities dotting the coasts of Macedonia and Thrace, both shores of the Dardanelles, the Sea of Marmora and the Bosphorus, and the sea-board of the Black Sea right up to the Crimea ; and all the Greek colonies westward, Magna Graecia in Italy, the Greek colonies in Sicily, Marseilles in France, Saguntum in Spain, and Cyrene on the coast of Africa. All Greek folk, wherever settled, who spoke some dialect of Greek, followed Greek customs, worshipped the Greek gods, and were organized in some kind of Greek polity, claimed to be Hellenes, the name by which the Greeks chose ultimately to call themselves and which their descendants still affect. But in another sense Hellas was the peninsula from the Cambunian Mountains to Capes Malea and Taenarum, together with the islands of the Aegean and Ionian Seas and Crete. The name Hellas itself belonged originally to a part of Thessaly, and in the *Iliad* is associated with the band of warriors called Myrmidons of whom Achilles was hereditary chief. Hellenes and Hellas were the names the Greeks came in the sixth century B.C. to use of themselves and their country. Greeks was the name by which the Hellenes became known to the Romans, and we get the names Greek and Greece from them. In earlier times, the times of the great epics, the Greeks appear to have been known as Achaeans : the chieftains in the Homeric poems are always Achaei ; while the names Argeii and Danai are also used of the common people. In historical times there were three distinct branches of the Hellenes, speaking different dialects of Greek, and of distinct stock, Ionians, Dorians and Aeolians. The Achaeans of this later time, though sometimes included with the Aeolians, may also be reckoned a distinct branch. These names are important ; for they involved differences of temperament and character as well as of speech, and the divisions of the Greek world followed mainly the lines of a rivalry between Ionians and Dorians. The Athenians were Ionian, the Spartans Dorian, the Thebans and other Boeotians, Aeolian.[1]

Common Race Characteristics.—All Hellenes had certain qualities in common. One was an instinct for political freedom, the adaptability for some type of state organism, or 'polis,' with a definite constitution and an ideal of political independence or autonomy. The Greek was a political animal in a very different sense from an Egyptian or Macedonian, or the subjects of one of the great oriental empires. Another was capacity for discipline, and mainly self-imposed discipline. There was the same marked contrast between Greek discipline, founded on self-respect and respect for law, and barbarian lack of discipline, as there was in India in the eighteenth century between European and Asiatic discipline—a contrast which, of course, holds to this hour. Thirdly, there was the Greek fondness for organized athletics. This was displayed in the great national athletic meetings of which the Olympic Games were the most famous. This institution is quite truly distinctive of the Hellenes, though to engage in athletic contests, especially wrestling and foot-races, is common to many warlike races. The Greek games were national festivals elaborately organized, and served other ends besides the opportunity of athletic rivalry and distinction. Men from different parts of Hellas met together, learnt to know each other and interchanged ideas. These meetings were something like our Fairs. But whereas fairs both in Europe and India were meetings where the main business transacted

[1] Of the "Coming of the Hellenes" Shuckburgh writes: "We cannot date the arrival of the Hellenes in Greece, nor the composition of the Homeric poems, the popularity of which did so much to fix the language and to secure unity. We can only say that about B.C. 800 they were there—in European Greece, the Islands and Asia Minor— and were beginning to send out colonies east, west and north; that the divisions of Greece had obtained the names which we know; and that among these Hellenes there were recognised three families or divisions distinguished by dialect, though of the same mother tongue, and by certain moral and political characteristics—Aeolians, Ionians and Dorians." *Greece to A.D. 14*, p. 37.

was commercial, the main business of the Greek meetings was athletic. All three alike had primarily a religious purpose. Fourthly, there was the common love of Homer and the common inheritance of the legends which had gathered round the names of heroes like Heracles and Perseus, Theseus and Bellerophon, or noble families like the house of Atreus and the house of Labdacus, and legendary episodes like the Voyage of the Argo and the Return of the children of Heracles. Fifthly, there was the ideal of Greek education as consisting in the equal training of mind and body. Some states like the Spartan overdid the bodily training and almost wholly sacrificed the training of the mind ; but a certain combination of the two was the accepted ideal. Another common characteristic, subtler than these and deeper, is the artistic temperament—a marked susceptibility to beauty in works of art and a certain sense of symmetry and rhythm, which distinguishes the Greeks from other races of men. The appreciation of beauty in literature, poetry and the graphic arts is, quite truly, a common possession of all men, but that the Greeks possessed this sense and this susceptibility in a higher degree than other men is proved, on the one hand, by the wealth of sculpture and painting with which their cities were adorned at the time when Greece came under Roman control, and by the unsurpassed excellence of their greatest masters ; and, on the other, by the amount of thought they brought to bear on the subject. The Greeks reasoned about the beautiful and laid the foundations of criticism both in the fine arts and in literature.

Underlying all this was the community of blood and speech and religion. The community of blood has to be qualified by the differences spoken of above, corresponding probably to successive migrations of men of kindred stock. The Dorians were certainly tribes of warriors who came from the North at a time within the memory of tradition, and conquered much of the Peloponnese. The community of speech has to be qualified by differences of dialect, which were as great as those between Northern

English (Scotch) and English of the South (Kent) or West (Somerset), and somewhat similar in character. The Doric like the English of the Scotch Lowlands was broader in sound than the other dialects. The community of religion consisted in the common worship of the greater gods, but this agreement is combined with innumerable peculiarities and differences of local worship. The great athletic festivals at Olympia, Delphi, Nemea and the Isthmus are, from this point of view, gatherings for common worship. Another religious bond was the oracles, the common shrines to which the Hellenes resorted in the belief that the answers given by the priests to their enquiries and prayers were inspired by the god. The best known and most influential of these shrines was the temple of Apollo at Delphi.

The Fifth Century B.C.—Our knowledge of the Greeks is carried by reliable tradition between seven and eight hundred years before the Christian era, and archaeological research has brought to light substantial evidence concerning early Hellenic civilization, which reaches far beyond 1200 B.C., the traditional date of the Trojan War. But the most vivid and eventful part of Greek history falls wholly within the century from 500 to 400 B.C., the outbreak of the Ionian revolt to 404 B.C., the surrender of Athens to the Spartan, Lysander. All that is most memorable of what the Greeks achieved in action falls within those ninety-five years, and great part of the most brilliant works of Greek genius in architecture, sculpture, and literature. Hellenic freedom ends with the victory of Philip of Macedon at Chaeroneia in 338 B.C. ; after that the Greek city-states were, first, politically subject to Macedonia, and then absorbed into the empire of Rome.

The Conquests of Alexander.—Yet the subjection of the Greek city-states by Philip of Macedon led at first to a vast expansion of Hellenic influence. Between 334 and 323 Alexander the Great overthrew the Persian Empire and conquered large part of the world, as master of the military strength of Greece and champion of Hellenic civilization. He regarded it as his mission to Hellenize the East, and this aim was in large measure carried out by the Macedonian dynasties which parted among them the vast territories he had united under one sway. Hellenic influences were carried over Western Asia to the borders of India ; and traces of these influences are found in Turkestan and the Punjab to this day.

The Achaean League.—After the death of Alexander the Great (in 323) the Greek states remained subject to Macedonia and the better minds felt the humiliation deeply. The old self-respect of the autonomous Hellenes was all but lost and the national character deteriorated. For a brief period the Hellenic passion for independence revived and lived on in the Achaean League renewed in 281 to resist the overlordship of Macedonia. For a hundred years this league maintained a vigorous life, and it is curious that the name Achaean, in which the heroes who fought at Troy had gloried, throws a parting radiance over the last struggles of Hellenic freedom. But meantime the Romans had appeared as the " Liberators " of Hellas. Rome first came into political relation with the Greeks in putting down piracy in the Adriatic. This was a few years before the Second Punic War. When Rome, thirty years later, broke the power of Macedon, she ostentatiously assumed the rôle of champion of Greek liberties. The consul, C. Flamininus, after defeating Philip V. at Cynoscephalae, roused wild enthusiasm at the Isthmian Games next year by publicly proclaiming freedom for all Greek cities. But fifty years later the League drifted into war with Rome and was destroyed. Corinth, then its leading city, where a mob had insulted the Roman commissioners, was taken after a short siege, plundered and left in ruins. The Achaean League has peculiar interest because as a federal union it offers, on a small scale, points of resemblance to modern confederations like the United States or the League of Nations, and had also attained to something like a representative system. With its dissolution Greek political independence ended finally ; the Hellenes were never again a self governing people till they rose against their Turkish masters, just a hundred years ago.

Greece under the Romans.—Soon after the sack of Corinth the city-states of Hellas were wholly merged in the Roman province of Achaia. A few cities, Athens in particular, enjoyed special immunities and privileges ; but the Hellas that repulsed the might of Persia was now only an administrative division of the Roman Empire. Intellectually, however, the influence of Hellenism was the wider for this subordination. As the Roman poet Horace wrote, " Greece, conquered Greece, her conqueror subdued." Athens became the recognized seat of literature and learning, to which men resorted to complete their education, the first university of the western world. On the other hand, a further decay of national character followed the total loss of national independence, till it was possible for Juvenal in the second century A.D. to satirize the Greeks as the worst of city pests : " Romans, I cannot stand a Greecized Rome." The starveling Greek, he complains, is everything to please everybody, a Jack-of-all-trades, pliant, servile and corrupt.

Constantinople.—Two centuries later a new era opened for the Greek race, when Constantine renamed Byzantium Constantinople and made this city of Constantinople the capital of the Roman Empire in place of Rome. The position of Constantinople at the opening of the passage from the Sea of Marmora into the Black Sea—with its matchless harbour, the Golden Horn, and its exceptional facilities for defence on the land side—was naturally adapted to be the site of an imperial city.[1] Already as a consequence of the conquests of Alexander and the absorption into the Roman Empire of the vast territories his successors had Hellenized, Greek was the language of half the Roman world. Even in Palestine when Christianity was first preached, Greek was the common

[1] So obvious were the advantages of its position that the Delphic Oracle referred to Chalcedon, founded a little earlier by Greek colonists on the Asiatic side of the Bosphorus, as the ' City of the Blind.'

medium of intercourse [1] for a population of divers tongues, like Hindustani in India. The Roman world was accordingly divided into a Latin-speaking and a Greek-speaking half, and the result by the end of the fourth century A.D. was the separation of the Eastern, or Byzantine, empire with Constantinople for its capital, from the Western empire. In correspondence with this division of temporal power, the Christian Church separated into the Roman, or Catholic Church and the Greek, or Orthodox Church, and this has ever since been the main division of Christendom.[2] The Western Empire was overwhelmed by barbarian invaders and came to an end before the close of the fifth century (in 476) A.D., fourteen hundred and fifty years ago ; but the Eastern Empire lasted to within five hundred years of the present time. It only came to an end when the Turks entered Constantinople in 1453.

The Byzantine Empire.—The Eastern Empire had been gradually weakened through the centuries by causes similar to those which ended the Western Empire in 476, slow internal decay and depopulation through misgovernment and war and the attacks of ever fresh swarms of warlike barbarians, Goths, Saracens, Huns, Avars, Russians, Bulgarians, Servians and Turks. Whether the Frankish host that turned aside from the Fourth Crusade to capture Constantinople should be numbered with these barbarians may, perhaps, be questioned, but without doubt their sack of the imperial city with every circumstance of horror in 1204 was one of the greatest crimes of history. It did more than anything else to weaken the defences of civilization in the Eastern Empire and led on to the final catastrophe of 1453. For a time a Latin Empire was substituted for the Byzantine and Frankish princes ruled in the homeland of the Hellenes.

---

[1] It is now recognized that it was the Septuagint, the Greek version of the Old Testament, not the original Hebrew, which our Lord quoted in his discourses to the people.

[2] ' Catholic ' is a Greek word meaning ' universal ' ; ' Orthodox ' has a meaning in contrast with ' heterodox,' which English has adopted. It implies the claim of the Greek Church to be the church of the true believers.

The Latin Empire never had any strength, and in little more than fifty years a Byzantine dynasty was again in possession of Constantinople. But Latin Princes of Achaia and Dukes of Athens added an interesting page to Greek history and lasted on till the coming of the Turk (1456). The traveller to-day is moved to a pleased surprise at lighting on a Frankish castle or a Lombard church in the heart of the Peloponnesus.

The Coming of the Turk.—It was towards the end of the thirteenth century that the Ottoman Turks, or Osmanli, in succession to the Seljuk Turks, began to secure a footing in Asia Minor ; and thence a little later crossed into Europe and came down through the Balkan provinces as conquerors. The battle of Kossovo in which the Servians lost their independence was in 1389. All Asia Minor was subject to the Turks by the middle of the fifteenth century ; little more was left of the Byzantine Empire than a strip of territory between the walls of Constantinople and the ' Great Wall ' across the neck of the Chersonese. At length Muhammad II., ablest of the Turkish sultans, made his preparations for the conquest of Constantinople itself. He attacked the city with over-whelming forces by land and sea, and after a gallant defence of fifty-three days the fortifications were stormed and Constantinople became the capital of the Ottoman Empire.

The New Discovery of Greek Literature.—The death agony of the Byzantine Empire and the loss of Constantinople to Christendom brought, however, one great compensating gain to western civilization. They were the direct means of bringing back to the western nations the vivifying energy of the master minds of Greece. Greek literature had been lost to Western Europe for nearly a thousand years, through the separation of the eastern and western halves of the Roman Empire and the overwhelming of the western half by barbarism. Boethius, author of the *Consolation of Philosophy*, in the fifth century A.D., was the last Greek student of eminence in Italy. Petrarch in the fourteenth century knew Homer through a translation, and lamented his inability to reach the music of these great poems in the original. His younger contemporary, Boccaccio, did acquire a knowledge of Greek, and made a literal translation of Homer into Latin, which Petrarch read. But it was not till the fifteenth century that there was any wide study of Greek by western scholars. Then, as the Turkish power advanced, men of letters, one by one, sought a refuge in Italy. It was these refugees who brought to Italy a full knowledge of Greek, and through Greek of the incomparable strength and beauty of Greek classical literature. Once more the men of the west read the *Iliad* and *Odyssey*, the tragedies of Aeschylus, Sophocles and Euripides, the histories of Herodotus, Thucydides and Xenophon, the speeches of Demosthenes, the dialogues of Plato ; and their eyes were opened. In these wonderful books they found the human mind working with a strength and freedom altogether new to them. It was the discovery of a new world not less momentous than Columbus' discovery of America in the same century. The result was a movement of ideas which transformed Europe. It began naturally in Italy, because Italy was nearest Greece ; and thence passed to France, Germany, England and the rest of Europe. Greek came to Oxford and Cambridge in the last years of the fifteenth century.[1] Printing which had been invented and brought into use early in the century helped greatly the diffusion of the new learning. For beautiful editions of the great classical writers were published, first at Milan, **Venice**, **Florence** and other cities of Italy, and then in other countries. The whole movement is known as the Renaissance, or Re-birth.

The Re-discovery of the Greek Land.—The knowledge of Greek spread and became in course of time, what it continued to be till the end of the nineteenth century, an

[1] William Grocyn began to teach Greek at Oxford in 1491. In 1518 Richard Croke became " the first public reader in Greek in the sister University." See Bywater, *Four Centuries of Greek Learning in England*, Oxford University Press.

essential part of a good education ; but to scholars in the west Greece long remained a distant land known only through books and through the renown of great names. It was so difficult of access, partly through mere distance, but more because it was under Turkish rule, that hardly anyone thought of going there and seeing for himself the famous places, the names of which fired his imagination. Englishmen travelled a good deal in Shakespeare's day and many visited Italy ; but none went on to Greece. Sir Philip Sidney made the Peloponnese the scene of his romance the *Arcadia*. Athens is the scene of Shakespeare's *Midsummer-Night's Dream*. Milton after spending a year in Italy had an eager wish to go on to Greece, but gave it up when he heard of the dissensions in England which led to the great civil war. A few Englishmen actually visited Athens and travelled in Greece in the seventeenth and eighteenth centuries, and two of them, Wheler (1675) and Chandler (1776), published books describing their experiences. The first English, indeed the first European, scholar to explore Greece systematically and spend time in identifying ancient sites, knowledge of which, and sometimes the very names, had perished, was Colonel William Martin Leake. Colonel Leake was in Turkey, variously employed, between 1799 and 1810, and used his opportunities to travel widely in Northern Greece and the Morea. After his return from Eastern Europe he published three volumes of *Travels in the Morea* and four of *Travels in Northern Greece*, besides a volume on Athens, all of which are valuable as pioneer work in Greek topography. The complete recovery of ancient Greece by travellers and archaeologists has been effected mainly since the deliverance of Greece from the Turks and the establishment of the Hellenic Kingdom. The most vivid descriptions of Greece in her desolation, as she was before the Greeks threw off their servitude to the Turks, are Lord Byron's.[1]

---

[1] Byron spent over a twelvemonth in Albania and Greece in the years 1809 and 1810. *Childe Harold* was published (Cantos I. and II. only) in 1812, *The Giaour* in 1813.

They will be found in the second canto of *Childe Harold* (especially stanzas 85 to 90), and in certain lines of his poem *The Giaour*. The work of exploration and excavation has been carried out with great thoroughness since, and is pursued with scientific precision by the various ' Schools at Athens,' French, British, German and American ; and by the Greeks themselves.

The Eleutherismos.—The valiant fight by which Greece was restored to civilized Europe was fought out between 1821 and 1829. April the 6th (in the Greek calendar, March the 25th) is observed by the Greeks as their ' Liberation Day.' It is the day on which Germanos, Archbishop of Patras, lifted a cross on high at the monastery of Lavra in Achaia as the symbol of revolt. The independence of Greece was finally secured by a Conference held in London during February, 1830. The Greek people fairly earned their deliverance by their heroism and endurance, but they were badly led. When Ibrahim Pasha, son of Mehemet Ali, Viceroy of Egypt, landed an army of regular troops in the Morea, the freedom won in the first months of the rising was nearly lost again. The whole Peloponnese was ravaged and its defenders driven to the mountains.[1] Then tardily Europe intervened, and the upshot was the Battle of Navarino, in which British, French and Russian warships destroyed the Turkish and Egyptian fleets. This was on the 27th of October, 1827. In August, 1828, a French army was brought to the Peloponnese, drove out the Egyptians and Turks, and occupied the country till 1834. Since that time the Hellenic Kingdom has been a land of free men.

Modern Greek.—Through all the ages of splendour and oppression, of national decay and national recovery,

---

[1] Venizelos, the patriot Premier of the Greeks during the Great War, said in a speech to the Greek Chamber on the 6th of May, 1920 : " In order that that small corner which constituted the independent kingdom of Greece might be freed, a struggle was waged, Gentlemen, which lasted ten years, in the course of which one-third of the population was wiped out, hardly a tree was left growing in the land or one stone upon another."

Greek has remained the language of the people. Greek is no dead language in Greece, but has been the speech of living men through the centuries continuously from the times of Solon, Pericles and Plato. It is the speech of the Greeks to-day. It is true that long before the nineteenth century it had greatly altered by reason of the loss of grammatical forms (just as Latin and English have), and debased by an intermixture of words from less noble languages. Nevertheless the language of the country has been Greek throughout, and always among the educated classes—and in the worst days of oppression the Greeks ever prized education—a more refined form of the language survived, and the great classics were read and studied. Since the liberation there has been a steady movement to purify the vocabulary and to restore some of the grammatical forms which had been lost. Anyone who has learnt Greek at school in France or England can soon read a modern Greek book or newspaper. Speaking modern Greek is more difficult, because the value of some of the vowel sounds has altered : for instance, ' u ' (Greek ' upsilon ') is now identical in sound with English ' e ' ; and Greek is pronounced strictly in accordance with the written accents. But it is exceedingly interesting to find that the accents, which are a tiresome and apparently unmeaning convention, as Greek is learnt at school, really have a definite meaning and purpose, and are a safe guide to pronunciation.

Modern Greece.—Greece is a land of infinite charm and of boundless historical interest, a land to read about and hear about, and above all to visit. The Greeks have their faults to-day (what nation has not ?), as they had in the best days of their greatness, but anyone who has been in Greece will agree that in the country districts they are delightful people, both men and women. It is a lively pleasure to see a Greek hillman, in white fusta-nella, stride along over some rocky track in Arcadia or Phocis, in the passes of Parnes or on the Boeotian plain. They are lithe and comely and frank and kindly these peasants of modern Greece, whether their blood be

IN ARCADIA.

Scene in Northern Arcadia looking S.E. over the bed of Lake Pheneos. Mount Cyllene, where Hermes was born (p. 47), rises on the left. The Styx (p. 53) is not far distant to the N

Albanian or Hellenic. And in Greece, if ever you are belated and fail to reach your inn by nightfall, you may rely safely on the hospitable instincts of the peasantry. They will give you a place by the hearth and a blanket to wrap round you, as freely as did Eumaeus to Odysseus, and ask no payment when in the morning you again set forth on your way. Of the pleasures of journeys in modern Greece, whether taken with the assistance of an ' alogon ' (or ' irrational ' beast), as modern Greek calls the horse, and as much material comfort as the simplicity of up-country life in Greece admits, or more freely on one's own feet, many have written with sympathy and insight ; but no one has more exquisitely divined and found expression for the fascination of Greece and of Greek travel than has Sir Rennell Rodd in his Greek poems, with one of which this chapter shall, by his permission, conclude.

In Arcadia.

" I think we shall keep forever in the heart of us, you and I,
That first Arcadian evening, till the day we come to die.

We had crossed from the rugged border, through the fierce Messenian hills,
And we came to the oak-wood pastures, to a ripple of mountain rills.

The late noon waned to the eventide and the gathering in of flocks,
The shepherd called with his uncouth cries to the goats far up in the rocks ;

While the kids leaped down with their startled eyes, and paused for a drink at the spring,
As he strode along in his kilted pride, with the gait of a mountain king.

The steep hills sloped to a narrow vale through willow and oak and pear,
To the gold-green sage on the further side, and the thyme that hung in the air ;

The corn-plots waved in the hollow, and the planes were marvellous green,
Where the young nymph-haunted Neda was a luminous thread between.

I C

The day went over the westward ridge too soon in the mountain
    world,
And the thousand frail sun-wearied convolvulus bells were furled.

A turtle cooed on the farther side, and the scented air of the vale
Was quick with tremulous throbbing of the song of the nightingale.

A mist rose up from the waters and the stream-nymph veiled her
    charms,
Where the mountain clasped her closest in the grasp of his purple
    arms.

It was red gold over the western peaks and pale gold over the sky,
It was middle May in the full moon time, and the land was
    Arcady !

And the scent of the thyme and the song of the bird drew a calm
    down over the breast,
The stream ran by with a soothing voice, and the note of it all
    was rest.

Ah, well with you, happy valleys, where the roar of the world
    is still,
Where the brain may pause in the battle of life, and the eyes
    may drink their fill !

And well with you, fair green isles, in your girdle of surf apart,
With never a rumor of march and change, Avalons of the weary
    heart !

The sunset over those gilded hills was more than an earthly name,
The moon was brighter than glory, the stars seemed better than
    fame.

And we, we shall keep, I know, in the heart of us, you and I,
That first Arcadian evening, till the day we come to die." [1]

[1] *In Arcadia*, Sir Rennell Rodd, *Myrtle and Oak*, pp. 80-82.

Note.—The quotations from the Homeric Hymns and Hesiod in this and the next chapter are from Evelyn-White's translations in the Loeb Classical Library.

CHAPTER III

GODS AND HEROES

1. The Gods of Olympus

" So in the shell of old Homeric lays,
    We hear hymned echoes from the world's prime,
    When gods were shepherding on hill and plain ;
    And though the simple faith, the glad surprise
    Of gods revealed, the glamour of old time
    Be far away, our hearts beat fresh again."

J. Edgar.[1]

ALTHOUGH in Greece Christianity has replaced the old polytheistic worship for more than 1500 years, the gods of the ancient Greeks are still familiar to us in common speech—Jupiter, Juno, Neptune, Pluto, Mars, Mercury, Apollo and Diana, Vulcan : only the names by which they are thus popularly known are, most of them, Roman, not Greek.[2] They are the Latin names by which the Romans called the Greek gods and goddesses when they learnt to admire and imitate Greek literature. Our poets and men of letters in the early Middle Ages in turn took over the Latin names, because Greek literature had been lost in Western Europe while Latin was well known. This has been unfortunate ; for the Roman deities were not by any means identical in attributes and character with the Greek to whom their names were transferred, only roughly similar ; and the identification is confusing. With the revival of Greek in the fifteenth century

[1] In the dedication of his translation of the Homeric Hymns.
[2] Of the above Pluto and Apollo are Greek ; the rest Latin.

35

the true Greek names were recovered, and it is these we shall use here. These Greek gods and goddesses were many in number ; not quite so numerous as the gods of the Hindus, which are said to number thirty thousand, but still very numerous. Some of these deities were worshipped only at special places ; those best known to us were worshipped in common by all Hellenes ; and twelve of these were recognized as surpassing the rest in honour and power, and as especially the objects of worship of the Hellenic race, the twelve great Olympian gods. They were called Olympian from Mount Olympus, the massive height (still called Elimpo) dominating the coast road from Macedonia into Thessaly, which the Greeks in early times believed to be the actual abode of these deities. Great mountain ramparts, as we have seen (p. 18), here bar the way from the north into the Greek land, and Olympus is the vast mass of rock in which the whole system culminates, rising into a lofty summit which soars high above the other snow-crowned peaks and stands out conspicuous. It is not far short of ten thousand feet above the sea. To the Greeks in the Thessalian plains, looking back towards the great barrier which their forefathers had penetrated, the peak of Mount Olympus was by far the most impressive object within view. As the Hindus placed the abode of their gods among Himalayan snows, so these Hellenes placed their heaven on Mount Olympus. The greater deities are spoken of in Homer and Hesiod as the Olympians, or the gods who dwell in the Olympian halls. Of these Olympian gods, Zeus, the father of gods and men, is chief. He has his palace on the topmost summit, and there the other Olympian gods assemble in council. It is worth while to pass in review the character and attributes Greek imagination gave to each of these Olympian gods.

Zeus.—Father Zeus (Ju-piter), first of the immortals in rank and power, and sovereign among them like an earthly king, is primarily god of the sky : lightning and the thunderbolt are his natural weapons. He is the ' cloud-gatherer,' the ' lightning-flasher,' the ' lord of thunder overhead,' the god who ' delights in the thunder-stroke.' But from these beginnings as an awe-inspiring nature-god he came in course of time to be regarded as the omnipotent ruler of the universe, supreme disposer of all things in earth and heaven. " I will sing of Zeus," says the ancient hymn, " chiefest among the gods and greatest, all-seeing, the lord of all, the fulfiller, who whispers words of wisdom to Themis as she sits leaning towards him." He is the ' all-wise Counsellor ' who ordains for man the law of righteousness ; " he watches over all men and punishes the transgressor." He is beneficent, the father of all ; and more especially he is the helper of those who are in distress ; the stranger, the suppliant and the beggar are under his protection. Kings enjoy his special favour, because of their authority and responsibility ; they are ' foster-children of Zeus.' Zeus is guardian of the family ; he sanctifies marriage and protects family life : his altar as Zeus Herkeios (Zeus of the Hearth) stood in the forecourt of every home. Zeus is protector of Greek national life ; he is Zeus Soter (Zeus the Saviour), and Zeus Eleutherios (Zeus the Giver of Freedom). Zeus represents Hellenic national unity, the community of free Hellenic states ; he is Zeus Hellenios, or Pan-Hellenios, Zeus of the Hellenic peoples.

Though the Greeks never became monotheists, there is certainly in their conception of Zeus as all-seeing, all-ruling, all-powerful, an approximation to monotheism. The conception of Zeus as beneficent and just is even more important and significant : the belief that Zeus had ordained a law of righteousness for men, and that he punished evil-doers, had a real influence on men's conduct, both public and private. To how noble a conception of the godhead a Greek could rise without breaking with the ancient polytheism, and how closely the language used approaches that of the great universal religions may be seen in the Hymn of the Stoic Cleanthes : [1]

" Most glorious of immortals, O Zeus of many names, almighty and everlasting, sovereign of nature, directing

[1] Cleanthes lived in the third century B.C.

all in accordance with law, thee it is fitting that all
mortals should address. . . . Thee all this universe, as
it rolls circling round the earth, obeys wheresoever thou
dost guide, and gladly owns thy sway. Such a minister
thou holdest in thy invincible hands—the two-edged, fiery,
ever-living thunderbolt, under whose stroke all nature
shudders. . . . No work upon earth is wrought apart
from thee, lord, nor through the divine ethereal sphere,
nor upon the sea ; save only whatsoever deeds wicked
men do in their own foolishness. Nay, thou knowest
how to make even the rough smooth, and to bring order
out of disorder ; and things not friendly are friendly in
thy sight. For so hast thou fitted all things together,
the good with the evil, that there might be one eternal
law over all. . . . Deliver men from fell ignorance.
Banish it, father, from their soul, and grant them to
obtain wisdom, whereon relying thou rulest all things
with justice." [1]

There were famous temples of Zeus at Olympia and at
Athens. That at Athens, like the cathedral of Cologne,
took many hundred years in building.[2] The fifteen
columns that are left of it form one of the most impressive
sights in Athens to-day. The temple at Olympia was
shaken down by an earthquake about 1500 years ago,
and the drums of the columns may be seen (since Olympia
was excavated in 1876) lying in rows as they fell, at an
angle to the temple platform. The statue of Zeus in
this temple, the work of Pheidias, was regarded in ancient
times as the perfect expression in sculpture of godhead's
noblest attributes. One who saw this ' Zeus ' in the first
century A.D. wrote of him : " His power and kingship are
displayed by the strength and majesty of the whole
image, his fatherly care for men by the mildness and
loving-kindness in the face ; the solemn austerity of the

---

[1] R. D. Hicks in the *Encyclopaedia Britannica* (11th Ed.) under
' Stoics : ' from Cleanthes' *Hymn to Zeus*, lines 1-3 ; 7-11 ; 15-21 ; 32-34.

[2] It was begun by Pisistratus in the sixth century B.C. and finished
by Hadrian in the second century A.D. The dates for Cologne Cathedral
are 1260 to 1880.

work marks the god of the city and the law . . . he seems like to one giving and bestowing blessings." [1]

Hera.—Hera (Juno) is the consort of Zeus and the partner in his greatness. She is " the glorious one whom all the blessed throughout high Olympus reverence and honour even as Zeus who delights in thunder." Because she is the wedded wife of Zeus, marriage as a religious institution is her special province ; she is " the wedded Hera, who is gay in all the bridal choirs and guards the keys of wedlock." [2] She is beautiful, and majestic in her beauty. With her beauty and her queenliness there goes a high spirit, quick to resent offences and vehement in anger. She is consequently violent and implacable in her hatreds : in Homer's poems and in the *Aeneid* she is the deadly enemy of Troy, who never forgives.

Argos was her favourite abode, and her temple there, the Heraeum, was exceedingly ancient. There was another very ancient Heraeum at Olympia, the foundations of which may still be seen. This temple dates from 1000 B.C. : it is much older than the temple of Zeus at Olympia, and probably the oldest Greek temple of which remains survive to this day.

Poseidon.—The Greeks, like the English, had much to do with the sea, and consequently had a great plenty of sea-divinities, male and female : Oceanus, Nereus, Triton, Proteus, sea-gods ; and sea-nymphs, Nereids and Oceanids (daughters of Nereus and Oceanus), some of whom had special names and functions, Amphitrite, Thetis, Leuconoe, Calypso ; besides strange supernatural creatures like the Sirens and the Harpies and Scylla. Chief among them all was Poseidon (Neptune), who had dominion over the realm of waters as Zeus in the sky, whose favourite dwelling-place was not on Mount Olympus, but in the depths of the sea. Poseidon was represented as riding

[1] Dion Chrysostom, Twelfth Oration, translated by Farnell, *Cults of the Greek States*, vol. i. p. 131. Dion Chrysostomus (the golden-mouthed) was born in the middle of the first century, and died at Rome A.D. 117.

[2] Aristophanes, *Thesmophoriazousae*, ll. 973-976.

over the waves in his chariot, with Amphitrite his queen,
attended by a train of sea-monsters and sea-nymphs.   In
his hand was the trident, the three-pronged fishing-spear,
the symbol of his sway.   Before him went his trumpeter
Triton, blowing on a shell, or conch, to still the waves.[1]
Poseidon's chariot is drawn by plunging white horses,
which seem to be a figure of plunging billows. He is himself, perhaps through a fanciful identification of the waves
with sea-horses, the horse-god, Hippios ; and the horse
was sacred to him.   In his contest with Athena for the
possession of Athens he is said to have created the horse,
as Athena created the olive. His worship was of high
account at Athens, though second to Athena's ; but the
chief seat of his worship was Corinth and the Isthmus,
where the Isthmian Games were celebrated in his honour.

Poseidon is called the Earth-shaker and the Earth-
holder, and is also ' lord of Helicon and wide Argae.'
One of the hymns says of him : " A two-fold office the
gods allotted you, O Shaker of the Earth, to be a tamer
of horses and a saviour of ships ! Hail, Poseidon, Holder
of the Earth, dark-haired lord !   O blessed one, be kindly
in heart and help those who voyage in ships."

Pallas Athena.—Of all the Greek gods and goddesses
Athena has the most marked individuality. She is no
mere personified abstraction, but in Homer and the
dramatists she speaks and acts like a person with a
vividly human character. What is her character is
significantly illustrated by the heroes whom she adopts
as her favoured champions and helps in their adventures—
Perseus, Bellerophon, Diomedes, and, most of all, Odysseus.
She tells Odysseus, when she makes herself known to him
on his first arrival back in Ithaca (see Ch. VIII. p. 159)
that she could not forsake him in his misfortune because
he is " practised in courtesy, quick-witted and steadfast
in mind." [2]   She prizes readiness of resource, tenacity of

[1] Wordsworth in a famous sonnet wishes that he might

" Have sight of Proteus rising from the sea ;
Or hear old Triton blow his wreathed horn."

[2] *Odys.* xiii. l. 333.

purpose, endurance and hardihood. She delights in warlike prowess. She is herself the Warrior Maid, good comrade of warriors though utterly aloof from love and marriage, for she is essentially Parthenos, the Virgin goddess, and her temple is the Parthenon. But her highest interest is the ordered life of the city-state. As Athena Polias, or Poliouchos, she is the guardian deity of many cities, and before all of Athens, her own city, to which she gave her name. Athens she won for her own in contest with Poseidon by the gift to mankind of the olive. She is mistress also of weaving and of all useful crafts in which women excel. In her great festival at Athens, the Panathenaia, the whole Athenian people march in procession [1] to the Acropolis to present in her temple the Peplos, the beautifully wrought robe, woven for her by women of the noblest families specially skilled in the art.

We discern in all this two sets of attributes proper to Pallas Athena, according as her sphere of action is peace or war. This is because she is the personification of the wisdom which builds and preserves cities and states. She is statesmanly wisdom, born without mother from the very mind of the supreme ruler, Zeus : or according to another image, her mother is Metis, Counsel—the counsel which governs states aright. But because in a world where rude force surges round every ordered polity, states can only be maintained by warlike virtue,[2] she has war-like attributes, and this aspect of her character looks superficially the more prominent. Her most familiar image presents her armed with spear and shield ; over her breast the wondrous *aegis*, fringed with serpents and with the Gorgon's head glaring in the centre ; on her head a great bronze helmet with lofty plume. The legend

[1] The Panathenaic procession forms the subject of the Parthenon frieze which may be seen at the British Museum in the Elgin Room ; slabs, to a length of 241 feet, are the original marble brought from Athens by Lord Elgin, 172 feet are plaster casts of slabs still in position on the walls of the Parthenon. The original total length was 522 feet 10 inches.

[2] Plato in the *Critias* calls her " a lover of war and of wisdom."

said she sprang thus armed in full panoply from the head of Zeus, when Hephaestus cleft it open with his axe ; and as the war-cry rang out from her lips all nature trembled. In this character she inspires heroes to deeds of valour and leads her Athenians into battle. But if in any sense she is a goddess of war, it is in a very different way from that in which other war-gods are conceived, and among them the Greek Ares. Ares is the god of war, savage and unrestrained, of war for war's sake : he breathes the fierce lust of battle and delight in bloodshed. Athena expresses the spirit of righteous and ordered war, the warfare of civilized men in defence of the sanctities of life. She inspires the warlike strength which saves civilization from savagery. A story was told how the goddess turned from Tydeus (father of Diomedes) because he savagely fastened his teeth in the head of his dead enemy, Melanippus, when it was brought to him as he lay dying. "It is civilized valour and the art of war, that was embodied in the goddess." [1] But the deeper and more abiding aspect of her nature is the wisdom that guides states to prosperity in peace. "When the war has been fought out . . . then it is that the goddess Athene reigns in all gentleness and purity, teaching mankind to enjoy peace and instructing them in all that gives beauty to human life in wisdom and art." [2] The Panathenaic festival celebrated the victory of Athena over the Giants, that is the conquest of savagery by civilization. For Athena is "the reflex of the civilized Hellenic polity." [3] It is quite in accordance with a true doctrine of origins to say that Athena embodies the spirit of Athens, her best beloved city. But while this is true, it is true also that Athena is ultimately more than the guardian deity of Athens ; she is a divinity of all the Hellenes, a personification of that Hellenic polity of which Athens gave to the world the noblest example.

[1] Farnell, *Cults of the Greek States*, vol. i. p. 309.

[2] Murray (A. S.), *Manual of Mythology*, p. 90.

[3] Farnell, *l.c.* p. 318.

The ideal of personal character which emerges from a review of these aspects and attributes of the goddess is one of resolved courage, careful foresight, and steady command of self. It is an ideal which has been expressed with a poet's insight and felicity by Tennyson in his *Oenone* :

> "Self-reverence, self-knowledge, self-control,
> These three alone lead life to sovereign power.
> Yet not for power (power of herself
> Would come uncalled for) but to live by law,
> Acting the law we live by without fear ;
> And, because right is right, to follow right
> Were wisdom, in the scorn of consequence."

Apollo.—Phoebus Apollo is very familiar in two characters : he is the god of the lyre or seven-stringed harp, the leader of the Muses (Musagetes), and with them the inspirer of all poets ; he is the god of the famous oracle at Delphi, where as the prophet, or interpreter, of Zeus he gives answers to those who consult him with due rites. Yet, again, he is the god of purification and of healing, the deliverer from calamity, Apollo the Averter : to Apollo in this character his worshippers raised the ' paean ' or song of deliverance, which became the Greek war-song and chant of victory. He is the god of the Silver Bow, the far-darter. All these characters are his, because primarily he is the god of Light, the Sun god. He is the Sun god, yet not to be identified physically with the sun, who for the Greeks was Helios Hypereion, a god originally quite distinct from Phoebus Apollo. Apollo is a personification rather of the sun's light than of the sun. He illumines and reveals like sunlight, he purifies like sunlight ; sometimes also he destroys, as do the sun's intenser beams. When men died mysteriously without suffering and without apparent cause, the Greeks said they were slain by Apollo's gentle arrows ; when they died of pestilence they were said to be slain by the arrows of his wrath.

Apollo, like Pallas Athena, is a personification of divine power characteristically Hellenic. It is through an imaginative refinement of the idea of light as illumination, spiritual as well as material, that he attains this char-acter. On one side this becomes the illumination of prophecy, the revelation of the divine will through oracles. On the other, it becomes the poet's inspiration ; it gives impulse to and regulates all forms of art. For Apollo is also the revealer of the principles of order, measure, harmony and symmetry, which comprise the special canons of Greek art. It was on the walls of Apollo's temple at Delphi that the precepts " Nothing in excess " and " Know thyself " were inscribed. Further, because Apollo was the teacher of moderation and good order, he was also the guardian of civil order in the state. When-ever bands of Greek settlers went out in search of new homes, they first took counsel of the Delphic oracle, and for this reason Apollo was sometimes called Archegetes, or Founder of Cities. In the highest conception of his attributes to which the Greeks attained he is the upholder of the moral order : on behalf of Zeus, his father, the supreme deity, he punishes sin and teaches the law of righteousness. Apollo became " the guardian of moral life, and the expression of moral purity and exaltation." " His pure and radiant nature constrained him to punish crime." " Apollo was to the Greeks from all antiquity the god of purity, far removed from wrong, from faults and sins ; he punishes the sinner and the wicked." [1] Finally, we may identify Apollo with enlightenment in all forms, artistic and spiritual. He is for the ancient Greeks the influence which purifies morality and religion, inspires noble art ; refines, civilizes, humanizes.

The extant representations of Apollo in Greek sculpture are disappointing. The image of Apollo should obviously unite the perfection of manly grace with the fire of a noble intelligence. But even the far-famed Apollo Belvedere fails by this standard. The poets do better. The Homeric Hymn to Apollo pictures him " playing upon his hollow lyre, clad in divine perfumed garments ; and at the touch of the golden key his lyre sings sweet." [2]

---

[1] Duncker, *History of Greece*, vol. ii. p. 230.
[2] Hymn to Apollo, ll. 183-185.

" What forms are these coming
So white through the gloom ?
What garments out-glistening
The gold-flower'd broom ?

. . . .

'Tis Apollo comes leading
His choir, the Nine.
—The leader is fairest,
But all are divine."

This is an English poet's vision [1] of Apollo and the Muses.

Artemis.—Artemis (Diana) is the huntress goddess,
twin-sister of Apollo, associated with moonlight as he is
with sunlight. All wild nature is her domain, and
especially the forests and woodland glades which are
haunts of wild animals. The wild creatures there are
under her protection and she takes cruel vengeance on
anyone who, like King Agamemnon, offends against her
forest law. She herself delights in the chase, and is as
skilful with the bow as Apollo, her brother. Her arrows
she lets fly sometimes at the wild beasts of the chase,
sometimes at human beings who have offended her. The
deaths of women who die suddenly and unaccountably
are ascribed to her gentle darts, as such deaths of men
to Apollo's. Her worship must at one time have included
human sacrifices, as the stories of Iphigeneia and Orestes
seem to show. Or possibly some more savage cult had
in certain places become merged in the worship of
Artemis. Like Athena she is a maiden unapproachable,
loving chastity for its own sake. She finds her happiness
in the free life of the open air, ranging over hill and valley
with her attendant wood-nymphs, all vowed to maiden-
hood and all in vigorous training like herself. She is
patroness, therefore, of all field sports. In appearance
she is tall and slender and beautiful. If a Greek wished
to pay a special compliment to a Greek maiden, he compared her with Artemis, as Odysseus does Nausicaa : " If
indeed thou art a goddess of them that keep the wide
heaven ; to Artemis, then, the daughter of great Zeus,
I mainly liken thee, for beauty and stature and shapeli-

[1] Matthew Arnold's in *Empedocles on Etna*.

ness." [1] " And even as Artemis, the archer," says the
poet in his own person, " moveth down the mountain . . .
taking her pastime in the chase of boars and swift deer,
and with her the wild wood-nymphs disport them, the
daughters of Zeus, lord of the aegis, and Leto is glad at
heart, while high over all she rears her head and brows,
and easily may she be known—but all are fair ; even so
the girl unwed outshone her maiden company." [2]

Hermes.—The infant Hermes (Mercury), in the hymn
which tells the story of his birth, is playfully called a
clever cheat, a robber, a cattle-lifter, a midnight spy, a
thievish hanger-about-doors, and the poem goes on to
relate how, before he was a day old, he had stolen and
successfully hidden a number of Apollo's cattle. Skilful
cunning always remained one of Hermes' accomplishments, so that he was regarded by rogues and vagabonds
as their patron deity—Hermes the Trickster (Dolios).
But he had other attributes more respectable. In the
hymn quoted above he is, indeed, the wondrous infant,
as Krishna is for the Hindus, astonishing and delighting
his votaries by his mischievous pranks. " Born with the
dawning," the hymn goes on, " at midday he played on
the lyre, and in the evening he stole the cattle of far-
shooting Apollo." He is described as climbing out of
his cradle and wandering out of doors. Just across the
threshold he found a tortoise and seized on it gleefully
as a plaything. The idea of a lyre made from the shell
at once flashed into his mind. Forthwith he killed the
tortoise, scraped clean the shell and fitted it with horns
and strings. Then he struck the strings with a key and
was enraptured with the musical notes produced as the
strings vibrated. Thus was the lyre invented, and next
day when Apollo had brought home to this precocious
child the theft of the cattle, Hermes gave him the lyre
as a peace-offering. And Phoebus Apollo received the gift
gladly and made a pact of friendship with Hermes, and
gave him in return some portion of his own prophetic art.

[1] *Odys.* vi. ll. 150-152.   Butcher and Lang, p. 97.
[2] *Odys.* vi. ll. 102-109.   B. and L., p. 95.

Hermes is most familiar to us in his office of herald of the gods, the messenger of Zeus.[1] Homer in the *Odyssey* describes him setting out on one of these errands : " beneath his feet he bound on his fair sandals, golden, divine, that bare him over the waters of the sea and over the boundless land with the breathings of the wind. And he took up his wand, wherewith he entranceth the eyes of such men as he will, while others again he awaketh out of sleep." [2] He is the intermediary between gods and men, and is even by one great poet represented as conveying prayer to the powers beyond the grave.[3] He is god of the roadside, the wayfaring god. Roads and boundaries,[4] as well as heralds, were under his protection. It is his function also to convoy the souls of the dead to the realm of Hades. He is god of the concourse of men in the market-place, and hence the god of eloquence. He was specially honoured in the palaestra, or wrestling-ground, and as Hermes Agonios (Hermes of the Contest) becomes the special guardian of athletic training. The place of his birth was fabled to be Mount Cyllene in Arcadia, and it appears that in origin he is the god of a pastoral people, Hermes Nomios, or lord of flocks. In this last character he is sometimes represented as carrying a ram or a calf upon his shoulders.

A statue of Hermes found at Olympia—the Hermes of Praxiteles—is one of the few pieces of statuary that have come down to us known to be the actual work of a great master. One sight of the Hermes of Praxiteles at Olympia will teach more about Greek sculpture than a whole treatise. No verbal description or photograph can reproduce the magic of this piece of sculptured marble. It must be seen where it now is, at Olympia itself. A sight

[1] In the *Iliad*, however, Iris (the Rainbow) is the messenger of the gods, not Hermes.

[2] *Odys.* v. ll. 44-48.

[3] Aeschylus, *Choephoroe*, ll. 124-126.

[4] Images of the god called Hermae were set up in the public thoroughfares of Athens. The mysterious mutilation of the Hermae caused intense excitement at Athens in a crisis of her history. See Bury's *History of Greece*, p. 467.

of the Hermes of Praxiteles is alone worth the pilgrimage
to the excavations.

Hephaestus.—Hephaestus (Vulcan) was the god of Fire,
the great artificer of Heaven. He had a workshop on
Mount Olympus, where he wrought all manner of curious
work for the Olympian gods : here, too, he made a suit
of armour for Achilles (see Ch. V. p. 91). But as it was
natural to connect the god of fire with volcanoes, the
poets also imagined Aetna to be his smithy, or Stromboli
in the Lipari Islands. The oldest seat of his worship was
in the island of Lemnos, near a volcano (Moschylos) now
extinct. It was on this island he fell, when, according
to the story to which Milton refers in *Paradise Lost*,[1] his
father Zeus in a fit of passion hurled him out of heaven :

> " from morn
> To noon he fell, from noon to dewy eve,
> A summer's day, and with the setting sun
> Dropt from the zenith, like a falling star,
> On Lemnos, th' Aegean isle. . . ."

Through the skill he teaches in metal-working and
various useful arts Hephaestus is associated with Athena
as a benefactor of mankind. " Sing, clear-voiced Muse,"
says the hymn in his honour, " of Hephaestus famed for
inventions. With bright-eyed Athene he taught men
glorious crafts throughout the world,—men who before
used to dwell in caves in the mountains like wild beasts.
But now that they have learned crafts through Hephaestus
the famed worker, easily they live a peaceful life in their
own houses the whole year round." In Homer any work
of art of special beauty of workmanship—like the silver
bowl which Menelaus gives as a parting present to Telemachus,[2] is called a work of Hephaestus.

Naturally as a smith Hephaestus has mighty strength
of arm, but he had been born lame and is afflicted with
a limp, which sometimes excites the laughter of the other
gods. In spite of this deformity he is married to Charis,
fairest of the Graces. Doubtless this is allegory, representing the union of artistic beauty with the smith's craft.

[1] Milton, *Paradise Lost*, i. 742-746.
[2] *Odys.* iv. ll. 615-617. B. and L., p. 67.

Hephaestus is, in fact, the element of fire deified. His limp-ing gait, it is suggested, symbolizes the flickering of flame.

Hestia.—Hestia, the Hearth-goddess, is more familiar to us as the Roman Vesta, to whose service the Vestal Virgins were dedicated. She has an important place in Greek life, both public and domestic, because her altar-hearth was found in every private house and in every public building ; and every act of importance, public and private, began with the pouring of a few drops of wine upon it. So the hymn to Hestia says : " Hestia in the high dwellings of all, both deathless gods and men who walk on earth, you have gained an everlasting abode and highest honour : glorious is your portion and your right. For without you mortals hold no banquet,—where one does not duly pour sweet wine in offerings to Hestia both first and last." In the Prytaneum, or Town Hall, of a Greek city perpetual fire was commonly kept burn-ing ; and if the city sent out a colony, fire from this altar was religiously conveyed to the new city and laid upon a new altar there. Should the fire on the public hearth of the new city chance to be extinguished at any time, fresh fire must be conveyed to it from the public hearth of the mother-city before it could be rekindled. All this illustrates the extreme importance of fire to primitive mankind and (before the invention of the lucifer match) the importance of the maintenance of fire once kindled. At Rome, if a Vestal virgin allowed the sacred fire to go out, the penalty was death.

The Greek Hestia, like the Roman Vesta, is a virgin goddess. In a hymn to Aphrodite it is said of Hestia : " God, the father gave her a fair boon instead of marriage, and ever she sitteth in the middle of the house, taking the fat of sacrifice and she receiveth honours in all temples of the gods, and among all men she hath been given the first place among divinities."

Aphrodite.—Aphrodite is the goddess of love and queen of beauty, dowered with every soft grace and charm. She was not in origin a national Hellenic divinity : her

I   D

worship was imported from Asia mainly through Phoenician agency and by way of the islands, Cyprus and Cythera. This eastern worship was that of the Semitic Astarte or Ishtar, a nature goddess, the source of life and fertility. Greek imagination refined and idealized the passion of love in the forms of Aphrodite (Venus) and Eros (Cupid). Cupid with his bow and arrows we owe to the Greeks. The Greek poets were well aware of the ruin that may be wrought in human life by the infatuation of love, as the story of the Trojan war and more than one of the great tragedies show. But it is rather of the loveliness of Love that they sing. " She gives kindly gifts to men," says the hymn in praise of Aphrodite, " smiles are ever on her lovely face, and lovely is the brightness that plays over it."

Demeter.—Demeter (Ceres), the Corn-goddess, by whose influence the earth yields fruits of increase, is interesting through the story of her daughter, Persephone (Proserpine), who was carried off by Pluto, god of the world of death, to be his queen. Milton compares Enna in Sicily, which he takes to be the scene of this carrying off, the *Rape of Proserpine*, with his Garden of Eden :

> " that fair field
> Of Enna, where Proserpin gathering flowers,
> Herself a fairer flower, by gloomy Dis
> Was gathered. . . ." [1]

The carrying off is thus related in the Hymn to Demeter : " Apart from Demeter, lady of the golden sword and glorious fruits, she was playing with the deep-bosomed daughters of Oceanus and gathering flowers over a soft meadow, roses and crocuses and beautiful violets, irises also and hyacinths and the narcissus, which Earth made to grow at the will of Zeus to please Polydektes, the Host of Many, to be a snare for the bloom-like girl—a marvellous, radiant flower. It was a thing of awe, whether for deathless gods or mortal men to see : from its root grew a hundred blooms and it smelled most

[1] Milton, *Paradise Lost*, iv. 268-271.

sweetly, so that all wide heaven above and the whole earth and the sea's salt swell laughed for joy. And the girl was amazed and reached out with both hands to take the lovely toy ; but the wide-pathed earth yawned there in the plain of Nysa,[1] and the Lord Polydegmon, Host of Many, with his immortal horses sprang out upon her, the Son of Cronos, He who has many names. He caught her up reluctant on his golden car and bare her away lamenting . . . and the heights of the mountains and the depths of the sea rang with her immortal voice." [2]

Demeter heard her daughter's cry of distress, though too late to save her, and sought her lost darling over all the world. Strange stories were told of the mother's wanderings ; how in grief and indignation she left Olympus altogether and travelled in mourning garments from city to city, seeking tidings of her lost one, until she came to Eleusis in Attica. There she was kindly received by the family of Celeus and Metaneira and found a resting-place as nurse to their late-born son, Demophoon.[3] And at first they knew not the goddess ; but afterwards she made herself known and bade them build her a temple. Thus it was that the Eleusinian mysteries, which play a part in Athenian history, came to be instituted. But when her temple was built at Eleusis, Demeter still sat there disconsolate, pining with grief for her daughter. Then to compel the gods to take notice of her great wrong, she stopped the growth of all kinds of corn and caused a grievous famine over all the earth. Fearing the extinction of mankind, and with that the loss of the sacrifices which were offered to the gods, Zeus sent twice to persuade her to relent. But she would not : on the contrary she declared that " she would never set foot on fragrant Olympus, nor let fruit spring

[1] The plain of Nysa is supposed to be in Asia but cannot be more exactly identified. There was a Mount Nysa in Thrace connected with the birth of Dionysus.

[2] *Hymn to Demeter*, ll. 4-20 ; 38 and 39.

[3] Triptolemus, whom the Athenians revered as founder of the Eleusinian Mysteries, sometimes takes the place of Demophoon in the story.

out of the ground, until she beheld with her eyes her own fair-faced daughter." [1] Then at last Zeus commanded Hermes to fetch Persephone from the realm of Hades. And Aidoneus, lord of the dead, was obliged to let her go up with Hermes to earth, to the place where Demeter waited for her. " And when Demeter saw them, she rushed forth as a Maenad [2] down some thick-wooded mountain, while Persephone on the other side, when she saw her mother's sweet eyes, left the chariot and horses, and leaped down to run to her, and falling upon her neck, embraced her." [3] But as the husband, Aidoneus, now too had his claims, a compromise was made : for one-third of the year Persephone dwelt with him in the dark underworld as queen of the realm of the dead, while the other two-thirds were spent with her mother among the gods of heaven.

This story is doubtless an allegory of the disappearance of grain from the fields at the coming on of winter and the reappearance of the young corn in the spring ; and indeed of that whole vivid drama of the seasons, the loss of all the brightness and beauty of the earth in winter and its recovery in spring, which has so deeply impressed both the psychology and the literature of Europe.

Hades.—Hades or Aidoneus, the Shadowy One, the husband of Persephone, was lord of the dark world below, and ruler over the dead. He was also called Pluto, because the riches beneath the earth were his possession. Men shrank from pronouncing his true name and used instead this other name Pluto, or some epithet like Polydektes or Polydegmon.

The realm of the dead, this House of Hades, the Greeks conceived as deep down below the surface of the earth. Mysterious openings in the ground led down to it, [4] like

---

[1] *Hymn to Demeter*, ll. 331-333.

[2] A Bacchante, or woman taking part in the wild rites in honour of Dionysus.

[3] *Hymn to Demeter*, ll. 385-389.

[4] Not far out of Delphi on the road to Arachova in the rock a little below the road is carved a double door supposed popularly to represent the Gate of Hades.

that in the cliffs of Cape Taenarum, by which Heracles entered to drag Cerberus, the watch-dog of Hell, up to the light of day. Orpheus and Odysseus, as well as Heracles, are said to have visited the realms of the dead and lived to return. The abode of the dead was encircled by the rivers of hell, whose names are given in Milton's sounding lines :

> " Abhorrèd Styx, the flood of deadly hate ;
> Sad Acheron of sorrow, black and deep ;
> Cocytus, named of lamentation loud
> Heard on the rueful stream ; fierce Phlegethon
> Whose waves of torrent fire inflame with rage.
> Far off from these, a slow and silent stream,
> Lethe, the river of Oblivion, rolls
> Her watery labyrinth, whereof who drinks
> Forthwith his former state and being forgets—
> Forgets both joy and grief, pleasure and pain."[1]

The souls of the dead were conducted by Hermes to the borders of Hades and conveyed across the waters by the ferryman, Charon, in his crazy boat. For this passage the fare was one obol ; and that the soul might not lack means of payment, a coin was placed between the lips of the dead before burial. It was believed that the soul could not be ferried across the Styx and allowed to repose in the abodes of the dead, unless the body had been duly buried or burnt, or at least a handful of dust had by some pious hand been flung over it. This belief had a firm hold on the minds of all the Greeks and powerfully influenced their conduct, as we see in the story of Sophocles' *Antigone* and in Euripides' *Suppliants* and *Trojan Women*. To this belief was due, in part, the Greek custom, amounting to a ' law of war,' by which, after a battle between Greeks, the bodies of slain enemies were always restored to their countrymen, when formal demand for their recovery was made by a herald.

The gates of Hades were guarded by Cerberus, a monster in the form of a dog with three heads and a serpent-tail : " on those who go in he fawns with his tail and both his ears, but suffers them not to go out back again, but

[1] *Paradise Lost*, ii. 577-586.

keeps watch and devours whomsoever he catches going out of the gates of strong Hades and awful Persephone." [1] The Greeks also imagined places of torment and of bliss, distinct from this House of Hades. The place of torment was Tartarus, a part of Hades deeper down, and darker, and more dreadful. The place of bliss was the Elysian fields, far removed from Hades and Tartarus, and often pictured as the Islands of the Blest, somewhere across far western seas :

> "Where falls not hail, or rain, or any snow,
> Nor ever wind blows loudly; but it lies
> Deep-meadow'd, happy. . . ."

Other Greek Deities.—These twelve were the chief deities worshipped by all the Hellenes. Of Ares there is nothing to add to what was said on p. 42, except that he is the Greek god of war and is identified with the Roman Mars. Dionysus, Pan and the Muses are characteristically Greek and deserve special notice.

Dionysus.—Dionysus, or Bacchus (the name Bacchus also was Greek before it was Latin), with his train of round-paunched Sileni, goat-faced Satyrs and intoxicated women (Bacchantes or Maenads), does not promise well as an object of a nation's adoration. And yet Dionysus is intimately associated with one of the noblest products of Greek genius, the tragic drama. In the great theatre at Athens, under the south-eastern cliffs of the Acropolis, the seat of honour is the throne of the Priest of Dionysus (we read the title of his office on his marble seat) : the altar of the god was the centre of the orchestra (or dancing space) round which the Chorus of a Greek play moved. "All the great Athenian tragedies were acts of worship dedicated to Dionysus." [2]

We think of Dionysus as the Wine-god, and so he was : this certainly became the popular conception of his attributes and character. But originally he was more than this ; he was a god of vegetation, of all the green life that bursts forth over the earth's surface with the

---

[1] Hesiod, *Theogony*, ll. 770-774.   [2] Dyer, *The Gods in Greece*, p. 135.

coming of spring. The ivy was sacred to Dionysus as
well as the grape. There are also clear indications that
Dionysus was not originally an Hellenic divinity, the
current myths plainly show that his worship was introduced with difficulty in the face of opposition, and that
it came from Thrace. In Thrace it was a wild religion,
associated with cruel rites and among these with the
eating of raw flesh. The object of the worshipper was
the escape from self, divine possession, the ecstatic or
trance-like state ; and wine appeared to be the most
direct means of inducing this state. To primitive man
intoxication was not ' drunkenness,' a degrading form of
self-indulgence, but a state of exaltation or ' elevation,'
which had something supernatural and wonderful about
it.[1] This state of exhilaration or mental exaltation
showed the miraculous power of the god, and to resist
the god could be honestly viewed as impious. The
ecstatic condition was, however, clearly out of keeping
with the Hellenic principles of moderation and self-
control ; hence the resistance offered to the introduction
of the worship of Dionysus with its orgies of excitement.
But the new religion supplied something which the
Hellenes wanted, and the march of Dionysus was a
triumphant progress. Stories were told of the dreadful
fate that overtook those who opposed his coming, like
Lycurgus, chief of the Thracians, and Pentheus, king of
Thebes. Lycurgus was blinded and with his own hand
lopped off his legs under the impression that he was
lopping a vine. Pentheus' end was even more dreadful ;
he was torn in pieces by his mother, Agave, and a troop
of women, who, in their Bacchic fury, mistook him for a
lion.

As in other cases this foreign worship was idealized and
beautified by the Greeks ; and by a fortunate con-

---

[1] " We have no clear record of the feelings of the aboriginal Thracian,
but probably the utterance of the Vedic worshipper, ' we have drunk
Soma, we have become immortal, we have entered into light, we have
known the gods,' expresses a religious perception in regard to the
mystery of alcohol, widely diffused in early religions."   Farnell, vol. v.
p. 122

junction of circumstances, in course of time, they wove into it high forms of artistic creation, both sorrowful and joyous, the one tragedy, the other comedy. Comedy belongs to that universal impulse to rejoice in the return of spring, which we see in the Holi festival in Northern India, and in our own May-day festivities. Tragedy is in origin a passion-play ; its ultimate source is the slaying of the beauty of the year by the on-coming of the dark season. Dionysus as the god of vegetation is the subject of that yearly tragedy, and from this passion of Dionysus come all other tragic dramas. The association with Dionysus gave play-acting at Athens and in all Greece a religious and solemn character. And yet all the time Dionysus in another aspect is just the god of wine. " The truth is that Dionysus was, from the outset, a god of contradictions. He represented death as well as life. . . . The leader and inspirer of the holy choral song, the god whose worship awakened and sustained the loftiest strain of sacred tragedy, was himself amid the brawls of drunkards, and his unreproving presence sanctioned all the worst excesses bred of unmixed wine." [1]

Pan.—Pan, the incarnation of the spirit of wild nature in the open country, is a peculiarly Greek divinity. How the Greek imagined Pan is shown vividly in the Homeric hymn in his praise : " Muse, tell me about Pan, the dear son of Hermes, with his goats' feet and two horns—a lover of merry noise. Through wooded glades he wanders with dancing nymphs who foot it on some sheer cliff's edge, calling upon Pan, the shepherd-god, long-haired, unkempt. He has every snowy height and the mountain peaks and rocky crests for his domain ; hither and thither he goes through the close thickets, now lured by soft streams, and now he presses on amongst towering crags and climbs up to the highest peak that overlooks the flocks." [2] It is difficult after reading these words to agree with those who say the Greeks had no appreciation for scenery, at least not for the wild scenery which appeals so strongly to modern sentiment. The very spirit of wild

[1] Dyer, *The Gods in Greece*, pp. 78, 79.   [2] *Hymn to Pan*, ll. 1-11.

nature is in this description—with the whimsical turn Greek genius gives it by endowing Pan with goats' feet and horns. Naturally the rustic god comes from the rustic highlands of Arcadia and is most worshipped there. He acquired a new national character at the time of the Persian Wars. For the Athenian Pheidippides, when he ran from Athens to Sparta and back again, declared that he met Pan while crossing the mountains and that Pan promised to help Athens (see Ch. XII. p. 286).

The Nine Muses.—Of all the Greek divinities, the Muses, the Sacred Nine, have most verisimilitude for us to-day. It is a literary ' convention ' when a modern poet appeals to the Muse for inspiration, and yet it is something a little more than a convention. The intensity of the poet's feelings, the exalted mood which we still speak of as ' inspiration,' give reality to the Muse, creature of the imagination though she be. The convention at all events lasted long among English poets : even Milton addresses the ' Heavenly Muse ' in the opening of *Paradise Lost*, and later professes himself

> " not alone, while thou
> Visitest my slumbers nightly, or when Morn
> Purples the East. . . ." [1]

To the Greek poet the Muses were living beings and the true source of the poet's song. Both the *Iliad* and the *Odyssey* begin with an invocation of the Muse : " O goddess sing the wrath of Achilles, son of Peleus, the ruinous wrath. . . ." " O Muse, tell of the many-sided hero, who wandered far. . . ." But it is Hesiod who is the most devout servant of the Muses. For they belong to his native Boeotia ; the chief seat of their worship is on Mount Helicon, and there are the Muses' sacred fountains, Hippocrene and Aganippe. To Hesiod the Muses make known their " power to invent stories like to truth, and also, when we will, to convey the truth itself in song." [2] This insight is the ground also of the poet's appeal at the beginning of the catalogue of the Greek

[1] *Paradise Lost*, vii. ll. 28-30. [2] Hesiod, *Theogony*, ll. 27 and 28.

host in Book II. of the *Iliad* : " Inspire me, Muses, you who dwell in the hall of Olympus. For ye are goddesses and are present everywhere and know everything, but we receive only what is handed down to us and know nothing of ourselves." [1]   The *Theogony* makes the Muses daughters of Zeus and Mnemosyne, or Memory. They were reputed nine in number and had distinguishing names and attributes. The best known are Calliope, the Muse of Epic Poetry, Clio, the Muse of History, and Terpsichore, the Muse of Dancing. The very name Muse seems to be connected etymologically with memory and mind. [2]   The Muses personify the powers of mind and memory. Places associated with the worship of the Muses, besides Mount Helicon and its fountains, are, the river Ilissus in Attica, the fountain Castalia and the town of Thespiae. Their worship came originally from Pieria in Thessaly on the eastern slopes of Mount Olympus.

[1] *Iliad*, ii. 484-486.

[2] " Their name, ' Mousa, Monsa, Mentia, the mindful one, is a word that belongs to the psychic domain, not to the world of things." Farnell, v. p. 435.

CHAPTER IV

GODS AND HEROES (*continued*)

2. MYTH AND LEGEND.

"The irresistible sound wholesome heart
O' the hero, more than all the mightiness
At labour in the limbs that for man's sake
Laboured and meant to labour their life long
. . . ."

BROWNING, *Balaustion's Adventure.*

The gods in a polytheistic religion like the Greek, the
Old English and the Hindu, are imagined as immortal
and endowed with superhuman powers, but in other
respects are exactly like human beings. They have their
loves and hates, their personal interests and rivalries.
They live in a society as men and women do, and are
described as related to each other by family ties. Greek
imagination invested the gods so vividly with personal
characters and was so active, that countless stories were
told by priests and poets about them and their doings.
The whole collection of these stories is Greek mythology :
mythology being a term we also owe to the Greeks.
'Mythos' just means in Greek a story, and from its use
by the Greeks has come to mean specially a story imagined
by people in early times concerning the divine beings of
their worship. These Greek myths do not always agree
with each other, nor do they make a consistent whole ;
the stories were differently told in different places and at
different times. But they are lively and interesting
beyond the similar stories of other races, and sometimes

exceedingly beautiful. They are broadly in character
with the god as popularly conceived and worshipped, but
with a wide margin of free invention. So long as the
distinctive characteristics of the deity were maintained,
the poets held themselves at liberty to invent details and
episodes as their fancy led them. Sometimes the story
is intentionally allegorical, that is to say, designed to
represent in a figure some truth of nature or life, as the
story of Proserpine symbolizes the disappearance of
verdure from the earth during the dark season of winter.
An attempt was also made to explain the origin of the
gods themselves and trace out the mystery of the first
beginnings of existence. For though Zeus and the
Olympian gods now ruled in heaven and on earth, they
had not, the Greeks were taught, so ruled from the
beginning. There was an earlier dynasty of gods whom
they dispossessed, the Titans : and the Titans only ruled
after overpowering their father Uranus.

The Theogony.—The Greek poet Hesiod [1] wrote a
poem called the *Theogony*, or ' Divine Origins,' which
combines a large number of these myths into a connected
narrative explaining the family relationships of the gods
and the first origin of existence. In the latter respect,
it does for the Greeks very much what the Book of Genesis
does for us, though in a different way. At first there
was Chaos, says the poet, and two other primaeval beings,
Gaea (Earth) and Eros (Love). From Earth came Uranus
or Heaven : after that Heaven and Earth became the
parents of the Titans, a family of divine beings twelve in
number, who ruled the universe in the Golden Age :
Cronos and Rhea were king and queen among them. Of
the brothers of Cronos, Oceanus (the Ocean stream),
Hypereion (father of Helios, the Sun) and Iapetus (father

---

[1] Hesiod was a native of Ascra, in Boeotia, not far from Mount
Helicon, and the devout servant of the Muses. This much we learn
from his poems ; and that he won a victory in a poetic contest at
Chalcis in Euboea and dedicated his prize, ' a tripod with handles,'
to the Muses of Helicon. Nothing else is known with certainty, but
the poems attributed to him, the *Works and Days* and the *Theogony,*
belong probably to the 8th century B.C.

of Prometheus and Epimetheus) are to be noted : of the
sisters of Rhea, Themis (Ordinance) and Mnemosyne,
mother of the Muses. Other children of monstrous kind
were afterwards born to Earth : the Cyclopes, huge beings
in men's shape with one round eye in the centre of their
foreheads : the Giants, Cottus, Briareus and Gyges by
name, each born with a hundred hands and fifty heads.
Of the Titan pair, Cronos and Rhea, were born six children, Hestia, Demeter, Hera, Hades, Poseidon and Zeus,
three goddesses and three gods or ' theoi,' destined to
found the second and more lasting dynasty of Heaven.
Fantastic stories are told of the jealous fears of Uranus
and Cronos, and how each in turn in spite of his precautions was overpowered and dethroned by his children.
The second revolution, the expulsion of the Titans by
the Gods, was only accomplished after a long struggle in
which Zeus and the Olympians gained their victory with
the help of the Giants. A fearful picture of this war in
heaven is painted by Hesiod : " The boundless sea rang
terribly around, and the earth crashed loudly : wide
Heaven was shaken and groaned, and high Olympus
reeled from its foundation under the charge of the undying gods, and a heavy quaking reached dim Tartarus
and the deep sound of their feet in the fearful onset of
their hard missiles. So, then, they launched their grievous
shafts upon one another, and the cry of both armies as
they shouted reached to starry heaven ; and they met
together with a great battle-cry. Then Zeus no longer
held back his might ; but straight his heart was filled
with fury and he showed forth all his strength. From
Heaven and from Olympus he came forthwith, hurling
his lightning : the bolts flew thick and fast from his
strong hand together with thunder and lightning, whirling
an awesome flame. The life-giving earth crashed around
in burning, and the vast wood crackled loud with fire all
about. All the land seethed, and Ocean's streams and
the unfruitful sea. The hot vapour lapped round the
earthborn Titans : flame unspeakable rose to the bright
upper air : the flashing glare of the thunder stone and

lightning blinded their eyes for all that they were strong." [1]
Finally the Titans were overwhelmed by the rocks which
the Giants hurled upon them, " three hundred rocks, one
upon another, they launched from their strong hands and
overshadowed the Titans with their missiles, and hurled
them beneath the wide-pathed earth." [2] Then " when the
blessed gods had finished their toil, and settled by force
their struggle for honours with the Titans, they pressed
far-seeing Olympian Zeus to reign and to rule over
them. . . . So he divided their dignities amongst them." [3]
The universe was accordingly apportioned between Zeus
and his two brothers : Zeus retained for himself the
regions of air ; to Poseidon he assigned the dominion of
the seas ; to Hades the realms below the earth.

Of the other great Olympians, Hestia, Demeter and
Hera are daughters of Cronos and Rhea. All the other
six claim Zeus as their father. Apollo and Artemis are
the twin children of Zeus and Leto (Latona) ; Hermes is
the son of Zeus and Maia ; Ares and Hephaestus are sons
of Zeus and his consort, Hera. Aphrodite is the daughter
of Zeus and Dione. Pallas Athena derives her birth from
Zeus and from no other. Starting from these beginnings
the Greek makers of myths elaborated a most complicated
series of family relationships, divine, semi-divine and
merely human. For instance, Dionysus (Bacchus) is the
son of Zeus and Semele ; Persephone is the daughter of
Zeus and Demeter ; Pan is the son of Hermes and a
wood-nymph ; the Charites, or Graces, are daughters of
Zeus and Eurynome ; the water-nymphs are daughters
of Oceanus or of Nereus. When, however, we come
to the human claim to divine descent the genealogy
becomes complicated. For all the noblest families in
the various Greek states aspired to trace their descent
from some divinity, and especially from Zeus. The most
renowned heroes, Jason, Perseus, Heracles, Theseus, were
all sons, or descendants, of Zeus. Agamemnon was

---

[1] Hesiod, *Theogony*, ll. 678-699.
[2] *Ib.* ll. 715-719.
[3] Hesiod, *Theogony*, ll. 881-885.

descended from Zeus through Pelops and Tantalus ; the royal houses of Sparta, Argos and Messenia through Heracles. It is all worked out with extraordinary ingenuity and precision. These genealogies have, of course, no value except as illustrating the strength of the temptation to flatter pride of birth, and the ease with which it was done. They had, however, one very unfortunate result. They inevitably resulted in placing Olympian Zeus in a ridiculous or odious light. For the myths took little account of the laws of decent human society. Though the Greeks were distinguished from Eastern peoples by being strictly monogamous, their supreme god Zeus figured as very far from a pattern of conjugal fidelity. Hera is naturally represented as bitterly jealous of the other mothers and as pursuing their children with relentless enmity. Thus she was the life-long enemy of the hero Heracles, and by a trick cheated him out of his inheritance. All this was extremely undignified as well as bad morals. The Greeks who reflected were shocked at it and protested against the traditional mythology. Without doubt this blemish contributed to the ultimate rejection of paganism. The Graeco-Roman world had lost all belief in the old religion before it found a new and better faith in Christianity. But the immorality was rather an accident of the myths than inherent in the old religion itself. It seems to have come about partly through the confusion in course of ages of tribal divinities with Zeus. The chieftain was descended from the tribal god, and when the tribal god was identified with Zeus, a new love story had to be invented connecting Zeus with some mortal princess. In spite of this and other blemishes, the world is permanently the richer for the Greek myths ; of some of them the beauty and charm are undying. This is true to some extent of the stories of the gods, of the myth of Prometheus, for instance, and the myth of Demeter and Proserpine : it is far truer of the legends of the Greek heroes, the stories of Perseus and Jason ; of Heracles and Theseus ; of Orpheus and Eurydice, and of Alcestis.

The Race of Heroes.—In Hesiod's other poem, the *Works and Days*, he describes the evils of the Iron Age, the age of all hardness of heart and unrighteousness into which he has had the misfortune to be born, and he contrasts it with four earlier ages, the Golden Age, the Silver, the Bronze [1] and between the Bronze and the Iron, the age in which lived " the god-like race of hero-men." " But when earth had covered this generation also " (the Bronze). " Zeus, the son of Cronos, made yet another, the fourth, which was nobler and more righteous, a god-like race of hero-men, who are called demi-gods, the race before our own." [2]   By this he means the warriors who fought in the Trojan War and those who warred against Thebes.   But there is a better sense in which we may speak of the heroic age of Greece, and in the most renowned of the heroes of the old legends we may discern something quite different from prowess in war.   Hercules and Theseus and Perseus and Bellerophon were heroes partly in that they had greater strength and greater courage and endurance than ordinary men, but still more because they used their strength not to oppress and hurt their fellow-men, but to deliver them and to help them. It seems as if in the legends of these heroes there lives on a memory of the ages when man's dominion over nature was insecure, and men lived in their villages in constant danger from monstrous beasts, lions and serpents, bulls and boars ; when human strength and cunning barely sufficed for the struggle.   The heroes are the champions of mankind in this struggle with the wild forces of nature.

Heracles.—Heracles, whose name is better known to us in the Latinized form, Hercules, is the most famous example of such a hero.   He is more than half divine,

---

[1] As an epoch recognized in the early history of mankind, the Bronze Age (following on the Stone Age) is reckoned to begin about 2500 years before Christ, and is passing into the Iron Age about the time of the Trojan War.   The Achaean warriors belong to the Bronze Age, but iron is beginning to be mentioned as the material for weapons of war in the *Iliad* and *Odyssey*.

[2] Hesiod, *Works and Days*, ll. 156-160.

the son of Zeus and Alcmena,[1] though Amphitryon, king of Tiryns, is reputed to be his father. The exploits attributed to him by the Greek legends are bewildering in their variety ; the most famous of them are his ' Labours,' the tasks or ' feats ' required of him by Eurystheus, the cousin who through Hera's craft had robbed him of his birthright. The obligation to attempt these dangerous enterprises was laid upon him by the Delphic oracle in expiation of the blood-guiltiness which he had incurred by killing his own children in a fit of madness. So Heracles went about the world, not only throughout Greece, but far beyond—as far as Spain and Africa, ridding the earth of monstrous pests at Eurystheus' bidding.

The Labours of Hercules.—The first of the tasks set by Eurystheus was to free the district of Nemea from the ravages of a terrible lion, huge of size and fierce, and believed to be invulnerable. This lion had its lair in the mountains through which passes the ' Tretus,' or pierced way, now called the Pass of Dervenaki,[2] between Corinth and the plain of Argos, and terrorized the district around. Heracles pursued the beast to its den in a cave (shown to this day) with two entrances. Heracles closed up one entrance and entered the other armed with his club. Then, since weapons could make no impression on the brute's hide, he seized the lion by the throat with his two hands and strangled it by sheer strength. He afterwards stripped off the skin and used it as a shield ; hence the lion's skin became a symbol of Heracles. The second task was the destruction of the Serpent of Lerna, the famous Hydra. Lerna is now a station on the railway from Argos to Tripolitza, and there is a stretch of marshland between the village and the sea, where every spot connected by Pausanias [3] with the episode can be identi-

---

[1] Alcmena also was descended from Zeus through Perseus.

[2] In this pass a Turkish army under Dramali Pasha was caught and cut to pieces, when the Greeks rose to fight for their independence.

[3] Pausanias, to whose authority we shall have occasion to appeal frequently, was a pious traveller who made a tour through Greece,

fied. The ' lake ' from which the terrible hydra took its
name is within view from the mountain haunts of the
Nemean lion. "At the southern outlet of the pass,"
writes Sir J. G. Frazer, " the whole plain of Argos, with
the mountains on either hand and the sea in the distance,
bursts suddenly on the view. On the left, nestling at
the foot of the hills, are Mycenae and Tiryns, with Nauplia
and its towering acropolis rising from the sea and bounding the plain on this side. On the right is Argos with
its mountain citadel, and beyond it the Lernean lake
glimmers faintly in the distance. In the centre of the
picture, beyond the long foreground of level plain, stretches
the blue line of the Argolic Gulf." The lake, when you
get to it, is still a place of horror—a dark pool of unknown
depth shut in by tall reeds and grasses. With luck you
may even see there some of the big water-snakes with
black and yellow markings, common in the neighbourhood. The hydra, however, was no common snake, but
a monster with nine heads, one of them immortal. It
preyed upon the country round, destroying crops and
cattle, and Heracles was sent to kill it. Having traced
it to the cavity in the ground where it lived, he forced it
to come out by shooting flaming arrows into the opening.
Then he seized it and put his foot upon its body easily
enough ; his difficulties began when he tried to cut off
the heads. For as soon as one of the heads was struck
off, two grew in its place ; so his labour was vain. This
difficulty he solved by directing his squire, Iolaus, to light
a firebrand, and as soon as a head was severed sear with
the flame the bleeding neck, so that no new head could
grow. In this way he disposed of eight heads. The
immortal head could not be similarly dealt with ; so this
he cut off and buried, and placed a great stone upon the
earth above it. Another labour was the cleansing of the

visiting all famous places and shrines, in the second century A.D. As
he has left a full and exact account in ten books of all he saw, his work
is of immense value to all students of things Greek. Of these ten
books of Pausanias' *Description of Greece*, Sir James Frazer completed
in 1897 a translation, in English, enriched with a commentary based
on his own extensive travels amid the scenes Pausanias describes.

stable-yard of Augeas, king of Elis. This vast enclosure
was deep in filth and refuse, for Augeas had large herds
of cattle and the stalls had not been cleaned for thirty
years. The task imposed was to cleanse the whole place
within a day. This Heracles accomplished by diverting
the course of the river Peneus, so that it flowed through
the yard and washed it clean. The proverbial phrase
' cleansing the Augean stables ' comes from this story.

It would take too much space here to go through all
the twelve Labours. Two others have special interest.
Heracles was sent to seize the cattle of a monstrous being
with three heads and a man's body called Geryon. Geryon
lived in Erythea, an island in the Atlantic Ocean, and
part of the difficulty of the task was to get there. On
his way Heracles passed through Spain and crossed into
Africa by the Straits of Gibraltar. As a memorial of his
visit he is said to have set down two mountains, one on
either side of the Straits, the promontories Calpe and
Abyla. These promontories have since been known as
the Pillars of Hercules. To sail beyond the Pillars of
Hercules was to sail out into the Atlantic. The last of
the Labours of Hercules was the strangest and most
difficult of all. It was to fetch Cerberus up from the
kingdom of Hades. This, too, the hero achieved. He
went down into the underworld by a passage that opened
into the earth (as mentioned above, Ch. III. p. 53) on
Taenarum, the rocky promontory in which the southernmost projection of the Peloponnese ends. He made his
way into the presence of Hades and Persephone, and from
them received permission to carry off Cerberus if he could,
but on condition that he used no weapon against him.
Heracles took the three-headed brute in his arms and
squeezed his throat till he lay quiet, but was himself
bitten by the serpent which served the monster for a
tail. However, in the end he carried Cerberus successfully up to earth, showed him in Eurystheus' palace, to
the terror of Eurystheus and the wonder of all beholders,
and brought him safely back to Hell.

Many other stories are told of Heracles, not all of them

profitable to tell ; for some of the acts attributed to him are violent and cruel. But through them all he fulfils in the main " the archaic conception of the hero's mission . . . he is purger of land and sea, the common benefactor of the Hellenes, who goes uncomplainingly whithersoever his fate leads him. Conscious of his origin, he fears no foe, and is stronger than everything except his own passions." [1]

The hero's death was as extraordinary as his life. His wife, Deianeira, fearing she had lost his love, sent him a magic garment smeared with the blood of Nessus, the Centaur,[2] whom Heracles had killed and who in dying had assured Deianeira that if ever her husband's love strayed from her, this charm would bring it back. But when Heracles put on the robe and the poison began to work, it ate into his flesh and drove him wild with torment. Unable to tear off the robe, or to find relief or cure, Heracles caused a lofty funeral pyre to be built on Mount Oeta, climbed to the top and lay down. The pyre was then lighted by his orders and Heracles passed from earth in the flames. But only the mortal part of him, men believed, was thus consumed : there was a divine Heracles whom Zeus raised to Olympus and married to Hebe.

Heracles was the national hero of Greece : he is the perfect " type of physical force, of dauntless effort and endurance, of militant civilization and of Hellenic enterprise." [3] " Ethically Heracles symbolizes the attainment of glory and immortality by toil and suffering." [4] This view of him is skilfully brought out in *Balaustion's Adventure*, Browning's version of Euripides' *Alcestis*.

Theseus.—Theseus, the hero of Athenian story, is in some respects a higher character than Heracles. Though not invincible, nor the equal of Heracles in bodily strength,

---

[1] Jebb, *Introduction to the Trachiniae of Sophocles*, p. xxxvi.

[2] Centaurs were mythical beings like horses with the heads and arms and bodies of men from the waist rising out of their necks. The fight between the Centaurs and Lapithae was a favourite subject of sculpture.

[3] Fennell in the *Encyclopaedia Britannica*.

[4] Jebb, *l.c.* p. xxxv.

he displays qualities not found in the legends of Heracles, intellectual power, ability to govern and political foresight. He is the statesman who made the greatness of Athens possible, by drawing the scattered townships of Attica into the unity of one strong city-state sheltered by the walls of Athens. Plutarch wrote a life of Theseus from this point of view and compared him with Romulus, founder of Rome. This is the Theseus of legendary history. There is also a Theseus of pure legend, of whose achievements stories very like those about Heracles were current. Theseus too is the champion of human kind, who rids the countryside of dangerous beasts and the highway of evil men. He was the son of Aegeus, king of Athens, but born at Troezen in Argolis, and brought up there by his mother Aethra, the king's daughter. When he reached manhood Aethra sent him to Athens to make himself known to his father by means of tokens which Aegeus had left with her for this purpose. The journey from Troezen to Athens is first through Epidaurus to the Isthmus of Corinth, and then through Megara and Eleusis by the coast road along which the traveller can pass to-day. This road was at the time beset by ruffians who ill-treated and murdered travellers, and Theseus deliberately chose to go this way rather than by sea in order to free the highway of these pests. His achievements on this journey are conveniently summed up for us by a writer of Julius Caesar's time, Diodorus the Sicilian, as follows :

" First, therefore, he killed Corynetes, who used to carry a club called Coryne, which he used as defensive arms, and with the same weapon knocked all passengers and travellers on the head.

" Then next he slew Scinis, who haunted the isthmus, and used to bend two pine-trees, one to meet another and bind one arm to one of the trees, and another to the other, of such as he took passing that way ; and when he had done, then to let them spring up on a sudden, which by their force and violence so rent in pieces the bodies of the poor miserable creatures, that they died in most horrid pain and torment.

"The third thing remarkable that he did, was the killing the Krommyonian sow, a most vast and fierce creature, which destroyed many.

"The fourth was the killing of Sciron who lay lurking amongst the rocks : his manner was that he would force passengers to wash his feet, and then kick them down headlong into the sea, near Chelone.

"Next he slew Cercyon at Eleusis, who killed all that he overcame in wrestling.

"Afterwards he killed one Procrustes, who resided in Corydallus in Attica : his custom was to force all that passed that way to lie down upon a bed, and if they were longer than it, to cut off so much of their legs as reached beyond the bed ; if they were shorter, then he racked and stretched out their limbs, till they reached the full length ; thence he was named Procrustes." [1]

When Theseus reached Athens he found the city in mournful commotion because seven noble youths and as many noble maidens were about to sail for Crete, there to be devoured by the Minotaur, a monster half bull, half man, who was kept confined in a mysterious structure known as the Labyrinth. This cruel sacrifice had been exacted by Minos, the monarch in whose reign Crete was mistress of the seas, as a tribute to be paid every tenth year in expiation of the death of his son, Androgeos, in Attic territory. Theseus made himself known to his father, then offered to go to Crete in place of one of the youths. His purpose was to slay the Minotaur and deliver Athens from the tribute. The enterprise seemed hopeless enough ; for the seven youths must go to Crete without weapons, and the Labyrinth in which they were shut up with the Minotaur was a maze of apartments and passages, and a captive once within it had little chance of finding his way out again unaided. Aegeus, who was overjoyed at the restoration of his son, consented with difficulty to this parting. It was agreed between them that if Theseus was successful and lived

---

[1] Diodorus Siculus, iv. ch. 4. Hence the adjective Procrustean, meaning ' forcing an unnatural uniformity by violent means.'

to come back, the ship in which the victims sailed should return with the black sails, which were used in sign of mourning, changed to white. Fortune favoured Theseus in an unexpected manner. When he reached Knossos, the capital of Crete in those days, Ariadne, the king's daughter, pitying his youth and manly beauty, secretly furnished him with a sword and a skein of thread. The thread Theseus unwound as he groped and turned among the passages of the labyrinth ; and when he came upon the Minotaur he slew him with the sword. Then by means of the thread he found his way back to the entrance from which he had started. Theseus sailed back victorious with the companions he had rescued, and with him sailed the princess Ariadne, whose love had saved him. But when they reached the island of Naxos and landed there, Theseus ungratefully stole away leaving Ariadne deserted. This ingratitude brought its retribution. For when the ship neared Athens Theseus forgot to hoist the white sail as he had promised, and Aegeus, who was anxiously watching for his son's return, seeing the sail was black not white, threw himself from the cliffs into the sea. And to this day the Aegean bears his name. Thus Theseus' triumphant return was changed to mourning.

Prometheus.—There is another heroic figure in Greek mythology, of one who dared and suffered for humanity —a god, not a man, Prometheus. When Zeus on his accession to power, in scorn of men's feebleness, was minded to extinguish the whole human race, Prometheus took pity on them, and endowing them with the gift of fire, which he brought to them from heaven in the hollow of a reed, made it possible for them, not only to survive, but to discover one by one the arts which improve man's lot on earth. For civilization has its beginning in the discovery of the uses of fire. Zeus, furious at this crossing of his will, and to punish Prometheus for what he regarded as the theft of fire from heaven, had him fastened by iron fetters to a rock upon a mountain on the distant borders of earth and ocean. There Prometheus remained in torment through long ages, till in accordance with prophecy he was released by Heracles. Such is this Greek myth, strange as it is to reconcile with the rest of Greek theology.

A work of the poet Aeschylus of which this binding of Prometheus is the subject is the most sublime drama in Greek tragedy. The English poet, Shelley, has written a *Prometheus Unbound*, which, though the work of a different kind of imaginative genius, has a beauty not inferior to Aeschylus' play. In Mr. Edwyn Bevan's translation of Aeschylus' tragedy, Prometheus cries :

> " O wretched,
> Entrammell'd in this web of agony,
> For that I gave good things to men ! I track
> Home to its hidden spring the flowing of fire,
> By stealth infringe it, drawing what doth charge
> A reed : the thing, reveal'd to man is mighty,
> Teacher of every art, the main of life,
> And lo, I have sinn'd !—and pay the forfeit so,
> A gazing-stock beneath untemper'd heaven."

Shelley concludes his *Prometheus* with these lines :

> " To suffer woes which Hope thinks infinite ;
> To forgive wrongs darker than death or night ;
> To defy power which seems omnipotent ;
> To love and bear ; to hope till hope creates
> From its own wreck the thing it contemplates ;
> Neither to change, nor falter, nor repent ;
> This, like thy glory, Titan, is to be
> Good, great and joyous, beautiful and free ;
> This is alone life, joy, empire and victory."

Religion and Conduct.—What, we may ask in conclusion, was the value of Hellenic religion as a guide to life. Religion is grounded in a sense of dependence, in a perception that man's life is set in the midst of forces and influences far mightier than he is, on which his well-being and suffering of ill depend. Then by a natural process he comes to think of these forces as personal and imagines beings like himself who have power over him. He begins by thinking of them merely as powers, often as evil and malignant powers, whom it is his interest to propitiate and satisfy. He comes later to think of them

as beneficent, as just and good and requiring righteousness from their worshippers. On the relation of these
two elements, the idea of power and the idea of goodness,
the value of a religion for conduct depends. For man
regarded as a moral being it does not matter how great
is the power attributed to God ; what matters is whether
God is conceived as good and as loving righteousness and
justice. The most important aspect of the ancient Greek,
as of other religions, is how it affected conduct. Now
many of the Greek divinities, as we have seen, are neither
good nor evil, but merely powers in certain spheres of
human interests, or aspects of the physical world. Such
are Poseidon, Ares and Hephaestus, Aphrodite and
Dionysus. To others moral ideas are certainly attached,
indirectly and incidentally as to Hestia, Artemis, Demeter,
Hades ; and directly as to Pallas Athena, Apollo, and,
above all, to Zeus, the ruler of the universe. The influence of the Greek religion on conduct was, we must admit,
somewhat uncertain and capricious. It cannot be said
that the whole weight of the Olympian deities was on
the side of virtue and justice. Some of the stories about
the gods were, as we have seen, distinctly immoral in
tendency. The cult of some deities, as of Dionysus and
Aphrodite, contained immoral elements ; and even
Hermes, so far as rogues might look to him for protection.
Yet, on the whole, we may say that the influence of the
Hellenic religious system was on the side of righteousness ; the prevailing popular view was that the gods
loved justice, favoured the good, and visited evil-doers
with punishment. We may go further than that, and
say that the worship of certain deities tended to introduce
higher moral conceptions ; we can trace the process of
a strengthening and refining of moral ideas in historical
times. The influence of poets and thinkers tended to
bring out more definitely the moral aspect of these deities,
and these higher conceptions of the deity in turn affected
ordinary opinion and conduct. It was thus that " Athena
became the type of a temperate and self-restrained disposition, of resolute bearing in the conflicts of life ; Apollo

the divine pattern of purity and elevation ; Heracles of persistent labour voluntarily undertaken in troubles and difficulties, of subordination and self-denial, of unshaken courage which does not flinch even before the terrors of the under-world." ¹   Above all, Zeus came to be thought of not merely as the highest in rank and strongest of the gods, but as the wise and just ruler of the universe, who, because he loves righteousness and hates iniquity, will surely bring to judgment those who work wickedness and exercise oppression.   " Listen to right and do not foster violence," exhorts Hesiod in the *Works and Days*.   " The better path is to go by on the other side towards justice ; for Justice beats Outrage when she comes at length to the end of the race." ²   " They who give straight judgments to strangers and to the men of the land, and go not aside from what is just, their city flourishes, and the people prosper in it. . . .   But for those who practise violence and cruel deeds far-seeing Zeus, the son of Cronos, ordains a punishment." ³   Heaven and all its powers are on the side of righteousness is, in fine, the faith he expresses : " for the deathless gods are near among men and mark all those who oppress their fellows with crooked judgments, and reck not the anger of the gods. For upon the bounteous earth Zeus has thrice ten thousand spirits, watchers of mortal men, and these keep watch on judgments and deeds of wrong as they roam, clothed in mist, all over the earth." ⁴

There is one other aspect of Greek religion which claims special notice, because it is peculiarly characteristic of the Greeks and has practical value for us to-day.   This is the association of religion with science, through the worship of Apollo and the Muses.   We owe to the Greeks the very conception of the Muses.   There are no divinities at all closely like them in any other religion.   They are, as we have noted (III. p. 58), a sort of deification of the

¹ Duncker, *History of Greece*, vol. ii. p. 216.
² Hesiod, *Works and Days*, ll. 213 and 216-218.
³ Hesiod, *Ib.* ll. 225-239.
⁴ Hesiod, *Ib.* ll. 249-255.

powers of mind, but they became very real persons to Greek imagination. They began as divinities of music and poetry, of the song and the dance ; but their sphere of inspiration became very much extended so as to include the whole world of art and intellect, as the modern meaning of Museum shows. The earliest ' Mouseia ' were places of education and lead on to the modern university. " The Muses are unique figures among the various ancient or modern systems of polytheism ; and though the popular faith in them may not have been very deep, or always real, they bear valuable witness, no less than Apollo, to this special religious gain of Hellenism." [1] " The study of this ' minor ' cult," says Dr. Farnell, " may serve to deepen our impression of the immense debt that modern education and culture owes to a religion like that of Hellas, which gave to the arts and sciences a stronger and more direct encouragement than any other religion in the world has ever given." [2]

Still more clearly Apollo was the inspiration of the artist, so that every work of art, great and small, had a religious value. It was an act of worship. So, too, with the investigation of truth by the thinker and the man of science. It was consecrate to Apollo because Apollo was the revealer, the god of light and truth. This is the unique achievement of the Apolline cult " that through it, more than any other ancient worship, the intellectual life and the work of the thinker and the artist were consecrated to God." [3]

[1] Farnell, *Cults of the Greek States*, vol. v. p. 437.
[2] Farnell, vol. v. pp. 436, 7.
[3] Farnell, vol. iv. p. 252.

CHAPTER V

THE TALE OF TROY

"To forget Homer, to cease to be concerned or even curious about Homer, is to make a fatal step towards a new barbarism."

Andrew Lang, *Homer and the Epic*, p. 2.

HELEN, daughter of Tyndareus and Leda, and sister of Castor and Pollux, was the most beautiful of mortal women. So wonderful was her beauty that men said she was not really the daughter of Tyndareus, but of Zeus. As she grew to womanhood all the foremost chieftains of the Achaeans (as the Greeks were in those days called) sought her in marriage, and the rivalry was so fierce that her father Tyndareus, fearing what might happen when he made choice among them, bound each of them severally by an oath, not only himself to refrain from violence against the husband chosen for her, but also to protect Helen from violence attempted by any other. He then married her to Menelaus, king of Sparta, whom Helen herself preferred. This Menelaus was brother to Agamemnon, the wealthiest and most powerful of the Achaean princes, who reigned at Mycenae in a fortress palace commanding the highway from the plains of Argolis through the mountains to Northern Greece. Helen was happy in her marriage, and a daughter was born to her and Menelaus whom they named Hermione. Then on a fatal day there came to Sparta a brilliant young stranger, named Paris. He was eldest son of Priam, the wealthy king of Troy, beautiful in person and able to dazzle the eyes of the queen and court at Sparta by the display of his riches. He had undertaken the voyage to Sparta because of the fame of Helen's beauty and with the base design of stealing her away in violation of the laws of hospitality. It happened that Menelaus was called away to Crete soon after Paris' arrival, and, fearing no evil, he left Helen to entertain his guest. Paris repaid his host's trust by using this opportunity to carry out his evil purpose, whether by force or guile is uncertain to this day. At any rate Paris sailed back to Troy with Helen on board his ship, and much wealth beside that was rightfully Menelaus' property.[1]

When this treacherous abduction of Helen was made known, there was hot indignation among the Achaean chieftains and princes. Agamemnon took up his brother's quarrel and reminded the other princes of their oath to Tyndareus. It was resolved to gather a great expedition and sail to Troy to demand the restoration of Helen, and, if the Trojans refused to give her up, to make war upon them and destroy their city. Aulis in Boeotia, a harbour a little south of the Euripus, the narrow channel between Euboea and the mainland, was appointed as the place of meeting. There nearly 1200 ships assembled in course of time, each manned by from fifty to a hundred and twenty warriors. Agamemnon was commander-in-chief, and with him were many famous chieftains, each a ruling prince in his own land. Of these the most renowned were Ajax, son of Telamon, from Salamis, Odysseus from Ithaca, Nestor of Pylus, a second and less famous Ajax, son of Oileus, from Locris, Diomedes, son of Tydeus, from Argos, Idomeneus of Crete, Palamedes, Philoctetes, and

[1] Greek fancy sought to explain the crime which provoked the Trojan War by the story of the Judgment of Paris. Hera, Athena and Aphrodite, each claimed the golden apple inscribed ' For the fairest,' which Eris (Strife) flung among the guests at the marriage feast of Peleus and Thetis. Paris was chosen to judge between the three goddesses. Hera tried to bribe him with the promise of sovereign power, Athena offered valour and wisdom, Aphrodite promised ' the fairest wife in Greece ' ; and Paris awarded the apple to Aphrodite. In fulfilment of her promise Aphrodite helped Paris to carry off Helen, while Hera and Athena became the bitter enemies of Troy. Tennyson's poem *Oenone* gives a modern version of this story.

above all Achilles, prince of the Myrmidons in Thessaly, along with Patroclus his foster-brother and friend.

The Story of Iphigeneia.—While waiting at Aulis for the gathering of the host to be completed, Agamemnon had recklessly shot down a stag in a grove sacred to Artemis. To punish this sacrilege Artemis sent adverse winds, which held back the sailing of the fleet. Calchas the prophet, when bidden to reveal the cause of this delay, made known the king's transgression and declared that, in order to appease the anger of the goddess and set free the armament, Agamemnon must offer his dearly loved daughter, Iphigeneia, in sacrifice. Agamemnon was horrified and at first refused. But he was hard put to it by the growing impatience in the Greek fleet, and at last reluctantly consented. Iphigeneia was taken from her mother Clytaemnestra under pretence of marrying her to Achilles and brought to Aulis; and there the horrid sacrifice was carried out.[1] But because this tale was too pitiful, men altered it and came to believe that at the last moment, when with uplifted knife the priest stood over his victim, Artemis herself intervened and substituted a hind for the maiden (as the ram was substituted for Isaac), and carried Iphigeneia herself away to the land once called the Tauric Chersonese and now the Crimea. However this may have been, the bereaved mother, Clytaemnestra, never forgave the deception practised on her by Agamemnon, and when,

---

[1] Lucretius, in the opening of his great poem *On Nature*, pictures the scene: "Soon as the fillet encircling her maiden tresses shed itself in equal lengths adown each cheek, and soon as she saw her father standing sorrowful before the altars and beside him the ministering priests hiding the knife and her countrymen at sight of her shedding tears, speechless in terror she dropped down on her knees and sank to the ground." (Munro's translation of Book I., ll. 87-92.)

In Tennyson's *Dream of Fair Women* Iphigeneia is made to say:

> " Dimly I could descry
> The stern black-bearded kings with wolfish eyes,
> Waiting to see me die.
> The high masts flicker'd as they lay afloat;
> The crowds, the temples, waver'd, and the shore;
> The bright death quiver'd at the victim's throat;
> Touch'd ; and I knew no more."

ten years later, her husband came home, exacted a terrible
vengeance.   (See below, p. 104.)

Landing in the Troad.—The grand fleet of the Greeks
now pursued its way to the Trojan land across the Aegean
Sea from island to island till they came to Tenedos.
Thence Menelaus and Odysseus were sent to Troy to
demand the restoration of Helen and surrender of the
stolen treasure.   One Trojan, Antenor, urged the wisdom
and justice of compliance ; but he was not listened to.
The demands were rejected.   Then the Greek fleet sailed
on to the Troad, which forms the north-west corner of
Asia Minor, at the very entrance of the Dardanelles.   The
Trojans had summoned to their assistance their Asiatic
neighbours, Mysians and Lycians and Phrygians and
Paphlagonians, as well as warlike tribesmen from the
opposite coast of Thrace (Turkey in Europe), and with
these allies endeavoured to oppose the landing.   In the
battle which followed, the Trojans were defeated and
driven within their walls.   The Greeks drew up their ships
along the shore and encamped by contingents.   But these
Achaean Greeks, though great fighters with spear and
shield, had small skill in attacking fortifications, and,
despite their command of the Trojan plain, they made no
progress towards the capture of Troy.   So from their
bivouac they conducted a series of expeditions by land
and by sea, in which they sacked many lesser cities and
took much booty.   The most daring and successful of their
leaders in these raids was Achilles, prince of the Myrmidons, renowned above all the other heroes for his
prowess.   Among the cities that Achilles sacked was
Thebe, the city of Eëtion, father of Andromache, Hector's
wife.   Hector was the bravest champion on the Trojan
side and the soul of the defence.   The Greeks believed
that this desultory warfare—it could hardly be called a
siege—went on for nine years ; and in the tenth year the
aims of the Greek host were almost completely defeated
through a quarrel between Achilles and Agamemnon.
This quarrel and all that came in its train is the subject
of Homer's *Iliad*, the world's greatest epic poem.

The Wrath of Achilles.—The quarrel arose in this way. After one of the Greek raids a captive maiden, Briseis, or daughter of Brises, had been given as a prize to Achilles, and Achilles had learned to love her well. To Agamemnon another fair captive had been assigned called Chryseis. Now Chryses, the father of Chryseis, was priest of Apollo, and he came to the Achaeans and offered a large ransom for his daughter's release. But Agamemnon refused Chryses' petition with roughness, and the priest in his distress prayed to Apollo ; and in answer Apollo smote the Greek host with a plague which slew mules and dogs and men. When this pestilence had lasted for nine days Achilles induced Agamemnon to call a council of chiefs, and appeal was made to the prophet Calchas to reveal the cause of the plague and how it might be stayed. Calchas made Achilles promise him protection before he would speak out, and then declared the pestilence to be due to Agamemnon's harsh repulse of Chryses ; atonement could be made, and made only, by the restoration of Chryseis and by sacrifices in expiation of the insult to Apollo's priest. Agamemnon had no choice but to give up Chryseis and make atonement as Calchas directed ; for he would have had the whole army against him had he refused ; but he was very angry and violently declared that compensation for the loss of Chryseis must be made to him. When, thereupon, Achilles reproached him with covetousness, he lost all self-control and rashly vowed that the compensation he would have should be Achilles' Briseis, even if he must himself go to Achilles' tents to fetch her. Now Achilles was the last man in the Achaean host on whom a monarch's arrogance could be safely tried. In a moment his hand was on his sword and he half drew it from its sheath with intention to strike Agamemnon dead. But the goddess Athena, who loved both Agamemnon and Achilles, stood behind him and laid upon him a restraining hand. Achilles turned and recognized Athena, though she was invisible to all the rest. Obedient to her admonition he thrust back the sword into the scabbard, but in scornful words he denounced

Agamemnon's high-handedness and swore a great oath that the king and all the host of the Achaeans should rue this ingratitude. When in accordance with the prophet's word Chryseis went back to her father, Agamemnon, as he had threatened, sent and took away Briseis. Achilles made no resistance ; but his resolve was taken. He would fight no more.

The Promise to Thetis.—Now Achilles had a goddess for his mother, Thetis, daughter of the sea-god Nereus : she had been given in marriage to Peleus, the Thessalian hero (and not to one of the immortals), through fear of a prophecy concerning the son that should be born to her. When Achilles grew up he was offered the choice of a long inglorious life, or a short life and great glory : and he had chosen glory at the price of early death. And now chafing under the wrong put upon him by Agamemnon and the inactivity to which he was condemned by his oath, he prayed to his mother, Thetis, reminding her how short his life was to be and begging her to take care that he did not lose the promised meed of glory. Thetis tried her best to comfort him, and undertook to obtain from Zeus a promise that without Achilles the Achaeans should be discomfited and brought low, and Achilles' glory be made to shine the brighter. And Zeus, when Thetis made her supplication, promised all that she asked.

Gods and Men in the Trojan War.—Now this promise of Zeus to Thetis inevitably brought his will into conflict with others of the Olympian gods who favoured the Greek cause. For the heavenly powers were keenly interested in the fate of Troy. Hera and Athena, in particular, were implacable enemies of Troy because of the judgment of Paris. Aphrodite was as decidedly on the side of the Trojans ; and with her was her lover, Ares, god of war. Apollo generally favoured the Trojans ; and Poseidon, who had an ancient grudge against the family of Priam, was for the Greeks. These deities are represented by the poet as ardently favouring the champions on either side, and sometimes as actually descending on to the plain of Troy to take part in the fighting. Zeus for a time laid strict command on all of them to abstain from active partizanship, but this order was evaded in various ways, and throughout the *Iliad* the gods take a forward part in swaying the fortunes of battle. In the end Troy's destiny must be fulfilled : meantime Zeus holds Hera, Athena and Poseidon in check till his promise to Thetis is redeemed and the Greeks are made by defeat and humiliation to learn the value of Achilles. This end attained, destiny resumes its course, and the fates of Hector and of Troy are sealed. But for a time it was decreed that for the greater glory of Achilles Hector should triumph.

Renewal of War : the Duel of Paris and Menelaus.— That night Agamemnon dreamt that the aged warrior, Nestor, stood by his bed and declared to him that the time had come when by the will of Zeus Troy should fall to his victorious arms. The dream was sent to delude him, but Agamemnon, believing it a divine assurance of victory, hastened next day to call a council of war, and, thereafter, set his whole host in array, contingent by contingent, for a great and final attack on Troy. And this time the Trojans accepted the challenge : for already they knew by report that they had no longer to reckon with Achilles ; and they poured forth from the city to do battle with the Greeks in the open plain. But just as the armies were closing in fight, Hector stepped forward, waved his spear and called a parley. He had obtained from Paris an offer to meet Menelaus in single combat for the possession of Helen and the treasure. Two heralds were despatched in haste to summon Priam. Now Priam was seated with the Elders of Troy hard by the Scaean Gates, on the ramparts of the Great Tower of Ilios, whence it was the custom of the women of Troy and the old men whose fighting days were past, to watch the conflict in the plain. And Helen also came thither, moved by a divine presentiment. And the Elders of Troy saw her coming and whispered one to another : " Small blame is it that Trojans and well-greaved Achaeans should for such a woman long time suffer hardships ; marvellously like is she to the immortal goddesses to look upon. Yet even so, though she be so goodly, let her go upon the ships and not stay to vex us and our children after us." [1] Now when Priam saw Helen he called her to him and with kind words made request that she would tell him the names of some of the Greek chieftains. Then came the heralds and delivered their message : and Priam drove off through the Scaean Gates, and came where Agamemnon and Hector were holding parley, and there solemn compact was made between the Greeks and Trojans to decide the whole issue of the war by this duel. In the combat which followed Paris was worsted and would have been made prisoner had not his helmet strap broken as he was being dragged away headforemost, and left the empty casque in Menelaus' hands, while Aphrodite by supernatural means spirited Paris himself safe back into Troy. But when Agamemnon, king of men (as Homer calls him), demanded the fulfilment of the compact and the surrender of Helen, an arrow sped from the bow of a Trojan named Pandarus and wounded Menelaus. After this treacherous breach of the agreement all was uproar and confusion, and soon the two hosts were locked in conflict.

Hector's Farewell.—Long time the battle swayed this way and that with no great advantage to either side. But presently the Trojans began to give way before the determined onset of the Achaeans, and to hearten them Hector went back into Troy and bade Hecuba and the Trojan women make solemn intercession to Athena. Before he returned to the battle-field Hector was fain to visit his home and speak with his wife, Andromache. Andromache was not in the house, for she too had gone to the Great Tower to hear news of the fight. Disappointed he turned back by the way he had come and was about to pass out by the Scaean Gates, when he saw Andromache hastening to meet him. That meeting, destined to be their last, shall be told as Homer tells it in the words of Dr. Leaf's translation :

" So she met him now, and with her went the handmaid bearing in her bosom the tender boy, the little child,

[1] *Iliad*, iii. ll. 156-160 (Lang, Leaf and Myers, p. 54).

Hector's loved son, like unto a beautiful star. Him Hector called Skamandrios, but all the folk Astyanax;[1] for only Hector guarded Ilios. So now he smiled, and gazed at his boy silently, and Andromache stood by his side weeping, and clasped her hand in his, and spake and called upon his name.

"'Dear my lord, this thy hardihood will undo thee, neither hast thou any pity for thine infant boy, nor for me forlorn that soon shall be thy widow; for soon will the Achaians all set upon thee and slay thee. But it were better for me to go down to the grave if I lose thee; for never more will any comfort be mine, when once thou, even thou, hast met thy fate, but only sorrow. Moreover I have no father nor lady mother: my father was slain of goodly Achilles, for he wasted the populous city of the Kilikians, even high-gated Thebe, and slew Eëtion; yet he despoiled him not, for his soul had shame of that, but he burnt him in his inlaid armour and raised a barrow over him; and all about were elm-trees planted by the mountain nymphs, daughters of aegis-bearing Zeus. And the seven brothers that were mine within our halls, all these on the selfsame day went within the house of Hades; for fleet-footed goodly Achilles slew them all amid their kine of trailing gait and white-fleeced sheep. And my mother, that was queen beneath wooded Plakos, her brought he hither with the other spoils, but afterward took a ransom untold to set her free; but in her father's halls was she smitten by the Archer Artemis. Nay, Hector, thou art to me father and lady mother, yea and brother, even as thou art my goodly husband. Come now, have pity and abide here upon the tower, lest thou make thy child an orphan and thy wife a widow . . . .'

"Then great Hector of the glancing helm answered her: 'Surely I take thought for all these things, my wife; but I have very sore shame of the Trojans and Trojan dames with trailing robes, if like a coward I shrink away from battle. Moreover mine own soul forbiddeth me, seeing I have learnt ever to be valiant and fight in the forefront

[1] The name means 'City King.''

of the Trojans, winning my father's great glory and mine own. Yea of a surety I know this in heart and soul; the day shall come for holy Ilios to be laid low, and Priam and the folk of Priam of the good ashen spear. Yet doth the anguish of the Trojans hereafter not so much trouble me, neither Hekabe's own, neither king Priam's, neither my brethren's, the many and brave that shall fall in the dust before their foemen, as doth thine anguish in the day when some mail-clad Achaian shall lead thee weeping and rob thee of the light of freedom. So shalt thou abide in Argos and ply the loom at another woman's bidding, and bear water from fount Messeis or Hypereia, being grievously entreated, and sore constraint shall be laid upon thee. And then shall one say that beholdeth thee weep: "This is the wife of Hector, that was foremost in battle of the horse-taming Trojans when men fought about Ilios." Thus shall one say hereafter, and fresh grief will be thine for lack of such an husband as thou hadst to ward off the day of thraldom. But me in death may the heaped-up earth be covering, ere I hear thy crying and thy carrying into captivity.'

"So spake glorious Hector, and stretched out his arm to his boy. But the child shrunk crying to the bosom of his fair-girdled nurse, dismayed at his dear father's aspect, and in dread at the bronze and horse-hair crest that he beheld nodding fiercely from the helmet's top. Then his dear father laughed aloud, and his lady mother; forthwith glorious Hector took the helmet from his head and laid it, all gleaming, upon the earth; then kissed he his dear son and dandled him in his arms, and spake in prayer to Zeus and all the gods, 'O Zeus and all ye gods, vouchsafe ye that this my son may likewise prove even as I, pre-eminent amid the Trojans, and as valiant in might, and be a great king of Ilios. Then may men say of him, "Far greater is he than his father" as he returneth home from battle; and may he bring with him blood-stained spoils from the foeman he hath slain, and may his mother's heart be glad.'

"So spake he, and laid his son in his dear wife's arms;

and she took him to her fragrant bosom, smiling tear-
fully. And her husband had pity to see her, and caressed
her with his hand, and spake and called upon her name :
' Dear one, I pray thee be not of over-sorrowful heart ;
no man against my fate shall hurl me to Hades ; only
destiny, I ween, no man hath escaped, be he coward or
be he valiant, when once he hath been born. But go
thou to thine house and see to thine own tasks, the loom
and distaff, and bid thine handmaidens ply their work ;
but for war shall men provide, and I in chief of all men
that dwell in Ilios.'

" So spake glorious Hector, and took up his horse-hair
crested helmet ; and his dear wife departed to her home,
oft looking back, and letting fall big tears." [1]

Rout of the Achaeans.—This parting over, Hector
straightway rejoined the fray, and led his Trojans
with such success that now the Greeks were routed
and chased across the plain and forced to take refuge
behind the defences which they had built to protect their
ships. For by reason of the defection of Achilles, the
Achaean leaders were less confident of their superiority
in the field, and they had built in all haste a wall with
high towers and strong gates to defend the space along
the shore on which they were encamped and where their
ships were beached several rows deep. And in front of
the ramparts was a broad trench strengthened by a
spiked palisade. When night came the Achaeans were
all cooped up within their wall and the Trojans instead
of withdrawing to the city bivouacked in the open plain.
Hector's hopes rose high of driving the hated enemy into
the sea, and by his orders the plain was lit up with
numerous camp-fires lest the ships should put to sea and
escape under cover of darkness. So disastrous to the
Achaeans was the difference made by Achilles' absence.

The Attempt at Reconciliation with Achilles.—Agamemnon was already so dispirited by this defeat that in
a war-council held that night he actually proposed an

[1] *Iliad*, vi. ll. 399-493 (Lang, Leaf and Myers, pp. 123-126).

abandonment of the whole enterprise and ignominious
flight. But the other chieftains, and especially Diomedes,
cried shame upon him. They urged instead that an
attempt should be made to appease Achilles' resentment
and bring him back into the fight. Accordingly Ajax
and Odysseus were sent as mediators to Achilles to offer
on Agamemnon's behalf full reparation, the restoration of
Briseis and ample gifts beside. Achilles received his
friends with all courtesy, but utterly refused to go back
from the oath he had sworn not to fight again till the
fleet was threatened with fire and his own ships in danger.
So the envoys returned baffled. The night was one of
restlessness and suspense on both sides. One story tells
how Diomedes and Odysseus stole out from the Greek lines
on a reconnaissance and by chance fell in with Dolon,
a Trojan warrior who had set forth on a similar errand
for his side. Him Odysseus and Diomedes took prisoner
and slew ; but before he was slain Odysseus craftily drew
from him information which enabled them to surprise and
kill a party of Thracian auxiliaries lately arrived and
encamped apart, and to make prize of the horses of
Rhesus their chief.

The Fight for the Ships.—Next day the struggle was
renewed at dawn, and in spite of their overnight discomfiture the Greeks fought well. After an obstinate
contest on equal terms Agamemnon with great spirit
headed a charge, and for a time spread slaughter before
him. But in the full tide of his success he is wounded
and compelled to withdraw from the field. Odysseus and
Diomedes rally their men against Hector's counter-charge
till both are wounded; Diomedes by an arrow shot by
Paris from the safe cover of a grave-stone that stood on
the battle-field, Odysseus by a lance-thrust. Fortune
now turns decisively against the Greeks. Machaon, so
valued in the host for his skill in healing, is wounded ;
and Eurypylus, Patroclus' friend. By degrees the
Achaeans are borne back (such is the will of Zeus), and
at length are driven once more to take refuge behind their
defences. Here, however, the Trojans were held in check

by the broad trench and the bristling stakes of the palisade. It was impossible to storm across in their chariots ; but on the advice of Hector's brother, Polydamas, the Trojan chivalry dismounted and boldly assailed the palisade on foot. A stubborn struggle ensued : for the rampart was strongly built and the Greeks knew well what was at stake. Missiles fell in showers, and many men were wounded on either side. The Trojans made furious efforts to tear down the defences ; the Greeks with locked shields closed their ranks to keep them off. Sarpedon, the Lycian prince, was first to make a breach : next Hector swung a huge stone with all his strength and burst open the main gate. Then the Trojans swarmed in. Yet even so the day was not won. A stand was made at the call of the two Ajaces, the Greater and the Less : Teucer and Idomeneus and Menelaus gallantly maintained the fight ; and a determined charge drove the Trojans back across the ditch. Only for a time, however. Hector in turn rallied the Trojans : once more the attack swept over the defences, and pressing on the Trojans fought their way right up to the first line of ships.

Patroclus to the Rescue.—Hard by the ships the fighting grew more furious than ever. The Trojans were inspired with the thought of their enemies' utter destruction ; the Greeks made desperate resistance, because all hope of escape was lost, if they could not keep the Trojans from their ships. For a time it looked as if Hector's utmost expectations were to be realized and the Greek fleet burned. Hector himself laid hold of the ship nearest to him—it was the ship in which Protesilaus had sailed to Troy— Protesilaus, who by gallantly leaping first on shore, had given his life for his countrymen's victory—and called for fire. Ajax alone of the Greeks sustained a stubborn defence, leaping from one vessel to another a long boarding-pike in his hands, and exhorting his men to save the ships. But even Ajax was presently overborne and forced to take shelter behind the bulwarks. Yet from this position he continued to strike down every Trojan who came within reach of his pike, till Hector with a sword-stroke sheared off its head. Then, all defence being at an end, the Trojans with their firebrands closed in on the ship and soon the stern was ablaze and the flames rose to the sky. When things had come to this desperate pass for the Greeks, help came to them in an unexpected way. Suddenly from the end of the lines where the Myrmidons were camped, there swept down a troop of fresh warriors, with a leader at their head whom the Trojans took to be Achilles. For all knew the fashion of Achilles' armour. This sight at once sent a thrill of dismay through the Trojan ranks, and though they turned to face the attack, they gave ground when the shock came. It was not, however, Achilles himself who was heading the charge, but Achilles' dear friend, Patroclus, clad in Achilles' armour. For Patroclus had followed the reverses to the Greek arms with increasing anxiety. He had never approved Achilles' implacability, and he was watching eagerly for an opportunity to bring him back into the fight. When he finds his friend, Eurypylus, among the wounded and learns how all the bravest and best of the Greeks are stricken and out of the fight, he goes to Achilles, his eyes streaming with tears, and begs that if Achilles cannot himself go to his countrymen's assistance because of his oath, at least he will lend his armour in order that he, Patroclus, may succour them in Achilles' likeness. To this appeal Achilles had listened and had sent his friend into the battle arrayed in his own armour. At first Patroclus carried all before him. He drove the Trojans from the ships, and back across the trench, and slew in single combat the noble Lycian prince, Sarpedon. A fierce struggle arose over Sarpedon's body, the Greeks endeavouring to carry it off, the Trojans to recover it.

Death of Patroclus.—This brings Hector into the mêlée, in the course of which Patroclus is first wounded by a Trojan named Euphorbus, then falls transfixed by Hector's spear. Menelaus, seeing Patroclus sink to the ground rushes up through the thick of the fight to attempt a

rescue, but knowing himself no match for Hector singly,
draws off to seek support. Then Hector strips off the
armour which Patroclus was wearing, the armour of
Achilles, and begins to drag the body away. Menelaus,
however, comes up again along with Ajax, and Hector
must perforce let go his prize. Whereupon Ajax steps
forward and throws in front of dead Patroclus his great
seven-fold shield, that no warrior but he can wield ;
Menelaus and Meriones together lift up the body and
begin a slow retreat, while Ajax, son of Telamon, now
supported by his lesser namesake, keeps the Trojans
at bay.

Achilles' Grief.—Meantime Antilochus, son of Nestor,
had sped from the field at Menelaus' request to carry the
bitter tidings to Achilles : to tell him that Patroclus, his
friend, was dead, slain by Hector ; that Hector had made
prize of the armour ; that the Greeks were doing their
best to save Patroclus' body from falling into the enemy's
hands, but were hard pressed. Achilles was overwhelmed
with grief, and in the violence of his distress flung himself
upon the ground, cast dust on his head and wept and
mourned together with all his company. And his goddess
mother heard him and came : and he told her all his
grief, and how his heart would know no rest until he had
avenged his dear friend's death by slaying Hector. Hearing this Thetis sorrowed ; for she knew that soon after
the slaying of Hector her own Achilles must die. Un-
deterred by this knowledge Achilles repeats his determination to seek and slay the slayer of his friend. And
Thetis promises to help him by procuring him a suit of
armour from the god Hephaestus. For his own armour
was now in Hector's possession.

Rescue of Dead Patroclus.—Meantime the sullen retreat
of the Greeks had brought the struggle for the body of
Patroclus nearer to the ships. Achilles heard the noise of
it and went, all unarmed as he was, and stood by the
trench, and shouted thrice. The Trojans saw him and
shrank back ; and then at last the body of Patroclus was

carried safely over the trench and laid on a bed in Achilles' tent. So the fighting ended for the day.

Polydamas' Advice to Hector.—Polydamas, that wise and valiant Trojan, strongly urged on Hector the prudence of withdrawing his troops within the walls and manning the city, now that Achilles had returned to the fight and hope of success in the open field was gone. But Hector refused to listen and rashly professed a readiness to face Achilles in single fight. " The war-god is alike to all," he said, " and a slayer of him that would slay." [1]

The Forging of the Armour.—All night long Achilles and the Myrmidons made lamentation for Patroclus : but Thetis went on her way to the dwelling-place of Hephaestus on Mount Olympus and made her supplication. And Hephaestus received her kindly, listened to her story, and straightway set to work. He made for Achilles a splendid suit of armour, a shield and a breastplate, a helmet and a set of greaves. The shield was a wondrous work of art ; a great round shield of metal, covered with intricate carving. In the centre were representations of sun and moon and stars, and about them in successive rings were scenes of city and country, of peace and war ; a marriage scene, a trial scene, a hunting scene ; fields, vineyards and battle-pieces. The whole was encircled about the rim by the stream of ocean. With this incomparable suit of armour Thetis returned to her son, and Achilles beheld the arms with a warrior's joy.

Achilles and Hector.—In the morning public reconciliation was made between Agamemnon and Achilles : each confessed himself to have been in fault. Agamemnon restored Briseis to Achilles and made satisfaction for the wrong according to his promise. Little cared Achilles for gifts now his friend was dead : one only desire consumed him, to rush into battle, find the man who had slain his friend, and slay him : but he had to hold in his impatience while the soldiery took food. " Take not fasting men into the fray," said Odysseus to him to check his eager-

[1] *Iliad*, xviii. l. 309 (Lang, Leaf and Myers, p. 375).

ness. When the Greeks were ready, Achilles put on the divine armour and prepared to seek Hector on the field of battle. Soon Greeks and Trojans closed once more in deadly strife and the battle surged forward and back : Achilles cared for nothing, but how he might avenge Patroclus' death on Hector. For a long time he raged up and down the battle, making a terrible slaughter, and chased the Trojans to their walls. Hector for his part was only too well aware that he was no match for Achilles in single combat ; yet he disdained to follow the rest of the Trojans within the walls. He stood alone outside the Scaean Gates and waited. Priam from the terrace along the walls saw him there and besought him to enter the city, and Hecuba, his mother, added her prayers. But he would not. He knew that his refusal to listen to Polydamas' advice had brought disaster on the Trojans, and he felt bound in honour to make good his word that he would face and fight Achilles. So repressing his own irresolution he stood his ground there by the gates. And Achilles came on, furious and terrible, his divine armour flashing as he came. Then, on a sudden, Hector's nerve failed : he turned and fled ; round under the walls of Troy he fled and Achilles exultantly flew after him : "They past the watch-place and wind-waved wild fig-tree sped ever, away from under the wall, along the waggon-track, and came to the two fair-flowing springs, where two fountains rise that feed deep-eddying Skamandros. The one floweth with warm water, and smoke goeth up therefrom around as it were from a blazing fire, while the other even in summer floweth forth like cold hail or snow or ice that water formeth. And there beside the springs are broad washing troughs hard by, fair troughs of stone, where wives and fair daughters of the men of Troy were wont to wash bright raiment, in the old time of peace, before the sons of the Achaeans came. Thereby they ran, he flying, he pursuing. Valiant was the flier but far mightier he who fleetly pursued him. For not for beast of sacrifice or for an oxhide were they striving, such as are prizes of men's speed of foot, but for the life of

horse-taming Hector was their race. And as when victorious whole-hooved horses run rapidly round the
turning-points, and some great prize lieth in sight, be
it a tripod or a woman, in honour of a man that is
dead, so thrice around Priam's city circled those twain
with flying feet, and all the gods were gazing on
them." [1] Even so is the scene imagined in Homer's
great poem. Three times round the circuit of the
walls went pursuer and pursued, and neither could
Achilles gain on Hector, or Hector out-distance Achilles
and escape. Then fearful lest some other should snatch
from him the sweetness of glory and revenge, Achilles, as
he ran, signalled to his Myrmidons not to interfere, but
to leave Hector to him. At length Achilles gave up the
chase and halted ; and then Hector stopped, too. And
courage returned to him and he came back resolved at
last to fight. The poet puts it that Pallas Athena, in
order to bring glory to Achilles, tricked Hector into
staying ; but this is only a poetic way of expressing the
change in Hector's mind. At any rate Hector now
turned and advanced upon Achilles. As he drew near,
he addressed his foe and offered to make a compact that
whichever of the two proved victor should treat his
enemy's body with respect. But Achilles glared upon
him and with implacable hate refused all terms of courtesy.
As he spoke he flung his lance, and missed : and Hector
exulted, for now he thought he had his mortal enemy at
his mercy. He cast his spear with sure aim and struck
Achilles full on the shield which Hephaestus had made.
But the spear only rebounded from it and fell harmless.
Then in turn Hector was at a disadvantage, for unlike
Achilles he had no second spear. So he drew his sword
and rushed in : but Achilles was too quick and met him
with a thrust of his lance full in the throat just above the
corslet. The spear entered Hector's neck and he fell
down in the dust, mortally wounded. Dying he made
one last appeal to Achilles to restore his body to Priam
for a fit ransom : but Achilles replied only with words of

[1] *Iliad,* xxii. ll. 145-166 (Lang, Leaf and Myers, pp. 438 and 439).

savage mockery. And when Hector lay dead, Achilles
stripped the body of its armour ; and his men ran up
and gazed upon it with awe and thrust and stabbed at
it as it lay there defenceless. And an evil thought came
to Achilles. He took thongs and drew them through
Hector's feet and fastened the other ends to his chariot.
Then he mounted the car, lashed his horses, and drove
away with Hector's body trailing after him in the dust.
This was the sight which presently greeted the eyes of
the anxious watchers on the city wall, Priam and Hecuba,
and Andromache, Hector's wife. And at the woeful sight
Andromache fell down in a swoon.

Achilles' dream.—Achilles, having in this way circled
the walls of Ilium, drove off to the Greek encampment
and took his chariot once round the place where Patroclus
lay ; and the chariots of the Myrmidons followed. Then
at last, having glutted his cruel hunger for vengeance, he
unyoked his chariot, lay down exhausted, and was soon
asleep. But his sleep was troubled : the spirit of Patroclus
appeared to him, reproaching him gently for neglect, and
beseeching him to hasten the performance of the last rites.
" Thou sleepest, and hast forgotten me, O Achilles,"
the phantom seemed to say. " Not in my life wast thou
ever unmindful of me, but in my death. Bury me with
all speed, that I pass the gates of Hades. Far off the
spirits banish me, the phantoms of men outworn, nor
suffer me to mingle with them beyond the River, but
vainly I wander along the wide-gated dwelling of Hades.
Now give me, I pray pitifully of thee, thy hand, for never
more again shall I come back from Hades, when ye have
given me my due of fire. Never among the living shall
we sit apart from our dear comrades and take counsel
together, but me hath the harsh fate swallowed up which
was appointed me even from my birth. Yea and thou
too thyself, Achilles peer of gods, beneath the wall of
the noble Trojans art doomed to die. Yet one thing
will I say, and charge thee, if haply thou wilt have regard
thereto. Lay not my bones apart from thine, Achilles,
but together, even as we were nurtured in your house,

when Menoitios brought me yet a little one from Opöeis to your country by reason of a grievous man-slaying, on the day when I slew Amphidamas' son, not willing it, in childish wrath over the dice. Then took me the knight Peleus into his house and reared me kindly and named me thy squire ; so therefore let one coffer hide our bones." [1]

Funeral Rites of Patroclus.—Achilles, perturbed by this vision, started out of sleep, and soon as day appeared the whole host of the Achaeans collected great quantities of wood, and with this they built up a great pyre, a hundred feet square and a hundred feet high, and on the top they placed the body of Patroclus with all customary ritual. The whole host of the Achaeans, in full armour, was gathered around the pyre, charioteers, horsemen and footmen. There they slaughtered many sheep and oxen, four war-horses, and two of Achilles' favourite dogs. Last they slew twelve Trojans of noble birth, captives of Achilles' spear. The whole huge mass was set alight and blazed through the night, while the great host stood looking on. When at length all was nearly consumed, wine was poured over the pyre to quench the flames, and the ashes of Patroclus were gathered from the centre and kept against the day when they should mingle with the ashes of Achilles according to Patroclus' prayer. Next morning funeral games were held on the shore in honour of the dead. Achilles brought prizes out of his tents, caldrons, and tripods, horses and mules, female captives and masses of iron. The chariot race came first and excited most emulation. Diomedes won, and the second prize was awarded to Menelaus, after that the judges had disallowed Antilochus for a foul. Then followed boxing and wrestling and the foot race. In conclusion a complimentary prize for throwing the lance was awarded to Agamemnon without a contest. With this the games ended.

Priam's Midnight Journey.—All this time and for some days more the body of Hector lay in the dust, and every

[1] *Iliad*, xxiii. 69-91 (Lang, Leaf and Myers, p. 452).

morning, when Achilles rose, he yoked his chariot and drove thrice round the sepulchral mound of Patroclus trailing the corpse behind him. But a marvellous thing happened ; though Hector had now lain many days unburied and though the unprotected body had been many times dragged over the plain, yet neither did the flesh decay nor was its comeliness marred. It was Apollo who watched over Hector's corpse, who day and night kept it from disfigurement and corruption. Hector's piety and courage and patriotism had indeed won the favour of all the immortals, and they now agreed with one consent to induce Achilles to relent and admit the body to ransom. Thetis was sent to incline her son's mind to mercy under pain of the divine displeasure, and Iris, Heaven's messenger, went at the express bidding of Zeus to inspire Priam with the daring purpose of begging the body from Achilles. It seemed a desperate enter- prise for the old king to undertake : to steal out of Troy by night, cross the plain and venture himself among the tents of the Achaeans ; but the plan once conceived, Priam carried it through. Hecuba, the queen-mother, shrieked when she heard of Priam's intention and entreated him to stay within the walls of the citadel, being sure that the journey must have a fatal ending. But Priam would not be turned aside from his purpose : he ordered his yet surviving sons to harness a mule-car and load it with treasure, gold and golden vessels and costly raiment, wherewith to win back the body of the best and bravest of his children. Accompanied only by one attendant, the aged herald Idaeus, the old king left his palace and passed out of the city into the darkness of the plain ; by the favour of heaven he crossed the space between the walls of Troy and the Greek entrenchment, passed through the outposts undiscovered, and at length found himself within Achilles' hut and in presence of the slayer of his son.

Priam and Achilles.—Achilles was sitting alone deep in thought after finishing his evening meal, and Priam came near him unobserved and, throwing himself on the ground beside him, clasped his knees in supplication and kissed his hands, " the murderous hands that had slain so many of his sons." Achilles looked down and saw him with astonishment. And Priam begged him for the sake of Peleus, his own father, an old man like Priam, to have mercy ; to pity his sorrows, and consent to the ransom of Hector's body. Then was Achilles moved to pity, remembering Peleus his father. He took Priam by the hand, disengaging himself gently ; and for a time they two wept silently, the old man and the young, each thinking of his own sorrows. At length Achilles sprang from his chair and raised Priam to his feet, pitying his hoary head and hoary beard and spake and said : " Ah hapless ! many ill things verily thou hast endured in thy heart. How durst thou come alone to the ships of the Achaeans and to meet the eyes of the man who hath slain full many of thy brave sons ?—of iron verily is thy heart. But come then set thee on a seat, and we will let our sorrows lie quiet in our hearts, for all our pain, for no avail cometh of chill lament. This is the lot the gods have spun for miserable men, that they should live in pain ; yet themselves are sorrowless. For two urns stand upon the floor of Zeus filled with his evil gifts, and one with blessings. To whomsoever Zeus whose joy is in the lightning dealeth a mingled lot, that man chanceth now upon ill and now again on good, but to whom he giveth out of the bad kind him he bringeth to scorn, and evil famine chaseth him over the goodly earth, and he is a wanderer honoured of neither gods nor men. Even thus to Peleus gave the gods splendid gifts from his birth, for he excelled all men in good fortune and wealth, and was king of the Myrmidons, and mortal though he was the gods gave him a goddess to be his bride. Yet even on him God brought evil, seeing that there arose to him no offspring of princely sons in his halls, save that he begat one son to an untimely death. Neither may I tend him as he groweth old, since very far from my country I am dwelling in Troy-land, to vex thee and thy children. And of thee, old sire, we have heard how of old time

thou wast happy, even how of all that Lesbos, seat of
Makar, boundeth to the north thereof and Phrygia
farther up and the vast Hellespont—of all these folk,
men say, thou wert the richest in wealth and in sons,
but after that the Powers of Heaven brought this bane
on thee, ever after are battles and man-slayings around
thy city. Keep courage, and lament not unabatingly in
thy heart. For nothing wilt thou avail by grieving for
thy son, neither shalt thou bring him back to life or ever
some new evil come upon thee." [1]

The Recovery of Hector's Body.—Upon this Priam preferred the request on which he had come ; and Achilles,
with difficulty curbing the impulse to an outburst of
anger, gave Priam rough assurance of his own intention
of giving Hector back. Thereat he went out with his
two squires and took the treasure out of the waggon, all
but two mantles and a finely woven tunic, which he left
to serve as wrappings for the dead. Next with courteous
considerateness he ordered his serving-women to wash
the body, that it might be made seemly for a father's
eye to see, and himself lifted Hector up and placed him
on a bier, and the bier was placed in the waggon. When
all was ready for the journey back, Achilles returned to
the hut and invited Priam to take food. And the two
men, so strangely brought together, looked long each
upon the other ; Priam marvelling at the strength and
stature of Achilles, Achilles admiring the noble mien of
Priam and his noble speech. Priam's strength was now
all but spent, and he begged to be allowed to sleep for a
little. This request also Achilles granted : couches were
arranged for Priam and Idaeus in a place where they
were not likely to be discovered by inconvenient visitors ;
and as a final favour Achilles offered to Priam an armistice
for such time as was required for Hector's obsequies.
Nine days were granted for mourning the dead, one day
for the funeral rites, and one day for the building of a
monument—eleven days in all : on the twelfth day hostilities would be resumed.

[1] *Iliad*, xxiv. 518-551 (Lang, Leaf and Myers, pp. 494 and 495).

Priam's Return to Troy. Funeral Rites of Hector.— Then Priam took his farewell of Achilles and lay down and slept. But before dawn came Priam and Idaeus rose, stole past the sentries again and crossed the plain by the road that skirted the ford of Scamander, and re-entered the city unscathed. Cassandra, Priam's daughter, so beautiful, and so pitiable for her vain gift of prophecy—it was her doom ever to prophesy true and never to be believed—was the first to see the waggon and to recognize her brother's body. And she cried out to the men and women of Troy to come and welcome the dead hero, whom so often they had welcomed living. And all Troy came out to meet Priam and Hector, and there was a great concourse and loud lamentation. With difficulty Priam induced the people to let the waggon pass and conveyed the body into the palace. There they laid Hector upon a bed, and the mourners stood around and Andromache led the wailing. Thereafter was all fulfilled according to the compact between Priam and Achilles. For nine days the Trojans mourned for Hector and gathered wood for the great funeral pyre ; and on the tenth they placed the body on the pyre and consumed it : on the eleventh day they quenched the fire and collected the ashes and raised a monument. And thus with the due performance of funeral rites to Hector the *Iliad* closes.

The Last Months of the Tenth Year.—But the tale of Troy goes on to its mournful ending. The defence of the Trojans was greatly weakened by the loss of Hector, and yet the Achaeans were still far from the conquest of the fortress city. New allies and new champions came to the aid of Ilium ; so the legends relate. First came Penthesilea, queen of the Amazons, from Thrace ; but after short-lived success she was slain by Achilles. Next it was Memnon, resplendent son of Tithonus and the Dawn-goddess, Eos, at the head of black warriors from Ethiopia. He drove back the Greeks for a time and slew Antilochus, bravest of Nestor's sons. But Memnon and Achilles engaged in single fight, and after a well-

matched contest Memnon was slain. A little later Achilles
himself met that early death which had been predicted
for him. One day when he had chased the Trojans into
Troy, he was wounded to death near the Scaean Gates
by an arrow shot by Paris. There was a fierce fight over
his body, but Ajax and Odysseus together bore it off.
Splendid funeral games were held in honour of Achilles,
at which Thetis offered the divine armour fashioned by
Hephaestus to the warrior who had done best service
against Troy. When the judges found it difficult to
decide between the claims of Ajax and Odysseus, they
consulted some Trojan captives who without hesitation
named Odysseus as their most formidable enemy. So
the armour of Achilles was adjudged to Odysseus. This
judgment had a tragic sequel. His defeat so preyed upon
the mind of Ajax that he went mad and made a murderous
onslaught upon a flock of sheep belonging to the army,
under the delusion that he was killing the chieftains who
had hurt his pride. When he came to himself and saw
what he had done, he went to a lonely place by the sea-
shore and threw himself on his sword. Paris, too, soon
after the lucky shot which ended Achilles' career of glory,
was smitten in his turn by an arrow and died of the
wound. And still Troy was not taken. Many stories
were told to account for these delays. It was said that
the Greeks could not take Troy without the help of two
other heroes : of Philoctetes, the great archer, who had
in his possession the bow of the hero Heracles ; and of
Neoptolemus, the son of Achilles. Philoctetes was
brought to Troy from Lemnos, then a barren island,
where he had been left since the voyage to Troy, suffering
from a festering wound in his foot ; and it was he who
shot the arrow which caused the death of Paris. Neoptolemus came from Scyros (another island), where he had
been brought up, and took part in the fighting and performed feats of arms worthy of Achilles' son. Yet still
Troy was not taken. Another story said that Troy could
not be taken as long as the Palladium, an ancient image
of the goddess Pallas Athena, was kept safe in the citadel.

Odysseus entered the city in disguise, gained access to the shrine by a secret passage and carried off the Palladium. And still Troy did not fall.

The Wooden Horse.—Troy was taken at last and burnt, as the walls uncovered at Hissarlik testify. Troy was taken not by force, but by stratagem. The fall of Troy is traditionally associated with the story of the Trojan Horse. Epeus constructed a huge horse made of wood, hollow within, and capable of holding a hundred men. The Greeks gave out that they were abandoning the siege and made ostentatious preparations for departure ; but a hundred of their best warriors entered the wooden horse and lay concealed in it. Then the fleet sailed away, leaving this huge image on the shore. Great was the joy of the Trojans when they saw the ships depart, and great their wonder when they found the horse on the sea-shore. A lively debate arose as to what was to be done with it. Some were for destroying it ; others suggested bringing it inside the city as a trophy of victory and dedicating it to the gods. While they were thus disputing, Laocoon, priest of Poseidon, more actively distrustful than the rest, struck the side of the horse with his spear, and, as he suspected, it rang hollow. But then occurred a terrifying portent : two huge serpents came out of the sea, enveloped Laocoon and his two sons in their folds and crushed them to death. Appalled by this sight, the Trojans thought no more of the hollow sound, but were only anxious now to bring the horse inside the city with all speed ; for they believed the deaths of Laocoon and his sons to be a punishment for impiety. And because the horse was too large to pass through the city gate, with their own hands they made a breach in the walls and dragged the horse within.

The Sack of Troy.— Great was the feasting and rejoicing that night, the laughter and the dancing, in celebration, as the Trojans thought, of their deliverance. At last, tired out with the excitement and the merry-making, all dispersed to rest. Then Sinon, a deserter from the Greek host, who had purposely entered Troy to play a traitor's part, unfastened the bolts which shut in the concealed foemen and secretly raised a fire-signal. For the Greek ships had sailed only as far as Tenedos, and when they saw the signal they returned at speed to their former stations on the shore of the Helles-pont, disembarked hastily and advanced upon the city. Then at dead of night the warriors hidden within the horse descended and began to enter the houses and slaughter the defenceless sleepers in them. About the same time the main body of the Greeks entered through the breach, so that massacre and pillage spread over all the city. Terrible was the awakening for the unhappy Trojans; terrible were the deeds done that night. Priam was murdered without pity by Neoptolemus before the eyes of Hecuba, at the very altar sacred to Zeus of the Hearth. Deiphobus was taken unawares and killed after a gallant resistance, and because he had claimed Helen in marriage after the death of Paris, his body was subjected to fearful mutilation by Menelaus. As at that time customary in the sacking of a city, every evil passion was let loose. Ajax, son of Oileus, committed dire sacrilege. He attempted to drag Cassandra from the shrine of Pallas, where she had sought sanctuary. The soldiery would have stoned him for it; but in the end the chiefs let him go unpunished, so that the heavy wrath of Pallas Athena was turned against all the host, as well as against Ajax. The slaughter went on in Troy till all the men found in the citadel and city were massacred; all but a few who, like Aeneas, managed to escape in the confusion, and Antenor, who was spared on account of his former friendly offices towards the Greeks. Nor did the atrocities at the capture of Troy end with that night of horror. Polyxena, another daughter of Priam and Hecuba, was barbarously sacrificed at the tomb of Achilles. Astyanax, Hector's baby son, was taken from Andromache's arms and hurled from the battlements. Andromache herself, Cassandra, Hecuba and the rest of the ladies of the royal house, were assigned by lot to the several chieftains as slaves: Andromache fell to Neoptolemus, Cassandra to Agamemnon, Hecuba to Odysseus. These calamities and the whole scene of insupportable misery have been represented most poignantly in Euripides' tragedy called *The Women of Troy*. This play is for all time a lively presentment of the unutterable tragedies which war brings in its train. Last of all Troy was fired. Then the Greeks put their captives on board their ships and sailed for home.

The Home-coming of the Chieftains.—And now the nemesis of the crimes committed by the Greeks at the sack of Troy, the burning of the temples and the violations of sanctuary, began to work itself out. Menelaus and Agamemnon quarrelled, some of the chieftains came drunk to the Council, and there were other unseemly doings. In consequence of the quarrel between the brothers, the fleet separated into two halves. One half of the ships sailed away at once with Menelaus ; the other half stayed with Agamemnon. Those who sailed first nearly all reached home safely—Nestor, Diomedes, Philoctetes, Idomeneus ; but Menelaus himself was driven out of his course and carried to Egypt where strange adventures befell him and Helen. He only reached Sparta after seven years of wandering in which he and Helen visited Cyprus, Phoenicia, and Africa. But dreadful was the fate that overtook many of the other chieftains who waited with Agamemnon. Ajax the Less was drowned on the rocky island of Gyaros, with words of impious boasting on his lips. Odysseus was doomed to ten more weary years of absence before he reach Ithaca ; and how at last he came home and what he found there, and how he made himself known and how he punished those who had wronged him in his absence, form the subject of Homer's other immortal epic, the *Odyssey*. Most dreadful of all was the fate of Agamemnon, the supreme commander. He landed on the shore of Argolis without misadventure, bringing with him his captive, Cassandra. But fire-signals had announced to Clytaemnestra, his queen, the fall of Troy, and she prepared for him an evil welcome. She had never forgiven her husband for the deceit by which he had taken Iphigeneia from her and given her over to death. Moreover, she had now formed guilty ties with Aegisthus, Agamemnon's cousin, and they two plotted death to Agamemnon when he should arrive. He was cut down ' like an ox in a stall ' at a banquet, to which Aegisthus invited him ; and Cassandra died also at the hands of Clytaemnestra. Afterwards Aegisthus, in spite of public execration, took possession of the throne of Mycenae. Greek legend told a dark tale how Orestes, son of Clytaemnestra and Agamemnon, escaped on that night of bloodshed, and some years later returned in disguise, and with the help of his friend, Pylades, and his sister, Electra, slew both Aegisthus and his mother, to expiate his father's murder. But for the murder of his mother, he was haunted by the Erinyes (Furies), and driven out of his mind. In the end, however, by the interposition of Apollo, he was acquitted of bloodguiltiness upon pleading his cause before the court of the Areopagus at Athens.

CHAPTER VI

ILIUM AND MYCENAE

1. ILIUM.

"The Burnt City would still have lain to this day hidden in the earth, had not imagination guided the spade."

R. VIRCHOW in Preface to Schliemann's *Ilios*.

THE story of the *Iliad* is a good story, and it would still be a good story if no such place as Troy ever existed, and we knew nothing more than what Homer tells us about the Achaeans who beleaguered Troy under the leadership of Agamemnon, King of Men. Yet it stirs most of us to be assured that Troy was a real stronghold which 3000 years ago dominated the Trojan plain and commanded the entrance to the Dardanelles ; that the massive walls of this fortress exist to this day and may be seen with our eyes, if we visit the site. If we cannot do this, we can at least learn how the fortress walls, long buried under the ruins of later buildings and the earth and débris heaped up over the great mound on which they stood, were uncovered to the light of day through the genius of Henry Schliemann and the labours of archaeologists who completed his work. The story is as wonderful in its way as the story of the Trojan War.

Henry Schliemann.—When Henry Schliemann, who was born in 1822, was a boy, the story of Troy took hold of his imagination, and he made up his mind some day to discover the true site of Troy and bring to light its ancient walls. Nothing could at the time have seemed more

unlikely than that he should ever be able to carry out
this purpose ; for his father, a Lutheran clergyman, was
too poor even to keep him at a classical school, and when
he was fourteen he had to go into business and earn his

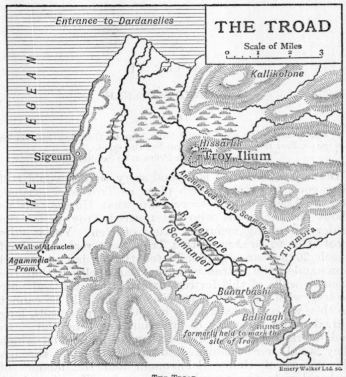

THE TROAD.

own living. The beginning was unpromising enough.
For years he had to serve as shop-assistant to a village
grocer, his whole time occupied in selling butter and
coffee and oil, herrings and tallow candles, and doing
whatever else was required of him in this employment.

Even this means of livelihood he lost by an accident, which, though a misfortune at the time, proved ultimately his first step to fortune. In dire straits he sailed from Hamburg as cabin-boy, was wrecked off Texel, and made a fresh start in business at Amsterdam. Here his capacity, industry and enterprise, and a remarkable gift for languages brought him advancement. He was sent to Russia by the firm he was serving, and there his success was rapid. By the time he was a little over forty he found himself master of a large independent fortune. Then he learnt Greek, travelled, and devoted himself to archaeology. His boyish ambition to discover Troy now became the guiding principle of his life. In 1870, when he was not quite fifty years of age, he was able to carry his purpose into action by starting the work of excavation on what he believed to be the site of Troy. His ultimate success was astonishing, but the work took long years of patient labour and was not fully accomplished when, in 1890, he died. His faith and enthusiasm were by that time amply justified, but it remained for others to complete the investigations which enable us to be sure that the walls of Homer's Ilium have in very truth been recovered for us.

Hissarlik and the Troad.—Unbroken tradition from the fifth century B.C., and earlier, connected the tale of Troy with a small plain at the north-west corner of Asia Minor, one side of which forms the Asiatic, or southern, shore of the Hellespont, the famous channel between Asia and Europe now known as the Dardanelles. This plain is about eight miles long from north to south, and three broad, and through it flows a river of some size, now called the Mendere, a name that may be taken to be a mere clipping of the name Sca-*mander*. Towards the lower, that is the northern, end of this plain, just three miles from the shore of the Hellespont, there juts out from the plateau bounding it on the east, a hill which, though of no great height (its top was about 120 feet above sea-level and its northern scarp rises steeply out of the plain), occupies a commanding position relatively to the lower ground. This height was in classical times the site of a town called Ilium, which was visited by Xerxes as he marched to invade Greece, and by Alexander the Great on his way to overthrow the Persian empire. This we know from Herodotus and Arrian. The Romans enlarged and beautified this Ilium in the belief that they were themselves descendants of the Trojans. Some inconsiderable remains of this Roman Ilium—a theatre and bits of the fortifications—were visible on the hill before Schliemann began to dig, but the city itself had long fallen into ruin and disappeared. For many centuries there had not even been a village there. But whether this hill, called Hissarlik, or ' Castle Hill ' by the Turks, was also the site of Homer's Ilium, had been disputed since the time of Demetrius of Skepsis, early in the second century B.C., when new Ilium was still a flourishing city ; and in Schliemann's day the weight of scholarly opinion actually lent to the view that ancient Troy must be placed on a hill called Bally Dagh, not far from the village of Bunarbashi, five miles further from the shores of the Dardanelles. Schliemann scouted this view, partly on the strength of the tradition which associated Ilium with the Hissarlik site, and even more because the position of Bally Dagh is inconsistent with the most vivid local touches found in the *Iliad*, whereas the position of Hissarlik agrees with these almost perfectly. Schliemann began to work, therefore, at Hissarlik with full confidence : " Ever since my first visit," he wrote in October 1871, " I never doubted that I should find the Pergamus of Priam in the depths of this hill."

Schliemann's Discoveries.—With characteristic thoroughness he began by cutting a great trench, fifty feet broad, across the top of the hill from north to south. His plan was to dig right down to the solid rock, and to do this it was found that his workmen had to cut through a mass of débris many yards thick. The virgin rock was reached at length at a depth varying from forty to forty-six feet. Long before this it had become clear that there was more buried within the

HISSARLIK
as seen from the Plain of Troy.

From a photograph by the Argonaut Camera Club.

mound of Hissarlik even than Schliemann had supposed
when he began. As the digging went down foot by foot
and yard by yard, evidence accumulated of not one
buried city but several. It became evident that in the
course of ages, not one or two but a long succession of
settlements had one after another occupied the site, each
built on the ruins of that which had gone before. Nine
such layers, or strata, have ultimately been distinguished ;
and it is now agreed that it is the sixth that must be
identified with Homer's Troy. Schliemann himself, however, died happy in the belief that he had found the
citadel of Troy, ' Priam's Pergamus,' in the Second City.
What persuaded him of this was, first, the great strength
of the walls and gates and towers that his digging had
laid bare at this level ; and, secondly, the plain evidence
he found that these remains had passed through some
great conflagration. Perhaps what even more strongly
inclined him to think he had found in this second stratum
the city of Priam and Paris was the discovery, in May
1873, of a miscellaneous hoard of treasure jammed together
in the mass of wall and débris on which his men were
working. The number and richness of the gold vessels
and ornaments in this treasure-trove called up a magnificent vision of ' wealthy ' Troy : and this treasure
appeared to belong to the Second City.

The Nine Strata.—Schliemann distinguished only seven
strata. More careful investigation since 1890 has increased the number of strata to nine ; and, as already
said, the Troy of Homer's *Iliad* is found in the sixth
of these. The strata were distinguished, of course, partly
by the position and character of the buildings discovered,
partly by the objects found at various levels and the
materials of which they were composed. Obviously one
would conclude that objects resembling each other in
style and character—pottery, for instance, and weapons
—belonged to the same age, whereas marked differences of
style would be taken to indicate difference of age, at all
events when the character was seen to vary in correspondence with the different levels. By degrees the notion of

different layers became more definite, and these were further interpreted as different settlements in successive ages. The task of distinguishing these was complicated and difficult. We readily see that if the supposition of successive settlements is true and several ' cities ' are built one above another, it would often in excavating be impossible to get at a wall or building at a lower level without displacing, or altogether destroying, structures belonging to one or more strata above it.[1] Obviously also the difficulty and complication become greater the lower you go. The result of Schliemann's uncovering process was inevitably ' an inextricable labyrinth ' of walls and buildings. Mistakes were easy to make, perhaps unavoidable. Moreover, while some of the settlements represented by layers were strong fortified places entitled to be called ' cities,' others were no better than villages or collections of huts. The main facts, however, stood out clearly. Hissarlik, the site of the Graeco-Roman Ilium, had in earlier ages been occupied by successive settlements, two of which were enclosed by formidable walls of wrought stone and defended by massive towers. Further, there were indications that both of these fortified places had been sacked and burnt. Such was Schliemann's achievement at Hissarlik : his faith that Troy would be found in the depths of the mound was more than justified.[2]

The Mycenaean Age.—The evidence which ultimately established the conclusion that not the Second, but the Sixth City is Homer's Troy, is the evidence of archaeology in a wider sense, the evidence of comparative archaeology.

[1] There has been notable improvement in the art of excavation since Schliemann's time, and there are now means of excavating lower levels without destroying anything of value above them. Sir Arthur Evans' excavations at Knossos (see p. 129) are a beautiful example.

[2] It is no detraction from Schliemann's just honours to recall that there was one earlier discoverer of the true site of Troy, Frank Calvert, an Englishman who owned an estate in the Troad which once included Hissarlik. At his farm, called by the Greek name Thymbra, near Bunarbashi, he entertained Dr. Schliemann in 1871 (as other visitors to the Troad since), and Schliemann owed to him the suggestion to excavate Hissarlik. See Manatt, *Aegean Days*, pp. 251 and 252.

In the twenty years during which Schliemann was digging at Hissarlik, archaeology moved on apace all over Greece, and especially in Argolis, the home of Agamemnon, Troy's conqueror ; later in the opening years of the twentieth century astonishing discoveries were made in Crete, the land of Minos and the Labyrinth. These excavations, and especially the opening of numbers of graves and of ' bee-hive ' tombs which were pre-historic monuments in the days when the Greek historians lived and wrote, have revealed the existence of an ancient civilization earlier than the Hellenic and in some respects differing from it. The characteristics of this civilization are so plainly distinguishable and so widely diffused, that it cannot be doubted that the objects which exhibit them are connected, and belong to one great epoch, to which the name Mycenaean is conveniently given because some of the most valuable and interesting finds were made at Mycenae. Vast numbers of objects were found in graves, or unearthed in the process of excavation, and these have been sorted and systematically arranged by archaeologists. The occurrence among them of articles which could only have come from Egypt, and the discovery of articles with the ' Mycenaean ' characteristics in Egyptian tombs, make it possible to infer the probable limits of the period during which this civilization flourished, that is from the seventeenth century B.C. to the twelfth. It is further possible to trace a process of change going on within the period, and to class objects as belonging to earlier and later stages of this civilization. Now the objects found in the Sixth Stratum at Hissarlik have the characteristics of the latest stage of this Mycenaean civilization, whereas the objects found in the Second Stratum have not. And the latest stage of Mycenaean civilization, from 1200 to 1100 B.C., actually agrees with the date traditionally assigned to the sack of Troy, B.C. 1184.[1]

[1] Another important consideration is that the Sixth City is more than double the size of the Second. The walls of the Second City enclosed a space of 8000 square metres ; the area of the Sixth City is 20,000. Even this space is only about five acres, so that Priam's Pergamos, if identified with it, must be thought of rather as a fortress

The Sixth City.—Enough of this Sixth City remains and has been uncovered by excavation to enable us to judge of its fitness to be accepted as the very Ilium of the *Iliad*. Unfortunately the most interesting parts of the city have perished beyond recall. The principal buildings stood on higher ground, which was all cut away in levelling the site for the new city which the Romans constructed : so we look in vain for remains of temples and of Priam's great palace. The fortifications, too, on the whole of the northern and north-western sides have disappeared completely : probably they served as a quarry for the building of Sigeum, a town of which Strabo, the geographer, records [1] that Archaianax of Miletus used the stones of Troy for building it ; and along with these walls went the Scaean Gates and the Great Tower which flanked it. But there are still long stretches of wall on the south and south-east sides of the hill, extending to nearly half the original circuit ; and this wall is exceedingly massive, being sixteen feet in thickness at the top, and reaching a height of twenty feet. This wall, moreover, appears to have been really a substructure or ramp. The actual defences of Troy were ramparts built on the top of this ramp. There are three gateways in this stretch of wall ; and on the south-eastern side it is strengthened by three great towers. The largest of the towers (called the Water Tower because it contains a reservoir) is of great strength ; it is sixty feet in breadth, and what is left of it is thirty feet high and gives some idea of what the Great Tower must have been like. The water supply is secured by a shaft or well, twelve feet square, which goes down into water-bearing rock. The masonry of the walls and towers and gates is constructed of squared blocks of stone carefully

than a walled city. Yet this restriction of size is not (allowing for some poetical exaggeration) inconsistent with Homer's narrative, or fatal to the identification of this Sixth City with Troy. We might compare it to the Tower of London, or better to the Fort at Agra or Delhi. How famous the siege of such a place of strength may become we may see from the story of the Residency at Lucknow.

[1] Strabo's *Geography*, xiii. 389.

cut and fitted, and is of great excellence. Defences on this scale must have made of Troy a place of almost impregnable strength in the age to which it belongs. " As it stands revealed to-day it justifies the muster of all Greece, and accounts for the ten years' siege. If those walls were ever mastered in a primitive age, we should say—what tradition avouches—that it was by fraud and not by force." [1]

The Plain from the Walls of Troy.—If we place ourselves in imagination on the battlements of this ' Sixth City ' and gaze northward towards the Dardanelles, or south-westward over the low hills that form the Aegean coast-line to Tenedos, the reality of the Tale of Troy comes home to us with new force. The stretch of plain between the city and the Greek ships lies full in view, and the distance is so moderate that we can understand how the battle rolls backwards and forwards from close under the walls of Troy to the Greek entrenchments in the course of a single day ; [2] and how easy it is for the chiefs to send a message to summon Priam to the battle-field (Ch. V. p. 82) when a solemn agreement is to be made to decide the quarrel by a duel between Paris and Menelaus ; for Priam to have his chariot harnessed and come to the meeting-place, perform the sacrifice and drive back before the combat begins. [3] We see how natural it is for the Trojans to keep a sentinel, Priam's son Polites, " seated on the top of the barrow of Aisyetes," to give warning of any onset from the Greek ships ; [4] for men could not be seen moving at a distance of three miles. This distance, again, makes Priam's midnight expedition perfectly intelligible ; for it was possible to drive three miles, penetrate the Greek lines, win back the body of Hector, eat and take rest, and yet get back before the walls of the city by early dawn. [5] The scene in Book III. (lines 153 to 242), where Helen comes to the Great Tower and dazzles the elders of Troy by her beauty, and

[1] Tsountas and Manatt, *The Mycenaean Age*, p. 362.

[2] *Iliad*, xi. to xv. [3] *Iliad*, iii. 116-313.

[4] *Iliad*, ii. 791-794. [5] *Iliad*, xxiv. 322-697.

I   H

thereafter, at Priam's request, names to him the leading
Achaean chieftains, Agamemnon, Odysseus, Ajax, gains
fresh vividness : we can see, too, the lists some distance
away, watch the duel and the shameful overthrow of Paris,
and see the treacherous arrow which wounds Menelaus, the
confusion which follows and the renewal of general battle.

The Great Tower and the Scaean Gates.—The great tower
of Ilium from which the elders of Troy and anxious wives
and mothers watch the battle was, we know from Homer's
narrative, close to the Scaean Gates. Of the Scaean
Gates which figure so largely in the most moving parts
of the story, and of the great flanking tower itself, no
traces are found for the reasons already given above
(p. 112). But we know from the data. Homer gives
where they must have stood. The Scaean Gates are the
main exit from the city through which passes the carriage-
way down to the plain. It is through the Scaean Gates
that Priam drives to meet Agamemnon in Book III. It
was these gates which by Priam's command were held
open to admit the fugitive Trojans, when chased by
Achilles to the walls ; [1] it was at the Scaean Gates that
Hector took his stand to wait for Achilles.[2] That the
Great Tower adjoined the gate is quite clear : Priam was
on the tower, when he saw Achilles pressing hard upon
the fleeing Trojans and went down to give his orders to
the warders of the gate. While Hector stands before the
gate waiting for Achilles, Priam and Hecuba from the
Tower beseech him to enter. It was by the Scaean Gate,
too, that Andromachè, who had been watching from the
tower, met Hector in that tender farewell which was to
be their last.[3] Now there is only one position on the
northern face of the hill where the physical facts fit the
given conditions. The tower must obviously have been
on the north-western side, looking down on the plain
between the city walls and the sea. Most of the northern
scarp, however, is steep ; but at one point near the

---

[1] *Iliad*, xxi. 526-538. See Ch. V. p. 92.
[2] *Iliad*, xxii. 5-6.   See Ch. V. p. 92.   [3] Ch. V. pp. 83-86.

north-western angle there is a small platform, nearly level, from which the ground descends at a slope gentle enough to admit of a carriage way. This we may be reasonably certain was the position of the Scaean Gates.

Hector's Last Fight.—It is a curious point that the scene of Hector's fight for life with Achilles was apparently out of sight from the battlements. The position is near the two springs described in *Iliad* xxii. ll. 147-156 (see above, Ch. V. p. 92), and these springs can with reasonable probability be located. But nothing was seen by the anxious watchers on the walls till Achilles' chariot trailing behind it the lifeless body of Hector came into view. Now the ground about the springs is nowadays quite visible from the platform where the tower must have stood. There seems at first a discrepancy; but further consideration shows that we have here a striking confirmation of Homer's accuracy.[1] For when the buildings of Troy were standing, they would have intercepted all view of the springs.

Reality of the Trojan War.—When the scenes so vividly described in the *Iliad* are placed once more in their local setting, it seems stupid to ask if the Trojan war ever took place. Yet the question has been asked, and the answers of scholars have represented every shade of belief and incredulity. There have been times when the whole story has been regarded as mythical and the very existence of Priam's Troy has been called in question. Since Schliemann's discoveries, however, and the careful study of the actual site by scholars, there has been a growing tendency to a revived belief in the historical reality of a struggle for the command of the entrance to the Dardanelles many centuries before the opening of Greek history, of which the Tale of Troy is the poetic version. We know how important the Black Sea route through the Dardanelles has been from the earliest times, which afford record down to our own day. It seems that the

[1] This explanation turns on l. 208 of Book xxii. Lang, Leaf and Myers, p. 439.

fortress-city on the hill overlooking the Trojan plain
commanded this Black Sea route in the days of sailing
ships. For, by reason of the prevailing winds and the
strong stream down the Hellespont from the Propontis
into the Aegean, trading vessels must needs cast anchor
in the neighbourhood of Troy before entering the Dardanelles. A fort commanding the plain could impose
conditions at the arbitrary pleasure of those who held it.
So the Greeks may well have had other causes of quarrel
with the princes who built the Sixth City on the site of
Hissarlik, apart from the special provocation of the rape
of Helen. It seems that the Achaean host of Agamemnon
fought in the Trojan plain for reasons not altogether
dissimilar from those for which the Allies in 1915 sought
to force the passage of the Dardanelles. " Given the
known data—the Hellespont an essential economic
necessity to Greece, but blocked by a strong fort, and the
expansion of Greece to the Euxine at the beginning of
the historical period—there must have been a point at
which that fort was taken by the Greeks. And it must
have taken place much in the way which Homer describes,
by a process of wearing down. A war of Troy therefore
is a necessary deduction from purely geographical conditions, and the account of it in Homer agrees with all
the probabilities of the case." [1] " My conclusion is,"
writes Dr. Walter Leaf after thorough exploration of the
Troad, " that there existed a real record of real events,
and that out of this the *Iliad* grew." [2] Nor does this
exclude an historical basis for the story of Helen. " What
was there, save actual history," Dr. Leaf pertinently
asks, " to locate at the mouth of the Hellespont the story
which of all that have ever been set down, has most
affected the imagination of succeeding generations ? "
" The Plain of Troy is certainly not picturesque. It
contains no natural features to attract the lover of
scenery, or stir the imagination of the poet. If no human
drama were ever acted there, it is hard to see why any
bard should have made it the stage for a story pieced

<hr>

[1] Leaf's *Troy*, p. 326.   [2] *Id.* p. 328.

together out of legend, or transferred to it the tale of battles fought among the steep and rugged hills and fertile plains of Greece itself." [1]

2. Mycenae.

If there is strong ground for believing that at Hissarlik we look upon the very walls which sheltered Paris and Priam, there is no doubt whatever that near the village of Charvati in Argolis we may climb to the citadel and palace from which Agamemnon went forth to the beleaguering of Troy.   For Mycenae has never been buried and lost like Ilium ; Mycenae was an inhabited city at the time of the Persian wars, though at that time its greatness was long past : warriors from Mycenae shared in the glories of Thermopylae and Plataea.   Not many years later (B.C. 462) an end was put to the political existence of the city by jealous neighbours ; the lower city was altogether destroyed, but not the citadel.   The traveller Pausanias visited the place in the second century A.D., and makes mention in his itinerary of the Cyclopean walls, the Lion Gate, and of certain " underground buildings of Atreus and his children where their treasures were kept "—all of which may be seen by the visitor to-day.   But much also which Pausanias cannot have seen has been uncovered on the site of Mycenae in recent times : through the sagacious guesses of modern men, and the labour of pick and spade, an amazing treasure, the existence of which he did not suspect, has been drawn from the rock itself in one corner of the area enclosed within the fortress walls.   And here again as at Hissarlik it was Schliemann who showed the way and who made the first grand discoveries.   Till Schliemann, in his tireless eagerness to bring to light what the earth held concealed of the life described in the Homeric poems, came to the site in 1874, Mycenae remained, what it already was when Pausanias visited it seventeen centuries earlier, a lonely ruin on a rocky hill in the midst of grim moun-

[1] Leaf's *Troy,* p. 24.

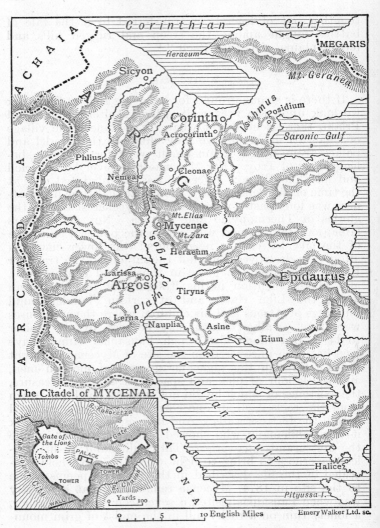

The Citadel of MYCENAE

THE PLAIN OF ARGOS.

THE DOUBLE CIRCLE OF STONE SLABS WITHIN THE CITADEL OF MYCENAE
with the mountains to the north-west beyond.

From a photograph by the Argonaut Camera Club.

tains. Pausanias had also made mention of royal tombs which he connected with names famous in the legends of Mycenae—with Atreus, Agamemnon, Cassandra and Aegisthus. It was these 'tombs' which Schliemann came to seek, strong in his instinctive conviction of the general trustworthiness of tradition. For he argued that Pausanias' words implied that the tombs were within the walls of the citadel, not outside. As at Troy, he met with extraordinary good fortune : his success went far beyond any expectations he had formed.

Schliemann's Excavations.—The whole space enclosed by the citadel walls has a circuit of a thousand yards. Schliemann began by sinking experimental shafts at various points over this area, thirty-four in all. There was one spot at the north-west corner, close to the Gate of Lions, where the immediate results were most encouraging, and here accordingly he set his men to dig. The ground all about this corner was heaped up with earth and débris to a height of ten feet above the rock-surface. In this mound Schliemann directed his workmen to cut an opening 113 feet square, and as they dug down towards the rock, they unearthed a rich variety of objects of interest, fragments of pottery, knives of bronze and of iron, iron keys, stone implements, terra-cotta images, and vases in great profusion, even one or two gems beautifully engraved. It was the number of such objects found in the preliminary digging which determined the choice of this particular spot for the main effort. Systematic excavation was started here on August the 7th, 1876. Before the end of the month discoveries had been made which began a new era in archaeology.

The Rock Tombs and what they held.—In digging through the mound the first really significant discovery was of two sculptured slabs which Schliemann at once recognized as tombstones. This was followed soon after by the find of two more of similar kind, and later of two of plain polished stone. At the same time the removal of loose material was gradually uncovering a curious double row of stone slabs, which were ultimately found to form two concentric circles of upright stones enclosing an area 87 feet in diameter. There was a space of three feet between the two rows, and there were evidences that the space between had been originally covered in by cross-slabs of the same stone : six of these cross-slabs were still in position.[1] From out this ring-wall at Mycenae, as from a magic circle, wonder after wonder issued in the months which followed. A series of five stone graves, cut in the living rock, was disclosed by Schliemann deeper down, and in the graves were the bodies of men and women covered with gold ornaments and surrounded by various articles which had been useful to them when alive—gold cups and weapons of war, diadems and hair-pins, rings and bracelets, and ornaments of all kinds. Schliemann's faith and zeal had again been rewarded by a marvellous find, a find even more remarkable than the treasure found at Troy embedded in the wall of the Second City (above, 1. p. 109). These rock tombs are mostly of considerable size, the largest 24 feet by $18\frac{1}{2}$ feet : one is as small as $11\frac{1}{2}$ feet by $9\frac{1}{2}$. The total wealth of relics which they yielded is immense. The whole collection has been removed to Athens and methodically arranged in cases in the Mycenae Room at the National Museum, where it may be seen ; but a fairly vivid idea of the wonder of Schliemann's find may be formed by merely enumerating the contents of one of the tombs. This is a list of what was taken from that known as the third tomb, in which were the bodies of three queens :

" To begin with the objects in gold : there were six diadems, among them the splendid gold crown with the flower-crest, which still encircled the head of one of the women ; a gold comb with bone teeth ; an ornate gold-headed hair-pin ; six gold spirals for the hair ; fifteen gold pendants ; eleven gold necklace coils ; six gold bracelets ; eight gold crosses and stars ; ten gold

[1] The most probable conclusion regarding the purpose of this double circle of stones is that it formed the substructure of a mound over the tombs. See Tsountas and Manatt, *The Mycenaean Age*, p. 108.

THE TWO-HANDLED GOLD CUP FROM TOMB IV.
with doves perching on the handles.

From Schuchhardt's *Schliemann's Excavations.*

With this may be compared Nestor's great golden Dove Cup described *Iliad*, xi. ll. 632-635 (Lang, Leaf and Myers, p. 222); only Nestor's cup was very much bigger and had four handles and eight doves.

grasshoppers hung from gold chains ; one gold butter-
fly ; four gold griffins—one flying ; four gold lions
couchant ; twelve gold ornaments, each with two stags
reposing upon branches of a date palm ; ten ornaments
with lions—one with two lions attacking an ox ; three
gold *intaglios* with vigorous figure-subjects ; fifty-one gold
ornaments embossed with cuttle-fish, butterflies, swans,
eagles, hippocampi and sphinxes ; four female idols in
gold, including two of Aphrodite with doves ; one gold
mask of child ; one gold goblet embossed with fishes
swimming ; five gold vases with lids ; and, finally, seven
hundred and one ' large, thick, round plates of gold, with
a very pretty decoration of repoussé work in fourteen
different designs—spirals, flowers, cuttlefish, butterflies,
etc.' In addition to this profusion of gold, there were
four silver vases and goblets, two silver rods plated with
gold ; a magnificent alabaster vase and cup ; one bronze
vase and three large bronze caldrons ; several engraved
gems ; and an enormous quantity of amber beads." [1]

The contents of the fourth and largest tomb, which fill
fi˘teen cases in the Mycenae Room at Athens, were even
richer and more varied. Among the more remarkable of
these are : three golden masks found on the faces of three
of the bodies in this tomb ; [2] a golden breastplate ; a
golden shoulder-belt four feet long ; a great silver bull's
head with golden horns and a rosette of gold set in the
centre of the forehead ; a three-handled vase of alabaster ;
a massive golden bracelet four inches in diameter ; two
signet rings exquisitely carved, one with the representation of a hunting scene, the other of a hand-to-hand
combat ; a massive two-handled goblet of gold weighing
four pounds, another with golden doves nestling on the
handles. Besides these there were taken from this tomb
nine more cups and goblets of gold, nineteen silver vessels
—goblets, bowls and flagons ; big copper jugs and caldrons

---

[1] Tsountas and Manatt, *The Mycenaean Age*, p. 88.

[2] There were altogether five bodies in Tomb IV., three known to be
men from the masks covering their faces ; the other two probably
women.

to the number of thirty-four in all. One of the caldrons is $2\frac{1}{2}$ feet across ; another was found to contain a hundred wooden buttons plated with gold. A large number of weapons of war was found in this tomb, lances, swords and knives. The shafts of the lances crumbled away as soon as they were brought into the air, so that only the lance-heads are left. The swords are mostly straight, two-edged swords tapering to a point, and therefore adapted for thrusting rather than cutting. Some of these blades were subsequently found on careful cleaning to be very beautifully inlaid with designs in gold. Small golden objects in a great variety of artistic designs were found in this tomb in hundreds : among them more than fifty tiny reproductions in gold of the great bull's head, which seems to have been a sort of mascot. A curious point to notice is that many of the golden objects in the tombs are made of gold beaten so thin that they cannot ever have been intended for real use. They were evidently made for the special purpose of being buried with the dead. The reason why such objects are found in graves at all is the prevalence in early times of the belief that the life after death is an exact copy of life on this earth, so that dead heroes and their women-folk need all the appliances of their earthly life for use in the spirit world. The warrior needs his spear and his drinking-cup, the lady needs her gem-box and her hand-mirror. At first the very things used in life are placed in the graves— solid articles of real value. Then it comes to be thought that shadows of the real things will suffice for the spirit existence, and so mere representations in gold-leaf are found in these royal tombs at Mycenae among the many objects of solid gold.

The Sixth Tomb.—Schliemann discovered and opened five tombs within the circuit of the double ring-wall. A sixth was discovered four years later by M. Stamatakes, a distinguished Greek archaeologist. The contents of this grave have been rearranged in the Museum at Athens precisely as they were arranged originally in the tomb itself. "The mere inventory," write Tsountas and Manatt,

" is enough to show the barbaric splendour which went with the Mycenaean to his tomb, but for a clear conception of ancient burial one should see the tomb itself with its tenants and their offerings about them. This every visitor to Athens may do, for in the National Museum, Grave VI (discovered by Stamatakes) has been reproduced (so to speak), and its occupants—two men— there lie outstretched on their pebble bed, with their drinking cups at hand and their armory in reach, while great vases are ranged about their feet." [1]

The Masks on the Kings' Faces.—The most interesting of all the objects found in these tombs are the golden masks, which undoubtedly represent the features of the dead persons on whose faces they were found. There were in all seven of these, two being masks of children. Of the five men's masks one has been so much crushed that the features can only be made out with difficulty. The other four have very distinct individuality. Two are from the fourth grave and two from the fifth. And of these the most interesting is the bearded mask from Tomb V (see Frontispiece), in which Schliemann believed he had recovered the very face and features of King Agamemnon. Agamemnon, legend tells (the story appears first in the *Odyssey*), was murdered immediately on his return from Troy together with the Trojan princess Cassandra, and all his train of attendants. [2] We know also that in Pausanias' time a tradition survived that the tombs of Agamemnon and those who perished with him were to be found within the walls. Dr. Schliemann was naturally inclined to believe that the tombs he opened in the rock within the double circle of stones near the Lion Gate were the very tombs of which Pausanias writes. If that conjecture can be accepted, we may well believe that in this bearded mask we do see the very lineaments of Agamemnon, king of men, who led the Achaean host to the siege and capture of Troy. But can it? Before we try and answer that question, we will first look round

[1] Tsountas and Manatt, p. 91.   [2] See Chapter V. p. 104.

and note what else is to be seen at Mycenae, and what later archaeologists have to say of the results of their efforts to ascertain the meaning of all the discoveries to which Schliemann's excavations have led. We will first make a rapid survey of the citadel itself ; next take more particular note of the palace and the Lion Gate, and from that go on to a brief description of the tombs outside the citadel once known as Treasuries. Then we will return to the question of the age and date of these various structures, and from that go on to try and find an answer to the question who were the kings who lay buried in the shaft-graves underneath that curious double circle of slabs in a corner of the citadel near the Lion Gate.

The Hill-fortress of Mycenae.—The citadel of Mycenae in the time of its greatness was a formidable stronghold. It occupies a triangular ledge of rock, which forms a bastion in front of the mountains just where, after converging from east and west, they close in the plain of Argos on the north. Deep ravines isolate this ledge on two sides ; the ravine of the Kokoretza running due west beneath the fortress platform, the ravine of the Chavos [1] running from north-east to south-west. The platform itself is about 400 yards in extent along its northern edge from east to west, and about 200 yards at its widest extent from north to south. The Cyclopean wall which Pausanias saw still defends the greater part of this circuit and is still of an impressive height, as much as thirty-five feet in some places. But it is not the height of the wall itself which contributes most to the effect of strength, but the wall when crowning the side of a steep ravine. In places there is a sheer drop of 150 feet. The wall is called ' Cyclopean,' because the Greeks gave this name to all ancient walls built of huge stones roughly hewn and fitted together irregularly ; ' Cyclopean,' because they could not conceive how these great stones could have been piled one on another by human hands, and therefore ascribed the building of the walls to the fabulous beings

[1] This name is the modern Greek form of the word which we have **adopted in English** in its older form ' chaos.'

THE PLAIN OF ARGOS

as seen from the Citadel of Mycenae looking south, with the mountains of Arcadia in the distance
on the right

called Cyclopes (like Polyphemus, see Ch. **VII. p. 154),**
who had more than human stature and strength. Most
of the wall encircling Mycenae has this Cyclopean character ; but portions of it are constructed of squared
stones laid in regular layers, other parts again of polygonal blocks of stone carefully shaped and closely fitted
one to another. Yet, in spite of ravines and wall, the
appearance of the fortress from the plain below is somewhat disappointing ; the line of the wall does not stand
out clear-cut as one might expect, but is hard to distinguish against the background of great mountains.
The height of the rock, though really 900 feet above
sea-level, is in appearance reduced by the swell in the
ground at the top of which the village of Charvati is
planted, and by the greater heights which soar above it
on the east. To the south is Mount Zara, over 2000 feet
high : to the north, the Prophet Elias 2500. On the
other hand, there is a really glorious view from the
platform itself over the whole plain of Argos to the sea—
a distance of nine miles.

The Palace and the Lion Gate.—The palace of the rulers
of Mycenae occupied the highest ground within the
citadel, approached by a series of terraces. The site was
excavated by Dr. Tsountas in 1886 and part of the
ground plan traced. The largest room discovered
measures 42 feet by 38. Investigation showed that a
Doric temple, dated in the sixth century, had been built
over the site of the palace, and the parts of it on that
side obliterated. The Lion Gate does not fall short of
its reputation. The sculptured lions from which it gets
its name are carved on a slab of grey limestone two feet
thick which fills a triangular space twelve feet by ten
above the lintel of the doorway. The lions, now headless, face each other on either side of a small pillar, with
their paws planted on the altar-like base on which the
pillar stands. These carved beasts must be at least three
thousand two hundred years old, dating from approximately 1400 B.C., and are without rival in Greece of that
early age. The heads were evidently fixed on separately ;

for the marks where they were attached can be seen,
and they were possibly of bronze, not stone. Perhaps
the most remarkable feature about the gateway (which
is roughly ten feet high by ten feet wide, narrowing
upwards by a few inches) is the enormous block of
stone which forms the lintel. The gateway is built,
nursery-fashion, of three single blocks, two uprights and
a cross-piece ; and the cross-piece, or lintel, is a slab
of stone fifteen feet long, eight broad, and eight feet thick.

The ' Treasuries.'—This stone which forms the lintel
of the Lion Gate is remarkable enough ; but there is
another stone, yet more remarkable, to be seen at Mycenae
outside the citadel, a few hundred yards to the south-
west. This greater stone is thirty feet long, sixteen and
a half feet wide ; three feet four inches thick, and is
calculated to weigh a hundred and twenty tons. How
this ponderous block was ever brought to the city of
Mycenae and hoisted into its place is an unsolved puzzle.
However it is there forming part of the lintel (for there
are in this case two slabs) of the great domed tomb called
the Treasury of Atreus. This, without doubt, is one of
the ' underground structures ' spoken of by Pausanias,
which are now known to be tombs. From their shape
they are sometimes called bee-hive tombs. There are
eight such tombs at Mycenae, and seventeen more have
been excavated in other parts of Greece. They are all
constructed in the same way : a domed chamber is
hollowed out inside a rocky hillock, or in the slope of a
mountain ; a passage is cut from outside through the
slope of the hill to the height of the door by which the
tomb was entered. The façade, or front, of the Treasury
of Atreus is 46 feet high ; the passage through the hill
leading to it is 115 feet long, 20 feet wide, and its sides
reach a height of 45 feet at the end next the entrance to
the tomb. A door about 18 feet high, and in breadth
8 feet 9 inches diminishing to 8 feet 1 inch at the top,
leads into the tomb itself.[1] This domed chamber is

_____

[1] The general appearance of this façade and door may be judged from
its exact reproduction in one of the Greek Rooms at the British Museum.

48 feet in diameter and 48 feet high. It is hollowed out of the very rock of the hill ; then carefully cased with rounded stones rising course above course to the number of thirty-three. On the right as one enters is a doorway leading to a smaller chamber, square in shape, 27 feet across and 19 high. Probably both these chambers were originally, like the shaft-graves, rich with the trappings of the dead. But if this was so, the tombs were long ago plundered ; for there was nothing in them when they were opened up in modern times. Schliemann cleared the ' dromos,' or approach to the Treasury of Atreus, and Mrs. Schliemann excavated another tomb scarcely less remarkable known as the Treasury of Clytaemnestra.

Hellas before the Achaeans.—A great deal more has been learnt of the site of Mycenae since Schliemann carried out his great work there in 1876, though nothing has been discovered to rival his first magnificent successes ; and a great deal more has been learnt by excavations in other places. The result in sum has been the extending of our knowledge of Greek lands backward into the past beyond the heroic age by several hundred years. A veil has been drawn aside, as it were, and a new vista of life in Hellenic lands before the Trojan war has suddenly been revealed. The things brought to light by archaeological research have demonstrated the existence of an earlier civilization in some respects resembling that depicted in the Homeric poems, but differing in others ; and this earlier civilization shows a greater advance in the arts of life, particularly in the fine arts, than that displayed by Homer's Achaeans. The art exhibited in the treasures of the rock-tombs of Mycenae is called Mycenaean, and similar art-forms found in excavating at other places are Mycenaean too. Comparative archaeology, chiefly by the aid of what has previously been concluded about Egypt, is able to date this earlier civilization at a considerably earlier epoch than that assumed for the Trojan war. Tradition places the Trojan war in the twelfth century B.C. Comparative archaeology assigns the building of the Lion Gate and of the fortress walls of Mycenae to the fourteenth, and infers that the shaft-graves within the ring-circle go back to the seventeenth century. At all events the shaft-graves and the ring-wall are clearly more ancient than the fortress wall. For this one simple piece of evidence is decisive. The citadel wall here, near the Lion Gate, is supported on an artificial terrace evidently constructed *to avoid breaking through the stone circle.* The fortress wall, no doubt, was built in this way so as to include within it the stone circle, because the walled circle enclosed a royal place of sepulchre which it would have been sacrilegious to disturb. But this one fact that the rock-tombs are more ancient than the Cyclopean wall is decisive against the identification of the bearded mask with Agamemnon (see p. 123). For the citadel walls are demonstrably older than Agamemnon.

The conclusion then is that within the double slab-circle we have the sepulchres of a wealthy dynasty that reigned at Mycenae some three or four hundred years *before* the Trojan war. Agamemnon, and Atreus his father, may have been later princes of this dynasty ; but more probably they belong to a later dynasty of different race, which displaced the kings of the rock-tombs and reigned in their stead. In any case the rich furniture in the rock-tombs is solid evidence of the wealth and luxury of Mycenae at an era earlier than the Trojan war ; and, therefore, by reasonable inference of the riches and power of the line of the Atridae which overthrew these earlier princes. For whether by succession or by conquest, the Atridae were inheritors of the wealth and power of these earlier kings. Mr. A. J. B. Wace, Director of the British School at Athens, who last year (1920) was working on the Mycenae sites and testing their witness to the uttermost, writes, in summing up the broad results of these, the latest, investigations there : "All these tombs and the other best known monuments of Mycenae, the Lion Gate, the massive Cyclopean walls of the Acropolis, and the Royal Grave Circle, may well have been built, if we may assume that the ancient Greek legends contain a kernel of historic truth, by the princes of the dynasty which culminated with Agamemnon. If we consider the wealth and power necessary for such gigantic constructions, we shall recognize how justified is Homer's epic description of the might and majesty of the Atridae." [1]

Crete and the Minotaur.—Schliemann's excavations at Hissarlik restored to the student of Greek history the very stones of Troy. His excavations at Mycenae brought to light material for the reconstruction of an earlier Mycenaean age hitherto unknown. There has been a third vital era of discovery in the Hellenic world, when, in the last years of the nineteenth and the first of the present century, excavations in Crete, at Knossos and elsewhere, revealed abundant evidence of an age yet earlier than the Mycenaean. And the hero of the excavations this time is an Englishman, Sir Arthur Evans, till recently Keeper of the Ashmolean Museum at Oxford. Though students of archaeology already surmised that Crete held secrets for the archaeologist worth the discovering, little systematic exploration was possible till Crete was made freely accessible to western scholars through the liberation of Crete from the Turk in the last decade of the nineteenth century. Sir Arthur Evans began work at Knossos, the city of the mythical king, Minos, in 1894. In the first six years of the new century discoveries were made not less momentous in their significance than Schliemann's at Troy and at Mycenae : Sir Arthur Evans at Knossos " has equalled Dr. Schliemann in good fortune and surpassed him in skill." [2] It is beyond the scope of this chapter to give any circumstantial account of the marvellous discoveries at Knossos, but it is apposite to our purpose to note that a more extensive and splendid palace has been excavated there than that at Mycenae—a palace so extensive and so intricate in structure that it at once suggests a new inter-

[1] Mr. A. J. B. Wace's article in the *Times Literary Supplement* for June the 24th, 1920.

[2] Hawes (C. H. and H. B.), *Crete the Forerunner of Greece*, p. 12.

pretation of the legend of the labyrinth. It now seems probable that the labyrinth, wherein, story said, Theseus fought the Minotaur, was really the palace of the kings of Knossos with its maze of apartments and passages. The labyrinth of legend was a fanciful embroidery of this reality. The name is probably derived from the ' labrys,' or double-axe, an emblem frequently found among the ornaments of the palace. This had quite certainly a religious meaning and may be supposed to have been also the cognizance of the Royal House. The Labyrinth means, therefore, the Place or Palace of the Double Axe. Even a rational explanation of the Minotaur is suggested by one art-subject found frequently among the relics of Knossos—that is—bull-baiting. If fierce bulls were kept at Knossos and war-captives forced to fight them, a story like that of the Minotaur might easily have been told at Athens.

The historian Thucydides preserves the tradition of an early Cretan power in the Aegean—a thalattocratia or sea-empire—which he associates with the name of king Minos.[1] The discoveries at Knossos testify that wealthy and powerful kings once reigned there, and it is quite credible that Minos really exercised a wide sway over the Aegean and could make his power felt at Athens.[2] The excavations at Knossos and several other places in Crete reveal a civilization even more elaborate than the Mycenaean and curiously modern in character.[3] It

[1] Thucydides, i. 4 and i. 8.

[2] There was a small island called Minoa close to Nisaea, the harbour of Megara near Salamis, which was probably originally a ' Minoan ' trading-station, or fort.

[3] " The finds of that first season's work " (1900) " were indeed marvellous. Besides the Throne and the Cupbearer, there were the long corridors with their rows and rows of long Aladdin's jars, twenty in a single store-room, many of them still standing in position and intact, as when they once held the wine and oil of King Minos. On the walls were frescoes of ' his minions and his dames,' in garden or in balcony ' viewing the games '; the men close-shaven and with flowing hair, the women with puffed sleeves and flounced skirts, frisées et décolletées, altogether ladies of fashion and the Court, of whom the French savant might well exclaim, 'Mais ce sont des Parisiennes.'" Burrows (Dr. R. M.), *Discoveries in Crete*, p. 3.

culminated in the rule of Minos in the fifteenth century B.C., but its beginnings can be traced at least a thousand years earlier. The earliest Minoan period, with which the Bronze Age begins, is put as far back as from 2800 to 2600 B.C. Eight more stages are distinguished between this period and the Siege of Troy, making nine Minoan periods in all : Early, Middle and Late Minoan, each subdivided into three periods. The Golden Age of Minos is technically known as Second Late Minoan and is dated by Sir Arthur Evans between 1500 and 1350 B.C. Destruction came to the palace of Knossos at the end of this period. There is neither written record nor tradition ; but the stones at Knossos themselves testify that this destruction was swift, sudden and complete. Knossos never revived. The sceptre of power passed from Crete to the mainland. And so we are led on to the overlordship of the princes of Mycenae and to the Trojan War.

Crete and Hellas.—The Minoan civilization is different from the Hellenic, and almost certainly the Minoan peoples were of quite a different race. Yet, in a sense, Greek history and Greek civilization begin with Crete. For in art and civilization Minoan leads on without a break to Mycenaean ; Mycenaean to Achaean ; Achaean to Hellenic. These Cretan origins have a very special interest to-day, when the ablest and best of the Greeks of modern time, the man who brought Greece safely through the Great War and raised her to an importance politically in the world, both east and west, which she has not reached since the fourth century B.C.—Eleutherios Venizelos—is a Cretan by birth. For our day the last word in Greek history, as well as the first, is Crete. And this remains true although Venizelos, like Themistocles, that other saviour of his country in the times of Persian invasion, is now an exile.

CHAPTER VII

THE STORY OF ODYSSEUS

1. HIS WANDERINGS

> " I am become a name ;
> For always roaming with a hungry heart
> Much have I seen and known. . . ."

ODYSSEUS was the son of Laertes, hereditary chieftain of Ithaca and overlord of the western isles of Greece—Same, Cephallenia and Zacynthus. When Agamemnon gathered the host of the Achaeans to war against Troy, he had not long been married, and reluctantly left his young wife, Penelope, and his newly-born son, Telemachus, to lead a squadron from the western isles to the Troad. When the story of the *Odyssey*, the other of the two great Greek epics, opens, he had been absent from home nearly twenty years. For ten years he had been fighting at Troy, and by his daring and sagacity had contributed more than any other hero, excepting only Achilles, to the ultimate success of the Greek arms. In the quarrel between the royal brothers he had sided at first with Menelaus ; then loyalty to Agamemnon took him back from Tenedos, where the ships following Menelaus had cast anchor. This was the last that was known about him among the Greeks who had reached home : and now, when another ten years had passed, he was still far from Ithaca, eating out his heart with longing for wife and child, detained against his will in the island of Ogygia by the nymph Calypso. The misfortunes which had befallen him in these years were due to the anger of Poseidon,

whom he had offended ; but the other gods were not
unmindful of the long trial of his patience, and Athena,
who had found in him a hero after her own heart, one
day took advantage of the absence of Poseidon in distant
Ethiopia to propose in the Council of the gods on Mount
Olympus a plan for his deliverance. Hermes should go
to Ogygia and lay on Calypso the strict command of Zeus
to devise means to send Odysseus home. Pallas Athene
herself speeds through the air to Ithaca in order that she
may breathe a new spirit into Odysseus' son, Telemachus,
now grown to manhood, that he may assert himself
against those who are wronging him. For now so many
years had passed since the fall of Troy that few people
could still believe there was any prospect of Odysseus'
return. Only Penelope, his wife, still clung to the hope,
and their son Telemachus, who had been brought up to
look for his father's return home as the one thing on
which all else in life turned. The young chieftains of
Ithaca and the neighbouring islands insisted on regarding
Penelope as free to marry again, and pressed her to
choose one of their number for husband in accordance
with custom. They flocked to Odysseus' palace in
Ithaca, and there, as guests uninvited and unwelcome,
they feasted and rioted, wasting the patrimony of Telemachus, as the weeks and months slipped by. The
Suitors were selfishly unscrupulous. Telemachus by
reason of his youth had no power to send them away ;
and since Odysseus' departure for Troy authority had
grown weak in the islands : there was no one strong
enough to check the Suitors.

Telemachus' Visitor (*Odys.* i. 96-324).—This is the
state of things which Athena finds in Ithaca when, in the
likeness of Mentes, chief of the Taphians, she stands at
the threshold of Odysseus' palace. In the portico before
the house the suitors were playing draughts, while the
servants were kept busy pouring wine, and their young
master sat apart brooding over his troubles. As soon as
Telemachus caught sight of the stranger he rose to welcome him. For always he was thinking of his father and

hoping whenever a ship put in at Ithaca that some
tidings might be learnt from those aboard. So he led
his unknown visitor into the house and set two seats
apart from the rest of the company where he might talk
with him, undisturbed by the noisy revelry of the Suitors.
And this time he was not disappointed. When the meal
is finished and the Suitors are listening to the songs of
the minstrel Phemius, Telemachus receives from this
supposed friend of his father assurance that Odysseus is
alive and will return ere long. This further advice the
stranger gives : let him on the morrow first call together
the assembly of the people and make public protest
against the injurious conduct of the Suitors. That done,
let him equip a ship of twenty rowers and set out over
the sea to enquire on the mainland for news of his father ;
first of Nestor at Pylus, and then at Sparta of king
Menelaus, since Menelaus was the latest returned of the
Achaean host. When she had thus admonished Telemachus Athena vanished : and Telemachus marvelled,
aware now that his visitor was more than seemed.

Telemachus' New Resolve (*Odys.* i. 325-444).—The
Suitors were still listening to the minstrelsy of Phemius,
and the lay he was singing was the disastrous homeward
voyage of the heroes from Troy. Penelope heard the
strain in the upper room where she was sitting and it
grieved her. So she came down attended by two of her
maidens and stood by a pillar holding the veil before her
face, and she reproached Phemius for choosing a subject
which distressed her sorely. Much to her surprise she
heard herself rebuked by her son for interfering outside
her woman's province ; and, marvelling at the new tone
of authority in his speech, she withdrew as he bade her
to her own chamber. Then Telemachus turned and
addressed the Suitors : " Wooers of my mother, men
despiteful out of measure, let us feast now and make
merry and let there be no brawling ; for, lo, it is a good
thing to list to a minstrel such as this, like to the gods
in voice. But in the morning let us all go to the assembly
and sit us down, that I may declare my saying outright,

to wit that ye leave these halls : and busy yourselves with other feasts, eating your own substance, going in turn from house to house. But if ye deem this a likelier and a better thing, that one man's goods should perish without atonement, then waste ye as ye will ; and I will call upon the everlasting gods, if haply Zeus may grant that acts of recompense be made : so should ye hereafter perish within the halls without atonement." [1]

The Suitors were both angered and astonished at the boldness of this speech, and Antinous, the leading spirit among them and the most unscrupulous, answered and said : " Telemachus, in very truth the gods themselves instruct thee to be proud of speech and boldly to harangue. Never may Cronion make thee king in sea-girt Ithaca, which thing is of inheritance thy right ! " And Telemachus made answer : " Antinous, wilt thou indeed be wroth at the word that I shall say ? Yea, at the hand of Zeus would I be fain to take even this thing upon me. Sayest thou that this is the worst hap that can befal a man ? Nay, verily it is no ill thing to be a king : the house of such a one quickly waxeth rich and himself is held in greater honour. Howsoever there are many other kings of the Achaeans in seagirt Ithaca, kings young and old ; someone of them shall surely have this king-ship since goodly Odysseus is dead. But as for me, I will be lord of our own house and thralls, that goodly Odysseus gat me with his spear." [2]

Telemachus' Appeal to the Ithacans (*Odys*. ii. 1-207).— Next morning the Agora, or public gathering, is duly summoned at Telemachus' command, and this made no small stir, because no meeting had been held since the day Odysseus left for Troy. Then Telemachus lays his plaint before his people. He begs them to use their authority to restrain the Suitors and free his home from their presence. Antinous boldly answers this challenge and lays the blame on Penelope, relating the story of the famous ruse which Penelope used to gain time : how she

[1] *Odys*. i. 368-380. Butcher and Lang, p. 13.
[2] *Odys*. i. 384-398. Butcher and Lang, p. 13.

began to weave a mantle and promised to make her choice and wed one of the suitors when it was finished ; but she unravelled at night the work she had done by day, till the trick was betrayed by one of her maid-servants. Telemachus has an easy remedy : let him send his mother back to her father's house, and then it will be her father's business to arrange a new marriage : but so long as she remains in the palace, the suitors, Antinous declares, will persist in their wooing. To this Telemachus replies that he cannot turn his mother out of the house against her will. He utterly declines to send her away by force. He bids the Suitors begone, and warns them that their unjust conduct may bring on them punishment from heaven. The sympathies of the people are with Telemachus, but they have not enough courage to oppose the party of the Suitors. One man alone, the aged Halitherses, speaks out and denounces the doom which will surely come, if these unrighteous courses are persisted in. For this Eurymachus assails him with abuse and threats. As for Odysseus—he is dead.

Telemachus finds help in Mentor (*Odys*. ii. 208-434).— Telemachus having failed in his appeal, now asks for a ship in which to start on his quest and for a crew of twenty men. Hereupon Mentor, a noble Ithacan, the trusted friend to whom Odysseus, when he sailed for Troy, had committed the charge of his house, rises and rebukes the people for their slackness in not restraining the Suitors, and for their ingratitude to Odysseus who had been to them a just ruler and protector. This excites Leocritus, another of the faction, to violent abuse : he even boasts that not even were Odysseus himself present would he and his friends refrain from doing as they pleased. Upon this the assembly broke up. But Tele-machus went to the sea-shore and prayed to Athena for help. And Athena came to him, this time in the likeness of Mentor, his father's friend, and promised to obtain a ship for him and a crew to man it. So Telemachus went back home ; and there the Suitors greeted him with mockery and derision. Telemachus, however, went his

way and induced Eurycleia, the aged housekeeper who
had been Odysseus' nurse, to supply him with the wine
and barley-meal required for his voyage. And he charged
her to say nothing as yet to his mother, lest she should
try to detain him. Accordingly, when night came, Athena
called the crew, man by man, and got them all on board,
then went to fetch Telemachus. The wine and the meal
were stowed in the ship and Telemachus put to sea, with
Athena, still in the guise of Mentor, as his companion.

The Visit to Pylus (*Odys.* iii. 1-384).—The voyage to
Nestor's country on the mainland opposite, somewhat
south of Ithaca, took just one night, and at dawn the
vessel came to shore close to the city of Pylus. It happened that the Pylians were that morning offering a great
sacrifice to Poseidon. Nine companies of men were
gathered on the shore, five hundred men to a company,
and to each of these bands nine bulls were apportioned for
sacrifice. Encouraged by Athena, Telemachus landed
and approached the parties seated on the shore. In one
of them sat Nestor and his sons making preparations for
the feast that was to follow the sacrifice ; some engaged
in roasting the meat, some putting slices on spits. As
Telemachus with Athena in the likeness of Mentor
approached, a crowd of people came forward to welcome
them, among these Pisistratus, youngest of Nestor's sons,
a bachelor of Telemachus' age, who took both by the
hand and made them sit down near Nestor himself upon
fleeces spread out on the beach for seats. They were
invited to share in the banquet, and when they had
feasted well, Nestor enquired who they were. Telemachus at once made known the whole object of his
journey. But of his father there is little that Nestor
can tell him ; for they had parted at Tenedos at the
beginning of the voyage home, when Odysseus went back
to rejoin Agamemnon at Troy, whereas Nestor sailed
on home with all speed. Since then Nestor had heard
no tidings of Odysseus, but he counsels Telemachus to
go on to Sparta and enquire further of Menelaus, for
Menelaus had but recently returned from a distant

country after long wanderings. At the same time he offers Telemachus a chariot and horses to make the journey by land, and tells him that Pisistratus shall go with him to bear him company. That night Telemachus at Nestor's invitation sleeps in the palace ; but Athena declines the invitation and vanishes.

The Journey to Sparta (*Odys*. iii. 404-iv. 36).—Next morning Pisistratus is ready betimes with the chariot and horses, and Nestor speeds the parting guest. By evening the two young men have reached Pherae, a township midway between Pylus and Sparta, and there rest for the night. By the evening of the next day they are approaching Sparta. There they find the household of Menelaus busied with the marriage of Hermione, Menelaus' daughter, Helen's only child. The wedding feast is at its height in the great high-roofed hall, and Menelaus' steward, Eteoneus, is sorely perplexed whether to bid them welcome or send them elsewhere for hospitality. But Menelaus rebukes him sharply, saying, " Eteoneus, son of Boethous, truly thou wert not a fool aforetime, but now for this once, like a child thou talkest folly. Surely our own selves ate much hospitable cheer of other men, ere we twain came hither, even if in time to come Zeus haply give us rest from affliction. Nay go, unyoke the horses of the strangers, and as for the men, lead them forward to the house to feast with us." [1]

The Palace of Menelaus (*Odys*. iv. 37-112).—" So spake he, and Eteoneus hasted from the hall, and called the other ready squires to follow with him. So they loosed the sweating horses from beneath the yoke, and fastened them at the stalls of the horses, and threw beside them spelt, and therewith mixed white barley, and tilted the chariot against the shining faces of the gateway, and led the men into the hall divine. And they beheld and marvelled as they gazed throughout the palace of the king, the fosterling of Zeus ; for there was a gleam as it were of sun or moon through the lofty palace of renowned

[1] *Odys*. iv. 31-36 (B. & L. p. 49).

Menelaus. But after they had gazed their fill, they went to the polished baths and bathed. Now when the maidens had bathed them and anointed them with olive oil, and cast about them thick cloaks and doublets, they sat on chairs by Menelaus, son of Atreus. And a hand-maid bare water for the hands in a goodly golden ewer, and poured it forth over a silver basin to wash withal; and to their side she drew a polished table, and a grave dame bare food and set it by them, and laid upon the board many dainties, giving freely of such things as she had by her, and a carver lifted and placed by them platters of divers kinds of flesh, and nigh them he set golden bowls. So Menelaus of the fair hair greeted the twain and spake: "Taste ye food and be glad, and thereafter when ye have supped, we will ask what men ye are. . . ." So spake he, and took and set before them the fat ox-chine roasted, which they had given him as his own mess by way of honour. . . . Now when they had put from them the desire of meat and drink, Tele-machus spake to the son of Nestor, holding his head close to him, that those others might not hear: "Son of Nestor, delight of my heart, mark the flashing of bronze through the echoing halls, and the flashing of gold and of amber and of silver and of ivory. Such like, methinks, is the court of Olympian Zeus within, for the world of things that are here; wonder comes over me as I look thereon." [1] But Menelaus overheard Telemachus' words and related how he had won his great wealth ' after many woes and wide wanderings.' He then went on to speak of the dreadful fate of his brother Agamemnon during his absence and of the deaths of other heroes at Troy, and this leads to remembrance of Odysseus: "Howbeit," said Menelaus, "though I bewail them all and sorrow oftentimes as I sit in our halls,—awhile indeed I satisfy my soul with lamentation, and then again I cease; for soon hath man enough of chill lamentation—yet for them all I make no such dole, despite my grief, as for one only, who causes me to loathe both sleep and

[1] *Odys.* iv. ll. 37-75 (B. and L. pp. 49 and 50).

meat, when I think upon him. For no one of the Achaeans toiled so greatly as Odysseus toiled and adventured himself ; but to him it was to be but labour and trouble, and to me grief ever comfortless for his sake, so long he is afar, nor know we aught, whether he be alive or dead. Yea methinks they lament him, even that old Laertes and the constant Penelope and Telemachus, whom he left a child new-born in his house." [1]

Helen of Sparta (*Odys.* iv. 113-305).—Upon this Telemachus could not refrain from tears, and Menelaus noticed his weeping, but hesitated to speak of it. At this moment Helen came in " like Artemis of the golden arrows," and with her came Adraste to set a chair for her ; Alcippe bare a rug of soft wool and Phylo a silver basket, a present to Helen from Alcandre, wife of Polybus of Thebes in Egypt. Polybus " gave two silver baths to Menelaus, and tripods twain, and ten talents of gold. And besides all this, his wife bestowed on Helen lovely gifts ; a golden distaff did she give, and a silver basket with wheels beneath, and the rims thereof were finished with gold. This it was that the handmaid Phylo bare and set beside her, filled with dressed yarn, and across it was laid a distaff charged with wool of violet blue. So Helen sat her down in the chair, and beneath was a footstool for the feet. And anon she spake to her lord and questioned him of each thing : " Menelaus, fosterling of Zeus, know we now who these men avow themselves to be that have come under our roof ? Shall I dissemble or shall I speak the truth ? Nay, I am minded to tell it. None, I say, have I ever yet seen so like another, man nor woman—wonder comes over me as I look on him—as this man is like the son of great-hearted Odysseus, Telemachus, whom he left a new-born child in his house, when for the sake of me, shameless woman that I was, ye Achaeans came up under Troy with bold war in your hearts." [2] Menelaus marks this likeness, too, when it is

---

[1] *Odys.* iv. 100-112 (B. and L. p. 51).
[2] *Odys.* iv. 128-146 (B and L. p. 52).

pointed out to him by Helen, and tells her how this young man had shed tears at the mention of Odysseus' name. But here Pisistratus breaks in and explains who they are and why they have come. There is then much rejoicing and sorrowing : of rejoicing because the son of a man whom Menelaus had greatly loved is come as a guest to his halls ; of sorrowing because each is reminded of some pain and loss. Helen and Telemachus and Menelaus, therefore, wept ; " nor did the son of Nestor keep tearless eyes. For he bethought him in his heart of noble Antilochus, whom the glorious son of the bright Dawn had slain." [1] Of this brother's fate he reminds Menelaus, at the same time urging the wisdom of moderating their grief. Menelaus readily agrees, complimenting him on his good sense, which well becomes a son of the wise Nestor. Moreover, Helen prepared a wonderful draught, putting into the wine " a drug to lull all pain and anger, and bring forgetfulness of every sorrow." Of this drug it is said that " whoso should drink a draught thereof, when it is mingled in the bowl, on that day he would let no tears fall down his cheeks, not though his mother and his father died, not though men slew his brother or dear son with the sword before his face, and his own eyes beheld it." [2] Long time they sat discoursing and telling stories : then beds are prepared for Telemachus and Pisistratus by Helen's orders in the portico, and there they sleep that night.

Menelaus' Tidings (*Odys.* iv. 306-619).—Next morning Menelaus comes and sits by Telemachus and enquires what has brought him to Sparta. Telemachus makes known his desire for news of his father and the troubles which beset his home. He beseeches Menelaus to tell him anything he knows, even though the news be bad news. In response to this earnest entreaty Menelaus relates the whole story of his own detention in Egypt and his adventures with Proteus, the sea-god of changing

[1] *Odys.* iv. 186-188 (B. and L. p. 54).
[2] *Odys.* iv. 220-226 (B. and L. p. 55).

form, in the island Pharos. From Proteus he had learnt that Odysseus was living, but was the prisoner of Calypso, pining in her magic island for his home in Ithaca. His tale ended, he invites Telemachus to make a longer stay at Sparta.

The Plot to kill Telemachus (*Odys*. iv. 621-847).—Meantime in Ithaca the Suitors, on learning that Telemachus has really sailed away as he said, plot to send a ship to lie in wait for him as he returns and kill him. Thus they pass from insolence to crime and fill up the measure of their iniquity. Penelope soon after discovers Telemachus' absence and at the same time hears from a faithful henchman, Medon, of the Suitors' plot. She is overwhelmed with grief and anxiety, but prays to Athena, and Athena sends her a comforting dream. But Antinous and the Suitors proceed to the stealthy execution of their plot. They choose out twenty of their number and launch a ship and put suits of arms on board of her, and moor the ship in the roadstead ready to sail. And when night came the twenty men went on board and sailed away to an island half-way between Ithaca and rugged Same. This island the poet calls Asteris. There they moored their ship and waited for Telemachus.

Odysseus and Calypso (*Odys*. v. 1-224).—And now the story leaves Telemachus and turns at last to Odysseus himself where he was pining still in Calypso's isle. Athena makes a fresh appeal to the gods of Olympus, and this time not in vain. Zeus straightway sends Hermes to Ogygia with exact instructions how Odysseus is to be transported on a raft to Scheria and thence conveyed to Ithaca through the friendly offices of the Phaeacians. Hermes finds Calypso in the cavern where she dwelt and lays strict command upon her to forward Odysseus' departure. Calypso murmurs, but obeys. When Hermes is gone, she searches the island for Odysseus, and finds him by the sea-shore weeping and straining his eyes over the sea. She promises to help him to get away if he will build himself a raft. Odysseus is incredulous at first

and requires Calypso to swear an oath that this is no
trap for his undoing. And Calypso replied : " Knavish
thou art, and no weakling in wit, thou that hast conceived
and spoken such a word. Let earth be now witness
hereto, and the wide heaven above, and that falling water
of the Styx, the greatest oath and the most terrible to the
blessed gods, that I will not plan any hidden guile to
thine own hurt." [1] Then Calypso took him back with
her and set mortal food before him while she herself ate
ambrosia [2] and drank nectar ; [2] and she reproached him
for leaving her for a mere mortal woman and warned him
of the distresses he must yet pass through before reaching
home. But Odysseus answered : " Be not wroth with
me hereat, goddess and queen. Myself I know it well,
how wise Penelope is meaner to look upon than thou in
comeliness and stature. But she is mortal and thou
knowest not age nor death. Yet even so, I wish and long
day by day to fare homeward and see the day of my
returning. Yea, and if some god shall wreck me in the
wine-dark deep, even so I will endure, with a heart within
me patient of affliction. For already have I suffered full
much, and much have I toiled in perils of waves and war ;
let this be added to the tale of those." [3]

The Voyage to Scheria (*Odys.* v. 228-493).—Next day
Odysseus built the raft under Calypso's direction. Four
days was the raft in making, and on the fifth Calypso
loaded it with abundant provisions and a skin of wine
and a great skin of water. Then Odysseus put off in the
raft and spread his sail to a fair wind, and steered his
course by the Great Bear as Calypso had directed. For
seventeen days the voyage continued without misadventure, and on the eighteenth there appeared to his
sight the shadowy mountains of the land of the Phaeacians, where it lay on the sea ' like unto a shield in the
misty deep.' And by ill chance Poseidon, newly returned

---

[1] *Odys.* v. ll. 182-187 (B. and L. p. 82).
[2] Ambrosia and nectar were the food and drink of the immortal gods.
[3] *Odys.* v. 215-224 (B. and L. p. 83).

from his business with the Ethiopians, caught sight of the hero voyaging tranquilly on his raft, and great was the wrath of the Earth-shaker. " Out on it," he cried, " the gods surely have changed their purpose regarding Odysseus, while I was away among the Ethiopians ; and now he is near the land of the Phaeacians where he is fated to escape the great issues of the woe which hath come upon him. Yet methinks even now will I drive him far enough along the path of suffering." [1] And then at Poseidon's will the skies darkened and the winds rushed down, East wind and South wind, and West, and North, confusedly ; and the billows rolled over the raft and tossed it about. One huge wave snapped the mast and swept Odysseus himself into the sea. As he came up he clutched the raft and scrambled on to it again ; and the raft with Odysseus upon it was tossed this way and that over the wild sea. Then in his direst need Leucothea, a sea-goddess who had once been a woman and a queen— Ino, the daughter of Cadmus—saw him and had compassion upon him, and gave him her veil with the promise, that if he wound it round his body and cast himself clear of the raft, he should be saved. Odysseus feared at first to leave the raft, because he was still a great distance from the land ; but another great wave came and broke the raft up, scattering its planks over the sea. Then he got astride one of the planks, stripped off his clothes as Leucothea had bidden, and having wound the veil about his body, slipped into the sea and began to swim. For two nights and two days he swam on, and at length the shore was near at hand. And then a new peril arose. When he was now within a short distance of land, he heard the boom of the sea upon the rocks and knew there was no safety that way ; for the water was everywhere deep close in shore, the cliffs rose up steep and sheer and below were jagged rocks. So he swam along by the cliffs in the hope of finding a possible landing place. Once he was almost dashed upon the reef and escaped only by clinging to a rock till the great wave had passed.

[1] *Odys.* v. 286-290

But still he swam on, and at last to his great relief he came over against the mouth of a river, where there was shelter from the wind and a beach free of sharp stones. And so at last he struggled into shallow water, and sank upon the shore breathless and speechless and with scarce strength left to move. When he had revived a little, he unwound the veil and, as the goddess had bidden him, dropped it into the river, whence it was carried back into Ino's hands.

So was Odysseus safe at last upon dry land after his terrible ordeal, but stark naked and utterly exhausted. With night coming on, a new apprehension seized him. If he stayed by the riverside, he feared he might be overcome by cold : if, on the other hand, he sought refuge in the thick brushwood on the slope above, he feared he might be attacked by wild beasts. In the end, choosing as he thought the lesser of the two evils, he crept up into the wood and found shelter between two thick bushes. There he sank down and covered himself with the fallen leaves. Soon he was sleeping the sleep of exhaustion.

Nausicaa (*Odys.* vi. 1-84).—While Odysseus lay in deep slumber in the shelter of the bushes, Athena was busy preparing for him a kindly reception by the Phaeacians. For the land to which he had been borne was the island of Scheria, where far removed from other men dwelt the Phaeacians in happy security under their king Alcinous and his wife Arete. Alcinous and Arete had a daughter now come to a marriageable age, the princess Nausicaa. She was sleeping in her chamber in the palace with two handmaidens at her door, one on either side. To her the goddess appeared in a vision in the likeness of a friend of like age with herself, the daughter of Dymas, admonishing her to carry all the clothes that needed washing to the washing-ground by the river mouth, since her marriage-day was near at hand, and it would not do to be taken unawares without good store of raiment newly washed. Should not Nausicaa next day ask her father for the mule-waggon and drive to the washing-tanks ? She her-

self would come too and help. Accordingly next morning
Nausicaa went to her father, king Alcinous, and made
her request; only she said nothing about her own marriage-
day, but gave as her reasons for asking, her father's need
of clean raiment for his council meetings and her brothers'
requirements for the dances they delighted in. Alcinous,
however, very well understood what she meant and
immediately assented. So the car was brought out, the
mules yoked, and piles of clothing, brought from the
house, were placed upon it. Arete, Nausicaa's mother,
supplied abundance of food and wine, and added a flask
of oil in case the girls liked to bathe after their work.
Then Nausicaa herself mounted the car, took up the
reins and drove off. And the hoofs made a lively clatter
as the waggon sped along the road.

Odysseus' Awakening (*Odys*. vi. 85-185).—In due time
they came to the washing tanks by the river, unharnessed
the mules and let them run free ; then set diligently to
their task. When the clothes were all washed and spread
out on the pebbles to dry in the sun, the girls bathed
and afterwards sat down to enjoy their picnic. After
lunch they played a game in which a ball was thrown and
caught to the rhythm of a song. Nausicaa was leader
and outshone all the others. As the time drew near to
end the game and think of returning, it happened (through
Athena's contrivance) that Nausicaa in throwing the ball
to one of her handmaids missed her aim, and the ball fell
into a pool of water. This caused an outcry, and the
outcry woke Odysseus. Greatly did the hero wonder to
what land he had come, and, pushing aside the bushes,
and using a broken branch as a covering, stepped forth
into view. The girls screamed and scattered, all except
Nausicaa, who held her ground. Odysseus marvelled at
her beauty and courage, and addressed her in carefully
chosen words : for a moment he inclined to clasp the
maiden's knees in supplication, but, fearing to offend, he
appealed for help in these words : " I supplicate thee,
O queen, whether thou art a goddess or a mortal ! If
indeed thou art a goddess of them that keep the wide

heaven ; to Artemis then, the daughter of Zeus, I mainly
liken thee, for beauty and stature and shapeliness. But
if thou art one of the daughters of men who dwell on
earth, thrice blessed are thy father and thy lady mother,
and thrice blessed are thy brethren. Surely their souls
ever glow with gladness for thy sake, each time they see
thee entering the dance, so fair a flower of maidens. But
he is of heart the most blessed beyond all other who
shall prevail with gifts of wooing, and lead thee to his
home. Never have mine eyes beheld such an one among
mortals, neither man nor woman ; great awe comes upon
me as I look on thee. . . . I wonder at thee, lady, and
am astonied and do greatly fear to touch thy knees,
though grievous sorrow is upon me. Yesterday, on the
twentieth day, I escaped from the wine-dark deep, but
all that time continually the wave bare me, and the
vehement winds drave, from the isle Ogygia. And now
some god has cast me on this shore, that here, too, methinks, some evil may betide me ; for I trow not that
trouble will cease : the gods ere that time will yet bring
many a thing to pass. But, queen, have pity on me,
for after many trials and sore to thee first of all am I come,
and of the other folk, who hold this city and land, I know
no man. Nay show me the town, give me an old garment
to cast about me, if thou hadst, when thou camest here,
any wrap for the linen. And may the gods grant thee
all thy heart's desire : a husband and a home, and a
mind at one with his may they give—a good gift, for
there is nothing mightier and nobler than when man and
wife are of one heart and mind in a house, a grief to their
foes, and to their friends great joy ; but their own hearts
know it best." [1]

Nausicaa's Kindness (*Odys*. vi. 186-250).—And Nausicaa
said in reply : " Stranger, forasmuch as thou seemest no
evil man nor foolish—and it is Olympian Zeus himself
that giveth weal to men, to the good and to the evil, to
each one as he will, and this thy lot doubtless is of him,
and so thou must in any wise endure it :—and now, since

[1] *Odys*. vi. 149-185 (B. and L. pp. 97 and 98).

thou hast come to our city and our land, thou shalt not
lack raiment, nor aught else that is the due of a hapless
suppliant, when he has met them who can befriend him.
And I will show thee the town, and name the name of
the people. The Phaeacians hold this city and land, and
I am the daughter of Alcinous, great of heart, on whom
all the might and force of the Phaeacians depend." [1]
Then she rebuked her maidens for their cowardice and
bade them minister to the stranger's needs, food and
clothing, and the requisites of the bath. And when
Odysseus had washed the brine from his skin and anointed
his body with oil, and put on the tunic and cloak which
the maidens had selected for him, he came forth looking
taller and younger and handsomer, and sat down by the
seashore. The maidens all marvelled at the change and
set before the hero the food and drink he needed so badly.

Nausicaa's Return to the Palace (*Odys*. vi. 251-vii. 13).—
After this the party prepared to return to the city. The
clean raiment was all folded and placed in the waggon.
Nausicaa took her seat again and bade Odysseus follow
with her maidens to the outskirts of the town ; but there
he was to wait by a poplar grove sacred to Athena till
they had time to reach the palace. Then he could easily
enquire his way on. She also told him to make supplication first to her mother, queen Arete. They reached the
grove as the sun was setting, and Odysseus sat him down
as he had been told to do, while Nausicaa drove on home.
There she was received by her brothers, who took out
the mules, unloaded the car and bore the raiment indoors.
She herself went to her chamber where her waiting-woman
Eurymedeia lit a fire and prepared supper.

Odysseus at the Palace of Alcinous (*Odys*. vii. 14-347).—
Odysseus offered a brief prayer to Athena, and, after
waiting a short time, went on into the city. And Athena
herself again came to his aid in the guise of a young girl
carrying a pitcher, and at his request showed him the
way to the palace. Then Odysseus entered the palace

---

[1] *Odys*. vi. 186-197 (B. and L. p. 98).

and marvelled greatly at the splendour which there dazzled his eyes. " Brazen were the walls which ran this way and that from the threshold to the inmost chamber, and round them was a frieze of blue, and golden were the doors that closed in the good house. Silver were the door-posts that were set on the brazen threshold, and silver the lintel thereupon, and the hook of the door was of gold. And on either side stood golden hounds and silver, which Hephaestus wrought by his cunning to guard the palace of great-hearted Alcinous, being free from death and age all their days." [1] And near the palace there was a wonderful orchard, four acres in extent. " And there grow tall trees blossoming," says the poet, " pear-trees and pomegranates, and apple-trees with bright fruit, and sweet figs, and olives in their bloom. The fruit of these trees never perisheth neither faileth, winter nor summer, enduring through all the year. Evermore the West Wind blowing brings some fruits to birth and ripens others." [2] Odysseus entered quickly and saw the hall full of leaders and counsellors sitting over their wine after a feast at Alcinous' table. And Odysseus, as he had been admonished, went straight to where Arete sat by the palace hearth with her husband king Alcinous, and he clasped her knees as a suppliant and made his prayer. And there was a hush throughout the hall, until presently an old counsellor, named Echeneus, was moved to exclaim at the delay. Thereupon Alcinous raised Odysseus from the hearth, and set him in the seat of honour next himself, and had meat and drink placed before him. Wine was served out to all, and before the company separated Alcinous laid proposals before them for the hospitable entertainment of the stranger and his safe convoy home. So far no questions had been asked ; but when the other guests were gone, and Odysseus was alone with Alcinous and Arete, Arete, who had recognized the garments he was wearing, questioned him about them ; and he told her of his voyage from Calypso's isle

[1] *Odys.* vii. 86-94 (B. and L. pp. 105 and 106).
[2] *Odys.* vii. 114-121 (B. and L. p. 106).

and the storm, of his escape from the sea and the meeting with Nausicaa, and of Nausicaa's kindness in befriending him. Alcinous listened benevolently to his explanations, and promised him a ship next day and safe-conduct home. A bed was then prepared for the guest in the portico of the house, and there after his tossing and privations Odysseus slept in peace that night.

The Banquet and the Games (*Odys*. viii. 1-384).—Next day high festival was held among the Phaeacians to honour their unknown visitor from the sea. Alcinous proposed in the public assembly that a ship with two and fifty oarsmen should be made ready to take Odysseus home to Ithaca, and he invited the chiefs of the people to a banquet. And all came, and with them the minstrel Demodocus " whom the Muse loved very dearly and gave him both good and evil ; of his sight she deprived him, but gave him the gift of sweet song." [1] Him the herald Pontonous led to a place of honour among the feasters close against a pillar, and hung his harp from a peg above his head within easy reach. And after the banquet Demodocus sang a song of the Trojan War, about a quarrel between Odysseus and Achilles, and hearing it Odysseus drew his cloak over his face and wept. Alcinous marked this, and, though he said nothing to Odysseus, he proposed, now the banquet was over, that all should go out and hold games. " Let us go forth anon," he said, " and make trial of divers games, that the stranger may tell his friends, when home he returneth, how greatly we excel all men in boxing, and wrestling, and leaping, and speed of foot." [2] So the company went out, and there was running and wrestling, and boxing and throwing the discus. And while this was going on, Laodamas, son of Alcinous, in a spirit of mockery invited Odysseus also to contend, and when Odysseus excused himself, a young Phaeacian named Euryalus, who had distinguished himself at the wrestling, treated him with insolence and taunted him as a mere trader unskilled in manly exercises. Whereat Odysseus turned sharply upon him and said :

[1] *Odys*. viii. 63 and 64.　　　[2] *Odys*. viii. 100-103 (B. and L. p. 118).

" Stranger, thou hast not spoken well ; thou art like a man presumptuous. So true it is that the gods do not give every gracious gift to all, neither shapeliness, nor wisdom, nor skilled speech. For one man is feebler than another in presence, yet the god crowns his words with beauty, and men behold him and rejoice, and his speech runs surely on his way with a sweet modesty, and he shines forth among the gathering of his people, and as he passes through the town men gaze on him as a god. Another again is like the deathless gods for beauty, but his words have no crown of grace about them ; even as thou art in comeliness pre-eminent, nor could a god himself fashion thee for the better, but in wit thou art a weakling. Yea, thou hast stirred my spirit in my breast by speaking thus amiss. I am not all unversed in sports, as thy words go, but methinks I was among the foremost while as yet I trusted in my youth and my hands, but now am I holden in misery and pains : for I have endured much in passing through the wars of men and the grievous waves of the sea. Yet even so, for all my affliction, I will essay the games, for thy word hath bitten to the quick, and thou hast roused me with thy saying." [1] This said, Odysseus seized a quoit larger and heavier than those used by the Phaeacians, and with a whirl sent it through the air far past the marks of all the competitors in the recent contest : the people crouched low as the quoit flew humming through the air. Then Athena in the form of a chance spectator set a mark on the place where it fell and cried out : " Yea, even a blind man, stranger, might discern the token if he groped for it, for it is in no wise lost among the throng of the others, but is far the first ; for this bout then take heart : not one of the Phaeacians shall attain thereunto or overpass it." [2] Odysseus was pleased at his success, and turned to the company in more genial mood and offered to meet the best of the Phaeacians in any other form of sport—boxing or wrestling or running or archery :

[1] *Odys*. viii. 166-185 (B. and L. pp. 120 and 121).
[2] *Odys*. viii. 195-198 (B. and L. p. 121).

excepting only Laodamas, who was his host. An awk-ward silence fell on the Phaeacians ; but Alcinous inter-vened and tactfully proposed an exhibition of dancing. "For," said he, with humorous disregard of the boasts he had made a little while before, "we are no perfect boxers, nor wrestlers, but speedy runners and the best of seamen ; and dear to us ever is the banquet, and the harp, and the dance, and changes of raiment, and the warm bath, and love, and sleep. Lo, now arise, ye dancers of the Phaeacians, the best in the land, and make sport, that so the stranger may tell his friends, when he returneth home, how far we surpass all men besides in seamanship, and speed of foot, and in the dance and song."[1] Then there was a pretty display of dancing in the fashion of the day, which Odysseus praised in courteous terms ; and all was once more harmony.

The Leave-taking (*Odys.* viii. 385-586).—The time had now come, Alcinous thought, to make arrangements for his guest's departure with the promised gifts. So he pro-posed that his twelve chief counsellors should each con-tribute a cloak and a tunic and a talent of gold ; and to this they all agreed, and Euryalus made atonement for his thoughtless speech by the gift of a bronze sword with belt of silver and an ivory scabbard. It was now evening, and the gifts were brought to the palace and placed before Arete, the queen, and Alcinous added a beautiful cup wrought of gold. Arete brought out a chest and packed the presents in it, and bade Odysseus himself make the lid fast with a cord ; and this he did, using a trick knot which Circe had taught him. Then, after bathing, Odysseus joined the company at table and sat down. And Nausicaa was there in her young beauty, standing by the door-post ; and she looked on Odysseus with kind eyes and bade him farewell, saying : " Farewell, stranger, remember me when thou art once more in thy native land ; for first to me thou owest the price of thy life." And Odysseus made reply : " Nausicaa, daughter of great-hearted Alcinous, now may loud-thundering Zeus

[1] *Odys.* viii. 246-249 (B. and L. p. 123).

grant me to reach home and see the day of my homecoming : so will I ever pray to thee there as to a god all
my days : for thou, maiden, hast given me life." [1]   Presently Demodocus the minstrel was led in, and Odysseus
sent him a portion of honour from the feast and begged
him to sing the tale of the Wooden Horse and the Sack
of Ilium, adding, " If thou wilt indeed tell me this tale
aright, I will declare to all mankind that the god hath
given thee abundantly the gift of divine song." [2]   Then
Demodocus complied and sang the whole story in order ;
and, as he sang, once more Odysseus was moved to tears
and hid his head as he wept.   But Alcinous again noticed
this and interposed and said : " Hear me, captains and
counsellors ;   now let Demodocus stay his hand on the
sounding lyre ;   for the song he sings is not giving pleasure
to all here :   from the time the feast began and the divine
minstrel's spirit was stirred within him, even so long
hath the stranger ceased not from woeful weeping ;   sore,
it seemeth, hath grief encompassed his heart.   Come,
then, let the minstrel stay his hand, that we may all
find delight, our guest and we who entertain him alike,
since it is far better so.   For indeed all we are doing is
for the sake of our worshipful guest, the convoy and the
kindly gifts, which we give him of our love.   In a brother's
place is the stranger and the suppliant, to one who
reacheth but a little way in understanding." [3]   Then he
turned to Odysseus and begged him to make known to
them who he was and why he wept when the minstrel
sang of the Trojan War.

Odysseus tells his Story (*Odys.* ix. 1-xii. 453).—Thus
pressed, Odysseus could not but comply, and at last
revealed to the Phaeacians his name and the place of
his birth :   " I am Odysseus, son of Laertes," he said,
" who am dear to all men for my cunning ;   and my
fame reaches unto heaven.   And I dwell in clear-seen
Ithaca, wherein is Neriton with the quivering leaves, a
mountain very plain to view :   many islands lie around
it close to one another, Dulichium and Same and wooded

[1] *Odys.* viii. 461-468.   [2] *Odys.* viii. 496-498.   [3] *Odys.* viii. 536-547.

Zacynthus. Now Ithaca lies low in the sea furthest towards the west (the rest are away towards the dawning and the sun) ; a rugged land, but a good nurse of sturdy sons : verily I for my part can imagine naught sweeter than a man's own land." [1] Then he began to tell the whole story of his adventures from the day he left the shores of the Hellespont with all his ships to the day when he was thrown upon Calypso's isle, a shipwrecked man clinging to a broken mast, sole survivor of all that company. He told how his men sacked Ismarus, a Thracian city, of the storm that caught his squadron rounding Cape Malea and drove his ships past Cythera and out into the unknown seas beyond. He told of his experiences and sufferings in the strange regions to which they were borne ; of the eaters of the Lotus, the drug that made those who tasted it forget all desire for home and friends, and all purpose in life ; of the horrible adventure in the Cave of the Cyclops Polyphemus ; of the blinding of the Cyclops' eye, which first brought upon him the vengeful anger of Poseidon (for Polyphemus was Poseidon's son). He told of his visit to an island where dwelt Aeolus, god of the winds, with his six sons and six daughters ; of the gift of a wallet in which all the winds were shut up except the fair wind which was to waft him homeward ; how, while Odysseus slept, tired out with ceaseless watching, his men in idle curiosity opened the bag and let out all the winds, when already they were near enough to Ithaca to see men tending the beacon fires ; how the ships were blown right back to the island, and how Aeolus when he heard the story would have no more to do with them. He told of the destruction of all his ships save one in the harbour of the Laestrygonians, a monstrous folk in the likeness of men, huge as mountain peaks and cannibals, who smashed the ships in the harbour with great stones and speared the men as they struggled in the water, as fishermen spear fish. He told of his strange fortunes at Aeaea, Circe's isle ; of how half his ship's company were trans-

[1] *Odys.* ix. 19-28.

formed into swine by the draught of Circe's cup, and
how with God's help he won their restoration to human
shape ; of his sojourn for a year in Circe's palace, and
how by her advice he visited the house of Hades, the
abode of the dead in the dark land beyond the stream
of Ocean. Strange were the means by which Odysseus
held commune with the dead, and strange was the knowledge he gathered from the lips of the spirits with whom
he talked. He spoke with his mother, Anticlea, who
had pined away sorrowing for his absence ; and with
Elpenor, one of his ship's company, who had fallen from
the roof of Circe's dwelling in Aeaea just before they
sailed, and who prayed Odysseus to speed his burial.
From Teiresias, the seer of Thebes, he obtained the
guidance and direction for which he had come. He
spoke also with Agamemnon and with Achilles, and saw
the wraith of Ajax striding into the gloom of the underworld in sullen silence. Also he had vision of the tor-
ments of the damned, of Tityos and Tantalus and Sisy-
phus ; he spoke with Heracles, and might have seen
others of the heroes of old but that, on a sudden, a panic
terror seized him of the thronging ghosts and their
strange cries, and he escaped back to his ship. Once, in
the course of this long narrative, Odysseus craved leave
to stop because of his weariness ; but the Phaeacians
begged him to go on and promised fresh gifts added to
those given already if he would continue his tale to the
end. So he told them also of his return to Aeaea, Circe's
isle ; of Circe's advice to him at parting and her warnings
of the dangers that still awaited him on the voyage to
Ithaca ; of the Sirens, of Scylla and Charybdis ; of the
rocks that clashed together and crushed the ship that
tried to pass between them. Above all she warned him,
as Teiresias had done already, of the danger of touching
the flocks of Helios Hypereion, the Sun-god. Odysseus
went on to tell how all happened as Circe had forewarned
him ; how they rowed safely past the Sirens, and escaped
from Scylla and Charybdis with the loss of six of his
best men, whom Scylla snatched out of the ship as it

swept by, and devoured alive. How, finally, they came to the island Thrinacria, and how Odysseus was for rowing by without anchoring there ; but his men were tired out and insisted on stopping to cook food and rest for the night. How in the night a tempest came on to blow, so that next morning they were obliged to draw up the ship and make her fast in a cavern by the shore. But the wind continued to blow that day and the next, and for many days more, till the store of food they had brought with them was exhausted, and scarcely could they keep themselves alive with the fish and water-fowl they were able to catch. This went on for a whole month ; and then one day, while Odysseus was away, the men listened to the evil counsel of one of their number, Eurylochus, and broke the oath they had sworn never to touch the sheep and kine on the island. They took the best of the kine of Helios Hypereion and slew them in sacrifice and prepared a feast by the seashore. And as Odysseus drew near on his return, the savour of the burning fat reached his nostrils, and he knew they were all undone. For six days his men feasted on the shore, and on the seventh the contrary wind abated and they put to sea in haste. But Hypereion in his anger had appealed to Zeus to punish those who had wronged him, and threatened that, if full atonement were not made, he would leave the heavens and carry his light to the underworld of the dead. To avert this catastrophe from gods and men, Zeus promised to destroy the ship with a thunderbolt. So soon after Odysseus and his men had started again, a dark cloud overshadowed the sea, and a fierce squall caught the ship and snapped the forestays, so that the mast fell down striking the helmsman and smashing his skull. Then came a crash of thunder : the ship shivered from stem to stern as the lightning struck her, and all the mariners fell into the water : only Odysseus was left alive. Then he went on to tell how soon after this the ship broke up and he was himself cast into the sea, but managed to hold on to the mast and keel which he bound together ; how clinging to this wreckage he drifted back through Scylla and Charybdis barely escaping destruction ; how finally, after nine days more, he was cast up upon Calypso's island.

Conveyance of Odysseus to Ithaca (*Odys.* xiii. 1-125).— He ceased, and for a time there was silence ; for the whole company were held spellbound by the story. At length Alcinous spoke proposing additional gifts for Odysseus, and all dispersed to their homes. Next day the ship was made ready, and in the palace banquet and song were renewed. But Odysseus was impatient to be gone, and often turned his head to see how near the sun was to his setting. Presently he begged Alcinous to speed his departure, invoking Heaven's blessing on himself and on all the Phaeacians. Then Alcinous called for a bowl of wine and sent it round as a farewell cup ; and Odysseus arose and placed the bowl in Arete's hands and spoke his farewell : "Well may it be with thee, O queen, all the days of thy life, till old age comes and death, which come upon all mankind. I depart now on my homeward way : may joy be thine in this thy house, in thy children and thy people, and in king Alcinous." [1] Thus having said, he crossed the threshold and made his way to the ship with one of the king's attendants to guide him. Three maids went with him also whom Arete sent, one to carry a change of raiment, one to carry the chest with the presents in it, and one with a provision of food and wine. When they reached the ship, the chest and the victuals were safely stowed, and a bed was spread for Odysseus on deck in the stern part of the ship, where his sleep might be undisturbed. Odysseus laid him down in silence : the rowers took their places on the benches, the cables were loosed, and as soon as the men bent to their oars deep sleep fell on Odysseus, ' a sound sleep, passing sweet and very like to death ' ; for he was utterly tired out with the two days' feasting and the fatigue of his long story-telling. Thus it came about that he was still fast asleep when, after a fair and speedy voyage through the night, the

[1] *Odys.* xiii. 59-62.

ship drew nigh to Ithaca. The Phaeacians steered straight for the harbour of Phorcys which they knew well, and ran the ship on to the beach half out of the water ; then lifted Odysseus out deep sunk in sleep, and laid him on the sand wrapped as he was in sheet and rug. And they took out the presents which the Phaeacians had given him and placed them in a heap together at the foot of an olive tree, a little out of the road for greater safety, then started back for Scheria.

CHAPTER VIII

THE STORY OF ODYSSEUS (*continued*)

2. HIS HOMECOMING

AFTER a time Odysseus awoke and looked about him;
and though he was in his native Ithaca all seemed
strangely unfamiliar, and he failed to recognize where he
was. He thought himself in some unknown land, and
was ready in his disappointment to blame the Phaeacians
for fulfilling their promises so badly. Yet he soon noted
that his possessions were all there near to him by the
wayside, the tripods and the caldrons, the raiment and
the gold. He could not understand what had happened,
and began wandering disconsolately along the shore.
There Athena met him in the guise of a young herdsman
of gentle mien. Odysseus accosted the supposed youth,
and learnt to his astonishment and delight that the land
was Ithaca. But of himself he gave a feigned account,
since it was dangerous to reveal his identity incautiously.
He was a fugitive from Crete, he said, a man who had
done murder and escaped on board a Phoenician ship :
but the ship had been driven from her course ; and in
the night, while he slept, the Phoenician seamen had set
him ashore with all his goods. Athena smiled at the
tale, and changing into a woman's shape made herself
known to Odysseus as his divine protectress. She promised to help him now, and with that took the mist
from his eyes, so that at last he recognized his native
Ithaca, and kissed the earth, and prayed in thankfulness
to the nymphs of the grotto by the harbour. Athena

next directed Odysseus to hide his wealth deep within the cavern : that done, she took counsel with him how the death they merited might be brought upon the Suitors. She told him of the three years' persecution of Penelope and of the Suitors' overbearing insolence in the palace. Odysseus protested his willingness to face any odds with Athena as his helper : " Yea verily I will be with thee," Athena made answer, " nor will I ever forget thee when we come to this toil." [1] But first, because it was necessary that his return should be kept secret, she told him she must make him " such-like that no one should know him," not even Penelope or Tele- machus. Thereupon she touched him with her wand, and in a moment he was changed from the hero of stately bearing, whom the Phaeacians admired, to a beggar old and feeble and in vile raiment, equipped with staff and scrip. First must he seek the swineherd Eumaeus, most faithful of his retainers, who has served Penelope and Telemachus with devoted loyalty. Eumaeus will be found watching over the swine by the spring, Arethusa, near the Raven Rocks, on the high lands above the harbour. She herself proposes to go to Sparta and recall Telemachus (*Odys.* xiii. 187-440).

Eumaeus the Swineherd.—During the long absence of Odysseus the loyalty of his dependents had been sorely tried. The younger among them only knew Odysseus as a great name. The Suitors were young and debonair, some of them free-handed : little was to be gained by loyalty to Penelope and Telemachus, if Odysseus never came back. And more and more people ceased to believe in the likelihood of his return ; very few realized what it would mean if he did come. Some of the women servants were flattered by the attentions of these young men of pleasure ; they had come to be their light-o'-loves, and were openly disloyal to their mistress. Many others, however, under the discreet guidance of Eurycleia, re- mained loyal. Among the men, too, there were some who wavered in their loyalty and some who remained

[1] *Odys.* xiii. 393, 394.

faithful. There was none so staunchly faithful as Eumaeus, Odysseus' chief swineherd. Eumaeus was of free birth, though all his life he had been a serf of the house of Odysseus. As a child he had been stolen by his nurse, a Phoenician woman, who had a Sidonian seaman for her lover, and to please him carried off her master's son and fled overseas. This child, Eumaeus, was bought from the Phoenicians by Laertes, Odysseus' father, who treated him kindly and brought him up with his own children. By Odysseus he was entrusted with the charge of the royal swine, and was the most devoted of all the retainers of the house, as deeply attached to Telemachus and to Penelope as to his absent master. It was to the hut of this faithful servant that Odysseus now made his way by a steep path through the woods.

Odysseus at the Swineherd's Homestead (*Odys*. xiv. 4-533).—Eumaeus the swineherd was sitting in the forecourt of the lodge he had built for himself with stones on the level hill-top. There was a clear view all round from this platform, and about the lodge Eumaeus had made a staked enclosure and had divided the enclosed space into twelve pens for his sows, fifty sows to a pen. The boars he kept outside, but these were much diminished in number through the daily feastings of the Suitors. Of his four under-herdsmen three were out watching the swine and the fourth had gone to the city with a boar for the Suitors' table ; so Eumaeus was alone as Odysseus approached, and he was busy cutting himself a pair of shoes from a strip of oxhide. His dogs were lying about him, and when they saw a stranger coming they rushed at him barking furiously. Odysseus dropped his staff and sat down ; for Greek dogs respect a suppliant and will not hurt a man who puts himself in this posture. Eumaeus, however, was quick to intervene : he shouted at the dogs, and drove them away with stones, then addressed the newcomer courteously ; and almost his first words recalled his absent master. " Here I sit," he said, " mourning and sorrowing for my godlike lord, and foster the fat swine for others to eat while he, craving, perchance, for food, wanders over some land and city of men of a strange speech, if haply he yet lives and beholds the sunlight." [1]   And with that he invited Odysseus to enter the hut.   Then he fetched brushwood and strewed it on the ground, and threw over the brushwood a shaggy goatskin.   And glad at heart was Odysseus at this welcome, and blessed Eumaeus in these words : "May Zeus, O stranger, and all the other deathless gods grant thee thy dearest wish, since thou hast received me kindly." [2]   Within the hut a meal was quickly prepared by Eumaeus, the flesh of two young sucking-pigs washed down with wine.   And when Odysseus had eaten and drunk, he made cautious enquiry of Eumaeus concerning the lord whose absence he lamented. And Eumaeus replied :   "Old man, no wanderer who may come hither and bring tidings of him can win the ear of his wife and his dear son, but lightly do vagrants lie when they need entertainment, and care not to tell truth.   Whosoever comes straying to the land of Ithaca, goes to my mistress and speaks words of guile.   And she receives him kindly and lovingly, and enquires of all things, and the tears fall from her eyelids for weeping, as is meet for a woman when her lord hath died afar.   And quickly enough wouldst thou, too, old man, forge a tale, if any would but give thee a mantle and a doublet for raiment.   But as for him, dogs and swift fowls are like already to have torn his skin from the bones, and his spirit hath left him.   Or the fishes have eaten him in the deep, and there lie his bones swathed in sand-drift on the shore.   Yonder then hath he perished, but for his friends naught is ordained but care, for all, but for me in chief.   For never again shall I find a lord so gentle, how far soever I may go, not though again I attain unto the house of my father and my mother, where at first I was born, and they nourished me themselves and with their own hands they reared me.   Nor henceforth it is not for these that I sorrow so much, though I long to behold them with mine eyes in mine own

[1] *Odys.* xiv. 40-44 (B. and L. p. 223).   [2] *Odys.* xiv. 53, 54.

country, but desire comes over me for Odysseus who is afar. His name, stranger, even though he is not here, it shameth me to speak, for he loved me exceedingly, and cared for me at heart ; nay, I call him ' worshipful,' albeit he is far hence." [1] Upon this the seeming beggar solemnly averred that Odysseus would surely come, and that soon. But Eumaeus would not believe it, and went on to lament further the absence of his young lord, Telemachus, and the danger that overhung his return journey. Nor would he believe the more, though his guest went on to tell a long story how after sundry adventures he had been the guest of Pheidon, king of the Thesprotians, and there had seen with his own eyes the treasure which Odysseus had brought from Troy and left in the king's care, while he went to enquire of the oracle of Zeus at Dodona concerning his return home to Ithaca. While they were thus discoursing, the other herdsmen returned, and Eumaeus prepared supper for all. This time a well-fattened boar of five years old was slain, Eumaeus the while not forgetting a prayer for his master's return as he cast the sacrificial bristles on the fire. When all was ready he cut the flesh into seven portions, one for the nymphs, one for Hermes, and five for the three swineherds, for himself and for Odysseus ; but to Odysseus he gave the portion of honour. And Odysseus was pleased and said : " Eumaeus, oh that thou mayst so surely be dear to father Zeus, as thou art to me, seeing that thou honourest me with a good portion, such an one as I am." [2] And Eumaeus made answer : " Eat, luckless stranger, and make merry with such fare as is here. And one thing the god will give and another withhold, even as he will, for with him all things are possible." [3] Then they prepared for rest. Eumaeus set a bed for Odysseus near the fire, and cast sheepskins and goatskins upon it, and because it was a cold and stormy night gave him a spare cloak of his own to wrap over

---

[1] *Odys*. xiv. 122-147 (B. and L. pp. 226, 227).
[2] *Odys*. xiv. 440, 441 (B. and L. p. 236).
[3] *Odys*. xiv. 443-445 (B. and L. p. 236).

him. So Odysseus slept warm by the fire and the young herdsmen lay near him. But Eumaeus himself, faithful to his trust, slung a sword over his shoulder, put on his warmest cloak to keep the wind off, and went outside to sleep in the shelter of a rock close to the herds which were in his charge.

The Journey back from Sparta (*Odys.* xv. 1-546).—On the day that the Phaeacians put Odysseus ashore in the haven of Phorcys, Telemachus was still at Sparta. But it was time now he should be back in Ithaca. Athena, therefore, appeared to him as he lay awake in anxious thought, and urged him to return home with all speed. At the same time she warned him of the ambush of the Suitors and how to avoid it. So strong was the impulse stirred by this vision that Telemachus gave Pisistratus (who was sleeping near him) a friendly kick and woke him, and was for then and there yoking the horses to the car and setting forward; it was with difficulty that Pisistratus persuaded him to wait till morning. Soon it was dawn, and when Menelaus and Helen came early to visit their guests, Telemachus made his request for a speedy leave-taking. Menelaus received the request in all kindness, and straightway went with Helen to his treasury and took out a beautiful two-handled cup and a silver mixing-bowl, while Helen chose out a richly embroidered robe which she had worked with her own hands, and gave it to Telemachus as a wedding gift for his bride. Then after the morning meal and kindly expressions of farewell on either side, Telemachus and Pisistratus drove away; and in the evening they came again to Pherae, where they were the guests of Orsilochus, son of Alpheus. An early start next day brought them by the afternoon into the neighbourhood of Pylus. In his haste to be gone, Telemachus begged his friend to help him to put to sea at once without entering Nestor's city; for he feared the old man's officious kindness and garrulity would delay him. So instead of following the road from the high ground to the city, Pisistratus turned aside and drove to the coast; and he warned Telemachus to hoist sail and get away before ever the chariot reached the city ; for Nestor, if he knew, would surely come in person and insist on his staying. So Telemachus and his men went aboard with all speed ; they were offering sacrifice and praying for a safe voyage when a stranger came up hurriedly and told them he was fleeing for his life with the avengers of blood close on his heels. He begged for a passage on their ship. It was Theoclymenus, one of a family of soothsayers, and a fugitive from Argos where he had slain his enemy. Telemachus granted his prayer. Forthwith the ship put out to sea, and to avoid the ambush of the Suitors sailed up along the coast of Elis, past Chronium, and Chalkis, and Phaeae, then crossed to Ithaca from the Pointed Isles, instead of taking the usual course through the Straits between Same and Ithaca, where the ship of Antinous lay. Nor did they stop at night, but pressed on, and by morning reached land in Ithaca at some distance from the city. Here Telemachus committed Theoclymenus to the care of his friend Piraeus, ordered the ship to proceed onward to the city and himself set off for the homestead of Eumaeus, where, unknown to him, his father was even then seated in conversation. For, after his first night at the lodge, Odysseus had tested the swineherd's goodwill by proposing to go on to the town and beg there. Eumaeus had earnestly dissuaded him and advised him to stay at the lodge till Telemachus himself should be back. That evening, they two, Odysseus and the swineherd Eumaeus, sat far into the night talking together, and it was near dawn before they lay down to sleep.

Visit of Telemachus to Eumaeus (*Odys*. xvi. 1-153).— It was on the morning after this that Telemachus ascended the mountain path and approached the hut. Odysseus heard his footsteps and noticed that the dogs did not bark, but ran out in a friendly way ; and he was remarking on this to Eumaeus, when his son—the son he had not seen since he was a baby in arms—entered the hut and stood before him. But it was Eumaeus who expressed joy and wonder. He leapt up in amazement so

hastily that the vessels out of which he was mixing wine
for the morning meal fell from his hands. He caught
Telemachus by the hands, he kissed his head and his
eyes with every manifestation of delight. For great had
been his fear that his young master would never come
back. Telemachus explains that he has come that he
may learn what has been happening in his absence, and
whether Penelope is still holding out. " Yea verily,"
replies Eumaeus, " she abides with patient spirit in thy
halls, and wearily for her the nights wane always and
the days, in shedding of tears." [1] Now as Telemachus
entered, Odysseus rose to give up his seat to the young
master, but Telemachus courteously refused to take it,
saying, " Be seated, stranger, and we will find a seat
some other where in our steading, and there is a man
here to set it for us." [2] Then these three sat down,
Telemachus and Eumaeus and Odysseus, and took food
together, roast meat and wheaten bread and ' honey-
sweet wine.' Presently Telemachus enquired of Eumaeus
who the stranger was, and Eumaeus replied in accordance
with the tale he had heard from Odysseus' lips, and
added : " But now as a fugitive from a ship of the Thesprotians has he come to my homestead, and I will put
him under thy protection : do with him as thou wilt ;
he claims to be thy suppliant." [3] But Telemachus
demurs, with a bitter sense of humiliation, that his power
is not strong enough to ensure his being able to protect
such a guest from the insolence of the Suitors. He
proposes instead that the stranger shall remain for the
present at the swineherd's lodge, while he himself will
send up food and other things necessary for his hospitable
entertainment. Odysseus affects astonishment to hear
of Telemachus's powerlessness in the very halls of which
he is the rightful master, and enquires the reason. Telemachus makes answer that it is because he is alone and
without kinsfolk to take his part, whereas the Suitors

[1] *Odys.* xvi. 37-39 (B. and L. p. 260).

[2] *Odys.* xvi. 44, 45 (B. and L. p. 260).

[3] *Odys.* xvi. 65-67.

are very many in number. Acrisius, his great-grand-father, he explains, had one only son, Laertes, Laertes no son but Odysseus, and he, Telemachus, is Odysseus' only son. Then he orders Eumaeus to go to the palace and make known to Penelope the tidings of his return from Pylus.

Odysseus made known to Telemachus (*Odys*. xvi. 154-320).—Eumaeus departs straightway, and then father and son, they two alone, are left in the lodge. Upon this Athena appears to Odysseus in the likeness of a woman fair and tall (but this sight was withheld from Telemachus' eyes), and gave him to understand by signs that the time has come to make himself known to his son. And she changed him back from the rags and squalor of the old beggar-man to the heroic form and proud bearing of a warrior in the prime of life. Then she vanished ; and Odysseus re-entered the house. Telemachus saw the change and exclaimed in his wonder, thinking himself in the presence of some god. But Odysseus looked upon him and said, " No god am I : why likenest thou me to the immortals ? Nay, I am thy father, on whose account thou mournest and sufferest sore trouble, exposed to men's outrageous violence." [1] Thereat he kissed his son and the tears ran down his cheeks. And Telemachus, scarce able to believe, spoke in turn and said : " Surely thou art not Odysseus my father, but this is some beguilement from the gods to make me mourn and lament more than ever. In no wise could mortal man contrive this by his wit, without the visitation of some god, lightly to make himself young or old at his pleasure. Verily but now thou wert old and vilely clad, but now thou art like the gods who dwell in the wide heaven." [2] But Odysseus comforted him and assured him that indeed he was Odysseus who had come back to his own land after twenty years of absence and suffering, as had been foretold. Then at length Telemachus was convinced and threw his arms round his father's neck, and they two wept long time together.

[1] *Odys*. xvi. 187-189.   [2] *Odys*. xvi. 194-200.

At length Telemachus enquired how his father had reached Ithaca, and Odysseus told him how the Phaeacians had brought him from Scheria, and had laid him wrapped in slumber on the shore ; and how it was by Athena's admonition that he had sought the swineherd's dwelling. It now behoved them to take counsel how vengeance on the Suitors might best be planned ; and the first thing to know is, how many Suitors there are to be reckoned with. One hundred and eight there are in all by Telemachus' count ; fifty-two from Dulichium, twenty-four from Zacynthus, twenty from Same, and from Ithaca itself twelve. Who is there to help them against so many ? "Athena and Father Zeus," replies Odysseus, "will that suffice for us twain ?" "Verily the best of champions," answers Telemachus, "are these two whom thou namest, though their seat is in the clouds : for they rule over all men and among the immortal gods."[1] Odysseus assures his son that they will have this divine help on their side when it comes to a fight with the Suitors. And then he begins to unfold his plan of action. Next day at dawn Telemachus must go home and associate with the Suitors as before. Later in the day he will himself come to the palace under guidance of Eumaeus in his wretched beggar's disguise, and even if he is roughly handled, Telemachus must endure to see it. Two charges in special Odysseus lays upon him : one is to find some pretext for removing from the great hall the weapons now in the stands, excepting only two swords, two spears and two shields ; the other, to let no one whatever, not even Laertes, or Penelope herself, know that Odysseus has come. All this Telemachus promises.

News of Telemachus' Return (*Odys*. xvi. 321-448).—Meantime the ship in which Telemachus had made his voyage had reached the city ; his presents were taken out and stored in a friend's house, and a messenger set out to announce to Penelope her son's safe return ; and it chanced that this messenger arrived at the palace at the same time as Eumaeus ; and Eumaeus, after deliver-

[1] *Odys*. xvi. 260-265.

ing his message to Penelope, went back. The news of
Telemachus' return came also to the Suitors and they
were cast down because their plot had failed. They
then went to the Agora and took possession of the hall,
suffering no one who was not of their party to join them,
either young or old. Antinous acknowledges the failure
of the attempt to intercept Telemachus on the sea, and
now openly proposes that they shall waylay and kill
him on land. But this infamous counsel is opposed by
Amphinomus of Dulichium and rejected. Then all return
to the palace. There presently Penelope came down
from her chamber and reproached them all, and especially
Antinous, for their wickedness in plotting Telemachus'
death. In particular, she lays ingratitude to Antinous'
charge ; for Antinous' father owed his life to Odysseus.
Eurymachus protested that no one should hurt Telemachus while he lived ; but his words were feigned.

Telemachus' Return to the Palace (*Odys.* xvii. 1-165).—
Next day, in accordance with the plan agreed upon,
Telemachus took his departure for the city leaving orders
with Eumaeus to follow him later in the day and bring
the stranger with him. Great was the rejoicing among
the women of Penelope's household, when the young
heir, the darling of the house, appeared, safe returned
from his journey abroad. The old nurse, Eurycleia, was
the first to see him and she wept for joy ; and there was
much embracing and kissing. Then came his mother,
and cast her arms about him and kissed his face and
eyes, and said : " Thou art come, Telemachus, sweet
light of my eyes : I thought indeed that I should never
see thee again, when thou didst steal away in a ship to
Pylus without my consent to seek tidings of thy father.
Come now tell me what sight didst thou get of him ? " [1]
But he put her off for the time and went to the Agora
to seek the stranger to whom he had promised protection.
When he had found him and settled matters with Piraeus,
he brought Theoclymenus back with him. Then he told
his mother the whole story of his journey, of his visits to

[1] *Odys.* xvii. 41-44.

Pylus and Sparta, and what he had learnt from Menelaus
concerning his father, and how Menelaus through the
spells of Proteus, god of changing shape, had had vision
of Odysseus sitting disconsolate in the island of Calypso.
Upon this Theoclymenus opened his lips and assured
Penelope that he knew of a surety through his prophetic
art that Odysseus was already in Ithaca and vengeance
about to fall on the Suitors.

Odysseus' Arrival at the Palace (*Odys.* xvii. 167-327).—
Soon after this it was supper time, and the Suitors trooped
in and sat down, and preparations were made as usual
for the feast. Meantime Odysseus and Eumaeus had
started for the city and were now close at hand. On
the way they fell in with the goat-herd Melanthius hard
by the waterfall and the spring from which the Ithacans
fetched their water. Melanthius was ill-affected to his
master's house and sworn enemy to Eumaeus. When
he saw, as he thought, an old beggar-man in Eumaeus'
company, he addressed insulting words to both, and as
he went by kicked Odysseus in the thigh. Hardly could
Odysseus restrain the impulse to strike him dead with
his staff, or lift him in his arms and hurl him to the
ground ; but with an effort he forbore, and only breathed
a prayer that Odysseus might return and punish insolence
like this. But Melanthius passed quickly on, and having
reached the palace, entered and sat down by Eurymachus in friendly wise. A little later Eumaeus arrived
with Odysseus ; and, as they had agreed, Eumaeus first
entered by himself. Outstretched in the forecourt lay
old Argus, who had been Odysseus' favourite hound
before he went away ; now he was very old and weak
and sadly neglected. But Argus recognized Odysseus in
spite of his disguise ; his ears dropped and he feebly
wagged his tail. Then, having seen his old master once
again, even as Eumaeus entered the hall, he lay down
and died.

Odysseus insulted by Antinous (*Odys.* xvii. 328-573).—
Telemachus beckoned to Eumaeus, when he saw him,

and Eumaeus brought a stool and sat down beside him.
Soon after Odysseus entered also in his beggar's guise
and sat him down on the threshold inside the doorway,
leaning his back against the pillar. Seeing him, Telemachus sent to him a loaf of bread and a portion of flesh,
and gave him leave to go about among the guests and
collect alms. Some of the Suitors took pity on him and
gave ; but Antinous replied to the beggar's appeal with
insult. And when Odysseus reproached him for his
hardness of heart he caught up a stool and struck him
on the shoulder. Odysseus bore the blow in silence and
went and sat down again by the pillar in the doorway.
Many of the other Suitors, however, were angry with
Antinous for his violence and rebuked him. As for
Telemachus he was deeply grieved, but knew that for
the present he must endure in silence. Penelope, however, when she heard of the outrage committed in her
halls invoked Apollo's vengeance on Antinous. And she
bade Eumaeus invite the stranger to speak with her, in
hope of hearing some tidings of Odysseus ; but Odysseus
thought it more prudent to wait till nightfall ; for then
the Suitors would have left the hall, and there would be
no danger of their insolent interference.

Fight with the Beggar Irus (*Odys.* xviii. 1-156).—As
evening drew on it happened that a well-known beggar
from the town, nicknamed Irus,[1] because he ran errands
for all and sundry, came loafing up to the house, and
seeing in the stranger a possible rival, began to pick a
quarrel with him. Antinous heard the wrangling, and
was delighted at this unlooked-for prospect of ' sport,'
a comic fight between two beggar-men, the young and
the old. " Friends," he cried, " never before has there
been such a thing : such goodly game has a god brought
to this house. The stranger yonder and Irus are bidding
each other to buffets. Quick, let us match them one
against the other." [2] So Odysseus seeing no way of

---

[1] Iris in the *Iliad* is the goddess who acts as messenger of the gods.
Irus is a male form of Iris.

[2] *Odys.* xviii. 36-39 (B. and L. p. 296).

escape, stripped and stood ready ; only first he asked a
promise that no one present would help Irus unfairly.
And the Suitors were astonished when they saw what
thews and sinews the beggar's rags concealed ; but Irus,
who was a coward and a braggart, had now to be dragged
to the encounter. Then the pair put up their hands to
fight. But the fight did not last long ; for Odysseus
struck one blow and caught Irus under the ear and
knocked him out. For Odysseus it was but a light blow,
yet Irus' jaw was smashed and blood gushed from his
mouth. The Suitors were like to die of laughter ; but
Odysseus dragged Irus by the foot out of the hall and
propped him up against the wall of the courtyard, and
put his staff into his hand and left him ; but he himself
went back to his seat on the step of the threshold. All
the Suitors now regarded him with favour and offered
congratulations, even Antinous ; Amphinomus actually
wished him happiness. And to Amphinomus, because
he was better than the others, Odysseus gave earnest
warning of the retribution that would overtake the
Suitors if Odysseus came home. He urged Amphinomus
to leave Ithaca and return to his own island. Amphinomus was touched with compunction, but his doom was
already fixed, and he went back to his seat among the
Suitors.

Penelope rebukes Telemachus and reproaches the Suitors
(*Odys.* xviii. 157-300).—All this time Penelope had no
suspicion who the beggar-man was in whom she had
begun to take interest. Her yearning for her husband
and her aversion to a new marriage were as great as
ever, yet something had to be done for Telemachus' sake.
This urgent need of action led to a new move on her
part. She washed away all signs of weeping, and went
down from her chamber into the men's hall, and openly
reproached her son Telemachus for failing to protect
their stranger guest from shameful usage. She looked
so handsome as she spoke that the Suitors were kindled
anew to admiration, and Eurymachus voiced the feelings
of all when he said that if all the Achaeans could see her

THE STORY OF ODYSSEUS

the number of her suitors would be even greater. Penelope replied sadly : " Eurymachus, verily my excellence
of face and form the gods destroyed when the Argives
embarked for Ilium, and my husband, Odysseus, among
them." [1] And she recalled his parting from her and
how he charged her, should he never come back, to watch
over the declining years of his father and mother, and
when Telemachus was grown a man, to take to herself a
new husband. " Even so did he speak," she continued,
" and now all these things have an end. The night
shall come when a hateful marriage shall find me out,
me most luckless, whose good hap Zeus has taken away.
But furthermore this sore trouble has come on my heart
and soul ; for this was not the manner of wooers in time
past. Whoso wish to woo a good lady and the daughter
of a rich man, and vie one with another, themselves bring
with them oxen of their own and goodly flocks, a banquet
for the friends of the bride, and they give the lady
splendid gifts, but do not devour another's livelihood
without atonement." [2] This taunt went home, and
before long the Suitors were rivalling each other in the
gifts they made. Antinous sent an embroidered robe
ornamented with twelve golden brooches, Eurymachus a
golden chain strung with beads of amber, Pisander a
handsome necklet ; each and all some beautiful gift.
Odysseus the while laughed within himself to see how
his Penelope had the wit to turn the infatuation of the
Suitors to profitable account.

Odysseus insulted by Melantho and by Eurymachus
(*Odys.* xviii. 301-427).—Penelope then returned to her
chamber, and the Suitors spent the rest of the day in
dancing and song. And when it grew dark three great
braziers were set flaring in the hall to give them light.
The maid-servants were for staying to keep up the lights,
but Odysseus bid them begone, undertaking himself to
look after the flares. And one of the maids named
Melantho, who cared nothing for her mistress's troubles,
and who was Eurymachus' paramour, mocked him and

[1] *Odys.* xviii. 251-253. [2] *Odys.* xviii. 271-280 (B. and L. p. 304).

abused him. But Odysseus cowed her with an outburst
of anger, and the woman withdrew in fear. And now
Odysseus was once more the mark of the Suitors' insolent scoffing, and when he answered with spirit, Eurymachus lost his temper and flung a footstool at him.
This time the missile missed its aim and struck a cupbearer, who straightway dropped the flagon he was
carrying and fell to the ground. There was uproar and
confusion then in the hall, which Telemachus with some
difficulty suppressed. Then at the suggestion of Amphinomus all dispersed for the night.

The Hiding of the Arms (*Odys*. xix. 1-52).—Odysseus
was now alone in the hall with Telemachus. Without
loss of time they set about removing the arms from the
arms-racks in accordance with the plans made in the
lodge of Eumaeus. As this must be done secretly,
Telemachus called Eurycleia and commanded her to
lock the maidservants in the women's apartments. Then
Telemachus and Odysseus carried all the arms—the
helmets and shields and spears—out of the hall into an
inner store-chamber : this done, Telemachus withdrew
to his own room for the night, and Odysseus was left
alone in the hall.

Penelope's Questions (*Odys*. xix. 53-569).—But
Penelope now came forth from her chamber and ordered
a chair to be placed for her by the fire, while the servants
cleared up the hall. She came expectant of the promised
conference with the mysterious stranger. So by her
command the housekeeper, Eurynome, brought a second
chair and threw over it a soft fleece ; and Odysseus sat
down by the fire and answered as best he could the
questions that Penelope put to him. It was still a
matter of life and death that Penelope should have no
suspicion of the truth. He was a Cretan, he told her, a
grandson of Minos ; he had once spoken with Odysseus,
he said, when Odysseus landed at Knossos on his way to
Troy. To test the truth of his story Penelope then asked
him to describe how Odysseus was dressed. " Lady,"

he replied, " it is hard for one so long parted from him
to tell thee all this, for it is now the twentieth year
since he went thither and left my country. Yet even so
I will tell thee as I see him in spirit. Goodly Odysseus
wore a thick purple mantle, twofold, which had a brooch
fashioned in gold, with two sheaths for the pins, and on
the face of it was a curious device : a hound in his fore-
paws held a dappled fawn and gazed on it as it writhed.
And all men marvelled at the workmanship, how, wrought
as they were in gold, the hound was gazing on the fawn
and strangling it, and the fawn was writhing with his
feet and striving to flee. Moreover, I marked the shining
doublet about his body, like the gleam over the skin of
a dried onion, so smooth it was, and glistering as the
sun ; truly many women looked thereon and wondered." [1]
And he told her also what manner of man Eurybates,
the herald who accompanied him, was in appearance.
This vivid picture called up Penelope's sense of loss so
sharply that she wept again. And presently she said :
" Now verily, stranger, thou that even before wert held
in pity, shalt be dear and honourable in my halls, for it
was I who gave him these garments, as judging from thy
words, and folded them myself, and brought them from
the chamber, and added besides the shining brooch to
be his jewel. But him I shall never welcome back,
returned home to his own dear country. Wherefore
with an evil fate it was that Odysseus went hence in the
hollow ship to see that evil Ilios, never to be named." [2]
Odysseus strove to comfort her with the assurance that
her lord was alive and would soon reach Ithaca from
the land of the Thesprotians, where his treasures were
laid up in the keeping of king Pheidon. He assured her
that Pheidon himself had told him this, and that he had
seen with his own eyes the wealth that Odysseus had
collected. Penelope still found it hard to believe ; but
she ordered her handmaids to wash the stranger's feet
and to prepare a bed for him. Whereat Odysseus pro-

[1] *Odys.* xix. 221-235 (B. and L. pp. 317, 318).
[2] *Odys.* xix. 253-260 (B. and L. p. 318).

tested : " O wife revered of Odysseus, son of Laertes, mantles verily and shining blankets are hateful to me, since first I left behind me the snowy hills of Crete, voyaging in the long-oared galley ; nay, I will lie as in time past I was used to rest through the sleepless nights. For full many a night I have lain on an unsightly bed, and awaited the bright throned Dawn. And baths for the feet are no longer my delight, nor shall any women of those who are serving maidens in thy house touch my foot, unless there chance to be some old wife, true of heart, one that has borne as much trouble as myself." [1]

Odysseus and Eurycleia.—And so it comes to pass that Eurycleia, Odysseus' old nurse, is commanded to do this service. And she at once remarked the likeness of the stranger to her master Odysseus, and Odysseus said : " Old wife, even so all men declare, that have beheld us twain, that we favour each other exceedingly, even as thou dost mark and say." [2] Now Odysseus in his youth had received a gash in his leg above the knee from the tusk of a boar, and suddenly misgiving seized him lest Eurycleia should see and recognize the scar of this wound ; and he turned his face away from the firelight. But Eurycleia saw the scar, and as she passed her hand over it she knew at once it was her lord, and in her agitation she let the foot drop and upset the footbath. And she was about to make a sign to Penelope when Odysseus, in mortal terror of discovery, laid his hand upon her throat to prevent her speaking, and drew her face near to him and whispered : " Mother, will you destroy me ?—you that nursed me at your breast, now that after sore travail I have returned in the twentieth year to mine own land." [3] And he charged her strictly on pain of death to keep silence. Eurycleia promised ; then fetched more water and quietly finished her task.

Penelope's Dream.—Then when Odysseus had drawn up his chair to the fire again, Penelope sought his advice

[1] *Odys.* xix. 336-347 (B. and L. p. 321).
[2] *Odys.* xix. 383-385 (B. and L. p. 322).
[3] *Odys.* xix. 482-484.

in her difficulties and told him how she had dreamt a dream. " Twenty geese I have in the house," she said, " that eat wheat coming forth from the water, and I am gladdened at the sight. Now a great eagle of crooked beak swooped from the mountain, and brake all their necks and slew them ; and they lay strewn in a heap in the halls, while he was borne aloft to the bright air. Thereon I wept and wailed, in a dream though it was, and around me were gathered the fair-tressed Achaean women as I made piteous lament, for that the eagle had slain my geese. But he came back and sat him down on a jutting point of the roof-beam, and with the voice of a man he spake, and stayed my weeping : ' Take heart, O daughter of renowned Icarius ; this is no dream but a true vision, that shall be accomplished for thee. The geese are the wooers, and I that before was the eagle am now thy husband come again, who will let slip unsightly death upon all the wooers.' With that word sweet slumber let me go, and I looked about, and beheld the geese in the court pecking their wheat at the trough, where they were wont before." [1] And Odysseus said : " Lady, none may turn aside the dream to interpret it otherwise, seeing that Odysseus himself hath showed thee how he will fulfil it. For the wooers' destruction is clearly boded, for all and every one ; not a man shall avoid death and the fates." [2] But Penelope only said : " Stranger, verily dreams are hard, and hard to be discerned, nor are all things therein fulfilled for men. Twain are the gates of shadowy dreams, the one is fashioned of horn and one of ivory. Such dreams as pass through the portals of sawn ivory are deceitful, and bear tidings that are unfulfilled. But the dreams that come forth through the gates of polished horn bring a true issue, whosoever of mortals beholds them. Yet methinks my strange dream came not thence ; of a truth that would be most welcome to me and to my son." [3]

[1] *Odys.* xix. 536-553 (B. and L. p. 327).
[2] *Odys.* xix. 555-558 (B. and L. p. 328).
[3] *Odys.* xix. 560-569 (B. and L. p. 328).

Penelope's Plan to bring the Suitors to the Trial of the Bow (*Odys.* xix. 570-587).—Then she told him one thing more, how she had appointed for the morrow among the Suitors a trial of skill which was to seal her fate. Twelve axes were to be set up in a row and the great bow of Odysseus brought out : he who of the Suitors strung the bow with most ease and shot an arrow through all twelve axes might claim her as his wife. And Odysseus answered : " O wife revered of Odysseus, son of Laertes, no longer delay this contest in thy halls ; for, lo, Odysseus of many counsels will be here, before these men, for all their handling of the polished bow, shall have strung it, and shot the arrow through the iron." [1]

Odysseus' Troubled Night and Awaking (*Odys.* xx. 1-121).—After this Penelope departed to her chamber, and Odysseus slept in the anteroom in front of the hall. And he tossed about where he lay, pondering deeply the problem how he might chastize the Suitors, when they were so many and he but one. And he saw the women of his household go by who had lightly given themselves to the Suitors ; and with difficulty he restrained himself from rising forthwith and slaying these wantons. Athena, however, appeared to him and comforted him and gave him sleep. But Penelope still lay awake, and she prayed to Artemis to end her life and save her from the fate which now seemed very near—that she, who was fast bound to the memory of her husband, Odysseus, should be forced into wedlock with one less noble than he. " Evil may be borne," she wailed, " when, though a man weep all day long in great sorrow of heart, yet sleep takes him in the night, for sleep makes him forgetful of all things, of good and evil, when once it has overshadowed his eyelids. But as for me, even the dreams that the gods send upon me are evil." [2] And Odysseus on his uneasy couch heard her weeping, and he prayed to Zeus for a sign, now that the dawn had come. And Zeus in answer to his prayer sent thunder from a clear sky, and a poor woman at work grinding meal for the household,

[1] *Odys.* xix. 583-587 (B. and L. p. 328).   [2] *Odys.* xx. 83-87.

having failed to complete her portion of the task, as the women, her companions, had done, owing to her lack of strength, invoked a curse upon the Suitors, saying : ", May the Suitors on this day feast for the last time in the halls of Odysseus. They have worn out my limbs with wasting toil in grinding meal for them, so may they now sup their last." [1] Greatly gladdened was Odysseus at these good omens, at the woman's speech, and at the thunder.

Morning in the Palace at Ithaca (*Odys.* xx. 122-239).— Meantime the maidservants under Eurycleia's superintendence were lighting the fire and clearing up the hall, cleaning the tables and washing up the bowls against the return of the Suitors. Telemachus passed through the hall, spear in hand, with two fleet hunting dogs at his heels, and went forth to the Market Place. Presently there arrived in succession Eumaeus and Melanthius, and each greeted Odysseus according to his character, Eumaeus with respectful courtesy, Melanthius with insolence. These were followed by a third retainer of the house, Philoetius the neatherd, who had crossed in the ferry from the mainland with a heifer and some goats for the feast. Philoetius was loyal like Eumaeus, and when he saw Odysseus he asked who the stranger might be, and on being told went up to him and welcomed him and said : " Father and stranger, hail ! May happiness be thine in the time to come ; but as now, thou art fast holden in many sorrows ! Father Zeus, none other god is more baneful than thou ; thou hast no compassion on men, that are of thine own begetting, but makest them to have fellowship with evil and with bitter pains. The sweat brake out on me when I beheld him, and mine eyes stand full of tears for memory of Odysseus, for he too, methinks, is clad in such vile raiment as this, and is wandering among men, if haply he yet lives and sees the sunlight. But if he be dead already and in the house of Hades, then woe is me for the noble Odysseus, who set me over his cattle while I was but a lad in the land of the Cephal-

[1] *Odys.* xx. 116-119.

lenians. And now these wax numberless ; in no better
wise could the breed of broad-browed cattle of any mortal
increase, even as the ears of corn. But strangers command me to be ever driving these for themselves to
devour, and they care nothing for the heir in the house,
nor tremble at the vengeance of the gods, for they are
eager even now to divide among themselves the possessions of our lord who is long afar. Now my heart within
my breast often revolves this thing. Truly it were an
evil deed, while a son of the master is yet alive, to get
me away to the land of strangers, and go off, with cattle
and all, to alien men, But this is more grievous still, to
abide here in affliction watching over the herds of other
men. Yea, long ago I would have fled and gone forth
to some other of the proud kings, for things are now
past sufferance ; but still my thought is of that hapless
one, if he might come I know not whence, and make a
scattering of the wooers in the halls." [1] And Odysseus
commended his loyalty and swore a great oath, assuring
him that Odysseus would come, and that his own eyes
should see the vengeance he would take on those who
had wronged his house.

The Signs of coming Doom (*Odys.* xx. 240-394).—The
Suitors now came trooping in and sat down at the tables ;
and preparations were made as on other days for their
entertainment. But that day the feast went not well.
Telemachus, with prevision of what was to come, had a
seat and a small table set for Odysseus near the threshold
of the door, away from the Suitors ; and there by Telemachus' command a portion was set before him as before
each of the guests. This gave offence to some of the
Suitors, and one of them, Ctesippus by name, a man of
evil disposition who came from the island of Same, took
up a bone and threw it at Odysseus telling him it was
a present for him. It missed, because Odysseus with
a grim smile moved his head aside and so avoided it.
But Telemachus was roused to anger and threatened
Ctesippus with condign punishment. Agelaus, another

[1] *Odys.* xx. 199-225 (B. and L. pp. 336, 337).

of the Suitors, better minded than the rest, supported
Telemachus in his condemnation of Ctesippus' outrageous
behaviour, but at the same time urged once more that
Telemachus should press Penelope to choose a husband ;
and once more Telemachus replied that he would not
drive his mother from her home.   And at this the Suitors
laughed out in derision.   But to Theoclymenus, through
his gift of second sight, the tokens of coming doom were
now made manifest : he saw the feasters shrouded as
it were in mist, their faces looked wet with tears, and
the walls of the hall and the roof dripped blood.   Yet
the Suitors only mocked at him, so that he left their
company and went to the house of Piraeus.   Upon this
the Suitors jested and laughed the more, condoling
ironically with Telemachus on his ill-fortune in the
guests he entertained.   But Telemachus said nothing ;
only watched his father and waited.   Penelope, too, in
the Women's Hall set her seat close up to the wall, so
that she might hear all that was passing.

The Bow of Odysseus (*Odys*. xxi. 1-117).—For now she
judged the time had come when she could bring out
the bow of Odysseus and invite the Suitors to a competition which should end the question of her marriage.
So she went upstairs to her room and took out the key
of the treasure-chamber, which was in the uppermost
part of the house ; for it was there that the bow of
Odysseus was kept, the great bow which Iphitus, son of
Eurytus, gave to him.   Penelope unlocked the treasure-
chamber and took the bow from the peg on which it
was hanging in its case ; and when she had wept over
it a little she went down into the hall and stood by the
doorposts and announced the conditions of the contest.
She invited all the Suitors to make trial of the bow,
and promised to marry him who should string it most
easily and send an arrow through the rings of the twelve
axe-heads.   Then Telemachus recited these terms in the
hearing of all and announced that he would himself also
take part in the competition.   If he succeeded in stringing
the bow and shooting an arrow through the axe-heads,

then must the Suitors all depart and Penelope might stay unmolested in her son's home ; but if he failed, then she would be given in wedlock to the man who achieved the feat most successfully.

The Trial of the Bow (*Odys.* xxi. 118-244).—This said, Telemachus put off his cloak and sword and set up the mark. All marvelled at the skill with which he fixed the axes in a line above a trench and stamped the earth about them. Then he stood by the threshold where the bow had been placed, and thrice he strove with all his strength to string it, and thrice he rested after the effort. And when he was preparing for yet another attempt, his father signed to him, and he forbore and said : " Lo you now, even to the end of my days I shall be a coward and a weakling, or it may be I am too young, and have as yet no trust in my hands to defend me from such an one as does violence without a cause. But come now, ye who are mightier men than I, essay the bow, and let us make an end of the contest." [1] And with this he laid down the bow and went back to his seat at the table. Then Antinous bade the Suitors to make trial of the bow, one after another, beginning from the left as they sat. The first to try was Leiodes the soothsayer, son of Oenops, most righteous of the Suitors, but he failed ignominiously and went back to his place. Vexed at his discomfiture and the want of spirit he showed, Antinous ordered a fire to be lit, and had the bow warmed and greased to make it supple. But the Suitors were no more successful for that ; one after another they failed in the trial, till only Eurymachus and Antinous were left. While this was going on Eumaeus and Philoetius chanced to go outside and Odysseus followed them, and said : " Neatherd and thou swineherd, shall I say somewhat or keep it to myself ? Nay, my spirit bids me declare it. What manner of men would ye be to help Odysseus, if he should come thus suddenly, I know not whence, and some god were to bring him ? Would ye stand on the side of the wooers

[1] *Odys.* xxi. 131-135 (B. and L. p. 348).

or of Odysseus ? Tell me even as your heart and spirit bid you." [1] And when they answered professing the utmost devotion, Odysseus made himself known to them and promised to reward them well if they stood by him in the fray which was now near at hand. He showed them also the scar to prove that his words were true, and checking their manifestations of delight sent them back into the hall to await the moment for action. He himself returned to the place near the threshold where a seat had been put for him.

Antinous' Proposal of Postponement (*Odys.* xxi. 245-273).—Eurymachus was now trying his strength, but he failed as the others had done to his exceeding chagrin. Then Antinous proposed a diversion. The Suitors were all failing, he said, because that day was the feast-day of the archer-god and not a suitable day for such a contest ; better to keep festival to-day and put off the decision till to-morrow, when better luck might be expected. His proposal was hailed with acclamation ; so once more revelry began in the hall and the wine-bowl went round.

Odysseus asks to make Trial of the Bow (*Odys.* xxi. 274-393).—Then spake Odysseus, still in his beggar's guise : "Hear me, ye wooers of the renowned queen, that I may say that which my heart within me bids. And mainly to Eurymachus I make my prayer and to the godlike Antinous, forasmuch as he has spoken even this word aright, namely, that for this present ye cease from your archery and leave the issue to the gods ; and in the morning the god will give the victory to whomsoever he will. Come, therefore, give me the polished bow, that in your presence I may prove my hands and strength, whether I have yet any force such as once was in my supple limbs, or whether my wanderings and needy fare have even now destroyed it." [2] This request made the Suitors very angry, and Antinous reviled the stranger

[1] *Odys.* xxi. 193-198 (B. and L. p. 350).
[2] *Odys.* xxi. 275-284 (B. and L. p. 353).

for his presumption. Penelope, however, intervened,
pleading for the stranger that their fears lest he intended
to be their rival for her hand were groundless. But
Eurymachus objected that their fear was of men's ridicule,
should a wandering beggar string the bow when the
nobles of the islands had failed ; and when his mother
rejoined on the stranger's behalf, Telemachus ended the
dispute by declaring the right of decision to be his. At
the same time he now charged his mother to withdraw
to her chamber. Then Penelope went out ; and Odysseus
was left facing the Suitors in the hall. Now Eumaeus
was already bringing the bow to his master ; but the
Suitors raised angry outcry, and Eumaeus would have
given way to their threats had not Telemachus called
out : " Father, bring hither the bow, soon shalt thou
rue it that thou servest many masters. Take heed, lest
I that am younger than thou pursue thee to the field
and pelt thee with stones, for in might I am the better.
If only I were so much mightier in strength of arm than
all the wooers that are in the halls, soon would I send
many an one forth on a woeful way from out our house,
for they imagine mischief against us." [1]   And the Suitors'
anger was turned to laughter. · Then Eumaeus crossed
the hall and placed the bow in the hands of Odysseus.
This done, he slipped out, called Eurycleia as Odysseus
had told him to do, and ordered her to close and bar
the women's quarters. At the same time Philoetius went
out and closed the outer gates, the gates that led into the
courtyard and made them fast with a ship's cable. Then
he returned to his seat and fixed his eyes on Odysseus.

Odysseus Strings the Bow (*Odys*. xxi. 393-434).—Odysseus the while was fingering the bow, turning it this way
and that. In a moment without effort he stretched the
bow and strung it, and lightly flicked the string to test
if it sounded true. The Suitors looked on in displeasure
and fear. Then Odysseus took up an arrow, fitted it to
the string, and took aim from where he sat by the threshold. The arrow passed through all twelve axes and

[1] *Odys*. xxi. 369-375 (B. and L. p. 356).

out on the other side ; and he cried exultantly : " Tele-machus, thy guest that sits in the halls does thee no shame. In nowise did I miss my mark, nor was I wearied with long bending of the bow. Still is my might stead-fast—not as the wooers say scornfully to slight me. But now is it time that supper too be got ready for the Achaeans, while it is yet light ; and thereafter must we make other sport with the dance and the lyre, for these are the crown of the feast." [1]

The Beginning of Vengeance (*Odys*. xxii. 1-41).—Then Odysseus stripped off his rags and sprang upon the threshold bow in hand ; the arrows he poured out of the quiver upon the ground at his feet. And he cried aloud : " Thus is this dread trial accomplished. And now I will take another mark for my aim, which no man yet hath shot at : haply, too, I may reach it, if Apollo grant my prayer." [2] Thereupon he pointed the shaft at Antinous even as he was raising to his lips a double-handled cup : the arrow struck him full in the throat and passed through his neck, and the cup dropped from his hands as he sank down. The blood poured in a stream from his nostrils and the table was overthrown as he lashed out with his feet in his death agony ; and all the food was scattered about and defiled. A great shout arose from the Suitors when they saw him fall : they leapt up from their seats reproaching and threatening the stranger : but even now they did not guess the truth ; they thought the shooting of Antinous to be accidental. But Odysseus quickly undeceived them and made him-self known. " Dogs," he said, " ye thought that I should never come home from the land of the Trojans, since ye devoured my house and lay with my women-servants perforce, and wooed my wife while I was yet alive, and had no fear of the gods who dwell in heaven, nor of retribution afterward from men. But now the ends of destruction have come on you all." [3]

[1] *Odys*. xxi. 424-430 (B. and L. p. 358).
[2] *Odys*. xxii. 5-7.   [3] *Odys*. xxii. 35-41.

The Slaying of the Suitors (*Odys*. xxii. 42-389).—Then cold fear laid hold on the Suitors, one and all, and they began to cast about for means of escape. Eurymachus alone faced Odysseus and attempted a parley. But Odysseus eyed him grimly, and said : " Eurymachus, not even if ye paid me all your heritage, both what ye now possess and whatsoever more ye might add thereto, not even so would I stay my hands from slaying till the wooers had paid for their transgression in full. Now ye must choose whether to fight against me, or to flee if death and fate may be avoided. Yet some there be, methinks, who shall not escape sheer destruction." [1] Then Eurymachus seeing there was no way out by conciliation, called on the others to draw their swords, and using the tables as shields assail Odysseus and force him from the doorway so that someone might get out and raise an alarm through the city. But even as he made his rush an arrow from the hand of Odysseus pierced his breast and he fell forward over the table in his death swoon. Amphinomus also sprang forward, but Telemachus struck him with a spear between his shoulders from behind, and the spear came through to his breast and he fell to the ground with a crash. This done, Telemachus ran swiftly down the hall and reached his father's side. Then after brief interchange of speech, he slipped out and fetched four shields and eight spears and four helmets from the armoury for Odysseus and himself and their two faithful followers. Odysseus meanwhile was shooting his arrows thick and fast among the Suitors, till the hall was piled with dead and no more arrows were left. Then swiftly he and the other two armed themselves with the weapons that Telemachus had brought. So far all had gone well. But now fortune took a turn which threatened to give the Suitors the advantage of their numbers. For Melanthius climbed by a gallery in the roof to the upper chamber where Telemachus had stored the armour from the hall. He brought back twelve shields and twelve spears with

[1] *Odys*. xxii. 61-67.

which the surviving Suitors armed themselves. Odysseus, however, saw what was happening and sent Eumaeus and Philoetius to waylay Melanthius should he attempt to fetch arms a second time. And they caught him unawares and bound him hand and foot, and left him in the upper chamber strung up to the ceiling. They then went back to support Odysseus and Telemachus in the fray ; four against many. Agelaus, son of Damastor, counselled the Suitors to aim their spears against Odysseus alone. And six of them hurled their spears together against him ; one hit the doorpost, another stuck in the door, another was fixed in the wall ; but Odysseus was untouched. Then the four threw their spears in turn, and each brought down his man. Again the Suitors threw ; most of their spears went wide ; but one wounded Telemachus slightly in the wrist, another struck Eumaeus high in the shoulder. Again the four threw their spears, and again four Suitors bit the dust. Odysseus next struck Agelaus at close quarters and slew him, while Telemachus drove his spear through Leocritus. Then panic seized those who yet remained and they fled, vainly seeking up and down the hall for some refuge, while Odysseus and his henchmen hunted and smote and slew. The ghastly moaning of dying men was heard throughout the hall and the floors ran blood. Leiodes, the soothsayer, caught Odysseus by the knees, protesting his own innocence and begging his life ; but there was no mercy for him, because, albeit a soothsayer, he had shared the Suitors' guilt. Two men only out of the whole number in the hall were spared, Phemius the minstrel and Medon the herald ; and when all the work of blood was done, these two only were left alive. The dead lay all about the hall heaped one upon another like fishes emptied on to the seashore out of fishermen's nets.

The Cleansing of the Hall (*Odys*. xxii. 390-494).—Then Odysseus bade call Eurycleia, the old nurse. So Telemachus smote at the door of the women's hall and called Eurycleia forth. Eurycleia obeyed and opened the doors of the women's apartments and followed Telemachus into the great hall. There she found Odysseus standing in the midst of all that slaughter, dyed in the blood of the slain and terrible to look upon. And when she recognized the bodies and saw what had been done, she raised a cry of jubilation. But Odysseus checked her : " Within thy heart rejoice, old nurse," he said, " and be still and cry not aloud : it is not right to exult over men that are slain." [1] After that he gave orders for the removal of the bodies of the dead, and for the washing and cleansing of the floors and tables in the hall ; and justice sharp and stern was done upon the wretched women guilty of disloyalty and upon Melanthius. Lastly, by Odysseus' orders, the fire was relit at the hearth in the great hall, and the whole house was fumigated with sulphur, the women's apartments, the great hall, and the outer court. And then Eurycleia went to call Penelope.

Odysseus and Penelope (*Odys.* xxiii. 1-372—the whole). —All this while Penelope had been quietly sleeping in her bed in the upper chamber : never since Odysseus left for Troy had she slept so soundly and well. So when the old woman woke her and eagerly told her wonderful tale, and how Odysseus had come home and was in the house, she was vexed at first and would not believe : even when informed of the slaughter of the Suitors she was still half-incredulous, unable all at once to believe her great happiness and fearful of some bitter disillusionment. " How," she asked, " if indeed Odysseus had come, had he been able to prevail in the fight, one against many." Eurycleia replied : " I saw not, I wist not, only I heard the groaning of the men slain. And we in an inmost place of the well-builded chambers sat all amazed, and the close-fitted doors shut in the room, till thy son called me from the chamber, for his father sent him out to that end. Then I found Odysseus standing among the slain, who around him, stretched on the hard floor, lay one upon the other : it would have comforted thy heart to see him, all stained like a lion

[1] *Odys.* xxii. 411-412.

with blood and soil of battle. And now are all the wooers gathered in an heap by the gates of the court, while he is purifying his fair house with brimstone, and hath kindled a great fire, and hath sent me forth to call thee. So come with me, that ye may both enter into your hearts' delight, for ye have suffered much affliction. And even now hath this thy long desire been fulfilled ; thy lord hath come alive to his own hearth, and hath found both thee and his son in the halls ; and the wooers that wrought him evil he hath slain, every man of them, in his house." [1]

Then Penelope went downstairs and entered the hall again ; and there she saw Odysseus sitting by the pillar near the fire, waiting for her coming. She longed to throw her arms about him, but still some strange shyness held her back, and she sat in the light of the fire by the further wall and watched him. Telemachus saw this coldness with impatience and chid his mother for her hardness of heart. But Penelope answered : " Child, my mind is amazed within me, and I have no strength to speak, nor to ask him aught ; nay, nor to look on him face to face. But if in truth this be Odysseus, and he hath indeed come home, verily we shall be ware of each other the more surely, for we have tokens that we twain know, even we, secret from all others." [2] Odysseus smiled and bade Telemachus leave him to this trial ; but because the danger was great when the slaying of the Suitors became known in the town, it was agreed that music and dancing should be renewed in the hall to turn away suspicion. While this was being done, Odysseus bathed and put on raiment more suited to his rank, and thus with strength and comeliness renewed came and sat down again by the fire opposite to Penelope. But when Penelope still gave no sign of recognition, he called Eurycleia and bade her prepare a couch for him alone in the porch. Upon this Penelope, to try the effect of her secret test, ordered Eurycleia to bring Odysseus' own

[1] *Odys.* xxiii. 40-57 (B. and L. pp. 377, 378).
[2] *Odys.* xxiii. 105-110 (B. and L. p. 379).

bedstead into the portico. Thereupon Odysseus cried out in protest and demanded to know who had moved from his bridal-chamber the bedstead he had wrought with his own hand, and how it had been possible to move it. For this bedstead had been built on to the trunk of an olive-tree rooted in the ground ; the tree formed one of the bedposts, and he knew the bed could not have been shifted without cutting through the trunk. At that word Penelope all but fainted ; for now at last she knew that it was Odysseus who had come, not some clever impostor : for none but Odysseus and she knew this secret of the olive tree. She burst into tears and put her hands about her husband's neck and kissed him, and begged forgiveness for her long disbelief, which was due only to her firm determination not to be deceived. And for Odysseus this moment was recompense for all the long years of wandering and waiting : to Penelope it was welcome as land to the swimmer escaping from a wreck. Long was the talk that they two held that night. Penelope told Odysseus of all the trials and sufferings of the long years ; Odysseus told the whole story of his wanderings and adventures, from the sacking of Ismarus and the episode of the Lotus-eaters to his escape from Calypso's Isle and his kind reception by the Phaeacians. But new cares came with the next day's dawn. For it was uncertain how the news of the slaying of the Suitors would be received in the city : Odysseus and his little band must be prepared, if necessary, to defend themselves.

Odysseus and Laertes (*Odys*. xxiv. 204-410).—First that day, however, Odysseus sought the farm where Laertes, his old father, lived sorrowing in retirement from the world. He found Laertes digging alone in his vine-yard : for all the farm hands were away gathering stones to build a wall. The old man was dressed in shabby clothes with oxhide leggings about his legs, and gloves to protect his hands from thorns ; and at the sight of his worn and sorrowful appearance Odysseus was smitten to the heart. He feared to make himself known too suddenly; so he entered into conversation with him, pretending to be a stranger newly arrived; he asked questions about Laertes himself and the garden, and about Odysseus, whom he claimed to have met in his own country. Laertes was sore stricken at the mention of Odysseus' name, and he took dust in his hands and cast it upon his grey head. This sight Odysseus could not endure, but he fell on his father's neck, saying: "Behold even I here am he, father, he of whom thou enquirest; in the twentieth year I am come to my native land. Therefore, stay thy weeping and tearful lamentation." [1] But Laertes could hardly believe and asked for proof. Odysseus showed the scar on his leg left by the gash of the wild boar's tusk, and told of the trees that Laertes had given to his little son when the boy had begged for a garden of his own: "Pear-trees thirteen thou gavest me," he said, "and ten apple-trees and forty fig-trees, and thou didst name the fifty rows of vines thou wouldst give me, each of which bore grapes at divers seasons—clusters of all sorts when Heaven's seasons loaded them from on high." [2] Then was Laertes fully convinced and threw his arms about his son; and Odysseus held him up half fainting. But when Laertes had recovered a little, he too bethought him of the danger there was that the people of Ithaca might rise against them because of the slaughter of the Suitors. Odysseus assured him that all this had been thought of, and that Telemachus and two faithful henchmen were already in the garden-house waiting for them. Laertes then washed and changed his raiment, and came forth renewed in strength and comeliness. Then they went back to the villa, and met there Laertes' steward, Dolius, and his six sons, all returning from their labours in the field. Old Dolius ran forward when he saw Odysseus and grasped his hand and kissed it, and said: "Beloved, since thou hast returned to us who sore desired thee, but no longer expected to see thee, and the gods themselves have led thee home, hail to thee and manifold

[1] *Odys*. xxiv. 321-323.   [2] *Odys*. xxiv. 340-344.

welcome, and may the gods give thee every blessing." [1]
Then all sat down and feasted.

Reconciliation (*Odys.* xxiv. 411 to end).—Meantime the
news of the slaughter had reached the city and spread
far and wide. Great indeed was the lamentation and
mourning around the palace of Odysseus where the dead
lay. The bodies of the slain were borne away by their
kinsmen ; those whose homes had been in the other
islands were conveyed across in fishing-boats. A great
concourse gathered in the market-place, and Eupeithes,
father of Antinous, harangued them : he called for an
immediate attack on Odysseus before he and his companions could escape overseas : Odysseus was accountable for the loss of all the warriors who had followed
him to Troy, and now for the slaughter of the Suitors.
" For shame it is, I ween, for them that come after to
hear, if we exact not retribution from the murderer of
our sons and kinsfolk." Medon the herald and Phemius
the bard, the two survivors from the slaughter in the
hall, opposed this counsel, declaring that the Suitors had
perished by the will of heaven : and Halitherses, the
seer, told the people that the fault was theirs because
they had not restrained their sons from their ill-doing.
But these protests were in vain ; for the greater part
of the assembly leapt up and followed Eupeithes. So
now a fresh conflict was impending, which would have
gone on to the bitter end, had not Zeus at Athena's
prompting decreed to stop it and reconcile Odysseus and
his people. The mob of Ithacans were now approaching
the farmhouse. Odysseus and his band of four, Laertes,
Telemachus, Eumaeus, and Philoetius armed themselves ;
Dolius with his six sons joined them—twelve spearmen
in all against the multitude. But Athena stood with
them in the likeness of Mentor. Odysseus knew her and
was glad, and bade Telemachus fight valiantly. " Thou
shalt see me, if thou wilt," replied Telemachus, " fired
as now I am, in no whit disgracing thy lineage." Laertes
rejoiced to hear these words and exclaimed, " What a

[1] *Odys.* xxiv. 400-403.

day is this for me, dear Heavens ! Vehemently do I rejoice : for I see my son and my son's son vying one with the other in valour." [1] Then Athena moved Laertes to begin the fight, and he hurled his spear, and the spear pierced the helm of Eupeithes ; and Eupeithes fell with a crash. Then Odysseus and Telemachus rushed upon the foremost rank of the rebels and smote them with spear and sword. And panic seized them and they fled. But when Odysseus sprang forward to pursue and slay, there came a flash of lightning, and a thunderbolt struck the earth by the feet of Athena. And Athena called on Odysseus and bade him stay his hands and make a covenant with his people. Odysseus gladly obeyed : and so with peace-offerings and reconciliation the poem comes to a close.

Epilogue.—Legend told of later wanderings of Odysseus —of which some hint is given in the *Odyssey*, and of his death in a foreign land. These further stories led an English poet to imagine one last adventure in which Odysseus sails with a crew of veteran seamen on a voyage over far western seas, from which he never returned. " I cannot rest from travel," Tennyson makes Odysseus say ; " I will drain life to the lees."

> " all times I have enjoy'd
> Greatly, have suffer'd greatly, both with those
> That loved me, and alone. . . ."
>
>   .   .   .   .
>
> How dull it is to pause, to make an end,
> To rust unburnish'd, not to shine in use !
> As tho' to breathe were life. Life piled on life
> Were all too little . . . .
>
>   .   .   .   .
>
>   " My mariners,
> Souls that have toil'd, and wrought, and thought with me
> That ever with a frolic welcome took
> The thunder and the sunshine, and opposed
> Free hearts, free foreheads—you and I are old ;
> Old age hath yet his honour and his toil ;
> Death closes all : but something ere the end,
> Some work of noble note, may yet be done,
> Not unbecoming men that strove with Gods."

[1] *Odys.* xxiv. 511-515.

PART II.

THE STRUGGLE WITH PERSIA

"Two several times Grecian civilization, which contained the germs of all subsequent European culture and progress, was within a hair's breadth of being swept away."

G. O. TREVELYAN, *A Holiday among some old Friends.*

CHAPTER IX

IONIANS AND DORIANS AND THE HELLENIC CITY-STATE

" Greek patriotism fused the emotions of school and family, of inheritance and early training, of religion and politics—all the best of boyhood with all the best of manhood—into one passionate whole. His city was the only city, and her ways the only ways."

Zimmern, *The Greek Commonwealth*, p. 65.

THE history of Greece, as distinct from legends and stories, can hardly be said to begin earlier than with the eighth century before Christ. It was from 776, when first the names of victors at the Olympic Games were recorded (the 1st Olympiad), that the Greeks in after times reckoned their chronology. We have good ground for believing that it was in the eighth century B.C. that most of the flourishing Greek cities of Sicily and Italy were founded. A few important events like the capture by the Spartans of Eira, the last stronghold of the Messenians, or· the attempt of Cylon to make himself master of Athens, can be assigned to approximate dates in the seventh century. With the sixth century something like a connected history of Greece begins to be possible : in particular, the history of Athens can be traced continuously and with some fulness of detail from the year 594, when Solon by his prudent legislation saved the state. But it is not till the fifth century that Greek history has any completeness. We then have the brilliant narratives of Herodotus and Thucydides to light up the period. Yet even so, it is only for the latter half of the fifth century that in Thucydides' history of the Peloponnesian War we at last have history written by a writer who was strictly a contemporary and actual witness of the events he describes. For Herodotus, our authority for the Persian Wars, was a child of four when the battle of Salamis was fought, and if, as is probable, he wrote his account of Marathon from material gathered at Athens when he became a resident there at thirty-seven years of age, the memories of the battle were already not far short of half a century old. It was as if the historian of the Battle of the Marne should begin to collect his materials about the year 1950. Broadly speaking, however, we can relate the history of Greece with fulness and approximate certainty from the fifth century onward. This fifth century B.C., as was said in our second chapter, includes a very large part of what is most interesting and worth remembering about the Greeks. It was then that the Greeks endured the great conflict which saved Europe from being engulfed in the Persian Empire. It was then it was determined that political freedom and the principles of responsibility and public law should be the guiding ideas of government in Europe, not the arbitrary will of one man. It was then that Greek genius ripened to produce the masterpieces in literature and sculpture which are still an inspiration to us and a model for the western world. To this century belong the names of Aeschylus, Sophocles, Euripides, Aristophanes ; of Herodotus, Thucydides and Xenophon ; of Pindar and Plato. To this century belong the Parthenon and the Propylaea, the Theseum and the gem-like temple of the Wingless Victory ; the temple of Zeus at Olympia ; the temple of Apollo at Phigaleia (Bassae). To this century belong the sculpture of Pheidias and the paintings of Polygnotus.

Change from Homeric to historic times.—This Hellas of history is a very different world from that of which the Homeric poems give us so vivid a picture. The chieftains with their palaces and princely hospitality, the Councils of Elders, and the loose gatherings of the freemen of the tribe in their Agora, have disappeared ; so have the easy social relations which made it possible for

Telemachus to journey to Pylos and to Sparta without any sense of leaving his own country ; and so have the simple conditions of family life which give us the delightful home pictures of Helen and Penelope and Arete ; of Nausicaa and her companions by the seashore ; of Eumaeus at the upland steading. In historic Greece these pleasing features of a society at once simple in its organization and of an engaging refinement of manners are gone, and in their place the Polis, or City-state, has become all in all, the support and frame of social and political life. Hellas is now a network of highly organized, but mutually repellent city-states, so numerous as to be counted with difficulty, each with its limited territorial domain, its peculiar constitution, its own customs and laws, its special religious cults ; each compact and sharply defined and separated socially and politically from all the rest. The ' polis ' is the organic whole which makes the political and social unit ; not the tribe or the nation, not Hellas at large. To realize what the political state of Hellas was like in the fifth century B.C. is a difficult matter for us who are born into the British Commonwealth and familiar with great national states like France, Italy, and Germany. We count ourselves British first, and only secondarily natives of Yorkshire, or Middlesex or Cornwall, citizens of Bristol, Birmingham, Manchester or London. But the Greek was first and almost wholly a citizen of Corinth, or Megara, or Athens, and only a long way after that a Hellene, much as he might pride himself in the last resort on his Hellenic birth and speech. He recognized acutely enough the distinction of Hellenic and non-Hellenic, Greek and Barbarian (and all men who were not Hellenes, however cultivated and civilized, were to the Greek barbarians). But his own special state, whether Argos, Thebes, or Sparta, was his peculiar fatherland, to which ordinarily all his patriotic devotion was paid, not Hellas. The people of other Greek city-states, though their claim to be counted Hellenes was exactly equal to his own, were foreigners (Xenoi), excluded alike from political privileges and the right of intermarriage. When a Greek state went to war, it was far more often with other Greeks than with barbarians. These Greek city-states varied in size from Sparta, which had for territory half the Peloponnese and Attica, which has an extreme length of fifty miles and an average breadth of five and twenty, to Megara, Plataea, or Corinth, whose lands would not have measured ten miles in any direction, or the townships of Phocis or Achaea with only a few thousand inhabitants and a few square miles of territory. Groups of these cities were in some instances banded into confederacies, as in Phocis, or brought under the influence and control of a powerful neighbour, as the Boeotian towns (except Plataea) under that of Thebes ; but all aspired and claimed by right to be independent sovereign states. That was autonomy and freedom (eleutheria). Anything else was servitude (douleia). In the Peloponnese, which is not much larger than Yorkshire, there were more than two dozen such independent states, although Sparta ruled over all the southern half : in Boeotia, which is not so large as Kent, there were nearly as many. It was as if Maidstone, Dover, Canterbury, Rochester and Tonbridge were not only sovereign states, each with its separate government and its surrounding belt of territory, but likewise Chatham and Ashford and many other smaller towns. Margate might be at war with Ramsgate, or Dover with Folkestone or Deal. Similarly York, Leeds, Bradford, Halifax, Scarborough and Hull (not to speak of Manchester and Durham) would be independent sovereign states, sometimes in alliance, sometimes at war. These Hellenic city-states, jealous rivals of each other and frequently at variance, led an intense political life, all the more intense because of its narrow concentration and the perilous issues at stake when it went to war. The penalties of defeat might in an extreme case mean the end of the state's existence, as it did, for instance, when the Argives put an end to Mycenae in 462, the Athenians to Aegina in 431. There was even an ultimate fear of a worse doom, the slaughter of all males capable of bearing arms, the

selling of all the rest into slavery. Further, these little
states were not only subject to the dangers of foreign
war, but were nearly always the battle-ground of rival
political parties. The full life of a man was conceived
by the Greeks as civic life, and the good man was first
and foremost the good citizen. For the good citizen, as
we noted in Chapter I. (p. 12), there could be no neutral
attitude towards party disputes. Still more, of course,
must the citizen of a Greek state be prepared to defend
his ' polis ' with his body by personal war-service. There
was no room in a Greek ' polis ' for any kind of ' con-
scientious objector.'

Origin of the City-state.—The importance of the city-
state in Greek history and the intensity of a Greek's
feeling for his ' polis ' may be attributed chiefly to two
causes. One is the long period of insecurity through
which the whole country had passed : the other, the
physical features of the Grecian land. The interval
between the reputed date of the Trojan War and the
fifth century is a long one, seven hundred years nearly,
as long a time back as from the present day to Magna
Charta (1920-1215) : obviously there is room for spacious
changes in such a length of time. Now, though there is
little that can be called history before the eighth century,
it is possible to argue back with reasonable probability
from the known facts of later times and the hints regarding
earlier traditions found in Greek writers, what the general
course of events must have been through the centuries of
which there is no written record. The most certain
inference regarding these earlier centuries is that of a
long-continued period of unsettlement lasting for many
generations, perhaps for centuries. Thucydides in the
opening of his history states clearly his own belief that
the Trojan War was followed by a prolonged period of
disturbance. " Indeed, even after the Trojan war," he
writes, " Hellas was still subject to migrations and in
process of settlement, and hence did not get rest and
wax stronger. For not only did the return of the Hellenes
from Ilium, occurring as it did after a long time, cause

many changes ; but factions also began to spring up very
generally in the cities, and, in consequence of these, men
were driven into exile and founded new cities. . . ." [1]
Even more significant are his reflections on the state of
Hellas in still earlier times : " For it is plain," he says,
" that what is now called Hellas was not of old settled
with fixed habitations, but that migrations were frequent
in former times, each tribe readily leaving its own land
whenever they were forced to do so by any people that
was more numerous. For there was no mercantile
traffic and the people did not mingle with one another
without fear, either on land or by sea, and they each
tilled their own land enough to obtain a livelihood from
it, having no surplus of wealth and not planting orchards,
since it was uncertain, especially as they were yet without
walls, when some invader might come and despoil them.
And so, thinking that they could obtain anywhere the
sustenance required for their daily needs, they found it
easy to change their abodes, and for this reason were not
strong as regards either the size of their cities or their
resources in general." [2] These passages confirm, what is
inferred on other grounds, that Greece was peopled by
successive waves of migration from the north, and that
for a very long period fresh bands of warriors continued
to press down, subduing or driving out the tribes that
had settled in the land before them. The insecurity
caused by this long-continued state of unsettlement was
further aggravated by the prevalence of piracy. On this
also Thucydides makes instructive comment : " It should
be explained that in early times both the Hellenes and
the Barbarians who dwelt on the mainland near the sea,
as well as those on the islands, when once they began
more frequently to cross over in ships to one another,
turned to piracy, under the lead of their most powerful
men, whose motive was their own private gain, and the
support of their weaker followers, and falling upon cities

[1] Thucydides, i. 12 (Foster Smith's translation in the Loeb Classical
Library, p. 23).
[2] Thucydides, i. 2 (L.C.L. pp. 3 and 5).

that were unprovided with walls and consisted of groups of villages, they pillaged them and got most of their living from that source. For this occupation did not as yet involve disgrace, but rather conferred something even of glory. This is shown by the practice, even at the present day, of some of the peoples on the mainland, who still hold it an honour to be successful in this business, as well as by the words of the early poets, who invariably ask the question of all who put in to shore, whether they are pirates, the inference being that neither those whom they ask ever disavow that occupation, nor those ever censure it who are concerned to have the information." [1]

It was during this long period of violence and insecurity, which is roughly comparable to the state of England at the coming of the Danes and Northmen, that the strong love of the ' polis ' took such hold on the Greek as to become with him an instinct. The physical peculiarities of the country contributed to bring about this result. Greece, we have noted (Ch. II. p. 19), is a land of high mountains rising steeply from small stretches of plain. In the plains an isolated rock often stands separate and dominates the low ground around. Such a rock, like the Acropolis at Athens or the Larissa of Argos, was easily defensible, and formed the nucleus of a city. Such a rock, when fortified, became a refuge in time of danger, and under its protection grew up the walled city. When times were at their worst, and we have reason to conjecture that for a long time they were very bad, the walled city was ever a sure defence and refuge for the primitive settler. " Inside the wall he could take breath. He could become for a time a man again, instead of a terrified beast." [2]

[1] Thucydides, i. 5 (L.C.L. pp. 9 and 11).

[2] Murray, *The Rise of the Greek Epic*, p. 56. Dr. Murray continues : " The wall was built, Aristotle tells us, that men might live, but its inner cause was that men might live well. It was a ship in a great sea, says a character in Sophocles (*Antigone*, 191), whose straight sailing is the first condition of all faith and friendship between man and man. The Polis became a sort of Mother-Goddess, binding together all who lived within its circuit and superseding all more personal worships. When this begins we have the germ of historical Greece."

The Return of the Heraclidae.—This development of the city-state clearly took place subsequent to the Trojan War. Now we know from strong and consistent tradition that a period of movement and violent change came very soon after the Trojan War. It would seem as if that combined effort of the old Achaean society, and particularly the long absence of the leading chieftains on the shores of the Troad, had everywhere weakened authority. The stories of the murder of Agamemnon by Aegisthus and Clytaemnestra and of the disorders in Ithaca illustrate this. At all events tradition very plainly asserted that Tisamenus, son of Orestes and grandson of Agamemnon, fell in battle against Dorian invaders of the Peloponnese eighty years after the destruction of Troy. These Dorian invaders were led by three chieftains, Temenus, Cresphontes, and Aristodemus, great-grandsons of Hyllus, son of Heracles ; they claimed to recover the Peloponnese as of right, because their ancestor Heracles had been fraudulently dispossessed by Eurystheus. This was the Dorian conquest of the Peloponnese, otherwise known as the Return of the Heraclidae. And here, as often happens, legend is the true interpreter of history. For the distinction of Dorian and Ionian is the key to Greek history in the fifth century. The Dorians were conquering tribes who established themselves in Sparta, Messenia and Argos ; in Corinth, Sicyon, Megara, Aegina and other places, but failed to dispossess the Achaeans from the strip of coast north of the mountains along the Gulf of Corinth, the Arcadians from the central highlands, or the Ionians from Attica outside the Isthmus. Consequently this Hellenic society in historical times is distinguished as Dorian and non-Dorian, and of the non-Dorian communities those claiming Ionian descent, which includes the Athenians, were far the most important. The Dorians founded kingdoms in Argos, Sparta and Messenia, each of which traced the descent of its kings from one of the Heraclid conquerors. Temenus, the progenitor of the Argive kings, was the eldest of the Heraclid princes ; therefore the Argives claimed the leadership in Hellas, and, when Sparta out-stripped them and became the foremost Hellenic state, they never forgot their deposition. This will be found to explain the behaviour of the Argives at the time of Xerxes' invasion. Somewhere between the ninth and the seventh centuries Sparta was transformed into a military brotherhood whose life and character was moulded by the rigorous Spartan discipline, and in the strength of that discipline prevailed so completely over the neighbour on her western border, the Dorian state Messenia, that the Messenians were reduced to the servile condition known as 'helotage.' Argos was more than once badly worsted in a trial of strength with Sparta and greatly weakened, but not conquered and annexed like Messenia. The migration of Aeolians, Ionians and Dorians, across the Aegean and the foundation of the numerous Hellenic cities along the coast of Asia Minor and beyond, is represented as an after effect of the Dorian invasion of the Peloponnese. The movement of expansion which resulted in the establishment of these Greek colonies in Asia Minor was in part due to other causes, but the pressure exercised by the Dorians in all probability contributed. In historical times these Greek cities fringing the eastern shores of the Aegean were combined into three groups united by race and speech. Most to the north, along the coast of Mysia and nearest to the Troad, was the Aeolian group, of which the island Lesbos with its capital Mytilene was the most important member. Ionia extended south of this along the shores of Lydia and Caria. It included the famous cities Ephesus and Miletus and the islands Samos and Chios. The Dorian group was southernmost, a confederation of six states, three city-states in the island of Rhodes, the island of Cos, and the cities Cnidus and Halicarnassus on the mainland, about the south-west corner of Caria. The Ionian was far the most important of these groups ; and since the Ionians were the Greeks who first became known to the peoples of the East, their name in the form Iavones became the common name in eastern countries to designate the Greeks. It is Yauna in Persian inscriptions, Javan in the English Bible, and Yunani in India.

Rivalry of Ionian and Dorian.—The people of Attica had once been called Ionian, and though by the fifth century the Athenians had ceased to use the name Ionian, and relations were actually so much reversed that the Ionians of Asia were reputed to be colonists from Attica and looked to Athens as their ' metropolis,' or mother-city, we find rivalry and antagonism growing between Ionians and Dorians. There was a difference in origin between Dorian and Ionian communities, a difference of speech, and a contrast of character which became more marked in process of time. The Dorians were tougher and hardier physically, but of hard moral fibre too, and intellectually stiff. The Ionians were quicker-witted and more versatile, but less stable morally ; and they were reproached with softness and effeminacy. This contrast was deepened when the cities of Ionia in the sixth century B.C. were made subject first to the Lydian monarchy and then to Persia. This contrast and rivalry not only prevailed in the homeland, but extended also to the colonies which between the eighth and the sixth centuries were planted by the Greeks on all the shores to which the seas on either side of Greece gave access.

Greek Colonization.—We have seen what influence the mountains of the homeland had in developing the political institutions and character of the Greeks. We have now to carry somewhat further than in Chapter II. our consideration of the influence of the sea in shaping the destinies of the Hellenic race. For this we need a map which takes in the whole of the Balkan peninsula and the seas on either side. It should, on the one hand, show the relation of central Hellas to Crete and all the coasts of the Aegean, and to the Dardanelles as leading through the Sea of Marmora and the Bosphorus to the Black Sea : on the other, it should include the Ionian Sea and show the relation of the western shores of Greece to Italy and

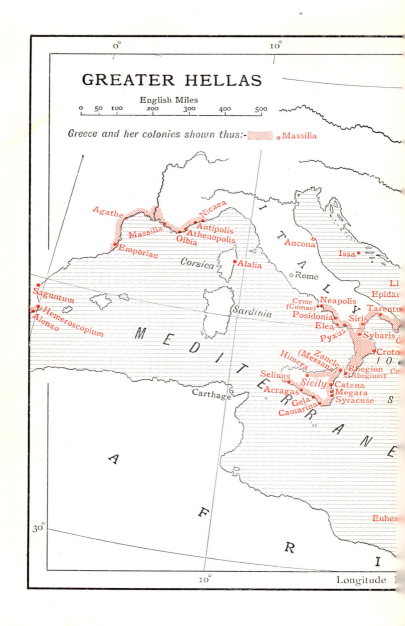

GREATER HELLAS

English Miles

0 50 100 200 300 400 500

Greece and her colonies shown thus:- ○ Massilia

Agathe

Nicaea

Antipolis

Massilia Athenopolis

Olbia

Emporiae

Ancona

Issa

Corsica Alalia

Rome

Li

Epidar

Saguntum

Cyme Neapolis Y

(Cumae) Tarentu

Hemeroscopium Posidonia Siris

Alonao Elea

Pyxus Sybaris

Sardinia

Croto

Zancle Ce

(Messana) 10

Himera Rhegion

(Rhegium)

M E D I T E

Selinus Catana

Sicily Megara

Acragas Syracuse S

Carthage Gela

Camarina R

R

A

A

N

E

F

Euhes

30°

R

I

Longitude

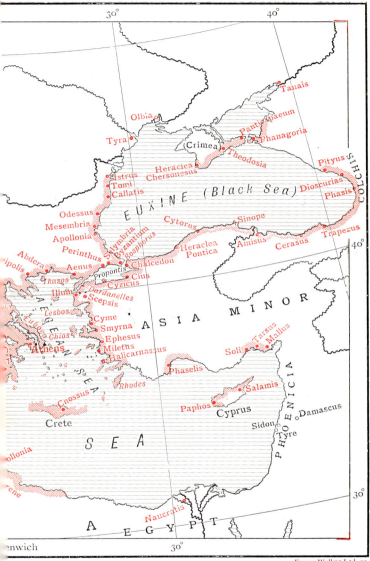

Sicily, and to all the western Mediterranean.[1] In looking at this map we are at once struck by a notable contrast between the eastern and western sides. The western, or Ionian, sea is a wide open sea entirely clear of islands, except for the few near the coast on either side of the Gulf of Corinth. The eastern, or Aegean, sea is strewn thickly over its southern half with the islands of the Grecian Archipelago, the groups called the Cyclades and the Sporades, while scattered more sparsely over the northern half are big islands like Chios, Lemnos and Thasos. When the places occupied by the Greeks in the fifth century B.C. are coloured red, as suggested in Chapter II., we see the Aegean as an oval basin, the edges of which are an almost continuous Greek land, while Crete and all the islands are fragments of this land scattered over the sea. And such in fact it was, though for a time the Asiatic Greeks and some of the islands were subjected to the rule of an eastern monarchy. Such it is to-day in spite of the long domination of the Turk. It is a striking example of the persistence of race. We may notice also that the eastern coast of Greece from Euboea to Cape Taenarum is more deeply indented by great bays than the western, except for the Gulf of Corinth. The Greeks, if we are right in supposing that for the most part they entered the Hellenic homeland from the north, were not originally a sea-faring people. They were turned into a sea-faring people by the character of the land in which they settled, and they came in course of time to be more than a match for the Phoenicians, those most daring navigators of prehistoric times in the Mediterranean, driving them not only out of Greek home waters, the Aegean and Cretan seas, but out of great part of the eastern Mediterranean. We can see from the map that, when the Greeks began to undertake sea adventures, they were drawn naturally eastward. For the earliest mariners preferred sailing along a coast within sight of land and were not easily emboldened to steer into the open sea, where, till the compass

[1] Only a map of Europe will show this last relation fully.

was invented, there was nothing except the stars to guide their course. But in the Aegean from Euboea and Attica and Argolis, the islands gleaming out of summer seas easily tempted even the timid navigator on from point to point, till he reached the mainland of Asia. Nevertheless, some of the western colonies carried the tradition of their origin as far back in the past as the tenth century B.C.

The Eastward Colonies.—There is no record of the earliest movement which peopled the whole coast of the Levant with Greek settlements. The settlements were there when Greek history opens. This is all we know certainly. But, as already said, it was in all probability a consequence, or rather a culmination, of the movement which brought bands of warriors from the north down into the Hellenic peninsula. When hard pressed by the invaders, the Ionians and Achaeans naturally passed on by the islands across to the opposite shores and there made new homes for themselves. Possibly the actual struggle for the possession of these new homes lent a vivid interest to the epic of the more ancient warfare in the Troad of which the poet of the *Iliad* sings. For without doubt the Homeric poems, if they originated in Thessaly, as some hold, took the later form in which we know them among the cities of Asia Minor. It is possible also that very early voyages were made through the Dardanelles and the Bosphorus to the Black Sea. There were ultimately Greek colonies, not only on both sides of the entrance to the Bosphorus at Byzantium and at Chalcedon, but all round the coast of the Black Sea and in the peninsula of the Crimea. The story of Jason's voyage to Colchis in the Argo seems to preserve the memory of an early adventure of this sort. Jason brought back the Golden Fleece as merchants later brought back precious merchandize.

The Westward Colonies.—But very early colonizing Greeks found their way west also to Italy and Sicily, in spite of the open sea on that side. Doubtless the islands along the western coast, Zante (Zacynthus), Thiaki, (Ithaca), Santa Maura (Leucadia), and Corfu (Corcyra), helped to bring this about. There is only an eighty mile stretch of sea from the north-west corner of Corfu to the nearest point of Italy, and this was the course Grecian navigators followed in the days of history, as did the Athenians when they sailed on their Sicilian expedition. The best known of all the Greek colonies in this direction is Syracuse in Sicily, which, according to data which Thucydides furnishes, was founded in 734. But much earlier than this was Cumae in Italy in the middle of Campania, the foundation of which is carried back to 1000 B.C. ; and from Cumae was founded a ' new city ' some few years later, which we know as Naples.[1] These two cities were founded by Euboeans from Chalcis and Eretria and by Achaeans from Cyme, one of the Aeolian cities in Asia Minor. Several other cities were founded by the Euboeans ; Catana and Himera were the chief of these in Sicily, and in Italy Rhegium. Syracuse on the other hand was Dorian, founded from Corinth ; and from Syracuse Camarina was founded in 595. Megara in Sicily (Hyblaean Megara) was a colony from Dorian Megara, and dated from 728 ; Selinus was another founded just a century later, in 628. Tarentum was a colony of the Lacedaemonians, the only colony Sparta ever planted. The famous rivals Sybaris and Crotona were both Achaean. But of all the Greek colonies westward, that which has played the greatest part in history is Marseilles. As Massilia it was founded by Ionians from Phocaea about 600 B.C.

Ties with the Metro-polis or Mother-city.—Although every Greek colony, when established, was an autonomous city-state, as independent as the city, or cities, from which its founders came, it was intimately bound by ties of religion and sentiment to the mother-city. When the resolution to found a new city was taken, the first thing for pious Greeks to do was to consult the Delphic oracle regarding the enterprise and the choice of a site. When

[1] The name Naples (Italian, Napoli) = Nea Polis, New Town.

this had been done, a leader, called oekist or founder, was chosen, whose name was ever after held in honour in the new city. Before the expedition sailed, fire was taken from the sacred hearth in the Town Hall (the Prytaneum) of the mother-city, and carefully kept alive through the voyage, so that the fire in the State-hearth of the newly founded colony might be kindled from it. Ties of affection were kept up between the colony and the mother-country by means of religious festivals ; any special form of worship peculiar to the mother-country would be conveyed to the colony ; representatives of the colony used to attend the religious festivals of the mother-country. If a fresh colony were in turn sent forth from the newly founded state, the leader (oekist) was supplied by the original mother-country. For a colony to go to war with its metropolis was regarded as impious and sacrilegious. Thus, although politically the Greek city-states, whether in the Hellenic peninsula, or on the shores of Asia Minor, or far away on the coasts of the Mediterranean or Euxine, in Sicily or Italy, on the coast of Africa or in the Crimea, were all alike independent sovereign states, they were still bound together by ties of religion and kinship, of custom and of speech. In spite of the jealously guarded political autonomy, in spite of the race difference between Ionian, Dorian and Aeolian, there were strong bonds of union holding in sympathy all Hellenes wherever resident. Two of the most notable were the Olympic Games and the Oracle of Apollo at Delphi.

The Olympic Games.—The Olympic Games, the most important of the four athletic meetings which attained a national character among the Greeks, were held in honour of Zeus at Olympia in Elis, the fertile district which forms the north-west corner of the Peloponnese. At Olympia were gathered once in four years men from every branch of Hellenic stock—from Europe, Asia, Africa ; from Sicily and Italy, from Thrace and the Crimea, as well as from the Peloponnese and central Greece—to celebrate this greatest of athletic festivals and

OLYMPIA.

Ruins of the Temple of Zeus from the N. under Cronos Hill, and looking on to the high

decide the championships of Greek athletics. Olympia is situated in the beautiful valley through which the Alpheus flows, and at a point where the Cladeus, after skirting the Hill of Cronus, joins the river from the north. This hill of Cronus is of no great height (some four hundred feet), and is easily climbed, though the ascent is steep. The scene below is one of great beauty, but only the bare skeleton of what was Olympia is visible there now, and that only since the German excavations between 1875 and 1881 uncovered the ruins that had been buried sixteen feet deep under the silt brought down by the Cladeus in flood. The Olympic running-ground, or Stadium, is eastward—with the slope of the hill forming one side of its enclosure ; along the base of the hill west-ward extends the sacred precinct, or *Altis* (the name means ' Grove '), in which were included the principal religious buildings connected with the celebration of the games—the temples of Zeus and of Hera, the shrine of Pelops, the great altar of Zeus, twenty feet high, built up with the ashes from the burnt thigh bones of the victims sacrificed. This altar was nearly the centre of the Altis ; the Pelopium was to the west of it ; the Heraeum, the most ancient temple known in Hellas, to the north of the Pelopium ; the temple of Zeus to the south. Beyond the Altis were other public buildings, the Council House, the Colonnade of the Echoes, the Wrestling-place and the Gymnasium.

When in its appointed season (the height of summer) the sacred month came round, the roads and mountain tracks leading to Olympia were thronged with parties of men (no women, for women were not admitted to see the games) travelling to the festival, some of whom had come across the sea to the nearest ports. To ensure security to the travellers a sacred truce was proclaimed a fort-night before the games began ; no traveller might be molested on his way to Olympia ; if any cities were at war they must refrain from all acts of hostility while the truce lasted ; that is, for a full fortnight before and after the meeting. To violate this truce was rank sacrilege.

Up to the time of the Persian wars the sports lasted only a day ; later they were extended to as many as five days. There were foot races of different distances, horse races and chariot races ; there was wrestling and boxing and throwing the quoit ; the mixed contest of boxing and wrestling called the Pancratium ; the five-fold event called the Pentathlum. There were in course of time separate contests for boys. The foot races took place in the Stadium, and so did the boxing and wrestling. The horse-racing was in the Hippodrome, which from Pausanias' description must have been further to the east beyond the Stadium. The length of the single course for running is exactly known ; for both starting line and goal-line in the Stadium have been uncovered, and the distance between is just 210 yards. This, then, for the Greeks was the length of their sprinting distance : the double course was very nearly equal to the Quarter Mile. The distance of the long course is not certainly known, probably between two and three miles. The pentathlum was a group of five events, running, long jump, throwing the discus (quoit), javelin-throwing and wrestling. The pancratium was a rough-and-tumble of boxing and wrestling. The horse contests, which took place in the Hippodrome, were four-horse chariot-racing, pair-horse chariot-racing and a mounted race. The events had been few at first and became more numerous as time went on. The prize in every contest alike was a wreath of wild olive leaves ; nothing more. Yet there was the keenest emulation among competitors and their supporters. For the Greek athlete contended for the honour of his native city, and by his native city no honour was prized more highly. The return of the victor to his home was a triumphal procession. The highest honours were showered upon him, and more substantial benefits also. At Athens the Olympic victor was entitled to receive his meals at the public expense in the Guild Hall of the city (the Prytaneum) for the rest of his days.

This was what the Olympic games were like in the days of Greek freedom, and such was the spirit in which the Greeks contended. The festival was so important that Greek men of letters came to date events by means of the Olympiads. The first recorded victory was that of Coroebus of Elis in the stadium or single course in the year 776 B.C., which is therefore the date of the 1st Olympiad. Mythical story carried the origin of the games much further back. According to one legend the games were instituted to commemorate the chariot race in which Pelops won his bride, Hippodameia, from her father Oenomaus ; and this is why the contest of Oenomaus and Pelops forms the subject of the principal sculptures which adorned the eastern front of the Temple of Zeus at Olympia. Another story made Heracles the first to run a race there and institute the Olympic Games. However they originated—and probably they began as a local festival of the Eleans in conjunction with the men of Pisa—the Olympic Games took a strong hold on the life of the Greeks, and were a practical expression of the Greek instinctive conviction that bodily strength and beauty is admirable and to be cultivated by training and competition. Pausanias, who visited Olympia in the second century A.D. when the greatness of Greece was long past, couples the Olympic Games with the rites of Eleusis for religious efficacy : " Many a wondrous sight may be seen, and not a few tales of wonder may be heard in Greece ; but there is nothing on which the blessing of God rests in so full a measure as the rites of Eleusis and the Olympic games." [1]

The Delphic Oracle.—The Greeks firmly believed that in the difficulties of life it was always possible to obtain supernatural guidance by consulting an oracle. Divination by means of oracles, that is through shrines where the answers delivered by priests to enquirers were regarded as inspired by the god worshipped there, was a peculiarly Hellenic institution, though, of course, divination by this and other means is common to many races. There were several Greek oracular shrines, but none so famous, or so widely consulted, as the Oracle of Apollo

[1] Pausanias, v. 10. 1 (Frazer).

at Delphi. Apollo's temple was there built on a wide shelving ledge of rock deep in the valley of the Pleistus under the heights of Mount Parnassus. Sheer walls of cliff, eight hundred feet high, meeting at a very obtuse angle, form the background of the scene. At the point where the two walls meet is a narrow gorge, down which falls a stream which in winter is a foaming cascade. This stream is the fountain Castalia. The cliffs were called Phaedriades, the ' Gleaming ' Rocks, because the sun at his rising darts shafts of light from them before his disc shows over the top. For some moments the rocks themselves appear to radiate light. Between 1500 and 2000 feet below, through a tangle of trees and grass and bushes, flows the Pleistus. The natural scene is one of wild beauty, and the effect was heightened in ancient times by the contrast with the sacred buildings which the veneration of the Hellenes for the awe and mystery of the place had raised there. Everything was calculated to exalt the religious feelings of the worshipper who came to consult the god. If he came from the Gulf of Corinth by the long road up from the port of Cirrha (now Itéa),[1] the splendid vision burst upon him at a sudden bend in the road. If he came by land through Phocis, he climbed for many hours through grand mountain scenery along the side of Parnassus till he came under the very gorge of Castalia.

This Delphi, the seat of Apollo's temple and of the Pythia, was lost to the knowledge of men for a thousand years and more. Over its site, till the year 1890, spread the primitive mountain village, Castri, and scholars had even been in doubt whether this village were the site of Delphi or not. Then the French dug, and by 1899 the complete plan of Delphi outlined in stone, precisely as it was described by Pausanias 1700 years before, stood revealed. You may now look from the platform of Apollo's shrine and call up some faint semblance of what Delphi was like in the days of its glory.

[1] The modern Itéa does not occupy the site of the ancient Cirrha. Cirrha was about a mile to the east.

The Greek who came to consult the oracle must first follow the appointed ritual to assure his personal purity ; then take part in a solemn sacrifice. If the signs were all favourable, he approached the temple, and the officiating priest, a member of one of the Delphian families, received his enquiry and disappeared into the sanctuary. In the chamber within [1] sat the priestess of Apollo, the Pythoness or Pythia, a woman of mature years, consecrated to this service. To prepare herself for the ordeal, she had fasted, and bathed in the Castalian spring, eaten of the leaves of the sacred laurel and drunk of the cold waters of the spring, Cassotis. Then she mounted the tripod, the three-footed stool of inspiration, and about her stood the priests of Apollo and the ' prophētes,' or interpreter, waiting for the inspired word that should fall from her lips. When the power of the god came upon her, the priestess writhed and twisted and threw out her arms and uttered strange cries. At last she poured out a series of more coherent sounds, which the attendant priest, or prophet, took down. This was the ' response,' which was subsequently given by the priest to the enquirer, generally in the form of two or more lines of hexameter verse. Sometimes the answer of the god was simple and plain, as when he forbade the men of Cnidus to cut a channel to turn the peninsula on which their city stood into an island.[2] More often it was expressed as a sort of riddle, which required an exercise of wit to interpret it and left an opening for error ; and it was from this that oracles became proverbial for their ambiguity. Well-known examples are the ' wooden wall ' which was to save Athens, and the reply which led Croesus to his destruction (Ch. XI. p. 261). However it is to be

[1] One would like to believe in the cleft or chasm in the rock beneath the sanctuary out of which rose a strange intoxicating vapour, and that it was above this that the tripod of the priestess was placed. Later tradition, beginning with Strabo, the geographer, is precise in describing all this. But certainly there was no trace of any such rift or cleft in the floor of the temple of Apollo when excavated by the French. It is all solid stone.

[2] Herodotus, i. 174.

accounted for (which does not concern us here), there can be no doubt that in the early days of Greek history the Delphic oracle enjoyed an extraordinary reputation. Its fame had gone out into all lands contiguous to the Greek world. It was consulted by the powerful princes of Lydia, and held in manifest respect by Persian kings and their servants. But while its influence thus extended beyond Greece, it was a peculiarly Greek institution, a possession in which the Hellenes might take pride. The Greeks of the fifth century B.C. consulted the Delphic oracle as private persons and as communities on all occasions of importance. There can be no doubt of the weight attached to the replies of the oracle and of the real influence it exercised. It was a potent instrument of Greek national life ; for, in matters of common interest, as the oracle spoke, the Hellenes could be swayed this way or that. Herodotus quotes an oracle which forbade the Spartans to attempt the conquest of Arcadia. It was the Delphic oracle which brought about the deliverance of Athens from the usurped rule of the sons of Pisistratus. For, whenever the Spartans consulted the oracle, whether in a public capacity or a private, the only reply they could get was an exhortation to free Athens. It is true a story was told at Athens that this happened because the priestess had been bribed, and that stories of such corruptibility already in the fifth century were beginning to undermine the old implicit faith in the oracle's truth. But there can be no question of the great influence once wielded by the oracle, or that, on the whole, this influence worked for good. It would seem that the central position of Delphi, and the resort to the temple of enquirers from all parts of the Hellenic world gave the priestly families unique opportunities of gathering information. The priestly houses were in touch with distant lands ; they had interests abroad and special sources of information. By these means also they acquired from generation to generation a sagacity in dealing with men and affairs which seldom led them astray. These powers of usefulness were shown most

widely and successfully in connection with Greek colonization. The founding of new settlements by the Greeks
may be said to have been carried out under the direction
of the Delphic oracle. Before a band of colonists set
out they invariably sought the advice of the oracle
(above, p. 209), so that Herodotus notes it as remarkable
when the Spartan Dorieus, " neither took counsel of the
oracle at Delphi as to the place whereto he should go,
nor observed any of the customary usages " ; [1] and
evidently regards this recklessness as the cause of his
failure. We can see good reason for this custom. The
Delphic priests from their knowledge of other lands were
in a position to give sound advice to intending emigrants.
For there can be little doubt that it was the priests, and
not the Pythoness, who really determined the substance
of the responses. The Pythoness in her ecstasy babbled
incoherent sounds ; the priests interpreted these sounds
in accordance with their judgment of what was fitting.
This may not account for all that is remarkable in the
history of the oracle, but it accounts for a good deal.

The oracle was a fountain of worldly wisdom and
practical sagacity to all Greece ; it was also a source of
moral guidance. There is a gradual refinement and
elevation of moral ideas in the course of Greek history,
and we can trace how the influence of the Delphic oracle
was prevailingly on the side of higher conceptions of justice
and humanity. " It is from Delphi that reverence for
oaths, respect for the life of slaves, of women, of suppliants, derive in great measure their sanction and
strength." [2] We had already occasion to notice in
Chapter III. the civilizing influence of the worship of
Apollo. This influence was exercised in part through
the Delphic oracle, which became " in a certain sense
the conscience of Greece." [3] A story which Herodotus
tells in his history is a good illustration of this influence.
In the times when Ionia was threatened by the rise of
the Lydian power a certain citizen of Miletus came to a

[1] Herodotus, v. 42.   [2] Myers, *Greek Oracles*, p. 45.
[3] Myers, p. 8.

Spartan named Glaucus, who had a great reputation for integrity, and begged him to take charge of a large sum of money, because the Peloponnese was so much safer than Ionia. Glaucus was to keep the money till some one came to claim it by producing tallies corresponding with those left with the deposit. Years went by, and after the death of the Milesian, his sons came to Glaucus, produced the tallies, and asked for the return of the treasure. Glaucus put them off saying that he had no recollection of the transaction. After they had gone away sorrowful, for they looked upon their money as lost, Glaucus went to Delphi to enquire of the god whether he might keep the deposit. The oracle replied in these terrifying words :

" Gainful it were for a time, O Glaucus, to have thy desiring ;
    Gainful to swear the oath and so make prize of the treasure.
    Swear then : death comes to him who keeps his oath when he
        sweareth,
    Yet there is one, Oath's son, without hand, without foot and
        nameless,
    Swift in his wrath to pursue, till wrath overtaketh the guilty :
    Then shall it whelm all his race and house in the doom of
        destruction.
    But they that keep their oath, these have fair sons to succeed
        them."

Glaucus in terror begged for pardon, sent for the sons of his Milesian friend and repaid the money. Nevertheless, the story concluded, in the third generation, not a single descendant of Glaucus was found surviving.[1]

[1] Herodotus, vi. 86.

CHAPTER X

SPARTA AND ATHENS

" And everyone who considers . . what children of his soul Lycurgus has appointed to be the guardians, not only of Lacedaemon, but of all Greece ; or what an illustrious progeny of laws Solon has produced . . . would choose rather to be the parent of such children than those in a human shape."

From Shelley's translation of Plato's *Banquet.*

ONE of the great services the Greeks were to render to western civilization was to provide a museum of the varying forms of constitutional government. The Greek city-states generally passed through a series of changes broadly exemplifying the same process of development,[1] while differing widely in points of detail. The starting-point is hereditary kingship, just the constitution we have presented to us in the Homeric poems. There the Achaean princes are leaders in war and have a good deal of arbitrary power ; but the arbitrariness of their power is limited (and here Greek kingship differs from oriental), first by the authority of the Council of Elders (the *Boule*), which the king is by custom obliged to consult regularly

---

[1] The great political thinkers, Plato, Aristotle, Polybius, discuss the different forms of constitution known in their day and the change from one form to another. Plato and Aristotle contrast perfect and imperfect forms of ' polities.' Polybius, who lived in the last days of the Achaean League and was the close friend of Scipio Africanus (the younger), sets forth a theory of the secular changes of the state from hereditary kingship through tyranny, aristocracy, oligarchy to democracy. There is a stage beyond democracy which it would greatly advantage political thinkers of our own time to study. He calls it ochlocracy (mob-rule). See Plato, *Republic,* Book viii. ; Aristotle, *Politics,* iii. 7 ; and Polybius, vi. 3-9.

on all matters of importance ; secondly, by the *Agora*, or gathering of free men, which is called together on occasions of special moment. Thus Agamemnon in the second book of the *Iliad* first takes counsel with his Boule, or Council ; then lays the question of peace or war before the host of the Achaeans in their Agora. Priam consults his Council on the question of the surrender of Helen. Telemachus appeals to the Agora in Ithaca against the overbearing conduct of the Suitors. Thus all the elements of the political developments of later times are found already in the society portrayed by Homer. Between the Homeric age and the fifth century, however, kingly power had either been greatly circumscribed or had altogether disappeared. Government by kings was first superseded by aristocracy, the rule of families of nobles ; as the rule of these nobles grew more close and selfish, aristocracy, the government of *the best*, was turned into oligarchy, the rule of *the few*. Then arose everywhere a struggle of parties, the people striving to acquire a larger share of political rights, the nobles seeking to maintain their exclusive privileges. In many of the city-states this struggle led for a time to a form of monarchical government which the Greeks called a ' tyranny.' This was the rise to sole power of some individual leader, generally in the guise of a champion of popular rights. The would-be ' tyrannus ' obtained command of an armed force on some plausible pretext, then used this force to make himself master of the lives and liberties of his fellow-countrymen. The ' tyrannus ' was not always a tyrant in the sense we now attach to the word ; but the word obtained that sense, because the tyrannus was very apt, when once he had command of irresponsible power, to show himself reckless of the rights of his subjects, and to act in a manner wholly arbitrary and tyrannical. The Greeks with their instinct for constitutional government had a natural hatred for the arbitrary rule of any ' monarch,' and branded that form of government as tyranny : and so the word ' tyrant ' acquired its present reproachful meaning. Tyrannies began to appear in Hellas about the middle of the seventh century B.C., and the period which follows is sometimes spoken of as the age of the tyrants. Such a tyranny was usually short-lived, rarely reaching to more than a second generation, and the age of tyrants had passed away (except in Sicily) before we come to the fifth century. But it had left its mark on Greek history, and not altogether for evil ; and tyrannies were always liable to recur : for a tyranny only meant the setting up of some new kinglike power, which had not the sanction of ancient and inherited right. The Greek world after the passing of the age of the tyrants is divided between oligarchy and democracy—the difference depending on the extent of the distribution of political privileges. If all the free men of the state, rich and poor, noble and simple, had equal political privileges, it was a democracy ; [1] if a class, or classes, had all, or most of the privilege and power, it was an oligarchy.[2] The Dorian states were mostly oligarchical, the Ionian democratic.

Sparta and Athens as Types.—When Croesus, king of the Lydians, was preparing to try conclusions with the rising power of Persia, he was advised by the Delphic oracle to ally himself with the most powerful of the Hellenes. And when he made enquiry, he learnt that the Lacedaemonians and the Athenians were reputed to have the pre-eminence, ' the former being of Doric stock, the latter of Ionic.' The primacy of Sparta and Athens was, then, already an accepted fact in the middle of the sixth century B.C. (of Athens, we note, as well as of Sparta), and we may conveniently take these two as contrasted types of the Greek city-state ; Sparta, Dorian and oligarchical in sympathy, Athens democratic and Ionian. It is true that both Sparta and Athens have a political character peculiar to themselves, and that the individuality of each, and variation one from another, is just the

---

[1] Democracy means ' power of the people.'
[2] Oligarchy means ' rule of the few.'

most significant fact about the Hellenic city-states. But as it is impossible to outline the history and constitution of more than one or two, Sparta and Athens are the two most convenient for our purpose, as being the two leading states, and because more is known about them. They were, moreover, contrasted types of the constitution resulting from the conflict of political ideas among the Hellenes. Greek history after the Persian wars tends to be resolved into a struggle between oligarchy and democracy. A sketch of the earlier history of Sparta and Athens should lead to clearer conception of the forces at work in Hellas, drawing the city-states together and driving them apart with the changing circumstances of the times.

1. SPARTA

We have seen [1] how the return of the Heraclids coincides with the Dorian conquest of the Peloponnese, and that the Dorian conquest of the Peloponnese was the culminating phase of a general movement of population taking place in the twelfth century B.C., not long after the Trojan War. The story of this conquest illustrates strikingly the natural strength of the Peloponnese ; for three attempts to effect a conquest by way of the Isthmus are represented as failing, and the Peloponnese is won at last by an attack from the western side across the mouth of the Gulf of Corinth ; and this attack was successful only with the help of the Aetolians. In the partition of the Peloponnese which followed, Elis the rich and comparatively level district on the western coast, was given to the Aetolian allies of the Heraclid princes : Temenus eldest of these princes, the sons of Aristomachus, took Argos ; Messenia fell to Cresphontes ; Lacedaemon went to the twin sons of Aristodemus. These stories of the fabled return of the Heraclidae are widely removed from history, but something as to the general course and character of the Dorian conquest may be inferred from known facts of later date. The subjection of the Achaean

[1] Chapter IX., p. 204.

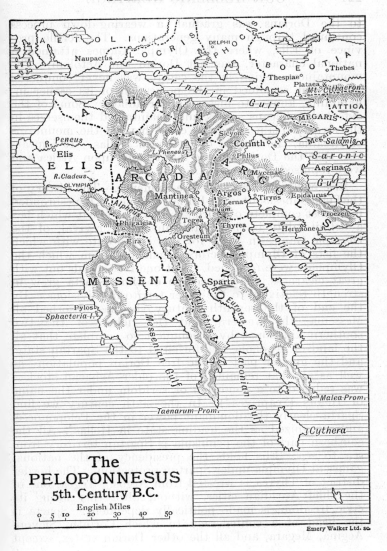

The
PELOPONNESUS
5th. Century B.C.

English Miles
0 5 10   20   30   40   50

Emery Walker Ltd. sc.

to the Dorians was gradual, a wearing-down process continued through many generations. The fertile province of Elis, where the Olympic Games attained a national character, was not Dorian but Aetolian. The mountainous region in the centre was never conquered at all, but remained in the possession of its earlier inhabitants, known to history as Arcadians. Some of the defeated Achaeans successfully maintained themselves in the strip of plain along the coast beyond the mountains of Arcadia, the Achaia of historical Hellas. It appears also that the Dorians made an attempt upon Attica and were repulsed.

Rise of Spartan Military Pre-eminence.—The history of the Peloponnesus after the Dorian conquest is long shrouded in almost complete obscurity. The first event which has a definite date is the establishment, or revival, of the Olympic Games in 776 ; for this is the date with which the lists of Olympic victors began and from which the Olympiads were reckoned. But one fact stands out with great clearness, that in course of time Sparta grew in strength relatively to the other territorial divisions. By the end of the seventh century she has absorbed all Messenia, the western, and the richer, of the two southern kingdoms, by a conquest so complete that all the land of Messenia was forfeited to the Spartan state, and the greater part of the free Dorian population—as well as all that remained of the older Achaean stock—was reduced to a condition of serfdom under the name of Helots (' captives '). In the sixth century we find Sparta clearly the dominant power in the Peloponnese, and recognized as the leading state in Hellas. All the southern part of the peninsula is Spartan territory from sea to sea. Elis holds the presidency of the national games at Olympia under Spartan protection. The border district of Thyrea is wrested from Argos. Tegea, one of the chief Arcadian cities, without altogether losing its civic freedom, is made politically dependent. Sparta is the head of a confederacy to which Corinth, Sicyon, Aegina, Megara, and all the other Dorian states, except

SPARTA AT DAYBREAK.

Scene in the valley of the Eurotas with the heights of Taygetus beyond.

Argos, belong. It was not exactly a formal league, as
there were neither regular meetings nor a definite constitution ; but it was effective for practical purposes,
since it could be counted on to act whenever occasion
arose. And outside this informal Peloponnesian alliance
the prestige of Sparta was such that everywhere her place
was cheerfully acknowledged to be first. This was not
merely respect for Sparta's military strength, though that
was looked upon as wellnigh invincible. It was also
spontaneous homage to certain excellences which other
Greeks discerned in Spartan institutions.

The Spartiatae and Sparta.—Not all the free inhabitants
of the Laconian land were Spartans. The Spartan name
belonged only to the ruling caste, the Spartiates (Spartiatae), or Dorian conquerors of pure blood, who lived in
the five open villages, which made up the city of Sparta,
in that part of the long Eurotas valley which in Achaean
times had been ' hollow Lacedaemon.' The Eurotas
valley is one of the most fertile parts of Greece ; the
scenery on all sides is magnificent.[1] All along its western
edge soars the mighty wall of Taÿgetus. The famous
river is broad, but usually very shallow and divided by
sandbanks into several streams.[2] It was the boast of
the Spartans that their city needed no walls : the valour
of her children was defence enough. Yet these Spartiates
cannot at any time have been very numerous. It is
doubtful if they ever numbered more than ten thousand

---

[1] " Sparta has the finest situation of any town in Greece. It lies in
the middle of the plain, which is equalled only by that of Messenia
for the luxuriance of its vegetation ; while on the W. rises the majestic
range of Taÿgetus more than 7000 ft. above the plain, and sloping
steeply down to the plain-level. . . . Sparta is surrounded by luxuriant
groves of oranges, figs, mulberries, olives and other fruit-trees. Beneath
the trees corn and fruit and vegetables are grown, especially melons
and pumpkins of excellent quality and enormous size." *A Handbook
of Greece*, published for the Admiralty by H.M. Stationery Office,
pp. 465 and 466.

[2] " The Eurotas at Sparta, with a bed from 200 to 300 yds. wide,
flows in several streams and the sandbanks between them are covered
with oleanders. In the height of summer the river is not more than a
foot deep. It floods in winter and is then often unfordable." *Ib.* p. 466.

fighting men.[1] The military force of the Spartan state was, however, very much larger. For the free Dorians of the rest of Laconia, who were not of Spartan race and who greatly outnumbered the Spartans, also furnished heavy-armed troops, and these fought alongside the Spartans, and in the wars of Sparta are usually included with them under the wider name Lacedaemonians. These other Dorians, who were called *Perioeci*, or Out-dwellers, had no share in the government, but do not seem to have resented this exclusion from political life, and throughout the period of Spartan greatness were in fighting value little below the Spartans themselves. Of light-armed troops, too, the Spartans could get as many as they chose from among their Helots. Yet how these ten thousand. or less, Spartans controlled so large a subject population, partly free, partly held down in bitter servitude—and withal made for themselves so great a name— remains a marvel.

The Spartan Government.—Outwardly the Lacedae-monian state retained down into the times of history a close likeness to that heroic polity we find in Homer ; Kings, Boule, and Agora (pp. 219 and 220 above). But at Sparta in historical times there were always *two* kings representing two distinct royal houses, co-equal in dignity ; and the kingly power had come to be little more than hereditary leadership in war.[2] The Boule at Sparta was called the Gerusia (Council of the Aged), and consisted of the two kings and twenty-eight councillors, all of noble family, and all over sixty years of age. The Spartan Agora was called the *Apella*. All Spartiate warriors on reaching the age of thirty had the right of voting in the Apella. It met once a month : its powers were to elect magistrates and vote on questions of peace and war But the real power at Sparta was vested in a board of five magistrates, called *Ephors*. The Ephors were elected

[1] Aristotle in the *Politics* (ii. 9. 17) is our authority for this estimate of 10,000 as a possible maximum.

[2] " This form of Kingship may be described as nothing more than an absolute and perpetual generalship." Ar. *Pol.* iii. 14. 4 (Welldon).

freely by the Apella and held office for one year. They had almost unlimited disciplinary authority over other Spartans ; they were an effective check on kings and magistrates at home, and controlled Spartan policy abroad. On them chiefly depended the maintenance of the institutions which gave Sparta her unique character.

Spartan Institutions.—Sparta has given us a word which has a recognized meaning in English, when we speak of *Spartan* fare, *Spartan* discipline, *Spartan* endurance : but there was more in Spartan customs than mere hardness. What most impressed the other Greeks in Spartan institutions was the consistency with which every detail was directed to one end, and that the welfare of the state. This welfare, too, must be understood, not in the narrowest sense of self-preservation only, though that necessarily had a good deal to do with it (for the Spartans lived armed in the midst of a subject population, once warlike, and many times more numerous than themselves), but in the sense also of worthy living. Narrow as it was in some respects, the Spartan life and discipline commanded admiration. The discipline was hard and painful, but the Spartan was intensely proud of it, and other men regarded it with approving wonder. The Spartan led a dedicated life all his days from infancy to old age. His life was not his own ; it did not belong to family or clan : first and last it was the state's. Therefore even from birth his relation to the state must be considered. No weakly man-child might be reared. The new-born babe was carried before a board of elders and must pass a test of bodily fitness before it was permitted to live. At seven years of age he was taken from his parents, and his regular education began in the great state school along with other boys of the true Spartan breed. This schooling lasted up to the age of twenty, and was a strenuous process, mainly physical and martial. " Of reading and writing, they learned only enough to serve their turn ; all the rest of their training was calculated to make them obey commands well, endure hardships, and conquer in battle." [1] Plentiful exercise, diet plain and limited, sparse clothing, common dormitories where the boy must not merely make the bed he slept on but gather materials for it from the riverside, games that were like battles and fagging for their elders. [2] 'Very like our English Public Schools,' is the natural comment ! And so it was.   The limited diet the Spartan boys were expected to supplement—in this unlike Public School boys—by stealing, how and whence they could.   To steal successfully was no fault ; but to be caught trying to steal entailed a flogging, not for dishonesty, but for ' slackness.'   The boys had their own leaders.   " The boy who excelled in judgment and was most courageous in fighting was made captain of his company : on him the rest all kept their eyes, obeying his orders and submitting to his punishments, so that their boyish training was a practice of obedience." [3] Above these ' prefects,' and in general charge of the training, were young men called *Eirens*, that is, the men between twenty and thirty years of age.   And over all was a ' Director,' of noble birth and high character, under whose supervision the best conducted and most warlike of the Eirens superintended the training.   When a boy was twenty he became an Eiren himself, and then his duties were military training, hunting excursions over the lonely heights of Taÿgetus, superintendence of his juniors in the state school, and sometimes employment on secret service. This last necessitated expeditions into rough and out-of-the-way places to observe the behaviour of the Helots (who always needed to be watched), and pick off any that seemed likely to prove dangerous.   At thirty years Eirens were admitted to the full rights of Spartan citizen-

---

[1] Plutarch, *Lycurgus*, 16 (B. Perrin in the Loeb Classical Library, p. 257).

[2] " This eiren, then, a youth of twenty years, commands his subordinates in their mimic battles, and indoors makes them serve him at his meals.   He commissions the larger ones to fetch wood, and the smaller ones potherbs."   *Lycurgus*, 17 (L.C.L. pp. 259 and 261).

[3] *Lycurgus*, L.C.L. p. 257.

ship and were called *Peers*. Every 'peer' had assigned
to him one of the estates or 'lots' which had been set
apart for the maintenance of the ruling caste : he and
his household were supported from the produce of these
lands which were cultivated by Helots ; the Helots might
make all they could after providing the state portion for
their lord. Often the young Spartan had been married,
but it was only now that he possessed a home of his own.
Though a free man of ripe age, he was no more free than
before to live a soft life or do as he pleased. The service
of the state claimed him as much as ever ; he was a
soldier of Sparta ; and even if there was no war, he must
keep in strict military training. There was no exemption
from these obligations : not only must he take exercise
and drill with the men of his battalion, but he must dine
every day at his mess. These common messes were one
of the most characteristic of Spartan institutions. The
messes were small, averaging fifteen members to a mess ;
they were formed by common agreement ; and, to ensure
that the members were congenial to each other, there
was a system of black-balling. Military service continued all through a man's life until he was sixty, when
the obligation ceased. "No man was allowed to live
as he pleased," writes Plutarch, "but in their city, as in
a military encampment, they always had a prescribed
regimen and employment in public service, considering
that they belonged entirely to their country and not to
themselves." [1] The cult of 'comfort' had no part in
their lives, nor were they out to 'have a good time.'
Certainly of the Spartan, if of any one, it was true, that
'to scorn delights and live laborious days' was the
watchword of his life. So much was this so that a real
campaign was to him a holiday. "Their bodily exercises
were less rigorous during their campaigns, and in other
ways their young warriors were allowed a regimen which
was less curtailed and rigid, so that they were the only
men in the world with whom war brought a respite in
the training for war." [2] At sixty at last they were free

[1] *Lycurgus*, 24 (L.C.L. p. 279).   [2] *Lycurgus*, 22 (L.C.L. p. 275).

of all this, and then the highest ambition of the Spartan was to become a member of the Gerusia.

A Spartan had not much home life, it will be seen (he always ' dined out ') ; but the home life he enjoyed was, perhaps, all the more valued for these enforced absences. At all events women were held more in honour at Sparta than in any other Greek state, and they had more liberty. Spartan women made good mothers : Spartan nurses were in demand in other parts of Greece. The State concerned itself also about health exercises for women, because they were to be the mothers of Spartans.

Lycurgus.—This peculiar social system, which made Sparta unlike any other society before or since, was regarded in after time as the work of Lycurgus. Lycurgus, tradition said, was the younger son of a Spartan king of the house of Procles and guardian for his nephew, Chari-laus. At that time government was very weak in Lacedaemon and great lawlessness prevailed : it was the most ill-governed state in Greece. Lycurgus was greatly troubled at this disorder and sought a cure in a deeply religious spirit. He claimed that his ordinances had the approval of the Delphic god and persuaded his country-men to adopt them, though they involved the recon-stitution of the whole political and social order. He believed that most evils in a state arise from covetousness and out of the inequalities of property that result from money-making, and his chief aim was the creation of a stable governing order by removing all temptations to the acquisition of riches. Accordingly he reserved for the state the whole of the cultivated land in Laconia. One portion of this land he divided up into small estates for the benefit of the Spartiate families of pure Dorian blood. The rest of the land was left to the free Dorian settlers in other parts of Lacedaemon and Messenia, the Perioeci (above, p. 226). Only the Spartiates were citizens of Sparta, and it is only to these Spartiatae that the full Lycurgean discipline applied. The aim was to preserve the Spartiatae, who were the governing class and the flower of Lacedaemonian military strength, in the highest state of efficiency. To this end all the corrupting influences of wealth were to be kept from them. The system of Lycurgus, therefore, aimed directly at the prevention of softness and luxury. The 'peers' were all provided amply with the prime necessaries of life from the produce of their estates, which were worked entirely by Helots. They were a military caste. National defence was their profession and they could have no other. They were expressly forbidden to engage in trade or any other occupation. The gathering of riches was further made impossible by prohibiting the use of gold and silver money, and permitting only an iron coinage of so little value and such ponderous weight that a waggon and a yoke of oxen were required to move fifty pounds worth of it from one place to another, and a large store-room was needed to keep it in. The institution of the common messes was effective against any temptation to over-indulgence in the pleasures of the table. A Spartan peer was not only required by law to dine at his mess, but expressly forbidden to dine at home as well. Luxury in the home was further checked by the ordinance that no tools might be used in the building of a house but the axe and the saw, the practical meaning of which was that a Spartan gentleman's house must be a log-cabin.

Alleviations.—This seems, and was, a hard regime. It was alleviated by the simple but solid comfort compatible with a log-cabin (as proved in British colonies), and by the spirit of good comradeship which was cultivated in a Spartan mess. The Spartan black broth and barley bread, and figs, and cheese, were seasoned by jest and song ; and though Spartans were famous for the brevity of their speech, their sayings were remembered as pointed and pithy. At the boys' meals verbal 'ragging' appears to have been not only permitted but encouraged. Nor are the Spartans to be thought of as altogether rude and uncultivated. Boys, we have seen, were at least taught to read and write. Music and poetry had a part in their lives. Tyrtaeus and Alcman were

famous Spartan poets. Alcman claimed for Lacedaemon :

" Flourish there both the spear of the brave and the Muse's clear
    message,
  Justice, too, walks the broad streets." [1]

And Pindar sings of Sparta :

" There are councils of Elders,
  And young men's conquering spears,
  And dances, the Muse, and joyousness." [1]

The Spartan Ideal.—It is plain on the surface that the
whole Spartan system aimed at military efficiency and
subordinated everything else to it. Plato says this of
the Spartan polity, and so does Aristotle ; and they
make it ground of blame. So to train the men of Sparta
that they should prevail over their enemies in battle was
certainly the aim, and it was very successfully attained.
But it is only fair to the Spartans to recognize that
victory in war was only part of the aim. The aim of
the Spartan system was good citizenship, the perfect
state as the Spartan law-giver conceived it. Order and
self-control and manly valour were to be its characteristics. [2]
This moral quality may be seen plainly in the Spartan
military temper. Whatever faults the Spartan state had,
it was not militarist. It did not pursue war for war's
sake. Rather of the two the Spartans were slow in
entering upon war. Their policy, as we meet it in history,
is notoriously hesitating and backward. They practised
war in peace to avoid war. In actual battle the temper
of the Spartan warrior was remarkably calm and self-
restrained. They had no admiration for the Berserker's
fury. Before they joined battle their king offered sacrifice
to the Muses, " reminding his warriors, as it would seem,
of their training, and of the firm decisions they had made,
in order that they might be prompt to face the dread
issue, and might perform such martial deeds as would be

[1] From the Loeb translation of Plutarch's *Lycurgus*, Ch. 21, p. 273.
[2] Müller, *Dorians*, Book III. ch. i. 10, vol. ii. p. 16.

worthy of some record." [1] They were moderate in
victory. "When they had conquered and routed an
enemy, they pursued him far enough to make their
victory secure by his flight, and then at once retired,
thinking it ignoble and unworthy of a Hellene to hew men
to pieces who had given up the fight and abandoned the
field." [2] War had a religious value for them ; they went
into battle as to a festival. "And when at last they were
drawn up in battle array and the enemy was at hand, the
king sacrificed the customary she-goat, commanded all the
warriors to set garlands upon their heads, and ordered the
pipers to pipe the strains of the hymn to Castor ; then he
himself led off in a marching paean, and it was a sight
equally grand and terrifying when they marched in step
with the rhythm of the flute, without any gap in their
line of battle, and with no confusion in their souls, but
calmly and cheerfully moving with the strains of their
hymn into the deadly fight. Neither fear nor excessive
fury is likely to possess men so disposed, but rather a
firm purpose full of hope and courage, believing as they
do that Heaven is their ally." [3]

There is another side to all this. The Spartan ideal
was narrow ; it left out of account much that is best in
human nature. Science had no part in it, and art very
little.[4] Spartan institutions were not fitted for the more
spacious world into which, through their very efficacy,
Sparta was drawn. But to the actual circumstances of
the Peloponnesus in the centuries with which Greek
history begins they were admirably adapted, and to

---

[1] Plutarch, *Lycurgus*, 21, pp. 273 and 275 (L.C.L.).

[2] Plutarch, *Lycurgus*, 22 (L.C.L. p. 277).

[3] *Ib.* 22 (L.C.L. pp. 275 and 277).

[4] Archaeological investigation on the site of Sparta (and this investigation was undertaken and carried out by the British School at Athens between 1906 and 1910) shows that in quite early times Sparta was as forward in the arts as any part of Greece, and that art declined there from the time when the Lycurgean discipline was established. "Within a generation of the division of the land," says Arnold Toynbee (*Journal of the Society for the Promotion of Hellenic Studies*, vol. xxxiii. p. 262. n.), "Spartan art was dead."

them Sparta owed her position and prestige in the fifth century. There was in them, too, an informing spirit peculiarly Dorian and Hellenic. The Dorian genius has made two notable contributions to the world's treasure of things beautiful—the Doric temple and the ' Doric lay.' In the Spartan life and discipline, as described by Plutarch, we may recognize a kinship to each of these.

2. ATHENS.

The history of Athens had been very different. The Athenians took a great pride in thinking of themselves as children of the soil, ' autochthones,' not immigrants ; and at one time their nobles wore golden grasshoppers in their hair in token of this claim. Attica does indeed seem to have escaped the stream of Dorian invasion, partly because Attica lies a little off the main route for a march through the Isthmus into the Peloponnese, and the land was not rich enough to tempt an invader to turn aside in that direction ; partly, perhaps, also through a certain aptness of the inhabitants for defending what was their own. We hear something of the repulse of two attempted invasions ; one of Boeotians from the north successfully stopped by the hero Melanthus, a descendant of Nestor of Pylus [1] and an Achaean refugee from Messenia, who slew the Boeotian leader in single combat and subsequently became king of Athens : the other from the south after the Dorian conquest of Peloponnesus, in which Codrus, the son of Melanthus, saved the country by the sacrifice of his life. But for the very reason of this comparative immunity from disturbance from without, Attica became a refuge for fugitives from the conquered Peloponnese (as for the Neleids from Messenia, of whom Melanthus was one), and in this way received a considerable accession of population. This, in turn, led to emigration.[2] The bands of adventurers,

[1] See Ch. VII. p. 137 ; cf. Ch. V. p. 82.
[2] Thucydides says : " for the most influential men of the other parts of Hellas, when they were driven out of their own countries by war or

who under leaders of the house of Codrus founded the Ionian cities in Asia Minor, started from Attica, and in after time their descendants looked on Athens as their mother-city (metropolis).

Attica and the Synoecia.—At some early time, but whether before or after the Dorian invasion we have no means of knowing, all Attica had been united into a single city-state, so that Athens and Attica were coincident. We are definitely told that this had been brough; about by the formal union of a number of separate communes or townships—tradition gave the number as twelve ; and the memory of this event was kept alive by the celebration of a festival at Athens called the Synoecia, or ' Joining of households.' There were in historical times other surviving traces of an earlier political condition in which Attica was divided up into several petty communities and groups of villages, each with its own government and practically an independent city-state. Marathon with three other villages formed a ' tetrapolis,' and we read of war between Athens and Eleusis. If we look into the map of Attica, we see how the Attic peninsula has on a small scale all the features we noticed in Chapter II. as characterizing Hellas as a whole. There are the flat plains encompassed by high mountains : there are the limestone hills, sometimes rising in single isolated heights (as Lycabettus and the Acropolis rock), sometimes extended in ridges many miles long (like Hymettus and Mount Aegaleos), and covering all the land to the north and north-east in the great barrier ranges of Cithaeron and Parnes, and the widely extended hill region which culminates in the shapely marble summit of Pentelicus. The plains of Athens and Eleusis are naturally marked out among these mountains

sedition, resorted to Athens as being a firmly settled community, and, becoming citizens, from the very earliest times made the city still greater in the number of its inhabitants ; so that Attica proved too small to hold them, and therefore the Athenians eventually sent out colonies even to Ionia." I. ii. translated by C. Foster Smith (L.C.L. pp. 5 and 7.)

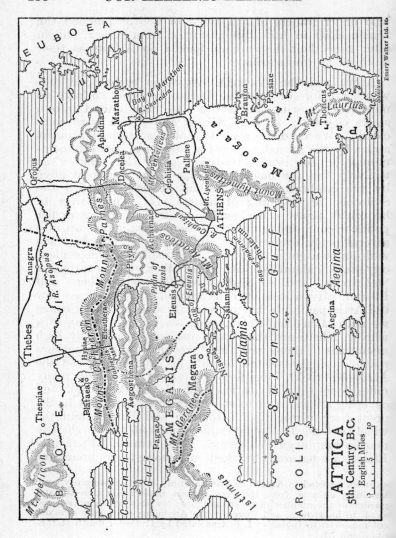

ATTICA
5th. Century B.C.
English Miles

as the areas of separate city-states. Aphidna, the Tetrapolis and Acharnae (that famous deme of later time),
though not to the same extent physically separate,
occupy well-defined areas. The extensive midland region
to the south, known as Mesogaia, an elevated plain of
varying level reaching from sea to sea, never formed a
single political whole, but the townships Brauron, Prasiae,
Thoricus, on its eastern side, were also once independent
civic communities. The union of all these and others in
Athens as the one common ' polis ' was conceived in later
times as the work of Theseus. It consisted, as Thucydides says, in abolishing the separate councils and magis-
tracies which they had possessed, and combining all, with
equal rights, in the one common government of Athens.
The people of Attica ceased to be citizens of Aphidna,
Eleusis or Brauron : all alike became citizens of Athens.
Attica formed one large city-state. A similar tendency
to the union of a number of small civic communities in
a greater Polis is discernible in other parts of Greece ;
for instance, in Boeotia.[1] In Attica alone did it end in
perfect unification. Had there been no union of Attica
in Athens, had all these petty states kept their autonomy,
the history of Attica, we may safely say, would never
have been worth the telling.

The Soil and the Atmosphere.—Because of its prevailingly mountainous character, Attica was far from
being naturally a fertile country. The greater part of
its surface is bare rock incapable of cultivation, and of
the area fit for cultivation the soil is generally thin and
light—except in the plains of Athens and Eleusis. Thucydides actually attributes to the poverty of the soil Attica's
freedom from invasion. Further, because the soil was
not rich enough to support a large population by agriculture alone, a class grew up interested in maritime

---

[1] Even Sparta had a synoecia of a sort in her early history, comparable to the union of Rome and Alba Longa in Roman history ; and
it is thought that her two royal houses, and co-equal kings, were a
consequence of this union. But it was a union of a different character
from the Synoecia of Attica.

enterprise. This was specially in the strip of coast on either side of Attica leading down to Cape Sunium, called Paralia or the sea-coast. One other physical feature is of importance. The visitor to Athens to-day, at least in spring and early summer, can confirm all that ancient writers say in praise of the climate. There is a lightness and briskness in the air which exhilarates all who breathe it ; and in the soft brilliance of the atmosphere objects appear with a peculiar beauty. The Athenians themselves ascribed to the influence of air and climate the keenness of their own intelligence : it was the fashion to contrast it with the heavy stolidity of the Boeotians. Milton combines these physical characteristics in his description of Athens in *Paradise Regained*,[1] as a city

"Built nobly, pure the air and light the soil."

Change from Kingship.—In early times Athens like other Hellenic lands had kings to rule over it. It is probable that the Synoecia took place under kingly rule. But very early the power of the nobles, called in Attica Eupatridae, put limits to the king's authority, and there was a gradual change from monarchy to aristocracy. The legend ran that after Codrus no kings reigned at Athens, because no one was thought worthy to succeed a king who had so nobly sacrificed his life for his country. This is not a very likely story. It is certain, however, that by the eighth century the kingly power had become much diminished, and the functions of kingship were shared among three magistrates, one of whom still bore the name of king, though he was the least influential of the three. The other two were the Polemarch (War-ruler) and the Archon, or Governor. The polemarch was the earlier instituted, we are told, because even while the kings had the sovereign power a king might have small talent for war and then a military leader was wanted to take his place. Some time later the Archon was substituted for the king as head of the state, and thenceforward archon became the title of the chief magis-

[1] Book IV. l. 239.

trates at Athens. The archon was elected instead of succeeding to the throne by hereditary right : but, at first, choice was limited to members of the house of Codrus, and the archon once chosen ruled to the end of his life. Some time later the period of office was limited to ten years ; a new archon was elected decennially. This change (according to tradition) came in the middle of the eighth century. Seventy years later (the traditional date is 683) the archonship became annual. Finally six more archons, called Thesmothetae (judgment-deliverers), were appointed to preside over the administration of justice, so that the whole number of archons was nine. The real sovereignty, however, seems to have passed to the Areopagus or State Council, doubtless the representative of the Council of Elders with which Homer makes us familiar, but possessing a character and powers developed in course of time at Athens.[1] This Council of the Areopagus was the one permanent authority in the state. It was a venerable body wielding a strong religious influence and respected as guardian of the laws and the constitution. It exercised judicial powers of wide range, having a recognized right to call to account any and all who transgressed against the weal of the body politic. All who sat in this Council of the Areopagus were members for life and they all came from the noble Eupatrid families. After a time the rule prevailed that the archons when their year of office was over became as a matter of course members of the Areopagus. The archons were by law always Eupatrids and were elected by Eupatrids. Athens was a strict aristocracy.

Rule of the Eupatrids.—This exclusive aristocracy appears to have governed Attica undisturbed through the greater part of the seventh century. Yet all was not well with the state. There was nothing to check the power of the nobles, who were the chief landowners and the only wealthy class. The unprivileged commons naturally resented this, and there was much discontent

---

[1] To be distinguished from Solon's Council of Four Hundred, changed subsequently into the Council of Five Hundred. See below, p. 251 ; cf. p. 246.

aggravated by economic causes. For the land of Attica was, as we have seen (above, p. 237), no land of teeming fertility like ancient Babylonia or the valleys along the coast of Asia Minor, or even as Boeotia and Thessaly. Except in the plain of Eleusis and the plain of Athens, the soil was light and gave no rich reward to the cultivator. Attica could not support a large population, and as the population increased the pressure on the land became great. Some relief had been obtained by the emigration which had peopled part of the Asiatic coast of the Aegean with Ionian colonies. But when this emigration ceased, the same causes, continuing, produced pressure on the land and poverty, with their natural accompaniment the indebtedness of the peasantry. Now the laws of Athens regarding debt in the seventh century B.C., like those of early Rome, were cruelly hard. The law was made by the Eupatrid landowners and permitted, if it did not compel, the distressed cultivator to offer his own body, or the bodies of his children, as security for his debt. If he failed to repay what he owed, his children, his wife, and finally he himself, might be sold as slaves. Towards the close of the seventh century this had become a very great evil. The peasantry were groaning under the tyranny of the rich landowners, who were the sole governing class, and the oppression had become unbearable. What profit was it that there were no serfs in Attica by right of conquest, if the free population were fast being reduced to a state of slavery through the laws of debt ? Partial efforts had been made towards the end of the seventh century to remedy these grievances by legislation associated with the name of Draco.[1] Draco extended political rights to all citizens who were able to serve as hoplites : that meant who were rich enough to provide at their own expense the arms and equipment of heavy-armed soldiers.

[1] Draco's principal work was to put the existing laws into written form so that people might know what the law was, but the laws of that day were so harsh that Draco's name has become a synonym of severity in a judge. In later times an orator once said that Draco's laws were " written not in ink, but in blood."

Twelve years earlier, about 630, a wealthy Eupatrid named Cylon, who had gained popularity by winning an Olympic victory for Athens, had seized the Acropolis and attempted to make himself despot. The attempt was a failure, but it left a painful mark on Athenian history through acts of sacrilege which attended its suppression. A number of Cylon's partizans surrendered —when their plight was already desperate—on a promise that their lives should be spared. In spite of this promise they were most of them killed on the way down from the Acropolis, some at the very altar of the Holy goddesses (the Erinyes or Furies), which stood by the wayside. Horror seized the people when the enormity of this sacrilege was realized, and of this Cylon's party took advantage. Megacles, of the rival house of Alcmaeon, one of the wealthiest of the Eupatrid families, was held accountable. After a period of fear and strife which lasted several years, the Alcmaeonidae were brought to trial before a court specially constituted for the purpose and found guilty. Megacles and all his house were declared accursed : the living were banished, and the dead who had died since the sacrilege were taken from their graves and cast beyond the borders of Attica. The Alcmaeonidae came back to all their former wealth and influence a generation later, but the memory of the sacrilege and of the curse remained to trouble Athens throughout all the most memorable period of her history.[1]

Solon.—Draco's legislation had failed to remove political discontents, and it had not touched the great social and economic evil of the indebtedness of the peasantry. Many of them had been reduced to the condition of serfs : many had been sold into slavery beyond the borders of Attica. The great majority of the free were still without any political rights at all. The discontent was not only loud, it was dangerous. The people were clamouring for a redistribution of lands.

[1] The Spartans used it to demand the expulsion of the Alcmaeonidae, including their leader, Cleisthenes, in 508 (see below, p. 250); and again in 432 against Pericles, who was an Alcmaeonid on his mother's side.

The nobles were fearing an outbreak. The whole state of things was critical, and no man could foresee the end. Athens was fortunate in finding a man who through his strength of character and complete integrity of purpose was able to guide her to a safe way through. This was Solon, the son of Execestides, an Athenian of the highest birth ; for he was not only a Eupatrid, but of the very lineage of Codrus. The property he should have inherited had been diminished by his father's generosity in helping friends in distress. Solon, therefore, became a merchant, and in that calling (not at that time held in any disesteem at Athens) gathered wide experience and a moderate fortune. As a young man he had won distinction by the part he played in recovering for Athens the island of Salamis, of which the Megarians had dispossessed her.[1] Through this public service and through his reputation for practical sagacity he was well thought of by all classes ; and in 594, when the tension between nobles and people was at its worst, a proposal was made that Solon should be elected to the archonship and invested with extraordinary powers as mediator and legislator.

Solon's Picture of his Times.—We are helped in a remarkable way to an understanding of Solon's times and of the troubles he had to adjust by certain poems of his, passages from which have fortunately been preserved by later writers. These verses form true contemporary documents—full two thousand five hundred years old : in reading them we see with his eyes the evils of his day and realize what he tried to do. These are a few of the verses in which he describes the greed and hardness of heart of the ruling caste and the sufferings of the people :

" Our townsmen through their foolishness will bring down to the
     dust
 Our glorious city, while they put in riches all their trust.
 The people's leaders' minds are set upon unrighteousness ;
 But their presumptuous pride will bring themselves to sore
     distress. .   .   .   .   .   .

[1] See below, pp. 252 and 253.

For when prosperity runs high, indulgence fathereth pride :
They spare not sacred things, the public plunder they divide,
Robbing the state on every hand. . . .

And many an honest yeoman, while these woes afflict the land,
Is carried off a bondsman slave to some far foreign strand,
Sold like a chattel for his debts, with shameful fetters bound." [1]

In the verses of another poem he appeals to Mother
Earth to testify how truly he has fulfilled his promise to
free her from the burden of the mortgage pillars which
recorded the peasants' indebtedness, and has redeemed
many of his countrymen from slavery.

"Thou, when slow time brings justice in its train,
O mighty mother of the Olympian gods,
Dark Earth, thou best canst witness, from whose breast
I swept the pillars broad-cast planted there,
And made thee free, who hadst been slave of yore.
And many a man whom fraud or law had sold
Far from his god-built land, an outcast slave,
I brought again to Athens ; yea, and some,
Exiles from home through debt's oppressive load,
Speaking no more the dear Athenian tongue,
But wandering far and wide, I brought again ;
And those that here in vilest slavery
Crouched 'neath a master's frown, I set them free.
Thus might and right were yoked in harmony,
Since by the force of law I won my ends
And kept my promise." [2]

The Seisachtheia.—The means by which Solon accomplished what he here claims were, firstly, that he put an
end once and for all to the wickedness of using human
flesh and blood as security for debt by making such
contracts illegal ; and, secondly, that he repaired as far
as possible the wrongs of the past by a measure appro-
priately called the Seisachtheia, or " Shaking-off of
burdens." This celebrated measure, much praised in
antiquity, was simply a general cancellation of debts.

[1] Solon, *Fragment* 13, ll. 5-8, 11-13 and 25-28.
[2] Quoted Aristotle, *Constitution of Athens,* 12 ; Sir Frederic Kenyon's
translation, pp. 19 and 20.

Aristotle, the philosopher, a very sober and trustworthy authority, plainly calls it " a cancelling of debts both private and public." [1] It is recorded moreover that the rich lost much good money by it. It was certainly a notable interference with the rights of property, such as could rarely be justifi d, but which, in the judgment of most ancient writers, had a justification in the circumstances of Solon's time. The state was very sick ; the condition of the whole class of cultivators was hopeless unless they were released from debt and started clear again. It was no time for half measures : Solon had the merit of going to the root of the trouble, and it was apparently accepted by the nobles as the lesser of two evils. It was at least preferable to what the people demanded and the nobles were dreading, a redistribution of land. Moreover, Solon's expedient was justified by success. What he did in the year 594 did not need to be done at Athens again. Political disputes and faction strife there were to be again soon enough : there was no recrudescence of this trouble of peasant indebtedness.

Solon's Constitution.—The other side of Solon's work was to make changes in the political constitution of Athens which caused him to be regarded afterwards as the founder of the Athenian democracy. He modified the existing constitution by giving a definite, though a strictly moderate, share of political rights to all free citizens, even to the poorest. Again what he did can best be described in his own words :

" I gave to the mass of the people such rank as befitted their need,
    I took not away their honour, and I granted naught to their
      greed ;
While those who were rich in power, who in wealth were
    glorious and great,
I bethought me that naught should befall them unworthy their
    splendour and state ;
So I stood with my shield outstretched, and both were safe in
    its sight,
And I would not that either should triumph, when the triumph
    was not with the right." [2]

[1] Aristotle on *The Constitution of Athens*, 6.

[2] Quoted Aristotle, *Constitution of Athens* ; Kenyon, p. 18.

Solon's attempt to effect a political settlement was to apportion privileges among four classes of citizens distinguished according to their means of serving the state. These classes apparently already existed at the time for the purposes of taxation and state service. The wealthiest called by the high-sounding name of "Pentakosiomedimni" (which, however, only means "Five hundred measure-men"), were the large landed proprietors whose revenues reached a minimum of five hundred measures [1] in corn and wine and oil. Next came the Hippeis, or Knights (so called because they could keep a horse for mounted war-service), who had at least three hundred measures; after these came the Zeugitae, or Yoke-men, small farmers who ploughed with a yoke of oxen, and whose income must be at least two hundred measures. From these three classes all state officials must be chosen, the highest officials from the highest class only. Outside these three propertied classes were all the people, free cultivators and free craftsmen, who had little property or none at all. Under Solon's constitution these 'Thetes,' as all were called whose income was less than two hundred measures, for the first time received substantial political recognition. They were not eligible for any public office, but they had two important rights. Firstly, they had the right of voting in the Ecclesia, or general Assembly of citizens, and hence now took part in the elections to all state offices. Secondly, they were admitted on equal terms to the new law courts which Solon instituted. These were the *dicasteries*, courts in which the judges (dicasts) were just groups of citizens selected out of the body of the people.[2] This latter was a most important right and in its ultimate effect extremely democratic, since it made everyone, the high and noble as well as the commonalty, subject to the jurisdiction of the people.

---

[1] A medimnus = 12 gallons or 48 quarts.

[2] These *dicasts* were judges with full powers, who not only gave their verdict as our jurors do, but pronounced sentence as well. In number, too, they were many more than twelve : five hundred was no unusual number.

Solon's Work as a whole.—Solon further connected the Council, or Boule, with the four ancient tribes into which the families of the nobility were aggregated by enacting that a hundred councillors should be elected by each tribe. The archons were to be chosen by lot out of forty candidates nominated by the tribes, ten from each. Here, too, we may see made good Solon's claim to have effected a moderate settlement. But in the political sphere his work was a beginning, not an ending. He had started Athens on a course of democratical development which continued after him, till all class privileges were abolished and Athens became the complete democracy. Solon also enacted a milder code of laws to supersede Draco's, and these were transcribed for all men to see on tablets which revolved in wooden frames. Many of these laws, recorded in Plutarch's *Life of Solon*, are curious. One, in particular, is worth recalling. Solon enacted that at a time of civil strife every citizen was required to take sides definitely, under penalty of the forfeiture of all political rights if he failed to do so.

Solon's legislation, though it did much to satisfy the aspirations of the people and has earned enduring approval, naturally roused a great deal of opposition and discontent at the time. For this and other reasons Solon, after laying down his office, left Athens and went travelling for some years. His work was done. His praise is that he discharged a very difficult and responsible task with scrupulous moderation and single-minded regard for the public good. Many of his friends, he tells us, counted him no better than a fool for not seizing despotic power, when he had it practically within his grasp. Quite surely Solon might, had he chosen, have made himself tyrant of Athens—as Pisistratus did thirty years later. He preferred the part of true patriotism without self-seeking, and he has his reward in the fair fame that keeps his name illustrious. There is no more gracious character in Greek history. And as Solon was not only a statesman and a patriot, but a poet and thinker also, we know him as we know few

men who lived two thousand five hundred years ago.
He speaks directly to us in the words of his poems, which
are largely autobiographical.

The ' Tyranny ' of Pisistratus and his Sons.—Solon's
work was in part completely successful. As we have
seen, it cured the social troubles he was primarily called
on to deal with. Attic peasants were never again overwhelmed with debt, still less sold into slavery.[1] But it
failed either to end party strife at Athens or to satisfy
the political aspirations of the people. As soon almost
as Solon had laid down his office, party conflicts broke
out again with fresh violence. The parties which emerge
have significant names, indicating that the interests in
conflict were largely regional, corresponding to the
natural divisions into which Attica breaks up. There
are the small fertile plains, the stretches of coast land on
either side of the midland region called Mesogaia, and the
widespread hill country to the north and east of Athens.
The parties were known as the *Plainsmen*, the *Shoremen*
and the *Uplanders*. They depended severally on local
interests and connections : there may even have been
some element of original difference of race. The rich
landowners of the plains, Eupatrids all, naturally formed
an aristocratic and conservative party. The poor cultivators of the hilly districts were the main strength of the
less privileged free men of Attica, and constituted therefore the extreme democratic party. Intermediate in
politics between these opposites was the party of the
new middle class interested in the growing sea-borne
trade of Athens ; and with this party the Alcmaeonidae
were associated. The hill-men also had their leaders in
a powerful Eupatrid family which had great estates in the
hill country, especially about the Tetrapolis (which includes Marathon). This family traced its descent (like
Solon) through the house of Codrus from Nestor of Pylus,
the Homeric hero, whose descendants, as we have seen,

[1] Some part in this result is now, perhaps rightly, put to the credit of
Pisistratus, who turned himself into a sort of agricultural bank for the
benefit of the small landowners (Aristotle, *Constitution of Athens*, 16).

took refuge in Attica ; and the head of the house at this time was called Pisistratus, after that younger son of Nestor who journeyed with Telemachus from Pylus to Sparta (Ch. VII. p. 138). A kind of three-cornered duel went on between these parties for many years. In 560—the year of the accession of Croesus to the throne of Lydia [1]—Pisistratus not only secured the predominance of his party, but as champion of the commonalty made himself master of Athens and ruled as tyrant. Though his authority was usurped and depended on force, he was popular with the multitude whose political cause he had represented, and the just and lenient character of his rule did much to reconcile the other classes to it. He ended his days in 527, still tyrant of Athens, and his sons, Hippias and Hipparchus, succeeded to his power without opposition. But his reign was not continuous through the thirty-three years from 560 to 527. Twice he was expelled by a combination of the other two parties. His second return was effected after an exile of ten years, during which he had strengthened his resources by mining enterprises in Thrace in the neighbourhood of Mount Pangaeum, and by political connections in Euboea, Thessaly and other places. With forces raised by these means, he landed in the Bay of Marathon, which adjoined the mountain region where his family estates lay, and thence advanced on Athens. The Athenians marched out to Pallene to meet him and were defeated. Pisistratus recovered thus his lost power and reigned quietly at Athens till his death. His sons reigned after him for seventeen years, and then tyranny at Athens was ended by the expulsion of Hippias.

Character of the Pisistratid Rule.—The Athenians like all other Greeks detested the arbitrary rule of one man, and so in after times the arbitrary rule of Pisistratus was put under the ban. But it is evident that Pisistratus himself used his power wisely and well in the interest of Attica, and showed himself a ruler of enlightened mind and far-seeing policy. Athens prospered under his

[1] See Chap. XI. p. 259.

government and began to be of more account in Hellas than she had hitherto been. The reign of Pisistratus was indeed the beginning of her greatness. He did much for Athens that was of lasting benefit. Two movements which owed their impulse to his initiative have been of permanent value in the realm of ideas. To one we owe our text of Homer ; to the other the Greek drama, and, through the Greek drama, our own. To improve the epic recitations at the Panathenaic Festival (Ch. III. p. 41), the splendour of which he greatly enhanced, he had the *Iliad* and the *Odyssey* arranged and written down. To increase the importance of the worship of Dionysus, the primitive cult of the country people of Attica, especially in his own hill districts, he instituted a new and more splendid festival in the City, known thenceforward as the ' Great Dionysia ' ; and it was in connection mainly with the Great Dionysia that drama in Athens took literary form.

The sons of Pisistratus, Hippias and Hipparchus, at first continued the mild and sympathetic rule of their father ; but in the end the house of Pisistratus went the way of all absolute governments and became in truth a tyranny. Hipparchus was killed as the outcome of a conspiracy originating in a private quarrel. After this bitter experience Hippias' rule changed its spirit : there were confiscations, oppressions, executions, and resentment grew. The Alcmaeonidae, who had been driven out a second time by Pisistratus, saw their opportunity. Their first attempts failed miserably, but at length, by the help of the Delphic oracle, the Alcmaeonidae secured Spartan support, and finally Hippias and all his family were expelled. Athens was freed and became a democracy again.

The Constitution of Cleisthenes.—This was in 510 B.C. At once the old division of parties showed itself, except that with the fall of the Pisistratids the ' Mountain ' was now eliminated. The ' Plain ' was led by Isagoras, the ' Shore ' by Cleisthenes, son of Megacles, the Alcmaeonid. Isagoras was worsted, because Cleisthenes now won the popular support by adopting a thoroughly democratic programme. Isagoras appealed to the Spartan king, Cleomenes, and came back through Spartan aid. But the people rose against the Spartans and compelled their withdrawal. Cleisthenes then carried through legislation which forms the decisive era in the history of Athenian democracy. For he at once introduced measures which transformed the constitution of Solon, in which the people (*demos*) was admitted to a limited share of political power, into a constitution which made the people in the fullest sense sovereign and supreme. Under the constitution of Solon the Eupatrids had retained the governing power exclusively. Cleisthenes saw that their political influence was bound up with the ancient social system of clans and families, closely associated as it was with local religious observances, and that the strength of the old parties rested on local ties with the districts from which the parties took their names. So by a clever stroke he substituted for the four ancient tribes, depending on birth, ten new tribes, put together on a system entirely artificial. By this means also he was able to confer the rights of citizenship on a great number of persons hitherto excluded from the tribes and brotherhoods (*phratries*) by the stubborn facts of birth ; and at the same time to annul effectually the dominance of local connection. The contrivance was this. He divided all Attica into three sections roughly, but only roughly, corresponding with the Plain, the Shore and the Mountain. Each of these sections he divided into ten parts consisting of groups of townships (technically called ' demes '). The groups of demes were called *trittyes*. Then he formed his tribes of sets of three ' trittyes,' so arranged that each tribe drew one of its three trittyes from each of the three districts. In this way no tribe contained two groups from the same district ; its constituent elements were widely separated in place. The expedient was successful. After the adoption of the new arrangement of tribes under the constitution of Cleisthenes nothing more was heard of Plain, Mountain or

Shore. At the same time the political influence of the old Eupatrid families was greatly lessened. In correspondence with the new system of tribes Cleisthenes re-constituted the Council or Senate also. In place of the Council of Four Hundred, a hundred from each tribe, he instituted a Council of Five Hundred, fifty from each of the new *ten* tribes. Further to facilitate administration, the year was divided into ten parts, and the fifty Councillors representing the several tribes formed by turns an executive committee which held office for one of these ten periods. The members of this Council of Five Hundred were appointed by lot out of a number of candidates elected directly by the demes. The Council henceforward became the chief executive power in the state. The ultimate sovereignty was vested in the people voting in their Ecclesia. But no measure could be brought before the Ecclesia except in the form of a ' probouleuma,' or resolution of the Council. The Boule, therefore, to a considerable extent controlled legislation. The military system again was reorganized in correspondence with the arrangement of tribes. From this time the military force of the state consisted of ten regiments, one for each tribe ; and over them were the ten tribal commanders, or strategi, though the polemarch continued to be commander-in-chief till the year 487, when the chief authority was transferred to the Ten Strategi as a War Council. To safeguard his new democracy Cleisthenes further introduced the curious contrivance known as *ostracism*. This measure was directed against the danger of a fresh revolution from the Pisistratids, or any other noble family of wealth and influence. It provided that at certain intervals the people should be invited to record an opinion whether, in the interests of good order and the safety of the state, it was expedient that some leader of mark should be required to withdraw from the country—not for ever, but for a period of years. Any citizen who pleased might then take an ' ostrakon,' or piece of earthenware, and write on it the name of a prominent political leader. If as many as six thousand

such votes were registered, the public man whose name
was written on the greatest number of shells was ordered
to leave the country for ten years.   The exile suffered no
other deprivation than the suspension of his rights as a
citizen.   Ostracism was not a punishment but a precaution.   It was an ingenious means of getting rid of
one of two rivals before party strife became dangerous.
Such was the constitution which Athens had reached by
the end of the sixth century B.C.

External History, 700 to 500 B.C.—The history of
Athens in relation to the rest of Hellas can be more
briefly told.   After the repulse of the Heraclids in the
eleventh century, no wars of Athens are spoken of till
the end of the seventh century, when Athens carried on
war with Mytilene over the right to plant a trading
settlement on the coast of the Troad at Sigeum.[1]   This
war was ended by arbitration.   About the same time, or
a little later, Athens fought a small war to recover possession of Salamis, which she claimed on the ground of
ancient alliance with the family of the Achaean hero,
Ajax, but had lost for a time to Megara.   How vital
Salamis was to Athens a glance at the map may convince
us.   Salamis lies right in front of the harbours of Athens.
Its straggling shape fits into the Bay of Eleusis like a
piece of a jig-saw puzzle.   Salamis was as essential to
the safety of Athens as Ireland to the safety of Great
Britain.   And at the time we speak of, not only had
Salamis passed into the keeping of Megara, but the
Athenians had fared so ill in attempting to reconquer
it—having as yet no sea power of any strength—that
a decree had been passed making it death even to propose
to renew the struggle.   But there were Athenians acutely
conscious of the ignominy of this decree and of the danger
that resulted for their country, and among these was
Solon, then a comparatively young man.   Being assured
that the recovery of Salamis was necessary for the welfare
of Athens, and that it was a disgrace to leave the Dorian
Megarians in possession, he feigned madness, dressed

[1] See p. 112.

himself up fantastically and went into the market-place. When a crowd collected he mounted the stone from which heralds made public announcements and recited a poem which he had composed to stir the hearts of his countrymen. This poem began :

" A herald am I, hither newly come from lovely Salamis,
   To offer you a song in ordered verse instead of speech."

It went on to reproach the Athenians with the disgrace of abandoning Salamis, and ended with a passionate appeal :

" To Salamis, to Salamis ! Up, up and fight for Salamis—
   The lovely island Salamis ! and roll away our shame ! "

This cleverly managed action was successful. The law was repealed, an expedition voted, and Salamis won back.[1] This was at the very beginning of the sixth century. There were no other foreign wars for Athens till near its end. Then, while Hippias was still in power, Athens became involved in a quarrel on the other side of Attica, the northern. The little Boeotian town, Plataea, repudiated the claim of Thebes to authority over the rest of Boeotia, and refused to make one of a Boeotian confederacy. When Thebes tried coercion, Plataea appealed to the Spartans. The Spartans declined to take Plataea under their protection, on the ground that the distance between Lacedaemon and Boeotia was too great. They advised the Plataeans to seek help from the Athenians who were very much nearer. The Plataeans accordingly turned to Athens in their distress, and did not turn in vain : the Athenians made good the protection they promised by marching against the Thebans and routing them in battle. This made Thebes the bitter enemy of Athens.

It was a consequence of the offence thus given to Thebes that when in 506, shortly after Cleisthenes' return

[1] This was not, indeed, the end. The contention between Athens and Megara went on for some time longer, and Salamis was ultimately assigned to Athens by arbitration. Both sides appealed to Sparta, and after a careful sifting of claims by five Spartan judges, the award was in favour of Athens.

to power, the Spartan king Cleomenes, repenting of his part in the ' freeing ' of Athens (above, p. 249), led an army of the Peloponnesian confederacy into Attica and camped in the plain of Eleusis, the Boeotians invaded Attica from their side and captured the border towns, Hysiae and Oenoe. Cleomenes' invasion came to nothing, because the allies, especially Corinth, refused to follow the Spartan lead in re-establishing a tyranny at Athens, and the other Spartan king, who was also present in the field, joined in opposing Cleomenes. So the confederate army broke up and the Spartans retreated. The Athenians were now free to deal with the neighbours who had gratuitously attacked them, the Boeotians and the Euboeans. For the Euboeans of Chalcis also, as old allies of Pisistratus, had crossed the straits from Euboea and were ravaging northern Attica. Against them the Athenians marched first ; but learning that the Boeotians were hastening up to succour their allies, the Athenians turned upon them, engaged them near the Euripus and inflicted a crushing defeat, capturing seven hundred prisoners. Then they crossed the Euripus into Euboea after the Chalcidians (who had by this time retreated across the straits), overtook them and defeated them, thus gaining two victories on one and the same day. It was a memorable day for democracy. Herodotus sees in it a proof of the invigorating effect of free institutions.

CHAPTER XI

THE PERIL FROM THE EAST

"An empire . . . which stretched from the burning sands of Africa to the ice-bound borders of China, vast but obedient. . . ."
Sir Percy Sykes, *History of Persia*, i. p. 180.

WHEN the confusion and anarchy, with which the second millennium B.C. ended and the first began for the Hellenic peoples, subsided, it was followed by a period of comparative tranquillity, during which Greek civilization was able to develop along the lines which the genius of the race gave to it, without interference from outside. It was then that Greek institutions gradually took on the distinctive forms which characterize them in historical times. By similar degrees the consciousness of the differences of their institutions from the ways and customs of other men deepened in the minds of the Greeks. They were Hellenes ; all other men were " Barbaroi " (Jabberers, as we might say)—barbarians : we have taken the word from them with all it imports of rough usages and intellectual inferiority. The word ' barbaroi,' in antithesis to Hellenes, is not used in the Homeric poems [1] : later the Greeks used it indiscriminately of all men who were not Hellenes, not only of the wild tribes of Thrace, or Sicily, or Epirus, and savage Scythians, but also of Eastern peoples with a civilization older and not less refined than the Greek. For such men had no understanding of life in a city-state, and no true self-respect.

[1] In one place in the *Iliad*, however (ii. 88), the epithet " *barbarophōnoi* " (of barbarian speech) is used of the Carians.

The Asiatic Greeks.—The Greeks who were on the eastern side of the Aegean, and nearest to the powerful civilizations of the East, for a long time shared this freedom from outside interference. They had had to fight for their new homes in Asia Minor, and in some cases they had intermarried with the peoples they dispossessed ; but once having wrested land enough for their original settlements, the strife was at an end, and they appear to have been left in undisturbed enjoyment of what they had made their own. Though not uninfluenced by their neighbourhood to the East, they were linked to the European communities from which they had gone out ; they belonged to the world which met in athletic rivalry at Olympia and resorted for guidance in perplexity to Delphi and other Hellenic shrines. So far as we know, from the eleventh century, when the migrations took place, to the beginning of the seventh, when the Lydians first became formidable, there was no strong military power near the coast to threaten the independence of the city-states founded according to the European model by Aeolians, Ionians and Dorians, weak and isolated though they were severally. The rich valleys along the coast in which they were planted were very fertile, and the Asiatic city-states prospered.

Ionia.—Especially is this true of the central group of cities, the Ionian. Of Ionia Herodotus writes : " Now the Ionians of Asia who meet at the Panionium, have built their cities in a region where the air and climate are the most beautiful in the whole world : for no other region is equally blessed with Ionia, neither above it nor below it, nor east nor west of it. For in other countries either the climate is over cold and damp, or else the heat and drought are sorely oppressive." [1] At the same time these cities of Ionia were favourably placed for trade ; the Ionians were a quick-witted race, and they were enterprising navigators. Miletus and Phocaea, in particular, took a leading part in extending Hellas further

---

[1] Herodotus, i. 142 ; Rawlinson, vol. i. p. 266.

by founding fresh colonies along the Hellespont and round the coasts of the Black Sea.[1] With these advantages of position and climate the Greek cities of Asia Minor, and especially the Ionian, went ahead, and for a time outstripped the cities of the Hellenic peninsula in wealth and prosperity. In all the arts which adorn life and bring refinement as well as comfort and ease, these Ionian cities were foremost in Greece. It would not be too much to say that at one time they were the most Hellenic of the Greeks. For progress in literature and the fine arts went along with progress in material comfort.[2] It was in Ionia seemingly that the stories of the Trojan War, which the immigrants brought with them from Europe, took shape as great epic poems. In Ionia professional bards, called rhapsodists, went about from city to city reciting these poems at festivals. Homer, if he really lived and wrote the *Iliad*, must have been an Ionian. The very language in which the *Iliad* and *Odyssey* have come down to us, the peculiar epic dialect, is Ionian rather than Aeolian. In whatever way scholars decide the Homeric controversy, the part assigned to the Ionians must be a considerable one. Again, the arts of sculpture and painting, afterwards perfected in European Greece, had in the sixth century B.C. made great advances in Ionia. The great succession of Greek thinkers which culminated in Plato and Aristotle, began in Ionia with Thales, Heraclitus and Anaxagoras. Hecataeus of Miletus was distinguished as a geographer and historian a couple of generations before Herodotus (who was himself an Asiatic Greek) wrote his history.

[1] No less than seventy-five of these Greek colonies looked to Miletus as their metropolis or mother-city.

[2] In the Homeric *Hymn to Apollo* there is a pleasant picture of the Ionian civilization as displayed in the festival held by the Ionians in honour of Apollo at Delos. "Delos," says the hymn, "where the long-robed Ionians gather in thine honour, they and their children and their honoured wives. With boxing and dance and song there in thy festival they celebrate thy name. Surely one who visited the gathering of the Ionians, beholding their fair beauty, would say they were immortal and free from eld : he would rejoice at heart to look on the men and the fair-girdled women, their swift ships and their great wealth." *Hymn to Apollo*, ll. 147-155.

Rise of Lydia.—About the middle of the seventh century this happy state of things for the Ionic Greeks was changed by the appearance in Lydia of a strong monarchy of oriental type. The Lydians had been neighbours of the Ionians from the first, and in fact it must have been at the expense of the Lydians that the Ionians originally acquired land to build their cities on. The explanation doubtless is that Lydia was weak at the time, and for long after no strong power appeared upon the coast. At last there came a line of princes, whom Herodotus calls Mermnadae, with ability enough to organize the wealth of Lydia into a strong monarchical state, whose military resources became a danger to Ionian independence. These princes, as they grew more powerful, naturally aspired to control the harbours on the coast which were all in the hands of the Greeks. They did not, however, attempt a sweeping conquest of Ionia. They kept on good terms with most of the cities, but picked a quarrel with one or another as occasion offered. Now the twelve Ionian cities were associated in a confederacy with a common meeting-place on Mount Mycale near Miletus, a Panionium or assembly of all Ionians. The wise course would have been for the members of this association to combine to defend each other from Lydian aggression. This they did not do : the association was religious, not political. For the sake of their much-prized autonomy they allowed the Lydian kings to attack and capture separately cities that were members of their league. Thus Gyges, founder of the dynasty, attacked and took Colophon. Ardys, his son and successor, took Priene. Alyattes, the next king, destroyed Smyrna,[1] but was beaten back from Clazomenae. This monarch also carried on a harassing war against Miletus, which ended in a compact of alliance. After Alyattes came Croesus,

[1] Smyrna is now the chief seaport of the Levant, while Miletus and Ephesus are desolate sites without inhabitant. Smyrna was revived as a city three hundred years after its conquest by Alyattes. Of all the famous Greek cities on the west of Asia Minor it is the only one to retain a high degree of prosperity in modern times. It is still a very Greek city.

whose name has become a synonym for one who has great riches. In Croesus the wealth and power of the Lydian dynasty culminated, and he felt himself strong enough to attempt the systematic reduction of all the Greek cities on the coasts of his dominions. He attacked them one by one on various pretexts, beginning with Ephesus, till all the Greek cities on the coast were reduced on terms which made them the vassals of Lydia. The Asiatic Greeks accordingly ceased to be independent and became the subjects of an oriental monarch. This result was brought about, not wholly by arms, but partly by diplomacy. Croesus deliberately courted the friendship of the Greeks by a Phil-Hellenic policy. He paid marked respect to Delphi and other Hellenic shrines. The gifts with which he loaded the temple of Apollo were one of the sights of Delphi in after time. All this helped to reconcile the Asiatic Greeks to Lydian overlordship. The yoke of King Croesus was not felt to be heavy ; for a large measure of local self-government was left to the cities individually. Nevertheless in the eyes of the Greeks of Europe, and in their own eyes, the Asiatic Greeks had suffered intolerable degradation ; they were no longer free men but ' douloi.'

Rise of the Persian Power.—Within a few years of his subjugation of Ionia Croesus himself had met with tragic disaster and the Lydian monarchy had fallen never to rise again. This had come about through the appearance to the east of Lydia of the far more formidable military power of Persia. The Persians were originally highlanders dwelling on the great mountain plateau of Iran between the Persian Gulf and the Caspian Sea. They were a hardy and a war-like race, in many respects as highly endowed as the Greeks, but in different ways. It was the Persians who in the sixth century B.C. entered upon the heritage of the great oriental monarchies which one after another arose in Western Asia—Chaldean, Assyrian, Babylonian, Median. In much earlier times the Persians had carried on a desperate struggle with the nomad tribes of Turkestan, vast hordes of Turkish or

Turanian horsemen. This was the age-long conflict of Iran and Turan, celebrated in Persian heroic legend.[1] Later the Medes and Persians were for a time numbered among the vassals of the Assyrian Empire, but the obedience they paid was intermittent, varying with the strength of the central power. About the middle of the seventh century B.C., along with their kinsmen the Medes, they finally threw off the Assyrian yoke, and not only maintained their independence, but destroyed the Assyrian Empire and built up a new empire on its ruins. There was no greater race difference between the Medes and Persians than between the Angles and Saxons who conquered Britain ; but at first the Mede was the pre-dominant partner, and the first dynasty of kings known to the Greeks was Median. Hence the Greeks used the name Mede of the Persians as well as the Medes, for they had come to hear first of the Medes. The Median kings extended their dominions westward and came into collision with the Lydians. War was carried on between the two powers with varying success. One battle between Lydians and Medes is specially memorable because it is recorded that it was stopped by an eclipse [2] and that the eclipse was predicted by Thales the Ionian. This battle was fought (in 585) between a Median king named Cyaxares and Alyattes, the father of Croesus. The eclipse was thought such a portent that peace was forthwith arranged between Lydia and the Medes, and Alyattes further gave his daughter Aryenis in marriage to Astyages, son of Cyaxares. Some time after this a domestic revolution took place in Media, from which it resulted that the Persians henceforward took the leading place instead of the Medes. This revolution is associated with the name of Cyrus (Persian *Kurush*), who thereafter was regarded as the founder of Persian greatness. But

---

[1] The noblest of these legends, the story of *Sohrab and Rustum*, has been given a noble English form by Matthew Arnold.

[2] As modern science enables astronomers to calculate eclipses back into the past, this fact is a valuable aid to determining the chronology of this period. It gives a fixed point for check.

Cyrus had deposed Astyages the Mede and Astyages was married to the sister of Croesus. This at once offered a *casus belli*. But Croesus was, apart from this, in dread of the growing power of the Medes and Persians and thought the occasion favourable to anticipate attack. He had already, in view of this contingency, allied himself with the kings of Egypt and Babylonia, and now, on the advice of the Delphic oracle, he added the Spartans to the alliance. Strengthened also by the answer the oracle had given to his enquiries, he crossed the Halys, the great river which divides Asia Minor into two parts. For this answer had been, " Croesus, when he crosses the Halys, will overthrow a great empire." Beyond the Halys a battle was fought at Pteria in the plains of Cappadocia, and though the battle was well contested and only broken off by night, it would seem that Croesus had the worst of it. For after waiting one day to see whether Cyrus would attack him again, he recrossed the Halys and led his army back to Lydia. Arrived in Lydia he at once dismissed large part of his army with orders to reassemble next year in greater force, never thinking that Cyrus, after his losses in battle, would venture to follow him into Lydia. But this is precisely what Cyrus did ; and he came on with such rapidity that he was close on Sardis before Croesus got intelligence of the invasion. In this extremity Croesus did what he could ; he led out his Lydians and gave battle to the Persians before the walls of Sardis. The Lydians fought bravely, but were outnumbered and defeated. Croesus with the remains of his army was shut up in Sardis : he prepared for a long siege, trusting that relief would come in time from his allies. He sent an urgent appeal also to the Spartans. But on the fourteenth day of the siege, Sardis was taken by escalade. On one side the rock on which the citadel stood was so precipitous that it was usually left unguarded. A soldier in Cyrus' army, named Hyroeades, happened one day to see one of the garrison clambering down the rock to recover his helmet, and it occurred to him that he might get up the same way. So he put himself at the

head of a small party, climbed up where he had seen the
Lydian soldier come down, and so effected the capture
of Sardis by surprise. The Spartans, Herodotus relates,
were actually fitting out an expedition to come to Croesus'
assistance, when tidings reached them that Sardis was
already taken and Croesus a prisoner.

Croesus and Solon.—The Greeks were deeply impressed
by the fate of Croesus the Lydian, seeing in it a signal
example of a sudden fall from greatness, and of the
' nemesis ' which so often waits upon extraordinary good
fortune. They weaved stories about him which Herodotus has preserved in his history. One is that Solon,
the Athenian lawgiver, while voyaging in the years of
his voluntary exile, came to Sardis and was hospitably
welcomed by Croesus. The story continues : " Two
or three days later, by Croesus' orders, his servants conducted Solon round his treasures and showed him all
their greatness and wealth. And when Solon had seen
and examined them all, as he had opportunity, Croesus
put this question to him. ' Stranger of Athens, many
stories have reached our ears concerning your wisdom and
your travels, telling how you have roamed far over the
earth from love of knowledge and a spirit of enquiry.
For this cause I am fain to ask if you have ever
met a man whom you would count of all men the most
happy.' This question he put in the expectation that
he was himself the happiest of men. But Solon answered
him without any flattery, declaring what he truly thought :
' Yes, Tellus the Athenian.' Croesus in surprise enquired
sharply what he meant. ' In what respect, pray, do you
judge Tellus to be happiest ? ' To which Solon replied :
' In this, first, that his country flourished in his time and
noble sons were born to him, and that he saw children
born to them and these were still alive : next, that while
he lived in good circumstances as comfort is counted
among us, his life came to a most glorious end. When
the Athenians were engaged in battle with their neighbours at Eleusis, he came up to their succour, routed the
enemy, and fell most nobly ; and the Athenians gave

him public burial on the field where he died and paid him great honours.' So when Solon had admonished Croesus by reciting all the happy features of Tellus' lot, Croesus enquired further whom he had seen next in happiness after him, thinking that he would certainly at all events take second place. But Solon said, ' Cleobis and Biton. They were Argives by race, had sufficient to live upon, and were in addition possessed of bodily strength such as I will describe ; both alike were victors in the Games, and this story also is told about them. The Argives were celebrating the feast of Hera and it was by all means necessary that their mother should drive to the temple in a waggon. Now their oxen did not come in time from the fields ; and as they could not wait, the young men put their own shoulders beneath the yoke and drew the waggon along ; and their mother rode in the waggon. They carried her thus for five and forty furlongs and reached the temple. And after they had performed this achievement in the sight of the assembled worshippers, their lives came to an end in a right excellent way : and the God showed therein how that for men death is better than life. For the Argive men who stood around were loud in admiration of the young men's strength ; and the Argive women extolled their mother for the sons she was blessed with. And then their mother, full of joy for what they had done and the praises it had brought, stood before the image of the goddess and prayed her to give to her sons, Cleobis and Biton, who had done her such great honour, the blessing best for men. After her prayer, the young men offered sacrifice and took part in the sacred feast, then lay down to sleep there in the temple and woke no more, but ended their lives so. And the Argives had statues of them made and set them up at Delphi, regarding them as men of heroic excellence.' To these youths then did Solon assign the second place in felicity. Then Croesus lost his temper and said, ' Stranger of Athens, is our felicity held by you in such contempt that you make no account of it at all in comparison with private

persons ? ' " [1]   To this reproach Solon replied with a
homily on the insecurity of human fortune, ending with
the admonition not to call any one happy until his life
was happily ended. It is only when a man's life has
ended well that he can safely be termed happy. " ' Men
must look to the end in every matter and see how it will
turn out. For to many a man god gives happiness for
a while, then casts him down in utter ruin.' " [2]   Croesus,
not a whit mollified by this sermon, let Solon go without
any mark of appreciation or honour, and thought no
more of his warning. But the story goes on to tell how
after the capture of Sardis a lofty funeral pyre was raised
by Cyrus' orders, and Croesus, loaded with chains, was
placed upon it. Then in the extremity of calamity he
remembered Solon and his warning, and called three times
on his name. Cyrus heard this cry, and, curious to learn
what it meant, sent to enquire. And Croesus related
the whole story of Solon's visit and what he had said.
Cyrus, struck with the truth of Solon's words, and smitten
with compunction, ordered the fire to be quenched,
released Croesus, and ever after treated him as a
friend.

Persian Conquest of Ionia.—And now fresh trouble had
come to the Ionians, and to all the peoples of the coast
who had been subjects of Croesus, Greeks and barbarians
alike. For when first Cyrus was leading his Persians
against Croesus, he invited the Asiatic Greeks to side
with him, but they refused. Now the Persians were in
possession of Sardis, the Ionian and Aeolian towns begged
him to allow them to become his subjects on the same
terms as they had served Croesus. Cyrus, however,
replied with an eastern fable. " A piper saw some fishes
in the sea and began playing on his pipe, thinking that
they will come out to him on to the land. When he was
disappointed in this expectation, he took a net, caught
a great number of fishes in it and drew it ashore. And
when he saw the fishes leaping, he said to them : Pray
stop your dancing now, since you did not choose to come

[1] Herodotus, i. 30-32.   [2] Herodotus, i. 32.

out and dance, when I played to you." [1] From this the Ionians concluded that they had nothing to expect from Cyrus's ' clemency ' ; and straightway they set to work to strengthen the defences of their cities. The danger was so extreme that this time, not only were the Ionians prepared to take common action, but the Aeolian cities also passed a resolution in their assembly to act with them. Only one city stood aloof : unfortunately the greatest, Miletus. For Miletus had already concluded a treaty of alliance with Cyrus and had nothing to fear. All the other Greek cities of the Levant sent an embassy to Sparta as the foremost Hellenic state asking for assistance. The Spartan government declined to send an expedition across the Aegean, but they nevertheless despatched a fifty-oared ship to Phocaea to report on what was happening. From Phocaea one of their officers took upon himself to go up to Sardis and there to warn Cyrus in the name of the Lacedaemonians not to interfere with any Hellenic city. Cyrus enquired of some Greeks who were standing by who the Lacedaemonians might be. When he was told, he turned to the Spartan envoy and said : " I never yet feared men, who have a place set apart in the middle of their city where they gather together to forswear themselves and cheat each other. If all goes well, these men shall have troubles of their own to talk about instead of the Ionians'." [2] In this crisis of their fate the Asiatic Greeks got no help whatever from their kinsfolk across the Aegean, either Ionian or Dorian. Cyrus himself went off to Ecbatana to deal with more formidable enemies ; the subjection of Ionia and the other cities and peoples of the western coast of Asia Minor he left to his generals. Nor did the alliance of Ionians and Aeolians for combined resistance come to much. Herodotus, in his brief account of these events, describes the resistance of the several cities as gallant in the extreme, but there are no signs of an effective plan for combined defence. The fortifications of the towns were strengthened, he says, and the citizens thereafter just

[1] Herodotus, i. 141.   [2] Herodotus, i. 153.

waited till Cyrus' generals came up, and took them, one by one, in succession. Resistance of this sort, however heroic, was useless ; for the Persian generals had command of unlimited numbers and resources. "They were defeated," writes Herodotus, "and on their surrender remained in their own country and obeyed the commands laid upon them." [1] The terms granted by Cyrus' generals appear to have been lenient ; of only one city, Priene, is it related that the inhabitants were sold as slaves. But to the Greeks trained in free political institutions, submission to this new master was more than ever ' servitude ' ; and servitude was abhorrent to the free-born Hellene. So strong was the aversion to ' servitude,' that is, the loss of political autonomy, that, rather than submit to it, the men of two Ionian cities, Phocaea and Teos, actually broke through all the ties which bound them to their city and sailed away to found new settlements across the seas, where they might again be free. The men of Teos fought on till the mound the Persian soldiery were building rose nearly to the top of their walls. Then they placed their women and children on shipboard together with their most valuable possessions, sailed to the coast of Thrace, and there founded the city of Abdera. Even sterner in resolution was the conduct of the men of Phocaea. The Phocaeans were the most enterprising of all the Ionians on the sea ; they were the first of the Greeks, Herodotus says, to make long voyages. It was the Phocaeans who founded Marseilles and made friends with Arganthonius, king of Tartessus (Tarshish) in Spain. Phocaea was now the first of the Greek cities to be attacked, and Harpagus, the Persian commander, offered them fair terms : " If they would throw down one battlement and dedicate one dwelling-house to the king," he said, "he would accept their submission." [2] But submission meant the forfeiture of their political liberties, and they could not bring themselves to that. They asked one day for deliberation and begged Harpagus to draw off his forces

[1] Herodotus, i. 169.   [2] Herodotus, i. 164.

from the walls. Harpagus replied that he understood what they intended to do, but nevertheless he would grant this request. As soon as the besiegers had drawn off, the Phocaeans manned their ships and put on board their wives and children and household goods, the images of their gods and the votive offerings from their temples. With these they sailed to Chios and tried first to buy from the Chians some small islands between Chios and the mainland, but the Chians would not allow it, for they were afraid of the commercial rivalry of the Phocaeans. On this refusal the Phocaeans determined to sail away to Corsica, where some years before they had founded a city called Alalia. But before they carried out this plan, they sailed back in their warships to Phocaea, surprised the Persian garrison, and put them all to the sword. With terrible oaths they then bound each other never to return to Ionia. Yet even so at the last—so great was the clinging of their hearts to their ancient homes—full half their number broke the oath, came back and reoccupied the empty city. So torn were the best spirits among the Ionian Greeks at this time between love of home and love of liberty. The rest sailed away to Corsica, and after many adventures and hardships ultimately founded the city of Elea in Italy on the shores of the Tuscan Sea beyond the Straits of Messina.

Irresistible Progress of the Persian Arms.—This was in 545 B.C., and for the next forty years the history of Ionia is a blank. But all that time the Persian kings were pursuing an almost continuous career of conquest, till the Persian empire was wider in extent and better organized than any yet known in the history of mankind. After the conquest of Ionia the reduction of the other cities and peoples of the western sea-board of Asia Minor was speedily effected. Babylon was taken by Cyrus in 538 : we know how the Hebrew prophets triumphed in its fall. Cyrus the Great ultimately came by his death in battle with the Massagetae, nomad tribes at that time strong in Central Asia ; but not till he had carried his conquering arms as far east as the Indus. Cambyses,

his son, conquered Egypt, led one expedition up the Nile
into the Soudan, and sent another into the Libyan
desert. The latter expedition never came back ; and of
the other but a remnant returned after terrible losses.
Cambyses, to whom the Egyptians imputed many strange
and sacrilegious acts, died by his own hand, and after
the brief reign of an usurper who personated Smerdis, a
brother whom Cambyses had ' put away ' out of jealousy,
was succeeded by Darius, a prince of the house of Achaemenes, who was as great an organizer of empire as Cyrus
had been conqueror and creator. Darius divided his vast
dominions into twenty satrapies (the number was subsequently increased to twenty-eight), and introduced a
system of government planned to maintain the Great
King's authority and make insurrection difficult. By a
careful assessment of tribute he augmented the material
resources of his empire ; he greatly increased its military
efficiency by a strict and equitable system of service ;
men, or ships, or munitions of war were requisitioned
from every province in accordance with its character and
resources ; internal communications were improved by
a system of posts along the ' Royal Road ' from Sardis
to Susa, a distance of over 1500 miles. Under Darius
the power of the Persian empire culminated : the Great
King's sway was extended across the Bosporus into
Europe through Thrace and Macedonia. And yet it was
against Darius that the Ionians revolted.

The Ionian Revolt.—For the ultimate causes of the
Ionian Revolt of 499 B.C. there is no need to look further
than to the natural restlessness of Greek city-states in
vassalage to an eastern despotism. The Ionians and
other Greeks of Asia had submitted to Cyrus' generals
after a brave resistance, and had remained the quiet
subjects of Persia for nearly fifty years. As such they had
to render military and naval service to the empire, and
they were employed both in the conquest of Eygpt and
in Darius' first European expedition. Yet without doubt
their submission must have been all along unwilling. To
be numbered among the ' slaves ' of a Great King,

capricious, autocratic, absolute, before whom men must prostrate themselves body and soul, was altogether abhorrent to Greek instincts, as it is to our own. The partial autonomy they enjoyed sustained in their minds a consciousness of what real independence was like, and the image of freedom was kept fresh by intercourse with their kinsmen the Ionians and Dorians of European Greece. Ever the contrast rankled ; they felt it as a reproach never far distant from the lips of their kinsmen, that, though of Hellenic blood, they were ' slaves,' not like Spartans and Athenians, Argives and Boeotians, free men. There must, however, have also been something in the circumstances of the time which made the prospect of successful revolt not altogether hopeless. This may well have been some loss of Persian prestige through the ill-success of one part of Darius' European expedition, his campaign into what is now Russia against the Scythians. The Bosporus had been crossed, indeed, and some parts of Thrace subdued by the king's generals ; but the outstanding fact was that the Great King himself had been forced to withdraw from the region beyond the Danube discomfited, and had barely escaped destruction. He had owed his safety only to the forbearance of the Ionian commanders, and of this the favour shown to Histiaeus of Miletus was an acknowledgment.

Darius' Scythian Expedition.—The Scythian expedition of Darius is one of the most extraordinary military enterprises in all history. Wonderful things are related of it by Herodotus, some quite incredible, some certainly true. It is no doubt true that Darius marched northward through Thrace and crossed the Danube with his army by a bridge of boats. It is not credible that his army numbered 700,000 men, or that it penetrated as far eastward as the Volga. Herodotus also relates that Darius left his bridge of boats across the Danube in charge of the Ionians, and that when his return was delayed beyond the appointed time, the Ionian leaders, who were the ' tyrants ' set up by Darius to rule their cities in the Persian interest, deliberated whether or not they should destroy the bridge as the Scythians begged them to do. Miltiades, tyrant of the Thracian Chersonese (Gallipoli), was for destroying it in the hope of thereby freeing themselves from Persian domination ; but the other chiefs were dissuaded by Histiaeus, tyrant of Miletus, who pointed out that their authority depended on Persian support. If the Persian power were overthrown, an end would be put to their own sovereignty too ; they would be expelled and democratic governments be established instead. Darius meanwhile had been vainly pursuing the nomad tribes over the Russian steppes, without ever succeeding in bringing them to battle. At last he was convinced, as other invaders have been since, of the futility of invading Russia, and led his wearied and famished army back to the Danube.

Outbreak of the Revolt.—Though Darius himself returned to Asia after getting back across the Danube, he left Megabazus in Europe with an army to complete the subjugation of Thrace. This Megabazus accomplished, and further induced the king of Macedonia to make submission to the Persian empire. For all this Herodotus' narrative implies that the campaign as a whole was looked upon as a failure, and it is possible that the excitement in Ionia from this cause helped to bring about the revolt. But what immediately led the Ionians to this daring attempt to win back their political freedom was an intrigue of Histiaeus with Aristagoras, his son-in-law and nephew. Histiaeus had received as his reward for services at the Danube bridge a district of land in Thrace for which he had asked. Here he began building fortifications and so came under the suspicion of Megabazus, who warned his master, Darius, of the danger of allowing a subject to make himself strong in a position of such natural advantage. Darius judged the advice good, and invited Histiaeus to leave Myrcinus and come to live at Susa as the king's personal friend and counsellor. Histiaeus had no alternative but to accept an invitation couched in such flattering terms, and went to reside at Susa. Aristagoras, his nephew, succeeded him as governor of Miletus. As time went on, Histiaeus wearied of this gilded captivity, and cast about for means of escape. Finding no better way, he schemed to incite Aristagoras to revolt, in the hope that if there were a rebellion on the coast he would be sent down to quell it. The difficulty was how to convey a message to Aristagoras without deadly risk of discovery. It is here the story is told of the slave whose head was shaved and tattooed with a secret message for Aristagoras. Time was allowed for the hair to grow again, and then the slave was sent from Susa to Miletus. When he came into Aristagoras' presence he asked that his head might be shaved ; and then Aristagoras read the message. Now it happened that at this time Aristagoras was himself in difficulties with the Persians owing to a rash undertaking which he had been unable to fulfil. He, therefore, jumped at the hopes the message suggested to him, and at once made plans to bring about the defection of all the Ionian cities. He began by laying down the power he exercised at Miletus as deputy for the Persian king and putting a democracy in its place. Next he effected similar revolutions in the other Ionian cities. Thirdly, he made an appeal for help to the leading Hellenic states on the European side of the Aegean. He went first to Sparta. There he met with no success at all ; for when he incautiously mentioned that Susa, the Persian capital, was three months' journey from the coast, the Spartan king Cleomenes abruptly broke off the conference and ordered Aristagoras to leave Sparta by nightfall. At Athens he had better fortune ; for the Athenians admitted the claim of blood kinship, and had naturally more sympathy with the Ionians than had the Dorian Spartans. After listening to an eloquent appeal from Aristagoras, the Athenians voted to send a squadron of twenty ships to his assistance. These ships, Herodotus remarks, " were the beginning of mischief both to the Greeks and the barbarians." But, whether it was prudent or not of the Athenians with their seven hundred square miles of territory and their thirty thousand citizens of military age to flout the might of Persia by so serious a provocation, it was certainly chivalrous to go to the aid of their Ionian kinsmen. Five ships from Eretria went with the Athenian squadron ; the Eretrians sent them out of gratitude for assistance which Eretria had once received from Miletus.

The Burning of Sardis.—When these twenty-five ships, five Eretrian and twenty Athenian, reached Miletus, they found an expedition planned by Aristagoras about to start for a surprise attack on Sardis, the seat of government in the coast satrapy. The combined fleet sailed along the coast to the neighbourhood of Ephesus, and there all available forces were landed for the march on Sardis. These forces marched up the valley of the Cayster, crossed Mount Tmolus and descended on Sardis by a road along the stream Pactolus. The town was occupied by the Greeks without resistance, the Persian garrison retiring to the citadel. But a house was accidentally set on fire and the fire spread ; and soon all Sardis was blazing. In the confusion caused by the fire the Persians rallied and attacked the Greeks, apparently with the support of the Lydian inhabitants. When night came the Greeks evacuated Sardis and began a hasty retreat to the coast. By this time other bodies of Persian troops had come together, and finding the invaders gone, started in hot pursuit. The Ionians and Athenians were overtaken near Ephesus, defeated and scattered. Those who escaped found refuge in friendly cities. The expedition had ended in disaster.[1] Sardis, however, the Persian provincial capital, had been burnt, and the effect of this dramatic event was seen in the rapid spread of the revolt ; northward to the cities on the Hellespont, and southward through Caria. All Cyprus, too—one city, Amathus, excepted—rose in revolt. It is not surprising if King

---

[1] This is Herodotus' account. Another account which happens to be preserved gives a reason for the attempt on Sardis which makes Aristagoras' plan not merely bold, but also well-conceived. According to this account the Persians were already besieging Miletus, and the march to Sardis was a diversion, and a successful diversion.

Darius was deeply incensed, and registered a vow to exact punishment from Athens and Eretria for this audacious deed.

The Struggle for Liberty.—For six years the Ionians maintained the unequal struggle, and that they held out so long is no slight proof of their endurance and valour. But the odds were too unequal. Athens after the loss incurred in the retreat from Sardis withdrew her succour altogether. Ionia is but a small land, and all the Greeks of Asia Minor were a handful compared with the millions who owned allegiance to the King of Persia. Worse even than that, the coast cities of Asia Minor were very unfavourably placed for combined action. These cities, speaking broadly, are planted in a series of rich valleys parallel to each other and at right angles to the coast. They were readily open to attack from the uplands of the interior, but were cut off from helping each other by the ranges bounding the valleys. A situation advantageous for communication by sea was fatally disadvantageous for communication by land. As it was in the sixth century B.C., so it is in the twentieth century A.D., and is a factor that must be reckoned with in any settlement of Asia Minor. With the whole of the interior under the authority of one strong central power, the cause of the Ionians was hopeless without strong aid from overseas. On the whole it was to their credit that they made so good a fight. Cyprus, the last to revolt, was first to be recovered for the Great King. The Ionians won a sea-fight, but the Cyprian princes, through the treachery of some of their number who went over to the Persians in the midst of the fight, were routed. " Cyprus," as Herodotus says, " after a year of freedom was enslaved for the second time." [1] Meantime the Persian generals on the mainland were again attacking and taking the little Greek cities one by one. Daurises took five cities on the Hellespont in five successive days : and then marched south against the Carians. The Carians made a fierce resistance. Three times they were defeated

[1] Herodotus, v. 116.

with great slaughter; yet again they rallied, and by a well-planned ambush and night attack destroyed the whole of the Persian army together with Daurises and two other Persian generals. But other commanders took the place of those who had fallen, and to them Cyme and Clazomenae surrendered in succession. The cause of the Asiatic Greeks was clearly on the wane; but all finally turned on the fortunes of Miletus. And now the Persian commanders were gathering their forces for an overwhelming attack on Miletus by sea and land. In face of this supreme danger the Ionians once more met in council at the Panionium. The question how best to use the strength of the league in defence of Miletus was debated, and it was resolved to stake all upon the fleet. To face the Persians on land was regarded as hopeless; no attempt was to be made to march the combined land forces of Ionia to the succour of Miletus. But on the sea every member of the league was adjured to send to Miletus its whole naval strength to the last ship, there to make a supreme effort for victory on the sea.

The little island of Lade, which then protected the harbour of Miletus,[1] was the station for the Ionian fleet. The total number of ships was 353, to which the large islands, Lesbos, Samos and Chios, contributed the biggest squadrons. The Chians furnished 100 ships, Samos 60, Lesbos 70; the Milesians themselves had 80 ships Phocaea (p. 266), once the most enterprising of all Greek maritime cities, could now only man three ships; but with them it sent a commander, who, had the Ionians steadfastly followed his leading, might have saved them —and so altered the course of history. This man Dionysius of Phocaea, told the Ionians plainly that victory could only be won by assiduous training and strict discipline; they must practise rowing and manoeuvring, and especially the manoeuvre of breaking the line But after seven days, Herodotus relates, " worn out by the hardness of the work and the heat of the sun," the

---

[1] This island no longer exists, having been joined to the mainland by the silting up of the channel between.

broke out into murmuring and removed Dionysius from the chief command. " Thenceforward all refused to obey orders ; they pitched their tents on the island just like a land force, took their ease in the shade and declined to go on board their ships, or practise." [1] And this indiscipline he represents as the cause of the ruin which befell a little later. For indiscipline bred want of confidence in each other, and want of confidence, treachery. The story, as Herodotus tells it, contains manifest improbabilities, but it may be a true representation in picturesque form of a real incapacity in the Ionian nature. Hard discipline was intolerable to them, and this proved their undoing. When the day of battle came, it ended in the complete defeat of the Ionians through base betrayal. No clear account of the battle has come down to us ; Herodotus preserves only the traditions that it was through the treachery of the Samians that the battle was lost, and that the Chians behaved with heroic courage, fighting on, in spite of the flight of the other squadrons, till more than half their ships were out of action. Dionysius, after making prize of three enemy ships, seeing the battle was lost, sailed away and made for himself a great name in Sicilian waters by preying upon the shipping of Carthage and the Tuscans. The Persian fleet probably greatly outnumbered the Greek. Herodotus puts it at 600 ships, made up of contingents from Phoenicia, Egypt, Cyprus and Cilicia. For the Persians, it should be kept in mind, were themselves no seamen. They never manned a single ship. The Persian fleet was always composed of the ships of Persia's maritime subjects, of whom the Phoenicians were the most skilful and the best affected to Persian interests.

The Fall of Miletus.—Thus was the fate of Miletus sealed. After their naval victory at Lade, the Persians pressed the siege by land and sea, and at length, in spite of desperate resistance, took both town and citadel. The town was destroyed and all the people of Miletus sold as slaves or carried into captivity. This was the end for

[1] Herodotus, vi. 12.

all time of the glory of Miletus ; for though the desolated
city was reoccupied later, it never attained anything like
its former prosperity. This utter ruin of Miletus was a
moral shock to the whole Greek world. The Athenians
especially took the catastrophe to heart, partly because
they looked upon the Ionians as near to them in blood ;
partly, perhaps, because they felt their own part in the
tragedy had been a sorry one. When Phrynichus, the
tragic poet, brought out a drama on the *Fall of Miletus*,
the Athenian audience burst into tears during the performance, and afterwards the people punished Phrynichus
with a fine for reminding them of their misfortunes.

End of the Revolt.—Histiaeus and Aristagoras, the
authors of the revolt, both met violent deaths as the
struggle neared its end. Aristagoras fell in a fight with
tribesmen in Thrace, where he had gone with a band of
volunteers from Miletus to try what could be made of
Myrcinus, the place Histiaeus had obtained as a gift
from Darius. Histiaeus himself came to a more evil
end. Darius had listened to his entreaties and promises
and given him leave to go down to the coast. When he
failed to persuade the men of Miletus to receive him
back, he found a refuge in Lesbos, and thence embarked
on various piratical adventures, in one of which he was
captured by the Persian commander, Harpagus. Harpagus struck off his head and had his body impaled ; the
head he had embalmed and sent to Darius ; and it is
said that the great Persian still retained enough regard
for this false friend to blame those who killed him. Of
the doom of the rest of Ionia, Herodotus uses these
terrible words : " And now the Persian commanders
made good the threats they had uttered against the
Ionians while awaiting battle. When they were masters
of the cities, they picked out the best looking boys and
had them mutilated to serve as eunuchs, and the fairest
of the maidens they tore from their homes and carried
off to the King. All this they did ; and moreover burnt
the cities with fire, temples and all. Thus for the third
time the Ionians were reduced to slavery : first by the

Lydians, then twice in succession by the Persians." [1]
Small wonder if the terror of the Persian name was
noised abroad through European Hellas, and to many a
brave man the might of the Great King seemed irresistible.

NOTE ON THE PERSIANS AND THEIR ACHIEVEMENT.

The Medes and Persians belonged to the eastern branch of
that Indo-European family of nations, to which Greeks and
Romans and most of the nations of modern Europe (Celts, Teutons
and Slavs) also belong. Their next of kin among the nations
are the Hindus, who in ages long before the dawn of history
occupied and civilized first the Punjab, and then the greater part
of the Indian peninsula. How well Eastern nations of this
stock can fight has been proved anew in our own times by the
records of Sikhs and Rajputs in France, Egypt, Palestine, the
Dardanelles and Mesopotamia. The Persians of 490 and 480 B.C.
were no weak Asiatics formidable only by their numbers. Probably Xerxes' boast to Demaratus (Herodotus, vii. 103) that,
man for man, his picked Guardsmen, called Immortals, were fit
to be matched with Spartans in single combat, was justified.
The Persians Cyrus led to conquest were a free, warlike and
manly race. Their loyalty to their chieftains and especially to
the royal house of Achaemenes was extreme, and seemed to the
Greeks with their stronger notions of individual worth and
dignity, to go beyond the bounds of reason. More than one
anecdote which Herodotus tells, illustrates the conviction the
Greeks had that the Persian subjects of the Great King reckoned
their lives as nothing, compared with the safety and comfort of
their king. Above all the Persians were a race of warriors, who
despised all pursuits except war and agriculture. Their contempt
for trade was even greater than that of the Greek aristocrats,
as Cyrus' taunt to the Spartans (above, p. 265) sufficiently shows.
Truthfulness and courage in war were their two cardinal virtues.

No estimate of the Persians is adequate which leaves out of
account their religion. The Persians of the fifth century B.C.
had a religion which invites comparison with the best religions
known to us. Some time before the Medes and Persians emerge
into the light of history as conquerors they had thrown off the
polytheism of their branch of the Indo-European stock, which
must once have been very like Hindu polytheism,[2] and adopted

---

[1] Herodotus, vi. 32.

[2] Both Persians and Hindus had two names for divine beings. In
Persian these are *Ahura* and *Daiva*; in Sanskrit *Asura* and *Deva*. Now

an ethical religion of universal appeal, at the teaching of Zara-
thustra (known to the western world as Zoroaster). This new
religion was in its essence the worship of Ahura Mazda (Ormuzd),
the Spirit of Light, of Wisdom and Beneficence. But since the
beginning of existence Ormuzd, the good spirit, has been opposed
by an evil spirit, Ahriman, the Spirit of Darkness, the inspirer
of all wickedness and cruelty. Every good thought and word
and work of man helps forward the final victory of Ormuzd ;
every evil deed and word and thought hinders it. This is a
very moral, and very morally helpful creed. It is doubtful
whether the Persians who built up the Persian Empire held fast
to this doctrine in its purity. Some elements of the earlier
polytheism had probably been revived, especially the adoration
of Fire and the Sun, as embodiments of the Divine Spirit ; and
this is how in after time the Persians came to be known as
' Fire-worshippers.' But something of the higher and purer
faith must have remained with the Persians of the fifth century B.C.
and it is curious that the Greeks of that age did not discover it.
The Parsis of modern India hold the ancient Persian faith to
this day in the form of a pure monotheism. In Persia itself,
since the Arab conquest in the seventh century A.D., the Persians
have been Muhammedans : the old religion was all but entirely
stamped out, and with it the early literature of Persia and the
record of early Persian history. The Parsis were Persians who
escaped from persecution to India, and were there granted asylum
by the Hindus ; and that is how it comes about that the religion
of Zoroaster, the religion professed by Cyrus the Great and Darius,
flourishes in India at the present time under the protection of
the British Raj.

in the Indian tongues Deva has retained the meaning ' god ' (we have
the word in *divine* and *deity*), while Asura has been degraded to mean
evil spirit or demon. Among the Persians this process of differentiation
was reversed ; Ahura retained the meaning good spirit or ' god ' (as in
Ahura Mazda), while Daiva came to mean demon, or evil spirit.

CHAPTER XII

MARATHON

" Age shakes Athena's tower, but spares gray Marathon."
Byron, *Childe Harold*, ii. 88.9.

FOR full three years more after the fall of Miletus the Great King nursed his wrath against the petty city-states that had dared to affront the majesty of Persia. Then at length in 490 B.C. a powerful armada was ready to sail across the Aegean with the direct purpose of punishing Athens and Eretria for their part in the burning of Sardis.

The Campaign of 492.—Two years earlier, in 492, immediately after the subjection and settlement of Ionia, Mardonius, a brilliant young Persian nobleman, high in Darius' favour and recently married to his daughter, had crossed the Hellespont into Europe with a large army and fleet. He had a wide commission from the king to recover and extend Persian dominion in Europe, and incidentally to wreak vengeance on Eretria and Athens. He proceeded victoriously westward along the coasts of Thrace and Macedonia, fleet and army acting in concert, until they reached the city of Acanthus close to the three remarkable promontories that jut out, like the prongs of a trident, from the district the Greeks called Chalcidice. There a great storm caught the fleet as it attempted to sail round the first of the promontories (Acte) and strewed the wrecks of ships and the corpses of men on the rocks beneath the steep precipices of Mount Athos. The loss was very great and the fleet was crippled : Mardonius' ambitious dream of conquest (he aspired to subdue all Hellas) had to be abandoned. Besides this the army suffered heavy losses from a night attack by Thracian tribesmen ; and though Mardonius made good this reverse by compelling the submission of these Brygi before his withdrawal, he returned to Asia a discredited man.

The Destruction of Eretria.—It was because of the disasters attending this campaign of 492 that an entirely different plan was adopted in the fateful year 490. The forces for the great punitive expedition were first gathered in the broad plains near the coast of Cilicia and embarked on board a fleet said to have numbered six hundred warships without counting transports for the horses of the cavalry. The fleet followed the coast of Asia Minor as far north as the island of Samos and then struck straight across the Aegean. Datis, a Mede, and Artaphernes, the son of Artaphernes a nephew of Darius, were in command. The Great King's orders were brief and peremptory : to reduce Athens and Eretria to slavery and bring the captives into his presence. About halfway across the Aegean the fleet reached the island of Naxos which had as yet maintained its independence. The Naxians did not even await the coming of the Persians, but fled to the mountains : [1] the Persians on their arrival made slaves of those whom they caught, and burnt with fire the city of the Naxians and its temples. In alarm at this news the inhabitants of Delos (which lies a little to the north) left their sacred island and sought safety in flight. But the Persian commanders had no hostile intentions against Delos, for the king himself had laid strict charge upon them to show all respect to the reputed birthplace of Apollo and Artemis. Datis therefore sent a message to the Delians assuring them of immunity ; he would not even suffer the ships of the fleet to anchor

---

[1] This is some measure of the terror caused by the failure of the Ionian revolt and the severities attending its suppression ; for in 500 B.C. the Naxians, when attacked, had resisted strenuously and successfully.

at Delos ; but he went on shore himself and offered sacrifice of frankincense upon the altar with lavish profusion. Leaving the neighbourhood of Delos, the fleet now sailed across the western half of the Aegean to Euboea : from every island passed on his course the Persian commander demanded hostages and a contingent of troops, so that Ionians and Aeolians, who were Greeks as much as the Athenians, formed a part of the hostile armada. When similar demands were made at Carystus, a town at the southern extremity of Euboea, the men of Carystus bravely refused to comply, saying that they would not give hostages neither would they join in an expedition against cities which were their neighbours. Thereupon the Persians ravaged the territory of Carystus and beleaguered the city, until the Carystians also bowed to the might of Persia and made their submission. From Carystus the Persian fleet sailed northward into the channel separating Euboea and Attica, till they came opposite to Eretria. There Datis and Artaphernes disembarked troops, both horse and foot, and prepared to attack the city. The Eretrians were not strong enough alone to face the Persians in the open field, but for six days they maintained a stout defence behind their walls. On the seventh the city was betrayed by two of its leading men. Eretria and its temples were plundered and burnt, the inhabitants were made slaves as Darius had commanded. Thus swiftly was one part of the charge given to Datis and Artaphernes carried out. It remained to deal with Athens.

The Landing in the Bay of Marathon.—If we look again at the map of Attica we see that its eastward coast begins almost opposite Eretria and runs a distance of some fifty miles down to Cape Sunium (Colonna). Athens is situated about the middle of the opposite side of Attica, which looks on the Saronic Gulf and faces south-west. The most direct way to Athens from Eretria lies across the triangle from the eastward side ; but the direct line from Eretria across Attica is blocked by the broad and lofty barrier of Parnes. However, twenty miles down the coast from the border town of Oropus (and about thirty-five from Eretria) is a crescent-shaped bay, with a sandy beach very suitable for landing troops, and protected at its north-eastern end by the sharply-jutting promontory called Kynos-oura (that is, Dog's tail), which forms one horn of the crescent. A semicircle of rocky hills looks down upon this bay, but leaves a stretch of level ground some two miles wide between the mountains and the sea. This is the Bay of Marathon. Fifty years earlier Pisistratus, as we have seen (Ch. X. p. 248), had landed at Marathon and thence made a victorious march on Athens, by which he recovered his lost power. Now Hippias, son of Pisistratus and successor in his tyranny, and afterwards long an exile at the Persian court, was with Datis and Artaphernes, looking to be restored to his throne and power when the Persians were masters of Athens. The plain extends some five miles along the curve of the bay, and the distance between the mountains and the sea varies from two and a half miles to a mile. There was room enough for the encampment of an army and for the movements of cavalry. From Marathon a smooth and level road leads along the coast and round the skirts of Pentelicus, by which the Persian host, both horse and foot, might march on Athens ; and the distance by this road is twenty-four miles from the city to the edge of the plain. Therefore, after a few days' stay at Eretria to repair losses and draw breath for the next effort, Datis and Artaphernes sailed on to the Bay of Marathon and there made a landing in full strength.

Alarm at Athens. The March out over the Mountains.— In Athens meantime it may well be believed excitement and anxiety ran high, as report after report came of the easy progress of the Persian fleet ; of the occupation of Naxos ; of the gathering of contingent after contingent from the islands ; of the forced submission of Carystus ; and finally of the ruin that had come upon Eretria. So far the power of Persia had proved as irresistible as in the Ionian Revolt. Each fresh success confirmed the prestige which the Persian power had won in Asia Minor.

And Eretria was little more than thirty miles away as the crow flies ; while the voyage round Cape Sunium was an easy two-days' sail (100 miles). The peril had come very near. What the people of Athens thought and felt in those days of anxiety and terror is not on record, but we have Herodotus' testimony that their spirit had been high since the expulsion of the Pisistratidae twenty years before this time. " Herein," he writes, " we may see demonstrated, not in one particular only but in every way, that political equality is an excellent thing : the Athenians, so long as they were ruled by tyrants, were no better in war than any of the neighbouring peoples, but when they were rid of their tyrants, were easily first." [1] It was in the strength of this new spirit that sixteen years before this time the Athenians achieved the feat of winning two victories on one and the same day, the first over the Boeotians, and the second over the men of Chalcis in Euboea (Ch. X. 2, p. 254). What is clearly recorded of this year 490 is that on receiving news of the landing of the Persians the fighting-men of Athens at once marched out in full force to meet the invaders at Marathon. Herodotus, who is our chief authority for the story of Marathon, does not tell us by which road they went. Since it was by the coast road that the Persians must advance on Athens, it might be argued that it was by this road the Athenians marched out to intercept them. But it is proved beyond reasonable doubt that the position occupied by the Athenians at Marathon before the battle was the high ground about the modern village of Vrana ; [2] and Vrana stands where a shorter and rougher mountain road from Athens, which

[1] Herodotus, v. 78.

[2] " At the south-west corner of the plain the small village of Vrana occupies a commanding situation. Backed by wooded mountains it stands on a height at the mouth of a wild and romantic glen." (Frazer, *Pausanias*, vol. ii. p. 436.) The mountain-road from Athens to the Bay of Marathon came down this glen, now called the Valley of Avlona. The site of the precinct of Heracles (the Heracleium) on which the Athenians camped has been identified with ground just above the modern village, now occupied by the church of St. George and a deserted monastery.

crosses the spurs of Pentelicus to the north, breaks
through the hills and comes in view of the plain. It
seems more probable that the Athenian hoplites made a
forced march through the mountains and emerged on to
the high ground dominating the plain and the Persian
camp. The advantage of this position, as the map shows,
is that at Vrana the Athenians commanded both routes

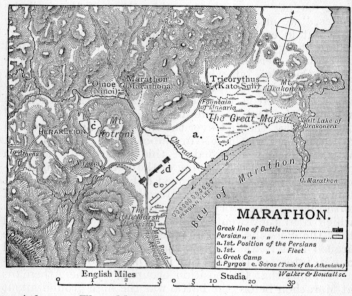

MARATHON.

Greek line of Battle ....
Persian „ „ ....
a. 1st. Position of the Persians
b. 1st. „ „ „ Fleet
c. Greek Camp
d. Pyrgos e. Soros (Tomb of the Athenians)

Walker & Boutall sc.

English Miles
Stadia

to Athens. They blocked the mountain path by which
they had come ; and they could take in flank from higher
ground any force which attempted to advance by the
coast road. At the same time they occupied a very
strong defensive position with all the advantages of the
ground in their favour should the Persians attack.[1] The

[1] " The Athenians were practically unassailable, or only assailable at
great disadvantage to the attacking force : right and left they were
protected from cavalry by the slopes of Agrielikia and Kotroni, while
the narrow valley would deprive superior numbers of their main advantage in attack." Macan, *Herodotus IV. to VI.* vol. ii. Appendix X. p. 240.

occupation of the high ground at Vrana was a masterly
stroke, and it is more probable that the Athenians chose
the rougher, but safer, road over the mountains rather
than the better road on which they might have encountered the Persians on level ground, and, moreover,
have been exposed to charges of cavalry. By their rapid
march and unexpected appearance on the high ground
above Marathon they foiled any hopes Hippias and the
Persian commanders may have entertained of an immediate and unopposed advance on Athens.

The Appeal for help to Sparta.—The decision that the
fighting forces of the city should march out and face the
Persians at Marathon was the decision of the free citizens
of Athens voting in their Ecclesia. The force that
marched was the full strength available for active service,
9000 hoplites, or heavy-armed spearmen, marshalled in
ten regiments, one for each of the ten tribes (Ch. X. 2,
p. 251). The ten strategi were at the head of these
forces, with the polemarch in chief command. Now
before they left the city, because the crisis was extreme,
the generals sent to Sparta to beg for help : for to the
Athenians, as to other Hellenes, Sparta was the foremost
of the Greek commonwealths and the champion of Hellenic
freedom. So the Athenians sent to carry their message
to Sparta a trained long-distance runner named Pheidippides.[1] Pheidippides made such speed that though the
distance from Athens to Sparta is close on 150 miles,
up hill and down dale, and often by rocky paths along
the sides of rugged mountains, he reached Sparta on the
second day after leaving Athens. To the Spartans he
delivered his message in these words : " Men of Lacedaemon, the Athenians pray you to come to their succour
and not to suffer our most ancient Hellenic city to be
reduced to slavery by the barbarians. Eretria, you must
know, has already been enslaved and Hellas has been
made the weaker by the loss of a city of renown." [2] The

[1] The name is properly Philippides ; but the mistaken form Pheidippides is consecrated in English by Browning's poem under that title.
See note at end of this chapter.

[2] Herodotus, vi. 106.

Spartans promised help ; but they must wait to march,
they said, till after the full moon : for by their law it
was not permissible in that month to march sooner.
With this answer Pheidippides sped back. But as the
full moon was on the 15th and it was now only the 9th,
and the Persians were already encamped on Attic soil,
it brought small comfort. A story was afterwards told
how Pheidippides nevertheless brought back with him a
promise of superhuman help more encouraging than this
message from Lacedaemon. As he ran on under the
dark cliffs of Mount Parthenium, where the railway from
Argos to Tripolitza passes to-day, he heard his name
called, and the god Pan with his horns and shaggy goats'
feet appeared to him and bade him assure the Athenians
that, though they had slighted his worship, he bore them
great goodwill and would help them in their present need.
For which cause the Athenians after Marathon built a
temple to Pan under the Acropolis,[1] and instituted yearly
sacrifices and a torch-race in his honour.

The Dilemma of the Persian Commanders.—The plan
with which the Persians landed was baffled, we see,
by the promptitude of the Athenians in marching
out, and their leaders' skill in seizing a position
which blocked the way to Athens. The Persian
commanders shrank from the attempt to dislodge the
Athenians from Vrana by direct assault. Yet it was not
safe to march past the outlet of the valley and risk a
sudden attack in flank or rear. They therefore waited.
We cannot know with certainty what their further plans
were, but it is extremely probable that they were all
along building on the chance of treachery. Lade had
been won through the defection of some of the Ionians ;
Eretria had been betrayed ; there had been partizans of
Persia ready to play traitor in every Greek city since
first the Persians had dealings with the Greeks. The
Persian leaders had every reason to believe that the
course of events in Attica would follow closely the course

[1] This cave may be seen in the face of the Acropolis rock at its north-
west corner, somewhat east of the Propylaea or main entry.

of events at Eretria ; that they could count on the betrayal of Athens by traitors among her own citizens, as Eretria had been betrayed by Euphorbus and Philagrus. There was even better ground for confidence in the work of treachery at Athens ; for was not Hippias with them, and Hippias had family connections and local ties in Attica to help him, and many a memory of the old party of the hill districts which Pisistratus, his father, had led. What more likely plan for them now than to hold the armed forces of Athens in play at Marathon while a strong squadron with all the cavalry transports sailed on round Cape Sunium and landed troops in Phalerum Bay, who might get into Athens through the connivance of Hippias' partizans, or even make a sudden dash across the plain and seize the city in the absence of the main body of its defenders ? The facts recorded, which in themselves make a very incomplete story, at all events fit in with this supposition.

Miltiades' Appeal to the Polemarch.—For the Athenian commanders, when the Persians made no attack, the problem was whether they should remain where they were and watch the enemy, or themselves venture down upon the level ground and fight. Of these commanders there were, as we have seen, eleven, ten strategi with equal powers, and the polemarch in chief command with a casting vote in a council-of-war should votes be equally divided. Five of the strategi were against offering battle to the enemy in the plain, on the ground that numbers were too unequal ; five were for fighting. Then Miltiades, one of the five who were for fighting, went to the polemarch, Callimachus of Aphidna, and said (so Herodotus relates) : " On you, Callimachus, it now depends either to bring Athens to slavery, or to make her free and leave a memory, as long as mankind endures, more glorious even than Harmodius and Aristogeiton. For never since the Athenians were a people have they stood in such sore peril as now. If they stoop to submission to Persia, they will be handed over to Hippias, and then it is surely decreed what they will suffer ; but if the city comes

through victoriously, it is like to become the first of
Hellenic city-states. How this may come about and how
it happens that on you devolves the power to determine
all, I will now indicate. Opinion is equally divided among
our ten commanders, some are for fighting, some against.
Now if we do not fight, I look for a sharp division of
factions, which will so shake the spirit of the Athenians
as to lead them to make terms with the Mede. But
should we fight before this rot spreads among our people
—if the gods will but hold the balance level—we are well
able to get the better in the fight. Accordingly, the
whole issue turns in your direction and rests upon you.
If only you give your support to my view, your fatherland shall be free,—yea and the first city in Hellas. But
if you support the opinion of those who would decline
the fight, then the very opposite of the advantages I have
rehearsed will ensue." [1] Callimachus was won over by
this appeal and gave his decision for fighting. The die
was cast, and the Athenian commanders, on the initiative
of Miltiades, made dispositions for attacking the Persians
in the plain as soon as there was a favourable opportunity. For this they still had to wait some days ; but
the opportunity came at last and altered the whole future
for Athens and for Greece.

Help from Little Plataea.—Meantime the Athenians
had received an accession of strength which, if not very
great in point of numbers, was most heartening for the
good courage and fidelity of which it was proof. While
they waited at Vrana, the whole military force of their
little ally, Plataea, marched up and encamped beside
them. This was out of gratitude for the protection
afforded by Athens against the Thebans (Ch. X. p. 253).
Thirty years before Athens had listened to the prayer of
the Plataeans and fought their battles, and now in the
hour of peril for Athens the Plataeans did not fail her.
This reinforcement raised the strength of the whole body
of hoplites under Callimachus to 10,000 men.

[1] Herodotus, vi. 109.

The Resolution to Attack.—The opportunity for which Miltiades was waiting came when information reached him that the Persians were re-embarking their cavalry on the transports and preparing to sail round Attica with part of their forces and attack Athens from the sea. It appears that the Persian commanders were expecting a signal which would tell them when the partizans of Hippias in Athens were ready to cooperate with them. This signal did not come, but it was expected at any time, and meantime the days were passing. After the full moon the Spartans would be free to march in accordance with their promise : this circumstance was probably also known to the Persian commanders and had to be reckoned with. They judged the Athenian position in the mountains too strong to be attacked ; they were afraid to attempt the march overland to Athens with a formidable force of heavy-armed troops on their flank ; yet something had to be done. So they began to embark the cavalry and part of their footmen in readiness to sail when the signal came, and drew up the rest of their infantry in formidable force between the Greek position at Vrana and the sea to cover the embarkation. These movements were in sight of the Greeks at Vrana, and Miltiades knew what they meant. This was the opportunity for which he had been waiting. He knew, too, what was to be feared from treachery at Athens. It was necessary to strike and to strike quickly.

The Athenian Charge at Marathon.—The Athenians were drawn up, tribe by tribe, in battle array, with the Plataean contingent on the extreme left. The post of honour on the right was occupied by the polemarch Callimachus. Then, because the Persians had still the advantage of numbers, although part of their forces were on shipboard, in order to extend the Athenian battle-front and make it equal to the Persian, Callimachus by Miltiades' advice deliberately weakened his centre, greatly reducing the depth there in ranks, while the wings were kept at full strength. Then the word was given and the solid array of Greek spearmen moved forward at a rapid

I   T

pace, which increased to a run, as, amid a shower of
missiles, they closed with the enemy. This world-famous
charge of the Athenian hoplites at Marathon is thus
described in the words of Herodotus, our sole original
authority : " Now when these dispositions had been
made for battle and the sacrifices were found propitious,
the Athenians, as soon as the word was given, went
forward at a run against the barbarians. The space
between the two armies must have been not less than
sixteen hundred yards. The Persians seeing the
Athenians come on at a run, made ready to receive them,
and thought in their minds that the Greeks were out of
their senses and must certainly be destroyed, seeing how
few they were in number and actually charging without
the support of cavalry or bowmen. This is what the
barbarians thought. But the Athenians as soon as the
whole line was fairly engaged fought with notable valour :
indeed they were the first of all the Hellenes of whom we
know to charge the enemy at the double ; they were the
first to endure to look upon the Median dress and the
men who wore it. For till that day the very name of
the Medes was a terror in the ears of the Hellenes. Long
time the fight at Marathon lasted ; and in the centre,
where the Persians themselves and the Sacae were posted,
the barbarians were victorious and broke the line and
carried the pursuit inland ; but on the two wings the
Athenians and Plataeans were victorious ; and when
they had thus gained the victory, they allowed the routed
divisions of the barbarians to escape, but themselves
drew together from either side and engaged the troops
who had routed the Athenian centre, and were victorious.
Then they pursued the flying Persians and cut them
down till they reached the sea ; and then they called for
fire and began to lay hands on the ships. In this part
of the conflict the polemarch Callimachus lost his life
after showing himself a valorous man, and Stesilaus, son
of Thrasylaus, one of the strategi, was slain. Cynegeirus, too, son of Euphorion, when he had laid hold on
the stern of one of the ships, had his hand lopped off by

an axe and fell ; and so fell many other Athenians of note." [1]

Panaenus' Picture.—In after years there were in the building called the Painted Portico (the ' Stoa Poekile ') at Athens, among other famous paintings, three frescoes, the work of Panaenus, brother of Pheidias, representing scenes of the battle of Marathon. These are described by the traveller Pausanias, who saw them there : " the Boeotians of Plataea and all the men of Attica are closing with the barbarians. In this part of the picture the combatants are evenly matched ; but farther on the barbarians are fleeing and pushing each other into the marsh. At the extremity of the picture are the Phoenician ships and the Greeks slaughtering the barbarians who are rushing into the ships. . . . Of the combatants the most conspicuous in the painting are Callimachus, who had been chosen to command the Athenians ; Miltiades, one of the generals ; and a hero called Echetlus." [2] We may place beside the vivid details, which these frescoes in the Stoa Poekile add to Herodotus' history, Byron's picture in *Childe Harold* :

> " As on the morn to distant Glory dear,
> When Marathon became a magic word ;
> Which utter'd, to the hearer's eye appear
> The camp, the host, the fight, the conqueror's career,
>
> The flying Mede, his shaftless broken bow ;
> The fiery Greek, his red pursuing spear ;
> Mountains above, Earth's, Ocean's plain below ;
> Death in the front, Destruction in the rear !
> Such was the scene. . . ." [3]

The Persian Dash on Athens.—Six thousand four hundred Persians fell in this rout. There was stiff fighting on the beach, but most of the fugitives succeeded in getting aboard the ships, and pushed off : seven ships only remained in the hands of the Greeks. The main fleet was apparently already at sea, or riding at anchor

[1] Herodotus, vi. 112-114.
[2] Pausanias, *Greece*, i. 15. 3 ; Frazer, vol. i. p. 22.
[3] Byron, *Childe Harold*, ii. Stanzas 89 and 90.

off the coast. At any rate soon after the embarkation the long-expected signal[1] was flashed from Mount Pentelicus by the traitors in the city. Consequently, all doubts for the Persian leaders were at an end ; their object now was to reach Athens before the Athenian forces who were in victorious possession of the field of Marathon. But the Athenians, fully aware of this danger, left Aristides and the men of his tribe in charge of the spoil on the battle-field and marched back with all speed by the coast-road. It was now a race between the Great King's fleet laden with troops and hindered by horse-transports, and the defenders of Athens flushed with their recent victory ; and the Athenians won. When the Persian fleet appeared in the Bay of Phalerum, the victors of Marathon were already in camp near the city ready for them. Thus baffled a second time, the Persian fleet, after hovering awhile within sight of the shore, drew off and sailed back to Asia Minor.

Athens saved.—So ended the first carefully planned attempt of the Persians on the liberties of European Hellas. The Spartans, true to their promise, set out from their city immediately after the full moon and made such speed that they reached Attica in three days. By that time the battle had been fought and won, but the men of Lacedaemon were eager to see the plain and the bodies of the Medes. So they marched on to Marathon and viewed the field and the slain, and gave generous praise to the Athenians for their valour : then marched back to Sparta. In Athens great was the exultation of victory and high the pride with which for ever after the Athenians looked back on Marathon. Reckoning by numbers[2]

[1] The flashing was done by means of the sun on a shield. Compare the modern heliograph.

[2] It is not easy to make any fair estimate of the numbers of the Persians at Marathon. In later times they were put very high. Herodotus does not say, but when all the probabilities are taken into account, it is not likely that the number was much higher than 20,000, if as high. The numbers in the Athenian charge are definitely estimated at 10,000.

THE TREASURY OF THE ATHENIANS.

The Athenian memorial of Marathon at Delphi discovered by M. Homolle in 1893. In front to the left is the Sacred Way leading up to the platform of the Temple of Apollo ; behind this appears the high road from the port of Itea, and beyond again Mount Kirphis on the further side of the valley of the Pleistus.

From a photograph by Alinari.

it was not a great battle, nor was the result an overwhelming defeat for Persia. It was but a check. The power of the Great King remained formidable as ever ; the menace of oriental despotism still overhung Greece. But the gallant charge of the Athenians at Marathon nerved the Greeks to resist the more formidable attack that was to come in ten years' time ; the victory at Marathon made possible the great deliverance at Salamis and Plataea.

The Monuments of Victory.—Great spoil must have been taken by the Athenians at Marathon, though Herodotus does not happen to say so. Plutarch speaks of the regiment of Aristides left in charge of the field, and it is natural to suppose that the Persian camp and rich camp-equipage fell into the victors' hands. We know that offerings, dedicated from the spoils of Marathon, were seen by Pausanias at Delphi. Chief of these was the Treasury of the Athenians, which was found by the French archaeologists in 1893 when they were excavating, and may be seen at Delphi to-day. It is in the form of a small Doric temple of Pentelic marble, 33 feet by 20, severe in style, but delicately beautiful.[1] The external sculptures, known as metopes, thirty in number, representing the exploits of Heracles and Theseus, and the battle of the gods and giants, remain in good condition.

A yet more intimate memorial stands to this day on the battle-field itself, the Soros, or sepulchral mound, built, as Pausanias informs us, over the bodies of the Athenians who fell in the battle and, as a mark of special honour, were buried on the field itself. " In the plain," he writes, " is the grave of the Athenians, and over it are the tomb-stones with the names of the fallen arranged

---

[1] M. Homolle, the discoverer, says of this shrine : " I hope that I do not exaggerate in describing it as a masterpiece of archaic art. I know no monument among the works of the beginning of the fifth century, of which the execution is more sharp, delicate and elegant. The sculptures have the same qualities of grace and precision. Their archaic severity is tempered by a softness of modelling rare in works of this date and by a richness that both surprises and charms us."

according to tribes. There is another grave for the Boeotians of Plataea and the slaves : for slaves fought then for the first time. There is a separate tomb of Miltiades, son of Cimon. . . . Here every night you may hear horses neighing and men fighting. To go on purpose to see the sight never brought good to any man ; but with him who unwittingly lights upon it by accident the spirits are not angry." [1] Of the tombs of the Plataeans, of the Athenian slaves, and of Miltiades, no traces are now found : only the Soros stands out of the spacious expanse of the plain, as you enter it from the coast-road, the only conspicuous object within view. It is a pleasant drive from Athens in the springtime and not an impossible day's walk, especially if you get the railway as far as Jerakas. The Soros helps greatly in determining the topography of the fight, since it is reasonable to suppose that it marks the scene of the actual fighting, possibly as Macan suggests, the very spot where the Athenian centre was broken and where the victorious wings wheeled together to win the fight.

The Plain of Marathon.—Coming by the coast-road, you enter the plain of Marathon along the edge of the Southern or Little Marsh, where the chief slaughter of the Persians took place as represented in the picture of Panaenus. The length of the plain along the coast, from the Little Marsh to the promontory of Cynosura, is just five miles. Two miles from the marsh it is divided in two by a water-course, or ' Charadra,' beyond which it extends another mile to the Great Marsh. This greater marsh stretches two miles further, leaving a narrow fringe of sandy ground along the coast. The Soros is just halfway between the Little Marsh and the Charadra in the southern half of the plain, and roughly halfway between the mountains and the sea. It is somewhat more than a mile from the high ground about Vrana where the Athenians lay, and somewhat less than a mile from the shore and the Persian ships. The plain to-day

---

[1] *Pausanias*, i. 32. 3 ; Frazer, vol. i. p. 49.

MARATHON FROM THE SOROS.

Looking N.W. towards the modern Marathóna and showing the olive trees and cultivated land in the plain : the asphodel flowers in the foreground are at the foot of the Soros.

From a photograph by Miss G. Crewdson.

is thick with corn in springtime, and part of the ground on which Greeks and Persians fought is covered with vineyards interspersed with olives. The flashing spearpoints as the Athenian lines charged down the slope must have been a splendid spectacle, the front lines of spears levelled, the rear lines held in air. Eight deep was the ordinary formation, and as this depth was lessened in the centre, this gives a front, probably, of fifteen hundred spears. It was no easy feat for these long lines of spearmen to advance at a quick pace for nearly a mile ; any disorder would have been fatal, and it was only discipline and steadiness which could maintain the formation over such a distance. The impressiveness of the charge of a mass of Greek hoplites is well illustrated by Xenophon's story of the review at which Cyrus's Ten Thousand Greeks (a century later) delivered a mock charge upon Persian troops and spectators, with the result that all present fled in panic dismay. At Marathon, however, the Persians stood their ground firmly enough, as is proved by their breaking the Athenian centre ; the final victory of the Athenians was due to hard fighting, to the superiority of Greek arms and discipline, and to the wise dispositions made by the Athenian leaders.

Miltiades.—Tradition assigned the chief personal credit for the victory to Miltiades. Miltiades was no ordinary Athenian, but head of a noble family, one branch of which, the branch to which Miltiades himself belonged, had for two generations ruled over that Thracian Chersonese now for ever linked with our own race under its modern name Gallipoli. When the systematic reduction of the Greek cities on the Hellespont was taken in hand after the suppression of the Ionian Revolt, Miltiades, son of Cimon, then the reigning prince, had put his treasure on shipboard and escaped to Athens. There he was admitted back to citizenship, and in the year of Marathon was elected Strategus by his tribe. The plan of battle, as well as the resolve to fight, if possible, at Marathon, was probably due to his genius, and Miltiades is rightly regarded as in a special sense the victor of Marathon.[1]

The Glory of Marathon.—The men who fought at Marathon were ever after held in high honour at Athens. The poet Aeschylus, who charged with the men of his tribe there, and whose brother was that other son of Euphorion (Cynegeirus) whom Herodotus immortalizes (p. 290), had this fact recorded in his epitaph, not his fame as a dramatist.[2] Marathon became for Athens the great memory of her history, the unique glory that was all her own. For in this glory no other Hellenic state had part save only little Plataea. It became a stock subject for her poets and orators. It was looked back to as a great and signal victory in which Athens in defence of Hellas overthrew the whole might of Persia. That on the face of it was an exaggeration; but deeply considered was not very far from the truth. For the civilization of Greece and the whole future of Europe really hung on the valour and discipline of the men of Athens that day. Not only for Athens and Greece may it be said, but for all Europe and for ourselves to-day, that " an halo of renown for ever hovers over the scene at Marathon, an undying interest belongs to the traditions associated with the name." [3] " The victory of Marathon was not only the first defeat of the Persians on Hellenic ground, but it saved Athens; and by saving Athens it saved Greece. For this reason it deserves a place among the great and decisive battles of the world." [4]

[1] The end of Miltiades was in painful contrast with the splendour of his services to Athens. After Marathon he was for a time a popular hero; but about a year later he was put on trial at Athens for deceiving the people and subjected to a heavy fine. This was because an expedition against the island of Paros (which had helped the Persians), undertaken on Miltiades' initiative, had failed disastrously. His son Cimon paid the fine; Miltiades himself died through the mortification of a wound incurred in the attack on Paros.

[2] The epitaph, turned into English prose, is as follows : " Aeschylus, son of Euphorion, the Athenian, this monument hides, who died in wheat-bearing Gela ; but of his approved valour the Marathonian grove may tell, and the deep-haired Mede who knew it " (Mackail).

[3] Macan's *Herodotus*, vol. ii. Appendix X. p. 149.

[4] Evelyn Abbott, *History of Greece*, Pt. II. p. 93.

Note on Pheidippides.

There was a sequel to Pheidippides' feat of endurance. Browning in his poem makes Pheidippides himself tell the story of his great race, and receive praise from Miltiades and promise of reward. Pheidippides fought at Marathon in the ranks of the Athenian hoplites. Then after the battle he ran once more to carry the news of victory to Athens. There arrived he cried once, " All hail! Victory is ours," and straightway fell down dead.

" So is Pheidippides happy for ever,—the noble strong man
 Who could race like a God, bear the face of a God, whom a
  God loved so well ;
 He saw the land saved he had helped to save, and was suffered
  to tell
 Such tidings, yet never decline, but, gloriously as he began,
 So to end gloriously—once to shout, thereafter be mute :
 ' Athens is saved!' Pheidippides dies in the shout for his
  meed."

CHAPTER XIII

THERMOPYLAE

"It was a desperate risk ; but there was just a possibility that by detaching half his force to stop the encircling body of the foe in the difficult path which they were travelling, he might still be able to maintain the pass."

GRUNDY, *The Great Persian War*, p. 316.

THE expedition of Datis and Artaphernes against Athens had miscarried through the valour of the Athenian spearmen at Marathon. But Darius was not one to be easily turned aside from his purposes. He was an able and enlightened ruler as well as an oriental despot. He has been called, not without reason, " the greatest Oriental that ever ruled in Western Asia." [1] He had good cause for anger against the Athenians for their interposition in the affairs of Asia Minor, and considerations of general policy required that the free Greeks on the other side of the Aegean should be compelled to own allegiance to the power of Persia, if they would not yield it voluntarily. The reverse to the Persian arms at Marathon merely supplied a new stimulus to action. Darius was, therefore, very far from relinquishing his schemes of punishment and conquest, and immediately began preparations for an expedition on a vaster scale. " Straightway," writes Herodotus, " he sent messengers throughout the empire with orders for the levying of forces, making the requisition from each province far more than before ; for warships also and horses and supplies and

[1] Grundy, *The Great Persian War*, p. 201.

transports." [1] Asia was in commotion, he says, by the space of three years. Then Egypt revolted. The Egyptians writhed always under a domination which outraged their religious feelings, and doubtless the fame of Marathon had reached them. This new crossing of his will, however, only fixed Darius more firmly in his resolves ; he was impatient to lead his armies in person both against the revolted Egyptians and against Hellas. But in the midst of his impatience death intervened. Darius the king died, and Xerxes, his son, reigned in his stead. This was in 485. Xerxes was the son of Darius' most royal consort, Atossa, daughter of Cyrus, founder of Persian greatness ; and with the throne Xerxes inherited, whether he would or not, his father's purposes and policy. He dealt first with Egypt. Within a year the rebellion was crushed, and Egypt lay prostrate in a servitude even more oppressive than before. Xerxes was free to concentrate all the resources of the Persian Empire on the conquest and humiliation of Hellas. How vast were those resources, how seemingly out of all proportion to the vigorous, but relatively petty, little Greek commonwealths, which had never yet combined effectively in a confederacy—unless it were in the Trojan War—may quickly be realized by observing that the Hellas of 480 B.C. covered no greater extent of territory than the Hellenic kingdom of to-day ; while Xerxes' dominions extended from what was then, and is now, Macedonia to the borders of India. The Persian Empire included, besides most of what till recently was Turkey in Europe— Asia Minor, Armenia, Persia, Mesopotamia, Afghanistan, Arabia, Syria, Palestine and Egypt. The Greeks with their training in athletic discipline, their heavy body armour, their strong spears and great shields, and their habit of fighting in ordered ranks, not each singly for his own hand, might be able to overthrow more than equal numbers of eastern troops with their unprotected bodies and lighter weapons and undisciplined way of fighting ; but what chance could their whole military

[1] Herodotus, vii. 1.

strength have against the countless myriads Xerxes
would lead against them from half Asia, supported by
the boundless wealth and vast mechanical resources
which the Great King could command. They must
surely be overborne and trampled under foot by the
sheer weight of Xerxes' marching hordes. So it seemed
to ordinary judgment in those days. No wonder there
was alarm and dismay amongst the free states of Hellas,
when the extent of the preparations being made against
them, in all the countries subject to Persia beyond the
Aegean, became known. No wonder, indeed, if before
Marathon, when Darius had sent envoys to demand
earth and water, Aegina and many another little state
had thought it prudent to comply.

Xerxes' Plans for the Invasion of Greece.—At the
Persian court the influence of Mardonius, who had led
Darius' armies into Thrace in 492, was now in the ascend-
ant, and the plan for invading Hellas overland through
Macedonia was taken up again. It involved a long
march for the army, even from the European side of the
Dardanelles, and without taking account of the difficulty
of getting vast bodies of troops across from Asia into
Europe ; a march through the peninsula of Gallipoli and
round the whole coast of Thrace and Macedonia by
Dedeagatch and Kavala and Saloniki (to recall names
familiar through the warfare of our own time), but, on
the other hand, this march would now be through friendly
territory right up to the mountain barriers between
Macedonia and Thessaly. For the Persian Empire, since
the Macedonians accepted a state of vassalage to Persia,
actually marched with Hellas, and it was only on passing
out of Macedonia into Thessaly that opposition had to
be reckoned with. Xerxes was much in the position of
Turkey in the war of 1897. There was even ground for
expecting there would be little or no resistance in penetrating the passes into Thessaly. Had not the princely
house of the Aleuadae, whose seat was Larissa, and who
aspired to rule all Thessaly and hoped to realize their
ambition with Persian help, repeatedly urged Xerxes in

pressing terms to undertake this expedition into Greece and promised their assistance ?

Preparations for the Great Expedition.—As soon as the reconquest of Egypt was completed, preparations were begun by Xerxes for an expedition on an even greater scale than that designed by Darius, his father. A vast army, made up of the choicest Persian troops and of picked contingents from every part of the empire, was to assemble in the interior of Asia Minor and march to the Hellespont : a great navy, formed of the fleets of the Great King's maritime subjects—Phoenician, Egyptian, Cilician, Asiatic Greek—was to meet the army there. From the Hellespont army and navy were to advance along the coast, keeping as far as possible in touch and acting in close cooperation. To facilitate this twofold advance by sea and land, the most lavish efforts were put forth. Roads were made, rivers bridged, harbours improved and immense quantities of stores accumulated at depots, of which Herodotus names the chief. Herodotus records further how in his own day the traveller came upon stretches of Xerxes' military roads in the wilds of Thrace ; the rude tribesmen, though they had little use for roads, looked upon them with awe as evidences of powers beyond their understanding, and refrained from driving their ploughs through them.[1] Two works in particular made a specially strong impression on the imagination of the Greeks as examples of the almost superhuman power of the Great King—which, nevertheless, free Hellas faced and overthrew. One was the Athos Canal, the other the bridging of the Hellespont. The object of the Canal was to prevent the possibility of another disaster like that which befell the fleet of Mardonius in 492. A canal was dug through the isthmus which joins the promontory of Acte to the district of Chalcidice, so that the fleet might sail through and altogether avoid the dangerous voyage round Athos. The bridging of the Hellespont was to enable the armies of Xerxes to march out of Asia into Europe by road, without the necessity of conveyance across the water by

[1] Herodotus, vii. 115.

boat. These great works were undertaken and carried out between 484 and 481. Herodotus has given a vivid description of each. His account of the cutting of the canal is as follows.

The Athos Canal.—" Triremes were moored at Elaeus in the Chersonese,[1] and thence as a base the digging was carried on by detachments of all the nations of the army, working under the lash ; and these detachments were relieved at intervals ; and the people who lived about Mount Athos also helped in the work. . . . Athos is a great and famous mountain, reaching out into the sea, and inhabited. Where the mountain ends on the landward side it forms a peninsula ; and the isthmus is about twelve furlongs across ; and here the whole extent of country from the sea of the Acanthians to the sea on the side of Torone is level plain except for a few low hills. . . ."

" Now this is how the barbarians dug the canal. They divided the whole distance into sections by nations and drew their line past the city of Sane. When the cutting grew deep, some stood at the bottom and dug, others received the earth as it was dug out and handed it up to others who stood on ladders ; these in turn passed it to others, till it reached the men at the top, who carried it out and threw it away. All the workers, except only the Phoenicians, had double trouble through the breaking away of the steep sides. This was the natural consequence of their making the top and the bottom of the cutting the same breadth. The Phoenicians showed their cleverness in this as in all that they do. On the section which fell to their lot, they made the top of the cutting double the breadth required for the canal, and gradually contracted the sides as the work advanced, so that when they got to the bottom the breadth of their section just equalled that of the rest." [2]

---

[1] Elaeus was just inside the Dardanelles, a little east of Cape Helles

[2] Herodotus, vii. 22 and 23. It is difficult to believe that those in charge of this canal-making, even if they were using unskilled labour really showed such a lack of intelligence as to begin by making perpendicular cuttings in the way Herodotus describes ; but his accoun

A succession of ponds " from two to eight feet deep, and from sixty to ninety broad " marks to this day the line of Xerxes' Canal, and can be traced almost from sea to sea. The soil is sandy, as Herodotus' account brings out, so it is not surprising that in the course of over two thousand years the cutting has been largely filled in, especially about the outlets at either end, which had originally been protected by breakwaters to prevent their being silted up. The distance across the isthmus from sea to sea is 2500 yards, which corresponds closely to Herodotus' estimate of twelve Greek stades, as a stade equals roughly 200 yards. Most of the ground is level plain, the surface nowhere rising to a height of more than fifty feet above sea-level. So apart from the sandy nature of the soil the work presented little difficulty and was well worth undertaking; for the Greek boatmen still dread the currents round Mount Athos, which are variable and uncertain, and the gales and high seas off its rocks. If the canal could be opened again it would be greatly to the advantage of local navigation.

The Bridging of the Dardanelles.—Xerxes' famous bridges—there were two of them—from Asia to Europe across the Hellespont have a new and poignant interest for us now. For they stretched from Abydos to Sestos; and the site of Abydos is close to Nagara Point, three miles above the forts of Chanak and Kilid Bahr, where the attempt to force the ' Narrows ' was made by our battleships in March 1915. The scene of Xerxes' feat of bridging the Dardanelles in the fifth century B.C. was one day to shake to the thunder of the guns of the *Queen Elizabeth* fired from across the Chersonese. It is not altogether easy to understand Herodotus' account of the construction of the bridges. He records that one was the work of Phoenician engineers and the other of Egyptian; and that the bridges first built were swept away by a storm. For this ill success the overseers of the work paid forfeit with their lives. Then orders were

at all events bears witness to the respect which popular belief paid to the technical skill of the Phoenicians.

given for a second attempt, and this time it was successful.
The distance, as stated by Herodotus, was seven furlongs ;
but by actual measurement now the Hellespont is nowhere quite so narrow as this. It is possible that the
channel has widened through the force of the current.
Across this distance, now some 2600 yards, a great number
of vessels were moored, triremes and penteconters,
anchored stem and stern and lying head on to the current,
which—as we know from our difficulties in 1915—runs
strongly.[1] There were 360 vessels in one bridge and 314
in the other, which seems to imply that the bridges were
of different lengths and crossed, not side by side, but at
an angle one to the other. Over these vessels strong
cables were extended as a foundation for the actual
roadway, six for each bridge. Planks were laid down
upon these cables over the whole length, side by side.
The planks were covered with brushwood and earth, and
the whole was stamped into a firm surface. Then to
complete the work a parapet was raised on either side
to a height sufficient to prevent the baggage animals
seeing the water and taking alarm. What is difficult to
understand is how cables of the length and weight described were swung and how they supported the bridge.
Herodotus records that pieces of these cables were afterwards taken to Athens as a trophy, and that one cubit's
length (18 inches) of one of the cables weighed a talent,
that is, about eighty pounds !

The Great King's Hosts.—The Greeks afterwards
boasted that forty-six nations had marched with Xerxes
to invade them ; and Herodotus gives a list of tribes

[1] " The strength of the current, which is variable, depends much
upon the direction and force of the wind, and, as will be easily understood, upon the heavy rains and snows of winter, which swell the large
rivers falling into the Black Sea. At that time, when it blows hard
from the northward, the violence of the current increases, especially
in the narrows, where it has been known to attain during the first few
days a rate of 5 knots between the old castles (Chanak Kalessi and
Kilid Bahr). . . . From Gallipoli to Kum Kaleh, the average strength
of the current may be estimated at 1½ knots for the whole distance.
Quoted from the " Black Sea Pilot " on pp. 359 and 360 of Leaf's
Troy.

and peoples, who took part in the great march overland,
not far short of this number. But most of the names
in Herodotus' list have little meaning for us. We get a
better idea of the disproportion between the sides in this
great struggle from the map. Greece from the borders
of Macedonia to the southernmost point of the Morea
looks small compared with Asia Minor, and Asia Minor
was but a small part of the vast territories of the Great
King in Asia. The utmost length of Hellas from north
to south was 250 miles, and the breadth of continental
Hellas is nowhere greater than 180 miles. Asia Minor
extends for 600 miles from the coast of Ionia to the
Euphrates. From the Euphrates to Susa, the capital of
the Persian Empire, was 700 miles more, and from Susa
the sway of the kings of Persia extended 1200 miles
further to the Indus, making a total distance of 2500
miles from the shores of the Aegean. From south to
north the Persian Empire reached from the Red Sea and
the Persian Gulf to the Euxine and the Caspian. And
besides all these Asiatic dominions, in Europe Persian
sovereignty was acknowledged in Thrace and Macedonia,
that is, roughly over the territories that made up Turkey
in Europe before the liberation of the Balkans in the
second half of the nineteenth century. In Egypt and
Asia Minor and Mesopotamia the Persian Empire included
the wealthiest and most fertile countries of the ancient
world. To form Xerxes' great armies of invasion troops
were recruited from all the inland nations, and to make
up his navy all the maritime territories were placed under
contribution. Every part of the empire was required to
furnish its quota according to its capability and natural
resources. " Some furnished ships ; some had to supply
infantry ; from others requisition was made for cavalry ;
some in addition to personal service must contribute
horse-transports ; others vessels for the bridges ; others
again provisions and ships." [1] The best and bravest in
every province were enrolled for military service. Emulation was excited by the offer of prizes for the best

[1] Herodotus, vii. 21.

I   U

equipped contingent of troops and the finest naval squadron. What importance was attached to personal service in the field by the Great King is shown by the story which Herodotus tells of Pythius the Lydian. This man was the wealthiest of all the subjects of the Great King, and when Xerxes on his march from Susa to Sardis passed through the city where Pythius lived, Pythius not only entertained Xerxes and Xerxes' army magnificently, but offered besides to give the king the whole of his wealth in gold and silver towards the expenses of the war, a sum calculated to amount to the value of five million pounds in our money, all but a few thousands. Xerxes was greatly pleased, and not only declared that Pythius should be enrolled in the number of the king's friends, but gave him also a substantial sum in gold to make up his five millions. A little later, when Xerxes was about to cross from Abydos into Europe, Pythius begged as a boon that the eldest of his five sons, all of whom were serving in the king's army, might be allowed to stay behind with his father. Xerxes was so indignant that, in spite of his former favour towards Pythius, he gave orders that this son should be sought out, arrested and cut in two, and that the two halves of his body should be placed, one on the right and the other on the left of the road by which the army was to march. And that was how the Great King's hosts marched out of Sardis.

The March from Sardis.—Sardis had been appointed to be the general place of assembly for the army, and thither in the spring of 480 B.C. Xerxes marched from Persia with the royal troops. By that time the troops from the eastern frontiers of the empire, from what is now the North-West Frontier Province of British India and the Punjab, had already come half across Asia, a distance of 2500 miles, and from Persia itself the march had been more than 1200. Other contingents came from other provinces. Herodotus estimates the total mass of fighting men that ultimately marched through Europe against Greece at upwards of two millions, and he calculated that the camp followers of all kinds were as many again. This is an impossible total, but there can be no doubt that the actual number was very great, and that Herodotus is justified in affirming that no other expedition up to his day had been on anything like the same scale. " What nation was there," he asks, " which Xerxes did not lead out of Asia against Greece ? What stream was there, whose waters did not fail—save only the big rivers —when his armies drank them ? " [1]

Ilium—Abydos and the Crossing into Europe.—On the march northward to Abydos, when the army passed through the Trojan plain, Xerxes visited the citadel of Ilium and offered a sacrifice of a thousand oxen to Athena. At Abydos, before crossing by the bridges into Europe, he held a review of his army and also of the fleet, which by this time had advanced to the entrance of the Dardanelles. The crossing took, Herodotus tells us, seven days and seven nights without pause. The fighting forces, infantry and cavalry, passed over by one bridge, the transport and camp-followers by the other. The Ten Thousand picked Persian guardsmen, called ' The Immortals,' led the way, crowned with garlands. On crossing to Sestos, the army was beneath Sari Bair and only ten miles from Suvla Bay. The head of the column turned right and traversed the length of the peninsula through the lines of Bulair ; then turned left and followed round the coast of Thrace, which in the Great War was Bulgarian territory. At Doriscus, some sixty miles along this coast, near the mouth of the Hebrus (Maritza), there was a great plain, and here after another review (according to Herodotus) the great army was numbered. The infantry, Herodotus states, were found to amount to 1,700,000. This total was reached by a curiously rough and ready expedient. A space was marked off which just held ten thousand men and was enclosed by a low wall. This space was then filled in succession with fresh troops, and the total calculated from the number of times it was filled and emptied. From Doriscus the army

[1] Herodotus, vii. 21.

marched on round the coast of Thrace under Mount Pangaeum (famous for its gold mines), passing the site of the modern Kavala, and crossed the Strymon (now the Karasu) at a place called ' Nine Ways,' near where the Athenians afterwards founded Amphipolis and not far from the town of Myrcinus which Histiaeus fortified. They then struck across the base of the peninsula of Chalcidice, reaching the sea again in the neighbourhood of Therma, which occupied the site of the city familiar to us as Saloniki, the true Greek name being Thessalonica. Here they were within sight of the great mountain barrier which separates Macedonia from Thessaly. From Saloniki, Mount Olympus, the home of the Olympian gods, is plainly visible, soaring to the height of 10,000 feet ; and Mount Ossa on the further side of the Peneus can also be discerned on a clear day at a distance of seventy miles. At Therma the army halted for some days ; for here they had reached the limits of the territories which owed obedience to Persia, and it was now to be put to the proof whether the passage into Thessaly would be opposed.

The Problem of Resistance.—At first the Greeks had planned to hold the pass which led down into the Thessalian plain by the gorges of Mount Olympus through the famous valley of Tempe. The preparations which had been going on throughout the Persian Empire had been known so long beforehand that they had had ample time to concert their means of defence. This time, at all events, there could be no doubt regarding the object of the expedition. It was plainly for the subjugation of all Hellas. Each free Hellenic community, small or great, had therefore now to make choice whether it would accept servitude to the Great King—gilded servitude it might be, yet servitude—or fight to preserve its liberties. Again, as in the time before Marathon, envoys had come from across the Aegean to demand ' earth and water ' ; only this time they did not come to Sparta or Athens. For when Darius' envoys had come to Sparta in 492, they had been thrown into a well and told to take earth and water for themselves, and Athens was outside the pale because of the burning of Sardis. For Athens and Sparta there could be no looking back : their part had been taken once and for all to resist the domination of an eastern king. But for the other Greek communities the path of submission by a simple act of symbolic surrender was open and easy. For the Greeks who refused to surrender their freedom it was first of all necessary to ascertain who was sound, how many of the free Greek communities could be relied on to combine for the common defence. Sparta stepped naturally into her place as leader, and Athens now stood with her in close alliance. A conference was held in the autumn of 481, to which came delegates from all the states interested in the defence of Hellas. The League of the Peloponnese (X. 1, pp. 224 and 225) was expanded into a Pan-Hellenic League under Spartan presidency. It included nearly every city-state in the Peloponnesus and most of the peoples of Central Greece—Boeotians, Phocians and Locrians ; and, of course, Athens. Thessaly was doubtful, but on the whole inclined to espouse the national cause. For though the powerful clan of the Aleuadae had been forward at the Persian court in pressing the invasion, this policy was due to their own ambitions and had not the support of the body of the people.

A Pan-Hellenic Policy.—The Greek city-states were so used to acting independently on their own initiative, that it was only by a great effort and through strong external pressure that they could be got for a time to act together ; and they were further distracted by rivalries and jealousies; some were even openly at war one with another. The first measure of the conference, therefore, was to put an end to existing enmities, and especially to reconcile Athens and Aegina, between whom a state of war had subsisted for some five or six years. Secondly, spies were sent across the Aegean to bring back an accurate report of the forces gathering against Hellas. Thirdly, attempts were made to rally to the national defence Argos (the only important state in Peloponnesus which had failed to send representatives to the conference), and certain of the more considerable Greek polities outside the Hellenic peninsula. It was hoped that some of these latter might be far-seeing enough to recognize that by joining in the defence of the homeland they would be fighting their own battle. In this hope the confederated Greeks were disappointed : no effective help came to Hellas in her life and death struggle with Persia from any of the cities of greater Hellas.[1] But at all events the policy of the Pan-Hellenic conference was wise and statesmanlike : " the aim they had in view," writes Herodotus, " was that, if possible, the whole Greek nation should become one, and that all should work strenuously for the same ends, seeing that the dangers that were coming threatened all alike." [2] Could this ideal have been realized, the military strength of united Hellas, efficiently directed, might have sufficed to defend the land against all the myriads that Xerxes could bring out of Macedonia. But the difficulty was first to get any union at all ; and when that was surmounted, there still remained the difficulty of providing effectively for common action. The very defensibility of the land was a source of distraction. We saw in Chapter II. how lofty ranges of mountains cross the breadth of Hellas from west to east in successive lines, forming so many barriers to invasion from the north ; and how the Isthmus of Corinth is like a draw-bridge connecting and disconnecting Northern Greece and the Peloponnesus. The Peloponnese, we have said, may be regarded as the citadel of Hellas, with the highlands of Arcadia as the central keep. It was this natural strength of the Peloponnese, however, which made the chief weakness of the Pan-Hellenic union. The isthmus is only four miles broad, and the Peloponnese could be made impregnable—*overland*—by building a wall across it. North of the isthmus and on the further side of Attica the ranges of Parnes and Cithaeron made a barrier

---

[1] Potidaea, in Chalcidice, a colony from Corinth on the isthmus of the promontory of Pallene, was the one exception.

[2] Herodotus, vii. 145.

between Attica and Boeotia. Beyond Boeotia the route from the north is crossed, as we have seen, by three lines of mountains, one on each side of the Thessalian plain : the great range which terminates in Mount Olympus to the north of Thessaly, Mount Othrys on the south ; and between the valley of the Spercheus and the Boeotian lowlands the continuous chain of rugged mountain masses which stretches right across Central Hellas from the west and reaches to the very margin of the sea in Malis. Of these four possible lines of defence, two, the lines of Othrys and Cithaeron, are not specially formidable ; they cannot readily be closed completely. The other two, the frontier range of Olympus and Mount Oeta in Malis were extremely strong—Mount Olympus because of the great height and mass of the range of which it is the eastern termination ; Mount Oeta because of the completeness with which the wall of mountains blocks the whole breadth of the land, leaving only a narrow roadway between high cliffs and the sea. The direct way for the invader from Macedonia into Thessaly was through the Pass of Tempe ; the way through Oeta into Boeotia was by the Pass of Thermopylae. Either of these passes could be readily held by a small force against a multitude.

Divided Counsels.—But the interests of all the members of the League were not identical ; and, in particular, there was sharp divergence between the interests of the Peloponnesians and the Hellenes outside Peloponnesus. The Peloponnesians fancied themselves secure in their citadel of the Peloponnese if only the isthmus were strongly held. It seemed practicable to build a wall across it from sea to sea which should prove an impassable barrier. But this was to ignore the interests of the Hellenes outside Peloponnesus ; first of Megara and Athens, and then, further to the north, the Boeotians, Phocians, Locrians and Malians. Finally, there was the question of Thessaly, the land first threatened by the Persian advance.

The Invasion by Sea.—So much for land defence. But

the practical question for the Hellenes, and not least for the Peloponnesians, was seriously complicated by the twofold character of the threatened attack, by sea as well as by land. Each of the positions distinguished above could be turned in succession if Xerxes was master of the sea. Obviously it was quite futile to build a wall across the Isthmus of Corinth if the Persian fleet was free to effect a landing in force anywhere round the coasts of Peloponnese. It was imperative from the first to take account of the double invasion by land and sea. The result of these perplexities was, that when the spring of 480 came and Xerxes' forces were already preparing to cross from Asia into Europe by the bridges the Great King had built, no definite plan of action had been agreed upon, but forces had been gathered at the isthmus and a second conference was being held there.

Embassy of the Thessalians.—Then it was that envoys came from Thessaly and said (so Herodotus relates): " Men of Hellas, we must guard the pass of Mount Olympus, in order that Thessaly and the whole of Hellas may be safe from invasion. Now we are ready to help in guarding it, but you too must send forces in strength ; because ye must know that, if ye fail to send them, we shall make our terms with the Persian. It is not meet that we, who by our position are exposed to the first attack, should be left unsupported and perish on your behalf." [1] The demand was fair enough, and was met by the despatch of a force of 10,000 hoplites to Thessaly. This force was conveyed by sea through the straits of the Euripus to the Pagasaean Gulf in the south of Thessaly (Gulf of Volo) and landed at the port of Halus. Thence they marched across Thessaly and down the valley of the Peneus with a view to holding the Pass of Tempe against Xerxes.

The Pass of Tempe.—The Pass of Tempe is the long rift between the precipices of Olympus and Ossa, by which the many rivers of the Thessalian plain, united in

[1] Herodotus, vii. 172.

the deep and broad stream of the Peneus, force their way to the sea. It is a mountain valley, four and a half miles long, so narrow in places that there is barely room for a roadway on one side of the river under steep cliffs. This defile is, moreover, so delightful to the eye from the contrast of the tall grey cliffs—some of them 1500 feet high—and the rich green vegetation below, and the plane trees which overhang the river, that it was famed in all antiquity for its beauty. It was now to be determined whether it was to become still more famous as the place where the Greeks made their great fight in defence of their freedom. As they marched down the valley of the Peneus the Greeks had about them scenes of mingled sublimity and beauty. " No view," wrote Colonel Leake, first of Englishmen to explore Greece in modern days, " can present a closer and more pleasing contrast of the sublime and terrific with the tranquil and beautiful ; the former represented by the precipices of Ossa and Olympus, the latter by the winding river and the villages of the valley, reposing amidst gardens, meadows, cornfields, scattered trees, and detached groves of oak and ilex." [1] The nearest and easiest way into Thessaly from the Macedonian coast is by this pass. For lofty highlands fill all the interior of the country westward, but leave a strip of comparatively level plain all down the coast. The road by which the Persians might be expected to advance lay through this level country, crossed the Peneus very near its mouth, then turned up into the Pass of Tempe. All Macedonia west of this was a wilderness of mighty mountains. It was confidently assumed that Xerxes would come this way ; and then along the narrow road overhanging the waters of the Peneus, where his cavalry would be useless, he could be met and stopped. But a few days after the Pan-Hellenic force had entered the Vale of Tempe, their commanders received information that there were other passes more to the west through which the Persians might come. Upon this they withdrew from Tempe, marched back to Halus and

[1] Leake, *Northern Greece*, iii. p. 385.

re-embarked for the isthmus. This at least is the opinion of Herodotus regarding the reason of the abandonment of the defence of Thessaly. There are indications, however, in his narrative that there were other reasons. It is clear that there were two parties among the Thessalians ; for we are told that the Aleuadae had actually pressed Xerxes to undertake this expedition. It seems unlikely, to say the least of it, that the Greeks should have been ignorant of the existence of other passes between Thessaly and Macedonia besides that of Tempe and the possibility of the Persians using them, or that it should have been thought impossible to hold these passes also with the support of the full fighting strength of the Thessalians. It is probable that the real reason for the abandonment of the line of Tempe was the want of any assurance of this support. If the Thessalian people were disunited, and could not be relied upon to fight with all their strength, the defence of Thessaly became impracticable, and there was nothing for it but to withdraw. All that we know certainly, however, is the fact of the brief occupation of the Pass of Tempe by a Pan-Hellenic force of ten thousand hoplites, and the fact of its withdrawal ; that as soon as the hoplites were gone the Thessalians lost no time in making terms with Xerxes, and that they were his good allies for the rest of the war. All this took place about the time when Xerxes was crossing from Abydos into Europe. The first plan of defence—to keep the invader out of Thessaly—had ended in fiasco.

Further Deliberations at the Isthmus.—The question where to make a stand had, therefore, to be decided anew. Othrys, the line of mountains which bounds the plain of Thessaly on the south, does not seem ever to have been thought of ; this range of hills, though lofty, offered no special advantages for defence. It was otherwise with the Pass of Thermopylae, which has been called ' the key of Greece.' Beyond the slopes of Othrys a wide plain opens out, through which flows the Spercheus. Beyond the Spercheus masses of mountains rise again, extending right across from Aetolia in the west and

eaching to the eastern sea under the name of Oeta.
Here the Gulf of Malis curves into the plain from the
channel which separates the north-western end of Euboea
from the south-west of Thessaly, and here two thousand
years ago, at two points some three miles apart, the
waters of the gulf almost lapped unscaleable rocks,
leaving only a narrow road, like a causeway, between
the cliffs and the sea ; while at a third point, halfway
between, the space from cliff to sea was similarly narrowed,
close to some hot springs from which Thermopylae took

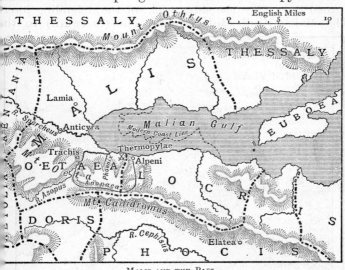

MALIS AND THE PASS.

name.[1] Through this pass led the highway from
Thessaly into Greece, and by this road an invader must
come. Thermopylae was the most favourable point at
which to try and stop him. The road was on the level,
it was true, so the defenders had no advantage of higher
ground, but the extreme narrowness of the passage at
three points, with precipitous mountains rising abruptly
on one hand and the sea lapping the road on the other,

[1] Thermo-pylae = Hot-Gates.

made it a place where a small body of men might confidently expect to hold in check an army many times
more numerous.

Artemisium.—Thermopylae had another great advantage for the Greek defence : it was close to the sea. It
was so close that just 200 years later (in B.C. 279), when
a swarm of half-savage Celts were trying to fight their
way through to the plunder of Greece, Athenian ships
steered close in and showered missiles upon the barbarians ; and when the pass was turned—as Xerxes
turned it in 480—the ships took off the defending force.
The Malian Gulf leads straight out (eastward) to the

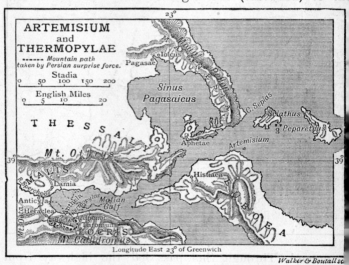

ARTEMISIUM
and
THERMOPYLAE
------ Mountain path
taken by Persian surprise force.
Stadia
0   50   100   150   200
English Miles
0   5   10   20

T H E S S A L Y

Mt. O l y m p u s

Iolcus
Pagasae
Sinus
Pagasaicus

C. Sepias
Sciathus
Peparethus

Aphetae
Artemisium

Histaea

E U B O E A

Lamia
Anticyra
Heraclea
Thermopylae
Malian
Gulf
Thronium
L O C R I S
Mt. Callidromus

39°   39°

Longitude East 23° of Greenwich

Walker & Boutall sc.

halberd-shaped end of the long island of Euboea. This
northern projection of Euboea faces the curious hook of
land in which the Thessalian coast district Magnesia ends.
The two shores are separated by a prolongation of the
channel from the Malian Gulf, which leads one way into
the Pagasaean Bay (Gulf of Volo) and another way out
into the Aegean. At the extreme northern corner of

Euboea is Artemisium, a promontory, named after a temple of Artemis there. It was an integral part of the Greek plan of defence that, while a Greek force blocked the advance of the Persian army through Thermopylae, the Greek fleet should meet and fight the Persian navies at Artemisium. The position at Artemisium, it may be seen from the map, was most convenient for the purpose. It covers the entrance to the Malian Gulf, and therefore also the entrance to the Euripus to which the Malian Gulf leads. If the Persian fleet continued to follow the coast-line, as it had all along been doing, after coasting down Magnesia under the heights of Ossa and Pelium, it would be intercepted by the Greeks at Artemisium. At the same time Artemisium was near enough to Thermopylae for the effective maintenance of communications by means of fire-signals from the heights of Euboea. The actual distance is rather over fifty miles. So when it became known that Xerxes was already entering the passes from Macedonia into Thessaly, the fleet at once sailed from the isthmus to take up position at Artemisium, and a small force of Peloponnesians under the Spartan king Leonidas marched to Thermopylae as the advance-guard of a much larger force which was to hold the pass.

The Persians in Thessaly.—The plan of Xerxes was for systematically combined operations by land and sea. So when the army set forth from Saloniki to enter and pass through Thessaly (now accepted as the complaisant vassal of the Great King), orders were given to the fleet to wait eleven days : this was to give time for the march across Thessaly and the arrangements consequent on Thessalian submission. The king's doings in Thessaly included horse-racing, in which the Persian horses were matched against Thessalian, and the king's horses won. From Thessaly Xerxes passed by Halus, where the country retained the old national name of Achaea ; and so through the passes of Othrys into Malis and within sight of Thermopylae. After passing through Lamia and Anticyra, and crossing the Spercheus, Xerxes encamped under the cliffs of Oeta in the neighbourhood of Trachis, about

three miles from the entrance to the pass ; and then
waited four whole days in full expectation that the
defenders would surrender or retreat. For he had heard
in Thessaly how scanty their numbers were.

Sea-fight and Storm.—The fleet had by this time sailed
on from Therma round the Gulf of Saloniki, past the
mouth of the Peneus and the outlet of the Pass of Tempe
and down the coast regions of Thessaly, already referred
to as Magnesia. All the way it is a rocky inhospitable
shore dominated by the great heights of Ossa and Pelium
without harbours or convenient anchorage. The fleet
was making for Aphetae in the Gulf of Volo, where there
is comparative protection from wind and storm through
the queer hook-like projection in which the coast of
Magnesia ends. But the entrance to the gulf was too
far to reach in one day's voyage, so at night the fleet
had to make what they could of the harbourage afforded
by the few small sandy beaches, which here and there
break into ' this coast of rocks and cliffs.' The night
passed safely, but early next morning it began to blow
from the east and a violent gale came on. Large numbers
of ships, both ships-of-war and transports, were caught
on the sea and wrecked. There was a very great de
struction. Herodotus says that at least four hundred
ships were reputed to have been lost, together with a
multitude of men and vast treasure. The storm lasted
three days, and when it abated, the ships that had been
beached in safety were drawn down and the fleet sailed
on to its destination, Aphetae, on the hook at the mouth
of the Pagasaean Gulf. Aphetae was on the opposite
side of the straits leading into the Malian Gulf and only
about twenty miles from the station of the Greeks at
Artemisium. A squadron of fifteen Persian ships, which
had been late in starting, sailed by mistake into the midst
of the Greek fleet at Artemisium and were captured.

Encouraged by this piece of luck and still more by the
report which reached them of the damage which the
enemy's fleet had suffered off the Magnesian coast, the
Greek ships boldly sailed out late in the afternoon despite

great disparity in numbers and offered battle. In describing the fighting which ensued on this and the two following days between the Persians at Aphetae and the Greeks at Artemisium, we will follow closely the account which Herodotus gives us in his history.

The First Greek Attack.—The Persian commanders on reaching Aphetae were eager to bring on an action without delay, but they were so confident in their numbers that their one fear was lest the Greek fleet should escape them. Therefore, either now, or some time a little earlier, they detached a squadron of 200 ships to sail round Euboea and enter the narrow straits between the island and the mainland from the south. The Greek line of retreat from the Malian Gulf lay through these straits, the Euripus channel, and if a Persian squadron occupied the Narrows, the Greek fleet would be completely bottled up. The news of this movement, Herodotus relates, was brought to the Greek fleet by a diver named Scyllias, the most expert professional diver of his day. A story was current that Scyllias swam under water the whole way from Aphetae to Artemisium across the straits, a distance of seven miles ! This feat Herodotus does not credit, and gives it as his opinion that Scyllias, who was deserting to the Greeks, crossed in a boat ! Scyllias brought also report of the damage done by the storm, and it was this news which encouraged the Greeks to sail out to the attack late in the afternoon. Some of the Greeks in Xerxes' Ionian contingent have left on record the feelings of anxiety with which they saw the comparatively few ships of their countrymen surrounded by a swarm of warships, which not only outnumbered them, but also sailed lighter and better. To the Persian commanders the attack seemed little short of madness. But the foremost Greek ships executed a manœuvre known as ' the globe.' A number of ships at a given signal drew together in a circle with their sterns close together and the prows pointing outwards ; then at a second signal the ships dashed out and engaged the enemy. They fought with such success that day that thirty Persian ships were captured ; but night came on while the victory was still undecided, and both sides returned to their moorings.

The Hollows of Euboea.—That night a second storm arose with squalls of wind and rain and caught the two hundred Persian ships sailing round Euboea on the most dangerous part of the coast, deep bays on the south-east side of the island, a place known as the Hollows, and drove them on to the rocks. Not a ship escaped. The winds and waves were fighting for Hellas against the Persian navies, as they fought for England against the Spanish Armada. Something had now been done to reduce the inequality in point of numbers between the hostile fleets. Tidings of this fresh disaster to the enemy reached the Greeks next morning, and about the same time fifty-three fresh ships sailed up from Attica. That evening the Greeks sailed out again late as on the preceding day. There does not seem to have been a general engagement ; but they attacked the Cilician squadron separately and sank several vessels. These two days Herodotus expressly informs us correspond with two unsuccessful attacks made by picked Persian troops to storm the Pass of Thermopylae.[1]

Indecisive Action between the Fleets.—Next day, in accordance with Xerxes' general plan, the Persians attacked. The whole fleet sailed out of the Pagasaean Gulf in order of battle, ranged in the form of a great half moon. The object of this formation was to encircle the Greek fleet and prevent their escape when defeated. The Greeks, on their part, met them with no less confidence, and a hard-fought engagement followed in which neither side gained a decisive advantage. The Persian squadrons were to some extent obstructed by their very numbers and sometimes got in each other's way. The damaged ships and wreckage and the corpses of the slain came into the possession of the Greeks ; but their own losses in men and ships were severe, and though the losses of the Persian fleets were numerically greater, the Persians

[1] Below, p. 322.

could bear them better. The Athenians who had fought with conspicuous bravery suffered specially severely, more than half their ships being disabled.

Bad News from Thermopylae.—Next day there came news of disaster from Thermopylae, which caused the admirals to give orders for immediate retreat. It was the news of the total destruction of Leonidas and the forces with him in the pass. The news was brought by a special messenger, Abronychus the son of Lysicles, an Athenian, who had been stationed off the coast near the pass in a swift-rowing thirty-oared boat for the express purpose of carrying news in case of emergency. This news altered the situation completely. As long as Leonidas held the pass, the fleet was bound to maintain its position at Artemisium. For if it withdrew, the Persian fleet had but to sail into the Malian Gulf, and further defence of the Pass of Thermopylae became impossible. For the pass in that case was turned, and troops could be landed behind it. But as soon as the pass itself was forced, there was no good reason for the fleet to hold its ground longer at Artemisium. There was the strongest reason against retreat, so long as Thermopylae was defended; there was overwhelming reason for retreat when Leonidas and all his men lay dead in the pass.

The First Two Days' Fighting in the Pass.—What had happened at Thermopylae, though a catastrophe for the Hellenes in that summer of 480 B.C., has made Thermopylae a name glorious for ever in all the world. Let Herodotus tell the story, for his is the only detailed account that has come down to us, and he lived nearest to the time.

" Four days Xerxes let pass, in constant expectation that the enemy will run away. On the fifth, when they did not move, but appeared firmly resolved to stay—a course which seemed to him sheer folly and impudence —he grew angry and sent the Medes and Kissians against them, with orders to take them alive and bring them into his presence. When the Medes rushed to the attack, many fell, but more came on and refused to give ground altogether, though they suffered great losses. Then it was made plain for all to see, and not least the king himself, that, while his fighting men were many in number, few of them were of any account. The conflict went on all through that day. And when the Medes had suffered very rough treatment, they were presently withdrawn, and there came on in turn the Persians whom the King called his ' Immortals,' under the command of Hydarnes, in the belief that they would make short work of clearing the pass. But when they encountered the Greeks, they fared no better than the Median division, but met with the same ill success, inasmuch as they were fighting in a confined space and were using shorter spears, and were unable to get any advantage from their numbers. The Lacedaemonians on their part were fighting magnificently, and they showed in various ways that they were trained men fighting with untrained ; for instance, from time to time they turned their backs and took to flight, and the barbarians seeing this came on with outcry and clatter ; but the Spartans, when nearly overtaken, faced round and after wheeling about struck down the Persians in numbers beyond count. A few of the Spartans also fell here, but only a few. And when for all their efforts the Persians could not win the passage after trying attack by divisions and every sort of device, they withdrew whence they had come. The story goes that as the King watched these attacks, he thrice leapt from his seat, in terror for his army. Thus the struggle was fought that day ; and, on the morrow, the barbarians fought with no better success. Seeing the fewness of the Greeks, they fought on in the expectation that the defenders would be worn down by wounds and at length be no longer able to hold up their hands in fight. But the Hellenes were marshalled by companies and by tribes and sustained the fight, turn and turn about—except the Phocians : the Phocians had been posted on the heights, to guard the mountain-path." [1]

[1] Herodotus, vii. 210-212.

The Betrayal.—After the failure of the Immortals, even under the eye of their emperor (like the failure of the Prussian Guards at Ypres), Xerxes was ' in a great strait.' His invasion seemed about to be brought to nothing through the valour of a few thousand men in the narrow roadway between Mount Oeta and the sea. Then a man of the country, a Malian Greek named Ephialtes, was brought into the presence of the king. This man offered to lead a detachment of the Persians over the cliffs above the pass by a rough mountain track known to him. Xerxes was highly pleased, and at once despatched Hydarnes and the Immortals with orders to make their way round by this path under the guidance of Ephialtes, and take Leonidas in rear. This force set out in the evening twilight, crossed the Asopus, and began to ascend the narrow and precipitous gorge by which that river reaches the plain. They climbed on through the night and at break of dawn were near the top of the ridge. Now Leonidas on his arrival at Thermopylae had provided against the danger which now threatened by entrusting the safekeeping of this track to the Phocians, who, to the number of a thousand heavy-armed men had joined him and the forces from the Peloponnese for the defence of the pass. The Persians were now nearing the place where the Phocians were posted. The approach of the Persians, though hidden from sight by the oak-trees which grow thickly over these heights, had been revealed by the rustling of the fallen leaves—distinctly audible in the stillness of the dawn—as the assailants tramped over them. The Phocians sprang up and seized their arms ; almost at the same moment the leading Persians came into view. The Persians on their part were as surprised to see the Phocians as the Phocians were to see them. Hydarnes enquired of his guide if these men were Spartans. When he heard they were not, he straightway gave the order to attack. Had the Phocians behaved with ordinary courage, they should have held their post easily. For here were a thousand of them and the path was a rough and narrow mountain track. But instead of holding their ground steadily, the Phocians after enduring a few flights of arrows retreated precipitately to higher ground, where they prepared to sell their lives dearly, as if they were themselves the main object of attack. But the Persians, whose sole aim was to get through and down beyond the pass, took no further notice of the Phocians, but pressed on with all speed to descend beyond Thermopylae.

Leonidas' Choice.—Leonidas had already had warning the night before of the intended movement over Callidromus. As this eventuality had been provided for in his original dispositions by posting the thousand Phocians to bar the way through, this news would not have caused him any very acute disquietude. But at early dawn scouts arrived who reported that the Persians had got past the Phocians and might be expected to appear at Alpeni in rear of the pass in a few hours' time. This was very serious news and a council of war was hastily called, the result of which was that the greater part of the defending force marched away out of the pass; but Leonidas and his three hundred Spartans remained, and with them 700 Thespians and 400 Thebans—1400 men-at-arms in all. It was believed later that the other troops departed under Leonidas' orders, but that he held himself bound in honour to remain and kept with him his own Spartans and the Boeotian troops from Thebes and Thespiae. At all events, when the rest of the troops from the Peloponnese had withdrawn, this devoted band of 1400 men remained in the pass to defend it to the end.

The Last Fight in the Pass.—The story of that last fight must be told in Herodotus' own words :

" At sunrise Xerxes offered libations ; then waited and made his attack about the time of the filling of the market-place. These were Ephialtes' directions ; for the descent from the heights is more rapid and the distance shorter than the way round and the ascent. The barbarians under Xerxes' command came on, and the Greeks under Leonidas, thinking that they were sallying out to death now advanced much further than at first into the broader part of the pass. So far they had been holding the barrier of the wall, and during the preceding days they had advanced cautiously into the narrow portions of the pass and fought, but now they joined battle outside the narrow roadway ; and the barbarians fell in great numbers. Behind them their commanders, whip in hand, smote right and left to urge their men to the attack. Many of them fell into the sea and so perished, a yet greater number were trampled to death by their comrades : indeed no account was taken of their losses. Knowing the hour of their death was at hand from the troops who were getting round the mountains, the defenders used their strength to the utmost against the barbarians, reckless of their lives and in a frenzy of desperation. Now by this time the spears of the greater number had been broken, so they slew the Persians with their swords. And at this crisis of the struggle Leonidas fell after displaying supreme valour and with him fell many other famous Spartans, whose names I have ascertained by enquiry on account of their high worth : in fact I have learnt the names of all the three hundred. And among famous Persians who fell there in numbers were two sons of Darius, Abrokomes and Hyperanthes, born to Darius of Phratagune, daughter of Artanes. . . . There was a sharp struggle between Persians and Lacedaemonians over the body of Leonidas ; in the end the Hellenes by their valour rescued it and four times routed their foe. So the fight went on, till the troops with Ephialtes were at hand. When the Greeks heard that they had come, at once the conflict changed its character. For the Greeks withdrew once more into the narrowest part of the road, and, passing beyond the wall, took post in a body upon the hillock—all except the Thebans.[1] This hillock is in the pass, where now the marble lion stands in memory of Leonidas. In this position they defended themselves with their swords—those who still had them ; or with hands and teeth, and were at last

---

[1] The Thebans by Herodotus' account (vii. 233) took the first opportunity to surrender, and their lives were spared.

buried beneath the missiles which the barbarians hurled
at them from all sides, some attacking in front after
tearing down the defending wall, others getting round
and ringing them in." [1]   Such was the end of the Spartans
and the men of Thespiæ at Thermopylae.

Leonidas and the Oracle.—The devotion of Leonidas
and his companions has won imperishable glory for the
Spartan name and made Thermopylae a watchword of
valour for all time.   A belief was current later that, when
the invasion of Xerxes was impending, the Spartans sent
to Delphi to seek guidance from Apollo's shrine, and that
the answer they received, couched as usual in prophetic
verse, was this :

> " O ye who in wide-meadowed Sparta dwell,
> One of two woes for you my words foretell :
> Either your glorious town shall be laid low
> By the rude ravage of the Persian foe ;
> Or, to avert this evil, ye must mourn
> A king of Heracles' right lineage born.
> For not the strength of bulls, the lion's might
> Avail against his onset.   In this fight
> Heaven's hand is with him ; and he will not stay,
> Till he have made or town, or king, his prey."

It was affirmed that in accordance with this oracle
Leonidas deliberately sacrificed his life at Thermopylae
in order that Sparta and Hellas might be saved.   That
was the official Spartan version.   What the true facts
were, what were the motives which really actuated
Leonidas when he took his great resolve to stay and
defend the pass to the last, we can never know with
certainty.   Beyond the narrative of Herodotus (and we
do not even know from whom he got his information),
all is conjecture.   Conjecture is very tempting where so
much is left to the imagination, and the need of rational
explanation is so great.   Dr. Macan holds that Leonidas
fought what in the phraseology of modern war is a rear-
guard action to cover the retreat of his main forces.
Bury suggests that the larger force which left the pass

[1] Herodotus, vii. 223-225.
[2] Herodotus, vii. 220.

was sent to occupy a position " some distance east of the point where the mountain path descended to the road, so as to take Hydarnes in the rear " ; [1] but were themselves routed by ' the Immortals.' If it be lawful to speculate at all, the theory which has most probability is Grundy's—that Leonidas, to meet the double attack on the pass, did indeed divide his forces in two, and sent the larger part to meet Hydarnes and his detachment as they came down from the mountains, but that the Peloponnesians, instead of turning and standing as ordered when they reached the position outside the pass, marched on towards the Peloponnese and basely left Leonidas and those with him to their fate. This would have been a very bad betrayal, as bad as the treachery of Ephialtes. Yet even worse than this was the larger betrayal which the whole story proves—the betrayal of the forces with Leonidas by the Peloponnesian command. For if Leonidas with his eight or ten thousand troops (if they were as many) so nearly maintained the pass against all the odds, it is evident that a force more in keeping with the full military strength of the confederate Greeks must have been entirely successful. It was in expectation of speedy reinforcement that Leonidas came. On his first arrival, Herodotus tells us, he issued a proclamation that his present forces were merely the advance guard of the main army sent forward to hold the pass in conjunction with local levies till the army of the Peloponnese followed in full strength. Why the full military forces from the Peloponnese and Central Greece did not march out to Thermopylae, we shall never know, though it may be conjectured that the cause was the selfish clinging of the Peloponnesian members of the league to their fortified line at the Isthmus of Corinth. That baseness has almost been forgotten, extinguished by the glory of Leonidas and his three hundred [2] who died there at their posts,

---

[1] Bury, *History of Greece*, p. 276.

[2] These three hundred appear to have been the bodyguard of three hundred picked men, who by custom attended a Spartan king wherever he went. Usually they were young men, but we are specially informed

faithful to the charge entrusted to them by Sparta. The simple epitaph inscribed over their place of burial in the pass is their best commendation :

> " Go tell the Spartans, thou that passest by,
> That here, obedient to her laws, we lie."

Thermopylae To-day.—You may travel to Thermopylae by the high road from Livadhia (Lebadaea) through Elatea by the coast to the eastern gate of the pass near Alpeni ; or you may come across the mountains from Salona (once Amphissa) and descend from behind Callidromus by the modern road to Trachis, past the heights over which Hydarnes and his Persians scrambled in order to turn the Greek defence. You will find, indeed, no pass to-day answering to Herodotus' description. The ' Hot Springs ' are there, and the Red Brook, ' Phoenix,' and the gaunt cliffs, and the hillock near the Phocian Wall, where the Spartans and the men of Thespiae made their last stand. The pass itself you will not find, because a change in the course of the Spercheus has so altered the physical features of the country that the ' Pass ' no longer exists. The points, three in number, where the sea almost met the cliff may be identified without much difficulty, but where once was the sea laving the narrow road, marshlands now spread. The scenery is magnificent to-day as when Greece and Persia clashed in the pass, and a walk through it from end to end, a distance of nearly four miles, is an experience to remember. The gorge of the Asopus, up which runs the foot-track Anopaea, opens grimly in the cliff wall three miles outside the west gate, " a magnificent chasm with perpendicular sides ranging from 700 to 900 feet in height." [1] " The scenery throughout," adds Dr. Grundy, " is most beautiful, finer, I think, than anything I have seen in Greece." And of all ways to see Thermopylae the best, to the present writer's mind, is to come over the hills from Salona by

by Herodotus (vii. 205) that on this occasion Leonidas took with him only men who were old enough to be fathers and had sons living.

[1] Grundy, *The Great Persian War*, p. 302.

the pleasant hamlet of Graviá. Then from the heights, before you descend into the pass by the modern road, you will suddenly catch a glimpse of the blue waters of the Malian Gulf, and presently find yourself overlooking the plain where the hosts of Xerxes lay encamped before they stormed into the pass at his command.

NOTE ON THE DEFENDERS OF THERMOPYLAE.

The figures which Herodotus gives (vii. 220) for the troops with Leonidas make up a total of 4200, exclusive of the thousand Phocians and the Opuntian Locrians who sent ' all the force they had.' The Phocians, who were separately posted on the heights behind the pass, need not be counted, so that the original defenders of the pass numbered some five or six thousand. The composition of this force also has an interest. Nearly half, 2120, were Arcadians, including 500 men from Tegea and 500 from Mantinea. There were 1100 Boeotians ; 400 from Thebes, 700 from Thespiae. A small contingent of 80 came from Mycenae. Only the men of Thespiae remained to the end with Leonidas, and they deserve to share more equally with the Spartans in the fame of Thermopylae.

CHAPTER XIV

SALAMIS

"The yoke of force is broken from the neck—
The isle of Ajax and th' encircling wave
Reek with a bloody crop of death and wreck
Of Persia's fallen power, that none can lift nor save!"

E. D. A. MORSHEAD, *Aeschylus' Persians*
(ll. 596-599), p. 85.

THERMOPYLAE immortalized Leonidas and has become one of the world's most glorious stories. But in July, 480 B.C., the bodies of the Spartan king and of the men who died with him, heaped in the narrow roadway and about the mound within the Phocian wall, were a dire calamity for Hellas. The Greek plan of defence had failed, and, unless the main army hurried from the Isthmus, all Central Greece, that is, Attica and the Megarid, as well as Phocis and Boeotia, lay open to the conqueror. The heroism of the Spartan defence of Thermopylae has obscured the fact that it was a complete Persian victory, at however great a cost it may have been bought. The abandonment of the naval position at Artemisium and the retreat of the Greek fleet through the Euripus (which the squadron wrecked on the Hollows of Euboea was to have forestalled) followed as a matter of course. Accordingly the Greek fleet sailed away next day towards Athens and the Peloponnese.

The Persians at Artemisium.—The news of the retreat of the Greeks was brought to Aphetae in the evening, but the Persian commanders were slow to believe. They sent out fast sailing-ships to reconnoitre; when these returned with the report that the Greeks were really gone, the whole fleet crossed next day at sunrise to Artemisium, and in the afternoon they went on to the Euboean city, Histiaea. There a messenger from Xerxes met them and announced that all who wished might have leave to cross to the shores of the Malian Gulf and view the scene of the slaughter of the king's enemies. The battlefield, Herodotus tells us, had been carefully 'arranged' for this purpose. The bodies of the Greeks were left heaped about the pass as they had died; of the 20,000 Persian dead all but a thousand had been buried. The crews of the Persian ships thronged so eagerly to take advantage of this permission that soon not a boat was to be had. Two days were occupied in sight-seeing and the return to the ships, and then the fleet sailed on for the coast of Attica.

Fire and Sword in Phocis.—At the same time Persian columns advanced through Phocis ravaging and burning. Twelve townships of the Phocians were destroyed; at one of them, Abae, the temple of Apollo, seat of an oracle and very rich in treasure, was plundered and burnt. Delphi, which was incomparably richer, was apparently left untouched; and the reason can be inferred from many signs. The great shrine of Apollo at Delphi was secure in the favour of Xerxes, who, Herodotus remarks, "was better acquainted with what there was worthy of note at Delphi, than even with what he had left in his own house." If the Delphians had not actually medized, they were tainted with Medism. The many oracles Herodotus puts on record show conclusively how faint-hearted was Delphic support of the Hellenic cause. Herodotus has preserved a romantic story, told at Delphi itself after the war, of the defence of the temple by supernatural means, which was held to prove that the god was " able without help to protect his own "; and two great rocks, said to have come crashing down from the cliffs above the road to overwhelm the sacrilegious assailants, were shown in Pausanias' day in proof of this legend.

Plight of the Athenians.—The defence of Hellas at Thermopylae having failed, the prospect was most critical for all the Hellenes north of the Isthmus, that is to say, for the peoples of Boeotia, Attica and Megara, and for the Phocians and Locrians. For the Boeotians, indeed, who—with the exception of the Thespians and Plataeans —had from the first inclined to make common cause with the invader, it was an easy matter, and even a welcome opportunity to some, to make their submission to Xerxes. For the Athenians it was of desperate moment to prevent the enemy passing from Boeotia into Attica. Their one hope was that, in face of this extremity, the Peloponnesians with all their forces would hasten north to offer battle to the Persians in Boeotia, or at least to hold the passes between Boeotia and Attica. They were very soon convinced of the vanity of this expectation. No army came from the Peloponnese ; only news came that the Peloponnesians were busy building their wall across the Isthmus. The intention of their allies was plainly to concentrate the defence at the wall. The only concession the Athenians could obtain was that the fleet in its retreat should put in at Salamis to give the Athenians time to provide for the safety of their women and children.

Great Resolve of the Athenians.—For now the men of Athens, seeing the impossibility of saving the land of Attica from invasion, and how slight the hope now was of a successful defence of their city, had come to a great decision. They resolved to abandon their whole territory, the homes they loved in the country districts and their beloved city itself, and carry the whole non-combatant population, the old and feeble, the womenfolk and children, to places where, for a time at least, they would be safe ; while all their men capable of service fought on for the Hellenic cause. When we recall how much their city was to them, how dearly they loved their country houses, and how they cherished the boast that they almost alone of the Hellenes had dwelt in their own land from time immemorial, we see this was a very hard resolution for

them. That such a resolve is possible, recent European
history has shown. For did not the Servian army in the
winter of 1915 march through the Macedonian and
Albanian mountains to the Adriatic and cross to Italy
from Durazzo and Scutari ? *Their* case was harder than
the Athenians', for they left their children and their
womenfolk at the mercy of merciless enemies. The King
of the Belgians and the Belgian army held fast by one
little corner of Belgium all through the four years of the
Great War, though all the rest of Belgium was in enemy
occupation. There were precedents, too, in 480 B.C. in
the behaviour of the men of Phocaea and the men of Teos
at the Persian conquest of Ionia (XI. pp. 266 and 267).

Athenian Refugees in Safety.—As soon as the fleet
arrived from Artemisium, proclamation was made that
every Athenian householder should make the best provision he could for the safety of his family. The family
no doubt included domestic slaves. A strange and busy
scene the shore of the Bay of Phalerum (now the Brighton
of modern Athens) must have presented, as these thousands of helpless people from Athens and all Attica
crowded on board the ships and were conveyed across to
the mainland or the neighbouring islands.[1] Troezen in
Argolis was the chief place of refuge, but many were
taken to Salamis and Aegina. This transportation of the
people was hurried, because the danger was pressing.
The natural reluctance of the people to go was mitigated

---

[1] Plutarch in his *Life of Themistocles* has some vivid touches : " When
the entire city was thus putting out to sea, the sight provoked pity in
some, and in others astonishment at the hardihood of the step ; for
they were sending off their families in one direction, while they themselves, unmoved by the lamentations and tears and embraces of their
loved ones, were crossing over to the island where the enemy was to be
fought. Besides, many who were left behind on account of their great
age invited pity also, and much affecting fondness was shown by the
tame domestic animals, which ran along with yearning cries of distress
by the side of their masters as they embarked. A story is told of one
of these, the dog of Xanthippus the father of Pericles, how he could
not endure to be abandoned by his master, and so sprang into the sea,
swam across the strait by the side of his master's trireme, and staggered
out on Salamis, only to faint and die straightway." (Plut. *Them.* x.
Loeb Classical Library, pp. 31 and 33.)

and their fears allayed by skilful appeal to an answer received some time before from Delphi, and by the wonder reported concerning the great serpent believed to live in a temple on the Acropolis. Every month the priests used to place in this temple a supply of honeycake as food for the serpent, and when the cake disappeared, as it always did, they gave out that the serpent had eaten it. This month, so the priests declared, the food remained where it had been put, and the people, when they heard this, were greatly comforted, for it was taken as a sign that the goddess Athena herself had left the Acropolis ; it was right, therefore, for her people to do the same.

The Answer from Delphi.—But this resolution of the Athenians to abandon their city, instead of defending it, had not been reached without great searchings of heart and a great conflict of opinion. Some time before the actual march of Xerxes began, probably in the autumn of 481, when, because of the ever-growing reports of the vastness of the Great King's preparations, men's hearts were failing them for fear, the Athenians, as other states were doing, sent special envoys to Delphi to ask counsel of the god in their distress. Hardly had the usual rites been completed when the priestess—her very name has been preserved, Aristonicê—chanted in the ears of the Athenian envoys, as soon as they had passed within the sanctuary of the god and taken their seats there, this truly terrifying prophecy :

" Poor wretches, why sit suppliant ? Rise and flee,
Flee to earth's utmost bounds, abandoning
Your homes, your circling city's fortress heights.
Neither the head, nor body, keeps its place,
Nor feet beneath, nor hands, nor aught between :
All is in dissolution. O'er them sweeps
Fire, and swift Ares in Assyrian car.
Full many a fencèd town shall he destroy,
Not thine alone ; and many, too, the shrines
Of the Immortals to devouring flame
Consign, that now methinks stand all a-sweat,
Quaking with terror, while from the high roof

The dark blood drips, token of woes to come.
Hence from my temple ! Bow your hearts to doom !" [1]

No wonder Herodotus writes that when the Athenian
envoys heard these words they were filled with the deepest
affliction. The doom of Athens was sealed, it seemed :
Heaven itself had turned against her. This discouraging,
and even hostile reply, delivered to the accredited envoys
of the Athenian people when the Persian invasion was
impending, certainly lends force to the suspicion that the
oracle itself, the very mouthpiece of the divine to the
Hellenes, was under the influence of pro-Persian agents.
This is by no means impossible ; already Asiatic monarchs,
Gyges, Astyages, Croesus, had been the most liberal donors
to the Delphic shrine, and Datis in 490 had quoted the
king's command that Delos was to be spared (Ch. XII.
p. 280). There may quite well have been a friendly
understanding between Delphi and Persian agents (a
form of ' peaceful penetration ' practised 2400 years ago) ;
that is to say, some of the priestly families which controlled the oracle—because, of course, the responses made
at Delphi to enquirers must have been composed and
dictated by the priests—were in collusion with Persia
and were of set purpose weakening the Greek defence.
A plausible excuse was not wanting. For had not Athens
been the aggressor ? Had she not by presumptuous interference in the affairs of Ionia provoked the calamities
now threatening all Hellas ? And was it not better that
Athens alone should suffer than all the Hellenes be
involved in a common ruin ? So the medizing priests
might have contended, and veiled their betrayal of Hellas
under the cloak of patriotic motives. But some at least
of the influential Delphians judged more truly. Herodotus goes on to tell how Timon, the son of Androbulus,
' one of the men of chief account among the Delphians,'
seeing how utterly cast down the Athenian envoys were,
" advised them to take branches in their hands and go
and consult the oracle a second time in the guise of
suppliants." The Athenians followed his advice and

[1] Herodotus, vii. 140.

said : " Lord, grant us a better response concerning our
fatherland, and have respect unto these branches of
supplication which we bring in our hands. Without it
we will not depart from thy sanctuary, but will remain
here till we die." This urgency and persistence at length
gained its object ; a second answer came from the lips
of the Pythoness, which, if not altogether favourable,
and though clouded with obscurity, at least gave some
clear ground of hope. It ran thus :

> " Pallas may not prevail with mighty Zeus,
> Neither by prayer incessant, nor deep wit.
> Yet mark the word I speak this second time,
> For stand it shall unshaken.—When all else
> Is taken, all that Cecrops bounds contain
> And the deep valleys of divine Cithaeron,
> *Her wooden wall Zeus granteth to the Maid*
> *Alone unravaged to the end.* And this
> Shall stead thee and thy children. Therefore heed !
> Stay not to meet th' advancing horse and foot
> That swarmeth overland, but turn thy back
> In flight : hereafter shalt thou face the foe.
> *O blessed Salamis !* thou, even thou
> Shalt slay men born of women, whether it be
> Demeter's scattering-time or garnering ! "

" This answer seemed to them (and was indeed) milder
than the first. So they wrote it down, and went back to
Athens." [1]

The interest of these lines obviously lies in the seventh
and the thirteenth. What was the ' wooden wall,' which
as a hard-won concession to Athena was to prove at the
last a sure defence for the children of Cecrops, when all
their fatherland was lost ? And what was the meaning
of the reference to Salamis and the carnage to be wrought
there ? As for the ' wooden wall,' there were two opposed
interpretations. One party held that the wooden wall
meant the Acropolis, because in former times the rock of
the Acropolis had been fortified with a wooden palisade.
This was the view of some of the older and more conservative of the citizens, who set most store by the

---

[1] Herodotus, vii. 141 and 142.

prowess of Athenian spearmen, and who clung passionately
to the site of Athens and the Acropolis. Others, however,
maintained that 'wooden wall' could only mean the
fleet. This was the view which Themistocles, whose name
is associated with Salamis as closely as that of Miltiades
with Marathon, was earnest in impressing on his countrymen. In contending for this interpretation Themistocles'
great care was to give a hopeful significance to the allusion
to Salamis. Some who were inclined to take 'wooden
wall' to mean ships were yet staggered at the reference
to Salamis; for it spoke of men's destruction and seemed,
they thought, to presage defeat. But Themistocles
pointed confidently to the epithet joined with 'Salamis.'
For, he argued, if defeat for the Greeks at Salamis had been
foretold, Salamis could never have been called 'blessed'
Salamis, it would have been 'wretched' Salamis. "He
therefore counselled his countrymen to make ready to
fight on board their ships, since *they* were the wooden wall
in which the god told them to trust." [1] Themistocles
prevailed; the Athenians used every endeavour to make
their fleet strong, and now the Persian hosts were advancing into Attica, the resolve was taken to remove all non-
combatants, abandon their homes and territory to the
enemy, but trust to their ships to recover, and more than
recover, all they were losing. So with their wives and
children and dependents pensioners on the bounty of
other Greeks, the Athenians prepared to fight on with
their full sea-power. This was now two hundred ships,
more than half the allied fleet. It is plain enough that
without these two hundred ships the Greek cause by sea
must have been lost, and then the Peloponnese could
never have been able to hold out permanently by land.
The counter-proposal, which Themistocles opposed and
succeeded in setting aside, was to put the whole population of Attica (or as much of it as was possible) on board
ship and seek new homes in Italy. It had been done
before by a Greek city in extremity, and Athens might
have done it. So the Athenians by choosing to stake all

[1] Herodotus, vii. 143; Rawlinson, iv. p. 117.

on their fleet, and Themistocles by persuading them to it, may truly be said to have saved Hellas.

The Athenian Navy.—This was one great service which in the hour of supreme peril Themistocles rendered to Athens. Perhaps an even greater was the foresight which in the years between Marathon and Salamis had placed Athens in a position to confide her whole national existence to her fleet. Only ten years before the great invasion Athens had been hardly strong enough on the sea to cope with her neighbour and rival, the island Aegina. In 487 Athens was at war with Aegina, and in spite of all the prestige of Marathon twice suffered a humiliating check. The war was still dragging on, as we have seen (above, p. 309, Ch. XIII.), when the call came for the Hellenes to combine and resist Xerxes. But in the interval something had been done which made all the difference. Athens had become far stronger on the sea through the wise prescience of Themistocles. It happened while the war with Aegina was in progress that the profits of the state-owned silver mines of Laurium had reached a substantial sum of money, which it was proposed to divide among the citizens of Athens, man by man. Themistocles after a tough fight induced his countrymen to forego this individual money gain and to build ships instead. In moving the decree which was to give effect to this purpose Themistocles used the argu ment that these ships would ensure victory to Athens in the war with Aegina, but there can be little doubt tha what he really had most in mind was the greater dange from Persia, which he knew must come. So it came t pass that when three years later the fleets of Xerxes se sail from Therma to assail Greece, the Athenians pos sessed a fleet of two hundred newly-built warships,[1] an contributed by far the largest contingent to the Gree fleet ; in fact, more than half. So there seems goo

[1] Triremes, or the battleships with three banks of oars, which at th period were a comparatively new departure. A few years before, v learn from Thucydides (i. 14), Greek warships were mainly fifty-oare long-boats, called penteconters.

ground for Herodotus' judgment that " It was the outbreak of this Aeginetan war which proved the saving of
Greece, by forcing the Athenians to develop their
sea power. The new ships were not used for the purpose
for which they had been built, but they were there to
help Greece in her hour of need." [1] Somewhat similarly
it might be said that the breaking out of the South African
War in 1899 proved the saving of Europe in 1914. For
it was then that the British learnt the powers of organization which enabled them to send the expeditionary
force to France with such promptitude in August of that
year.

Themistocles.—Themistocles, to whom Athens and
Greece owed so much, had to win his way to influence
at Athens in the face of prejudice and opposition. He
did not belong to the ancient Eupatrid nobility, like
Solon and Miltiades ; his father, Neocles, was an Athenian
of middle station ; his mother was a Thracian. It was
only by grace of the liberal legislation of Cleisthenes
that he was reckoned an Athenian citizen at all. And
yet it was to this ' outsider,' this half-caste, that Athens
now owed her salvation, and, with Athens, Hellas. His
position was, however, by this time quite assured as
leader of the popular or democratic party. He had commanded the Athenian contingent in Thessaly in the spring
of 480, and he was admiral with (seemingly) full dis-
cretionary powers at Artemisium. Nay more, the influence of his large and statesmanlike ideas is traceable in
all the actions of the Athenian State throughout this
critical time.

The Refugees at Troezen.—The removal of the women
and children was carried out under desperate pressure,
but was safely accomplished. The State allowed a small
sum of money to every citizen needing help ; but some
few—Herodotus says—mostly of the poorer sort, were
left behind, and these now garrisoned the Acropolis. It
appears that there was a minority who were still genuinely

[1] Herodotus, vii. 144.

convinced that the interpretation of the ' wooden wall '
as barricades to defend the Acropolis was the right one,
and these, too, stayed with the hope and intention of
holding the citadel in despite of all the Persian king's
power. As to the Athenian refugees it is pleasant to
find it recorded that they were kindly treated, especially
at Troezen, the reputed birthplace of Theseus. There
the State treasury made them a small daily allowance
for each person's support ; and even provided schooling
for the children.[1]

Persian Advance to Athens.—By this time the Persian
armies had advanced in one or more columns through
the passes from Boeotia into Attica after burning Thespiae
and Plataea. They marched straight on, ravaging and
burning as they went. They were soon at Athens. The
Persians occupied the empty city without opposition and
at once began to lay siege to the citadel. For this purpose Mars' Hill (the Areopagus), which rises beyond a
slight hollow opposite the western end of the Acropolis,
was the most favourable ground. This position was
accordingly occupied, and attempts were made from it
to set fire to the wooden fortifications by shooting at
them arrows to which pieces of lighted tow were fastened.
The garrison were hard put to it to prevent their wooden
wall being set on fire, but they maintained a stout resistance and refused to surrender, though the Pisistratidae
came and offered terms. They repelled the Persian
assaults on the gates by rolling masses of stone upon
the assailants, and for a time it looked as if the faith of
the elders in these wooden walls was to be justified. But
this was not to be : the oracles which pointed to the
conquest and devastation of all Attica were to be literally
fulfilled. Some enterprising spirits among the besiegers
found a place on the northern face of the Acropolis rock
where it was possible to climb. There are caves on this

---

[1] Plutarch, *Themistocles*, 10 (L.C.L. pp. 29 and 31). " They actually
voted to support them at the public cost, allowing two obols daily to
each family, and to permit the boys to pluck of the vintage fruit everywhere, and besides to hire teachers for them."

side which are easily enough reached, but above the caves the cliff appears to rise sheer. The soldiers managed to scale this cliff, which was unguarded, and scrambled over the top.[1] As soon as they appeared, the defenders in a panic either fled to the temples for sanctuary or threw themselves down the precipices. The Persian soldiers rushed to the gates, opened them, and the Acropolis was won. The defenders were all massacred, even those who had taken refuge at the shrine of Athena. Thus for the time being Sardis was fully avenged and Darius' purpose at length accomplished by his son and successor. In little over three months Xerxes had crossed from Asia Minor with his vast army by the Bridge of Boats, had marched round all the coasts of Thrace and Macedonia and on through Thessaly, had forced the Pass of Thermopylae, swept on through Boeotia and over Mount Cithaeron and now was master of all Attica—of the whole plain of Athens and of the Acropolis itself. As soon as Xerxes was completely master of Athens, a horseman was despatched to carry the glad news all the way back to Abydos and Sardis, and thence by the Royal Road to Susa.

Xerxes had triumphed ; Athens was low in the dust. Her shrines were burnt and desecrated. The Medes were in possession of the city and the plain and of the mainland shore of the Straits of Salamis. But looking across from the rocks under Mount Aegaleos, where now the ferry starts which will take you to the island, might be discerned in the shelter of the harbour of Salamis the ships of the Hellenic fleet from Artemisium, and among them the two hundred triremes of Athens with the flower of her citizens on board, still undaunted in spirit and prepared to fight for a city which some held no longer existed. In spite of Xerxes' triumph these men were to prove what Aeschylus afterwards proclaimed—that while her men still lived, she was defended by firm bulwarks. The

[1] Any visitor to Athens may, if he pleases, test the possibility of scaling the rock here and climbing to the platform of the Acropolis. It is not a difficult feat.

story goes that the day after the sack of the Acropolis, while the buildings of the citadel were still smoking, Xerxes called together the Athenian exiles who had accompanied his army and bade them ascend to the top of the Acropolis and there offer sacrifice. These men reported on their return that when they entered the temple and looked for the sacred olive which had been burnt in the general conflagration, they found that it had given forth a new shoot, a cubit in length.

The Council of the Captains.—News of the capture of the Acropolis and the massacre of the garrison reached the Greek fleet at Salamis, at a moment when the naval commanders were assembled at the invitation of the admiral, the Spartan Eurybiades, to discuss where to fight the Persian fleet. A majority were found to be in favour of fighting at the Isthmus of Corinth, where they would be close to the Peloponnese. While the question was still in debate, the news came of the capture of the Acropolis. The effect of this news on the Greek commanders was so disturbing that some of them actually left the council, went on board their ships and began to make preparations for sailing away. A formal vote was taken from those who stayed, and it was for fighting at the Isthmus. Then the council separated for the night.

Themistocles' Perplexity.—This decision Themistocles knew to be fatal. To fight with abundant sea-room at the Isthmus would be all to the advantage of the Persians : the narrow straits between Salamis and Attica were to the advantage of the Greeks. On the ground of numbers alone wide sea-room was advantageous to the Persians, and disadvantageous to the Greeks, for it enabled the Persians to make use of their superiority in this respect. But more than that, speaking generally, the ships in the Persian navies were lighter-built and better handled : the Greek ships were more heavily built but stronger, and in close encounter the fighting men on the Greek ships could beat the Persians on board Xerxes' ships. In the confined waters between Salamis and the shores of Attica the Greeks would fight under the conditions most favourable to their success : whereas at the Isthmus these advantages would be lost ; and, conversely, the Persians could make full use of their greater numbers and their superiority in manœuvring. There was even something worse to be feared, if once the Greek fleet left Salamis : seeing what was the state of mind of the Peloponnesian seamen, there was fear that the several contingents from the Peloponnese might disperse to the defence of their homes.

Mnesiphilus.—As Themistocles, his mind oppressed by these thoughts, climbed on board his ship, he was met by an Athenian, by name Mnesiphilus, his friend and teacher, who enquired what the decision of the Council had been. On hearing, Mnesiphilus said : " If these men take their ships from Salamis, you will have no fatherland left to fight for ! They will return each to his own city, and neither Eurybiades nor any one else will be able to stop them from scattering the fleet to the winds ; and Hellas will be ruined by foolish counsel. But do you go and by any and every possible means try and upset their decision, and see if you may haply persuade Eurybiades to reconsider his plans and stay here." [1] On thus hearing his own forebodings more than confirmed, Themistocles straightway re-entered the ship's boat in which he had come from the council and rowed back to the admiral's ship, begged an interview, and argued so persuasively that Eurybiades at once left his ship and personally summoned the captains once more to a council. Themistocles now made his appeal to Eurybiades and the other commanders in the following terms : " It lies now in your power to save Hellas, if you will follow my advice and stay and fight here, and not follow the advice of those who bid you withdraw your ships to the Isthmus. Only listen and weigh the one course against the other. If you join battle at the Isthmus, you will fight in the open· sea, which is least of all to our advantage, since our ships are heavier, and fewer in number. In the second

[1] Herodotus, viii. 57.

place you will lose Salamis and Megara and Aegina, even if all else goes well for us. Further, this land army will advance along with their fleet ; you will draw them on against the Peloponnese and so imperil the whole of Hellas. But if you do as I say, you will find in that course all the following advantages : first, by fighting in a narrow strait, few ships against many, on an ordinary reckoning of chances, we shall win a great victory ; for to fight in a narrow sea is to our advantage, to fight with wide sea-room is to their advantage. Secondly, Salamis is saved, where our children and our women have taken refuge. Moreover this point is secured of which ye make so much account ; by staying here you fight for the Peloponnese as much as by fighting at the Isthmus, nor will you, if you are well advised, draw them upon the Peloponnesus. And if what I expect comes to pass and we conquer at sea, the barbarians will never reach your Isthmus ; they will not advance beyond Attica, but will retreat in disorder ; and we shall gain by the preservation of Megara, and Aegina, and of Salamis, about which we have an oracle that we shall get the better of our enemies there. When men follow good counsels, for the most part things come to pass according to their mind ; but when they follow ill counsel, god's will refuseth to fall in with human judgments." [1] A somewhat heated discussion followed, but in the end Themistocles prevailed by a last personal appeal to the Spartan admiral : " If you will stay here," he said, " by so doing you will prove yourself a man of worth. If you will not, you will ruin Hellas, since on our ships hangs the issue of the war. Only be persuaded. But if you will not do as I say, we will forthwith put our households on board ship and sail to Siris in Italy, which has been ours from of old to this day, and which, oracles say, is destined to be colonized by us. And when you have lost us as allies and find yourselves alone, you will remember my words." [2] Upon this Eurybiades gave his decision for remaining and fighting at Salamis.

[1] Herodotus, viii. 60.   [2] Herodotus, viii. 62.

The Persians at Phalerum.—It was now close on morning : the Council broke up and, in accordance with
Eurybiades' decision, the Greek commanders prepared
their ships for battle. Herodotus relates that there was
an earthquake shock just as the sun was rising : whereon
the Greeks invoked the gods in prayer and sent for the
images of Ajax, Telamon and Aeacus from Aegina, even
as the Israelites sent for the Ark of the Covenant. The
Persian fleet meantime had come on from Artemisium
and lined the whole coast of Attica as far north as Phalerum so as to hide from view the neighbouring shores.
Xerxes, on his part, held a council of the commanders
of his fleets : and the decision was to attack the Greeks
at Salamis. It was then too late to engage that day,
and the battle was fixed for the morrow. That same
night the Persian army in Attica began its march towards
the Peloponnese. News of this reached the Greek fleet,
and once more a wave of anxiety spread from ship to
ship. It was known already that the land forces at the
Isthmus were working with feverish energy to complete
the cross-wall. This knowledge and tidings that the
great host of Xerxes was now on the march for the
Isthmus produced among the Peloponnesian crews a
state of excitement bordering on mutiny. " For a time,"
writes Herodotus, " talk went on in whispers, each man
commenting to his neighbour, and expressing astonishment at the folly of Eurybiades : but presently the discontent broke out openly. They gathered together and
disputed on the whole subject as before, the one part
saying that they must sail off to the Peloponnese and
risk their lives in battle there, and not for a country
already conquered ; while the Athenians and Aeginetans and Megarians were for fighting where they
were."[1]

Sicinnus.—It was then that Themistocles, convinced
that the Peloponnesian captains would now carry a
resolution to abandon Salamis and fight at the Isthmus,

---

[1] Herodotus, viii. 74.

and knowing surely that this course of action would be
fatal to the Greek cause, played a daring stroke, which
ensured that the purposed withdrawal should be forestalled and his countrymen compelled to fight at Salamis.
He sent a secret message to the Persian admirals by
means of Sicinnus, a slave of his household who was tutor
to his sons, informing them that the Greek ships were

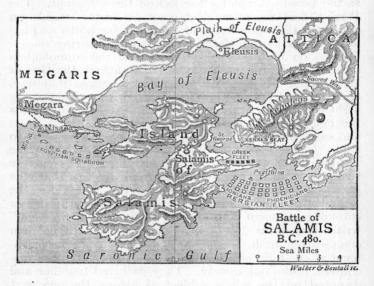

Battle of
SALAMIS
B.C. 480.
Sea Miles

Walker & Boutall sc.

meditating flight and would escape before morning unless
prevented. The Persian commanders, eager for the
capture of the whole Greek fleet, swallowed the bait and
at once took the measures necessary to close both outlets
of the channel within which the harbour of Salamis lies.
What these measures were, a glance at the map makes
clear. The island of Salamis is very irregular in shape,
but has roughly the form of a flattened horseshoe, and
this horseshoe is wedged sideways into the Bay of Eleusis
on the Attic coast, between Piraeus and Mount Aegaleos

on one side, and Nisaea, the harbour of Megara, on the other. Round the northern half of the horseshoe winds a land-locked channel, which broadens out in the Bay of Eleusis, but is narrow at both ends and obstructed by islands. Salamis, where the Greek fleet lay, is just within the eastern opening of this channel, behind the sharp projection running out from the island which contracts the opening and was called (like the similar projection at one end of the Bay of Marathon) Cynosura (that is, Dog's-tail).[1] Between Cynosura and the opposite coast is the low rocky island of Psyttaleia (now Lipso-kutali), about three-quarters of a mile long and between two and three hundred yards broad, which divides the eastern channel into two. The orders were that at night-fall the whole fleet should put to sea ; the Egyptian squadron numbering two hundred ships was sent round the island to block the western channel ; the main fleet, in three lines, was to patrol outside the eastern entrance on both sides of Psyttaleia. The utmost vigilance was enjoined, on pain of death, should the Greeks slip out and get away. About the same time a large body of picked Persian troops was landed on Psyttaleia where, should there be fighting within the channel, they would be able to save alive men of their own fleet who escaped to land from sunk or disabled ships, and kill or capture Greek seamen in a similar plight.

Aristides' Message.—News that the enemy had closed with his ships both outlets of the narrow straits was brought to the Greek fleet while the captains were still debating the question of withdrawal, and words had grown high and fierce. Then it was that a message called Themistocles from the Council. He went out and found awaiting him his great political rival Aristides, chief of the opposing party at Athens, who had been banished by ostracism three years before, but had re-turned under an amnesty, like other patriotic exiles, when the danger from Persia grew acute. Aristides now

[1] See p. 282.

brought word that the question of retreat had no longer any meaning, since the Greeks were surrounded and shut in by the Persian fleet. Themistocles thanked him and expressed lively pleasure at the news, at the same time explaining his own part in bringing about what had happened. He begged Aristides to go in and repeat the news to the Council, since if Themistocles himself told them, they would not believe. So Aristides went in and reported that he had come from Aegina and had barely escaped capture by the ships blockading the western channel. The Greek fleet, he said, was entirely enclosed, and he advised them to make ready to fight. Even so, many of the captains would not believe. While the discussion was still going on a trireme from Tenos sailed in, which had deserted from the Persians and came to fight for Hellas. Her ship's company fully confirmed Aristides' report, and the doubters were at length convinced. Without more ado all rejoined their ships and made ready for battle. The fighting men serving on the ships were first called together on shore and harangued by their leaders according to Greek custom. Of the speeches made, Herodotus tells us, Themistocles' was by far the best and most inspiriting. Then the whole fleet put to sea in good order.

Salamis.—It was now early morning. The main Persian fleet had been up all night patrolling outside the eastern channels. The men were tired and disappointed : nothing had been seen of ships trying to slink out of the narrow waters. And now orders came to enter the straits. This could only be done in column of ships, and in this formation accordingly the three divisions went forward into the two narrow channels, one on either side of Psyttaleia. Suddenly a burst of sound broke the morning stillness, the war-cry of the Hellenes, the paean that told not of flight, but of readiness for battle. A trumpet rang out and was followed by the plash of many hundreds of oars striking the water in time with the boatswain s song. For a while the long spit of Cynosura concealed the Greek ships from sight. Then first the right wing

THE STRAITS OF SALAMIS.

The entrance to the straits viewed from the coast of Attica, W. of Piraeus. Psyttaleia (1) and the spit of Cynosura (3) appear to the left, with Salamis town (2) in the bay behind Cynosura. _____ Bay of Eleusis (4), the har_____ _____ Mount Aegaleos (5) and the

came into view, and then the whole fleet advancing in
battle formation. The cry rang out :

"On sons of Hellas ! Free your fatherland,
Free wives and little ones ; free shrines where dwell
Your country's gods ; graves where your forefathers
Are sepulchred ! To-day your all's at stake ! "

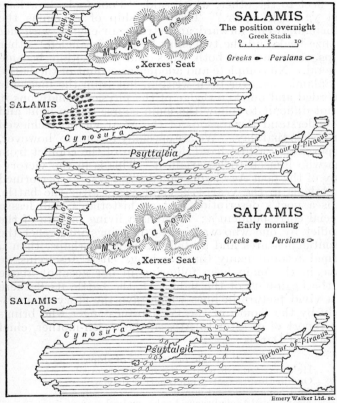

Emery Walker Ltd. sc.

In spite of their surprise, in spite of their night-long
vigil and disappointment—for they had been promised
victory without fighting for it—the fleets of Xerxes

responded with shouts of defiance and pressed on past Psyttaleia into the channel. For a few moments the Greeks recoiled ; but perhaps it was only to lure the enemy further into the straits. One report in later times declared that a woman's form appeared to the eyes of the Greek mariners and a voice was heard from one end of the fleet to the other, which said, " Poor fools, how long will ye back water." Then the ship of Ameinias the Athenian swept forward and struck an enemy with her bronze beak and the two ships became entangled ; other ships came up on both sides and the action became general. No complete and adequate account of the battle of Salamis has ever been written, but from the incidents recorded and our knowledge of the physical conditions it is not difficult to follow the main course of the fight and to understand the reasons of the great victory achieved for Hellas that day. We are specially fortunate, however, in possessing a first-hand description of the conflict from one who himself took part in it. This is in the victory-play of the poet Aeschylus called *The Persians*, performed at Athens in the year 472, eight years after the battle. It is a poet's description, not an historian's, still less a special correspondent's ; but it is a living picture of the conflict by one who was in it ; it brings into relief the essential features and so tells us more, perhaps, than a formal account many times as long. It is Aeschylus we have in the main been following in our account above of the beginning of the fight. Of the battle itself there is a vivid picture in lines which give the story dramatically by the mouth of the Persian messenger who brings the report of disaster to Atossa, the queen-mother, chief consort of Darius :

> " Awhile our stream of ships
> Held onward, till within the narrowing creek
> Our jostling vessels were together driven,
> And none could aid another : each on each
> Drave hard their brazen beaks, or brake away
> The oar-banks of each other, stem to stern,
> While the Greek galleys, with no lack of skill,
> Hemmed them and battered in their sides, and soon

The hulls rolled over, and the sea was hid,
Crowded with wrecks and butchery of men.
No beach nor reef, but was with corpses strewn,
And every keel of our barbarian host
Hurried to flee, in utter disarray.
Thereon the foe closed in upon the wrecks
And hacked and hewed, with oars and splintered planks,
As fishermen hack tunnies or a cast
Of netted dolphins, and the briny sea
Rang with the screams and shrieks of dying men,
Until the night's dark aspect hid the scene." [1]

Causes of the Persian Overthrow.—It is not difficult to understand why the Persian fleets were utterly defeated in spite of their great superiority of numbers, the technical skill of the Phoenicians, and the stubborn courage with which, by the testimony alike of Aeschylus and Herodotus, the Great King's servants fought. They went into battle unbreakfasted after a night of wearisome patrol work. The Greeks, though their leaders may have had a sleepless night, were comparatively fresh and were probably able to get their morning meal before standing to quarters. There was an element of unexpectedness in the way the Persian ships came upon the Greek, though the encounter was not exactly a surprise. But most of all, the formation in which they entered the straits and the confined space in which they fought, when once they were within them, put the Persians at a disadvantage. If we look at the map with a little imagination—still more, of course, if we look across at Salamis from the Attic coast—we see at once that the Persian fleets, entering the straits in column (as Aeschylus actually describes their doing), were exposed to a flank attack from a fleet advancing in order of battle out of Salamis Bay. The Persians would endeavour to deploy into line to receive this attack, and were quite right in doing so, but the attempt in that confined space only resulted in confusion. The Athenian and Aeginetan ships on the left of the Greek line (we may gather from what Herodotus says) charged the Phoenicians as they were forming, and the battle became a mêlée in

[1] Aeschylus, *Persae* (ll. 414-430) ; Morshead, pp. 78, 79.

which the greater weight of the Greek vessels, the heavier armament of the fighting men aboard, and the well-ordered formation of the Greek line, all told in their favour. The heads of the Persian divisions were thrown into disorder on their first entry into the straits, and the disorder was rapidly increased by the number of ships crowding in behind, while the leading squadrons were giving way and were actually being pressed back into the passage. The result was great destruction and slaughter before the remnants of the Persian fleet extricated themselves from the straits and withdrew to Phalerum. Not that the victory was easily won : there was plenty of hard fighting, and there were individual feats of valour on both sides which Herodotus illustrates by lively anecdotes. But the battle went against the king's ships from the first, and by the afternoon the victory of the Hellenes was complete.

The Tragedy of Psyttaleia.—Besides the heavy losses of ships and men in the sea-fight, a further disaster overtook the Persians in the slaughter by the Greeks of all the men who had landed on Psyttaleia. At some time in the course of the fight Aristides, who was apparently in chief command on land, noticed the Persian troops on Psyttaleia and saw his opportunity. He collected a mixed force of hoplites and light-armed troops (javelin-men and bow-men), landed on the island, and overwhelmed the Persians there after a fierce resistance. Of this episode also Aeschylus gives a vivid, and somewhat lurid, description :

> " On every side,
> Battered with stones, they fell, while arrows flew
> From many a string, and smote them to the death.
> Then, at the last, with simultaneous rush
> The foe came bursting on us, hacked and hewed
> To fragments all that miserable band,
> Till not a soul of them was left alive.
> Then Xerxes saw disaster's depth, and shrieked. . . ." [1]

Xerxes on Skarmanga.—On the slope of Mount Aegaleos (Skarmanga), the range of hills, one end of which faces

[1] Aeschylus, *Persae* (ll. 461-467) ; Morshead, pp. 80 and 81.

Cynosura along the first reach of the inner channel, is a low hillock, the top of which has been artificially levelled. It is a reasonable guess that this platform was the position from which Xerxes viewed the fortunes of the fight, as described by both Aeschylus and Herodotus. Herodotus writes : " During the whole time of the battle Xerxes sat at the base of the hill called Aegaleos over against Salamis ; and whenever he saw any of his own captains perform any worthy exploit he enquired concerning him, and the man's name was taken down by his scribes together with the names of his father and city." Aeschylus, on his part, describes imaginatively the agony of mind in which the Great King saw with his own eyes the massacre going on upon Psyttaleia. For the troops landed on Psyttaleia included many of the noblest Persians in the host.[1] Alike to Herodotus and Aeschylus this overthrow of the Persian armada at Salamis was an example of the retribution which overtakes human pride and power in excess. For Hellas it was a day of glorious deliverance : all the shores of the narrow strait were strewn with the wrecks of the ships of Xerxes' fleets and the corpses of his men. For Persia it was a day of dire calamity, preluding disaster to come, yet more terrible.[2]

[1] It has been suggested, but not very convincingly, that the Persians on Psyttaleia were not a mere *corps d'élite*, as Herodotus implies, but the staff directing the naval operations. This would account for the high rank of the slain, but is not probable on general grounds. See Caspari in *Journal of Hellenic Studies*, vol. 31 (1911), p. 108.

[2] The French, quick to see the parallel between Xerxes and the Persian defeat at Salamis and the failure of the Kaiser to break through and force his way to Paris, produced a French version of *The Persians* in Paris in 1919. A few lines may be quoted by way of illustration, a rather free rendering of lines 467-473, lines immediately following those translated into English on p. 352 :

> " Et le roi, cependant, pousse de longs sanglots.
> Car, assis sur un trone, au haut d'un promontoire
> D'où bientôt il devait contempler sa victoire,
> C'est la mort qu'il contemple à terre et sur les flots,
> Pleurant et gemissant et déchirant sa robe,
> Il donne le signal de la retrait ; et lui,
> Lui-même, sans honneur, brusquement se dérobe ;
> Reine, pleure deux fois ; le Roi des Rois a fui ! "

" Land of the East," wails the Chorus in *The Persians* :

> " Land of the East, thou mournest for the host,
>   Bereft of all thy sons, alas the day !
> For them whom Xerxes led hath Xerxes lost—
>   Xerxes who wrecked the fleet, and flung our hopes away." [1]

[1] Aeschylus, *Persae* (ll. 550-555) ; Morshead, p. 84. The numbering of the lines of the *Persæ* in this and preceding notes is Paley's.

CHAPTER XV

PLATAEA

"Si le crime fut grand, la peine vaut le crime ;
Dans l'abîme des maux ils roulent malheureux.
D'autres maux, sous leurs pieds, jailliront de l'abîme."

AES. *Pers.* ll. 809-811.

THE victory of the Greeks at Salamis was complete ; how complete they did not themselves at first realize. It decided the war on the sea, and by deciding the war on the sea, it really decided the war on land, too. But at first the Greeks expected a renewal of the Persian attack ; and next day, after taking possession of the damaged ships abandoned by the enemy, made ready to meet it. No attack, however, took place either this day or the next, and then came the surprising intelligence that the Persian ships were no longer on the coast of Attica, but had fled. The Greek fleet at once started in pursuit, and went as far as the island of Andros in the Aegean, south of Euboea. As there were no signs of the enemy, the chiefs held a council of war to determine on their course of action. Themistocles was for sailing straight to the Hellespont and destroying the bridge of boats ; but Eurybiades strongly opposed this, declaring it to be far better policy to leave the way of retreat by land open to Xerxes. The land forces were as yet undefeated, and if Xerxes of necessity remained in Europe he would be compelled in desperation to carry on the war with the greatest vigour possible. There was something to be said for this view, and it prevailed ; but it is probable

355

that if Themistocles' bolder plan had been followed, it would have been justified by success.

Xerxes' Return to Asia.—All Greek accounts agree in representing the Great King's state of mind after witnessing the defeat of his fleet at Salamis as wanting in manly firmness. It is certain that within a few days of the battle Xerxes and all his host evacuated Athens and retired through the passes into Boeotia, and thence by Thermopylae into Thessaly ; and that, soon after, Xerxes made over command of his forces in Europe to Mardonius and returned overland to Asia Minor. Herodotus relates that Mardonius himself suggested to the king the advisability of his return to Persia, along with the greater part of the army, and offered to complete the subjection of Greece if allowed to choose out the troops which he judged most serviceable. Xerxes readily assented ; and when Mardonius had made his choice, he set out for the Hellespont with the residue of his ' grand army.' Both Herodotus and Aeschylus represent the actual retreat as calamitous ; and bearing in mind the probabilities, and the known hardships of other great retreats, it is likely enough that it was so. " All along their line of march, in every country where they chanced to be," writes Herodotus, " his soldiers seized and devoured whatever corn they could find belonging to the inhabitants ; while, if no corn was to be found, they gathered the grass that grew in the fields, and stripped the trees, whether cultivated or wild, alike of their bark and of their leaves, and so fed themselves. They left nothing anywhere, so hard were they pressed by hunger. Plague too and dysentery attacked the troops while still upon their march, and greatly thinned their ranks. Many died ; others fell sick and were left behind in the different cities that lay upon the route, the inhabitants being strictly charged by Xerxes to tend and feed them." [1] It is said to have taken Xerxes over six weeks to reach Sestos ; and when he got there after all he found the Bridge of Boats destroyed. He had

---

[1] Herodotus, viii. 115 ; Rawlinson, iv. p. 348.

no difficulty in crossing by ship to Abydos. Thence he went on to Sardis and there made long stay.

Plans of Mardonius.—Xerxes may have quailed at the sight of the havoc wrought on his fleet in the narrow straits of Salamis and the slaughter of many of his noblest Persians on the rocks of Psyttaleia, but Mardonius remained undaunted and supremely confident of his ability to conquer all Greece with the troops left with him. He shared the belief of the Persians, which neither Marathon nor Thermopylae had greatly shaken, that they were the best and bravest fighting men on earth, and invincible by land. The sea was not their element. What mattered the loss of a few planks or the misconduct of Phoenicians, Egyptians, Cyprians, or Cilicians ? The strength of Persia lay in her matchless steeds and horsemen. But to secure victory he must be careful to choose a battle-ground where he could use his cavalry effectively. He had kept with him all the Persians and the most warlike of the troops of other nations. Horse and foot together made up the formidable total of 300,000 men, without counting the Greeks who would be fighting on the Persian side. The picked troops of which his army now consisted were a far more efficient military instrument than the unwieldy host with which Xerxes had marched to Thermopylae. The half was more than the whole.

The Embassy to Athens.—On these grounds Mardonius was full of confidence. Nevertheless, when winter was over and the spring of 479 brought the time for a new campaign, he attempted to detach the Athenians from the cause of Hellas by offers as flattering as they were advantageous. He sent Alexander, son of Amyntas the king of Macedonia, to make the offer and persuade the Athenians to accept it. The Spartans were so alarmed when they heard of this that they despatched a special mission to Athens to counteract Alexander's influence. The Athenians gave audience to the Macedonian prince in presence of the Spartan envoys. Mardonius in his message enlarged on the vastness of the Great King's power, the hopelessness of resistance and the liberality of the terms offered—nothing less than equal alliance and compensation for the injuries suffered by the Athenians in the Persian invasion. Not only was the king willing to restore to the Athenians their own land and rebuild their temples, but to add as a free gift any territory they liked to choose. " Do not," the message concluded, " by matching yourselves against the King wilfully entail upon yourselves the loss of your country, with the risk all the time involved to yourselves ; but rather come to terms. This you may now do in the most honourable way, since the King makes the first overtures. Make close alliance then with us, clear of deceit and fraud, and keep your freedom." " The King's power," Alexander added, " is more than human, and his hand reaches far. If then you will not at once agree to peace, when this great offer is made to you, I am in terror for your sakes, since of all the allies you lie directly in the path of invasion and must ever in your isolated state suffer devastation, since your land is the natural battleground. Consent then. It is a great thing that the King pardons your offences and would fain be your friend." [1]

The Lacedaemonian envoys endeavoured to combat these arguments by reminding the Athenians of their responsibility for bringing this war upon Hellas and appealing to their love of liberty and their sense of honour. They acknowledged all the Athenians had themselves suffered, and, as some mitigation of their losses, offered to undertake the support of the whole non-combatant population of Attica for the duration of the war.

Then the Athenians made answer to Alexander the Macedonian, bidding him cease his efforts to persuade them since they would not listen and sending this reply to Mardonius' offer : " So long as the sun keeps his course, we shall never make peace with Xerxes ; rather will we march out and resist him, relying on the help of the gods and heroes for whom he showed no reverence,

[1] Herodotus, viii. 140.

but burnt their temples and their images." And they
warned Alexander never to bring such proposals to them
again : " You are the guest and friend of our nation, we
would not that you should suffer aught ungracious at
our hands." [1]

Then, Herodotus relates, they turned to the Spartan
envoys and made reply in words which remain the noblest
eulogy of the conduct of Athens in the fiery trial of the
Persian War : " 'Twas natural no doubt," they said,
" that the Lacedaemonians should be afraid we might
make terms with the Barbarian ; but nevertheless 'twas
a base fear in men who knew so well of what temper and
spirit we are. Not all the gold that the whole earth
contains—not the fairest and most fertile of all lands—
would bribe us to take part with the Medes and help
them to enslave our countrymen. Even could we any-
how have brought ourselves to such a thing, there are
many very powerful motives which would now make it
impossible. The first and chief of these is the burning
and destruction of our temples and the images of our
gods, which forces us to make no terms with their destroyer, but rather to pursue him with our resentment to
the uttermost. Again, there is our common brotherhood
with the Greeks : our common language, the altars and
the sacrifices of which we all partake, the common character which we bear—did the Athenians betray all these,
of a truth it would not be well. Know then now, if ye
have not known it before, that while one Athenian
remains alive, we will never join alliance with Xerxes.
We thank you, however, for your forethought on our
behalf, and for your wish to give our families sustenance,
now that ruin has fallen on us—the kindness is complete
on your part ; but for ourselves we will endure as we
may and not be burdensome to you. Such then is our
resolve. Be it your care with all speed to lead out your
troops ; for if we surmise aright, the Barbarian will not
wait long ere he invade our territory, but will set out so
soon as he learns our answer to be, that we will do none

[1] Herodotus, viii. 143.

of those things which he requires of us. Now then is the time for us, before he enters Attica, to go forth ourselves into Boeotia, and give him battle." [1] So the Spartan envoys went back reassured.

Second Occupation of Athens.—When Mardonius learnt from Alexander the Macedonian that the Athenians rejected his overtures and were steadfastly resolved on resistance, he lost no time, but set his armies in motion once more and advanced swiftly southward upon Attica. The Athenians had dared all in trust that Sparta would lead the whole strength of the Peloponnese to their assistance. When day after day passed and no succour came, while the Persian forces were reported to be advancing rapidly and already to have entered Boeotia, they abandoned their city again after sending their families and their valuables across the sea, this time chiefly to Salamis. So when in course of time Mardonius once more took possession of Athens, he found the city deserted and empty. This second occupation of Athens by the Persians happened ten months after the first capture by Xerxes, and Mardonius at once had the news flashed across the Aegean by means of a system of fire signals from island to island which he had arranged. The Athenians on their part were deeply angered at this betrayal. They sent ambassadors to Sparta to make known their indignation and put pressure on the Spartan government. Since Boeotia was now lost, they suggested the Thriasian plain, inland from Eleusis, as a suitable field of battle. Even now the Spartans delayed : day followed day, till ten days had gone by, and still no forces marched. At last the Athenian envoys, of whom Aristides was one, tired of this incorrigible procrastination, had recourse to threats, and announced that they would forthwith leave Sparta and return whence they came. Upon this the Ephors declared on oath that their troops had started and were already at Oresteum in Arcadia on their way to fight the barbarians. Finding on enquiry that a force of 5000 Spartan hoplites really had started,

[1] Herodotus, viii. 144 ; Rawlinson, iv. pp. 370 and 371.

the Athenian ambassadors hurried off with all speed to overtake them. Another force of 5000 Lacedaemonians, " all picked men and fully armed," though not Spartans, but Perioeci, started at the same time. The route followed was not the most direct route from Sparta to the Isthmus, perhaps with the object of lessening the danger of interference from Argos. For Argos, though she had not medized openly, had, seemingly, a secret understanding with the Persians. And now when the march of the Spartans in full force became known, the Argives with all speed sent a courier to Athens to inform Mardonius that the Spartans were on the march and the Argives were not strong enough to stop them.

Mardonius' Strategic Retreat to Boeotia.—Mardonius on receiving the tidings judged it expedient to fall back on Boeotia, because there the country offered better opportunities of using his cavalry. He was also influenced by the consideration that if the fortunes of war went against the Persians when fighting in Attica, their only way of retreat would lie through the passes of Mount Cithaeron. Before he began this withdrawal, however, he gave orders for the complete destruction of Athens. Not a building was to be left standing. Then the whole army retreated at leisure into Boeotia. One division—probably cavalry —was at the same time detached to make a raid into the territory of Megara. This force ravaged the Megarid, but when news came that the whole Greek army, consisting of the united forces of the Peloponnese, had already reached the Isthmus, it hastily retreated. Herodotus notes that this raid into the Megarid marks the furthest point southward reached by the Persians. On receiving news of the Greek advance, Mardonius made haste to quit Attica by the Pass of Decelea (Tatoi). Thence he marched by Tanagra to Thebes, and from Thebes as a base made his dispositions for the coming struggle. He posted his army behind the Asopus along the river bank westward from the high road between the Oakheads' pass and Thebes. He then gave orders for the construction of an immense fortified camp one mile square. To provide wood to build it, great numbers of trees were cut down in the Theban plain. About this time also the troops of the Greek states now subject to Persia joined Mardonius, Boeotians, Thessalians and others. Among these was a contingent from Phocis a thousand strong ; but the submission of Phocis had been unwilling, and bands of their fighting men still maintained themselves on the heights of Parnassus, and made raids on the Persian lines of communication, thereby rendering substantial service to the Hellenic cause. Mardonius' Greek auxiliaries Herodotus estimates at 50,000 men, which would bring his total forces up to 350,000. An element of weakness on the Persian side was that Artabazus, son of Pharnaces, who had escorted Xerxes to the Hellespont with 60,000 men, seems to have held a practically independent command, though nominally he was under Mardonius' orders.

The Greeks at the Isthmus.—When the Spartans reached the Isthmus they were quickly joined by troops from all the principal Peloponnesian states (except Argos). Herodotus gives the total Greek forces at Plataea as exactly 110,000 men, of whom 38,200 were Greek regulars, or hoplites. Of these latter the largest contingent was the Lacedaemonian, 10,000 strong, half being Spartans and half Perioeci. The Athenian force, which later crossed over from Salamis and joined the main army at Eleusis, numbered 8000. Corinth sent 5000 hoplites ; Megara and Sicyon, each 3000. Contingents of a thousand came severally from Troezen and Phlius ; 1500 men came from Tegea. The remainder of the 38,000 was made up of smaller contingents from other places within the Peloponnesus and a few from outside. Mycenae and Tiryns together supplied 400 men. Two hundred came from Cephallenia, one of the islands which in the *Odyssey* own Odysseus' sway. A small contingent also came from Leucadia, which some scholars now identify with Ithaca. The most distant place from which forces were sent was Potidaea, a colony of Corinth in the peninsula of Pallene.

The rest of Herodotus' total was light-armed. Herodotus reckons that seven Helots (serving as light-armed troops) accompanied each Spartan, and that one light-armed soldier may be counted for every heavy-armed ; but it is possible that this is very much of an over-estimate, for light-armed on the Greek side play very little part in the story of the battle. In any case, however, this was by far the largest army the Greeks ever mustered in the days of their freedom. Pausanias, son of Leonidas' younger brother, Cleombrotus, was in supreme command, being regent for his cousin Pleistarchus, Leonidas' son, who was quite a boy.

The March over Cithaeron.—This Greek army, assembled under the command of Pausanias at the Isthmus, shortly after advanced through Attica in pursuit of the retreating Persians. Their object was to bring the enemy to battle and overthrow him, thus ending once for all the peril of the Persian invasion. The Athenians had suggested the Thriasian plain as a suitable battle-ground : this was no longer possible as the Persians had evacuated Attica altogether and Pausanias must follow them. He did not, however, follow them through Decelea by the route taken by Mardonius in his retreat, but after reaching Eleusis (where they were met by the Athenian division), they turned north and took the direct road over Cithaeron by Eleutherae, which was and is the main highway between Athens and Thebes. This highway is thus described by Sir James Frazer (1898) : " From Eleusis the road to Eleutherae, which is at the same time the high-road from Athens to Thebes, goes north-west across the plain. The olive trees begin to appear soon after we have left Eleusis, and the road runs for three miles through thick groves of them to the large village of Mandra situated on a small height at the entrance to a valley ; for here the mountains which bound the plain of Eleusis begin. The native rock crops up among the houses and streets of the village. The hills that rise on both sides of the valley are wooded with pine. Beyond the village the valley contracts, and the road ascends for a long time

through the stillness and solitude of the pine-forest." [1]
This is the road by which the Greeks under Pausanias
marched in 479 B.C. till they came to the entrance of the
pass, "a narrow rocky defile, up which the road winds
tortuously between high pine-clad slopes on either hand.
In the very mouth of the pass . . . a steep conical, nearly
isolated hill rises up as if to bar the road. Its summit
is crowned with the grey walls and towers of Eleutherae." [2]

The road winds on and up under the ruins of this castle
for some miles further till it reaches the top of the pass,
and then a spacious view of the plain of Boeotia unfolds
itself to the eye " stretching away to the line of far blue
mountains which bounds it on all sides." " Below us,
but a little to the west, at the foot of the long uniform
slope of Cithaeron, the red village of Kokla marks the
site of Plataea. Thebes is hidden from view behind the
dip of a low intervening ridge. The sharp double-peaked
mountain on the west, beyond the nearer fir-clad de-
clivities of Cithaeron, is Helicon. The grand mountain-
mass, which, capped with snow, looms on the north-west,
is Parnassus." [3] This was the view on which the eyes of
Pausanias and the other Greeks rested as they came out
of the pass close to the little Boeotian town, Erythrae.
Here they learnt, Herodotus says, that the army of Mardonius was encamped upon the Asopus ; indeed they had
no need to ' learn,' for the whole country lay open to
view and they could see the long front of the Persian
position stretching parallel with their own bivouac on
the slope of Cithaeron. The enemy were in the plain a
few miles below them—only on the further side of the
Asopus.

The Passes and the Battle-ground.—To understand the
decisive battle of Plataea and the indecisive skirmishes
which led up to it, three points have to be clearly grasped.
The first is the difference between Greek and Persian
equipment, which naturally determined the tactics of
Mardonius and Pausanias to an equal extent but in

[1] Frazer's *Pausanias*, ii. p. 515.   [2] Frazer, *Pausanias*, ii. p. 516.
[3] Frazer, *Pausanias*, ii. pp. 516, 517.

opposite ways. The second is the nature of the ground between Plataea and the Asopus over which the struggle was to take place. The third is the general character of the Cithaeron range and the position of the passes between

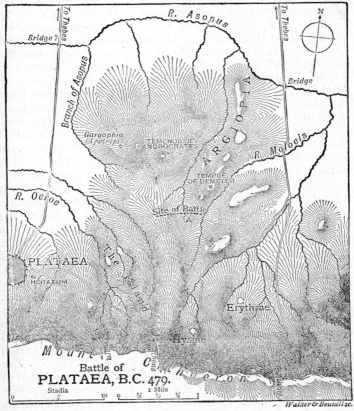

Attica and Boeotia. It is more convenient to take these points in reverse order. Cithaeron with its eastern continuation in Mount Parnes is a lofty range of hills averaging 3000 feet high and rising at its highest to 4620: it

stretches almost from sea to sea along the southern border
of Boeotia and makes a formidable barrier between
Boeotia and Attica. It is formed of rugged limestone
mountains, many of them thickly covered with pines, as
Frazer's descriptions have shown. So conspicuous is this
last feature that its name in modern Greece has come to
be *Elatias* or ' Pine mountain.' There are altogether six
passes across this barrier. Three of these do not concern
us here.[1] The three which concern us closely are the
pass from Plataea to Megara, the pass from Plataea to
Athens, and the pass on the main route from Athens to
Thebes along which Sir James Frazer's descriptions have
taken us. The outlets of these three passes all lie within a
short distance of each other along the slopes of Cithaeron ;
the easternmost, the main road past Eleutherae, was called
the Oak-heads (*Dryos-kephalae*) by the Athenians, and
by the Boeotians the Three Heads. From the heights
outside the passes the Boeotian plain appears a wide
expanse of one uniform level ; but when you get down
into it this impression is found to have been misleading.
That part of the plain which lies immediately below the
passes—over which the fighting was to take place—is
really very uneven, and some of the ridges by which it
is crossed are high enough to conceal the movements of
troops from each other in different parts of the plain.
The ridges—low outlying spurs of Cithaeron—run mostly
north and south with shallow streams flowing between ;
and halfway between the foot of the hills and the Asopus
(a distance of four miles) is a depression beyond which
the ground rises again towards the river. The ground
between the passes and the Asopus is thus very varied
in level and is much intersected by small streams. The
Greeks, as they deployed out of the pass, occupied a
position along the slope of the mountain (directly opposite
the position of the Persians in the plain) from Erythrae,
where the pass emerged, westward along the ridge towards

---

[1] These are the extreme eastern pass by Decelea, which was used by
Mardonius in his retreat ; the extreme western pass on the side of the
Gulf of Corinth by Creusis and Aegosthena to Pagae, the port of
Megara ; and the route from Athens by Phyle.

Plataea. This was a good defensive position, for it covered the main pass from Thebes to Athens, and was difficult of attack from the plain below. On the other hand these advantages were of no avail if Mardonius refused to attack. The strength of the Persians lay in their cavalry ; the strength of the Greeks in their heavy-armed infantry. The lightly garbed eastern soldiery were no match for the panoplied Greek hoplites fighting in serried array : both Thermopylae and Marathon had shown this. On the other hand, the Persian cavalry were largely horse-bowmen and their tactics were very much those employed by the Parthians (their kinsmen) some centuries later against the Romans. They could ride up to heavy-armed infantry, shower in their missiles and wheel off before the armour-clad spearmen could get to close quarters. More than that : in suitable country they could ride *round* heavy-armed infantry and attack them in flank and in rear. But for this the country must be suitable : it could not be done over rough stony country, still less on the steep slopes of a mountain range. Consequently the evolutions which followed between the emergence of the Greek columns from the Oak-heads' Pass and the final decisive struggle near Plataea resolve themselves into a contest of patience between Pausanias and Mardonius ; the Persian commander trying to induce the Greeks to attack him in positions where he could make full use of his cavalry ; the Greek commander seeking to provoke the Persians to a general engagement wherein the superior weight of the ranks of hoplites might have its full effect.

Repulse of the Persian Horse.—Accordingly the Greeks at first took up this strong defensive position on the slopes of Cithaeron. Mardonius does not seem to have made any attempt to assail the Greeks as their columns extended on coming out of the pass ; still less was he minded to leave his fortified camps on the Asopus and make a general attack on the Greek position. But he did send his cavalry to see what they could do. They were commanded by Masistius, a splendid figure on a

Nisaean charger magnificently caparisoned and with a golden bit. Now there was only one part of the Greek position assailable by cavalry, that over the lower ground on either side of the high road out of the pass. Over this ground the Persian horsemen charged by squadrons in successive waves, partly because the front was narrow, partly expecting in this way to wear down the enemy's resistance. For each squadron could ride up at the gallop in turn, discharge its arrows, then wheel round to make way for the squadron next following. The troops holding this part of the Greek line—it was near the centre—were those from Megara. The Megarians soon found themselves hard beset and sent a message to the general asking to be relieved. Pausanias called for volunteers, and, according to Herodotus, only the Athenians responded. They sent a body of three hundred picked hoplites and all the bowmen in their force. The action which followed is thus described by Herodotus : " As the cavalry kept charging by squadrons the war-horse of Masistius (which was in front of the rest) was hit in the flank by an arrow, reared in agony and threw his rider. When Masistius was down, the Athenians instantly rushed upon him. They captured his horse, and when Masistius himself offered resistance, proceeded to kill him. This they were at first not able to do, the reason being the nature of his defensive armour ; he had on a golden corslet of chain mail below his tunic, and the scarlet tunic outside. While their blows fell on this corslet, they produced no effect ; but presently a soldier noticed why this was and thrust him through the eye." [1] When the horsemen discovered the loss of their leader, they rallied and with loud cries charged upon the Athenians in a mass. The Athenians were at first borne back by the rush, and for a time the Persians got possession of the body. But in answer to an appeal for assistance other reinforcements came up and after a fierce fight the horsemen broke and fled. They came to a halt a quarter of a mile off, but instead of attacking again, withdrew and

[1] Herodotus, ix. 22.

reported the loss of their leader to Mardonius. When Mardonius and the Persians heard the ill tidings they made great lamentation : " they shaved their heads and cut short the manes of their horses and their baggage animals, and filled the air with cries of grief. All Boeotia echoed with the sound of their mourning, for the leader they had lost was esteemed of most account after Mardonius both by the Persians in general and by the King." [1]

Advance of the Greeks.—The first encounter in Boeotia had thus gone in favour of the Greeks : they had repulsed the attacks of the Persian cavalry. But as yet they were no nearer their real object, a general engagement and the defeat of the enemy's main forces. Pausanias therefore determined, in consultation with the other Greek commanders, to descend the slope of Cithaeron and take up a position nearer the Persian army, which was in bivouac on the further side of the Asopus with its left resting on the fortified Persian camp. The Greeks were in good spirits for fighting after their initial success against the Persian horse ; on the lower ground they could camp in greater comfort, and, in particular, would be better off for water. Accordingly orders were given to strike camp and the whole army marched a couple of miles westward, past Hysiae and towards Plataea ; then descended into the plain and took up the new positions marked out for them, " partly along some hillocks of no great height, and partly upon the level of the plain." The Greek right, held by the Lacedaemonians and the men of Tegea, was on the higher ground in front of the spring Gargaphia, the chief water supply of the whole army ; the Athenians were on the extreme left where the ground was lowest.

The Days of Waiting.—Their object, of course, was to bring the Persians to battle ; there may even have been some expectation of effecting an outflanking movement and taking the enemy by surprise ; but, if so, the expectation came to nothing. Neither did the Persians cross the Asopus and attack. Mardonius when apprised

[1] Herodotus, ix. 24.

I

2 A

of the advance of the Greeks into the Plataean territory,
moved his whole army into new positions further up the
Asopus and opposite the Greek encampment, but still
with the main stream of the Asopus between. The two
armies in full array were thus facing each other on
opposite sides of the Asopus, but neither crossed to the
attack. Mardonius, though eager to fight, was desirous
of fighting on his own terms. He had deliberately placed
his front behind the Asopus, and he wished to force the
Greeks to attack him under the disadvantage of having
first to cross the river. This, however, the Greek commanders were nowise minded to do. Their plan was to
wait for Mardonius to attack. Consequently for some
days—Herodotus says for eight—there was a deadlock.
Each side waited for the other to begin. Each army
had offered sacrifice in accordance with Greek ritual to
see if the signs from heaven were favourable ; and to
each the answer of the sacrificing priest was the same ;
the signs were unfavourable, if they crossed the river to
attack ; they promised victory alike to Greeks and
Persians, if they remained on the defensive. In such
wise we see the sacrificial divination of the ancients was
often a means of giving weight to a general's judgment
of military expediency. For the Greeks this waiting was
not wholly disadvantageous, for their numbers were
strengthened from day to day by fresh arrivals from the
Isthmus, contingents of troops that had come too late
for the general rendezvous. On the other hand, Mardonius, through his overwhelming superiority in cavalry,
had it in his power to make the Greeks very uncomfortable in their exposed position ; and this accordingly he
proceeded to do, when he found they refused to cross to
the attack. If the Greeks had any cavalry it was not in
such number as to be able to afford any effective check
on the movements of the Persian horse, and the Persian
horse, who swarmed all over the open plain, were practically free to work round the Greek positions at their
pleasure. They were thus able to threaten to intercept
all the supplies which were coming to the Greek army

from the Peloponnese by raiding the passes—one of their exploits was to destroy or capture the whole of a large convoy of five hundred animals at the Oak Heads ; and they harassed and distressed the Greek forces by incessant attacks. This did not, however, satisfy Mardonius, whose impatience grew day by day, especially when he perceived the Greek numbers steadily growing. So he took his colleague, Artabazus, into council, pressing his own wish to take the offensive forthwith. Artabazus, however, was altogether against risking a general action. He advised a withdrawal to the secure protection of the walls of Thebes, where they had provisions and fodder in abundance ; and then an attempt to bring over the leaders of the Greek states by a liberal use of money. In this way he thought the subjection of Greece might be effected without any more fighting at all. But Mardonius would have nothing of this. The Persian army, he declared, was far stronger than the Greek ; they ought to join battle at once and not suffer the numbers gathered against them to grow greater. As for Hegesistratus (the Greek soothsayer) and his sacrificial victims, no heed was to be paid to them ; instead of straining the interpretation of omens, they should follow their own customs like true Persians and fight. Then he charged all his officers to prepare for battle.

Alexander's Warning.—That night, the eleventh since the advance of Pausanias to the Asopus, when the watches were set and both armies deep in slumber (Herodotus relates), a solitary horseman rode up to the Athenian outposts and asked to speak with certain commanders whom he named. When these officers came he informed them that Mardonius was fully prepared to attack next day. " Had I not greatly at heart the common welfare of Greece," he said, " I should not have come to tell you : but I am myself a Greek by descent, and I would not willingly see Hellas exchange freedom for slavery. Know then that Mardonius and his army cannot obtain favourable omens ; had it not been for this, they would have fought with you long ago. Now, however, they have determined to let the victims pass unheeded, and, as soon as day dawns, to engage in battle. Mardonius, I imagine, is afraid that, if he delays, you will increase in number. Make ready then to receive him. Should he, however, still defer the combat, do you abide where you are : for his provisions will not hold out many more days. If ye prosper in this war, forget not to do something for my freedom ; consider the risk I have run, out of zeal for the Greek cause, to acquaint you with what Mardonius intends, and to save you from being surprised by the barbarians. I am Alexander of Macedon." [1]

Successes of the Persian Cavalry.—There was no general attack next day, but the Persian horse were active again. They rode up to the Greek lines and made attacks as they pleased, pouring in arrows and javelins, but keeping their distance carefully. Probably there were attacks on flank and in rear as well as in front. The Greek troops were sorely distressed, enduring fatigue and losses in the dust and heat, without being able to retaliate ; for whenever they tried to get to close quarters the horsemen eluded them. Worst of all, the cavalry made a successful attack on the water springs which Herodotus calls the Fountain Gargaphia and left them choked and useless. This meant the loss of their main water supply for practically the whole army. For though the Greek left rested on a branch of the Asopus and the main stream was in front not far away, this was of no use to them, for the Persian horse kept them off with their missiles.

Greek Withdrawal on Plataea.—The whole Greek army was now in a bad way. Their water supply was gone ; their store of provisions was exhausted, and the passes by which alone fresh supplies could come from their base at the Isthmus were now, it appears, in the hands of the enemy : for we hear of convoys blockaded in them. The infantry, too, had been put to severe distress by the ceaseless attacks of the enemy's horse. That nigh-

---

[1] Herodotus, ix. 45 ; Rawlinson, iv. pp. 412 and 413. This inciden makes a pretty story, but it does not fit in very well with the rest c Herodotus' narrative.

THE RIDGE OF CITHAERON FROM THE BOEOTIAN PLAIN.

Looking from the plain across the battlefield of Plataea to Cithaeron.

Pausanias held a council of war at which it was agreed that, if the general engagement expected did not come off next day, the whole of the Greek forces should retire to new positions adjoining the city of Plataea, and that from this new position one-half of their available forces should be despatched to recover the command of the passes and relieve the convoys. This retirement was to be made silently and secretly in the night, to avoid harassment by the Persian cavalry while their forces were on the move. Through all the day following, the attacks of the Persian cavalry continued without cessation, but there was no general engagement. Accordingly at nightfall all dispositions were made for retreat as agreed. But the 'morale' of the whole army had been shaken and the retirement was not carried out as planned. What exactly happened in the night it is difficult to understand from Herodotus' narrative, our only original authority. It is precise and detailed, but the parts do not hold together consistently. The result, however, is clear enough. When morning came, the Greek army which had made one front on the Asopus was broken up into three detachments. The Athenians were moving from their old position on the extreme left along the depression distinguished on p. 366 ; the Lacedaemonians and the men of Tegea who held the right were retiring over the high ground further east ; the whole of the centre was out of sight under the walls of Plataea.

The Battle.—When morning dawned—it was the fourteenth day since the Greeks came down into the plain—the Persian horse rode out as on previous days to repeat their harassing tactics. They discovered, of course, that the positions were empty, and at once dashed off in pursuit. About the same time tidings that the Greeks had abandoned their positions and were in retreat were carried to Mardonius. Mardonius, elated at the news and believing that the Greeks were beaten and in flight, at once led his Persians over the Asopus. They were followed by other divisions of troops in rapid succession. The Lacedaemonians and Tegeans were in plain view retreating over the ridge ; the Athenians, though really nearer, were hidden by the swell of the plain ; the divisions forming the Greek centre were right out of sight. Consequently the whole brunt of the first attack was borne by the Lacedaemonians and the men of Tegea. The barbarians rushed forward at their best speed with little regard for order : " on they went with loud shouts and in a wild rout, thinking to swallow up the runaways." [1] The Spartans were hard pressed and sent a horseman to summon the Athenians to their assistance. But Mardonius' Greek allies had now come up and were attacking the Athenians ; it was not possible for them to comply. The main battle, accordingly, resolved itself into a duel between the Lacedaemonian troops supported by the Tegeans and the whole army of Mardonius excepting the renegade Greeks. Herodotus computes the combined force of Lacedaemonians and Tegeans at fifty thousand.[2] What proportion of Mardonius' three hundred thousand is to be reckoned as actually engaged is difficult to say ; possibly about half that total. At first the Lacedaemonians merely stood their ground ; the victims were still unfavourable ; for while they waited they once more sought to learn the will of heaven by sacrifice. Many fell on the Spartan side during this delay and many more were wounded : " For the Persians made a barrier of their wicker shields, and from behind this poured in their arrows so that the Spartans were in sore distress ; and when the sacrifices still proved inauspicious, Pausanias turned his eyes towards the Heraeum of the Plataeans and called upon the goddess, beseeching her not to let them be cheated of their hopes. And while he was still praying, the men of Tegea were first to move forward and advanced upon the barbarians ; and immediately after Pausanias' prayer the sacrificial signs became favourable for the Lacedaemonians. And when this at last

---

[1] Herodotus, ix. 59 ; Rawlinson, iv. 421 and 422.

[2] But of the 50,000, if Herodotus' estimate may be accepted, all but 11,500 were light-armed. Of the 11,500 men-at-arms, 5000 were Spartans, 5000 other Lacedaemonians and 1500 Tegeans.

happened, they too went forward against the Persians,
and the Persians let go their bows and met them face to
face. Then first there was a fight about the barrier of
shields. And when this had gone down, the battle grew
fierce hard by the shrine of Demeter and lasted long time
till it came to a close struggle hand to hand. For the
Persians took hold of the spears and broke them off
short. In martial spirit, indeed, and in bodily strength
the Persians were not inferior to the Greeks ; but they
were without shields, and further were untrained and not
equal to their antagonists in military skill ; and so dashing
forward one by one or ten together, sometimes fewer in
number, sometimes more, they closed in combat with the
Spartans and perished. They pressed their enemies
hardest in the part of the field where Mardonius himself
was, riding a white charger, and with the thousand picked
Persians, the flower of their nation, about him. And as
long as Mardonius was alive, they held their ground
stoutly and struck down many of the Lacedaemonians :
but when Mardonius was slain and those about
him, who were the best strength of the Persian
host, were all fallen, the rest of the forces gave way
before the Lacedaemonians and took to flight. What
most put them at a disadvantage was their light equipment, and, in particular, their not having shields ; for
it resulted from this that they were like men without
armour contending with men fully armed." [1]

Such is Herodotus' description of the great fight between Spartans and Persians which decided the battle of
Plataea. He adds : " Then was the warning of the oracle
fulfilled ; and the vengeance which was due to the Spartans for the slaughter of Leonidas was paid them by
Mardonius—then too did Pausanias, the son of Cleombrotus . . . win a victory exceeding in glory all those to
which our knowledge extends." [2] He records also that
Mardonius was slain by a Spartan named Arimnestus.

Once routed, the Persian forces fled confusedly from
the field down the valleys towards the Asopus and took

[1] Herodotus, ix. 61-63.   [2] Herodotus. ix. 64 ; Rawlinson, iv. p. 425.

refuge in their fortified camp. The Persian cavalry at this stage once more showed their usefulness by covering the fugitive footmen and checking the pursuit. Meanwhile the Athenians had fought with Mardonius' Greek contingents from Boeotia, Thessaly and Macedonia and defeated them. With the exception of the Thebans these Greeks and semi-Greeks fought with no heart, or even declined to fight at all. But the Thebans fought fiercely and stubbornly, and were only beaten after heavy loss. Some of the other Greeks, who hurried up to support the Athenians in somewhat loose order, were caught in the plain by the Theban cavalry and cut up. The Theban infantry in their flight made for Thebes; the rest of the medizing Greeks dispersed.

The End of the Great Invasion.—The Athenians thus freed joined the Spartans in their attack on the Persian camp. It was an elaborately constructed fortification with ramparts and high towers, and for a time the defenders resisted vigorously. Presently a breach was made and the victorious Greeks poured through, the Arcadians of Tegea leading. A terrible carnage ensued. All resistance ceased, but no quarter was given, and with the exception of fugitives who escaped to the open country all Persia's myriads perished in that slaughter-house. Only 3000 survived. That is, out of those who fought with Mardonius on the field of Plataea. It is related that Artabazus with his separate army, now reduced to some 40,000 men, was absent from the battle, and finally effected a retreat through Thessaly and Thrace to the Hellespont; but only after considerable losses through famine and the attacks of Thracian tribes. So ended Xerxes' great invasion. The Greek losses were comparatively inconsiderable, though they cannot possibly have been so light as Herodotus makes them—91 Spartans, 16 Tegeans, 52 Athenians, apart from 600 Megarians and Phliasians caught in the open by the Boeotian horse. The dead were buried nation by nation on the field of battle. The body of Mardonius disappeared the day after the battle.

The Four Phases of the Battle.—In the battle of Plataea, which was rather a campaign than a battle, there were, as we have seen, four distinct stages or phases. The first was the skirmish on the slope of Cithaeron where the road from the Pass of the Oak Heads led down to the plain. Here the Persian cavalry, which attacked the Greek lines soon after they had taken up their position on emerging from the pass, were repulsed and their leader Masistius was slain. In the second phase the two armies lay for some days opposite each other, with the Asopus between them, each waiting for the other to attack. But here Mardonius, though he did not as yet venture on a general engagement, was able to use his cavalry with effect, and by cutting off convoys and harassing the Greek troops by attacks at various points on the front and flanks and in rear, finally ruining their water supply, rendered their position untenable. The third and decisive action was fought while the Greeks were in the midst of the withdrawal necessitated by the attacks of the Persian cavalry. It resolved itself mainly into a duel between Mardonius and the best Persian troops on one side and the Spartans under Pausanias on the other. In this duel the Spartans and Tegeans were victorious after a hard-fought struggle and Mardonius was killed. Finally, there was the fight in the Persian fortified camp, which, as soon as the Greeks had stormed the ramparts at one point, was turned into a massacre. Not merely was the whole of the Great King's army worsted at Plataea, it was annihilated.

CHAPTER XVI

THE GREAT DELIVERANCE

" The invasion of Hellas by the myriads of the Persian Empire and their ultimate repulse constitute an event in the history of the world which is unsurpassed alike in importance and in dramatic grandeur."

SYKES, *History of Persia*, i. p. 198.

" Marathon, Salamis and Plataea were victories not only for Greece but for mankind. It was the triumph of the higher ideal."

Ib. p. 225.

IN the At Meidan at Constantinople (once the Hippodrome of Constantine), in front of the Mosque of Sultan Ahmed, there stands to this day a bronze column not much short of twenty feet high, formed of three entwined serpents, on the lower coils of which are engraved the names of the Hellenic states which fought at Plataea and Salamis. This column was originally the base on which stood the golden tripod dedicated from the tenth of the spoils taken at Plataea, and was set up at Delphi. The gold was melted down by the Phocians in the Sacred War, a hundred and thirty years after the battle of Plataea. The serpent column was removed from Delphi by the Emperor Constantine and placed in the Hippodrome of his new capital, where it served to support the mechanism of a fountain. The serpent heads have been broken off and lost (one is said to have been severed by Muhammed II. with an axe), but the pillared coils have survived the conquest of the Turk, and most of the inscriptions have been deciphered. This was the chief of the offerings dedicated to the gods by the Hellenes in commemoration of their great deliverance, and its scarred and mutilated remains are one of the most interesting memorials in the world.

A greater memorial, omnipresent, is incorporated into the very texture of our civilization : into our literature and science, and our political institutions, which would never have been shaped to their present form had the issue of the conflict been different. " A battle so great and so important," says Dr. Grundy, " must necessarily excite the imagination of any student of history. It is hardly an exaggeration to say that much of the environment of our daily life at the present day owes its existence to the issue of that struggle in the hollow beneath the temple of Eleusinian Demeter. Had the great battle turned out differently, as it so very nearly did, the whole history of the fifth century might have been altered." [1] Salamis was the supreme crisis, the victory which made the final repulse of the Persian conqueror possible, but Plataea was needed to consummate the great deliverance. With the victories of Plataea and Mycale, [2] the menace of submergence under the levelling flood of oriental despotism, which for twenty years had threatened the free life of Hellas, was at length completely removed. The flood was rising when the efforts of the Ionians to regain their lost liberties were crushed at Lade ; it rolled onward in full force when Xerxes' myriads poured across the Hellespont bridges and surged past the barriers of Olympus and Oeta. It was stayed by the brave onset of the Greek warships at Salamis and by the disciplined

[1] Grundy, *The Great Persian War*, p. 511.

[2] On the same day that the conflict between Mardonius and Hellas was fought out in Boeotia, the Greek fleet won a signal victory at Mycale, the hilly promontory on the coast of Asia Minor opposite the island of Samos, which was the seat of the Pan-Ionic festival. The fleet had by this time crossed the Aegean to raise Ionia. The King's fleet shunned any further encounter by sea, beached their ships and built a stockade to defend them. The Greeks landed, defeated the troops who opposed them, then carried the stockade with great slaughter of the Persians and burnt all the ships.

valour of the hoplites at Plataea. The Persian wars went on for many years more, but they were waged in Asiatic, not European, waters ; never again did a Persian invader set foot on the soil of Hellas.

Critical Retrospect.—When we get to the end of the story as recorded in the pages of Herodotus, perhaps, for the moment, our uppermost feeling is of wonder that Hellas came safe through at all : the mistakes, the weaknesses, the hesitations, the selfishness, the disabling jealousies—the treacheries even of the Hellenes, seem so many and so serious. Amid such timidities, misunderstandings and errors of narrow vision, how were the Greeks able to make a successful resistance ? Their victory would be incomprehensible were not their faults and errors compensated by high qualities which more than redress the balance, and were not the account to be further balanced with the mistakes and weaknesses of the Persians.

Faults and Weakness of the Greek Defence.—The outline of events we have followed has shown how painfully lacking were the Hellenes as a whole in the ability to take a large and generous view of the necessities of combined Hellenic defence, if Hellas was to escape subjugation by a military power so overwhelming as was that of the Great King. There was, indeed, a perception on the part of the leading Greek states of the mainland, on the part of Athens and Sparta at all events, of the imperative necessity of unity of plan and purpose and of loyal devotion to the cause. Yet twice the considered plans of Hellenic defence were wrecked : once when no sincere effort was made to meet the Persians in Thessaly ; a second time, and more disastrously, when no Peloponnesian army went to Thermopylae, as had been promised, in support of the slender vanguard with Leonidas. From what actually happened at Thermopylae it is clear as daylight that, with half the force which next year gathered to fight Mardonius in Boeotia, the Greeks could have held Thermopylae, both the pass and the track above it by which it was turned, so that, provided the Greek fleet kept the sea, Xerxes' myriads would have beaten against the gates of Hellas in vain. The military chiefs at Sparta cannot be absolved of responsibility for this failure, whether it was due to calculated duplicity (the secret disinclination to fight at all north of the Isthmus), or merely to slowness and want of enterprise. All the Peloponnesian states appear to have been guilty of the stupid selfishness which narrowed their conception of the national interest to the Peloponnesus. In blind confidence that, if only they built their wall across the Isthmus strong enough, the Peloponnese was secure, they had no regard or care for the fate of the Hellenic states outside, too dull for all their Hellenic quickness of mind to see that the only real security for each and all, both within the Peloponnesus and without, was to meet and overcome the invader as far from the Isthmus as possible. The case of the disloyal Hellenes who accepted the Mede for their master and, willingly or unwillingly, joined forces with him against their countrymen was worse. Of such there were too many. The wilful traitors were worst, the Thessalian Aleuadae, the Thebans and the Argives ; but the Thessalians and Boeotians and the other Greeks who gave earth and water showed but a poor spirit and deserved the servitude they ultimately escaped through the constancy of better men. Strangest of all is the Medism of Delphi. For it hardly admits of question that the utterance of Apollo's prophetic shrine, which should have been a trumpet call to Hellas, was a voice of doubt and wavering and coward fear. All the greater honour to the undaunted Hellenic patriots who upheld the national cause, when even the national god, who claimed to interpret the very will of Heaven, seemed to counsel despair and submission.

Again, the path over Anopaea by which Thermopylae was turned should have been secure from any and every assault with its thousand Phocians to hold it : it was only through the Phocians' unpardonable want of vigilance and their failure to do their duty when surprised,

that **Hydarnes** and his Immortals slipped by. Thermopylae was lost by a twofold betrayal : first, the betrayal
of Leonidas and all with him by the war-chiefs in Peloponnesus ; secondly, by the incompetence, or cowardice,
of the Phocians, who at the mere sight of an enemy
abandoned the narrow track they were posted to keep.
It almost seems that a people who between them were
responsible for such a miscarriage of well-laid plans did
not deserve to be saved.

The Qualities which saved Hellas.—Yet saved they
were : and more than anything else what saved the
Greeks and enabled them after all to come victoriously
out of the struggle, was their downright courage and
skill as men-at-arms when it came to fighting at close
quarters. In the actual clash of battle the stout spear
and the broad shield, wielded as Greek hoplites learnt to
wield them, were more than a match for the bows and
javelins and mail corslets of the Persians, even with the
advantage of their numerous and mobile cavalry to
support them. The phalanx of spearmen was like a
rock against which the waves of Persian chivalry, horse
and foot alike, beat in vain. This superiority of the
Greeks in battle depended on training, and on training
in two senses. It depended on the formal military training which made the Greek man-at-arms a disciplined
soldier instead of a ' brave.' For as Demaratus said to
Xerxes : " The Lacedaemonians, fighting in single combat, are as good men as any ; but, when they fight in a
body, are the best in the world." [1] The Greeks were
disciplined soldiers in a sense in which the Persians with
all their bravery were not, nor any of the levies Xerxes
brought with him from Asia. This is one of the immemorial differences of east and west. It is found in an
incipient form already in the Tale of Troy, where in the
third *Iliad* Homer describes the noise and outcry of the
advancing Trojans as contrasting with the steady silent
march of the Achaeans.[2] It is the same difference which
enabled Wellesley's army to scatter swarms of Mahratta

[1] Herodotus, vii. 104.   [2] *Iliad*, iii. 2-9.

horse and foot, many times more numerous, at Assaye.[1]
So in the accounts of Thermopylae and of Plataea we see
how the Persians come on with splendid impetuosity,
but not in any set order. They fight as single warriors
or a few together, but not as drilled men united by a
common discipline. " Dashing forward one by one or
ten together, sometimes fewer in number, sometimes
more, they closed in combat with the Spartans and
perished," writes Herodotus of Plataea. What a steady,
disciplined thing a Greek phalanx was we know ; it even
seems to us stiff and unwieldy ; but its whole efficacy
rested on steadiness combined with skilful management of
weapons. It was only by assiduous drill and constant
practice in the use of their arms that the warrior-cham-
pions of the heroic age were transformed into the powerful
engine of war which the phalanx of hoplites became. It
was drill and discipline and steady practice which enabled
the hoplite to use his short spear and heavy shield with
such force and dexterity as gave him the victory over
all ' barbarians.' But no less did Hellenic disciplined
warfare depend for its efficacy on training in the other
sense—athletic training and bodily fitness (let it not be
forgotten that ' athletics ' is a Greek word)—or what the
Hellenes called ' gymnastic.' Every citizen of a Greek
state who bore arms was in hard training, or something
approaching to it. Greek ' gymnastic ' was directed to
developing general bodily fitness as much as our games :
and when it came to real war, this counted. The Persians
were fine men physically ; Dr. Grundy even suggests
that, man for man, they were probably better than the
Greeks in physique and courage.[2] But they had not the
regular bodily training of the Greek gymnasium and
palaestra, and that made a difference.

The mental side of such discipline and training is,

[1] The Mahrattas were 50,000 ; the British 4500.

[2] The elements of Persian liberal education were (Herodotus affirms)
to ride, to shoot with the bow and to speak the truth. A polo match
between Persians and Turks is described in Firdausi's *Shah-nama* as
being played, eight a side, in the days of the legendary hero Siawush
and of Afrasiab, king of Turan.

however, more important than the bodily. It was the ordered support of his comrades to right and left, on which the Greek shield-bearer could count, that was his strength in the day of battle. It was not the prowess of individual warriors that decided the fight now as in epic combats; it was the capacity of the phalanx to act together as a complex unity, the actions of all its members coordinated to the common end. There were higher things still which upheld the Greek citizen-soldier and made him terrible in fight. There was his inborn love of freedom and belief in a free mån's dignity. Above all, there was his patriotism, his intense love of his own city. It was mostly a narrow patriotism, but it was the more intense for that; and for many—as we may believe, for instance, of Themistocles—it was expanded into love of Hellas. The Hellenes in many a feud between neighbours had learnt to fight and die for their 'polis,' and when the great invasion came they showed they could fight and die for Hellas.

Causes of Persian Defeat.—The Persians, though they had pride of race and courage and physical prowess and personal devotion to their king, had no 'patriotism' like this. They had no such intense feeling for their country as the Greeks had severally for Sparta, or Athens, or Plataea. We have seen in Chapter XI. what formidable antagonists the Persians were, not alone for the numbers they could bring with them into the field, but for their own good qualities, too. Individually the picked Persian guardsmen were no bad match for the Spartans. Of the conflict at Plataea Herodotus expressly testifies that " in martial spirit and in bodily strength the Persians were not inferior." [1] The strategy of Mardonius compares not unfavourably with the strategy of Pausanias. In organization the Persians showed themselves greatly superior. For the organizing powers required for the transportation of the vast armies and fleets of Xerxes from the Hellespont to Attica, and to keep armies and fleet in touch, were something out of all proportion to any organizing faculty

[1] Quoted above, p. 375.

shown by the Greeks ; and up to Salamis—except for the
storms which were beyond human control—all had gone
without a hitch. The Persians had the great advantage
of nearly absolute unity of command ; land forces and
sea forces alike obeyed without question the will of the
king. Whatever the king ordered was sedulously carried
out, and there seems to have been throughout army and
fleet keen emulation to gratify Xerxes personally, an
emulation by no means confined to the king's Persian
subjects. Why, then, were the Persians beaten ?

Contrast of Discipline.—It was not wholly on account of
the inferiority of Persian arms and equipment. Herodotus
himself makes too much of this : " What most put them
at a disadvantage was their light equipment, and, in
particular, their not having shields ; for it resulted from
this that they were like men without armour contending
with men fully armed." [1] That is true, but it is not
the whole truth, nor the most important part of it.
Steady discipline—Hellenic discipline—counted for more
than big shields and heavy spears, though, to be sure,
the two went necessarily together. For without training
and discipline the heavy equipment of the hoplite would
have been no use at all, only an encumbrance. But
more than discipline was the patriotism which nerved
the Greek to stand firm in the defence of his *polis*, and
the spirit of comradeship which bound him to the fellow-
citizens who stood beside him in the ranks.

Persian Character.—The Persians were brave and energetic, generous and hospitable, but along with these good
qualities they had, and have to this day, certain defects of
character. These are said by one who knows modern
Persia intimately to be lack of self-control, intense
vanity and love of luxury. [2] These same faults certainly appear conspicuously from time to time in
Herodotus' narrative. The Persian luxury which impressed the Greeks so strongly is well illustrated

[1] Herodotus, ix. 63, part of the passage quoted, Ch. XV. p. 375.

[2] See Sir Percy Sykes, *History of Persia*, i. ch. xv. p 182.

I   2 B

by a story which Herodotus tells of Pausanias after Plataea. " When Xerxes fled from Greece he left his camp-equipage with Mardonius. Now when Pausanias saw Mardonius' tent furnished with gold and silver and richly embroidered curtains, he ordered the cooks and the bakers to prepare a dinner exactly as they would have done for Mardonius. When they did as he commanded, Pausanias, beholding the gold and silver couches with beautiful coverlets laid over them, the tables of gold and of silver, and the sumptuous provision for the repast, was amazed at the good things before him, and, with mocking intention, ordered his own servants to prepare a Spartan dinner. And when the great difference between the two banquets was manifested, Pausanias laughed and sent for the Greek commanders. When they had come he pointed to the two tables and said : ' The reason I called you together, gentlemen, is that I wish to show you the folly of this Median general, who, when his daily fare was such as you see, came against us to rob us of our poverty.' " [1]

Persian Luxury.—The Persian grandee went to war attended by all the paraphernalia of luxury to an extent that did not conduce to military efficiency. Rich furniture, couches plated with gold and silver, and golden drinking vessels were found in great number among the booty in the Persian camp on the Asopus. Elsewhere in describing the arms and accoutrements of all the various tribes and peoples in Xerxes' host, Herodotus concludes : " Of all the troops the Persians were adorned with the greatest magnificence, and they were likewise the most valiant . . . they glittered all over with gold, vast quantities of which they wore about their persons. They were followed by litters, wherein rode their concubines, and by a numerous train of attendants handsomely dressed. Camels and sumpter-beasts carried their provision, apart from that of the other soldiers." [2]

[1] Herodotus, ix. 82.
[2] Herodotus, vii. 83 ; Rawlinson, iv. p. 71.

Persian Conceit.—Persian vanity is brought out vividly in various places in Herodotus' narrative ; when, for example, he says that the Persians estimated the valour of other nations by the distance of their country from Persia, reckoning themselves the most valiant of mankind. We may recall that when the Persians saw the Athenians charging at Marathon they took them for men demented, so confident were they in their own superiority. It was a similar vanity which led the naval commanders to fall so easily into the trap set for them by Themistocles before Salamis. But it is in Xerxes himself that this self-conceit of the Persians is exhibited in its most inordinate form. Xerxes is Persian vanity personified. The stories in which Herodotus revels of Xerxes scourging the Hellespont ; of Xerxes sitting on a white throne and watching the review of his armies and fleets ; of Xerxes waiting three days before Thermopylae for the Spartans to run away, all illustrate this point and serve to lend piquancy to the contrast of Xerxes traversing Thrace followed by a disorderly and demoralized rout of men, or (as Aeschylus pictures) arriving at Susa travel-worn, his royal robes soiled and ragged. With this inordinate vanity and overweening pride went an infatuated belief in the efficacy of numbers and of material resources. It was this which made it impossible for Xerxes to believe the Greeks would ever offer any serious resistance to his marching myriads. It was this which made him deaf to Artabanus' warning that two of the mightiest forces in the world were inimical to his success. " Strange man," said Xerxes, " what are these two mighty forces you mean ? Would you find ground for cavil in the number of my army, and think you the Greek host will be more numerous than ours ? Or is it our fleet which will fall short of theirs ? Or do you find both deficient ? If in this respect our strength appears to you defective, it were easy with all speed to gather fresh forces." But Artabanus answered and said : " O king, no one who had any sense would find fault with your army, nor

with the number of your ships. Nay, if you gathered
more, the two things of which I speak would become far
more hostile still. These two are the land and the sea.
In all the sea there is not, I suppose, anywhere a harbour
large enough, should a storm arise, to receive your fleet,
and ensure its safe preservation. And yet not one such
harbour only ought you to have, but harbours along all
the coasts of the mainland by which you voyage. But
if there are not harbours to receive your ships, remember
that men are ever at the mercy of accidents. And now
that I have explained one of the two dangers, I will
go on to speak of the other. The land is your settled
foe in this way : even if no opposition is offered to your
advance, it becomes more hostile in proportion as you
advance further, lured on by success ; for men are never
satisfied with their achievements. So even though no
one at all opposes your advance, I say the lengthening
distance, as time goes on, must at last produce famine." [1]

The Sin of Presumption.—To the thoughtful Greek the
overthrow of the fleets and armies of Xerxes was a
sublime manifestation of the chastisement which the
moral forces governing the universe mete out to the
overweening pride of man. Aeschylus and Herodotus
alike are impressed with the poignant contrast between
Xerxes setting out in the fulness of his splendour as the
Great King, marching in the midst of armed myriads and
his swarming fleets, digging a trench across the neck of
Mount Athos, bridging the Hellespont, draining rivers
dry with the multitude of his host ; and Xerxes scurrying
like a fugitive through Macedonia and Thrace, his fleets
destroyed, his pride lowered. Herodotus calls this chastisement which overtakes the sin of presumption the
divine ' indignation,' or Nemesis. He shares with Aeschylus the belief that human power and pride, when they grow
excessive and wax insolent, surely bring down God's wrath
and end in calamity. In this they only express a common
Greek opinion which seemed to find impressive confirmation from time to time in the great reversals of fortune

[1] Herodotus, vii. 48 and 49.

in human story—the " Falls of Princes," as our mediaeval
men of letters entitled them.   Xerxes was to the Greeks
the supreme example of such a reversal.   In him " the
haughtiness of men was made low," and it was the vain
presumption of man and the nothingness of his pride to
which the Greek chiefly looked.   So Aeschylus puts the
moral into the mouth of Darius, appearing as a spirit at
the summons of Atossa, his queen, in the hour of Persia's
humiliation :

> " Let not a mortal vaunt him overmuch.
>   For pride grows rankly, and to ripeness brings
>   The curse of fate, and reaps, for harvest, tears." [1]

Moral Causes in History.—And, certainly, we may so
far accept this Greek view of the nemesis of pride as to
recognize in the result of the Great War of five hundred
years before Christ an example, many times confirmed
since, of the importance of moral issues in history.   The
Persian failed against Hellas, because his cause was a
worse cause, because the principles his power stood for
were lower principles than the principles in which Hellenic
life was rooted.   It is by no means inevitable that, in the
clash of opposing forces in this world, the higher principles must always win ; but it is a fact, verified again
and again, that moral principles count for a great deal
and may often be the determining factor.   So it was in
the crisis of conflict for Hellas in 480 and 479 B.C., and
so it has been in the Great War from 1914 to 1918 A.D.
In spite of the immense resources of the Persian monarchy,
in spite of the high qualities of the Persian race as warriors
and administrators, the higher ideals, the nobler personal
qualities were with Hellas—and Hellas won.

The Conflict of Principles.—For it is here in the conflict
of principles that the value for us of the story of this
great deliverance of other days is to be found ; and this
is because we have an intimate concern in what has come
of the issue of that conflict.   Expressed in its widest
terms, it was a conflict between the small autonomous

[1] Morshead, p. 96 (*Persae*, lines 816-818).

city-states of Hellas and the vast loosely organized political system over which one man, the Great King, ruled despotically ; in other words, a conflict between free institutions and autocracy. The Greeks had not solved the problem of free government, of government in which all men are equal before the law, and a reasonable share of protection and liberty is secured to every one ; but they had set the problem, and by the way in which they had set the problem, and by the many examples of constitutions in active working with which they furnished the world, they made possible an ultimate solution : a solution which, in spite of twentieth-century democracy, is not yet found. What, we may ask, is the essential difference reduced to its simplest expression ? Under constitutional government laws are impartially administered, and the aim is the common good, as determined by the reasoned choice of the people themselves. Law is above king and minister ; above magistrate, and police, and army. In an autocracy all depends on the will of the sovereign, which may at any moment be no better than arbitrary caprice. The king's will is law ; and the king is a fallible human being, swayed by whims and overswept by passion. The Great King could cut a man in two because his father begged him off military service, or decapitate his master-engineers because a storm carried away part of the bridge they had constructed. The ' tyrant ' embodied, in Greek imagination, the extreme evils of autocracy. "There is nothing in the whole world so unjust, nothing so bloody as a tyranny," said the Corinthians, when protesting against the proposals of King Cleomenes to restore at Athens the rule of the Pisistratids. It was the arbitrary character of such rule, with the consequent liability to the furious outbreak of the tyrant's passions, that Hellenic reason condemned. Oriental despotisms, in fact all forms of absolute government, have approximated to this type. The king's arbitrary pleasure is everything. He raises the slave to-day to be his minister ; to-morrow he abases him in the dust or delivers him over to the executioner. You have it all illustrated in a fascinating way in the *Thousand and One Nights*.[1] You may read of it in Bernier's accounts of the Moghul Court in the seventeenth century, or in the annals of Turkish misrule. Under constitutional government it is different. The rights of all men are pre-scribed and secured by legal enactment. The magis-trates are appointed by orderly process, either by election or by some duly constituted authority. Promotion is the reward of merit. We are speaking of types, ideals. Actual governments approximate only to these ideals. Constitutional governments are never quite so good as the ideal; despotisms not quite so bad. But the main contrast holds good, the tendency makes an essential difference.

Along with the exaltation of the will of the sovereign in a despotism goes the degradation of the subject through subservience. For all men are as dust beneath the feet of the king. Hence the genuflections and prostrations of the oriental court, the ' kow-towing.' It was abhorrent to the reason of the free Greek that one man should so abase himself before another. Signs of respect, saluta-tions, and the use of titles of honour are not lacking in a constitutional state ; they are points of courtesy ; there need not be anything degrading in them ; but under despotic government these signs of respect go beyond reason. It was so when the Roman Republic was trans-formed into the Empire. A due sense of personal dignity, of the value of man as man, is preserved under constitu-tional government ; it tends to be lost under autocracy. Similarly, freedom of speech, the right to individual opinion, and the influence of public opinion, are cherished under constitutional government ; they dwindle and pine under despotic government. This holds whether the

---

[1] For instance in the *Story of the Three Apples*, when the body of a murdered woman is found in a chest drawn from the Tigris, the Khalifa Harun-Al-Rashid says to Jaafar, his chief minister, " If thou do not bring to me him who killed this woman . . . I will crucify thee at the gate of my palace, together with forty of thy kinsmen." And the Khalifa is habitually accompanied on his sportive midnight adven-tures by Mesrur, his executioner.

despotism is that of one autocrat or of several. The essential difference is not the difference of one and many, but of law and arbitrary caprice. The gist of the matter is contained in that story which Herodotus tells of Xerxes and the exiled Spartan king, Demaratus. Demaratus, of the house of Procles, had been stripped of the honours of kingship at Sparta on the pretext that he was not true-born ; he took refuge at the court of Darius and accompanied Xerxes on his march into Hellas. Herodotus describes how at Doriscus in Thrace, after the numbering of the host, Xerxes questioned Demaratus and asked him whether in his opinion the Greeks would dare to offer any resistance. And when Demaratus replied that the Spartans most certainly would, whatever the odds, Xerxes laughed and pressed him further, and said : " How possibly could a thousand men, or ten thousand, or even five times ten thousand, stand against an army great as mine, especially if they were all free alike and not the subjects of one lord. Why even if they were five thousand we should have more than a thousand for every one of theirs. Now if they were the subjects of one lord after our fashion, they might through fear of him show themselves brave beyond their nature and might go forward, few against many, under the compulsion of the lash ; but left to their own freedom of action they would do nothing of the sort." [1] But Demaratus held to his point in spite of Xerxes' derision, and gave to the Great King the reason of his faith in these words : " For though they are free, yet are they not free in all respects ; they have a master over them, their country's laws, which they hold more in dread than thy subjects hold thee. And whatever these laws bid, they do ; and what they bid is ever the same ; they permit them not to flee from battle before any multitude of men, but bid them stand firm in their ranks, and conquer or die." [2] Willing obedience to a code of civic duty as against submission to the coercion of force ; these are at bottom the principles contrasted—law versus fear.

[1] Herodotus, vii. 103.   [2] Herodotus, vii. 104.

The Persian system broadly represented the one, the Hellenic the other.

Therefore it has been to the lasting advantage of Europe, and of mankind, that Hellas prevailed in the great struggle with Persia. It has meant in the long run for us the preservation of a distinctive European civilization and the emancipation of the human spirit. For in Hellas, redeemed by the heroic constancy of Athens and the might of the "Doric spear," Hellenic literature, art, and thought reached their perfection ; and on these the culture of Europe on its intellectual and artistic sides has been built. We owe to the Greeks who fought at Salamis and Plataea the salvation of the ideals of personality, of human dignity and political freedom. We owe to them spiritual freedom also—the power and right to work out that advance in the material and moral conditions of human existence which we call 'progress.' For out of Greek thought came modern science with its possibilities for good. It is for these reasons that the story of Troy, the rise of the city-state and the great war of the fifth century B.C. are of such close and intimate concern to us. These are not alien things, but our very own. They are not parts of a story, strange and dim, and remote from our modern world. They form an early and a glorious chapter of our own history. They are the very stuff of which our minds are built, the medium through which our lives are lived to-day.

INDEX.

n refers to footnotes.

OUR HELLENIC HERITAGE

MACMILLAN AND CO., Limited
LONDON · BOMBAY · CALCUTTA · MADRAS
MELBOURNE

THE MACMILLAN COMPANY
NEW YORK · BOSTON · CHICAGO
DALLAS · SAN FRANCISCO

THE MACMILLAN CO. OF CANADA, Ltd.
TORONTO

ATHENS AND THE ACROPOLIS.

As seen from the high ground to the south-west, with Mount Lycabettus showing over

OUR HELLENIC HERITAGE

BY

H. R. JAMES, M.A.

SOMETIME PRINCIPAL, PRESIDENCY COLLEGE, CALCUTTA

VOL. II.

PART III.   ATHENS—HER SPLENDOUR AND HER FALL

PART IV.   THE ABIDING SPLENDOUR

WITH MAPS AND ILLUSTRATIONS

New York

THE MACMILLAN COMPANY

1927

PREFACE

THE scope and purpose of this volume was sketched in the
Preface to Vol. I. The aim as there explained is the communication not of critical results, but of some part of a
very wide content. The method therefore, it may be
emphasized again, is necessarily selective ; and in the final
subdivision of the work selection has been peculiarly difficult. For almost each chapter in Part IV. deals with a
subject to which a fully equipped specialist devotes a life-
time of study. The method of condensation and summary
was here evidently more than ever out of place, and what
has been attempted is something quite different. The
endeavour is to present some part or aspect of each subject with such fulness as may produce an effect, within its
limits, definite and complete. In the chapters on drama
the attempt is to make Greek tragedy and comedy intelligible to the modern reader through the presentation of
certain plays in the concrete. In dealing with history the
standpoint has been the personality of the great historians.
Similarly under " oratory " the life-story of Demosthenes,
and, to a secondary extent, of Isocrates, has been taken
as the most effective means of showing what Greek oratory
was, and what power it had. In the yet harder enterprise
of bringing to the ordinary reader some realization of the
significance of Greek philosophy, it has seemed best to
attempt this through the personal side of the teaching of
Socrates, Plato and Aristotle. It is, however, in the
chapters on art that the difficulty has been most acutely
felt. Here I have tried to use the means most ready to
hand in England, and to create, where it is not already

present, a sense of the greatness of Greek temple architecture and architectural sculpture through the Parthenon and the Elgin Marbles. For in the Greek Rooms in the British Museum there are opportunities of a first hand appreciation of Greek sculpture unique in their amplitude. I have simply tried to make full use of these opportunities.

How much this method leaves out needs no showing. One or two out of many omissions I specially regret. I have not been able to include any estimate of the achievement of the ancient Greeks in Mathematics and Astronomy and Medicine, though each is a fascinating subject and quite recently has received brilliant illumination through the work of Sir Thomas Heath and Sir Clifford Allbutt. I have had reluctantly to leave out any sketch of the development of early Greek thought from Thales to Heraclitus, Empedocles and the Atomists. On the side of art it has not been found possible to supplement sculpture with vases, terra-cottas and painting.

Another self-denying ordinance has been necessary in respect of illustrations. Architecture and sculpture invite liberal illustration by photographs. But to illustrate sculpture, at all events fully and effectively, was too costly to be practicable. It has therefore seemed better to leave sculpture almost without illustration in the text, and, while referring the reader to books where good illustrations may be found, to insist that the best and most adequate illustration is to be sought among the marbles and casts of the British Museum.

In the final revision of this volume I have had the help and stimulus of *The Legacy of Greece*, published over two years ago, almost simultaneously with my first volume. That is, of course, a book in which the most accomplished Hellenist finds profit and pleasure, and in my very different task I run no risk of appearing to court rash rivalry. All I have had to do has been to make grateful use of this work of ripest English scholarship. My indebtedness to other books is more conveniently acknowledged—so far as what is in its nature infinite can be acknowledged—in the *Note on Books* appended to each Part of the present volume. But I take this opportunity of thanking Mr. J. T. Sheppard for his personal kindness in telling me things I wanted to know about the performance of the *Oresteia* at Cambridge in 1921, and for much other helpful suggestion bearing on my chapters on the Greek drama. To Mr. Penoyre, and to my brother, my obligations have been what they were for my first volume. Mr. G. A. Macmillan has not only been as before a sure source of wise counsel in difficulties, but was good enough to spare time for a critical reading of Chapter XVIII. both in manuscript and in proof.

H. R. JAMES.

PREFACE TO PART III

THE story of the Athenian empire is not, like the story of the Persian War, swift, clearly defined, straight-forward, and inspiring throughout, with a direct and simple interest which rises to a climax. It is a complex and tangled piece of history, long-drawn and chequered, closing in catastrophe. It is an essential tragedy, and a tragedy of the right Aristotelian pattern, for the hero, the Common-wealth of Athens, is illustrious and of noble dignity, but not free from fault. There is thrilling action in it and a height of splendour, followed by a poignant reversal of fortune. In Greek History it is only one episode ; but it is an episode which has largeness and unity and en-during significance. It has not often—since Thucydides left the story of the culminating tragedy to be " a posses-sion for all time "—been separately handled as a dramatic whole.[1] The drama ends with the Peloponnesian wars and the downfall of Athenian dominion ; and good reason

[1] Bulwer-Lytton began, but did not finish, a history of Athens ; and there is also in English a history of *The Athenian Empire* by Sir George Cox in the series *Epochs of Ancient History*, published by Messrs. Longmans.

may be shown for regarding that downfall as a calamity for Hellas and for European civilisation.   There were really two wars.[1]   In the first war from 431 to 421 B.C. Athens was victorious ; and but for the rash adventure of the Sicilian Expedition her empire might have continued. Peace in the year 421 B.C. must have seemed as well secured as peace in Europe after the Treaty of Versailles, 2,300 years later.   In the second war, 413 to 404, Athens was beaten.   She who had won Salamis and the Eury-medon, was overthrown by her own errors not less completely than was the Mede by his.   The story of the rise and fall of the Athenian power will, therefore, always be one of the most vivid chapters in human history, and one of the most instructive ; and the inheritors of Greece and Athens—and these are all who participate in western civilisation all the world over—have in it a personal concern.

[1] Bury with much justice speaks of *three*, extending the duration of the struggle back to 459.

CONTENTS

ix

CONTENTS

PART IV.   THE ABIDING SPLENDOUR

CONTENTS

LIST OF ILLUSTRATIONS

LIST OF MAPS AND PLANS

NOTE ON TRANSLATIONS USED IN PART III.

Translations from *Thucydides* have been taken at discretion from Jowett, Crawley and the Loeb Classical Library *Thucydides* (C. Foster Smith). Translations initialled L. J. are by Lionel James, Head Master of Monmouth.

Translations of *Plutarch* and *Xenophon* are mostly from the Loeb editions :

> *Plutarch's Lives* by Bernadotte Perrin ;
> *Xenophon's Hellenica* by Carleton L. Brownson.

In quoting from the anonymous tract on the *Athenian Polity* the translation used is Dakyns'.

PART III.

ATHENS—HER SPLENDOUR AND HER FALL

"Athens has a place in the inner history of man which no other spot on earth can rival."

FREEMAN, *History of Sicily*, Vol. I. p. 330.

CHAPTER I

ATHENS IN THE PERSIAN WARS

"The History of Mankind contains few nobler pages than those which record the conduct of the Athenian people during the entire period of the Persian invasion."

ROGERS, *Introduction to the Clouds of Aristophanes*, p. xx.

MARATHON, Thermopylae, Salamis are imperishable names ; their glory is renewed from generation to generation. Plataea does not ring down the ages with a renown equal to theirs, but no student of history can miss its importance. It is otherwise with the battle of Mount Mycalê, which, according to a belief which Herodotus shared, was fought in the afternoon of the day on which Pausanias, the Spartan, shattered the strength of Mardonius at Plataea. Yet the victory at Mycalê was scarcely less important than Plataea or Salamis : for it signified definitely the transfer of the struggle between Greeks and Persians from Europe to Asia.

The Battle of Mycalê.—After Salamis, in 480 B.C., the Greeks had not ventured to carry the pursuit of the enemy further than Andros, the island immediately south-east of Euboea. Early in the spring of the following year (B.C. 479) the Greek fleet, commanded now not by Eurybiades, the high admiral of the preceding year, but by the Spartan King Leotychides,[1] advanced to Delos in the centre of the Cyclades, half-way across the Aegean. The Persians had stationed their fleet at Samos,

---

[1] This Leotychides belonged to the younger of the two Spartan royal houses, the house of Procles, not to that from which Leonidas and Pausanias came.

which lies close off the promontory of Mount Mycalê where the Ionians had their place of assembly, the Panionium.[1] Obviously after the defeat of the King's fleet at Salamis the Persians were nervous about the loyalty of the Asiatic Greeks, and Samos was a convenient station from which to watch Ionia. The King's fleet there assembled numbered 300 ships of war; the Greek fleet at Delos only 110. But the Persian fleet included an Ionian squadron, and it was much in doubt whether reliance could now be placed by the Persian admirals on any Ionians.

While the Greek fleet lay inactive at Delos a deputation of three men came secretly from Samos and promised that all Ionia would break into revolt, if the Greeks did but show themselves off the coast. Leotychides gave ear to them and sailed for Samos.[2] Thereupon the Persian fleet was withdrawn to the mainland opposite Samos, where it would have the support of the Persian land forces, 60,000 in number, which were in occupation of Ionia. These forces were now concentrated under Mount Mycalê on the promontory which looks towards Samos. When the ships reached the coast the crews disembarked, the ships were dragged ashore and a strong rampart of wood, strengthened in places with stones, was built round them. The Greek fleet disappointed of finding the enemy at Samos, after some debate, continued the pursuit to Mycalê, and seeing on arrival how things were, the commanders disembarked their men and prepared to attack. The Persian admirals, embarrassed by their distrust of the Ionians, made no attempt to oppose the landing, but, drawn up in front of their palisade, awaited the Greeks' onset. At the same time they took the precaution of disarming the Samians who were serving

[1] Herodotus, i. 148. See vol. i. pp. 256 and 274. The channel between Samos and the shore under Mount Mycalê is hardly more than a mile wide.

[2] At first Leotychides was disinclined to any bold action; but he happened to ask the spokesman of the envoys his name. 'Army leader' (Hegesi-stratos) replied the Samian; and Leotychides hailed the omen, and gave orders forthwith for the fleet to proceed to Samos

with them. Then they planted their shields in front of them, as Mardonius' men had done at Plataea, and prepared for resistance. The Greeks rushed forward to the attack with extreme eagerness. Herodotus relates that as they advanced a rumour spread through the army, passing quickly from rank to rank, that their fellow-countrymen at home had fought and won in Boeotia. This report excited the various contingents to intense emulation. The Athenians reached the enemy first as their line of advance lay along the shore ; the Spartans had hilly ground to impede them and a torrent bed to cross. For a time the Persians made a good fight : but the Athenians charged fiercely and beat down the barricade of shields. Then the Persian line gave way, and all fled to the stockade. The Athenians followed so closely that some of them entered the defences along with the fugitives. Inside the stockade the Persians, alone of all the royal troops, kept up the fight for a time : but when the Lacedaemonians and the rest of the Greeks came up, all resistance ceased as it had ceased in the fortified camp on the Asopus—and the stockade became a shambles. A few survivors escaped into the hills above the shore. All the ships were burnt by the victors, together with the wooden ramparts. The victory was complete, and was followed by the revolt from Persia of the islands, though not yet of Ionia.

It was found by subsequent enquiry, says Herodotus, that the battles of Plataea and Mycalê had been fought on the same day ; Plataea in the morning, Mycalê in the afternoon. The pious Greek of the fifth century B.C. saw in this double victory on one and the same day the manifest hand of Providence. About the time that the rumour of the victory at Plataea reached the Greeks at Mycalê, a herald's wand was found lying mysteriously on the beach. "Many things prove to me," writes Herodotus, "that the gods take part in the affairs of man. How else, when the battles of Mycalê and Plataea were about to happen on the self-same day, should such a rumour have reached the Greeks in that region, greatly cheering the whole army, and making them more eager than before to risk their lives ? " [1]

Athens the Saviour of Hellas.—The conflict at Mycalê had the effect of raising still further the prestige of Athens, already heightened greatly by her behaviour throughout the two years of the war. In a remarkable passage of his seventh book [2] Herodotus, in introducing the story of the response of the Delphic oracle to the Athenians, says : " Here I am constrained to affirm an opinion which I know will be unacceptable to very many, nevertheless, inasmuch as it appears to me to be the truth, I will not keep it back. If the Athenians, through dread of the danger which was approaching, had abandoned their country, or if, though they did not abandon it but stayed, they had made submission to Xerxes, there would have been no attempt at all to oppose Xerxes by sea. And if no one had tried to oppose Xerxes by sea, this is what must have happened on land. Though line beyond line of fortifications had been carried across the Isthmus, the Lacedaemonians must have lost their allies (not by wilful desertion but as a necessary consequence of the cities being reduced in detail one after another by the fleet of the barbarians) and been left to fight alone ; and left to fight alone, they would have died nobly after making a gallant resistance. Either this is what would have happened to them ; or, before this befell, they would have seen the other Greeks going over to the Persians, and made their own terms with Xerxes. So in either case Hellas would have come under the Persian yoke. What good the wall across the Isthmus would have been, when the King had command of the sea, I am unable to discover. If then we now said that the Athenians were the saviours of Hellas, we should not err from the truth. The conditions were such that the scale was bound to incline to the side to which they attached themselves. When they had made their choice that Hellas should remain free, it was they who roused to action the rest of the Greeks who had not

---

[1] Herodotus, ix. 100 ; Rawlinson iv. p. 451.   [2] vii. 139.

submitted, and, next to Heaven, it was they who repulsed the King."

When Herodotus was writing, Athens, imperial Athens, had lost much of the admiration won in the Persian wars, and become an object of detestation as well as of jealousy throughout great part of the Greek world. But we at once recognize the truth of his statement and it must have been patent to all the confederate Greeks in the year after Salamis. Every one knew it was the fleet of Athens that had saved Greece, the number of her ships, the skill and courage of her seamen and the sagacity of her admiral, Themistocles. But it was not alone her material share in the victory, though that could not easily be overstated, that now raised Athens high in the estimation of all Hellas. It was at the same time the moral qualities the city and her people had shown, the dauntlessness, the indomitable will, the self-control, the devotion to the national cause, the spirit of self-sacrifice. Sparta and the Peloponnesian states had made mistakes, had failed the common cause again and again, if they had not, like some other of the Greek name, stood aside altogether or gone over to the Mede. Athens had made no mistakes, had never faltered ; called to the extremity of endurance she had borne the test and come triumphantly through it. She had seen her land overrun by the enemy, her city itself occupied, its buildings razed to the ground, its sacred places desecrated ; had seen her people scattered homeless to find refuge as they could ; had seen her interests betrayed once and again by the selfishness or slowness of her allies. And she had not wavered, but endured the utmost with serenity, and at the height of her trial had rejected the offer of a noble enemy to win her to his side. She had shown, too, the less heroic, but not less useful, quality of a capacity for subordination in loyalty to the common interest. Herodotus has a story —which may or may not be true—of a dispute before Plataea between the Tegeans and the Athenians for the place of honour in the battle line, next after Sparta. And he makes the spokesman of the Athenians con-

clude the presentment of their claim with these words :
" Nevertheless, Lacedaemonians, as to strive concerning
place at such a time as this is not right, we are ready to
do as you command, and to take our station at whatever
part of the line, and face whatever nation, you think
most expedient. Wheresoever you place us, 'twill be
our endeavour to behave as brave men. Only declare
your will, and we shall at once obey you." [1] Even if
the story is not literally true, it has value as showing the
spirit which could be thought in character with the
Athenians at this time.

Ionia ' Irredenta.'—As soon as the allied fleet had won
its brilliant success at Mount Mycalê,—with all Ionia
looking on and quivering with new hope—the question
what was to be the future policy of the victors on the
eastern coast of the Aegean at once became acute. Was
there to be a new Ionian revolt ? Were Ladê and
Miletus to be avenged ? Were the confederate Greeks
to undertake the liberation of all the Greek cities of Asia
Minor, held in subjection to the Mede ? If so, and if the
Greek towns in territories owning the Great King's sway
were to be encouraged to rise against their Persian
masters, what was the prospect of their being able to
maintain their independence, when the Pan-Hellenic
fleet was withdrawn again to Europe and dispersed ?
Leotychides and the other Peloponnesian leaders answered
with no uncertain voice that there was no such prospect ;
and it did not come within their mental horizon to conceive of an allied fleet kept permanently on a war footing
for the protection of the Greek cities in Asia Minor.
" It appeared to them an impossibility," writes Herodotus,
" that they should stay for ever on guard to protect
the Ionians ; yet if they did not protect them there was
not the slightest expectation that the Ionians would
come off scatheless at the hands of the Persians." [2] They
therefore made—quite seriously it would appear—an
astounding proposal. They proposed that the Ionian

---

[1] Herodotus, ix. 27.6 ; Rawlinson, iv. p. 395.

[2] Herodotus, ix. 106.2.

land should be abandoned to the Persians, and the Ionian Greeks—and presumably the Aeolian and Dorian Greeks with them—be transplanted back across the Aegean, reversing the process of emigration which had taken place some five hundred years earlier. New homes were to be found for them by declaring forfeit the seaport towns of the European Greeks who had traitorously joined forces with the invader, or had betrayed the cause of Hellas by failing to aid the Pan-Hellenic League in repelling him. Thus at one and the same time the Greeks who had medized would be punished, and a solution be found for the problem of Ionia. But the Athenians would have none of this. The Ionians were their kinsmen, and the Ionians were unwilling to leave the land which for centuries now had been their home. At the same time Athenian interests were closely involved ; for to the Athenians it was of vital necessity that the trade route from the Black Sea through the Hellespont and the Bosphorus should be in friendly keeping. The Peloponnesians gave way, and Samos and the other islands were admitted into the Pan-Hellenic alliance. Then the fleet sailed to the Hellespont with the object of destroying Xerxes' bridges. They occupied Abydos, but found the bridges destroyed already by the winds and waves. Leotychides and the Peloponnesian squadrons hereupon sailed for home ; but the Athenians under the command of Xanthippus, the father of Pericles, together with their new allies from the islands, crossed the channel of the Dardanelles and laid siege to Sestos. This city, which had been the European end of Xerxes' bridges, was held by a strong Persian garrison reinforced by refugees from the Chersonese (the Gallipoli peninsula). Summer passed into autumn and still Sestos held out. The men of Athens who were serving in the fleet grew impatient and demanded to be led home : for they had left Athens a city of ruin and their minds were haunted by remembrances of their devastated farms and home-steads. But Xanthippus stood firm, declaring that he would not withdraw from the siege without orders from

Athens. Meantime the garrison were hard pressed for food, and presently were in the grip of famine. The Persian defenders then left the city and made an attempt to escape : whereupon the Greeks inside Sestos opened the gates and let in the Athenians. Within the town, of which they obtained possession in this way, the Athenians found the shore-cables which had been used to support Xerxes' bridges : these they conveyed as trophies to Athens. The effect of all this was to raise the prestige of the Athenians yet higher.

Misconduct of Pausanias.—Next year (478) the Spartan government sent out Pausanias, the victor of Plataea, with twenty ships, to take command of the allied fleet. To this fleet the Athenians, on their part, sent thirty ships under Themistocles' rival, Aristides. Pausanias sailed first to Cyprus, and drew most of the Greek cities in that island into the League. Thence he sailed on to the Hellespont, passed through the Sea of Marmora to the Bosphorus, laid siege to Byzantium and took it. The Greeks had now command of the entrance to the Bosphorus as well as of the passage of the Dardanelles. But the fair hopes that these successes opened out to the Hellenic League under Spartan leadership, were spoilt by the behaviour of Pausanias himself Either his head was turned by the glory he had won at Plataea, or there was some congenital strain of madness in him which the excitements of the times had brought out. He began openly to imitate the bearing, and even the dress and equipment, of a Persian satrap, and while so doing managed to give offence to all the allies, officers and men alike. The rank and file he angered by the severity of the punishments he imposed for breaches of discipline ; the commanders he provoked by the haughtiness of his demeanour and the open contempt with which he treated them. He soon had all the allied forces seething with indignation. When Aristides, as admiral of the Athenians, tried remonstrance, Pausanias turned his back on him. The truth was, he was indulging the evil dream of becoming literally a Persian satrap and the Great

King's son-in-law, and to realize this ambition he was willing to sacrifice the fair fame won at Plataea and undo the work he had there done for Hellas. The proof of this is found in a letter which, about this time, he had addressed to the King, the curiously worded text of which Thucydides has preserved.[1] It was the first example of what afterwards became notorious,—the failure of the admired Spartan discipline to fit those trained in it for novel responsibilities in a wider sphere than Lacedaemon or the Peloponnese. This criminal folly led ultimately to Pausanias' ruin and death,[2] but the more immediate effect of his misconduct was to open for Athens further opportunities of action and achievement. For, in disgust at the overbearing manners of Pausanias and his Spartans, the Ionians came to Aristides and openly urged that Athens should undertake the leadership against Persia in place of Sparta. They proposed to form a new confederacy with Athens at its head, an organized league, both defensive and offensive, against Persia. It was thus that the great opportunity of her destiny came to Athens, and the Confederacy of Delos was formed.

---

[1] Among the Persian prisoners captured at Byzantium were some relatives of the King. It was given out soon after that these persons had escaped ; but the truth was that they had been secretly sent by Pausanias to Xerxes with a letter couched in the following terms : Pausanias, the Spartan commander, wishing to do you a favour, sends you back these men whom he took with the spear. And I make the proposal, if it seems good to you also, to marry your daughter and to make Sparta and the rest of Hellas subject to you. And I am able, I think, to accomplish these things with the help of your counsel. If any of these things please you, send a trusty man to the sea, and through him we shall in future confer." Thucydides, i. 128; Loeb, vol. i. p. 217.

[2] The Ephors some years later obtained proof of his treasonable designs and were preparing to arrest him, when Pausanias received warning in time to take sanctuary in a small building within the sacred enclosure of the temple of Athena at Sparta, known as the Temple of Athena of the Brazen House. The Ephors used no force against him, but they stripped the roof off the building and built up the doors so that no food could possibly reach him, and there Pausanias slowly died of starvation. When he was at the point of death, the Ephors had him carried out, thinking in this way to avoid the guilt of sacrilege. But in popular belief the guilt was already incurred, and the story was remembered as ' the curse of Athena of the Brazen House.' See also i. v. p. 129 below.

Aristides.—Athens was extraordinarily fortunate in the man who at this crisis was entrusted with the command of her fleet. We have met Aristides already, as Themistocles' political rival, who had been banished by ostracism three years before the invasion of Xerxes and had returned just in time to inform Themistocles that all retreat from the narrow straits was blocked ; and that, whether they would or not, the Greeks must fight at Salamis.[1] Aristides was leader of the conservative party at Athens, the party opposed to the further advance of democracy. He was himself of noble birth, an Eupatrid, but far from wealthy : indeed his honourable poverty is part of his title to remembrance. For Aristides' lasting fame is an integrity pure and unsullied throughout his life ; in ancient Athens unfortunately a rare integrity. His name comes down to posterity as Aristides the Just. At the time when the vote which sent him into exile was being taken at Athens, a peasant who had come in from the country to vote and who could not write, stopped him in the street and asked him to write a name for him on his voting tile. "What name shall I write ? " asked Aristides. "Write Aristides," said the man. "Why friend, has Aristides done you wrong ? " "Oh no only I am tired of hearing him called the Just ! " But Aristides' justice was a solid quality, and now in 478 B.C. it stood Athens in good stead. Aristides' fairness of mind and moderation were in marked contrast with the arrogance and violence of Pausanias. It was the attractive personal qualities of Aristides, and of his noble colleague Cimon, son of Miltiades (who was beloved at Athens as a prince of good fellows), which in large measure induced the newly liberated Eastern Greeks to beg Athens to put herself at the head of a new organization for the assertion of Hellenic freedom. Above all it was their confidence in Aristides' 'justice.' If a permanent union for defence was to be organized, it would be necessary to assess carefully the contribution—whether in ships, or money, or both—to be made by each community

[1] See vol. i. pp. 347-8.

so that none should be taxed out of proportion to its
resources and none get off too lightly : obviously a difficult
and delicate task. But this delicate task the allies were,
one and all, ready to entrust to Aristides, and pledged
themselves to accept his assessment. The people of
Athens consented and lent the services of Aristides.
And so for a year or more, Aristides, with a staff of assist-
ants, went about among the islands and the continental
cities, carefully enquiring into and estimating the resources
of the several members of the League and rating their
contributions proportionately. His success was complete.
" Aristides," writes Plutarch,[1] " being made responsible
for this large exercise of authority, Hellas in a sense
putting her entire administration in his sole hands, poor
as he was going out came back yet poorer, after making
his assessment not merely with absolute integrity and
fairness but also with consideration for the wishes and
convenience of all." This assessment of Aristides was
accepted with contentment at the time and remained
substantially unchanged for fifty years.

The Confederacy of Delos.—Athens accepted without
hesitation the call of the Eastern Greeks to organize a
machinery of defence in the struggle which still had to be
fought out after Salamis and Plataea. Sparta, with a
spirit less high than might have been expected, acquiesced
in this transfer of responsibility without resistance, and
even without protest. Many circumstances contributed
to this complaisance. About the time that the newly
liberated Greeks of Asia Minor were pressing their request
on Athens, Pausanias had been recalled to Sparta. The
scandal of his behaviour had reached the Spartan government and he was sharply ordered home to answer the
charges brought against him. Next year other leaders
were sent out, but in a half-hearted manner ; and when
the new admiral found the confederate Greeks disinclined
to accept his authority, he and his lieutenants went
home. It was a little ignominious ; but, after her experi-

[1] Plutarch, *Aristides*, 24 (L. J.).

ence of the conduct of Pausanias, Sparta was afraid of
the effect of distance and relaxed control on the character
of her commanders. And the truth was that Sparta had
no real heart in this business of liberating the Asiatic
Greeks—mostly Ionians : any more than she had when
Aristagoras pleaded for assistance in 500 B.C.[1] Her
interests were all on the western side of the Aegean and
centred in the Peloponnese. There was excuse for her
in her geographical position and the character of her
polity. Sparta, moreover, had no navy ; and the
Spartan government was aware that Athens was better
equipped to continue the war against Persia, which must
necessarily be based on sea-power. The feeling of the
Spartans at the time was, as Thucydides has recorded,
relief at being quit of the Median war.[2] The path,
therefore, was every way clear for Athens to step into the
leading place among the Greeks who were actively
continuing the contest, a place she had fairly earned by
her conduct in the years of Xerxes' invasion and repulse.

Objects of the League.—The Confederacy of Delos was
primarily a union for defence and protection of all the
Greek polities in the islands of the Aegean and on the
coasts of Asia Minor, Thrace, the Hellespont and beyond,
which by their position were exposed to the hazard of
the Great King's vengeance if they had revolted, or which
wished to revolt if they were still in subjection. But
it did not stop at that. It looked also to the prospect of
reprisals on the Persian empire and of making good, by
plundering the King's territories, some of the loss incurred
through Xerxes' invasion. Thucydides plainly says :
"the avowed object being to compensate themselves
and the allies by devastating the King's country."
The work of organizing a confederacy on this scale was
very great : the mere extent of territory, if we trace on
the map the number of states included, is considerable :
and that it was done by Athens in an enduring form—it
lasted for over seventy years, 477 to 404—was no mean
achievement. The Confederacy of Delos was by far the

[1] See vol. i. p. 271.   [2] Thucydides, i. 95. 7.

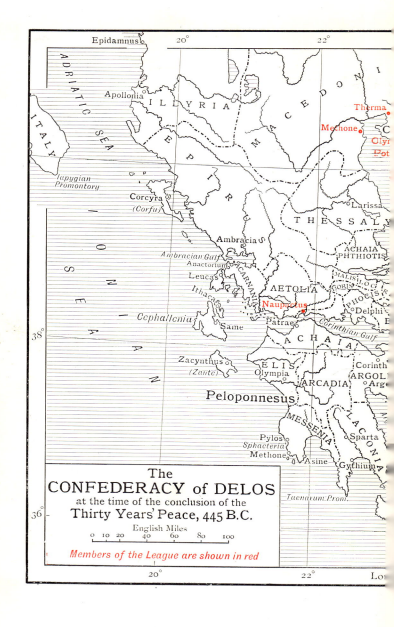

The
CONFEDERACY of DELOS
at the time of the conclusion of the
Thirty Years' Peace, 445 B.C.

English Miles
0 10 20   40   60   80   100

Members of the League are shown in red

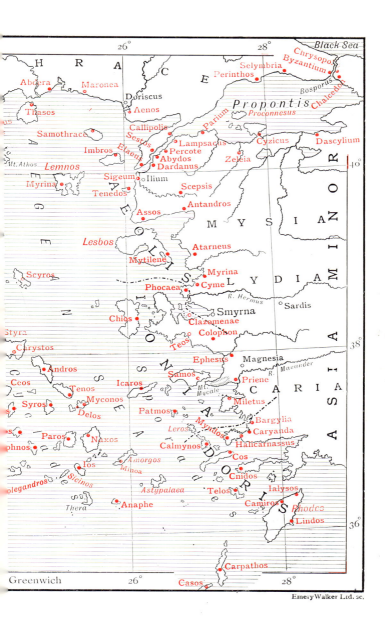

Black Sea

26°   28°

H   R   A   C
Abdera   Maronea   E   Perinthos   Selymbria   Chrysopolis   Byzantium
Doriscus   Bosporus   Chalcedon
Thasos   Aenos   *Propontis*   Proconnesus
Samothrace   Callipolis   Parium   Cyzicus   Dascylium
Imbros   Sestos   Lampsacus   Zeleia
Mt. Athos   Lemnos   Elaeus   Percote   Abydos   Dardanus   R   40°
Myrina   Sigeum   Ilium   Scepsis   O
Tenedos   Antandros   N   I   A   M
Assos   M   Y   S   I   A   Z   I
Lesbos   Atarneus   M
Mytilene   Myrina   Y   D   I   A
Scyros   Phocaea   Cyme   L   Sardis   A
Chios   *R. Hermus*   Smyrna
Clazomenae   Colophon   38°
Styra   Teos
Carystos   Ephesus   Magnesia   I
Andros   Samos   *R. Maeander*   A
Ceos   Icaros   Priene   C   A   R   I   A   S
Tenos   Mt. Mycale   A
Syros   Myconos   Miletus
Delos   Patmos   Bargylia
Paros   Naxos   Leros   Caryanda   A
phnos   Calmynos   Myndos   Halicarnassus   S
Amorgos   Cos   A
Ios   Minoa   Cnidos
Sicinos   Astypalaea   Telos   Ialysos
olegandros   Camiros   Rhodes
Thera   Anaphe   Lindos   36°
Carpathos
Greenwich   26°   Casos   28°

most extensive union of Greek states ever formed in ancient times. No exact account of its constitution and working has come down to us. Thucydides tells us only (1) that the total amount of the original assessment was 460 talents ; (2) that the island of Delos was chosen for the treasury of the league ; and (3) that the synod or council of the league held its meetings in the temple there.[1] One authentic and most interesting source of information we owe to archaeological research in Athens. Fragments of broken marble, slabs and pillars found on the Acropolis have been pieced together with infinite pains (in one case the fragments are as many as thirty) and, though when put together still mutilated and imperfect, have been sufficiently deciphered to show that they contain accounts of moneys received from numerous states which were members of the League. They are just lists of contributing cities with the amount paid by each inscribed beside the name.[2] By this means the names of between two and three hundred contributing states have been certified, some very familiar names like Ephesus and Miletus, some like Belbina and Pholegandros, quite obscure. To combine this prodigious number of individual autonomous states, varying greatly in size, character and resources, into a stable and efficient working whole, was a task demanding rare political sagacity, originality and tact ; and, above all, honesty of purpose. And this is what Athens, through the wise and conciliatory mediation of Aristides, accomplished in the years 477 and 476.

Constitution and Working.—Although the recorded details of the constitution, working and history of the

---

[1] Thucydides, i. 96. 2.

[2] With one exception these inscriptions are lists not of the actual contributions paid by the several states, but of the proportion due to the temple for its use as a treasury. As, however, this proportion is always one sixtieth, the total contribution can in any case be reached imply by multiplying the amount given by 60. The one exception is he inscription of a decree of the year 425 which gives the actual contributions laid by assessment on the communities named. See also note at the end of this chapter, p. 20.

Confederacy of Delos are few and fragmentary, nevertheless these, taken with their implications, suffice to enable us to reconstruct the main outlines with reasonable certainty. All the members of the League were originally independent and autonomous city-states, which entered the confederation voluntarily and undertook the obligations necessary for the fulfilment of its purpose. The island of Delos was chosen as the seat of the League on account of its central position and sacred character. The temple of Apollo and Artemis was the Treasury and there also the meetings of the Council were held. Each member of the Confederacy had one vote in the Council. The Council was the authority which guided the policy and acts of the League : and by common consent, not only was the presidency of the Council and the practical leadership assigned to Athens, but also the duty of enforcing the decisions of the Council. Athens was thus at one and the same time a member of the Confederacy, the equal and no more than the equal of each of the rest ; and she was more than a member. She was organizer, president, and responsible executive. The officers who collected the revenue, ten in number, were called *Stewards of the Hellenes* (*Helleno-tamiae*), but they were also Athenian citizens, accountable to the government and people of Athens. Her position in relation to the League was from the first unique, and there were dangers latent in this both for her and for the other members, which were not, perhaps, clearly discerned in the beginning, but which inevitably showed themselves in course of time. The success of the League necessarily depended on the loyalty, fidelity and energy with which the individual members carried out their obligations ; and on the combined strictness and self-restraint with which Athens exercised her controlling function.

Relation of Athens and the Allies.—The obligations laid upon Athens by the express desire and will of the allies are plain from what has just been said. Her duty and responsibility were to see that the League did its work and to administer its revenues. The obligations of her numerous associates were determined by the survey and assessment of Aristides. The ultimate obligation was to wage war upon the Persians ; and for this three things were necessary—men, ships and money. From Thucydides we learn that from the beginning some of the members furnished ships and personal service, and some money in lieu of these. " The Athenians," he says, " assessed the amount of their contributions, both for the states which were to furnish money for the war against the Barbarians and for those which were to furnish ships." [1] The reason why some contributed money payments instead of personal service is not far to seek. ' Most of the members," Bury says, " were small and poor ; many could not equip more than one or two ships ; many could do no more than contribute a part of the expense to the furnishing of a single galley. To gather together a number of small and scattered contingents at a fixed time and place was always a matter of difficulty ; nor was such a miscellaneous armament easily managed. It was therefore arranged that the smaller states, instead of furnishing ships, should pay a yearly sum of money to a common treasury." [2] Such an arrangement was, we can see, in the general interest, and in the circumstances of the several states, even inevitable.

Achievements of the Confederacy. (1) Redemption of Ionia.—No full history of the warfare with Persia following the constitution of the Confederacy of Delos was ever written. This is much to be regretted, for it must have been interesting and full of incident. There must have been a second, and this time a successful, Ionic Revolt. But for this we have not even so much as Herodotus' incomplete and confused account of the Ionic Revolt of 99. We know only that at the time of the Battle of Mycalê all Ionia was still part of a Persian province and all the Greek cities of the Aegean coast were Persia's vassals. Thucydides gives us bare particulars of two or three

---

[1] Thucydides, i. 96. 1.   [2] Bury's *Greece*, p. 328.

II   B

striking incidents—the recovery of Sestos, the capture of
Byzantium, the desperate defence of Eion on the Strymon [1]
when besieged by Cimon in 476. And we know the broad
result, that from this time no tribute was paid to Persia
by the Greek cities of Asia so long as the imperial strength
of Athens remained unimpaired. We may say with
assurance that this deliverance could not have been
effected without a good deal of fighting of which there is
no record : " It is certain," says Grote, " that the first
ten years of the Athenian hegemony must have been
years of the most active warfare against the Persians." [2]
In 478 the Persians were in occupation of Thrace and the
shores of the Hellespont and Propontis. We learn from
Herodotus [3] that even as late as the reign of Artaxerxes
(464-425) the Persians still held possession of the fortified
town Doriscus in Thrace, where Xerxes had numbered
his host on the march into Greece.

(2) **The Freedom of the Seas.**—When the Greek cities
which had been subjects of the Persian empire had been
freed, it was the task of the Confederacy of Delos, firstly
to keep them free, and, secondly, to make the Aegean
safe for the navigation of the Greeks. The conquest
of the island of Scyros illustrates this second task, for the
people of Scyros were given to piracy and it was a boon
to the commerce of the Aegean when Cimon, in 474,
rooted them out and the Athenians occupied the island
with their own colonists. This much comes from Thucydides and Plutarch ; [4] but no other details are on record
of what it cost to maintain the freedom of the seas for
Greek commerce. That the policing of the Aegean was
done effectually may reasonably be inferred from the
flourishing state of the Greek communities in the Aegean
and on the route to the Black Sea. It must have been
an exacting task requiring constant vigilance. For

[1] Boges, the Persian governor, rather than surrender when starved
out, slew his children and the women of his family and threw the bodies
on to a great funeral pyre : then he cast all his treasure into the river
and himself leapt into the flames.

[2] Grote, Part II. ch. 45.   [3] Herodotus, vii. 106.

[4] Thucydides, i. 98.2. Plutarch, *Cimon*, 8.

apart from the permanent danger of renewed activity
on the part of the fleets of Persia, which means first and
foremost of the Phoenicians, the untiring rivals of the
Greeks, the piratical habits which Thucydides alludes to
as prevailing widely in early times,[1] lingered long among
the Greeks themselves, so that at the beginning of the
Peloponnesian war we find the Athenians establishing
a naval port off the coast of Locris to check the pirates
who sailed out of Locrian harbours to plunder Euboea.

Battle of the Eurymedon.—Fragmentary as is the story
of the later phases of the struggle with Persia, we know
that it culminated in another big fight by sea and land,
the battle of the Eurymedon. The Eurymedon is a
river which flows into the Mediterranean out of Pamphylia and Pisidia. Here Cimon, son of Miltiades, in
the year 468, brought to battle a Phoenician fleet of
200 sail and destroyed them all. After the sea-fight,
as at Mycalê, the troops disembarked and routed the
Persian forces on land also. Immense booty was taken.
This victory," writes Bury, " sealed the acquisition of
southern Asia Minor, from Caria to Pamphylia, for the
Athenian federation." [2] This was not quite the end of
the war of liberation. For eighteen years later—in B.C.
450—Cimon led an expedition to Cyprus (it was his last
campaign). The siege of Citium was begun : and there
Cimon died. But the fleet sailed on to Cyprian Salamis,
and here once more a double victory by sea and land was
won by the Athenians over Phoenician, Cilician and
Cyprian forces. And after this there was peace to all
intents and purposes between Hellas and Persia for many
years, though it is improbable that any formal peace was
ever definitely made.[3] By mutual agreement two small
groups of islands, one in the Black Sea just outside
the Bosphorus, the other in the Mediterranean off the
south-east corner of Lycia, were accepted as boundaries
beyond which the war-vessels of the Great King must not
sail. For the rest, as Plutarch writes in his *Life of Cimon*,

[1] Thucydides, i. 5.   See vol. i. p. 202 and 203.   [2] Bury's *Greece*, p. 337.
[3] See note below on *The Peace of Callias*.

" Asia from Ionia to Pamphylia was entirely cleared o
Persian arms " : [1] and also of Persian tax-gatherers
" not one of whose scribes, nay, not so much as a horse
had been seen within four hundred furlongs of the sea."
This, too, was the achievement of Athens in the Persia
war, her last and greatest.

NOTE ON THE PEACE OF CALLIAS.

It is an extraordinary thing, yet nevertheless true, that it ha
never to this day been determined whether peace was mad
between Persia and Hellas in 448 B.C., or not.   Certainly neith
Herodotus nor Thucydides mentions any such peace.   Bu
later, famous orators, Lysias, Demosthenes, Lycurgus, refer t
the peace as something well known ; and Plutarch in his *Life*
Cimon[3] speaks of the peace as made after Cimon's earlier victor
at the Eurymedon.   Callias, son of Hipponicus, is said to hav
been sent to Susa to negotiate it, and a reference in Herodot
vii. 151, to the actual presence of this Callias at Susa is a curio
confirmation.   But the balance of evidence is against any form
conclusion of peace.

NOTE ON THE TRIBUTE LISTS.

The lists which record the sums dedicated to Athena as fir
fruits of the allied contributions stored in her temple, have be
recovered from a number of marble blocks found among hea
of broken stone once scattered over the Acropolis.   They for
an almost complete series from B.C. 454 to B.C. 432.   The lists a
very imperfect, because the blocks were found in fragments a
have only by great labour been pieced together, but they suppl
ment each others' defects.   The contributing states named ma
a total just short of 290.   From the year 443 (the 12th in orde
the contributing states are arranged in five groups which evident
formed divisions of the Athenian empire.   These groups are t
Ionian, Hellespontine, Thracian, Carian and Island.   Later agai
from B.C. 439, the five groups became four through the mergi
into one of the Ionian and Carian groups.   The reference to t
Corpus is C.I.A. i. 226-272 (Kirchoff).   All the Quota lists are giv
in full in Hill's *Sources for Greek History* B.C. 478-431, pp. 43-
Sample years will be found in Roberts and Gardner's *Introducti
to Greek Epigraphy*, Part II., pp. 288-298, or in Hicks and H
Manual of Greek Historical Inscriptions, 33, 43 and 48, pp. 48-5
70-73 ;   80-83.   For the decree of B.C. 425 see Hicks and H
64, pp. 112-122 ;   or Roberts and Gardner, pp. 45-50 ;   a
Hill's *Sources*, pp. 426-430 (Addenda et Corrigenda).

[1] Plutarch, *Cimon*, 12.   Loeb, ii. pp. 439 and 441.
[2] Cimon, 19.   Loeb, p. 467.   [3] Plutarch, *Cimon*, 13.

CHAPTER II

THE PATH OF EMPIRE

"This dominion of ours was not acquired by force. . . . Circumstances from the first compelled us to advance it, till it reached its present extent :—it was fear more than anything else that swayed us ; the motive of honour came in later ; and finally also the consideration of our own advantage."

Thucydides, I. 75.

The Re-building of the Walls.—As soon as the peril of another invasion was over, the people of Athens set about the building up again of their ruined city, and to this task they brought the same fortitude and energy as that with which they had helped to crush the enemy. The ruin they found on the site of Athens was pretty complete. Walls, temples, dwelling-houses had all been destroyed : only a few of the larger buildings, which had sheltered Persians of high rank, were left standing. The work of restoration began as soon as the Athenians were once more in possession of the site of their city. And their first thought was for the rebuilding of their city's defences. By the direction of the government, in which the influence of Themistocles was still paramount, the lines of the new city wall were traced out so as to increase considerably the area enclosed ; and the whole population, bond and free alike, was set to work upon it. Scarcely had the building of the wall begun when an embassy arrived from Sparta to urge upon the Athenian government the wisdom of stopping it. It would be far better, the Spartans argued, that there should be no fortified towns outside Peloponnese which an invader might occupy

21

and use for a base, as Mardonius had used Thebes. They
therefore counselled the Athenians not only to give up
their own purpose of re-fortifying Athens, but to join
Sparta in pulling down the fortifications of other walled
towns [1]—outside Peloponnese. The Peloponnese itself
they contended, would always be a sufficient place of
refuge and base of operations for the rest of Greece
This unsought advice was extremely unwelcome to the
Athenians. It was not difficult to see through the
pretence of Pan-Hellenic interest and find the real motive
in the newly-awakened jealousy with which the Pelo
ponnesians were already regarding Athens, because of
the strength she had put forth in the defence of Hellas
But in the present unfortified state of their city it was
scarcely prudent to give to the Spartans the straight
forward reply they would have wished. After their
experience of two years of close alliance they had no
great faith in Peloponnesian friendship. It was possible
if they simply told the Spartan envoys that they would
not stop the re-building of their city wall, that the army
of the Peloponnese would soon be over the border in
such force as to make resistance hopeless. They there
fore made answer to the Spartan embassy that they
would send a mission to Sparta to discuss the ques
tion. In this way they got the Spartan envoys out of
Attica.

Thucydides ascribes the whole conduct of this business
to Themistocles and tells at length the story of what
followed. And this is the story he tells. Themistocles
urged the Athenians to appoint him a member of their
mission and despatch him forthwith to Sparta, but to
delay as long as possible the departure of the other envoys
Meantime the whole people, men, women and children
were to unite in a supreme effort to get the walls built
to a height that admitted of defence. Accordingly
Themistocles went to Sparta, and when he got there
used all his ingenuity to avoid an official audience

[1] It will be recalled that Sparta was herself a city without wall
See vol. i. p. 225.

When his friends—at this time he had many admirers
and friends at Sparta—asked him why he did not get his
audience, he replied that he was waiting for his colleagues ;
that he expected them every day and was surprised that
they had not come. At first the Spartan authorities
accepted these explanations ; but presently people
began to arrive who declared positively that the new
walls of Athens were rising rapidly and had already
attained a fair height. Themistocles begged them not
to give credence to reports, but to send commissioners
of their own who might see for themselves how things
were at Athens : and the Spartans sent commissioners,
as he advised. But Themistocles himself sent secret
word to the Athenians to contrive the quiet detention of these envoys, and not to let them go until he
and his fellows of the Athenian mission were safe out
of Spartan territory. These fellow-commissioners had
by this time arrived in Sparta, and the fear was that the
Spartans, when they learnt the truth, would decline to let
them go. When Themistocles received word that the
Spartan mission had reached Athens and were virtually
hostages for his own and his colleagues' safety, he threw
off the mask and spoke out. He told the Spartan
authorities that the walls of Athens were high enough now
to be defended, and that if the Lacedaemonians or their
allies wished to negotiate further, they must for the future
treat with the Athenians as with a people able to judge
what was for their own interest, and for the interest of
Hellas. "When the Athenians came to the resolve to leave
their city and embark on their ships, they had, he said,
reached the decision to brave the danger without Spartan
help ; and in all subsequent deliberations they had shown
themselves second to none in judgment. For their part
they considered it was better at the present time that their
city should have walls : this was most for their own
advantage and for the advantage of all the confederates."
The eyes of the Spartans were opened, but they did not
find it expedient to show outwardly the anger they felt.
Themistocles and his two colleagues were allowed to

return to Athens. But the slow resentment of Sparta was one day to cost Themistocles his rights as a citizen of the country he had served too well.[1]

This is the story, and thus it was that the walls of Athens and the defences of the Acropolis were thrown up in hot haste, irregularly and of any materials that came to hand—rough stones, fragments of columns, broken slabs, sepulchral stelae, bits of ornamental work from houses and temples : solid stone of some sort to face the structure and a jumble of rubble inside. Even so you may see it with your eyes to-day in the stretch of the wall still standing between the Dipylon Gate and the Street of Tombs.[2]

The Harbours of Athens.—On his return to Athens Themistocles was free to mature his plans for the future safety of the city. The next step was to secure harbours for the fleet, which had by its achievements in the war acquired a new and vastly greater importance. The open Bay of Phalerum,[3] which was all the harbourage Athens had up to the time of Salamis, was both inadequate and unsuitable now Athens stood pledged to defend with her naval strength the newly liberated cities of Ionia. But west of the Bay of Phalerum there projects into the Saronic Gulf a rocky promontory with a rounded head, which by turning further westward encloses between its northern end and the coastline of Attica a spacious sheet of water, 1400 yards long by 800 broad. This sheet of water was, and is, the harbour of Piraeus. There are two smaller basins on the outer side of the promontory,

[1] See Note at end of the chapter, pp. 47-49.

[2] The exact account of Thucydides (i. 93. 2) is : " the lower courses consist of all sorts of stones, in some cases not even hewn to fit but just as they were when the several workers brought them, and many columns from grave monuments and stones wrought for other purposes were built in."—Loeb, i. p.157.

[3] Phalerum Bay is the nearest part of the coast from Athens and is visible from the city. Moreover, the open shelving beach there was suitable enough for the earlier kind of war-vessels such as the pente-conters or fifty-oared galleys used before triremes came in.

which are the harbours Munychia and Zea.[1] Of this magnificent suite of harbours Athens, up to the time of the Persian invasion, had made no use; but at least one Athenian had realized the great natural advantages of the position. Themistocles, when archon in 493, three years before Marathon, had gained the assent of the people to a scheme for the fortification of the whole peninsula. This much Thucydides tells us. And now that the city itself was again safely enclosed within walls, Themistocles resumed his great scheme for providing Athens with harbours suitable for the first sea-power in Hellas. A wall was carried from the edge of the Bay of Phalerum round the complete circuit of the rocky peninsula, a total length of seven miles, to fortify and protect both the two outer basins on the east and south, and the great basin of Piraeus on the west. The wall was planned on a mighty scale : it was to be of a breadth and height to defy all attack. The whole was constructed of solid blocks of stone clamped together by metal. These harbour walls were exceedingly strong, stronger than the walls of the city itself. And within the space between the harbours, the outer and the inner, a new town sprang up a generation later, more commodious and well-arranged than the ' City '—with wide straight streets diverging from a central market-place, which occupied much the same positions as the market-place and streets to-day. On one side, the eastern, nearest Athens, the rock rises to a height of 200 feet, thus forming a natural fortress,

[1] It will be seen that this account does not follow Professor Ernest Gardner(*Ancient Athens*, ch. xiv., and especially Note xiv *a*, pp. 562 and 3) in making Munychia the midmost of the three Piraic harbours (the modern Pasha Limani) and calling the most easterly (modern Fanari) Phalerum. The argument based on M. Angelopoulos' measurements has much force. But against the identification of Phalerum with Fanari are these considerations : (1) On any plain reading of Thucydides and Pausanias—and especially of Pausanias (i. 1. 2), Phalerum is *separate from and contrasted with the three Piraic harbours* and cannot also be one of them ; (2) Phalerum is described by Pausanias as in the part of the coast nearest the city ; and again as twenty stades (4000 yards) distant from the city (Paus. viii. 10. 4). Either of these descriptions applies aptly to the open Bay of Phalerum, or to the Chapel of St. George where Frazer places the ancient township of Phalerum, but not to the rocky basin now called Fanari.

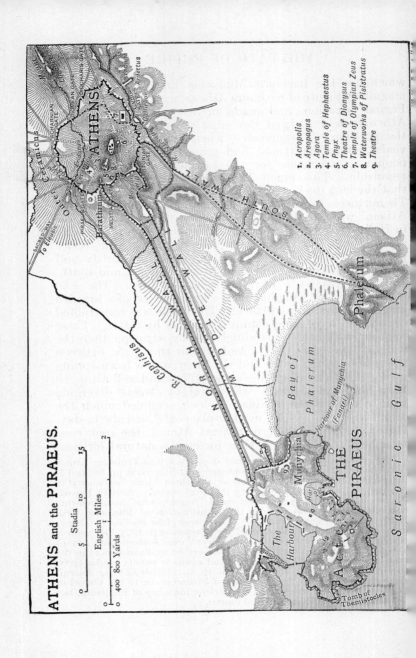

ATHENS and the PIRAEUS.

Stadia
0   5   10   15

English Miles
0   1   2

0   400   800 Yards

1. Acropolis
2. Areopagus
3. Agora
4. Temple of Hephaestus
5. Pnyx
6. Theatre of Dionysus
7. Temple of Olympian Zeus
8. Waterworks of Pisistratus
9. Theatre

ATHENS

CERAMICUS

To Eleusis

SACRED WAY

PIRAEIC GATE

MELITE

Barathrum

COLLYTUS

ACHARNIAN GATE

DIPYLON GATE

DIOCHARIS GATE

Cape Xypetè

MUSEUM HILL

CONE

COELE

R. Ilissus

To Eleusis

NORTH WALL

MIDDLE WALL

R. Cephisus

SOUTH WALL

Phalerum

Bay of Phalerum

Saronic Gulf

THE PIRAEUS

Munychia

Harbour of Munychia
(Fanari)

Aphrodisium

The Harbour

Tomb of Themistocles

the hill Munychia.   Themistocles was so convinced of the
advantages of this harbour site that he counselled his
countrymen to leave Athens and move to Piraeus.   But
this advice the Athenians could not follow ; the feelings
which attached them to Athens and the Acropolis were
too strong.   Piraeus increased and flourished, outstripping
in civic amenity the ancient city : but the systematic
laying out of Piraeus as a town and the ample provision
of shipbuilding yards and dockyard equipment which
went with it, belong to a somewhat later time, when
Pericles was the ruling spirit.   Ultimately there were
three war-harbours, with docks for nearly four hundred
triremes, the foundations of the slips down which the
triremes slid into the water from covered sheds (the roofs
of which rested on a colonnade of pillars) may be traced
along the water's edge in several places.   The entrances to
the harbours, Piraeus itself, Munychia, and Zea, were
protected by moles, and could be closed with a chain.

The sea at Phalerum is three miles from the Acropolis
rock ; Piraeus is rather less than five.   A railway line
nowadays connects Athens with Piraeus ; for the pedes-
trian it is a dusty walk of six miles, and so it was in
ancient times.   The ground near the peninsula was
marshy and the road had to be carried over this by a
causeway.   So even when the whole Piraic peninsula
was fortified there was still danger that Athens might
be cut off from the sea and starved.   This danger was
eliminated when, some twenty years later, Piraeus and
Athens were made into one city by the building of the
Long Walls.   One wall stretched from the Piraic Gate
of the city to the great engirdling wall of the peninsula ;
the other to the north-eastern corner of the Bay of
Phalerum, where ancient Phalerum was.[1]

[1] Later, some time before 431 B.C., a second Long Wall was built
almost exactly parallel to the northern Long Wall, at a distance of some
200 yards and known as the *Middle* Wall : and after this the northern
or Phaleric wall became of less account and was allowed to fall out of
use.   See Bury, p. 377.   Some writers, however, now deny that any
Phaleric wall ever existed.   This is contrary to the natural meaning
of what Thucydides writes, though it is probable that in the Peloponnesian War the Long Walls meant the two parallel walls as described above.

New Strength of Athens.—When these walls and harbours were built, the new Athens arising out of the ruins of the old was a very different Athens, and far more powerful. She was powerful already and endowed with the potentiality of much greater power. Destiny had called her to be champion of maritime Greece and chief of a widely extended confederacy. This extension of her influence eastward across the Aegean was simply a development of tendencies which were in operation before the Persian War. As early as the time of Pisistratus Athens had developed interests north-eastward across the Aegean and in the direction of the Hellespont. And the reason was a fundamental one, the need of her people for food. Attica, though the home of the olive and the vine, is as a whole too bare and rocky to support a large population from her own soil.[1] But the population of Attica grew and there was more and more need to seek the means of buying corn through the commerce which Solon helped to foster. It is a sign of this that early in the sixth century B.C. the Athenians seized and occupied Sigeum by force of arms, and fought a small war with the Mytileneans for its possession. Now Sigeum,[2] we see from the map, is near the entrance to the Dardanelles on the Asiatic side. Towards the end of the same century Miltiades, afterwards victor at Marathon, was an independent prince in the peninsula of Gallipoli, as his father and uncle had been before him. Thus Athenian influence was at that time strong on both sides of the Hellespont channel, which means that Athens had control of the passage through the Dardanelles to the Black Sea. With the advance of the Persian power and the failure of the Ionian Revolt the Athenians no doubt lost to a great extent their command of the Dardanelles. We notice that as soon as the Persian fleet was destroyed at Mycalê it is to the Dardanelles that the Greeks straightway sail : Abydos is occupied, Sestos taken after a siege ; and next Byzantium, which commands the Bosphorus,

[1] Cf. vol. i. p. 237 and p. 240.

[2] It was the town, we may remember (vol. i. p. 112), which Archaianax of Miletus built out of the stones of Priam's Troy.

is captured. When the Spartans withdrew from the leadership of Hellas in Eastern waters, Athens naturally reaped the full benefit of these acquisitions. The trade route to the Black Sea was once more secured to her. We may recall also Pisistratus' interest in the coast of Thrace and in the gold mines in the region of Mount Pangaeum. All through the story of Athens we shall see how important to her was the control of the Hellespont. The Athenian ' empire ' begins with the siege of Sestos, and ends with Aegospotami ; the one at the mouth of the Dardanelles, the other half-way down its winding channel and not far from the modern town of Gallipoli.

Athens and the Confederate Greeks.—When the Greeks of the islands and of the Asiatic coast invited Athens to organize with them a league, defensive and offensive, against Persia, interest as well as honour urged her to take up the task. In all good faith she accepted as allies all the separate states, large and small, that were eager to join, Lilliputian units like Pholegandros and Belbina, as well as Lesbos, Chios and the other large islands. All alike took the oath of fidelity to the league and sealed it by the symbolic sinking in the sea of a mass of hot iron. Athens took her place among the rest in the Synod of the Confederacy at Delos and exercised her right of voting as one among equals. But in another aspect she was not, and could not be, merely an equal, nor did the Confederacy so regard her. They made her chief and president of the Synod. They asked her to accept the responsibility of assessing the proportion in which each member of the League was to contribute to its support, and they expected her to enforce by her preponderant strength the decisions of the League in council. The executive officers of the Confederacy, appointed to apportion and collect the revenue of the League, the *Helleno-tamiae*, were Athenian citizens.[1] It was thus from the first a fellowship unequally yoked, and as such in danger of insidious transformation into something other than the free and equal alliance which it was in theory. There had

[1] See ch. i. p. 16.

been a time when the larger islands had possessed stronger
fleets than Athens herself. The Chians had sent 100
ships to Ladê, Lesbos 70, Samos 60 : Naxos was able to
resist successfully a Persian fleet of 200 vessels in the
year before the Ionian revolt. On the other hand Athens,
in 487 B.C., three years after Marathon, was glad to
borrow twenty ships from Corinth to fight Aegina. The
balance of naval power had greatly changed since then,
and Athens now kept the seas with a fleet of 200 triremes,
while the fighting strength of the islands had dwindled :
the smaller islands and cities had no fighting ships at all.
In order that all might contribute to the common cause,
it was, therefore, as we have seen, agreed that the smaller
states should make a money payment proportionate to
their resources. It had been Aristides' task to estimate
how much in each case this should be. There were also
other states, which, though they were able to provide
ships, by their own choice made a money payment instead. So from the beginning of the League there were
two classes of members, (1) those who like Athens and
Chios and Samos contributed ships ; and (2) those
who commuted service for a money payment. The
policy, conduct and strategy of the League depended
upon Athens, and her lead was so energetic and so prudent
that by the year 468, with Cimon's double victory at the
Eurymedon, all fear of successful Persian aggression
passed away—*provided the League itself was kept in being.*

The Ionian Temperament.—But there was another
difference between Athens and her allies, more charged
with destiny for both, than even the difference of size
and strength. It is unjust to stigmatize the Ionians and
other Asiatic Greeks as altogether enervated and cowardly.
They made a good fight for the recovery of their liberties
in the years between 500 and 494 B.C.[1] But we have seen
also that there was in them a strain of slackness and
indiscipline which was their undoing at Ladê.[2] They
were the same Ionians still. They were pleasure-loving,
and disinclined to war-service with the discipline it called

[1] See vol. i. p. 273.   [2] See vol. i. pp. 274 and 275.

for. They preferred to get their fighting and training done for them. They liked to stay at home and have a good time. The Athenians, braced by the domestic freedom they had worked out for themselves, lifted above their nature by the remembrance of Marathon, steeled and tempered to endurance by the Persian invasion, were urged on to action and adventure as only perhaps the Northmen, the Spanish Conquistadores, and the English Elizabethans, have been at other times in the history of mankind.[1] Their greatest praise comes from the mouths of their enemies : " Their bodies they devote to their country as though they belonged to other men ; their true self is their mind, which is most truly their own when employed in her service. . . . To do their duty is their only holiday, and they deem the quiet of inaction to be as disagreeable as the most tiresome business."[2] So said the Corinthian ambassadors at Sparta. Compare this temper with that of the Ionians, who said of the training imposed by Dionysius the Phocaean, their chosen admiral : " We had better suffer anything rather than these hardships ; even the slavery with which we are threatened, however harsh, can be no worse than our present thraldom. Come, let us refuse him obedience."[3] Not only is it obvious that Athenians and the eastward Greeks were unequally yoked in alliance, but it might have been prophesied that more and more the real power of the League would pass to Athens, and more and more the weaker members would lean upon her strength. In what way could such a process end, but in the transformation of Athenian leadership into Athenian lordship, while the allies were gradually lowered to the status of dependants ? It was not long before the course of events brought a critical turning-point.

The Question of Secession.—In 469, within ten years of Mycalê, the large island of Naxos tired of the alliance

[1] The conquering energy of the Arabs after the death of Mohammed was more wonderful still, but had more special causes.

[2] Thucydides, i. 70. 6 and 8 (Jowett).

[3] Herodotus, xi. 12. 3 (Rawlinson).

and attempted to break away. Athens refused to permit this and used the forces of the League to coerce Naxos. " Then the Naxians revolted," writes Thucydides, " and the Athenians made war against them and reduced them by blockade." When the Naxians surrendered, they were not restored to their former position of independent allies, but as a punishment were made a dependency of Athens, a subject state. Thucydides does not scruple to use of the condition in which they were placed the detested word ' douleia,' enslavement. " This was the first of the allied cities which was *enslaved* contrary to Hellenic right ; the turn of the others came later." [1] The issues involved are debateable. Were the members of the Confederacy of Delos, all of whom had joined the League of their own free will, equally free to secede from it at their pleasure ? Athens emphatically said, ' No ! ' [2] and apparently the other confederates were with her. Every member had taken an oath of fidelity, and the obligations of the League might be taken to last as long as the existence of the Persian Empire constituted a menace to Hellenic freedom, active or potential. But the strict application of this principle, combined with Ionian slackness, did certainly lead before very long to the conversion of the Ionian Confederacy into an Athenian ' empire.' In the years which followed, one by one the numerous members of the League came into conflict with the controlling power, were reduced by force, and then became subject cities of Athens instead of independent allies. Thucydides sums up the process in a few pointed sentences : " Among the various causes of defection the most serious were failure to furnish the contributions due in money and ships, and in certain cases refusal of service. The Athenians were strict in their insistence on the discharge of obligations, and gave offence by applying coercion to men unaccustomed to severe effort and averse to it. In other ways, too, Athenian leadership

[1] Thucydides, i. 98. 4.

[2] So also said Abraham Lincoln in A.D. 1861 when certain of the ' United States ' broke away from the Union.

was no longer as welcome as it had been : they no longer
shared service on equal terms with the allies, and it was
becoming easy to reduce any who seceded. For this the
confederates were themselves to blame, because most of
them through dislike of military service compounded
their share in the upkeep of the navy by a money payment ; and consequently . . . when it came to seceding,
found themselves without the necessary equipment and
without training for war." [1] But if we grant the fitness
and even the necessity of the maintenance by force of
arms of the cohesion of the Delian League as a whole,
and recognise Athens as rightfully its armed executive,
there remains the further question whether the forfeiture
of independence was the just and reasonable penalty
of insubordination or secession. And that is much more
doubtful, whether the question is regarded as one of
equity or of expediency.

Allies or Subjects ?—A few years before the attempted
secession of Naxos (probably in 472) Athens had made
war at her own initiative against Carystus in Euboea—
the city which in the year of Marathon had resisted for
a time the whole power of Datis and Artaphernes [2]—
and compelled the Carystians to join the Confederacy.
This was a coercion which seems to have less justification.
Yet all the Euboean towns but Carystus, it appears, had
entered the Confederacy, and it might pertinently be asked
why Carystus should get all the benefits which the League
secured and make no sacrifice for them. This much,
however, is clear : if once the principle of coercion was
admitted in these two cases : (1) that states might be
compelled to join the Confederacy, and (2) be punished
if they seceded from it or failed in some point of obligation,
Athenian domination was bound to come in time. For
the penalty of subjugation after resistance was, as we saw
above, that the state subjugated was no longer a free
member of the League, but a subject state ; and a subject
state not of the League but of Athens. The consequence

---

[1] Thucydides, i. 99.   [2] See vol. i. p. 281.

of this was that by the time of the Peloponnesian war, just fifty years after Salamis, only two members of the Confederacy were left in the position of free allies, the islands Chios and Lesbos. All the rest were dependencies. The Confederacy of Delos had been transformed into an Athenian empire.

At every step probably a fair case could be made out for the action Athens took : but the net result was to place her in a position fatally opposed to the deep-rooted Hellenic sentiment for autonomy. Yet for a long time this result was not foreseen either by Athens, who was passing without any deliberate intention into the position of a ' tyrant ' state ; nor by the allies, who, by their slackness and folly, themselves brought about the loss of their independence. It was all so easy and convenient. The small states wanted to be protected from the Great King, but they did not like service on ship-board. It suited them to provide money instead, and let Athens build the ships and find the men to man them. They were quite content that the Athenians should do their fighting for them. They did not realize that they were thereby forging chains for their own binding. On the other hand it suited the Athenians to accept money contributions in place of personal service, because with the money they built ships and these ships formed part of their own navy and strengthened it. At the same time the ships gave employment to a large part of the growing population ; ship-builders to build them and seamen to man them. So, while things went smoothly, both the allies and Athens were well pleased with the arrangement It was only when disagreement arose that the fatal error of the small state was revealed. For then, whatever the merits of the dispute, the small state was helpless. It was too late, when the appeal to force came, to attempt to make good on a sudden the lack of ships and the want of experience and training. This transformation of the Confederacy of Delos into the Athenian empire came about, as we may see, gradually, almost insensibly. It was not formally completed by the time that the Peloponnesian war began, but it was practically a reality long before that. The transference of the Treasury of the League from Delos to Athens was a definite outward mark of the change. The exact date of this transfer is not recorded. It is inferred on general grounds, and on the evidence of the quota-lists that it was in 454 B.C. or a little after. About the same time, too, the Federal Synod or Council must have ceased its meetings—there was so little of it to meet by this time that the only members left—besides Athens—were the islands, Chios, Lesbos and Samos, and the cities of Euboea.

A Divided Hellas.—Along with the growth of this arbitrary power of Athens over subject Hellenic communities there went on a deepening and hardening of the differences which tended to divide Hellas into two hostile aggregates. There was on the one side the confederacy over which Athens presided, the Confederacy of Delos, or, as the enemies of Athens preferred to call it, the *arché* or dominion of Athens ; and on the other a new Peloponnesian confederacy, the nucleus of which was the old Peloponnesian League under Sparta. Such a rivalry and division was foreshadowed when the Peloponnesian contingents withdrew from the Hellespont after Mycalê, and when two years later the Spartans acquiesced in yielding to Athens the further conduct of the war with Persia. The division followed in the main the racial distinction of Ionian and Dorian, and, politically, democratic sentiment on the whole swayed the one, oligarchic the other. The causes of this cleavage lay deep in the past of Hellas and arose out of the historical relations of her peoples to each other. Athens was Ionian—that after all was the head and front of her offending.

Dorian Jealousy of Athens.—How quick the Dorians of the Peloponnese were to conceive a jealousy of the naval power of Athens is shown in Thucydides' account of the rebuilding of the walls of Athens. It was the Peloponnesians who urged on Sparta the proposal to stop the restoration of these defences, because already they had

begun to dread the strength of Athens' fleet and the daring
spirit her people had shown in the war. The Spartans
for their part seem to have conceived a genuine admiration
for Athenian prowess, and for Themistocles personally.
They had been offended, indeed, by the success with which
Themistocles had " bluffed " them over the rebuilding of
the walls, but their anger was directed rather against
Themistocles than against Athens. The transfer to
Athens of the leadership against Persia does not seem to
have disturbed good relations between Athens and
Sparta and, so far as we know, good relations continued
for the next ten or twelve years. The first active hostility
we hear of is in 465, when a dispute about the working
of the gold mines of Thrace had arisen between Athens and
the island of Thasos, which lay just opposite their settlement. The people of Thasos were defeated in battle and
shut up within the walls of their town. When hard
pressed in the siege they sent an appeal to the Spartans,
begging them to invade Attica and so create a diversion.
The Spartans are said to have given a promise that they
would, but to have been unable to make it good owing
to a calamity which befell Sparta in the year following
the year 464. There was an earthquake, the most terrible
in human memory at the time. The ground yawned,
the whole town of Sparta was levelled and there was much
loss of life.[1] At once the Helots rose in revolt. The
immediate danger was averted by the presence of mind
of King Archidamus.[2] But, though their first attack

---

[1] Plutarch writes (*Cimon*, 16) : " In the fourth year of the reign of
Archidamus, the son of Zeuxidamus, king of Sparta, there happened
in the country of Lacedaemon, the greatest earthquake that was known
in the memory of man ; the earth opened into chasms, and the mountain Taÿgetus was so shaken that some of the rocky points of it fell down
and except five houses, all the town of Sparta was shattered to pieces."
(Clough).

[2] When Sparta was in a turmoil of confusion, and most of the citizens
were busy rescuing what property they could from their wrecked
homes, he had the assembly sounded. The Spartans rushed to arms
and gathered in a body. So when the bands of Helots swarmed down
on Sparta, he was able to meet them with a body of troops in good
order and put them to rout.

failed, the revolted Helots seized Mount Ithomê, the ancient stronghold of their race, and there held out. The situation was still critical, and Sparta appealed to her allies for help. At this time at Athens Cimon's influence was very strong, and he was an admirer of Spartan institutions and a firm advocate of friendship with Sparta. When a Spartan envoy came and made a special appeal for help, he persuaded the Athenians to send a force of 4000 men to co-operate in the siege of Ithomê, and himself went in command. This friendly succour was, however, so far from drawing Athens and Sparta closer together that it led to a fatal estrangement. For the Spartans credited the Athenians with special skill in the conduct of sieges and looked for the speedy fall of Ithomê after the arrival of the contingent. When this expectation was not fulfilled their disappointment was keen. In their vexation they believed that the Athenians were purposely failing them, and even began to suspect that there was some secret understanding between the Athenians and the rebels. In this state of mind they suddenly intimated to the Athenian commanders that they had no further need of their assistance. The Athenians were mortally offended and showed their resentment by immediately breaking off their alliance with Sparta and allying themselves with Sparta's traditional enemy, Argos. This, according to Thucydides, was the beginning of the enmity which culminated in the Peloponnesian War. Meantime Thasos, after a two years' siege was forced to surrender. The penalties of defeat were severe. Her walls were pulled down, her fleet confiscated. A heavy indemnity was laid upon her and a yearly tribute. Her territory on the mainland, which Athens coveted, was declared forfeit. Athens had even sought to further her designs in this region by establishing a settlement three miles inland from Eion on the Strymon. The settlers numbered ten thousand, partly from Athens, partly from the allied states. All went well at first ; the settlement was planted at Nine Ways, where later the Athenians founded Amphipolis. Then came appalling

calamity. In attempting an advance further inland the
settlers came to a place called Drabescus. There they
were overwhelmed by a combined attack of all the tribes
in that part of Thrace and perished to a man. The
settlement at Nine Ways was wiped out. It was a heavy
blow : but it hardly checked the astonishing activity
that Athens was now showing in every direction.

The Crowded Years.—The twelve years from 459 to
448 are the years which most vividly illustrate the extraordinary energy put forth by the Athenian people in the
period following their great deliverance. The wonder
of it is the greatness of the output relatively to the
numerical strength of the people, the extent of their
home territory and the total of their fighting forces. At
the outbreak of the Peloponnesian War, that is in 431
B.C. the land forces of Athens have been calculated to
reach a possible total of some 70,000 men,[1] infantry,
cavalry and light-armed—approximately the strength
of the British Expeditionary Force to France in 1914—
they cannot well have been more thirty years earlier, and
may have been considerably less. Her fleet at its greatest
strength was 400 ships of war, and, reckoning a ship's
company at two hundred, the *personnel* of this fleet
would be 80,000 men. But Athens never had so many
ships in commission at one time : the largest total we
have the means of calculating is 300 ; so the figure for the
fleet is nearer 60,000 than 80,000. These land and sea
forces were her active service forces, her first, second
and third lines of defence. There were no reserves behind
them. The total population of Attica was under half
a million—perhaps a tenth of the present population of
London : and of the half million, probably nearly half
were slaves. Out of these limited resources in man power
Athens had to provide all that was necessary for active
service abroad and for garrison duty at home. In the
year 459 B.C. an Athenian fleet won a victory off the
island of Cecryphalae in the Saronic Gulf near Aegina

[1] See Zimmern. *The Athenian Commonwealth,* p. 414. Cf. pp. 172
175.

her land forces suffered defeat at Halieis on the eastern
shore of the Gulf of Argolis. Naupactus [1] in Aetolia,
at the mouth of the Gulf of Corinth, was captured from the
Locrians and in it were planted the survivors of the
gallant band of Messenians who had defended Ithomê for
five years against all the efforts of Sparta. Megara,
that Dorian city which tradition said had once been
Attic, and which from its position commanding the gate
of the Peloponnese through the Isthmus of Corinth was
of such fateful importance to Athens, was at her own
request admitted into the Athenian alliance ; and the
Athenians built for the Megarians walls a mile long to
join Megara to Nisaea, her harbour on the Saronic Gulf.
Most memorable of all, an Athenian expedition to Egypt,
at that time in revolt against Persia, had sailed up the
Nile to Memphis and captured the city with the exception
of the citadel, known as *White Castle*. It was the *annus
mirabilis* of the rising Athenian empire. A vivid memory
of this year survives in a slab of marble, now at Paris,
in the Louvre, which has inscribed upon it the names of
176 men of the tribe of Erectheus, who in this year fell
in battle for Athens, " In Cyprus, in Egypt, in Phoenicia,
at Halieis, at Aegina, at Megara," [2] evidently just one of
ten such slabs, one for each of the ten tribes.

In the next year (458) the Aeginetans and their Peloponnesian allies were defeated on the sea with a loss of
70 ships, and Aegina itself was besieged ; the building
of the Long Walls of Athens was begun, and Myronides
with an army made up wholly of the older and the youngest
classes of military age (because all the best troops were
away fighting in Aegina and Egypt) twice defeated the
Corinthian levies who had made a raid into the Megarid,
in the confidence that Athens would be unable to find
men to meet them without raising the siege of Aegina.

---

[1] Naupactus, Ship-building-town, got its name from the belief that
it was here the Heraclids built the fleet that conveyed their armed
bands across the Gulf before the successful Dorian invasion of Peloponnese. See vol. i. ch. ix. p. 222.

[2] See Hicks and Hill, 26, pp. 36-39, or Roberts and Gardner, 359
pp. 498-500. *C.I.G.* i. 165.

In 457 the Athenians, after being worsted at Tanagra
in a stubbornly contested battle by the army of the
Peloponnesian League, two months later marched into
Boeotia led by the same Myronides, routed the Boeotians
at Oenophyta near Oropus, and, as a result, gained
complete political control over all the Boeotian land.
About the same time the Long Walls were finished. The
surrender of Aegina followed next year : the Aeginetans
agreed to give up their ships, dismantle their walls and
pay a contribution to the Delian Confederacy. In the same
year (456) the Athenian admiral Tolmides sailed round the
Peloponnese and burnt the Lacedaemonian dockyards
at Gythium in Laconia. This was the moment when
the fortunes of the Athenian empire reached their highest
point.

Two of the episodes of these years of strenuous effort
and enterprise, the expedition to Egypt and the conquest
of Boeotia, are of such striking significance as to repay
more detailed treatment.

Athens and Egypt.—The connection of the Greeks with
Egypt dates from the beginning of Greek history and even
earlier ; for instance the name of Egypt figures four times
in the Odyssey.[1] Greek soldiers in the pay of an Egyptian
king voyaged up the Nile as far as Abu Simbel (which
is on the left bank between Korosko and Wadi Halfa).
Of this we may be sure because their names are found
there scratched on the gigantic figure of Rameses II.
in front of a great rock-hewn temple. At Naucratis,
near the western mouth of the Nile, the Greeks, some
fifty years earlier had been allowed to form a settlement.[2]
And earlier again (B.C. 635) Greek mercenaries had helped
to set Psammetichus, founder of the 26th dynasty, on
the throne of Egypt. Egypt with its strange customs

---

[1] Odyssey, iii. 300 ; iv. 351 ; xiv. 275 ; xvii. 426.

[2] Excavations on a site conjectured to be that of Naucratis, undertaken for the Egyptian Exploration Fund, 1884 to 1886, by Dr. Flinders
Petrie, resulted in the discovery of the remains of several Greek temples
and of a large fortified enclosure. The site was further investigated
for the British School at Athens by Dr. Hogarth in 1899.

and stranger deities, its stupendous monuments and venerable antiquities had a strong fascination for the Greeks, as it has for many moderns. Thales, Pythagoras, Solon, Plato were said to have visited Egypt and learnt of her wisdom. So, when in 459, while a powerful Athenian fleet of 200 sail was engaged in another attempt to win Cyprus for Hellas,[1] news was brought that Inaros the Libyan, who had raised successful revolt in Egypt, asked for assistance, it seemed to the Athenian commanders (their names are not recorded) too good an opportunity to be missed. What advantages might not accrue to Athenian commerce from an Egypt delivered out of the power of the Mede, not to speak of the blow such a loss would be to Persian prestige ? The fleet sailed straight from Cyprus to the Nile, swept up the river to Memphis (which is fourteen miles south of Cairo), got possession of the whole of the town, but could not capture the citadel, known as the *White Castle*. For two years the Persian garrison, supported by a pro-Persian party among the Egyptians, held out stubbornly, beating back every attack. For two years the Athenians pressed the siege. Then there was a dramatic reversal of the position. Megabyzus, son of Zopyrus, came with a great army across the Sinai desert (over which British airmen flew in the advance on Palestine in 1916), defeated the Egyptians in a pitched battle, raised the siege of White Castle, and so turned the tables on the Athenians that they were shut up in an island lower down the Nile, which Thucydides calls Prosopitis. Here for a year and six months the Athenians held out. Then Megabyzus diverted the water which defended the Athenian position, so that their ships were left high and dry and the island was joined to the river bank. This accomplished, the Persians had nothing to do but march straight upon the Athenians and overwhelm them by force of numbers. Before, however, the final assault was made a capitulation was agreed to and a remnant of the Athenian forces

[1] Phoenician influences were strong in Cyprus and the island was never brought effectually into the Hellenic confederacy.

withdrew across the Libyan desert and found a refuge in Cyrene. All the two hundred ships were destroyed. It was a very great disaster. Nor was this the end, for, unaware of what had happened, a reinforcing squadron of fifty Athenian and allied ships came sailing up and entered the Nile. They were attacked from the river and from the shore : most of the ships were destroyed, only a few escaped. How Athens bore up under so heavy a loss of men and material will never be known.

Athens and Boeotia.—The part of Boeotia in the Persian War had been one of mixed glory and shame. Seven hundred Thespians died with Leonidas at Thermopylae, though the caprice of tradition has given all the praise to Sparta. The Plataeans had a prime share in the glories of Marathon and Plataea. But Plataeans and Thespians were a minority among the Boeotians. All the rest had medized. Now Boeotia in contrast with Attica is a wide plain surrounded by hills. This plain is divided by a low hilly ridge into two parts, of which the southern is the plain of Thebes, containing besides Thebes, the towns of Thespiae, Leuctra, Plataea and Tanagra. Chaeronea, Lebadea, Coronea, Haliartus and Orchomenos are in the northern section, a large portion of which is taken up by the great marsh formed by the river Cephisus, and known as Lake Copais.[1] Thebes, a city whose mythical renown[2] rivals that of Mycenae, was by far the strongest of the Boeotian cities and claimed through the historical period to be the rightful head of a Boeotian League. It was the support Athens gave to Plataea in resisting this claim that made Thebes so long the determined enemy of Athens. And because of this enmity Thebes gladly made common cause with the Mede. The penalty Thebes paid for the defeat of Mardonius was that she lost for a time her supremacy in Boeotia. But as

[1] Much of the area of the ancient lake (estimated at 61,750 acres) has been drained by a British Company and brought under cultivation.

[2] With Thebes are connected the legends of Semele (mother of Dionysus), Cadmus, Amphion, the terrible tragedy of Oedipus, and the stories of the two sieges of Thebes, the first of which happened a generation before the Trojan War.

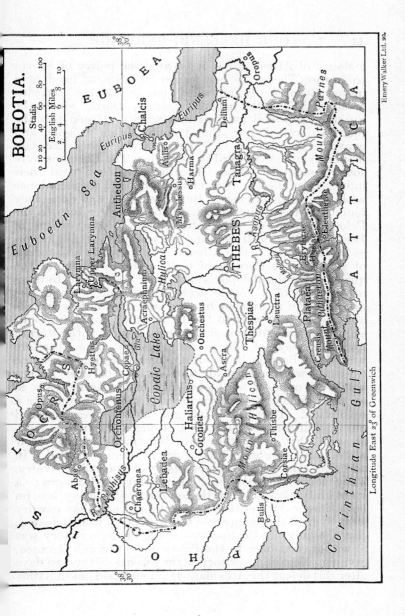

BOEOTIA.

Stadia
0 10 20 40 60 80 100

English Miles
0 2 4 6 8 10

EUBOEA

Euboean Sea

Euripus

Chalcis

Aulis

Anthedon

Larymna

Upper Larymna

Harma

Mycalessus

Tanagra

Delium

Oropus

Mount Parnes

ATTICA

THEBES

Hyliea

R. Asopus

R. Thespius

Acraephnium

Copae

Copaic Lake

Onchestus

Thespiae

Ascra

Leuctra

Erythrae

Hysiae

Plataea

Cithaeron

Eleutherae

Mount Cithaeron

Crensis

LOCRIS

Opus

Hyettus

Orchomenus

R. Cephisus

Abae

Chaeronea

Lebadea

Coronea

Haliartus

Mount Helicon

Thisbe

Corsiae

Bulis

Corinthian Gulf

PHOCIS

Longitude East 23° of Greenwich

38° 30

38° 30

Emery Walker Ltd. sc.

jealousy of Athens grew, it became the policy of Sparta to restore Thebes to her former position as head of a united Boeotia. It happened that in 457 the Phocians attacked the little neighbour state, Doris, which the Spartans regarded as their mother-city. Upon this the Spartans called out the Peloponnesian League and conveyed a force of 11,500 men (1500 being Lacedae-monians) across the Gulf of Corinth. The Phocians were soon brought to terms. The Spartans then used their influence to effect a settlement of Boeotia in accordance with their own interest. But when this was done they found themselves in difficulties about their return to the Peloponnese. For this interference in the affairs of Boeotia might well be—and was—regarded at Athens as hostile action. The Athenians had already a squadron of ships in the Corinthian Gulf, and it was out of the question for the Peloponnesian army to attempt to cross in presence of a hostile fleet. On the other hand, the difficulties of retirement by land were hardly less formid-able. The only road to the Isthmus lay through Mount Geranea, and Athens since her alliance with Megara had possession of the passes. The Spartans therefore waited in Boeotia, and all the more willingly because overtures were being made to them by a party in Athens who were opposed to the building of the Long Walls as an ultra-democratic enterprise, and were scheming for a revolution. To stop this intrigue the Athenians marched out in full force : their total strength was 14,000 men-at-arms, that is together with the troops sent by their allies, among whom 1000 Argives were included. In addition, they had with them a body of Thessalian cavalry. They found the Peloponnesian army at Tanagra ; a stubbornly contested battle followed with heavy loss on both sides. At a critical moment the Thessalian cavalry went over to the enemy and the Athenians were defeated. But the only use the Spartans made of their victory was to withdraw at once to the Peloponnese through Geranea, ravaging Megarian territory as they went. Sixty-two days after this defeat the Athenians again marched out of Attica in full force under Myronides. At Oenophyta, between Oropus and Tanagra, they gained a complete victory over the forces of the Boeotian confederacy. This victory made Athens for the time being complete mistress of Boeotia, and seemed to foreshadow a land dominion for Athens complementary to her sea-dominion.

Athenian Empire at its Height.—This astonishing career of success was soon to suffer a severe check, but the power of Athens was now at its height (from 455 to 447). On the western side of the Aegean Athenian influence extended over all Boeotia and Phocis, as well as Megara, Aegina and Euboea. Naupactus, garrisoned by refugee Messenians, who were the mortal enemies of Sparta, gave her a commanding position at the mouth of the Corinthian Gulf. When in 453 Achaia also came into the Athenian alliance, Athens had almost as strong a position in the Corinthian Gulf as in the Saronic. The Isthmus was securely hers through alliance with Megara ; Argos and Thessaly were her allies. Her land empire, or confederacy, bade fair to be as powerful as her sea confederacy, which embraced the islands of the Aegean (except Melos and Thera) and all eastward Hellas. Her sea-power was by this time complete and undisputed. Already it was true that " the whole expanse of water, from Crete to the Crimea, with insignificant exceptions, had been converted into an Athenian lake." [1] It was still in name the Confederacy of Delos, but already for all practical purposes it was the Athenian empire.

Jurisdiction.—Another aspect of the transformation of the Athenian confederacy into an Athenian dominion was the judicial. It was natural enough, and a matter of public convenience, that early in the existence of the League questions in dispute between Athens, or individual Athenians, and the allies should be tried at courts in Athens. Athens in her law courts had all the required machinery, and through practice in these courts the ordinary Athenian citizens acquired a remarkable judicial

[1] Zimmern, *The Greek Commonwealth*, pp. 374 and 375

competency. By degrees the custom hardened into a
rule, and ultimately all legal business between Athens and
her allies was transacted at Athens as a matter of obligation, not of choice. It was but an easy extension of this
principle that cases between any two members of the
Confederacy came to be tried by Athenian judges in
Athenian courts. Finally, other cases came to be tried
at Athens, even when both parties to the suit belonged
to the same state. We find an example from an inscription of a convention between Athens and Chalcis in
Euboea, which happens to have survived,[1] that cases
involving the death-penalty could be tried only at Athens.
This, however, was when the allies of Athens had become
practically her subjects. And as the system extended,
and the first acquiescence changed into protest and discontent, it became one of the grievances of the confederate states that so much of their legal business must
be done at Athens. It was one of the causes contributing
to the conversion of the confederacy into an empire and
also one of the results of the change.

Revenue.—Legal business brought employment to the
Athenian law-courts (and how large a proportion of the
citizen-body had a share in this we shall see later) ;
it brought fees to Athens and it brought business in
the wide sense to harbour-town and city, through the
number of litigants who were forced to come to Athens
and spend their money there. The maintenance of the
confederate navy gave employment and pay to an
increasing number of the less wealthy citizens, though a
proportion of the seamen in the Athenian navy were
mercenaries or slaves. The building and repairing of
the warships kept large numbers of workmen and
their overseers busy. Athens thus profited in various
ways through the discharge of the onerous duties she had
undertaken when the League was constituted in B.C. 478.
And in addition she controlled the spending of the 460
talents, the sum total of allied contributions under

[1] Hicks and Hill, *Manual of Greek Historical Inscriptions*, 40. p. 65,
ll. 71 to 76 ; *C.I.A.* vol. iv. p. 10, 27a, ll. 71-76.

Aristides' assessment. Even when the Treasury was at Delos, the control of the expenditure was Athenian, since the ' Stewards of the Hellenes ' who administered it, were all citizens of Athens. But at some time later, probably, as we have noted, in 454, after the Athenian disaster in Egypt, the treasury was removed from Delos to Athens and stored in the temple of Athena Polias. Whatever the reasons for this transfer, the result was to make Athenian control of the allied funds unchecked and absolute. " Ostensibly this meant no more than a change of banker, Athena taking the place of Apollo. But, practically, the result was to remove it once for all from the control of the Confederate Parliament, and to make every one see and feel, what they had known in their hearts long ago, that it was the money of Athens, with which she could do what she liked. The world is still blessing her for what she did with it." [1]

Note on Themistocles.

When Pausanias the *traveller* came to Athens in the second century A.D. he saw, as he sailed from Sunium round the peninsula of Actê into Piraeus, an ' altar-like structure ' behind which was a rock-hewn grave believed to be the grave of Themistocles. It was a fitting site for the tomb of the man who had seen the vision of the dock-yards and shipping, of the three harbours, and of the sea-power Athens was to found upon them, while the waves still lapped the bare rock :

> " Fair lies thy tomb
> For it will speak to merchants everywhere ;
> It will behold the seamen sailing out and in,
> And mark the contests of the ships." [2]

But Themistocles—the true founder of the imperial greatness of Athens—himself died in exile, a pensioner on the bounty of the son of the Persian king, to foil whose attempt to conquer Hellas he had done more than any other Greek. For the enemies of Themistocles in Lacedaemon contrived to implicate him in the treason of Pausanias the Spartan (above p. 11 note), and had he not escaped by flight he would have been tried on a charge

[1] Zimmern, *The Greek Commonwealth*, p. 192.

[2] Frazer's translation (Pausanias, ii. p. 21) of the lines by the comic poet Plato, quoted by Plutarch, *Themistocles*, 32.

of Medism and perhaps put to death by his own countrymen. Thucydides and Plutarch tell a romantic story of this flight and escape. Themistocles was living at the time at Argos, having been ostracized some time after 474 (probably in 471). When the charge was made against him at Athens by envoys sent from Sparta, Athenian officers set out along with the Spartans to effect his arrest. Themistocles learnt of the peril in which he stood in time to escape out of the Peloponnese. He went first to Corcyra because he had a claim on Corcyraean gratitude. But the Corcyraeans had not the courage to run the risk of offending both Sparta and Athens : so they conveyed him across to the mainland opposite their island, the country of Epirus. There the ruler was Admetus, prince of the Molossians, a chieftain whom Themistocles had some time before this thwarted in his plans for alliance with Athens. It was therefore doubtful what reception he had to expect. Admetus himself was away from home: so Themistocles made his appeal first to the chieftain's wife, as did Odysseus to Aretê (vol. i. pp. 148, 9). She told him to take in his arms her little son, Admetus' heir, and sit as a suppliant at the king's hearth. Themistocles did as she advised, and when Admetus returned, appealed to his generosity to befriend him, not keeping in mind old causes of resentment, because Themistocles was now in danger of his life. Admetus raised him from the hearth ; and when soon after the pursuers came and demanded his surrender, the king refused to give him up, and afterwards for safety sent him across the mountains to Pydna in Macedonia. Ultimately, after other hair-breadth escapes, Themistocles passed by sea to Ephesus and thence into the territories of the Great King. The Great King was now Artaxerxes, who not long before had succeeded to the throne of Xerxes his father. From him Themistocles claimed protection on the singular ground of services rendered to the royal house. Artaxerxes on his part was flattered at the prospect of having Themistocles to be his servant, received him into favour and gave him for maintenance the revenues of three great cities, Magnesia Myus and Lampsacus. Themistocles died not long after at Magnesia and was buried there with great magnificence. His bones were afterwards brought to Attica by his kinsfolk, either secretly (as Thucydides says), or because (as Pausanias suggests the Athenians " repented of what they had done." [1]

The charge against Themistocles of treasonable correspondence with Pausanias the Spartan and the Persians was never proved and we are under no obligation to believe it. The probabilities are strongly against it ; because, though Themistocles was no Aristides, and may have acquired wealth by doubtful means, he was no fool : he had no motive for intrigue with the Persians

---

[1] Pausanias, i. 1. 2.

There can be no question of the extraordinary quality of his genius. His character has been drawn by the one writer formed by nature to do it justice. Thucydides' character-sketch of Themistocles remains a consummate example of the expressive power of the Greek language. It is the despair of translators : the translation with which this note concludes is at all events the matured result of many years' trial.

"Themistocles gave the strongest proof of force of genius, of which he is a surprising and unique example. By his own mother-wit, to which neither education nor study contributed, he was an admirable judge of an emergency on a moment's consideration, and could forecast with rare insight the most distant future. With a gift of clear exposition when his plans were formed he combined an adequate power of decision in unforeseen contingencies ; when completely in the dark he could still foresee more surely than any one the better or worse plan. In a word, by strength of natural genius he could in a flash of intuition extemporise better than any man the required expedient." [1]

[1] Thucydides, II. 138 (L. J.).

CHAPTER III

THE CITY BEAUTIFUL

> " . . . Athens, diviner yet,
>   Gleamed with its crest of columns, on the will
> Of man, as on a mount of diamond, set ;
>   For thou wert, and thine all-creative skill
> Peopled, with forms that mock the eternal dead
>   In marble immortality, that hill
> Which was thine earliest throne and latest oracle."
>
> SHELLEY, *Ode to Liberty*, stanza v. ll. 9-15.

" That which brought to the city of Athens its most agreeable adornment and struck the world with wonder, that, too, which now alone bears witness for Hellas that the ancient power and splendour of which men speak was no mere fiction, was his construction of memorial temples."

" A man may be not at all points free of reproach, yet one of a noble spirit and of a soul that coveted honour."

PLUTARCH, *Pericles*, 12 and 10.

MODERN ATHENS is a city worth visiting for the beauty of its situation, its fine streets and public buildings, the variety and interest of its life as the capital of an alert minded and energetic modern people, who are playing a leading part in South-Eastern Europe to-day and are likely to play a greater. It is most of all worth visiting for the surviving memorials it contains of a greater glory in the past ; for these cannot be equalled anywhere else in the world. The Parthenon, the Propylaea, the Temple of Athena Niké, the Erechtheum, belong to Athens, peculiarly, but they belong not to her alone. They belong to the whole world. They are part of our own inheritance. They belong to all who have the faculty to understand

50

and admire : for in those shattered buildings and the sorely misused fragments of sculpture found in them, the principles of beauty in architecture and sculpture may be studied as nowhere else. This is the unique glory of modern Athens, though among present-day capital cities she ranks high by right of her existing amenities. She reached her height of greatness in the fifth century B.C., and she has seen strange vicissitudes of fortune since. Her material prosperity, her reputation as a seat of learning and of the arts, (except for the havoc wrought by Sulla's siege and sack in 86 B.C.) increased rather than diminished under Macedonian and Roman ; Athens enjoyed the favour of a succession of Roman emperors and was adorned by them and by her own wealthy citizens with sumptuous buildings. She lost much of her wealth and dignity through the triumph of Christianity, especially when in the sixth century A.D. Justinian suppressed the schools of the philosophers on which her vogue as a university town depended. Yet she retained a moderate degree of prosperity down to the time of the Frankish Dukes of Athens. Then, with the coming of the Turk she sank into utter decay, so that when visited again in the seventeenth century by travellers from western Europe she was little better than a miserable village huddled under the north side of the Acropolis.

Athens to-day.—You may go to Athens all the way from Marseilles by sea, landing at the Piraeus after passing between the moles built to protect the harbour by Themistocles ; or by railway overland from Patras, skirting the Achaean land between the mountains and the Gulf of Corinth and crossing the Canal by a railway bridge. Not many, perhaps, have entered Athens for the first time on foot from Corinth, but there is much to be said for this manner of approach. You follow the road to Megara by the Scironian rocks, as did Theseus when he journeyed from Troezen to Athens to find his father,[1] first winding along by the blue waters of the

[1] See Vol. I., pp. 69 and 70.

Saronic Gulf, with the musical tinkle of goat-bells to cheer you on your way, and a profusion of wild-flowers by the wayside instead of adventures with evil men and monsters. You may even find a quiet beach to bathe from, if the day is hot. And from Megara you wander on by the sea to sacred Eleusis ; then strike inland to the Pass of Daphni and the highroad into Athens. It is a not-to-be-forgotten experience to enter unknown Athens in the deepening twilight, a little uncertain of the way to a night's lodging.

But by whatever means you come, you awake next morning to an astonishing combination of new and old. For Athens, north of the Acropolis is a thoroughly up-to date modern town, with electric trams, broad thorough fares, good modern shops and handsome public buildings. But when you round the Acropolis to the south-west you are in ancient Athens : not in ancient Athens humming with life as vivid and as varied as the modern, but the silent ruined shell of ancient Athens. For while the encircling walls of Themistocles' day formed a ring round the Acropolis, modern Athens has grown up almost entirely on the north and east. So now on the east and north you have the interlacing thoroughfares and street of modern Athens, narrow and tortuous near the citadel rock, broad and spacious more to the north-east toward Lycabettus, where lies the most modern quarter, extending beyond the limits of the ancient city on that side : west and south you have a wide unoccupied space, including sites memorable in the life of the ancient city, the Areopagus, the Pnyx, and the Hill of the Muses, mostly empty now, not built over and not much strewn with ruins, but marked extensively with the traces of the excavator.

The Acropolis.—Between the two regions, joining the very old and the very new, and still the chief centre of interest, is the Acropolis rock with its monuments. The Acropolis, we may say, far more than any other part of Athens to-day, *is* ancient Athens. For through the sagacious diligence of archaeologists during the last

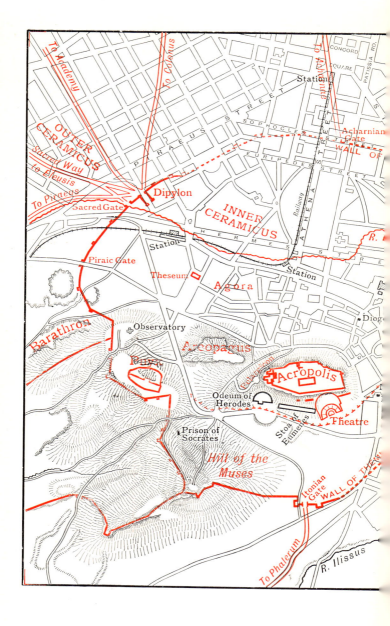

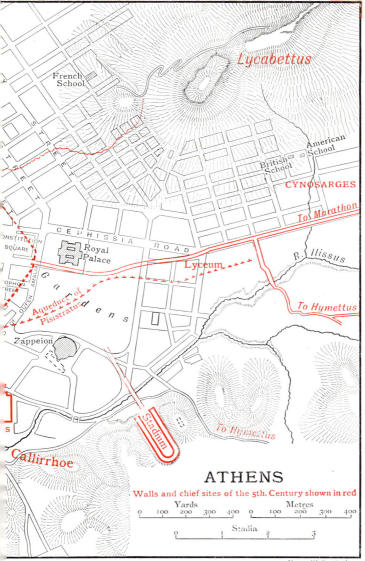

French
School

Lycabettus

American
School

British
School

CYNOSARGES

To Marathon

C E P H I S S I A   R O A D

ONSTITUTION
SQUARE

Royal
Palace

Lyceum

R. Ilissus

To Hymettus

Aqueduct of
Pisistratus

G a r d e n s

OPHON
REET

QUEEN AMALIA

S

Zappeion

Stadium

To Hymettus

S

Callirrhoe

ATHENS

Walls and chief sites of the 5th. Century shown in red

Yards
0   100   200   300   400

Metres
0   100   200   300   400

Stadia.
0   1   2   3

Emery Walker Ltd. sc.

sixty years the accretions of her later history have for the
most part been cleared away,[1] and the traveller of the
twentieth century sees the Acropolis more nearly as it
was in the days of Pericles than it has been at any previous
time since the dissolution of the classical world. More
nearly—yet with how great a difference, since the Acropolis
we see is but a ruin and a relic, the petrified body with
the life gone out of it. Yet how beautiful in its desolation !

If, as in all likelihood, your hotel is near Constitution
Square and the King's Palace, you will make your approach to the Acropolis by the handsome Boulevard
named after Queen Amalia.[2] This takes you between
the Palace Gardens and a well-to-do residential quarter,
past, on the right, the English Church and on the left,
the Arch of Hadrian and the stately columns of the
Temple of Olympian Zeus, till presently it brings you
under the S.E. corner of the Acropolis with the sweeping
circles of the Theatre of Dionysus climbing high up under
the bare rock. You pass along the whole of the south
face and, curving round by the Odeum (Music Hall) of
Herodes Atticus, you approach the ascent to the Acropolis
by a modern road which partly follows the line of the
ancient Panathenaic Way from the Market-place.

The Approach to the Propylaea.—The Acropolis rock
is one of those limestone ridges rising abruptly out of a
plain which are so characteristic of Greece.[3] It is of
rugged, dark-coloured stone, and its top is between 250
and 300 feet from the ground below, and 512 feet above
sea-level at its highest point. It extends nearly 350
yards from east to west, just short of 150 yards from
north to south where it is broadest. Its shape is an
irregular oblong ; but the rock has been so built up and
cut away and filled in and buttressed out in the course
of successive fortifications, that little of the original

---

[1] Prints of mediaeval Athens will probably convince doubters of the
immense gain of this clearance.

[2] Wife of Otho, first King of the Hellenes after the constitution of the
monarchy in 1834.

[3] See vol. i. p. 203.

curved and indented outline is left to view ; and the sides
are crowned with a mighty face of walls which tower
above the natural rock and—more especially on the
east and south sides—sweep in long straight lines, and
give the fortress its aspect of impregnable strength. It
is the flat top which makes the Acropolis so suitable for a
fortress-city, but the flatness is largely the result of successive levellings dating back from prehistoric times and
continued to the building of the Parthenon. In fact the
Acropolis, as we see it to-day, owes scarcely less to art
than to nature. The cliffs below the walls are on three
sides almost perpendicular ; they can only be climbed
in places, and that with difficulty. The fourth side, the
western, is less steep, and has its height diminished by the
rock shelving up to it. This western end was, therefore,
always the natural way up to the top, and when the
Acropolis became a citadel was the side which most
needed defence. Accordingly, in very early times, the
times associated with the people known to the Greeks as
the Pelasgians, there was an outwork at this end called
later the *Pelargicon*,[1] and a system of nine gates, arranged
possibly one above another, like the seven gates of the
hill-fortress of Gwalior.[2] And so things continued til
the time of the invasion of Xerxes.[3] When Athens was
re-fortified by Themistocles, so strong a wall was buil
about the lower town, that the Acropolis was no longe

[1] This outwork is called by Thucydides ' Pelargicon,' which mean
' Fort Stork.' For a most interesting discussion of the position an
extent of this earliest Athens see Dr. Jane Harrison's *Primitive Athen
as described by Thucydides*, pp. 5-36. Frazer (Pausanias II. pp. 356 an
357) cites convincing evidence for placing the Pelargicon at the foot o
the N.W. angle of the Acropolis only, not with Dörpfeld (whom Mis
Harrison follows) giving it a wide sweep round all the west and south
west ends.

[2] Gwalior is one of the Mahratta states. The fort of Gwalior is a roc
of approximately the same height as the Acropolis (300 feet above th
plain), but with a vastly more extensive area on the top, 1¾ miles b
half a mile.

[3] The Acropolis, it will be remembered, was captured by the Persian
not by direct assault through the gates, but by escalade of the pre
cipitous rock on the north side, at a point which was left unguarded
See vol. i. pp. 340 and 341.

THE ACROPOLIS OF ATHENS.

South-east angle, viewed from the Boulevard of Queen Amalia.

regarded as a fortress ; and in the middle of the fifth century B.C. a grand hall of entry was constructed across the west end for splendour of architectural effect not defence, and called the *Propylaea*. But it is not the Propylaea that we come to first as we ascend the Acropolis rock to-day. What first meets the eye is a dull and heavy Roman gateway, called after the French archae-ologist who dug it out, the Beulé Gate. A narrow opening six feet wide lets us in : immediately above, up over shelving rock and a long flight of steps, is the outer portico of the Propylaea, a row of six Doric columns leading into what was once a spacious hall.[1]

The Propylaea.—It is not difficult to apprehend the scheme of the Propylaea—no doubt Pericles' ; and to see that it was magnificent. The rock at its western ex-tremity is about 220 feet wide, and it was Pericles' design to occupy the whole breadth with a superb structure consisting of a central hall and two wings, the wings slightly thrown forward and faced with porticoes flanking the approach. This design was not carried out in its entirety : one wing is little more than a pretence to save appearances. Each wing should have consisted of a side-chamber with a porch in front of it facing inwards to the main ascent : in the southern wing, that on our right, the side-chamber is wanting ; there is just the porch and a back-wall a few feet behind it. This incomplete corre-spondence of the two wings is, however, very little felt in approaching the Propylaea from below. For one thing the eye is drawn by the brave aspect of the little Temple of Victory, boldly planted on the precipitous bastion to the right, nearly thirty feet above, which more than compensates for the comparative weakness of the right wing of the Propylaea. At the same time the non-conformity of the two wings is concealed by the appearance

[1] This central portion of the Propylaea ought not, perhaps, to be called a ' Hall,' yet it is difficult to know what else to call it. Its front is open columns, and columns flank the central roadway on both sides. It is therefore a porch rather than a hall,—but a porch with the dimen-sions of a great hall. Gardner calls it " a great covered hall, divided into three aisles by rows of Ionic columns." (*Ancient Athens*, p. 224)

of correspondence which the portico gives. What mars the effectiveness of the Propylaea now is the ruin wrought by an explosion in the middle of the seventeenth century, when the eastern portico was being used by the Turks as a powder magazine.[1] The hall is roofless, the columns are without their capitals, some of them mere stumps. We pass within the outer portico and on between two rows of Ionic pillars which once supported a rich ceiling ; then through a lofty door, one of five, up a few steps, and out through the upper portico on to the sloping rock which leads to the summit. If we here pause, and turn, the view back through a vista of columns over the plain of Athens and the sea is entrancing ; but the Propylaea halls and columns themselves in their present state are less impressive than their fame.

The Parthenon.—It is otherwise when you ascend the slope and, turning slightly southward, come into full view of the Parthenon, a little to your right. There is a majesty in the wreck of the Parthenon, as it now stands, roofless and rent and broken, that even the Parthenon in its first glory, with its columns complete and the sculptures that adorned its front and sides clear-cut and fresh, could hardly have exceeded. Shattered and muti-lated as it is, grace and strength emanate from its form and outlines, proclaiming it the perfection of symmetry. The first full view of the Parthenon must affect with awe those who come to it with any feeling for human aspiration and achievement ; some even without that stimulus for the sheer graciousness of its lines and proportions.

We can walk round the temple and identify the frag-ments of original sculpture still in position. We may stand on the temple platform and on the pavement of its

---

[1] The magazine was struck by lightning one night in the year 1656, and the Greeks had a story that the storm was sent by St. Demetrius, whose church, some 500 yards S.W. of the Acropolis, was threatened with destruction by the Turkish governor, who had guns ready trained upon it and intended to fire them next day. The governor, who had his residence in the Propylaea, himself with all his family perished in the explosion. The church has since been known as the Church of St. Demetrius Loumpardaris, that is, of St. Demetrius the Bombardier.

THE PARTHENON.

As seen in ascending from the upper Portico of the Propylaea.

From a photograph by the English Photographic Company.

THE ERECHTHEUM.

cella, the shrine of Athena—exactly a hundred Attic feet in length, like the old temple of Athena which was called on that account the *Hecatompedon*. Grievously little—practically nothing—is left of the noble figures sculptured in the round with massive, yet exquisite, art (as the surviving fragments show) ; the best of the Metopes have been taken away ; the slabs that remain are so broken and defaced that the subjects can scarcely be more than guessed at. But a good many of the most spirited and best preserved sections of the frieze are still in their places, especially on the western front of the temple, where all remain but one.

The Erechtheum.—The ruined Parthenon is the greatest of all the sights in modern Athens, but the Parthenon and the Propylaea do not exhaust the architectural glories of the Acropolis. North of the Parthenon, and close to the northern edge of the rock, is the Erechtheum, a temple, or rather a group of associated shrines, like nothing else in Greece, excelling in the rich elaboration of its decorative work as the Parthenon excels in the majesty of simple outlines and proportions. The form of this building is most unusual. A Greek temple is usually a plain rectangle, with either rows of columns at its eastern and western ends, or a portico of columns on all four sides. The shape of the Erechtheum departs widely from this norm. There is the usual portico at the east end ; but at the west end there projects on the north side a large portico which actually extends beyond the wall of the main building ; and on the south side a smaller portico. It is not for the symmetry of its shape that we are drawn to the Erechtheum ; its beauties are different. We study the Erechtheum for the marvellous richness and exquisite finish of its incidental decoration, the bands of carving along its walls, and on the capitals and bases of its columns—carving in stone " so delicate that modern hands, even with modern tools, have never been able to reproduce the fineness of the original." [1] Perhaps

[1] Mrs. Bosanquet, *Days in Attica*, p. 138.

its supreme beauty is the little portico projecting on the south side, the Caryatid Porch. The Caryatides, those gracefully poised female figures, types of patient and serene endurance,[1] catch the eye as one advances from the Parthenon. There are six of them, shapes of women serving as pillars (four in front, with a second figure behind each of the two outer ones), which support on their heads the entablature of this S.W. portico. The name is taken from Caryae, a town in Laconia on the Arcadian border and signifies merely ' the women of Caryae'. Fifth century Athenians, as inscriptions show, called them more simply ' the Maidens,' that is the hand-maids of Athena.

The Temple of Athena Nikê.—And then there is the Temple of Athena Nikê, commonly called the Temple of Wingless Victory, which we saw above us to the right as we ascended the Propylaea, as perfect in miniature as the Parthenon is in the grand style. Its platform is only 27 feet by 18, whereas the platform of the Parthenon is 228 feet by 102. The Temple of Nikê has four Ionic columns at each end, east and west, and the columns are $13\frac{1}{2}$ feet high. The Parthenon has 58 Doric columns (double rows of 8 at each end, east and west, and 17 along the sides), and these are more than 34 feet high. It is to the Parthenon as the carved jewel to the marble statue. It is as gem-like among Greek temples as the Pearl Mosque at Agra is among Indian mosques. An astonishing fact in its history is that towards the end of the seventeenth century (A.D. 1684), the Turks pulled it all down in order to build a new battery, this point being from of old a vantage point for the defence of the Acropolis.[2]

---

[1] R. L. Stevenson writes in *Our Lady of the Snows* :

" For those he loves that underprop
With daily virtues Heaven's top,
And bear the falling sky with ease,
Unfrowning caryatides."

[2] It was originally an outwork planned in conformity with the early art of defensive fortification, so as to compel assailants, as they advanced, to expose their right sides, the sides not covered by their shields (carried on the left arm), to the missiles of the defenders.

THE TEMPLE OF ATHENA NIKÊ.

From the north-east, with view of the Bay of Phalerum and Munychia to the south-west,

From a photograph by the English Photographic Company.

But the stones were not destroyed, only built into the defences. In 1835 this battery was in turn removed and the stones discovered. Then the little temple was carefully built up again stone by stone from the original materials by three German archaeologists,[1] with what success the visitor may see to-day.

If the view back from the Propylaea is good, that from the narrow bastion of the Temple of Victory is better. Looking south-west, you see outspread beneath you a fine panorama of the plain of Athens, Piraeus, Phalerum and the sea, the islands in the Saronic Gulf and the mountains of Argolis.

One beautiful decoration which the Nikê bastion once had is absent to-day—a protecting parapet wall a little over three feet high, very richly sculptured. A large number of fragments (about forty in all) have been recovered and are all now in the Museum on the Acropolis. The subject is some ceremony connected with the celebration of victory. Some of the Victory figures are of exquisite beauty : one of them, the Victory stooping to adjust a sandal strap is, perhaps, the very loveliest fragment of Greek sculpture extant.

The First Splendour.—This, briefly and imperfectly sketched, is what we experience in ascending the Propylaea and moving over the levelled summit of the Acropolis to-day. But if we could call up the vision of it in its newly-finished splendour, how incomparably more brilliant would not the spectacle be ? We should see the Propylaea, not as a vista of broken and roofless columns, but as a stately vestibule and entrance-hall, fifty feet deep by sixty broad, covered in by a panelled ceiling at a height of forty feet above the pavement, its fluted columns fresh from the chisel and glowing with colour. Left and right would be the porticoes of the northern and southern wings, the former leading to a picture gallery (which contained paintings by Polygnotus and other famous artists). In front of the central hall is a wall

[1] Ross, Schaubert and Hausen. Ludvig Ross was at the time chief conservator of antiquities at Athens.

pierced by five doorways, the great door in the middle twenty-four feet high, leading through to the upper portico (less deep than the western or lower, only thirteen feet) and out on to the slope of the rock. Here directly in front, but slightly to the left of the roadway, would be the Promachus, the colossal brazen statue of Athena, the Defender ;—her helmet's top and the point of her spear could be seen, when the sun caught them, from the decks of Attic ships on the homeward voyage after rounding Cape Sunium. And when we turned our eyes to the Parthenon, the fearsome rent beyond the sixth column [1] would be filled up and the temple would stand with its roof and gable end and incomparable sculptures whole and complete, the most magnificent work of the greatest artists in stone who have ever lived. The eye would first be caught by the splendid figures of the western pediment, grouped to represent the contest between Poseidon and Athena for the possession of Athens, the figures carved boldly in the round and standing out with striking effect. Below the pediment, but above the columns of the portico, in the intervals between the triglyphs would be the metopes, portraying Theseus' fight with the Amazons. If we walked forward, ascended the steps to the level of the temple platform, passed under the first row of columns and looked up, we should see— a little dimly in the lack of light from above—the beginning of that marvellous succession of figures which extends along the top of the side walls of the sanctuary and above the inner columns at both western and eastern ends :

[1] The Parthenon stood whole and complete and little injured by time (for it was successively a Christian church and a Mohammedan mosque), till near the end of the seventeenth century. Then the Venetians besieged Athens, and their leader, the Christian Francesco Morosini, opened fire on the Parthenon, because he had information that the Turks had stored their powder there. One of his shells struck the Parthenon, exploded the powder and made the havoc of the centre of the structure which we see to-day. Morosini did further irreparable injury to the Parthenon by attempting to remove the central sculptures of the eastern pediment and doing it so badly that the figures crashed to the ground and were shattered. The battery from which the shot was fired is said to have been near the church of St. Demetrius, the Bombardier (above, p. 56 n).

it represents in low relief the great Panathenaic procession :
—not as now, just fragments of it in broken sequence
with the marble slabs that are still in position (only a
third of the original number) most of them worn, mutilated
and imperfect, but a continuous band of sculpture—
all vivid, clear-cut, fresh from the artist's hand—figuring
in marble the stream of worshippers as it moved in
procession from the western end along the two sides of
the temple north and south, to unite in the imagined
presence of the gods in front of the eastern entrance to
Athena's shrine.

There was all this ; and there was besides the rich
colouring which the Greeks (like the Christian builders
and image-makers of the Middle Ages) used profusely
to sharpen and deepen the lines of their temples and
statuary, alike in column and architrave, triglyph and
metope. There was the gold and ivory statue of Athena,
the Maiden, within the Parthenon shrine ; there were the
treasures behind the sealed doors of the back-chamber.
There was life and movement round about the sanctuary ;
the priests, the animals for sacrifice, the temple guards,
the throng of worshippers coming and going.

When we realize all this and contrast the present with
the past, we discover a deep pathos in the words of
Plutarch, so often quoted : " Each one of them, in its
beauty, was even then and at once antique ; but in the
freshness of its vigour it is, even to the present day,
recent and newly wrought. Such is the bloom of perpetual
newness, as it were, upon these works of his, which makes
them ever to look untouched by time, as though the
unfaltering breath of an ageless spirit had been infused
into them." [1]

Pericles and Pheidias.—These buildings made Athens
architecturally the noblest of earth's cities. They were
the work of the Athenian people, a thank-offering and
memorial dedicated to the gods who had delivered Hellas
from the invader. But as it was to Themistocles and

[1] Plutarch, *Pericles*, 13. Loeb, iii. p. 41.

Aristides, two of her citizens, that Athens owed her great achievements in the Persian wars, so it was to two of her citizens, Pericles and Pheidias, that she owed the glory of works of art which have long outlived her political greatness. It was the mind of Pericles which conceived the possibility of making the whole Acropolis one vast shrine of Hellenic religion, a monument of Athenian action and endurance. It was the artist soul and the artist hand of Pheidias which wrought out this sublime thought of Pericles in forms of surpassing beauty.

Pericles.—Pericles was by birth a Eupatrid ; on his mother's side an Alcmaeonid ; on his father's also of a very noble Athenian family. He is the most illustrious of all Athenian statesmen, perhaps the most lofty-minded of all the Greeks. He did great things for Athens in his life-time and would have done one greater thing for Hellas, had not the narrow political ideals of the Hellenes stood in the way. In his public career Pericles followed the example of his great-uncle Cleisthenes and carried through measures which may be said to have completed democracy after the Athenian model. Here, however, we are concerned only with the part he took in adorning Athens with splendid buildings and works of art.

Pericles first comes prominently into Athenian political history in connection with that struggle of parties at Athens which ended in the banishment by ostracism of Cimon, and the taking from the Council of the Areopagus,[1] the last stronghold of aristocratic privilege at Athens, all its remaining political influence. Cimon's banishment was in 461, and when Ephialtes, who had led the democratic attack, was assassinated,[2] Pericles, though still comparatively young,[3] was left not only the leading statesman of the democratic party, but also the only statesman of great influence in Athens. Cimon came back in the year of the battle of Tanagra (457), but he no

---

[1] See vol. i. p. 239.

[2] Probably by some who resented as sacrilege the violence done to the venerable Council of the Areopagus.

[3] It is probable that the birth of Pericles was in 493 B.C.

longer took any active interest in domestic politics. Consequently Pericles may be said to have guided the destinies of Athens, as her foremost citizen and chosen leader for over thirty years [1] (461-429). For nineteen of these years there was still a strong conservative opposition headed by Thucydides, son of Melesias ; [2] and this opposition was largely a personal opposition to Pericles' 'imperial' policy. But in 442 Thucydides was ostracized, and then for the rest of his life Pericles swayed Athens without a rival. Year after year he was chosen one of the ten *strategi*, and as strategos, or general, he frequently exercised command of the military and naval forces of Athens. Thus in 453 we find him in command of an expedition to the Gulf of Corinth which obtained substantial successes. He is said by Plutarch to have set up trophies of victory nine times in all. But he was not a brilliant war-leader like Cimon. The Ecclesia was the scene of his greatest achievements. Pericles was a statesman and a thinker, and his greatness was shown most of all in the largeness and perspicacity of his views for Hellas and for Athens. At one time in his life he had seen the vision—a vision that mocks us across the centuries—of an organized and united Hellas, able not only to keep the Persian at bay, but to assume, as was her due, an undisputed preeminence among the nations of the world. The proof of this is that soon after the double victory of 449 in Cyprus had put an end to the fear of renewed Persian aggression, Pericles was the author of a memorable attempt to assemble at Athens a council, in which all Hellas east of the Ionian Sea should meet to discuss matters of common interest to the Hellenic race. The proposal came to nothing, for success depended on the spontaneous assent and sympathy of all the communities invited ; and Peloponnesian jealousy of Athens stood fatally in the way. But the interesting thing is that such an invitation should have been issued

[1] Plutarch (*Pericles*, 16) says for forty.

[2] To be carefully distinguished from Thucydides, the son of Olorus, the historian.

and that the thought of it was Pericles'. We owe our knowledge of the incident to Plutarch only : Thucydides has no word of it. Now, though Plutarch was writing in the second century A.D., five hundred years after Pericles' death, and Plutarch's narrative lacks confirmation, it is not otherwise than credible in itself, and, there being no obvious motive for the invention of such a story, it may be regarded as probably true. It is, therefore, worth while to see exactly what Plutarch says. The passage is in his *Life of Pericles* : he writes " When the Lacedaemonians began to be annoyed by the increasing power of the Athenians, Pericles, by way of inviting the people to cherish yet loftier thoughts and to deem itself worthy of great achievements, introduced a bill to the effect that all Hellenes, wheresoever resident in Europe or in Asia, small and large cities alike, should be invited to send deputies to a council at Athens. This was to deliberate concerning the Hellenic sanctuaries which the Barbarians had burned down, concerning the sacrifices which were due to the gods in the name of Hellas in fulfilment of vows made when they were fighting with the Barbarians, and concerning the sea, that all might sail it fearlessly and keep the peace." [1] He goes on to describe how four deputations, each of five members, all men above fifty years of age, were sent in different directions ; and adds : " But nothing was accomplished, nor did the cities come together by deputy, owing to the opposition of the Lacedaemonians, as it is said, since the effort met with its first check in Peloponnesus. I have cited this incident, however, to show forth the man's disposition and the greatness of his thoughts."

The failure of this enterprise may well have convinced Pericles of the futility of hoping for a permanent union of Hellas by persuasion and a recognition of the common interest ; it probably confirmed him in his suspicions of Sparta and a determination never to trust her or let Athens yield to her for the sake of peace any point of grave importance. But he did not relinquish his ultimate

[1] Plutarch, *Pericles*, 17. Loeb, iii. pp. 55 and 57.

aim, only modified profoundly the method of its accomplishment. Athens should more than ever embody the Hellenic ideal and set up a pattern for the rest of Hellas. The means, if other methods failed, must be the strengthening and extending of the Athenian *arché*. It is at all events certain that Pericles' mind was exalted and filled with this conception of the worthiness of Athenian institutions, and it became the main purpose of his life to fit Athens in all possible ways for the high rôle which was her destiny. If the other states of militant Hellas would not come together at her bidding to deliberate concerning the Hellenic sanctuaries, and the fulfilment of vows made when they were fighting against the Barbarians, Athens should do these things for herself first ; and in some sort, should take on her to do them for all Hellas—the Hellas she had saved from the Mede. This is, as Bury explains,[1] the true key to the understanding of the great public works that were executed at Athens during the administration of Pericles, roughly between 447 and 431. Plutarch comments on the wonder of their swift execution. " Each one of them, men thought, would require many successive generations to complete it, but all of them were fully completed in the heyday of a single administration." [2] This is not true without qualification, but it is true enough to make good Plutarch's point. Pericles himself was filled with a lofty sense of the religious meaning of his great undertaking, and this zeal and enthusiasm were communicated to the Athenian people who voted the works, and to the masons and artificers who were set to work upon them. " So then the works arose," says Plutarch, " no less towering in their grandeur than inimitable in the grace of their outlines, since the workmen eagerly strove to surpass themselves in the beauty of their handicraft." [3] This

---

[1] Bury's *Greece*, p. 367. " We shall miss the meaning of the architectural monuments which now began to rise under the direction and influence of Pericles, if we do not clearly grasp their historical motive, and recognise their immediate connexion with the Persian war."

[2] Plutarch, *Pericles*, 13. Loeb, iii. pp. 39 and 41.

[3] Plutarch, *Pericles*, 13. Loeb, iii. p. 39.

is the secret of the perfection of the Parthenon and the Temple of Victory, of the Erechtheum and the Propylaea : a united [1] people who had endured and conquered, and were still filled with the fervour of great striving and achievement, set about the building of them with one mind and purpose. The buildings they wrought illustrate the truth which Ruskin preached to his generation, that architecture is the expression of national life and character. The ruins on the Acropolis are an abiding witness to the high temper and capacity for action of the people of Athens in the fifth century B.C. They express their passionate devotion to their city, their belief in their own powers and their zeal for their religion so closely bound up with both. For the building of the Parthenon and the Erechtheum was a new and more comprehensive consecration of the whole area of the Acropolis. The Propylaea formed a portal on a scale suited to the grandeur of the dedicated area ; nor is the position of the Temple of Victory on a forward bastion just in front of the Propylaea without significance. For it is victory over the Persian invader who had desecrated the Acropolis and its shrines, which the new consecration commemorated. How deeply the Athenians felt the destruction of their sacred places may be judged from the words used by Herodotus in giving their reasons why it was utterly impossible they should accept the tempting offers of Mardonius : " The first and chief of these," they are made to say, " is the burning and destruction of our temples and the images of our gods, which forces us to make no terms with their destroyer, but rather to pursue him with our resentment to the uttermost." [2] The Mede had been discomfited, and Athens was once more in possession of her citadel and its consecrated ground. But as yet there had been no restoration of the shrines that had been destroyed. It was time the vows and promises made in the hour of victory and

---

[1] The unity has to be qualified, however, by what is said later in this chapter, p. 72, of the opposition to Pericles' schemes.

[2] Herodotus, viii. 144. Rawlinson. Quoted vol. i. p. 359.

thanksgiving should be carried out. There was peace with the King of Persia since 448—at least there was a cessation of active hostilities. And in 445 there was peace also between Athens and the enemies of Hellenic blood and speech, with whom she had been at strife since 459. The moment was every way opportune.

Storm and Stress.—The pacification of 445 B.C., known as the Thirty Years' Peace, was only reached after the Athens of Pericles had passed through an ordeal which left the main fabric of Athenian power, her sea federation, firmer than ever, but ended the predominance in Northern Greece which ten years before she seemed to have secured. This period of stress began in 447 with a serious reverse to Athenian arms in Boeotia. News had come that bands of exiles from the Boeotian cities were gathering head in Northern Boeotia. Tolmides, the hero of the raid on Gythium, hastened with insufficient forces to crush them. He was attacked on the march by superior numbers and his whole force annihilated. Many were killed, Tolmides himself among them ; and many were made prisoners of war. To recover these prisoners Athens agreed to evacuate Boeotia. Oligarchical governments, unfriendly to Athens, were once more established in all the Boeotian cities, with Thebes dominant among them. This was a blow to Athenian prestige ; and next year (446) Euboea revolted. Strong forces at once crossed into Euboea under the command of Pericles ; but no sooner were they there than further news came that Megara had again changed sides, that the Athenian troops occupying posts in the Megarid had been cut off and destroyed, all but a remnant that had escaped to Nisaea ; lastly that the army of the Peloponnesian League was about to invade Attica. Pericles at once conveyed his army back to meet the danger of invasion ; and the Peloponnesians, after laying waste the country as far as Eleusis, retreated. Pericles and the Athenians were then free to deal with Euboea. When the Euboeans made their submission, conventions were made with the cities individually, and, on the whole, the terms were

lenient.[1] One town, Histiaea, was treated with greater
severity : the inhabitants were expelled and their territory
divided among Athenian settlers. The name of the city
was changed to Oreus. Plutarch gives as the reason
for this that the Histiaeans had put to death the crew of
an Attic ship which had fallen into their hands.

The Thirty Years' Peace.—Athens was, on the whole,
well out of Boeotia and her 'land empire' ; but the
treachery of Megara was a permanent disaster and left
bitter memories. With Megara as an ally, Attica need
have no fear of invasion from the Peloponnese. With
Megara hostile, she was always open to invasion on that
side. It was this consideration, doubtless, together with
a certain exhaustion after the almost superhuman effort
of the preceding fifteen years—when she had practically
been fighting Persia and the Peloponnesian League at
the same time,—which induced Athens, still under the
auspices of Pericles, to make peace in 445. She had to
make sacrifices for it. She gave up Nisaea and Pegae,
the harbours of Megara, which she still held, and Troezen,
and Achaia. She renounced, in fact, all claim to territorial influence outside Attica. It was humiliating ;
but she was the stronger for it. The treaty was for thirty
years : and the peace is known therefore as the Thirty
Years' Peace, though it did not last quite fifteen. The
allies of both Athens and Sparta were included, that is
the whole of the two confederacies ; and it was expressly
provided that neither Athens nor Sparta might form an
alliance with any state which at the time of the making
of the treaty was on the other side : but this clause did

[1] Two extremely interesting inscriptions illustrate these events in
Megara and Euboea.   One is a tombstone commemorating a Megarian,
Pythion by name, who did Athens signal service by guiding an Athenian
force out of Megarian territory safe back to Attica.   It seems that on
the outbreak of the Megarian revolt three tribal regiments had marched
into Megara and been cut off there by the advance of the invading
Peloponnesian army.   Pythion had then guided the troops back by
a roundabout route.   The other is a copy on stone of the convention between Athens and Chalcis one of the Euboean cities.   This
convention has been already referred to above, ch. ii. p. 46.   The
inscriptions are Nos. 38 and 40 in Hicks and Hill, pp. 61-65.

not apply to neutral states which were left free to ally themselves as they pleased.

Pericles' Peace Schemes.—One of the motives that swayed Pericles in making this peace may well have been his longing to concentrate the resources of the city on his great plan for her adornment. The building of the Parthenon was begun in 447 : extant inscriptions establish this with approximate certainty. A full generation had passed since the sack of the Acropolis and the restoration of the temple of the guardian goddess had been too long deferred. A beginning had indeed been made in the time of Themistocles. Plans of a new temple had been designed on an ample scale, a new site was chosen ; and, because the rock there was not level, a mighty substructure was built. Then there was a check and the work ceased, till Pericles in the fulness of his power took the matter in hand. And Pericles thought of the glory of Athens as well as of what was owing to the gods. The design he adopted went beyond the design of that earlier time and was all that the most consummate architects of this culminating epoch of Hellenic architecture could make it. The substructure was modified to suit the new plan ; for the new temple was to be of a better proportioned shape, broader and a good deal less long : the marks of the necessary alteration in the substructure are visible there. On these foundations Pericles built the Parthenon. In nine years (447 to 438) the structural work was finished [1] and the image, the great gold and ivory Athena, dedicated.

The building of the Propylaea was begun immediately after the dedication of the Parthenon, that is in 437, and the work continued to the outbreak of the Peloponnesian war. It was intended solely as a splendid forecourt to the consecrated area of the Acropolis. We have had occasion to notice already that the Propylaea was not built altogether in accordance with the architect's original design (above p. 55) : one of the two wings is much smaller

[1] Inscriptions, however, show that work on the *sculptures* of the Parthenon was going on as late as 433.

than the other, in fact just a hollow front to give the appearance of symmetry. But how greatly the existing Propylaea fell short of the architect's grand conception has only been discovered through detailed study of what is left of it. The walls as they stand have a tale to tell, and their tale is of a vast design thwarted and cramped by narrow prejudices. There are plain indications that it was at first intended to build two large eastern halls, one on each wing, on the further side of the western halls actually built. Mnesicles' original design for the Propylaea was thus at once simple and sumptuous : a central hall of entrance with porticoes at either end, upper and lower ; and double wings on either side, each consisting of two halls, a western and an eastern. Only one of these four halls was built in accordance with this plan, the north-western hall or Picture Gallery. The south-western hall is contracted in size, as we have seen. The north-eastern and the south-eastern halls were never built at all. But the cornices running along the top of what are now exterior walls [1] bear witness to the ampler project of the architect. Magnificent as was the Propylaea, and great as was the Athenians' pride in it,[2] it was an unfinished work, a fragment, a noble instalment of a mighty whole,—like some great things in our literature, Spenser's *Faerie Queene* and Chaucer's *Canterbury Tales*.

It is not difficult to conjecture what the hindering causes were. We may see on any plan of the Acropolis how the Propylaea wing on the south side impinges on the precinct of Brauronian Artemis. The southern wing could not be carried out according to plan without cutting into this precinct : because of religious opposition based on this ground the original design had to be abandoned. The architect modified his plan and did the

---

[1] The point of course is, that only *interior* walls want cornices and that these exterior walls would have become interior had the eastern halls been built.

[2] The Thebans are reported to have said (in the middle of the fourth century) that the only way to abate the pride of the Athenians was to remove the Propylaea bodily from the Acropolis to their own citadel, the Cadmeia.

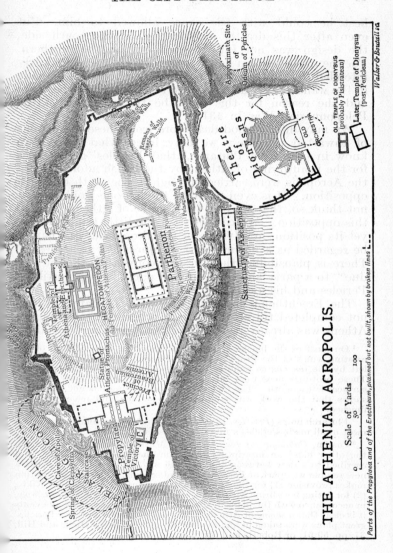

THE ATHENIAN ACROPOLIS.

Scale of Yards

0   50   100

Parts of the Propylaea and of the Erechtheum, planned but not built, shown by broken lines

OLD TEMPLE OF DIONYSUS (probably Pisistratean)

Later Temple of Dionysus (post-Periclean)

Walker & Boutall sc

best he could with the space allowed to him. But even after this drastic modification on the south side, the design was not fully carried out on the northern. For the north-eastern hall was never built, though clearly intended (for on this side there are even holes ready made in the walls above the cornice to receive the roof-beams) : and the reason for this must be the outbreak of the Peloponnesian War in 431.[1]

We may infer a good deal more from these indications of thwarted purpose : we may infer, what indeed we know in part from Plutarch,[2] that Pericles' great plans for the beautifying of Athens by the lavish adornment of the Acropolis were carried through in the teeth of a stiff opposition. It is even possible, though one would rather not think so, that we owe the Temple of Athena Nikê to this opposition. We cannot wish the little temple away, yet its position, in advance of the Propylaea, can hardly be regarded as a natural part of Mnesicles' great design. There is plausibility then in the conjecture that it was due " to a party and to a wave of party feeling hostile to Pericles and his ideals." [3]

The Erechtheum is admittedly of later date ; it was not completed till after 395 B.C., when the splendour of Athens was already past. We cannot with any certainty

---

[1] On most of the blocks of stone built into the walls of each of the existing wings of the Propylaea are to be seen the knobs, which were left by the masons as handles to help placing the stones in position. These protuberances were intended to be chipped off later and the surfaces left smooth. The fact that this smoothing has not been done shows that the work was stopped on a sudden and never properly finished.

[2] Plutarch notes (*Pericles*, 12) that it was his great public works which most of all made Pericles a mark for abuse and slander.

[3] Casson, *Catalogue of the Acropolis Museum*, Part II. p. 12. On the other hand an inscription found on the Acropolis in 1896, and ascribed to a date between 460 and 446 B.C., appears to prove that a new temple was part of Pericles' original scheme. For this inscription makes provision (1) for the appointment of a priestess of Athena Nikê ; (2) for fitting her shrine with a door ; and (3) for building a new *temple*, in accordance with the plans of the architect, Callicrates. At all events it is clear that a *shrine* of Athena Nikê existed on the site *before* Pericles' great plans were taken in hand. For the inscription see Hicks and Hill, 37, pp. 59-61, or Roberts and Gardner, pp. 8-10.

know how far this temple, or another temple on the same
site, found place in Pericles' original scheme. But here
also in the problems which a study of the remains of the
Erechtheum raises we encounter indications of the same
conflict of ideals. The shape of the Erechtheum, as we
noted, is puzzling. It is like no other Greek temple ;
and as it stands it is glaringly unsymmetrical. It has
been surmised that the Erechtheum, too, is an unfinished
building ; that the original design, whether part of
Pericles' great plan, or a project initiated by the conservative opposition out of rivalry, included an extension
of the structure westward to balance the larger chamber,
or shrine, to the east. The north and south porticoes
would then find place in the middle of the north and
south sides, not at one end. This cannot be proved,
but it solves the puzzle of the existing shape of the temple ;
and assuming that such had been the original design the
obstacle to carrying it out would again be found in a
religious scruple, for immediately west of the Erechtheum
lies the Pandroseum, ground consecrate to Pan-drosos
(*All-dew*), daughter of Cecrops, and a prolongation of the
Erechtheum westward must have trenched upon this
ground.[1]

The duality of this building known to us as the Erechtheum is a fact of extraordinary interest. It is not only
the Erechtheum but the temple of Athena Polias, and its
character as the shrine of Athena Polias is far more
important than its character as the shrine of Erechtheus.[2]

[1] This theory about the plan of the Erechtheum was propounded
and worked out in detail by Professor Dörpfeld.

[2] This duality is also after all a unity ; for according to the oldest
religious tradition, in the Iliad and Odyssey, the House of Erechtheus
was the only place where Athena had her habitation. In the Odyssey
(vii. 80 and 81), Athena, when she vanishes from Odysseus' sight in the
streets of Phaeacia, is described as going to ' wide-wayed Athens '
and entering ' the strong built house of Erechtheus.' Now Erechtheus
was born of Earth and is described as adopted by Athena and reared
as her foster-son. He is also Ericthonius, who in the form of a snake
lived in the temple of Athena and was regularly fed by the priests on
sweet cakes. In the *Catalogue of the Ships in the Iliad* (ii. ll. 546-549)
the Athenians are called " the people of Erechtheus—Erechtheus
whom erstwhile Athena, daughter of Zeus, reared (though the bounteous
Earth was the mother who bore him) and set him in her own rich temple."

The Erechtheum is a small building compared with the Parthenon (its length is 71 feet against the Parthenon's 228), yet as the seat of the worship of Athena Polias it was the more deeply venerated shrine of the two. Though not built on the exact site of the old temple of Athena burnt by the Medes, it yet seems in the esteem of the Athenians to have represented that earlier and supremely venerable seat of worship. The Erechtheum, not the Parthenon, contained the most sacred image of Athena, the image of olive wood that men said had fallen from heaven. It was to this image in the Erechtheum, and not to the gold and ivory Athena in the Parthenon, that the Peplos carried in the Panathenaic procession was presented. Other objects of special religious interest were either in the Erechtheum or near it : the olive-tree created by Athena in her contest for Athens with Poseidon, the ' sea ' the production of which was Poseidon's rival feat and the marks of his trident in the rock.[1] In the Erechtheum, too, were preserved the golden breastplate of Masistius and the scimitar of Mardonius ; a foot-stool made by the artist Daedalus (first of mortals to experiment in flight) and a wonderful lamp, the work of Callimachus, which went on burning for a whole year when it was filled.

There were thus really two temples of Athena on the Acropolis, and of the two, if the Parthenon was the more magnificent, the Erechtheum was the more revered. The Parthenon is the proud memorial of the imperial power of Athens, but it was to the shrine of Athena Polias that the religious emotions of the people were most deeply attached. For us the splendour of artistic achievement may be the dominant consideration ; for the Athenians it was the traditional associations. We can trace in all the buildings reared on the Acropolis of Athens in Pericles' age evidence of contending ideals. The ultimate result—however it was brought about—was to make the whole Acropolis an area consecrated

---

[1] The trident marks were in a crypt under the north porch, and a hole was left in the floor of the porch, through which the pious could look down and see them.

to the glory of Pallas Athena. Of the two splendid temples on the summit, one, the Parthenon, was dedicated wholly to Athena Parthenos, the Maiden Athena; the other, the Erechtheum, was primarily the shrine of Athena of the City (Athena Polias) and only secondarily the shrine of Erechtheus, her foster-child, or of Poseidon, her defeated rival. And in front of the Propylaea was planted, like a sentinel, the little temple of Athena the Victorious. Athens was Athena's city, and on the Acropolis all lesser cults were absorbed into the worship of Athena.

Pheidias.—Ictinus is named as the architect of the Parthenon and Mnesicles of the Propylaea. They are names immortalized by the master works attributed to them, but beyond that nothing is known of either. Callicrates, who is said also to have laid out the Long Walls, is associated with Ictinus for the Parthenon, and is named in the inscription referred to above (p. 172 n.) as the architect of the Temple of Victory. The architect of the Erechtheum is not known. But by general tradition and the express assertion of Plutarch, the great inspiring mind in the carrying out of Pericles' comprehensive scheme for the Acropolis was Pheidias. "His general manager and general overseer was Pheidias," says Plutarch, "although the several works had great architects and artists besides." Pheidias, too, is only a name transcendently great; of the circumstances of his life or personal characteristics little is recorded. He was an Athenian by birth, the son of Charmides, and he had a brother Panaenus, who painted the scenes of Marathon in the Stoa Poekilê.[1] We know also that he was the personal friend of Pericles as well as his director of works. He was the maker of the famous gold and ivory image of Athena in the Parthenon, and of the yet more famous gold-and-ivory Zeus at Olympia:[2] also of the colossal Athena Promachos, which crowned the Acropolis. These are the only facts about him definitely authenticated. There is besides some poor gossip related by Plutarch

[1] Vol. i. p. 291.　　　　[2] Vol. i. p. 38.

and two contradictory stories (both unhappy) concerning
his death.   Much of the sculpture for the decoration of
the Parthenon which survives is ascribed to him—or
at least to his design and inspiration ; but of no single
piece of it can it be affirmed with certainty that it is
his handiwork.

The School of Pheidias.—In a general sense Pheidias
is the author of all the Parthenon sculptures, of the
pediment groups, the metopes and the Panathenaic
frieze.   But it is calculated that frieze and metopes
together, without reckoning the great figures in the
pediment groups (of which there must have been between
forty and fifty) covered 4000 square feet of marble
surface.   Obviously all this cannot possibly have been
the work of one man's hands.   Some of the fragments
of the East pediment group, now to be seen in the British
Museum among the Elgin Marbles,[1] show such mastery
over stone (notably the drapery of the seated figures and
the horses' heads in the right-hand corner) that it is
tempting to call them the work of Pheidias.   That work
displaying such marvellous inspiration and dexterity
should be left nameless, when an illustrious name offers
so readily, is tantalizing.   The same impulse must be
felt when we look on many of the slabs of the frieze
whether it is the still grace of the processional figures
or the lifelike action, inexhaustible in its variety, of the
prancing horses.   But it has to be acknowledged that no
warrant—except this inner feeling—exists for calling
any particular piece among these sculptures the work of
Pheidias.   Undoubtedly, however, this much we may say
on the authority of Plutarch, who was in touch with direct
tradition, that the inspiring genius of all the decorative
work of the Parthenon was the genius of Pheidias.   His
was the general responsibility for all that was done.
And he had under him, we are told, ' great architects and
artists besides.'   We must conceive of what might well
be called a school of Pheidias, a group of sculptors, who
worked under his inspiration and guidance, and the

[1] See Note at end of the Chapter.

marvel is—almost the greatest marvel of all—that a sufficient number of 'great artists' was found to catch the inspiration and carry out the ideas of the supreme master mind with such unity of effect that they appear to us (such at least would be the hypothesis that best explained them) the work of one great master-craftsman of infinite resource and inexhaustible energy. We have in this a substantial proof of the high standard of taste and culture and capacity attained at this period by the body of the Athenian people.

The Athenians of Pericles' Day.—For we must be careful to qualify our statement that Athens owed her splendid adornment in the third quarter of the fifth century B.C. to Pericles and Pheidias. This is true in so far as these great men directed and shaped the impulses which urged the Athenians to incorporate in the gleaming marbles of Pentelicus the force and energy and spiritual strength which had animated their commonwealth during and after the agony of their 'great war'; but it is only one side of the truth. These great achievements in architecture and plastic art were not possible without the active sympathy of the rank and file of the Athenian democracy, who voted the moneys, approved the expenditure and placed the work in the hands of the men most capable of giving beautiful and stately form to the temples which were to be a monument at once of the greatness of their polis and of their gratitude to the gods. These matchless buildings bear their witness to the intellectual and moral endowments of the Athenian people, as much as do the dramas of Aeschylus, Sophocles, Euripides and Aristophanes. For only in a highly gifted community could such works have found scope. " The golden age of Greece is, properly speaking, a golden age of Athens," says a scholar, writing recently of Athenian 'imperialism'; and he goes on to indicate that the decisive factor in producing this golden age at Athens was—along with the intensity of the national life—" an unrivalled facility for great leaders to get into effective contact with the masses under conditions in which there was the fullest opportunity for men in general to use their natural powers to the utmost." [1] And he adds, " This happy combination of creative genius and receptive multitude arose in the main from the democratic institutions of Athens." We are thus led on naturally from a consideration of the City Beautiful to a consideration of the forms of government and social institutions which the people of Athens had shaped for themselves.

NOTE ON THE ELGIN MARBLES.

For those who live in England it is possible to get vivid impressions of the sculptures of the Acropolis buildings, and some measure of the splendour of their setting, without ascending the Propylaea or leaving England at all. A large proportion of the surviving remains of the Parthenon sculptures, pediment groups, metopes and frieze are in London, in the Elgin Collection, housed since 1816 in the British Museum and arranged in their present positions in 1869. And in the Elgin Room at the British Museum, along with these priceless treasures, there are drawings, pictures, photographs, a model of the Parthenon in its present ruined state, and a model of the whole Acropolis, all helpful to the imagination and all conveniently handy to each other and to the original marbles.

Of the Parthenon Frieze there are in the Elgin Room more than 50 original slabs, casts of the 14 still in position at the west end of the temple and of the 22 in the Acropolis Museum at Athens : 413 feet of sculptured relief out of a total length of 523 feet, 241 being the original marble. Of the metopes which were set above the architrave of the Parthenon on all four sides, 92 in number, 15 are in the Elgin Room, all taken from the south side of the temple and representing combats between Centaurs and Lapithae. There are casts of five others, making 20 metopes in all. Practically *all* the remains of the Pediment groups—the exceptions being comparatively unimportant— are in the British Museum. In the Elgin Room they may be seen and studied at leisure, safe, one may hope, from further risk of injury.

It is no exaggeration to say that even in their maimed and battered state, these fragments of the pediment figures merit, on purely artistic grounds, the closest attention and study. There is not, it is true, one single whole figure among them : bodies without heads, heads and trunks without hands and feet, these are all the pediment sculptures have to offer. And yet !

[1] W. Scott Ferguson, *Greek Imperialism*, p. 41.

. . . Look well at the folds of drapery and the graceful pose of the seated figures on the left side of the East pediment (E and F) recognized as Demeter and Persephonê ; of the three associated figures on the right (K, L, M), called conjecturally the Three Fates. Was loose drapery, and the rounded limbs beneath, ever rendered in marble with such miraculous grace ? Note the vitality, the lithe agility of the fragment (N) interpreted as Iris, on the right of the West Pediment. Note the sensuous ease of the reclining figures (D on the East Pediment and A on the West), identified the one with Theseus, the other with the river Ilissos. Marvel at the fire breathed from the cold marble nostrils of the horses of the Sun ; the more subdued energy expressed in the other horse's head, the head from the chariot-team of Selenê. " I shall never forget the horses' heads—the feet in the metopes," wrote the painter, Benjamin Haydon, in 1808 when taken to see the marbles on their first being opened to private view. " I felt as if a divine truth had blazed inwardly upon my mind, and I knew that they would at last rouse the art of Europe from its slumber in the darkness." [1]

The story of the acquisition of the Marbles and their conveyance by sea to London reads like a romance. In 1799, Thomas Bruce, seventh Earl of Elgin, at the time a comparatively young man, was appointed ambassador to Turkey. In the seventeenth and eighteenth centuries western Europe had been discovering Athens. Travellers journeyed to Greece, came back and wrote books, as did Sir George Wheler in 1682 and Richard Chandler in 1776. Stuart and Revett, the one a painter, the other an architect, had made a careful study of the existing remains of architecture and sculpture at Athens, and brought out a book in 1762, which has since been a classic. Lord Elgin went to the East imbued with a keen interest in the works of art which had made Athens famous above all other cities, and he formed a plan " to measure and to draw everything that remained and could be traced of architecture, to model the peculiar features of architecture." [2] With this end in view, while in Sicily on his way to Constantinople, he took into his service a small band of artists, a draughtsman, two architects, two *formatori* or moulders of casts—and put them under the orders of the painter Lusieri (' the first painter in Italy ' Lord Elgin calls him). These artists he sent on to Athens in 1800, when he went to his post at Constantinople. At first Lusieri and his associates met all kinds of opposition and obstruction in Athens, and the work of measuring and drawing proceeded slowly. But in July 1801 Lord Elgin obtained a firman ' from the Porte which gave him practically *carte blanche*

[1] *Life of B. R. Haydon,* vol. i. p. 85.

[2] Report of the Committee of the House of Commons, p. 40, quoted on p. 189 of the *Journal of Hellenic Studies for* 1916.

to do as he pleased with old stones of every kind at Athens.[1]
The Turks themselves had no interest whatever in the remains
of Athenian art, and set not the slightest value on them. Their
only motive in granting the firman was to gratify the British
ambassador : and no doubt the victory of the Nile and the
success of British arms against Napoleon in Egypt had a good
deal to do with that. It was not, however, till he had observed
what injuries the sculptures were exposed to and how real was the
danger of their continued destruction that Lord Elgin entertained
the idea of any wholesale removal. The marbles were suffering
year by year, partly from exposure and neglect, partly from the
depredations of travellers who broke off pieces to keep as relics.
The Turks in their very indifference were capable at times of
working havoc as extensive and irreparable as if it had been due
to malice : they would pound up fragments of marble statues
to make mortar, and they made a clearance of the Temple of
Victory to use its site as a battery position. Moved in part by
these considerations Lord Elgin was fired in the end with the
project of removing all the best to England, so as to preserve
what was best and greatest in Greek art for the delight and
instruction of western Europe. This project he carried out with
a thoroughness to which the collection in the British Museum
bears witness. The work went on through the years 1801 to
1803. At every stage the difficulties to be overcome were great
first, the irrational obstruction of the Turks in possession of the
fortress (the Greeks unfortunately did not count and were not
consulted) : then the critical task of detaching and lowering
heavy masses of stone from their position high on the Parthenon
carrying them to the harbour and shipping them for the voyage
to England.[2] The voyage, too, was not without its dangers
One ship, the *Mentor*, a brig specially purchased by Lord Elgin
was wrecked with seventeen cases of marbles off the island o
Cythera : the cases were ultimately, at great cost and after long
continued efforts, recovered by divers. The largest consign
ments were carried by the *Braakel*, which sailed for Malta i
February 1803 with forty-four cases, and on the *Prevoyante*, whic
voyaged with fifty cases from Malta to England in 1804. Arriva
in England began in 1803 and continued till as late as 1812.

Lord Elgin himself visited Athens in 1801 and made an ex
tensive tour in the Peloponnese and other parts of Greece. H
returned to Constantinople by way of the islands and the coas

---

[1] A clause in this *firman* (the second of two granted to Lord Elgi
says : " that they be not molested and that no one meddle with the
scaffolding or implements, *nor hinder them from taking away any piec
of stone with inscriptions or figures.*"

[2] From three to four hundred workmen were kept employed fo
several months ; and in special crises Lord Elgin was able to call i
the aid of the crews of British warships at Piraeus.

of Asia Minor ; not long after he was recalled. In passing through France on his way home, in May 1803, he had the ill fortune to be seized, like other English travellers, by Napoleon's orders on the sudden renewal of war, and was detained a prisoner in France till 1806. Consequently he was not in England when his cases arrived. They were unpacked, and the contents were first stored in the cellars of Lord Elgin's house in Park Lane ; and afterwards displayed at Burlington House. In 1816 the collection was purchased by the nation for £35,000, a sum considerably less than what it had cost Lord Elgin to bring it.

There were those who passed severe judgment on Lord Elgin for removing the best of its surviving sculptures from the Parthenon and conveying them to England. Byron denounced it in five bitter stanzas of *Childe Harold* [1] and in a satirical poem entitled *The Curse of Minerva*. And indeed the whole transaction is open to question. Any such removal of works of art from the country which has an historic claim to them would be intolerable now. Had it been possible to foresee the resurrection of Hellas within twenty years, it would have been intolerable in 1801. The case was different, when Athens was in the power of the Turk, and no other prospect was discernible than that Athens should remain in the power of the Turk indefinitely. On the whole the fair and sober judgment seems to be that Lord Elgin's action was both enlightened and patriotic, and that he performed a magnificent service to European art.

For a first study of the Elgin 'Marbles' the *Short Guide to the Sculptures of the Parthenon*, obtainable for a shilling at the British Museum, gives just the skilled assistance needed. For the serious student the great works are *The Sculptures of the Parthenon* published by the Department of Greek and Roman Antiquities in 1910, and Michaelis' *Der Parthenon* : and, of course, the relevant chapters in Gardner's *Ancient Athens*, or Weller's *The Acropolis and its Monuments*. The magnificent work of Stuart and Revett—in five large folio volumes—*The Antiquities of Athens*, is still unsurpassed both in historic interest and for the beautiful reproduction of architectural detail. The whole story of *the Elgin Collection* is told exhaustively in A. H. Smith's admirable monograph in the *Journal of Hellenic Studies* for 1916.

[1] *Childe Harold*, Canto II., Stanzas 11 to 15.

CHAPTER IV

THE COMPLETE DEMOCRACY

" Let there be light ! " said Liberty ;
And, like sunrise from the sea,
Athens arose !

SHELLEY, *Hellas*, ll. 682-4.

" The Athenian community during the Periclean time mus
be regarded as the most successful example of social organizatio
known to history. Its society, that is, was so arranged . . . a
to make the most and the best of the human material at it
disposal. Without any system of national education, in ou
sense of the word, it ' drew out ' of its members all the power an
goodness that was in them."

ZIMMERN, *The Greek Commonwealth,*
Note pp. 365 and 366.

" the city where men learnt to put the fair debate and the fr
vote instead of the brute force of tyrants, mobs, or oligarchs."
FREEMAN, *History of Sicily*, iii. p. 3.

WHEN an Athenian spoke of democracy, he understood k
the word something very different, at all events supe
ficially, from what people mean (if indeed they mea
anything), when they talk of ' making the world safe f
democracy.' By derivation the word merely signifi
' power of the people ' ; and in the last resort the princij
of Athenian and of modern democracy is the sam
namely, that the ultimate authority in the state resid
in the whole people, not in any particular person, or cla
of persons. But the manner in which effect is giv
to the principle differs greatly. In a modern democra
effect is given to the sovereign will of the people throu

what we call representative institutions. The Greeks, and in particular the Athenians, never explored the capabilities of the representative principle for the solution of the problem of popular government.[1] In their experience and belief the sovereignty of the people must be exercised directly and personally by the people themselves. With them every free-born citizen of age to share in the defence of the commonwealth was a member of the Ecclesia, or sovereign assembly of the Athenian people.

Principles of Democracy at Athens.—The Athenians carried out their idea of the sovereignty of the people with a logical thoroughness which is at first rather disconcerting. The ideas on which their fabric of democracy was reared were : (1) All citizens have equal rights ; and therefore, not only must all have equal votes in the Ecclesia, but must also be alike eligible for all offices with the exception of military command and of one or two others, for which special gifts and special training were seen to be indispensable) ; (2) Political duties must be performed directly and personally by the individual citizen.

(1) **Equal Claims to Office.**—At first sight the length to which the doctrine of equal eligibility for office was carried at Athens is barely credible. At Athens literally every citizen was eligible for every post in the civil administration with the exception of the very few just mentioned ; and a sweeping efficacy was given to this doctrine in practice by the almost universal employment for all appointments of election by lot. The ten *Strategi*, the Military Treasurer, the Superintendent of Water-springs, were elected by open vote ; but with these exceptions all magistrates, *all civilian officials*, from the nine archons

---

[1] This does not mean that the Greeks never had recourse to ' representation ' in practice. In some of the federal unions formed in the course of their history,—especially in the Aetolian and Achaean leagues, and in the religious federations called *amphictyonies*, there were rudiments of representative institutions. For an interesting discussion of the point, see Zimmern, *The Greek Commonwealth*, p. 157 and p. 159 *n.*

to the Market Commissioners and the Superintendent
of Games, were selected simply by drawing lots among
the candidates. There was further a rule that no citizer
might fill the same office more than once, except tha
any one might, if the lot fell on him, be *twice* a membe
of the Council. It was much as it is in those clubs and
associations in which all members hold office (Secretary
President and so on) *in turn* : only instead of there bein
a score or so of members there were between twenty and
thirty thousand. The principle in both cases was th
same, namely that every member of the association wa
adequately qualified for the discharge of the ordinar
duties of office and that it was good for him to tak
his turn. At Athens the incumbents of all state office
were in theory chosen by lot out of the whole bod
of 25,000 citizens. Doubtless in practice the choic
was very much more limited ; for presumably, thoug
this is nowhere definitely stated, candidates wer
limited to those who voluntarily came forward, and
for reasons which will shortly appear (p. 86), no citize
would be likely to come forward for an office th
responsibilities of which he was totally incapable
sustaining.

(2) The personal sovereignty of the Demos or Con
monalty of Athens was exercised through two institution
the one found in some form in every Greek state, t
other peculiar to latter-day Athens. At Athens, as
have seen,[1] the *Ecclesia* corresponded to the Agora
heroic Greece, which in some form or another surviv
in all or nearly all Hellenic polities. Only whereas
Sparta (for instance) the *Apella* numbered some five
six thousand members and had very limited power
the Athenian Ecclesia had three or four times as ma
members, and had powers relatively unlimited. Mo
over, at Athens there was besides a distinct organizati
wherein and whereby the sovereign people discharged t
judicial functions it had first had secured to it by Solo
legislation. In this judicial capacity the people w

[1] Vol. i. p. 245, cf. p. 220.

alled the *Heliaea*.[1] Solon organized the dicasteries or
popular courts,[2] and gave the poorer citizens equal rights
o serve on these courts. But it is probable that in so
loing he was only giving a more democratic character
o some primitive form of trial before the people, or the
ribe, such as we find conspicuous in Roman history.[3]
'ericles gave new efficacy to the principle of popular
ight in the Jury-courts by instituting payment for
ttendance. The amount paid was not large : it was
hree obols [4] at the time when Aristophanes was making
un of it in his comedies (about five shillings perhaps in
resent money values) ; not enough to compensate the
vell-to-do for their time and trouble, but large enough to
nable poorer citizens who depended on their day's work
or their livelihood, to serve in the courts instead of work-
ng. In theory the Dicastery-courts were, each of them,
he sovereign Demos sitting in the seat of judgment ;
ut for convenience sake, instead of the trial taking place
efore the whole body of citizens in the Ecclesia, it took
lace before a section of the whole body, from 200 to 2000
r more in number, selected for the purpose by the im-
artial discrimination of the lot. Every year 6000
itizens above thirty years of age were registered in lists
or the performance of these duties, and the whole number
o chosen and registered was called the *Heliaea*.

Responsibility of Magistrates.—There was a third
rinciple, subsidiary to these two, for securing the com-
lete sovereignty of the people. This was the direct

[1] By derivation the word Heliaea appears to be connected with a
erb meaning to gather or assemble, so that its significance is ultimately
he same as that of Agora and Ecclesia.

[2] Vol. i. p. 245.

[3] The right of popular trial was enshrined in the *Lex Valeria de Pro-
ocatione*. See Myres, *History of Rome*, p. 68.

[4] Six obols went to a drachma. *Obol* means by derivation ' spit ' ;
nd *drachma* meant originally a ' handful.' The explanation is that
on *spits* were an early form of money, and six of them were treated as
aking a *handful* of spits. The modern Greek drachma about equals
franc. But money had in the fifth century at least ten times the
urchasing power it has now.

subordination of all magistrates and officials to the Démos. The people of Great Britain are credited with a healthy distrust of officials as such ; but British jealousy of official persons and powers is mild compared with the Athenian The Athenian safeguards against the abuse of official position were so rigorous that it is rather surprising that any one was found at Athens courageous enough to seek office at all. " All magistrates," writes Aristotle " whether elected by lot or by open vote are examined before entering on their office." This was the *Dokimasie* or Testing. When his year of service was over the magistrate must render strict account of his conduc as an official to one board and submit his money account to audit by another, and while this *Euthuna,* as it was called, was in progress it was open to any citizen who considered himself aggrieved to lodge a complaint Further, once every month at the first of the regular meetings of the Ecclesia called *kuria,* or ' sovereign meeting, the conduct of all officials was passed in review and a vote taken on their continuance in office. Doubt less in most cases review and vote were formal : but it is obvious that public servants in the Athenian democrac were looked after by the public they served in a truly awe-inspiring manner. There was a test before they wer admitted to office, an examination once a month durin their year of office, and most formidable of all, a stric scrutiny before they were quit of their responsibilitie This strictness of account has to be weighed along wit the rule of election by lot in judging of the efficiency of the Athenian democratic system.

The Sovereign People in their Ecclesia.—It is difficu at this time of day to form a conception of a deliberativ assembly on the scale and with the powers of the Athenia Ecclesia in the latter half of the fifth century B.C. Ever free-man in Attica of the age to bear arms (that is eighteen years of age and over) was a member of this bod We have no exact census of the number of such citize in Pericles' time, but we can infer that it must have bee not less than 20,000, and may have been very muc greater. A Parliament of twenty or thirty thousand, all equally entitled to vote and to speak, the very notion seems preposterous ; and yet that is what the Athenian Ecclesia was, at least potentially. In practice, of course, so many as that never came together. Some were on active service abroad, or serving in the fleet ; some were unable to leave their farms in the country and come into Athens ; many more would keep away from slackness or disinclination. At ordinary meetings there may have been no more than three or four thousand (we have hardly any figures at all to judge by,[1] it is mainly guess work) : for an ostracism six thousand votes was the *quorum* required. But even an ordinary sitting of the Ecclesia must have been very like a Trafalgar Square meeting : only instead of listening to speeches and perhaps passing a fiery vote that means nothing, the great meeting in the Pnyx at Athens had tremendous powers. They voted war and peace ; they voted treaties ; they voted the life or death of public servants (ministers and generals) impeached before them ; they voted on the subsidies to be paid by subject communities ; they voted on the expulsion of undesirable aliens. The House of Commons does some of these things in England, but not a mass meeting of citizens. It seems a surprising system, open to damaging criticism—and indeed it had its weak points : yet under it Athens attained to that height of power and splendour at which we have been contemplating her, and under it she achieved and suffered much which we shall presently pass in review, before the days of her greatness were over.

The Council of Five Hundred.—There was no limit to the constitutional authority of the Ecclesia. So far as concerns sovereign power the Athenian constitution was a single-chamber constitution, and a majority of the Ecclesia could do anything whatever that it pleased. But in practice there were safeguards. Firstly by custom

[1] Thucydides uses words in one place (viii. 72) which imply that during the Peloponnesian war meetings of the Ecclesia never reached so high a total as 5000.

having the force of law nothing could come before the
Ecclesia which had not previously been considered by the
Boulê or Council. The Council (or Senate) of the fifth
century B.C. was a very different body from the Council
of Solon's time or even of Cleisthenes', and still more
unlike the ancient Council of the Areopagus. All these
were bodies of an aristocratic complexion. The later
Council of Five Hundred was a thoroughly democratic
institution ingeniously devised to ensure its being an
epitome of the whole Demos. It was to all intents and
purposes a Standing Committee of the Ecclesia with wide
executive powers in addition to deliberative : in fact
it was the most important part of what we should call the
government. The Boulê unlike the Ecclesia (which met
at intervals) was in permanent session : but because
for practical purposes the whole five hundred was too
large a number, subdivisions of the Boulê carried on the
business of the state in turn. The Boulê itself was made
up of ten bodies of fifty, each elected by lot out of one of
the ten Athenian tribes.[1] Each of these groups of fifty
discharged the active duties of the Boulê for one tenth
of the year (roughly a month, actually thirty-six or thirty-
five days) and were called during their period of office
Prytaneis. A president was appointed by lot out of these
fifty and held office for one day. A fresh president was
elected daily ; and no councillor might hold office as
president more than once.

The functions of the Boulê were both deliberative and
executive. The most important of them was that already
mentioned just above—to prepare business for the
Ecclesia. No business whatever could come before the
Ecclesia which had not previously been discussed in
the Boulê. The result of this discussion was then placed
before the Ecclesia in the form of a preliminary resolution
of the Boulê, or *probouleuma*. On the executive side
the Boulê was the permanent co-ordinating agency in
the government. "The Council," says Aristotle, "*co-
operates with* the other magistrates in most of their duties."[2]

---

[1] See I. p. 251.   [2] Aristotle, *Constitution of Athens*, 47 (Kenyon).

Some of the functions which Aristotle specifies are un-expected. The Council exercised a general supervision over the ships of the fleet and their equipment : the Council built new ships. The Council looked into the condition of the cavalry horses provided by the state. The Council inspected public buildings : at one time it had examined and passed building plans. The Council received foreign ambassadors. It is not surprising that with these varied activities the importance of the Athenian Boulê grew ; yet it never attained to anything like the dominant position in the state at one time occupied by the Senate of Rome.

The Magistrates.—The Boulê, we are told by Aristotle, ' co-operated ' with the other magistrates. He is speaking of civil affairs, and the most important magistrates of all in Pericles' time, the *Strategi*, bore a military title, though their influence extended into civil administration also. Other public functionaries in great variety are enumerated by Aristotle and most of them were probably in existence a century earlier. They were usually organized in Boards of ten, elected by lot one from each tribe, all holding office for one year only. There were City Com-missioners, Market Commissioners, Corn Commissioners, Commissioners of Weights and Measures, Superintendents of the Mart, Commissioners of Repairs, Commissioners of Roads, Commissioners of Games, Commissioners of Public Worship. All these were boards of ten and their functions are suggested by their names. There were several Financial Boards also :—Treasurers of Athena, Commissioners for Public Contracts, Receivers-General, Auditors, all boards of ten and appointed by lot. An exception in point of number was the ' Eleven,' the dread board known by that name, who had charge of prison management and, incidentally, of executions. Elected also in the same way and for the same period were certain special officers ; a Clerk to the Prytaneis, a Clerk of the Laws, a Demarch for Piraeus, an Archon for Salamis. The *nine* Archons were still elected annually and were still invested with the prestige of their title, but they had only a shadow of their ancient power. The year still took its name from the Archon Eponymus. The King Archon discharged the religious obligations once associated with royalty. The Polemarch had become a sort of Protector of Immigrants. The Thesmothetae worked the machinery of the Dicastery Courts, but no longer themselves acted as judges. Aristotle gives a total of seven hundred officers of the Civil Service of Attica and as many again for the Civil Service of Athens abroad in her colonies and empire. All these officials were directly accountable to the sovereign people and must pass the ordeal of the *Euthuna* before they were freed from responsibility. There was a monthly checking and confirming of all officials (as we have seen) through the Ecclesia : but accountability to the sovereign people was mainly brought home to officials through the Euthunae, which were connected with the organization of the Demos of Athens in its judicial capacity as the *Heliaea*.

The Heliaea.—Five of the six thousand Athenian citizens enrolled for the judicial work of the sovereign people, and known as the Heliaea, were divided up into ten bodies of 500. These were distinguished by the first ten letters of the Greek alphabet, A, B and so on down to K, and told off for work in the courts, while the remaining thousand dicasts were held in reserve to make good casual vacancies in the ten batches of five hundred. There were ten Dicastery Courts, and the next ten letters of the alphabet after K were used to distinguish them. To ensure freedom from undue influence the method of assigning judges to the several courts was curiously elaborate. No judge knew till the day on which a trial took place to which court he would be assigned, who his colleagues would be, or what case would come before him. In the morning of each day on which legal business could be done the Thesmothetae decided what courts should sit, what cases should be taken in them and how many judges should be allotted to the several courts. The number of judges might vary from 201 (there was always an odd number of dicasts) to as many as 2501. The minimum for a public case was 501, but 201 or 401 was usual in a private suit. For each court a proportion of the judges was taken by lot from each of the ten sections, so that each court, whether of two hundred judges or two thousand, was representative of the whole body of citizens forming the Heliaea, which again represented the whole Athenian People. Each court further was marked with a distinctive colour ; and every day counters of these various colours in number corresponding to the number of judges required for the several courts (201, 401 and so on) were placed in an urn. Then the individual Heliasts came up, one by one, and drew a counter : the colour of the counter drawn determined the court in which he was to sit that day. He received a staff or baton of a corresponding colour, and a ticket. At the end of the day's sitting he gave up his ticket at a pay office and received his three obols. The same process was repeated the next day the courts were open and for every day throughout the year.

The business of the Athenian dicastery-courts grew to be very heavy, since—in addition to the mass of home-bred litigation—legal cases from the allies were brought to Athens in ever increasing volume, till the delays of the courts became one of the grievances of the subject states.

The Heliaea and Legislation.—Moreover, the Heliaea had another most important function of a *regulative* nature, in its capacity as guardian of the constitution. The Ecclesia had deliberative and executive powers. It was the final authority for state action and there was no limit but one to its initiative. " It was the deliberate intention of the Athenians," writes Ferguson,[1] " that the ecclesia should consider everything it wanted to consider." And all decisions of the Ecclesia were final. The one exception was new legislation. The Ecclesia passed decrees but had no strictly legislative function, that is no power to make new laws (nomoe). New *laws* could only be brought in by a legal process in *judicial* form, and that

[1] *Greek Imperialism*, p. 54.

process took the shape of a trial before a committee of the Heliaea.[1] The law in regard to which change was proposed was formally indicted, pleas were heard for and against, and judgment was delivered by the dicasts. This procedure dates from the end of the fifth century, when a form of indictment was introduced by a statute to be used against any one who proposed a new law which infringed any existing law, an indictment for illegality—a *graphê paranomôn*. This statute made it a hazardous thing to introduce any new legislation at all : for it was a hard matter to propose any new law which did not touch some existing law in a way that might be represented as infringement, and a vexatious law suit might ensue.

The Strategi as heads of the Executive.—The institutions we have passed in review provide an ample organization for the conduct of routine administration, but we are conscious of something still seriously wanting for the effective government of a great state : a central executive and leadership, such as is found in cabinet government in England, in the President of a republic, in a king and his ministers. At Athens this active ministerial function, once vested in the archons, was in the age of Pericles most nearly discharged by the Strategi. In title the function of the Strategos was military ; but in practice the Strategi for the year were the supreme ministers of the State, with functions civil as well as military, like the Consuls at Rome. There were ten such Strategi at Athens, usually, though not necessarily, one from each tribe, and elected not by the lot but by open voting. The ten strategi formed a board ; and there is reason to conjecture, though it cannot be fully proved, that one of the ten each year was permanent president.[2]

The Chief of the People.—Moreover, in Athenian history down to the times we are now considering, there had always been some leader who had stood out as virtual,

---

[1] Called in this capacity ' nomothetae ' or law-makers.

[2] See Greenidge, *Greek Constitutional History*, pp. 181-2 and Appendix pp. 253-5.

if not titular, chief of the state. There is a succession of great names, Cleisthenes, Miltiades, Themistocles, Aristides, Cimon, Thucydides (son of Melesias), Pericles. In Pericles the succession culminates. Thucydides (the historian) and Aristotle both give the name ' Chief of the people ' (*Prostatês tou demou*) to such a natural leader, guiding the counsels and decisions of the ecclesia by force of character and the strength of his personal reputation. Of Pericles in particular, Thucydides writes that in his time Athens was in name only a democracy, but in reality the rule of the first man in the state.

National Defence.—*Strategos* (army-leader) is a military title. It is not a little significant that at the height of her political development the title of the chief officers of the Athenian commonwealth was military. This emergence of the Strategi as the chief officers of state dates from a little before the Persian war.[1] With the formation of the Delian League and the assumption by Athens of responsibility for the defence of the Greeks of Asia, military, and still more naval, organization naturally gained in importance, though it never assumed so relatively large a place in state economy as it did at Rome. It goes without saying that every Athenian youth, as he came to man's estate (and this was reckoned at eighteen years of age) aspired to be enrolled in the national militia. For two years he received military training among youths of like age (the Ephebi from 18 to 20) serving on outpost and garrison duty on the frontiers ; and through his prime of manhood and up to the age of sixty he was liable to go on active service when called upon.[2] Every Athenian citizen at all well-to-do, and able to provide himself with a full outfit as a man-at-arms, served as a hoplite or shield-man. The sons of wealthier citizens were, to the number of 1200, privileged to serve in the cavalry, and were called *Hippeis*. They formed a crack

[1] B.C. 487 See I. p. 251.

[2] Citizens' names were kept in a ' catalogos ' or roll, and whenever an expedition was voted by the ecclesia, a certain number of citizens ' on the roll ' were called up to serve.

corps and were permitted (like our Cavaliers in the seventeenth century) to wear their hair long and to put on a good deal of swagger. They figure as chorus in one of Aristophanes' comedies called after them the *Hippeis*, or ' Knights.' The poorer sort of citizens served as light-armed infantry, or in the fleet.

The Navy.—The manning of the fleet was, of course, in the fifth century B.C. a matter of supreme importance for Athens. The marines (*epibatae*), who were the fighting force on shipboard, archers and javelin men mostly, were through the most flourishing period of the Athenian navy, no more than ten.[1] This was because the effective value of a trireme in naval war depended much more on the skill of the oarsmen who propelled it, and who were perfected by hard training in the difficult art of rowing in time under the given conditions : and these oarsmen, with ' spare oars ' nearly 200 in number,[2] were in large proportion free men of Athens. Usually they were citizens of the lowest of Solon's four classes, the Thetes. But, if the need were great enough, Athenians of every class were apparently ready to serve. At the time of the Persian invasion Athenian citizens of all classes hurried on board ship and served as rowers. It is expressly related [3] to the glory of Cimon, son of Miltiades, that when Themistocles made his appeal for volunteers to man the fleet, Cimon as a Knight, for the sake of example, carried his bit and bridle to the Acropolis, and laid them up before the altar of Athena, as a sign that to help the state in her need he forsook land-service for sea-service. And in the latter half of the fifth century B.C. it appears that a large proportion of Athenian citizens had experience of sea-voyages, had acquired a measure

[1] See Thucydides, iii. 95, and Dr. Arnold's note.

[2] There were 62 Top-bench oars (Thranitae), 58 Middle-bench (Zeugitae) and 54 Lowest-bench (Thalamitae)—fewer on the lower benches because the cut of the trireme gave less length below. The *Trierarch* was captain of the ship. Other officers were the *Helmsman* or Pilot ; the *Look-out Officer* or ' Prow-man ' ; a *Piper* to give the time to the rowers, and a *Boatswain* to shout orders.

[3] Plutarch, *Cimon*, 5.

of seamanship and learnt how to row. The unknown author of the treatise on the Athenian Polity expressly says : "A man who is perpetually voyaging is forced to handle the oar, he and his domestic alike, and to learn the terms familiar in seamanship. . . . So that the majority of them are able to row the moment they set foot on board a vessel." [1]

To the less wealthy citizens naval service was made attractive by high rates of pay, a drachma a day, as against the three obols of the dicastery fee (just double). This high rate of pay was attractive also to foreign seamen, that is Greeks of other city-states. The *personnel* of the Athenian fleet at the height of her sea-power has recently been put as high as 100,000.[2] This is hardly an over-statement if we must suppose that Athens kept the 400 war-vessels of her full naval strength (above, ch. ii. p. 38) continually on a war footing. But as this is not probable, an estimate of about half that total is nearer the mark. In the Peloponnesian war a considerable number of foreign seamen served in the Athenian fleet : we do not know in what proportion. But the obligation of personal service was universally recognized at Athens in the fifth century : of the highest classes in the cavalry, of substantial burghers and yeomen in the hoplites, of the artizan classes among the light-armed infantry or on shipboard, every man according to his ability. But so vital was the navy to the very existence of Athens, that in an emergency every man from the highest to the lowest was prepared to serve in the fleet. Thucydides records more than one instance of this.[3] And in this willingness for personal service lay the safety of the state. Later there was a decline in public spirit and in the fourth century Athens waged her wars mainly by means of mercenaries. We find Demosthenes again and again lamenting this shirking of personal service and exhorting his fellow-countrymen to return to the braver practice

[1] *The Polity of the Athenians*, i. 19 and 20. Dakyns vol. ii. pp. 281-2.
[2] Stevens and Westcott, *A History of Sea Power*, p. 39.
[3] Thucydides, iii. 16; viii. 94. 3.

of former days.[1] By that time the splendour of Athens had passed : but universally we may lay down that the military power of any state (whether kingdom, republic or empire) is doomed in no long time to pass away, when its people are no longer willing—all classes alike according to their ability—to bear arms in her cause.

Class Distinctions.—There were wide differences of wealth at Athens and nobility of birth carried appreciable weight in public life. But there were no rigid class distinctions, either politically or socially. In particular there was no class privileged *politically.* " There never was a people which made the principle that all its citizens were equal a more live reality than the Athenians made it." [2] In Athenian social life there was little, if any, of the spirit we have come to call ' snobbery.' It is significant, for instance, that the same Greek word means both a stone-mason and a sculptor. " The Greeks," says Zimmern, " never recognized any distinction between a craft or ' trade ' and a profession." [3] The only valid class distinctions at Athens were distinctions of obligation. The high-born had religious duties to discharge in relation to the state ; the rich had costly public burdens to shoulder. One distinction, however, there was, which fashion and common speech recognized, a distinction of manners and education, rather than of wealth or birth, a distinction comparable to the discrimination of character and status implied in the English use of ' gentleman.' People assumed to recognize certain higher standards of conduct and behaviour were called *Kaloikagathoi,* literally the ' noble and good.'

State Services or ' Liturgies.'—It was a recognized custom at Athens to require the well-to-do to undertake on behalf of the state certain public duties involving considerable expense. These forms of costly state-

[1] Demosthenes, 1st *Philippic,* 21, 24, 44, 47 ; 2nd *Olynthiac,* 24, 27, 31 ; 3rd *Philippic,* 70.

[2] Ferguson, *Greek Imperialism,* p. 39.

[3] *The Greek Commonwealth,* p. 257.

service were called *Leitourgiae,* from which we get our word
' Liturgy.' The most important of these was that of
fitting-out a trireme and commanding it on service ;
and this was called a *trierarchy.* There were four hundred
trierarchs appointed every year.[1] Other kinds of state
service had to do with public festivals and games, musical
contests, races. One which occupied a very conspicuous
place in Athenian life was the *Choregia,* the duty of training
the chorus required for the dramatic contests held in the
course of the celebration of the Great Dionysia.[2] It is
not, perhaps, quite accurate to call these liturgies or
state-services voluntary, since there was no choice in the
matter. If you were a well-to-do Athenian citizen and a
liturgy was assigned to you, you had to perform it whether
you liked it or not.[3] But it is a point very well worth
remembering that so far as evidence goes these liturgies
were not only willingly but zealously and gladly undertaken. There was a keen spirit of emulation in the discharge of some of them, and particularly in the presentation
of choruses for the tragic stage or for comedy.[3] The
working of the system of liturgies in its relation to public
finance at Athens is admirably summed up by Dr.
Zimmern : " A large part of the public expenses of the
Athenian State, the mounting of its plays, the equipment
of its ships, the arrangements for its games and festivals,
its chariot and horse and torch races, its musical contests
and regattas both in city and township, were defrayed
by private citizens, who came forward voluntarily, and
took pride in vying with their predecessors or with a
crowd of rivals in their performance of the task." [4] It
was found that the choregus who fitted out a play was as
eager as the poet who wrote it, that the play should win
the prize for the dramatic contest for which it was pre-

[1] See below p. 102.

[2] See vol. i. pp. 55, 56 and 249.

[3] People at Athens did not theorize about the obligations and responsibilities of wealth, but rich and poor alike assumed them as a
matter of course, and acted on the assumption without fuss or controversy.

[4] *The Greek Commonwealth,* pp. 287 and 288.

pared, and in later times a whole street in Athens, the Street of Tripods, took its name from the monuments which successful choregic competitors put up to celebrate their success. One of these monuments, the Choregic Monument of Lysicrates (a little east of the Theatre of Dionysus) is an object of interest for the visitor to Athens to-day.

Life in Democratic Athens.—We may now in the light of the preceding paragraphs try to form some picture of what it was to be a citizen of Athens in the days of Pericles, and to be moulded by the institutions described. We will ask first what were, under the constitution, the advantages and opportunities of every citizen, even the meanest, apart from the adventitious aid of riches and nobility of birth. " All citizens sit in parliament ; every office from commander-in-chief to civil service clerk is open to talent ; an aristocrat, a grocer, an artisan may equally become premier : he has only to persuade parliament to elect him." [1] This is a vivid summary of the result ; but we see that it is true with some little qualification ; for provided a man's claim to full citizenship was undisputed, neither lowly birth nor narrow means was a bar to his candidature for office, and the lot was no respecter of persons. The qualification is that wealth and birth at Athens, as everywhere else in the world, were elements in the making of a successful career in politics. Pericles the son of Xanthippus, or Nicias the son of Niceratus, apart from natural endowments, had a better chance of rising to be a power in the Ecclesia than Ephialtes who lived and died a poor man, or Hyperbolus who could always be reproached with his low birth, or Lamachus who was only a good soldier. Further every citizen of Athens was certainly born to extraordinary advantages, quite apart from the brilliant opportunities that were open to him in politics if he had the sort of ability that told in the Ecclesia. Even if he were born in too low estate to enjoy the full training in Music and Gymnastic which was peculiarly Greek, he

[1] Livingstone (R. W.), *The Greek Genius*, p. 209.

received a liberal education of wide scope through the social and political institutions of his native city. Pericles when addressing to the people of Athens in the presence of the kinsfolk of the dead, at the close of the first year of the Peloponnesian war, his famous *Funeral Speech*, reminded them of the succession of public entertainments and spectacles with which the year at Athens was diversified : " we have not forgotten," he said, " to provide for our weary spirits many relaxations from toil : we have regular games and sacrifices throughout the year." [1]

The Athenian Festal Year.—There were some thirty festivals spread over the twelve months of the Athenian year which began in July with the month Hecatombaeon, and a good many of these lasted for more than one day ; some for as many as five days. It has been reckoned that the number of holidays at Athens came to seventy, which is appreciably in excess of the total which our Sundays make together with the other holidays recognized by law (Christmas Day, Easter Monday, Whit-Monday, Boxing Day and the other Bank holidays). But whereas there is a certain sameness about our Sundays, all the Athenian holidays were different, and had a distinctive character. Some celebrated great victories. There was a Marathon day and a day in memory of Plataea. Some were deeply grounded in social and political history, like the Synoecia,[2] the Theseia, the Apaturia, the Thesmophoria ; some were associated only, or mainly, with the cult of some particular god, the Diasia and the Diipolia with the worship of Zeus ; the Thesmophoria and the Eleusinia with the worship of Demeter ; the Delphinia and the Thargelia with the worship of Apollo. Processions, games (that is, ' athletic sports '), musical contests, torch races, boat races, variously accompanied these festivals. Above all there were dramatic contests at two of the festivals of Dionysus, the Lesser and the Great Dionysia. The boat-racing in which trireme raced trireme from Piraeus to Munychia, one for each of the ten tribes, took place on the last day of the Panathenaea. Torch-races were a feature of the

<hr>

[1] Thucydides, ii. 38.   [2] See vol. i. p. 236.

Theseia and the Bendidaea : [1] and of the Panathenaea
also. There were processions at the Lenaea, the Great
Dionysia, the Thesmophoria. the Eleusinia and most
splendid of all at the *great* Panathenaea, once in four
years.

The chief events of the whole cycle were the Panathenaea and the Great Dionysia, each occupying not less
than five days. The Panathenaea may have taken eight,
it is thought by some. For us the Great Dionysia have
most interest because of their connection with Greek
drama. It was for the prize competitions in the Great
Dionysia that all the tragedies of the Attic drama were
written and most of the comedies. To see these dramas
acted the whole free population of Athens crowded to the
Theatre of Dionysus in the early morning and stayed
there till sunset, watching play after play ; and it remains
an astonishment to all time how this great mixed concourse of Athenian citizens, high and low, rich and poor
(women probably among them), had minds to follow and
appraise dramas of such elevation of thought and language
as Aeschylus' *Agamemnon*, *Eumenides*, or *Persians*,
Sophocles' *Oedipus at Colonus* or *Antigone*, or Euripides'
Women of Troy. When we contrast this with the difficulty which any play of more than ordinary intellectual
quality has in keeping the stage of any of the many
theatres of London, astonishment grows. The comedies
of Aristophanes demand for their appreciation mental
endowments scarcely less high, and intelligence at least
as quick as a Gilbert and Sullivan musical comedy or the
Beggar's Opera.

But for the Athenian of the fifth century B.C. the
greatest festival of all was the Great Panathenaea : this
came once in four years, in the third year of an Olympiad.
Every resource, spectacular, artistic, literary, religious,
was used to heighten this, the culmination of the Athenian
festal cycle. First came the competition between
trained choirs of men and of boys (as in an Eisteddfod) ;

---

[1] A festival in honour of Bendis. a Thracian goddess sometimes
identified with Artemis.

next athletic contests, and horse and chariot races. There
was a ' manhood ' competition (Euandria) between representative teams of two competing tribes : the prize
was the honour of walking in the Panathenaic procession.
There was a competition between bands of youths in war-
dances, and, as we have already noted, a torch-race.
These competitions took up four days of crowded interest.
Then came the fifth and great day, the 28th Hecatombaeon.
It began with an all-night vigil, and then with morning
came the great Panathenaic procession, the representation
of which is seen in the Parthenon frieze ; and after the
procession high sacrifice. It was on the day after this
that the people crowded down to the Piraeus to see the
regatta and the race between picked war-ships.

These festivals, with their processions, musical competitions and dramatic performances, which were attended,
and meant to be attended, by the whole body of the
people, were an education of a potent kind, and in the full
sense national. Nor was that all the education which the
ordinary citizen got from the State. He received valuable
education, political and practical, from the mere discharge
of his duties as a citizen. And to the fulfilment of these
political duties he was urged and even driven. If he
lingered in the market-place on a day when the Ecclesia
was sitting, or in the streets adjoining the Pnyx, he was
swept into it by officers of the City Police holding the
ends of a rope well plastered with red powder, and there
in the Pnyx, hour after hour, he listened to the discussion
of important public questions, and one day by good luck
might hear a speech from Pericles. He spent many a
long day in the Dicastery Courts, and besides earning his
poor wage of three obols—which might or might not be
a consideration with him—he became familiarized with
a great variety of legal business and a multiplicity of
matters of general interest, public and private. " Here
are some of the cases which have to be decided on,"
writes the author of the treatise on the Athenian State,
commonly printed with Xenophon's works, but not his,
" someone fails to fit out a ship : the case must be

brought into court. Another puts up a building on a piece of public land : again the case must be brought into court. Or, to take another class of cases : adjudication has to be made between the choragi for the Dionysia, the Thargelia, the Panathenaea, year after year. Also as between the trierarchs, four hundred of whom are appointed each year, of these, too, any who choose must have their cases brought into court, year after year. . . · There are various magistrates to examine and approve and decide between ; there are orphans whose status must be examined ; and guardians of prisoners to appoint. These, be it borne in mind, are all matters of yearly occurrence ; while at intervals there are exemptions and abstentions from military service which call for adjudication, or in connection with some extraordinary misdemeanour, some case of outrage and violence of an exceptional character, or some charge of impiety. A whole string of others I simply omit ; I am content to have named the most important part with the exception of the assessments of tribute which occur, as a rule, at intervals of five years." [1] We see from all this that frequent attendance in the law-courts, if it had other more questionable aspects, certainly gave the ordinary citizen a wide familiarity with practical legal business. Ferguson justly claims that " the normal town-meeting of the Athenians was, from one point of view, an assembly of experts . . ." [2]

The citizen's war-service, military or naval, may count for something, too. As a young man from eighteen to twenty he learnt the rudiments of drill and the routine of frontier duty. If called on later in life to go on a military expedition over the frontier or across the seas, he received liberal pay. In peace time he enjoyed spacious social advantages in the public resorts at Athens, in the wrestling-grounds and gymnasia, in the market-place and even in the public streets. Among men at any rate—and perhaps because society at Athens, at least

[1] *Athenian Polity*, iii. 4 and 5.   Dakyns, ii. p. 289 (slightly altered).
[2] Ferguson, *Greek Imperialism*, p. 57.

respectable society, was an exclusively masculine society —social relations were easy and free. Life at Athens was lived largely in the open air, and abroad in the streets and exercising grounds and market-place you might talk with whom you would free of obstruction by irksome social conventions. Greek social life is aptly compared to club life—but *without the rule of silence*.

The wealthy and high-born at Athens shared in all these advantages, and, in addition, though the laws gave them no special privileges either in political rights or in the national amusements, wealth and rank were an important supplement to natural ability, if they chose to follow a political career. For the rest they enjoyed precisely the same privileges as poorer citizens. There is no sign of jealousy of wealth or birth as such in the Athenian democracy. For this the system of liturgies is largely responsible : the obligations of wealth to the state were thereby discharged automatically but in a way that made it easy to win popularity and that stands in poignant contrast to the thankless and ungracious way of an Income Tax, however artfully graduated. On the other hand there was extreme sensitiveness to anything that looked like disloyalty to democratic principles, and suspicion of any desire to narrow political privileges and substitute oligarchy for democracy. And for this suspicion of oligarchical intriguing the history of Athens shows there were good grounds. But in spite of this the prestige of a great name still counted for very much in the Ecclesia. Without doubt it helped Cimon in his public career that he was son of Miltiades, and Pericles that he mingled the blood of the Butadae and the Alcmaeonidae. Again young men of wealth at Athens in the fifth century B.C.—a Callias[1] or an Alcibiades, a Glaucon or a Critias—could resort to the foreign teachers (Gorgias, Protagoras, Prodicus, Thrasymachus) who came to Athens and professed to endow those who sought their society with wonderful practical capacities, of which the

---

[1] Xenophon, *Symposium*, i. 5.

art of public speaking was one. The young men of the
wealthier classes were able to serve as *Hippeis* in the
cavalry, and they probably had a better chance of becoming infantry officers, *lochagi* or captains and *taxiarchs*
or colonels : as officers they would acquire some tincture
of military science and so stand a better chance of being
ultimately elected *Strategos*. But the true privilege
of birth and wealth in democratic Athens was to be sought
in the *liturgies,* the inestimable privilege of the opportunity
for superior service to the State as trierarch, as choregus,
as gymnasiarch.

The Opposition at Athens.—But freedom to use and
enjoy what was theirs, along with the reality of democratic equality in the essentials of political life, by no
means contented all the well-born and wealthy at Athens.
Continuously throughout Athenian history we trace the
activities of a not uninfluential oligarchical minority,
working sometimes in the open, but more often beneath
the surface. These people had a way of arrogating
to themselves the title ' the noble and good ' which had
more properly the ethical significance we gave to it on
p. 96. This opposition at Athens had two forms which
we may distinguish as the loyal opposition and the
revolutionary. There was the lawful conservative opposition, represented by Aristides, Cimon, Thucydides
(son of Melesias), and Nicias ; in Cimon and Nicias
combined with mild Lacedaemonian sympathies ; which
cherished the old ideals associated with the landed aristocracy, war service with spear and shield and memories
of Marathon, and disliked the later developments of
democracy, especially the growth of the power of the
Dicastery-courts.[1] And there was the revolutionary
oligarchical faction, seeking the overthrow of the democracy and always in a state of passive or active conspiracy.
We see this disloyal oligarchical opposition intriguing
with the Spartans before Tanagra (above, ch. ii. p. 44),

---

[1] Three of the comedies of Aristophanes—the *Acharnians,* the
Knights and the *Wasps* (especially the last)—express the standpoint of
such honest conservatives with all the poet's vigour and wit.

coming into the open in the oligarchical revolution of 411, and in 404 triumphing for a time in the tyranny of the Thirty.

Freedom in Athens.—But though this oligarchical opposition was sometimes formidable in Athenian politics, and never negligible, on the whole democracy, as understood in Athens, was rooted firmly in the hearts and lives of the people. The great charm of living at Athens was freedom. Probably there was never a community in which there was less interference with men's thoughts, words and actions—outside the indispensable requirements of law and order—than in the Athenian democracy between 479 and 429 B.C. All Hellenes had a passionate love of liberty ; but at Athens liberty was clothed in more gracious forms and acquired a deeper meaning. The Athenians made it their boast that they were lovers of freedom in a richer and finer sense than other Hellenes.

Atossa in Aeschylus' *Persians* asks about the Athenians

" And who is shepherd of their host and holds them in command ? "

And the answer is returned

" To no man do they bow as slaves, nor own a master's hand." [1]

Theseus in Euripides' *Suppliants* makes the same claim :

> Our state is ruled
> Not of one only man : Athens is free.
> Her people in the order of their course
> Rule year by year, bestowing on the rich
> Advantage none ; the poor hath equal right.[2]

This is more than the autonomy which all Hellenes craved ; it is equality before the law, justice alike for Eupatrid and lowly-born. And in the same speech Theseus makes a claim beyond this :

> Thus Freedom speaks :—" What man desires to bring
> Good counsel for his country to the people ?
> Who chooseth this, is famous : who will not,
> Keeps silence. Can equality further go ? " [3]

[1] Aeschylus, *Persians*, ll. 243 and 4 (Morshead).

[2] Euripides, *The Suppliants*, 404-8 ; Way's translation, i. p. 381.

[3] *Ib.* ll. 438-441 ; Way, p. 382.

This is equality of political privilege and the right of free speech. There is an anticipation of this note, too, in the triumph-song in *The Persians* : [1]

> The whole land o'er
> Men speak the thing they will. . . .

But freedom, and freedom of speech, in imperial Athens went deeper than that. Nothing, perhaps, shows more astonishingly how deep than the ' Old Comedy ' as illustrated by plays written by Aristophanes between 430 and 410. Five that have come down to us have definitely political subjects (*Acharnians*, *Knights*, *Wasps*, *Peace*, *Lysistrata*). Like all Aristophanes' comedies they include a good deal of very plain-spoken indecency : but this, of course, is not the freedom that is meant. They contain much daring criticism of personages and events of the day—of Pericles, Cleon, Lamachus, the war, the sovereign Demos, the Dicastery-courts, along with noble patriotic sentiment, much wholesome advice and at least one superb appeal for peace and goodwill among Hellenes, which we shall notice in its place.[2] These plays of Aristophanes are contemporary documents of extraordinary interest, the veracity of which cannot be questioned. They carry us into the live atmosphere of fifth century Athens ; and in them we breathe air as free as blows in Great Britain or France to-day, or in the United States of America. In some respects it is freer.

A proof of the reality of Athenian freedom, no less telling than Aristophanes' presentment of its effects in thought and speech, may be found in the censure of philosophical critics who do not like it. Plato's gibe in the *Republic*,[3] " a charming form of government, full of variety and disorder, and dispensing a sort of equality of equals and unequals alike," is possibly not quite apposite to the present point. But the satirical descrip-

---

[1] Aeschylus, *Persians*, ll. 594 and 5 (Morshead).

[2] Chapter vi. p. 165.

[3] Plato, *Republic*, viii. 558 ; Jowett, vol. iii. p. 265 (3rd ed. 1892).

tion, a little further on in the same book—of liberty at Athens—is very much so : " no one who does not know would believe, how much greater is the liberty which the animals who are under the dominion of man have in a democracy than in any other State : for truly, the she-dogs, as the proverb says, are as good as their she-mistresses, and the horses and asses have a way of marching along with all the rights and dignities of freemen ; and they will run at anybody who comes in their way if he does not leave the road clear for them : and all things are just ready to burst with liberty." [1]

Most significant of all is the mock praise of Athenian liberty in the political tract found among the works of Xenophon to which we have more than once referred already : " Another point is the extraordinary amount of license granted to slaves and resident aliens at Athens, where a blow is illegal, and a slave will not step aside to let you pass him in the street." [2] This is not praise, but satire : we, however, see things differently and recognize with satisfaction that democratic Athens admitted slaves to be human beings with human claims and human rights in a fuller degree than other Greek communities.

All these considerations bear out the claim which Pericles makes for Athens in the Funeral Speech : " And not only in our public life are we liberal, but also as regards our freedom from suspicion of one another in the pursuits of everyday life ; for we do not feel resentment at our neighbour if he does as he likes, nor yet do we put on sour looks which, though harmless, are painful to behold. But while we thus avoid giving offence in our private intercourse, in our public life we are restrained from lawlessness chiefly through reverent fear, for we render obedience to those in authority and to the laws, and especially to those laws which are ordained for the succour of the oppressed and those which, though unwritten, bring upon the transgressor a disgrace which all

[1] Plato, *Republic*, viii. 563 ; Jowett, iii. p. 271.
[2] *The Polity of the Athenians*, i. 10 ; Dakyns, ii. 277 and 278.

men recognize." [1]   So when Nicias at a moment of extreme danger makes a last appeal to his sea-captains before going into action, the note he plays upon is just this : " He reminded them that they were the inhabitants of the freest country in the world, and how in Athens there was no interference with the daily life of any man." [2]

Pride in the City.—This many-sided freedom was one source of the pride which the Athenian felt in his city ; its new architectural glory was another ; but most of all it was her achievements—all that Athens had done and suffered since the Persians ventured to set foot on the shore of the Bay of Marathon.   This pride was intense and concentrated to a degree difficult to realize in this day of more diffused patriotism.   It was keen as a Public School boy's feeling for his school along with something of the largeness of patriotic English devotion to the ideals of the British Commonwealth.   A complete expression of this pride is recorded in the Funeral Speech of Pericles,[3] from which quotation has been made more than once. Passionate pride in the beauty and worthiness of Athens throbs through the quietest sentences in that speech and rings out in memorable phrases.   " I say that Athens is the School of Hellas."   " We love the fine arts, but study thrift withal : we love free speculation, but do not allow this to enervate our minds."   " For we have compelled every land and every sea to open a path to our valour ; and have everywhere planted memorials of our friendship or of our enmity."   " I would have you day by day fix your eyes upon the greatness of Athens, until you become filled with the love of her ; and when you are impressed with the spectacle of her glory, reflect that this empire has been acquired by men who knew their duty and had the courage to do it, who in the hour of conflict had the fear of dishonour always present to them, and who, if ever they failed in an enterprise, would not allow their virtues to be lost to their country, but freely

[1] Thucydides, ii. 37. 2 and 3.   Loeb, pp. 323 and 325.

[2] Thucydides, vii. 69. 2.   Jowett, vol. ii. p. 316 (2nd ed. 1900).

[3] Thucydides, ii. chs. 35 to 46.

gave their lives to her as the fairest offering they could make to her." [1] And in his last exhortation to the Athenians a short time before his death Pericles said : " Know that our city has the greatest name in all the world because she has never yielded to misfortunes, but has sacrificed more lives and endured severer hardships in war than any other ; wherefore also she has the greatest power of any state up to this day ; and the memory of her glory will always survive." [2]

Splendour of Athens.—Looking back across the score of centuries that have passed since Aeschylus, Thucydides and Aristophanes were writing their praise of Athens we can see that the most fervent expressions of this admiration and pride had their justification. We can see this, perhaps better than an average Athenian of Pericles' day, far better than Greeks of other cities, who, some with good reason, were stirred only to enmity. Zimmern in his *Greek Commonwealth* does not hesitate to speak of these great days of Athens as " perhaps the greatest and happiest period in recorded history." It is a high claim, greatly daring. He repeats it in his last chapter, restates his reasons with an eloquence as moving as it is true ; and indicates the crisis to which Athens was brought in her endeavour to maintain her course along the pathway into which her destiny had led her. " For a whole wonderful half century," he writes, " the richest and happiest period in the recorded history of any single community, Politics and Morality, the deepest and strongest forces of national and of individual life, had moved forward hand in hand towards a common ideal, the perfect citizen in the perfect state. All the high things in human life seemed to lie along that road : ' Freedom, Law, and Progress ; Truth and Beauty ; Knowledge and Virtue ; Humanity and Religion ! ' Now the gods had put them asunder. Freedom, Law, Virtue, Humanity and all the old forces of city life lay along one road : Beauty, Knowledge, Progress, and all the new

[1] Thucydides, ii. 43 ; Jowett, i. p. 132.
[2] Thucydides, ii. 64 ; Jowett, i. p. 147.

world of Civilization to which Riches and Empire held the key, along another. The gods had put them asunder. The gods have kept them asunder. Twenty-three centuries have passed ; the world has grown wiser than ever Greeks hoped, kinder than ever they dreamed, and richer far than ever they would have desired ; yet man has not learnt how to reunite them." [1]

NOTE ON CHAPTER IV.

There is no intention to shirk recognizing that there was another side to the picture of the Athenian commonwealth, or that there were blemishes in the social and political life of fifth century Athens—in particular slavery, and the position of women (leading to the degradation of chivalrous love). These things are not included, because they do not come into the scheme ; they are no part of what we inherit from Hellas. Far and away the best discussion of this part of the subject will be found in the *Spectator* for April the 29th of this year, 1922, in a letter signed ' Outis,' p. 522, under ' Correspondence,' and the editorial comment on this letter in the article, p. 519, bearing the same title as the letter, *Apologia pro anima Graeca.*

[1] Zimmern, *The Greek Commonwealth,* p. 430.

CHAPTER V

THE LEAGUE AGAINST ATHENS

" If our place were taken by others, we fancy they would afford the best possible proof of our moderation. Indeed it is from our very fairness that, so far from winning credit, we have most unreasonably got a bad name."

From a *Speech of Pericles* in Thucydides, i. 76.

" Yet if in other days they showed themselves good men against the Mede, but are now behaving badly towards us, they deserve double punishment, because they have turned to bad from being good."

From a *Speech of the Spartan Sthenelaidas*,
Thucydides, i. 86.

The Price of Empire.—We have seen how Athens in fifty years of heroic action, and with many vicissitudes of fortune, had won undisputed control of a sea-power extending—to use Aristophanes' phrase—" from Sardinia to Pontus." But the price she had had to pay for it was heavy. The tax on her people's moral energies had been very great and the actual loss in men through the toll of war serious enough to make us wonder how the wastage was made good. The loss of life in regular warfare of the Hellenic type was not, it is true, usually more than moderate, and sometimes curiously slight. But we have always to remember that the total Athenian man-power, though large for an Hellenic city-state, was narrowly limited. The total of 70,000 men suggested in ch. ii. is an outside estimate ;[1] and during these fifty years

[1] This is taking no account of any separate estimate for the fleet. It is impossible to reconcile satisfactorily the military and naval requirements of Athens with the given total of 30,000 male citizens of full age. The balance, no doubt, is made up of privileged alien residents (metics), allied contingents, hired seamen and (sometimes even) slaves ; but in what proportions we have only scanty means of judging.

Athens was often waging war simultaneously in several quarters. The ' roll of honour ' for the year 459-8, which was also cited in ch. ii. (p. 39), contains 176 names, but it is the list for one tribe only out of ten ; and if the roll for the other nine was in proportion, the total would be 1760, which is two and a half per cent. of 70,000, the estimated number of free men capable of bearing arms. If, however, we take for comparison the 30,000, which is the accepted upward limit of the total of full citizens, 1760 is one fifteenth, or nearly seven per cent. The grounds of inference are here, admittedly, very uncertain, but unless the indications found are altogether misleading, and if the year 459-8 may be taken as typical of *some* even of the ' crowded years,' we see at once how excessive was the drain on the manhood of Athens. But over and above the toll taken year by year through the waste of ordinary war, we read of disasters on a more calamitous scale. The loss in slain at Coronea (447) was especially heavy. In the disaster at Drabescus in 465 ten thousand colonists are said to have perished. These were not all Athenians, but, whatever the proportion of citizens of Athens, all were killed. In Egypt in the destruction of the great expedition on the island of Prosopitis by Thucydides' account nearly the whole of that great armament perished ; there were two hundred ships without counting the fifty of the reinforcing squadron, most of which were likewise destroyed, ' a few ' ships only escaping. The crews of two hundred ships, we may remember, amount to 40,000 men. A good many of these would be allied ships, manned by islanders and others, but a large proportion would have been Athenians and the loss to Athens alone must have been, relatively to her population, enormous. Again, at the revolt of Megara in 446 nearly the whole Athenian garrison was slaughtered, and its number must have run into hundreds. We see the tax on Athenian manhood in the half century following Salamis must have been prodigious ; and those who were taken were in great proportion her best. It would not be surprising if the quality of those who were left was deteriorating. Well might Pericles claim that Athens had "sacrificed more lives and endured severer hardships in war than any other Greek city." [1]

But more disastrous than the drain upon her strength in men and their valour was her loss of moral prestige through the insensible transformation into an Athenian 'arché' or 'dominion' of the free confederacy of which she was the chosen head in 478. Then for the part she had played in the repulse of the Mede, Athens was the admired of all Hellas. Jealousy on the part of the Dorian states was indeed already making itself felt. But Sparta had been won to honest admiration and had conceded to Athens the leadership in the continuance of the war in Asia. As for the Ionian and other Asiatic Greeks, there was no limit to their appreciation of the power and valour of Athens, and of the moderation and urbanity of her commanders. Best of all was the inner strength which Athenians felt in themselves as champions of Hellenic freedom. Among the Hellenes ideals counted for much. It was different in 440 B.C. Little by little Athens had not only lost this brilliant popularity, but more and more had incurred odium and ill-will. This had happened, as we have had occasion to remark already, not either wholly through her own fault, nor yet through the fault of her allies, but largely through the inevitable drift of circumstances. Under the given conditions, if the Delian League was to work at all, it was impossible but that offences should come : "for in various ways Athenian leadership was no longer as welcome as it had been." [2] The course of events inevitably roused and fostered Athenian ambitions by forcing them to act arbitrarily in their conduct of the League, if they were to act with any effect at all. This ambitious temper, once stimulated, passed insensibly into high-handed dominance and the habit of command. What Athens had once received at the wish and request of friends who trusted her and desired to shelter in her strength, she now took as claims due to her superior power. She did not forget her duty of safe-

---

[1] Thucydides, ii. 64. 3.   [2] Thucydides, i. 99. 2.

guarding Hellenic interests against Persian aggression, but as the price of this protection she exacted a submission to her orders which bore an ugly likeness to the vassalage from which she prided herself on having delivered the Asiatic Greeks. The jealous Dorian states began to protest, and the lax Ionians and Islanders to whisper among themselves that Athens was herself now the tyrant city and was imposing on Hellenic city-states, which by natural Hellenic right were autonomous, a subjection as dishonouring as any imposed by the barbarians. The last stage was, when Athens, hearing herself so often called ' the tyrant city,' and seeing no way of escape from her existing commitments by any means which would not involve her in disaster, began herself to glory in the title, so that we find Pericles (as interpreted by Thucydides) arguing in the first crisis of the Peloponnesian War : " your hold of your empire is like a tyrant's of his power : men think it was wrong to take it but it is perilous to let it go." [1] If this argument could fairly be put into the mouth of Athens' leading statesman and champion, small wonder if the enemies of Athens had no lack of material for the indictment they framed against her.

The Enemies of Athens.—It is surely, however, something to the credit of Athenian statesmanship that the enemies who were most clamorous against her in the years preceding the outbreak of the Peloponnesian war were not her ' down-trodden ' subjects, Ionians of Miletus or Ephesus, Chalcidians from the Chersonese, or Hellenes from the distant cities of the Black Sea, but Dorians of the Peloponnese, who were not her ' subjects ' at all, but who feared her power. Broadly one might say that all the Dorians of the Peloponnese (Argos, Sparta's sullen rival, only excepted, and perhaps Troezen, Theseus' native place) were Athens' enemies, and in a sense we might say that Sparta was her chief enemy. But Sparta, though ultimately the protagonist on the other side, and always since the Persian war the recognized rival of Athens, was not the bitter enemy of Athens, nor always

[1] Thucydides, ii. 63. 2.

her enemy. The chief enemies of Athens were the Boeotians, Megara and Corinth.

The Boeotians.—The Boeotians, and more particularly the Thebans, were the oldest enemies of Athens, partly just because they were her next neighbours. There was an invasion of Attica by Boeotians in epic times, when Melanthus (of the house of Pylian Nestor) slew the Boeotian leader in single combat.[1] But the more special hostility of Boeotia, or rather of Thebes as head of Boeotia, to Athens dates from the end of the sixth century B.C., a generation before Marathon, when Plataea asked the Athenians for protection against Thebes, and the Athenians marched out and routed the Thebans in battle, thus earning the undying gratitude of Plataea, but the lasting resentment of Thebes. Thebes tried in 506 to pay Athens out, but herself suffered a costly reverse.[2] Enmity to Athens may, in part, account for the conduct of Thebes in the Persian war : hatred of Athens made Thebes the zealous ally of Xerxes and Mardonius. We have seen (above, ch. ii. p. 45 and iii. p. 67) how more recently Athens for a time had won political control of all Boeotia by the victory of Myronides at Oenophyta, and had lost it again through the disastrous overthrow of Coronea. Since Coronea in 447 Boeotia had been free of Athenian influence, but jealousy of the power of Athens and fear of renewed alliance between Athens and the democratic parties in Boeotian cities kept Boeotian animosity alive. Boeotia was not free from political divisions because the oligarchies had been restored and the partisans of democracy were kept under.

The Boeotians were not Dorians, but Aeolians ; and they had migrated, Thucydides relates,[3] from Thessaly. There appears to have been a special antagonism between the Athenian and Boeotian temperament. Boeotia is very different in climate and character from Attica, and this contrast was reflected in Boeotian manners. Hence the reproachful significance which the adjective ' Boeotian ' even now sometimes retains, as meaning, ' rude,'

---

[1] Vol. i. p. 234.   [2] Vol. i. p. 254.   [3] Thucydides, i. 12. 3.

' stolid,' ' rustic.' But if we ever use Boeotian in this sense we should remember that Hesiod, the poet of the *Works and Days*,[1] was a Boeotian, and so was Pindar, and that Thebes produced two of the finest characters in Greek story, Pelopidas and Epaminondas. Throughout the fifth century Thebes figures as the irreconcilable enemy of Athens ; but a day was to come when Thebans and Athenians should stand shield to shield on the field of Chaeronea and go down together in the last fight of free Hellas. But that was long after the dream of Athenian empire had been dissipated.

The Megarians.—Megara, her next neighbour on the other side, was another enemy of early times : for in the seventh century Megara had disputed with Athens the possession of Salamis. The recovery of Salamis by Athens belongs to the story of Solon.[2] A century later for a short time Athens and Megara had been close allies, a union of such importance to Athens that she had gladly built Long Walls to connect Megara with her harbour, Nisaea. But this short-lived love was changed to bitter hate, when in 446 Megara broke this new connection and slew most of her Athenian garrison. The Athenians felt the loss, and the treachery, very keenly ; for Megara controlled the passes, and security on the side of the Isthmus meant so much to her. Her anger ultimately took a form which helped to precipitate the Peloponnesian war. But by the time the war came, and throughout the second half of the fifth century, the most active and malignant of the enemies of Athens was Corinth.

Corinth.—The position of Corinth, planted just within the Isthmus, on the one overland trade route between the interior of the Peloponnese and Northern Greece,[3] and with a port on either sea,[4] was one very favourable for commerce. Above ancient Corinth to the south towered Acrocorinth, a fortress which dwarfs every other acropolis

[1] Vol. i. p. 60 *n*.   [2] Vol. i. pp. 252 and 3.

[3] We saw, vol. i. p. 76 and p. 65, how the trade route from Argolis in epic times passed up by Mycenae through the Tretus Pass.

[4] Cenchreae on the Saronic Gulf, Lechaeum on the Gulf of Corinth.

in Greece—close on 2000 feet high, with fortifications on the top one and a half miles in circuit ; an acropolis one would have thought impregnable, if it had not as a matter of history been so often surrendered. The trade of Corinth at one time extended widely both east and west. Eastward it had been much diminished by the rise of the Athenian empire ; but westward, towards Sicily and Italy, Corinthian trade still flourished. The gulf named after her Corinth naturally regarded as her own home waters. Her colonies, Leucas, Anactorium, Ambracia, Corcyra, Apollonia, Epidamnus, fringed the Ionian Sea. Syracuse in Sicily was a Corinthian colony. Up to the beginning of the fifth century Corinth was the commercial rival of Aegina and good friends with Athens. In 506 when Cleomenes had invaded Attica with a Peloponnesian army for the purpose of driving out Cleisthenes and restoring Isagoras,[1] the Corinthians refused to follow him and were the cause of the break-up of his army. A little later when the Lacedaemonians held a session of their league at Sparta and proposed to restore Hippias as despot of Athens, the Corinthians strongly opposed the plan and frustrated it.[2] And in 487 we find the Corinthians actually helping the Athenians against Aegina by the loan of twenty ships.[3] But after the Persian war the expanding sea power of Athens was a real menace to the commerce and prosperity of Corinth. The trade of Corinth had extended both west and east, and both west and east it had been more extensive than the Athenian. With the new dominance of Athens in the Aegean Corinthian trade naturally dwindled on that side, especially when after 459 there was war between Athens and Corinth. But Athens was not satisfied with the lead in commerce with Asia Minor and the Black Sea. She aspired to commercial expansion westward also, as the whole policy of Pericles shows. Between 459 and 445 we see Athens gradually attaining a position of command on the trade route to Italy and Sicily, which Corinth regarded as peculiarly her sphere. Naupactus,

[1] Vol. i. p. 254.   [2] Herodotus, v. 75 and 92.   [3] Herodotus, vi. 89.

garrisoned by Messenians (ii. p. 23), gave Athens a commanding port at the mouth of the Gulf of Corinth. We have seen her gaining control for a time of Achaea and Troezen. It is not strange that Corinth watched all this with growing anxiety, and that even after the set-back to Athenian ambitions involved in the terms of the Thirty Years' Peace she still looked on Athens with suspicion and resentment. It needed but some new offence to rouse Corinth again to violent hostility. Causes were not long wanting.

Foes of her own Household.—Athens was hated by Thebans and Corinthians and Megarians ; and Sparta was her enemy. It is not true to say that she was also held in detestation by the allied cities and states of the Delian Confederacy, most of whom were subject to the sovereign will of the Athenian democracy. Certain passages in Aristophanes' *Wasps* and *Peace*,[1] and some sharp satire in the anonymous tract on the Athenian Commonwealth [2] would lead us to conclude that abuses in the administration of the empire existed and, in particular, that unscrupulous politicians at Athens were able at times to use the dicastery courts as a means of extortion. The allies had, it appears, grievances which the enemies of Athens could exploit for political purposes.[3] But there is no evidence of any very deep-seated or wide-spread discontent. There was, so far as we have evidence,

[1] Aristophanes, *Wasps*, 288, 9 ; 669-671. *Peace*, 639-647

[2] *The Athenian Polity*, i. 14-18 ; Dakyns, ii. 279-281.

[3] One hardship there undoubtedly was of which a great deal might be made—the necessity the allies were under of serving in distant wars, not against the Persian empire, as required by the constitution of the League, but on any military service into which the democracy of Athens chose to lead them. After 450 this was exclusively against other Greeks, either the Peloponnesian enemies of Athens or rebellious members of their own confederacy. We have no information about the principle on which contingents were furnished, but mention is repeatedly made of allied contingents in the accounts of the larger Athenian expeditions. There is no evidence tending to prove that such service was unwilling ; but in reading of an Athenian disaster, we may well wonder how the allies bore their share of it, when they had not patriotic devotion and a proud imperial spirit to uphold them.

no oppression comparable, for instance, to that which Cicero denounces in his speeches against Verres. Athens had indeed enemies in every one of these subject states and cities, but they were mainly oligarchical minorities who were ever on the watch for an opportunity to seize the reins of power, if they were not already the dominant party, and if they were in power, to break away from the association with the arch-democracy and assert their complete autonomy. In the more notable cases of revolt of which Thucydides gives the full story, it was a faction of the wealthier citizens who made the revolt, not the whole people. So far as we have means of judging, the general body of the people was in sympathy with democratic Athens.[1] These oligarchical factions in the several states of the confederacy were to Athens ' foes of her own household.' Much more so was the oligarchical faction in Athens itself, the faction that opposed the building of the Long Walls and had been ready to betray Athens in 457. In all the dependent cities we may say with assurance that there were enemies of Athens, and also a party, usually a majority of the population, who were friendly to Athens. We shall find the *people* of Mytilene —when Lesbos revolted—as soon as they got arms in their hands insisting on coming to terms with Athens : the revolt of Lesbos had been the work of the oligarchy. In fact, all through the course of the struggle between the Athenian and the Peloponnesian confederacies, it is never a simple issue between Athens and Sparta, or even between Ionian and Dorian. There is a cross division which enters always as a factor in determining the side taken, the division of parties, in every Greek state. It would not, perhaps, be too much to say that this was the strongest factor of all. In every Greek city-state, whether ruled

---

[1] In Thucydides, iii. 47, a speaker in the Athenian Ecclesia is made to say : " At the present time the populace of all the cities is well disposed to you, and either does not join the aristocrats in revolting, or, if forced to do so, is hostile from the beginning to those who stirred up the revolt ; and so, when you go to war, you have the populace of the rebellious city as your allies." (Speech of Diodotus in the Mytilenean debate, Loeb, vol. ii. p. 83.) See also Greenidge, pp. 203 and 204.

democratically or by an oligarchy, there was an opposing faction, always ready to betray their country and join forces with the enemy, if only thereby they could secure the controlling power in their own state. Greek history in the fifth century B.C. cannot be appreciated without taking account of this duality in every state. It was this which principally raised up for Athens enemies in every city of her empire. It was this which caused the Revolt of Samos in 440 B.C.

Samos in Revolt.—Samos is one of the largest Aegean islands. It lies close to the coast of Asia Minor, separated from the mainland only by a narrow strait, and across the narrow strait is Mount Mycalê.[1] Miletus is on the next headland a little further to the south. It was at Samos that the second revolt against Persia had begun. Earlier Samos had been for a short time the seat of a considerable sea-power, which reached its greatest strength under the tyrant Polycrates, shortly before the Persian conquest of Lydia. Samos, as a free member of the Delian Confederacy, retained sufficient naval force to go to war on her own account with Miletus five years after the conclusion of the Thirty Years' Peace, that is in 440. This waging of private war between two members of the League was certainly contrary to the spirit of the Confederacy of Delos, whether or not it transgressed any definite rule or provision. At any rate, when the Milesians got the worst of the fight they lodged a complaint against the action of Samos, and so also did certain Samians who wished to effect a change in their own government. Athens listened to the Milesians and to the Samian malcontents, sent a fleet to Samos, put down the existing government and established a democracy in its place. The leading oligarchs fled to the protection of the Persian satrap Pissuthnes, and with his help levied mercenary forces. With these they returned to Samos and effected a counter-revolution. On the news of this the Athenians sent Pericles with a fleet of sixty ships to Samos. With

---

[1] See ch. i. p. 4 n.

forty-four of these ships (sixteen having been detached to keep watch against the expected appearance of a Phoenician fleet) Pericles intercepted a Samian fleet of seventy ships recalled from Miletus and defeated them. After this battle forty more triremes came from Athens and twenty-five from Chios and Lesbos. The Samians were shut up in their city and Samos was eventually reduced, but not till after the Athenian arms had suffered one serious reverse and many more warships had come to take part in the siege, two squadrons from Athens, one of forty the other of twenty ships, and thirty more ships from Chios and Lesbos. The Athenian defeat took place during Pericles' absence ; for on a report of the approach of the Phoenician fleet he had himself sailed with sixty ships to look for them. Samos surrendered after a siege of nine months. The terms granted to the Samians were that they should dismantle their walls, surrender their fleet, give hostages, and repay by instalments the cost of the war. Byzantium had revolted along with Samos and now also made submission, resuming her former position without other penalty. The part played by the Persian satrap and the Phoenician fleet in this story shows that the danger to Greek independence from Persia was not altogether extinguished.

And now that Samos had lost her perilous independence and her fleet, Chios and Lesbos were the only ' allies ' of Athens left in the confederacy members on an equal footing. We may note, however, that Chian and Lesbian warships took part in the reduction of Samos, and no hint is given in the pages of Thucydides that the service was reluctant.

Causes of the Peloponnesian War.—The conflict between Sparta and Athens which came a few years later must always have a profound human interest. It was a struggle not merely between Sparta and Athens, between a Peloponnesian League and a Delian, or between Dorian and Ionian confederations, but a conflict which shattered the older system of Hellas made up of numberless small autonomous city-states forming a world to themselves ;

warring one with another, gathering into allied groups for temporary ends, but not capable of permanent national union. The Peloponnesian war set seal to the impracticability of the development out of this welter of small autonomous states of an organic whole uniting the free states of Hellas into a true commonwealth of nations. There were too many of them, and separatist interests were too strong. The Delian Confederacy under the headship of Athens for a short time made the contingency seem possible : the Peloponnesian war, by disabling Athens for the national rôle her most far-seeing statesmen had marked out for her, made that impossible, and so paved the way for the conquest of Hellas successively by Macedonia and Rome. The Peloponnesian war, in which this momentous issue was decided, arose, not so much out of the rivalry of Sparta, as out of the enmity of Corinth. Sparta had no quarrel of her own with Athens beyond a jealous regard for her claim to primacy among Hellenic cities and a touchiness about her relation to other Peloponnesian communities. Her policy was conservative and unaggressive, and she was forced into war, as we see from Thucydides' careful narrative, by the importunity of Corinth and a rather reluctant acceptance of her responsibility as head of the Peloponnesian League and the traditional guardian of Dorian autonomy. She did not really care about the liberation of islanders and other Ionian ' trash ' : she hardly even pretended to ; and when the opportunity came blandly handed them back to bondage under the barbarian. But she did care very much about her own position in the Peloponnese and the course of events as between Athens and members of Sparta's own confederacy. Thucydides distinguishes between the causes of the war and the occasion of its outbreak ; and is the first to make this important distinction. The ultimate cause of the Peloponnesian war was Dorian jealousy of the Athenian empire. The immediate cause, or occasion of the outbreak, was the exasperation of Corinth at the intervention of Athens in a quarrel which arose between her and her undutiful colony, Corcyra ; and that was quickly followed by a second collision even more serious.

1. The affair of Epidamnus.—The first specific action leading to this conflict with Corinth was the conclusion by Athens in 433 B.C. of a defensive alliance with Corcyra, the island-state lying off the coast of Epirus which was a colony of Corinth, but at variance with the mother-city. Corcyra is the rich island of Corfu, with a traditional claim to identification with the happy kingdom of the Phaeacians,[1] and still an earthly paradise.   Corcyra was colonized from Corinth in the eighth century B.C. and was early a rebellious daughter.   There was remembrance of a sea-fight between Corcyra and Corinth in 664 B.C. ; Thucydides calls it " the earliest sea-fight of which we know " :   and the hostility between mother-city and colony had continued since.   In 433 the Corcyraeans, who hitherto had prided themselves on their freedom from treaty entanglements, and had played a double game at the time of Xerxes' invasion,[2] were driven to seek an alliance with Athens owing to the disadvantage in which they found themselves in a new war with Corinth : for Corinth had allies who supplemented her strength, whereas in her isolation Corcyra had none.   Corinth and Corcyra were now at strife over Epidamnus (afterwards Dyrr-hacchium and now Durazzo), a colony founded by Corcyra, in which, however, Corinth, as mother-city to Corcyra, had by Hellenic custom also an interest.   Corinth had undergone a humiliating defeat at Epidamnus and was making prodigious efforts to avenge it.   The defeat was in 435.   For two years the Corinthians matured their preparations, building ships and hiring seamen ;   and these preparations were so formidable that the Corcyraeans began to repent of their isolation and sent envoys to

[1] Thucydides, i. 25 4.   See vol. i. ch. vii., esp. p. 145.

[2] When envoys came to Corcyra asking for help against Xerxes, the Corcyraeans spoke them fair and promised assistance.   But when their fleet of 60 ships sailed southward in 481, it was with orders to wait to hear the issue of the conflict by sea before rounding Cape Malea. Herodotus, vii. 168.

Athens begging for an alliance. The Corinthians also sent envoys to oppose this request. The Corcyraeans based their proposals frankly on interest : they needed support themselves, and the Athenians would, they argued, find it to their advantage to have the Corcyraean fleet with them rather than against them in that conflict with Sparta and the Peloponnesians which all men saw to be impending. The Corinthians opposed them on the ground that such an alliance was contrary to the spirit, if not to the letter of the treaty of peace. They reminded the Athenians of services which they claimed to have rendered to Athens in the past, and of one recent service in particular. When Samos revolted and appealed to the Peloponnesian states for assistance, Corinth had opposed in the counsels of the League the proposal to interfere on their behalf. In the end the people of Athens decided to make an alliance with Corcyra, but a *defensive* alliance only.[1] In so doing they were within the letter of the Treaty : for the Treaty left it to the discretion of neutrals to join either alliance, or neither, as they pleased. But considering the state of feeling between Corcyra and Corinth it was certainly provocative and dangerous.

The Corinthian armament sailed none the less against Corcyra. Ten ships had by that time been sent from Athens, with orders not to engage unless the Corinthians were actually sailing against the coast of Corcyra with intention to land. The fleet sent by Corinth numbered 150 ships, 90 only of these being Corinthian. The Corcyraeans mustered 110. The battle which followed was stubbornly contested : on one wing the Corcyraeans were victorious, chased the defeated ships to land and burnt and plundered a Corinthian camp. On the other wing the Corcyraeans were well beaten. But when the Corinthians sought to press their advantage, the small Athenian squadron sailed up and by their appearance and threatening attitude helped the defeated Corcyraean ships to get away. A little later there was a rally of both fleets ; the Corinthians were preparing to renew the

[1] Thucydides, i. 44.

attack when a fresh fleet was sighted coming up from the south-east. They were Athenian ships ; and though there were only twenty of them, the Corinthians, unable to gauge their number, drew off without further fighting. Athenian and Corinthian ships had actually met in hostile encounter, and this was an act of war.

2. The Revolt of Potidaea.—The second proximate cause of war arose out of the first. If Corinth and Athens were not yet openly at war, acts of war had taken place between them. The Corinthians were angry, and anxious to pay Athens back for this, as they held, gratuitous interference in their private quarrel with Corcyra. Now, Corinth had one colony on the other side of Greece, in the Aegean, Potidaea, planted just at the neck of the peninsula of Pallenê, with a harbour on each of two seas like Corinth herself. And at the same time Potidaea was a member of the Delian Confederacy, paying her quota into the Athenian treasury like other members and taking orders, on occasion, from Athens. On the other hand, as a colony of Corinth, Potidaea, this relation to Athens notwithstanding, received yearly by ancient prescription two officials, whose authority perhaps was ceremonial only, but who were Corinthian citizens. Up to this date the Athenians had raised no objection to this time-honoured custom ; but now they not unnaturally became anxious about the loyalty of the Potidaeans to the League. Potidaea had a good record for war service. When besieged by Artabazus after Salamis she had repulsed the Persian attack, and had sent a force of three hundred hoplites to fight at Plataea.[1] There was now fear that out of sympathy with Corinth, their mother-city, the Potidaeans might revolt and set in motion a general rising among ' Thrace-ward cities.' Affairs were already critical in that region owing to the recent hostility of Perdiccas, son of Alexander, king of the Macedonians, who was trying to make trouble for Athens. In these circumstances the Athenian people took strong measures. They sent a demand that the Potidaeans should demolish the wall which protected their

[1] See vol. i. p. 310 *n*, and p. 362.

city on the side of the peninsula of Pallene, give hostages for good behaviour, send away the magistrates from Corinth, and for the future decline to receive them. In vain the Potidaeans strove to avert the blow by negotiation. The Ecclesia refused to reconsider their demand. It is possible they had already certain intelligence of a treasonable understanding between the Potidaeans and Perdiccas. And when the Potidaeans failed to comply with these demands the Athenians sent a squadron of warships to enforce their order. Thereupon the Potidaeans entered into alliance with other cities of Chalcidicê who were nursing grievances against Athens, and revolted. This was in 432. As soon as the revolt became known at Corinth, Aristeus, son of Adeimantus, one of the citizens of most distinction there, who had close ties with Potidaea, called for volunteers, and with a force of 1600 hoplites and 400 light-armed men sailed with all speed to Potidaea to reinforce the garrison. A fleet of forty ships with 2000 hoplites arrived in the Thermaic Gulf soon after from Athens and proceeded first to act along with a force of a thousand hoplites and thirty ships which had been previously sent against Perdiccas. In a short time these forces had brought Perdiccas to terms, then they turned their attention to Potidaea. There was a battle just outside the isthmus on which the city stood : Aristeus the Corinthian, after some initial success, was defeated, the Potidaeans were chased within their walls and the siege of Potidaea began. Soon after the Athenians were further reinforced, and built walls on either side of the isthmus from sea to sea, thus completely blockading Potidaea. When this happened Aristeus escaped by sea to the mainland with the purpose of raising war there, and so helping Potidaea more effectually than by remaining cooped up within the town.[1]

The Question of Peace or War.—Both parties had now a new grievance : " the Corinthians being aggrieved because the Athenians were besieging Potidaea, a colony

[1] Potidaea held out for over two years and was then (in 430) forced by starvation to surrender on terms.

of theirs with men in it from Corinth and the Peloponnesus; the Athenians, because the Peloponnesians had brought about the revolt of a city that was an ally and tributary of theirs, and then had come and openly fought with the Potidaeans against themselves."[1]   The Corinthians forthwith set to work to stir the Peloponnesian League to action.   For this purpose they sent envoys to Lacedaemon to denounce the conduct of the Athenians as a breach of the Thirty Years' Peace and to demand war.   They were seconded by emissaries from Aegina who came secretly, since as subjects of Athens they dared not come openly. The complaint of the Aeginetans was that the clause in the treaty which assured their autonomy remained a dead letter.   After this the Spartans issued a summons to all the members of their league who considered themselves wronged by Athens.   A number of delegates arrived and were called to a meeting of the Spartan assembly, the *Apella*,[2] and bidden to lay their grievances before it. The most prominent of the accusers were the Megarians and the Corinthians.   The Megarians had a sheaf of complaints to make, but that which they pressed most was that by a recent decree of the Athenian Ecclesia they were shut out of all the ports within the Athenian Confederacy, and thereby reduced to the utmost straits for the very necessaries of life.   But the most virulent attack was that of the Corinthians, who did not spare Sparta herself, charging her with slack leadership and neglect of the just interests of her allies.   When the Corinthians had finished their vehement harangue, some Athenian ambassadors, who happened to be in Sparta on other business and present at this meeting of the Apella, asked leave to speak ; and leave was given.   Thucydides has represented at full length in his history [3] the arguments of both Corinthians and Athenians, and these speeches help greatly to an understanding of the conflicting interests and passions which led to the Peloponnesian War.   When all the complaints and the reply of the Athenian envoys

---

[1] Thucydides, i. 66. 1.   Loeb, pp. 107 and 109.
[2] See vol. i. p. 226.   [3] Thucydides, i. 68-78.

had been heard the speakers were required to withdraw
and the Apella proceeded to debate the momentous
alternative of peace or war. One voice was raised for
peace, or at least for patience and moderation and the
exhaustion of every pacific means of getting redress before
plunging into a war of which the limits could not be
foreseen. This was the voice of Archidamus the king,
now well advanced in years, he who as a young man had
saved Sparta at the time of the earthquake by rallying
the Spartans before the revolting helots swooped down.[1]
He was swayed partly by a clearer discernment of the
strength of the Athenian empire and the difficulty for the
Peloponnesians of assailing it without a navy more fit
to cope with the Athenian, and without money to provide
the sinews of war ; partly by an uneasy feeling that the
Athenian offer to submit the questions in dispute to
arbitration was just and ought to be accepted. But the
temper of the Apella as a whole was bellicose, and, after
Archidamus, the Ephor Sthenelaidas made a brief harangue
in the approved 'laconic' style, meeting Archidamus'
arguments and bluntly recommending war. Then a vote
was taken. The method of the Spartan *Apella* was the
method of the English *folk-moot*—'acclamation.' When
the 'Ayes' and the 'Noes' rang out, Sthenelaidas, who
was presiding, took the unusual course of 'dividing' the
assembly. "Whoever of you, Lacedaemonians," he said,
"thinks that the treaty has been broken and the Athenians
are doing wrong, let him rise and go to yonder spot, and
whoever thinks otherwise, to the other side." [2] There
was a large majority who voted that the treaty had been
broken. And after this vote had been taken the allies'
representatives were called in. They were told that by a
vote of the Apella the Athenians were adjudged to have
broken the treaty, and that it was the intention of the
Spartans to call a full meeting of the Peloponnesian
Confederacy in order that the decision for war, if judged
necessary, might be taken with all formality and after due

[1] See above, ch. ii. p. 36 *n*.
[2] Thucydides, i. 87. 2.   Loeb, i. p. 147.

deliberation. A full conference of the Peloponnesian
League was accordingly held later in the same year (432).
The Corinthians were again the most vehement advocates
of war. They canvassed the delegates beforehand to
vote for war, and they urged war upon the conference in a
carefully argued speech. A vote was taken of all the
states represented at the conference, small and great
voting on equal terms, and the majority voted for war.[1]

Diplomatic Fencing.—There was still an interval before
the actual outbreak of hostilities. The Athenians had
no wish to begin—they were on the defensive ; the
Peloponnesians, who had willed the war, were not ready.
In this interval the Spartan government was busy devising
pretexts to give a plausible colour to their declaration
of war. They first sent heralds bidding the Athenians
drive out of their midst " the curse of the goddess."
This was going back to the old story of Cylon's conspiracy [2] and the violation of sanctuary, the guilt of which
was fastened on the House of Alcmaeon—for Pericles
was an Alcmaeonid on the mother's side. The Athenians
retorted with a demand that the Lacedaemonians should
drive out ' the curse of Taenarus ' and ' the curse of
Athena of the Brazen House.' For the Lacedaemonians
also had their tales of sacrilege. The sacrilege of the
Brazen House was the violation of sanctuary attending the
death of Pausanias, the victor at Plataea : [3] the sin of
Taenarus was the violation of sanctuary perpetrated in
putting to death certain helots who had revolted and fled
for refuge to the temple of Poseidon. Nothing, of course,
came of this interchange of religious pretexts, which was
merely vexatious. Then the Lacedaemonians made their
real demands : (1) that the Athenians should raise the
siege of Potidaea ; (2) restore to Aegina her promised
' autonomy ' ; (3) rescind the decree against the Megarians.
Later they gave the Athenians to understand that war
might be avoided if only they would withdraw their decree against the Megarians. To all these demands the

---

[1] Thucydides, i. 119-125.   [2] Vol. I. p. 241.   [3] Ch. i. p. 11 *n.*

Athenians, acting under the advice of Pericles, returned a steady refusal. At last came an ultimatum quite differently worded : " The Lacedaemonians desire peace, and there will be peace, if you give the Hellenes their independence." [1] The Athenians replied once more, as Pericles counselled, that they would yield nothing to dictation, but, as they had said all along, were ready, in accordance with the treaty, to submit disputes to arbitration.

The Attempt on Plataea.—War was now all but inevitable ; but there was not yet a state of open war : " the two parties continued to have intercourse with one another during these recriminations and visited each other without heralds, though not without suspicion ; for the events which were taking place constituted an annulment of the treaty and furnished an occasion for war." [2] The actual outbreak of hostilities happened in a dramatic and unexpected way. Early in the spring of 431 a body of men-at-arms, 300 in number, set out by night from Thebes and marched to Plataea. Arrived beneath the town walls they obtained entrance through the treachery of a party in Plataea friendly to Thebes and oligarchy, who opened one of the gates. They marched through the darkness to the market-place quietly and unopposed, and there grounded arms. Then they made proclamation by herald, inviting the Plataeans to embrace alliance with Thebes like the other Boeotians ; and they took this course trusting that conciliation would be effective, but contrary to the advice of the faction leaders at whose invitation they came : these wanted to hunt out their enemies one by one and slay them. The Plataeans, taken completely by surprise—for they had gone to rest in seeming security—were at first inclined to accept the offer of the proclamation. But while negotiations were proceeding, they became aware how small the number of the invaders really was. They took counsel together again and recovering their confidence made dispositions

---

[1] Thucydides, i. 139. 3.   [2] Thucydides, i. 146 ; Loeb, i. p. 255.

for attack. To communicate more easily and collect
together without attracting the enemy's attention, they
broke a passage through from house to house. Then
near the first dawn, but while it was still quite dark,
they suddenly made their onset. The Thebans, though
taken by surprise, closed their ranks and beat back the
first attacks. But the Plataeans came on in increasing
numbers and a shower of missiles rained down from
above : for women and slaves came out on the roofs
of the houses and with yells and screams began hurling
down stones. The noise and uproar was bewildering, and
to add to the difficulties of the Thebans a heavy storm
of rain came on, beating in their faces and turning the
road into mud. Seized with sudden panic they now gave
way, and soon were being chased through the dark
streets vainly seeking for means to escape. Some were
struck down fighting ; some were pursued into corners
and done to death ; some in desperation scaled the city
wall and leapt down, only in most cases to perish. But a
considerable number kept together and rushing along
saw before them open doors, which the foremost took to
be the gates of the city. They were really the doors of a
large building near the wall, which happened to be open :
the doors closed upon them and they were trapped.
There was then debate among the pursuing Plataeans
whether to set light to the building, or what to do. In
the end these, and any other Thebans who still lived, were
allowed to surrender at discretion.[1]

Morning was now at hand, and with morning light came
a larger body of Thebans, who ought to have arrived in
support during the night, but had been delayed at the
crossing of the Asopus owing to the heavy rain. On
learning what had happened in the night, they were
proposing to take prisoner all the Plataeans they could
catch without the city and hold them as hostages for the
lives of their own Thebans captured in Plataea. The
Plataeans, in alarm for their fellow-townsmen and for their
property without the walls, opened negotiations with the

[1] Thucydides, ii. chs. 2-4.

new arrivals ; an agreement was reached, as a result of which the Thebans marched away at once without doing any damage. The Theban story—and the probabilities support it—was that they agreed to withdraw without doing any harm to property or person, on condition that their Theban comrades, prisoners in Plataea, were restored whole and sound, and that the promise given by the Plataeans was sealed with an oath. The Plataeans, in their version of what took place, contradicted this story in the crucial particulars of the promise and the oath. Be that as it may, what happened was that as soon as the Theban forces were gone, the Plataeans in all haste removed their property from the country into the city —and then put their prisoners to death. Scarcely had this rash and bloody deed been done, when a herald arrived from Athens with an urgent message charging them to do nothing about the prisoners without a reference to Athens.[1]

Revenge is sweet ; the Plataeans had their revenge ; but they were to pay dearly for it in the end.

War.—After these doings at Plataea, which involved both Thebes and Plataea in guilt—the imminence of war could no longer be in doubt. Both sides pushed forward their preparations to the utmost, collecting money, building ships, urging their allies to zealous assistance. A Peloponnesian army, two-thirds of the fighting forces of each community, assembled at the Isthmus, ready to invade Attica. But Archidamus, who, as king of Sparta, was in command, first sent a Spartan named Melesippus, in hope that even now fresh negotiations might be opened. The Athenians sent him back without a hearing, and with a warning to cross the frontier before sunset. On reaching the frontier Melesippus is reported to have exclaimed, " This day will be the beginning of woe for the Hellenes."[2]

[1] Thucydides, ii. chs. 5 and 6.

[2] Thucydides, ii. 12. 3.

CHAPTER VI

THE LOST OPPORTUNITY

" For mercy is the highest reach of wit,
　A safety unto them that save with it."
　　　　Fulke Greville, Lord Brooke, *Mustapha.*

"The last thing war does is to proceed according to rule."
　　　　　　Thucydides, i. 122.

Ruined Homes.—The war so long dreaded, and by many
deemed inevitable, had come ; and once more Athenian
country gentlemen and peasant farmers left their pleasant
farms and homesteads and the life amid fields and vineyards that they loved, as they had done fifty years
before at the coming of the Mede.　This time, however,
it was not to take refuge overseas, but to crowd within
the circuit of the walls of Athens and its harbour-town ;
and the enemy was not the Great King and his myriads,
who had come to subdue Hellas, but their own kinsfolk
from the Peloponnesus, led by the Spartans, in close
amity with whom Athens had faced the perils of that
earlier time.　Archidamus and his host came on slowly.
Archidamus was a Hellene at heart, conscious of the enormity of the fratricidal struggle which was beginning, and
he clung to the hope that the Athenians would even now
make some concession to save their beloved fields from
ravage.　He first spent some time (his Peloponnesian
critics said ' wasted ') in an attempt to carry by assault
the strong border fortress, Oenoe.　When all efforts
proved abortive and no herald came from Athens to
negotiate, he gave orders for an advance into the Thriasian

plain which lies westward of Mount Aegaleos between
Eleusis and Mount Parnes ; and the whole army sat down
to systematic destruction.   Then he advanced to Acharnae
(now Menidhi), a township only seven miles from Athens,
and again paused before giving orders for the havoc to
begin.   For Acharnae was a populous place : it furnished
three thousand hoplites to the city's forces ; and Acharnae
was almost in sight of the city walls.   The men of
Acharnae were noted for their fiery courage : the sight of
their homes and crops burning before their eyes must
surely be more than flesh and blood could stand.   And
since the hope of accommodation had failed, Archidamus'
aim was, if possible, to bring on an engagement in which
the superior strength of the Peloponnesian militia must
necessarily tell.   His expectations were well enough
founded.   Thucydides gives a vivid description of the
excitement of the fighting men cooped within the walls
of Athens.   " When they saw the army in the neighbourhood of Acharnae," he writes, " and barely seven miles
from the city, they felt the presence of the invader to be
intolerable.   The devastation of their country before their
eyes, which the younger men had never seen at all, nor
the elder except in the Persian invasion, naturally
appeared to them a horrible thing, and the whole people,
the young men especially, were anxious to go forth and
put a stop to it.   Knots were formed in the streets, and
there were loud disputes, some eager to go out, a minority
resisting. . . .   The excitement in the city was universal,
the people were furious with Pericles, and, forgetting all
his previous warnings, they abused him for not leading
them to battle, as their general should, and laid all their
miseries to his charge." [1]   Then more than ever Pericles'
strength of mind and purpose shone conspicuous, and his
wonderful hold on the Athenian demos.   He stood
firm, and even used his position as *Strategos* to prevent
any meeting of the ecclesia being held, lest the people
" coming together more in anger than in prudence, might
take some false step."   As a slight outlet for pent-up

[1] Thucydides, ii. 21 ; Jowett, 2nd ed. (1900), vol. i. p. 118.

emotions, he sent out bodies of the Athenian horse (knights) to check plundering near the city, and did what else he could to allay the popular anger. A measure on a more effectual scale was the despatch of a hundred ships-of-war, with 1000 hoplites and 400 archers aboard, to carry out round the coasts of Peloponnese reprisals for the ravaging of Attica. And when the summer was over and the invaders had withdrawn, Pericles himself as general, led out the whole of the city's forces, citizens and settlers alike, joined with the crews of the hundred ships returned from the Peloponnesus into the territory of Megara, and there they burned and harried and destroyed everything they could see, and sated their fierce anger for the injuries they had themselves suffered. And so they did year after year while the war lasted.

A Crowded City.—Thanks to the slow advance of Archidamus the Athenians had time to get their families and movable property into safety. Their families and household goods (and even, Thucydides relates, " the woodwork of their houses ") were brought into the city ; their flocks and cattle and beasts of burden they transported into Euboea and other islands. But when these immigrants arrived within the protecting walls their position, as may be imagined, was one of intense discomfort. Only the few had houses of their own, or relatives and friends with whom they might live. The great mass of them had to find makeshift shelter, in any ground there might be not built over, in the turrets of the walls, in temple precincts, under the shelter of the Long Walls, wherever and however they could. The inconveniences of such accommodation were very great. On a sudden, without any adequate provision or preparation, the population of the city was doubled. It was an appalling state of things. And the distress was all the greater because most of the refugees were utterly unused to city life, and would have detested it even under favourable conditions : " for the Athenians," Thucydides tells us, " had most of them been always accustomed to reside in the country. This mode of life had been characteristic of them more than of any other of the Hellenes, from very early times." [1] The Synoecia, the union of the townships of Attica in Athens, had made little difference to the people in this regard. Though united in a single city, " they and their descendants, down to the time of this war, from old habit generally resided with their households in the country where they had been born. For this reason, and also because they had recently restored their country houses and estates after the Persian War, they had a disinclination to move. They were depressed at the thought of forsaking their homes and the temples which had come down to them from their fathers and were the abiding memorials of their early constitution. They were going to change their manner of life, and in leaving their villages were in fact each of them going into exile." [2]

Plague.—Next year the Peloponnesian army again invaded Attica, carrying their ravages not only over the plains as in the preceding year, but also passing down the whole length of the peninsula to Laurium and its silver mines, laying waste first one side of Paralia and then the other. But this year, hard on the heels of invasion came a more dreadful visitant—Plague. Plague !—many Englishmen in the last twenty-five years have made acquaintance with plague in India. But when plague broke out in India in 1897—as in the previous great visitations famous in history, the Plague of London, the Plague of Florence, the Black Death—the best way of combating plague was to flee before it : for the unstricken to take to the open country or to some hill refuge ; and to segregate the stricken areas and let no one come forth from them or enter in. In the Plague of Athens a whole population, 300,000 human beings or more, were from the first shut in within the walls of their fortified city. There was no escape to the open country, there was no possibility of segregation. The whole city was one colossal segregation camp, hideously overcrowded. This was the

[1] Thucydides, ii. 14 and 15.
[2] Thucydides, ii. 16 ; Jowett, vol. i. p. 115.

supreme horror of the Plague of Athens, making it like no other plague : no one could escape from it ; there was no getting away from Athens. Thucydides has described the plague at Athens, how it came about, what the symptoms were and how fatal was its usual course ; what numbers perished and what horrible demoralization resulted. All this is to be read in the pages of his history, and it is not pretty reading ; but his clear and precise descriptions of the disease and its course [1] have been useful to modern physicians when called upon to face similar terrors. Thucydides himself suffered and recovered. The mortality in the city was so dire that the Peloponnesians at last hastened their withdrawal ; but their occupation of the country this year continued forty days, a longer time than any other invasion during the war. There was one exception to the impossibility of getting out of Athens. It was possible to send troops away on service, and in the midst of the invasion Pericles despatched one hundred ships with 4000 hoplites on board and 300 horsemen. And this year the fleet acted with more vigour, making descents on the territory of Epidaurus, Troezen, Halieis, Hermionê, and capturing and plundering Prasiae in Laconia.

This plague was an incident of warfare outside Pericles' reckoning, and it did more damage to the power of Athens than many invasions, not only, or so much, because of the calamitous loss of life, but most because of the demoralization. Athens was never quite the same again.

The Death of Pericles.—A little later Pericles died, while the clouds of misfortune still hung over Athens, yet with his own faith in the soundness of his policy undiminished. For a time the sufferings of the people had overborne their better judgment : they had brought Pericles to trial and subjected him to a fine. Then in a short while they repented of their anger and made him again their Strategos ; and it was in this high office

[1] Thucydides, ii. 47-53.

that Pericles died.   Thucydides pays eloquent tribute to
his wisdom and integrity as a statesman : " For so long
as he presided over the affairs of the state in time of
peace he pursued a moderate policy and kept the city in
safety, and it was under him that Athens reached the
height of her greatness ; and, after the war began, here
too he appears to have made a far-sighted estimate of
her strength.   Pericles lived two years and six months
beyond the beginning of the war ; and after his death
his foresight as to the war was still more fully recognized." [1]
And he goes on to point out why Pericles' influence kept
the Athenian people from mistakes which later proved
fatal.   " And the reason for this was," he says, " that
Pericles, who owed his influence to his recognized standing
and ability, and had proved himself clearly incorruptible
in the highest degree, restrained the multitude while
respecting their liberties, and led them rather than was
led by them, because he did not resort to flattery, seeking
power by dishonest means, but was able on the strength
of his high reputation to oppose them and even provoke
their wrath.   At any rate, whenever he saw them un-
warrantably confident and arrogant, his words would cow
them into fear ; and, on the other hand, when he saw
them unreasonably afraid, he would restore them to
confidence again.   And so Athens, though in name a
democracy, gradually became in fact a government ruled
by its foremost citizen." [2]

A Lesson in Sea Power.—In this year 429 a remarkable
demonstration was given to both contending parties of
Athenian naval superiority.   The Athenian admiral,
Phormio, with twenty ships brought to battle a fleet of
forty-seven enemy ships and defeated them severely.   When
the Peloponnesian fleet was raised by reinforcements
to seventy-seven ships, Phormio achieved the feat of
engaging the whole seventy-seven and again beating them.
It came about in this way.   Phormio with his squadron was

[1] Thucydides, 65. 5 and 6 ; Loeb, p. 375.
[2] Thucydides, ii. 65. 8 and 9 ; Loeb, p. 377.

stationed at Naupactus,[1] and it was his business to watch over the entrance to the Gulf of Corinth, so that ships of the Peloponnesian League might not pass in or out without molestation. This was important because of the trade with Sicily, in which Corinth had a large share. It happened that at this time the Peloponnesians, at the instigation of the Ambraciots, were attempting to reduce

THE GULF OF CORINTH.

Acarnania, the firm ally and friend of Athens in western Hellas. Their fleet was to assemble at Leucas; and to get there, the contingent from Corinth and other towns within the Gulf must needs pass Naupactus and Phormio's twenty ships: Naupactus is on the north shore of the Gulf. Phormio knew of the sailing of this contingent, and waited for them outside the entrance straits: for

[1] Naupactus is *Lepanto* in the Middle Ages; and besides being the scene of Phormio's victories the mouth of the Gulf of Corinth was to be the scene of the Battle of Lepanto in 1571 A.D. when the Venetians and Spaniards broke the naval power of the Turks.

he relied upon his trained crews and their skill in manoeuvring. The tactics of the Athenian navy had changed
since Salamis. Athenian seamen, with their regular
training year after year, now trusted to their speed and
to the clever handling of their ships. The object of the
captain of an Athenian warship was by a sudden turn to
strike an enemy ship in the side, and either sink her by
ramming, or disable her by breaking off the oars. This
manoeuvre required plenty of sea room, and Athenian
naval strategy was therefore now just the reverse of
Themistocles' before Salamis; that is, it was to avoid
straits and fight always in the open sea. Now, the Corinthian squadron did not want to fight at all, but to get
out of the gulf and join the rest of their fleet : and they
did not think that Phormio with so great an inferiority
of numbers would attack them. So they first tried
sailing close along the coast of Achaea and slipping out
unnoticed. When they found that Phormio had seen
them, and that his ships were moving parallel with them
along the opposite coast, and further, that when they
turned north-westward and steered across the open gulf
for Leucas, the enemy followed, they realized that a
battle was inevitable. Upon this they drew together
in the formation known as the globe, their light craft
in the centre and the warships in a circle round them,
with their prows pointing outward. Phormio's ships
came on in single file, one behind another, and circled
round the ' globe,' [1] threatening every moment to ram, but
never quite driving the charge home. In this way they
gradually forced the mass into a smaller space, so that the
ships jostled each other and began to lose their formation.
Phormio's men had orders to look to his signal before
charging : for he was waiting for the morning breeze to
spring up, which he knew would add to the difficulties
of the enemy. Round and round the ships of Phormio
circled, never giving the enemy a chance because his
ships were the slower. Thucydides' description of the
sequel is too good to miss : " When presently the breeze

[1] See vol. i. p. 319.

began to blow, the ships which were already too close
together soon began to be in difficulties, partly through
the force of the wind, partly through the small craft
getting in their way. Ships ran against each other and
were fended off by poles ; what with shouts and cries
of ' keep away ' and abuse the crews could not hear a
word of their orders, nor the boatswain's voice giving
the time ; while the failure of their untrained rowers
to clear the water in the heavy sea made the vessels
unmanageable. This was the moment which Phormio
was waiting for ; he gave the signal and the Athenians
thereupon charged home. First they sank one of the
admirals' ships, then proceeded to disable the rest, where-
ever they were found, and so disordered them that no
ship offered resistance any longer, but all fled to Patrae
and Dyme in Achaia. " [1] The total Peloponnesian loss
in this fight is not given ; but in the pursuit the
Athenians, we are told, captured twelve ships, crews
and all.

The authorities at Sparta were very angry. They
could not believe that the Athenian superiority at sea was
so great, and put down this signal defeat to want of a
resolute spirit in their own fleet. Accordingly they sent
out a board of three officers as ' advisers ' to Cnemus who
was in command of the Acarnanian expedition, with
peremptory orders to fight again and win. Great efforts
were made to collect more ships, with the result that in a
short time a Peloponnesian fleet of seventy-seven ships
was waiting at Rhium on the Achaean coast, just within
the straits, while Phormio, still commanding only the
twenty ships with which he had won his victory (for
reinforcements despatched from Athens at his request
had not arrived), was watching on the opposite coast
from a position just outside. To understand what
followed, it is necessary to get a clear idea of the relative
position of the two fleets to the mouth of the Gulf of
Corinth and to Naupactus. The straits by which the
Gulf of Corinth is entered from the west are not much

[1] Thucydides, ii. 84. 3.

more than a mile wide at their narrowest,[1] which is between
two headlands both known to Thucydides as Rhium,
and distinguished, that on the southern coast as the
Achaean Rhium, that on the northern as the Molycrian
Rhium (also known later as Anti-rhium). Naupactus
is on the northern coast, six miles further within the
straits. Phormio's object was to keep out in the more
open water and fight there as in the first engagement.
The Peloponnesians wished to avoid fighting in the open
water. For six days the opponents watched each other,
the Athenians declining to enter the narrow waters, the
Peloponnesians fearing to trust themselves outside.
Then Cnemus tried a new move. He ordered his fleet to
put to sea and sail—not westward out into the open sea,
but north-eastward within the straits along the Achaean
coast. Now this was the direction of Naupactus, and
seeing this Phormio in all haste also put to sea and began
sailing along the opposite side of the straits to cover
Naupactus. This was the opportunity Cnemus wanted.
His fleet was proceeding in column four abreast, with the
twenty fastest-sailing ships leading. Suddenly on a
given signal the whole fleet turned and in four lines bore
down on the Athenian line in single file on the opposite
shore, every ship rowing at topmost speed : for in this
way they hoped to cut off the whole Athenian fleet in
the narrow waters. This manoeuvre was almost completely successful : but not quite. The eleven leading
Athenian ships by an effort of speed just rowed clear of
the advancing right wing of the enemy, and got into the
wider waters further within the straits ; the remaining
nine were intercepted, forced ashore, and disabled.
Some of the seamen swam to land, some were killed.
The empty hulls were mostly saved by Messenian soldiers
who had been marching parallel with the fleet along the
shore, and who fought the Peloponnesians off them, as
they were actually being towed away. Meantime the
twenty fast-sailing Peloponnesians on the right wing

[1] A mile and a half wide now ; but Thucydides makes it rather less
than one mile.

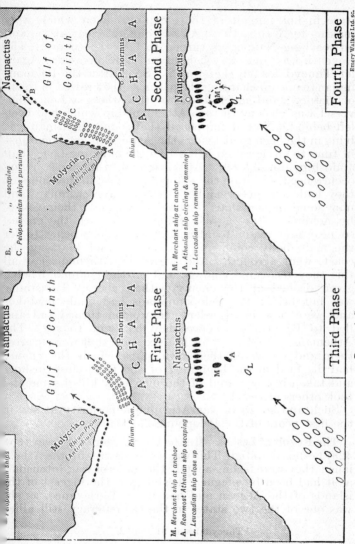

PHORMIO'S SECOND SEA-FIGHT IN 429 B.C.

were in hot pursuit of the escaping eleven which were making for Naupactus. All but one got clear away, and on reaching Naupactus turned to face the enemy. The eleventh was some way behind and hard pressed. Again let Thucydides tell the story : " Soon after the Peloponnesians came up chanting the paean as they rowed in token of victory ; and much ahead of the others a Leucadian vessel was chasing the one Athenian ship which had been left behind. Now it happened that a merchantman was lying in the open roadstead : the Attic ship got home just in time to circle round her, strike the pursuing Leucadian amidships and sink her. At this unlooked-for and startling occurrence fear fell on the Peloponnesians : in their pursuit they had kept no order because they were winning, and now some of the ships' companies checked their course by holding water—a rash thing to do with the enemy so near and ready to attack—their object being to let the main body come up ; and others not knowing the coast, went aground. And when the Athenians saw all this they recovered courage and on the command being given dashed at the enemy with a cheer. Resistance was but brief : the Peloponnesians had made mistakes and were now in disorder : they soon turned tail and fled to Panormus, whence they had put to sea. The Athenians gave chase, took the six ships that were nearest them and recovered their own ships which the enemy had disabled in the beginning of the fight close inshore and taken in tow ; and of the men they killed some and took others alive." [1]

Such and so great was Athenian superiority at sea in the first years of the Peloponnesian War.

The Revolt of Lesbos.—In the fourth year of the war (B.C 428) Lesbos revolted. This was a sore matter for the Athenians : they were feeling acutely the stress of war, intensified as it had been by plague : Lesbos was the biggest of the islands of the Aegean and had no real grievance, as she was one of the two states in the Confederacy still allied

[1] Thucydides, ii. 91 and 92.

to Athens on equal terms. So unwelcome was the information that the people of Mytilenê, the chief city of the Lesbians, were planning this revolt, that at first the Athenians refused to believe it : when there was no longer room for doubt, they acted promptly. A fleet of forty warships was despatched, in some expectation of taking the Mytilenaeans by surprise. But the Mytilenaeans got warning of this in time to put the fortifications they were repairing into a rough state of order, and they met the demand of the Athenians for complete submission—which meant that they must surrender their fleet and pull down their city walls—with a refusal. But they were really ill prepared for resistance and, on the failure of a feeble attempt at facing the Athenian fleet at sea, they had recourse again to negotiations. A truce was made while envoys went to plead their cause at Athens. Nothing, however, was effected, and hostilities were resumed. The Mytilenaeans made a sortie and held their own in an attack on the Athenian camp : but they retired again within their walls. On the other hand the Athenian forces were not strong enough to occupy the country effectively. All they could do was to hold positions in strength on either side of the town and shut the Mytilenaeans from the sea. On land the Mytilenaeans controlled the open country and even made an attack on the town of Methymna which had remained true to the Athenian alliance. But the real hope of the Mytilenaeans was in the coming of help from the Peloponnese. They had intrigued for Spartan aid even before the war, and at once on the arrival of the Athenian fleet, before a complete blockade was established, a ship had stolen out to ask help from Lacedaemon. By direction of the Spartan government the Mytilenaean envoys laid their request before the assembled Greeks at the Olympic Games which were being held that year) and the decision was to help them. Attica, it was arranged, should be invaded a second time ; ships be carried across the isthmus on rollers for a simultaneous naval attack on Athens from the sea. This danger stirred the men of Athens to a special effort.

They manned another hundred ships with volunteer crews of citizens and foreign residents, to show they were strong enough to meet the crisis without withdrawing a single ship from Mytilenê. This display of power disconcerted the Spartan plans and had a decisive influence on the ultimate fate of Mytilenê. A Peloponnesian squadron of forty ships did at last sail for Lesbos, but so tardily and cautiously that the fate of the city was settled before it arrived. For a time the Mytilenaeans kept command of the land, but in the autumn the Athenians despatched, under command of Paches as general, a thousand more hoplites, who themselves rowed the ships out to Lesbos. On the arrival of this fresh force the Mytilenaeans were driven within their walls and lines of investment were completed, so that by the time winter set in Mytilenê was close shut in by land and sea. At this critical moment a Lacedaemonian named Salaethus crossed to Lesbos and managed to make his way into the beleaguered city, bringing assurance of the invasion of Attica and of the coming of a relieving fleet from the Peloponnese. The invasion of Attica duly took place next spring and was peculiarly rigorous. "They destroyed," says Thucydides, "any new life that had sprung up in the parts of Attica that had been devastated before, and all that had escaped ravage in previous invasions." [1] Yet this helped Mytilenê very little. For no fleet came from the Peloponnesus and supplies were failing. In this extremity Salaethus attempted a remedy which proved fatal. He called to arms the body of the people. His object, of course, was to strengthen the defence ; but the effect was opposite. For the mass of the people, the demos, were friendly to the Athenian democracy ; and now they had arms in their hands they demanded that the government should bring out corn for distribution, threatening that if this were not done they would make terms with the Athenians and surrender the city. Upon this those in power, in a panic, themselves made an agreement with Paches. For they knew their

[1] Thucydides, iii. 26. 3.

position would be desperate if an agreement was concluded and they, the leaders of revolt, had no part in it.
The agreement was that they should yield themselves at
the discretion of the Athenian people. They were to
open their gates to the Athenian forces and send envoys
to Athens ; and until the envoys returned and declared
the will of the Athenian people none of the Mytilenaeans
should receive any hurt either by imprisonment, enslavement or death. On these terms the Athenians entered
Mytilenê. But all who had taken an active part in
bringing about the revolt were now in great fear, and
many took sanctuary at the altars. These Paches,
without using force, removed to Tenedos, and subsequently
to Athens, along with Salaethus who had been found
in hiding and made prisoner, and all others whom Paches
thought to be implicated in the guilt of the revolt.
Salaethus the Athenians put to death immediately, and
then it was for the Ecclesia to settle the fate of the rest
of Mytilenê. The Athenians were in no mood for clemency : they were angry and they had reason to be angry,
for they had suffered grievously through the revolt of
Lesbos. Their anger found vent in a decree which they
themselves next day saw to be monstrous : they decreed
that all adult males in Mytilenê (not only those sent by
Paches for trial) should be put to death ; the women and
children sold as slaves. A trireme was despatched
forthwith to Lesbos to convey orders to this effect to
Paches. But night brought reflection to the better-
minded ; and next day " a feeling of repentance came
over them and they began to reflect that the design they
had formed was cruel and monstrous, to destroy a whole
city instead of merely those who were guilty." [1] The
friends of Mytilenê, both the envoys who had come to
plead their cause and Athenians who were acting with
them, were quick to note this change in public feeling, and
they induced the authorities to summon the Ecclesia
and bring the case of the Mytilenaeans before it a second
time. Thucydides has set out in full the chief arguments

[1] Thucydides, iii. 36. 4 ; Loeb, ii. p. 57.

used on either side, putting the plea for ' justice ' into the mouth of Cleon, the son of Cleaenetus, the plea for mercy into the mouth of Diodotus ; with the result that the opinion of Diodotus prevailed, but only by a narrow majority. Then began a desperate race for the lives of the Mytilenaeans : for the first trireme had twenty-four hours' start. Great rewards were promised to the rowers if they reached Mytilenê in time ; and as they rowed, they were fed with barley soaked in wine and oil to keep up their strength, and in turns they snatched a little sleep, while the rest rowed on. Fortunately no adverse wind met them, and as the crew of the first trireme had little heart for their mission, their progress was slow. In the end the second trireme made the harbour of Mytilenê very shortly after the first had anchored there ; and while Paches, after reading the despatches, was making preparations to have the orders carried out. " So narrow was the escape of Mytilenê from destruction."

The prisoners who had been brought to Athens, more than a thousand in number, were all put to death.

The Betrayal of Plataea.—In this year also (427) was consummated the crime by which Plataea—the site consecrated for ever as a memorial of Hellenic deliverance from Persia—was blotted from the map of Greece. The men of Plataea had stood by the Athenians at Marathon and now in the Peloponnesian war Plataea was still found ranged by the side of Athens. In 429 Archidamus instead of invading Attica, turned the whole force of the Peloponnesian alliance to the reduction of Plataea No doubt this was largely due to the importunity of Plataea's irreconcilable enemy, Thebes. Plataea was but a little town, how small we are not told ; but the garrison that held it was under 500—just 400 Plataean and 80 Athenians : the women and children, and non combatants generally, had been removed for safety to Athens immediately after the Theban attempt on Plataea in 431. On the arrival of the Peloponnesians before the walls, King Archidamus made the Plataeans an offer if they would undertake to be neutral in the war, they should not only be unmolested but protected in their rights. The Plataeans sent to Athens to consult the Athenians, and the Athenians made this reply : " The Athenians assure you, Plataeans, that as in times past, since you became their allies, they have never on any occasion deserted you when you were being wronged, so now they will not suffer you to be wronged, but will assist you with all their might. They therefore adjure you, by the oaths which your fathers swore, not to break off the alliance." [1] Accordingly the Plataeans rejected the Lacedaemonian offer, and hostilities began. After exhausting what skill they had in siege operations without success, the greater part of the Peloponnesian forces went home. A certain proportion of each contingent was left, and these set to work to build walls in a double circuit round the town. There was a space of sixteen feet between the walls and this space was roofed in, so that the structure had the appearance of a single wall of great strength. There were battlements all along the top and high towers at intervals, and the space between the walls was divided up and used as quarters for the troops. When the building was finished most of the troops were withdrawn and only a garrison left to maintain the blockade. The blockade of Plataea then continued through the winter of 429 and the whole of the following year. Towards the end of the year supplies were failing, and in the summer of 427, when they were altogether exhausted, the Plataeans surrendered themselves to the Lacedaemonians, on condition that they would be their judges, and that no one should be punished contrary to justice. Not all the original garrison thus surrendered ; nearly half of them—to the number of 220—had made a daring escape in the preceding winter. Five commissioners came from Sparta to hold the trial, but when the prisoners were brought before this tribunal, they found that in place of any form of legal procedure, they were each, man by man (Athenians included), to be asked a single

[1] Thucydides, ii. 73. 3 ; Loeb, p. 393.

question : had they done any service to the Lacedaemonian cause in the war. They protested vigorously
against the unfairness of this question, but their protest
was overruled, and the trial proceeded in this form.
" So they caused them to come forward again, one at a
time, and asked them the same question, whether they
had rendered any good service to the Lacedaemonians
and their allies in the war, and when they said ' no '
they led them off and slew them, exempting no one." [1]

This judicial murder was a black crime to be set to the
account of Sparta. But it may be doubted whether the
crime of Athens was not even worse. For there is no
indication whatever in the record that the Athenians made
any effort, at any time, summer or winter (though Plataea
was within a day's march of the Athenian border), to
break the cordon and rescue these faithful allies, and that
despite the assurance quoted above (p. 149). It is a
sorry story, relieved only by the stirring episode of the
escape of half the garrison in the winter of 428.

A Bid for Life and Liberty.—When supplies were getting
low and all hope of relief from Athens had been abandoned,
the bolder spirits in Plataea matured a plan for breaking
out over the besiegers' wall and escaping. A stormy
night and ladders of a proper length were seen to be the
conditions of success. The length for the ladders was
arrived at by counting and recounting the number of
bricks in a bit of wall that happened not to have been
whitewashed like the rest, and so calculating the height
of the wall : and then, having made all other dispositions
necessary, they waited. The plan originally was for the
whole garrison to make the attempt, but afterwards
about half thought the risk too great and drew back.
This in the end helped materially the success of the escaping party, because those who stayed were able to make a
diversion at the critical moment. At last the night came,
a wild night, tempestuous with wind and rain, in the dark
of the moon, and those who were resolute to make the

[1] Thucydides, iii. 68. 2 ; Loeb, ii. p. 123.

attempt set forth.   The leaders got safely across the space
between the moat outside the wall of Plataea and the
besiegers' lines, and planted their ladders against a
stretch of wall between two of the towers.   Those who
went up first were armed only with corselet and dagger,
or with short spears, in order that their movements might
be unimpeded.   When a few only had got up, one of the
party happened to dislodge a tile and it fell to the ground
with a clatter.   An alarm was raised : guards and sentinels
rushed to their posts, but on account of the darkness
and the uncertainty of what was happening, stayed where
they were without attempting to reach the point of
danger.   At the same moment the part of the garrison
remaining in Plataea made an attack on the Peloponnesian
wall at a point facing the opposite side of the town, and
so effected a most timely diversion.   Meanwhile those
who were first up, turned right and left along the wall,
made their way into the flanking towers and killed the
guards.   More ladders were brought up and the main
body crossed the wall as rapidly as they could, while
their comrades held the towers on either hand, and got
down the other side.   By this time the defenders were
everywhere astir, and a picked band of three hundred
men kept always ready for emergencies came advancing
along the foot of the wall in all haste, carrying lanterns.
But their lanterns did them no good, only made them a
readier mark for the missiles of the Plataeans and
Athenians.   In the end the escaping party got over the
wall and away, the last men with some difficulty : all
at least but one, an archer, who was made prisoner.
Once clear of the walls the fugitives moved off as fast as
they could, not in the direction of Cithaeron, toward
Attica, but in the opposite direction along the road which
was the last the enemy would expect them to take, the
road to Thebes ; and from this road they could see the
lights of their pursuers glimmering along the road which
led to the Oak-heads,[1] the main pass through the mountains.   After following the Theban road for a time they

[1] For the Oak-heads Pass see vol. i. p. 366.

turned off along another road leading over Cithaeron, and ultimately got clear away.[1]

The Depravation of Hellas.—The wholesale slaughtering of the Mytilenaean prisoners by the Athenians, and of the garrison of Plataea by the Spartans, were acts of savagery, which the moral feeling of thinking Greeks condemned. Nor were these the worst atrocities perpetrated in Hellas in the course of the Peloponnesian war. The most horrible of all—and they are scarcely exceeded in all the blood-stained records of mankind—were done at Corcyra in a struggle between the oligarchical and democratic factions there, which had begun before the war, were intensified after it broke out, and ended only with the massacre of the whole of the oligarchical party. Thucydides relates the story in full and makes one of his rare comments. He is not of those who believe in the refining and purifying effects of war : from his experience he regards war as demoralizing and depraving : " For in peace and prosperity," he says, ".both states and individuals have gentler feelings, because men are not then forced to face conditions of dire necessity ; but war, which robs men of the easy supply of their daily wants, is a rough schoolmaster and creates in most people a temper that matches their condition." [2]

A Lucky Turn of Fortune.—The war went on from year to year with varying success, each side inflicting hideous damage on the other without, seemingly, bringing the conflict any nearer to a conclusion. There can hardly even be said to have been a clearly conceived and far-sighted plan of operations on either side. The struggle dragged on as a series of badly connected episodes, breaking out now on this side of Hellas, and now on that. Only year by year, regularly, Attica was invaded, and year by year an Athenian naval squadron went round Peloponnesus, wasting and plundering. And every year the Athenians further sated their anger at the damage done in Attica by the Peloponnesians on unhappy Megara, by burning and destroying in the Megarid, right up to the

---

[1] Thucydides, iii. 20-24.   [2] Thucydides, iii. 82. 2 ; Loeb, ii. p. 143.

city walls. Neither side had made any real progress
towards victory. And then in 425 a dramatic change
came over the scene, when suddenly, more by accident
than design, Athens found herself in a position to dictate
to Sparta almost any terms she pleased. This was
because by an extraordinary stroke of luck the Athenians
got into their hands as prisoners of war nearly three
hundred Lacedaemonians, a good proportion of them
Spartans of good family. The story is worth setting forth
with some fulness, but no re-telling can approach the
story as first told in Thucydides' pages.

High Adventure at Pylos.—On the west coast of Peloponnesus, in the southern half of the district that was once
the kingdom of Messenia, is the Bay of Navarino, where
in 1827 the Turkish and Egyptian fleets were destroyed
by the attack of British, French and Russian warships,
and the Greeks rescued from Turkish oppressors. In
front of the Bay of Navarino lies the island of Sphagia,
anciently called Sphacteria, about 2¾ miles in length
and half a mile broad, with a wide channel into the bay
at its southern end and a narrow channel at the northern.
Opposite the northern end of Sphacteria, with just the
narrow channel between, is another mass of rock, not
quite a mile in length, joined to the mainland coast by
a very narrow neck and with a shallow lagoon to the
east of it. This rocky peninsula was in the fifth century
B.C. called Coryphasion by the Spartans and by the
Athenians Pylos : [1] and the lagoon, which has been gradually
formed in the course of countless centuries by the deposit of
silt, was then still practically part of the bay. It happened
in 425 that an Athenian squadron under orders to sail
to Sicily passed by this coast and that it had on board an
enterprising Athenian commander who was a great
friend of the exiled Messenians and was eager to serve
his country by some valiant stroke. Demosthenes had

[1] The Homeric Pylos, the home of Pylian Nestor, was somewhere
along this coast, but the probabilities are against the identification of
Coryphasion with Nestor's Pylos. See for Telemachus' journey to
Pylos, vol. i. p. 137.

no official position in the fleet,[1] but he was allowed to
sail with it on the understanding that he should be
supported in any service of which he saw opportunity,
and it may be conjectured that he had all along a particular opportunity in view. He had started, we may suppose,
with a clear purpose in his own mind of making a landing and seizing Pylos ; but at first it seemed that he would
have no chance of carrying it out. He put his request
to the admirals in command, Eurymedon and Sophocles, but they would not hear of it. A storm, however,
did for Demosthenes what Eurymedon and Sophocles
would not do : it obliged the Athenian fleet to take
shelter in the harbour. Even so for some time Demosthenes was no nearer the accomplishment of his purpose, for neither commanders nor men would help him
to fortify the position. Then further chance brought
what he desired. The bad weather continued and kept
the fleet at Pylos. The sailors had nothing to do, and to
pass the time began to turn this headland of Pylos into a
fortified post. This was easy ; for stones and wood in
abundance were lying about and there was sand to serve
for mortar. Warming to their work they ultimately
made a creditable job of it, and by the time the fleet was
able to sail Coryphasion was a defensible post. It may
be seen from the map and illustration that the position
was one which naturally lent itself to defence. The
rock slopes steeply up from the channel separating
Pylos and Sphacteria to a height of 450 feet ; then falls
away abruptly to the isthmus, the curious sand-bar
which in crescent shape joins the peninsula to the mainland coast on the north. The top forms a natural keep,
where there are now extensive remains of a mediaeval
castle built by the Venetians, and traces of an earlier
stronghold which may possibly date from Mycenaean
times. A cliff edge running continuously from east to
west forms a line convenient to hold on the north. Nearly

[1] The words used by Thucydides are curious : " Demosthenes also,
. . . at his own request, had permission, if he should wish, to make
use of the ships in the course of the voyage round Peloponnesus " (Thuc.
iv. 2. 4.)

the whole of the eastern side (above the lagoon), and
great part of the western (towards the sea) are secured

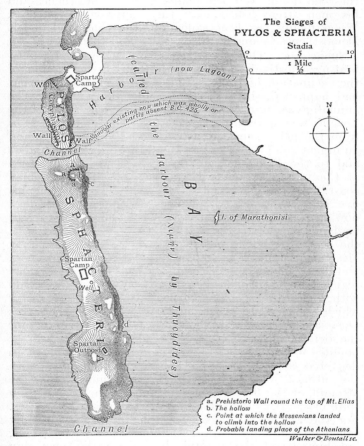

The Sieges of
PYLOS & SPHACTERIA

Stadia

1 Mile

a. *Prehistoric Wall round the top of Mt. Elias*
b. *The hollow*
c. *Point at which the Messenians landed
   to climb into the hollow*
d. *Probable landing place of the Athenians*

Walker & Boutall sc.

from attack by precipitous cliffs. There were only two
places where attack was practicable : a strip of rock-
strewn shore at the south-west end, and the western

side of the northern cliff where a lower level makes approach from the sandy isthmus relatively easy ; and these no doubt were the points which Demosthenes and his men strengthened with their improvised defences. When finally the fleet sailed on, the commanders left Demosthenes behind with five ships and their crews.

Sphacteria.—The Lacedaemonians—they were celebrating a festival—at first made light of the rumour of the occupation of Pylos. But when they realized what had happened, there was something like a panic. The annual invasion of Attica was going on ; the army of the League was hurriedly recalled ; Lacedaemonian troops from the neighbourhood marched to Pylos at once, and an urgent summons was sent to all the allied commanders and to the Peloponnesian fleet which was at the time at Corcyra to hasten with all speed to the Messenian coast. Demosthenes meantime had sent two of his five ships to report the danger to the Athenian fleet now arrived at Zacynthus : his remaining three ships he hauled ashore and prepared to hold the post with the scanty forces at his disposal. He had only forty Messenian hoplites besides the crews of his three triremes, and most of his crews, of course, were just unarmed seamen. The seamen he armed as well as he could with wicker targes, obtained from a Messenian privateer which happened to be at hand.[1] The bulk of his forces Demosthenes posted to defend the northern end : for the defence of the strip of rocky shore he took sixty hoplites only and some bowmen. The Lacedaemonians delivered attacks at both points simultaneously with the utmost vigour. Especially determined was the attempt of the fleet to force a landing on the rocks, in spite of the risks the ships ran of being dashed to pieces. For the gallant Brasidas [2] was there, and he not only called on the ships' captains not to spare their vessels, but himself set the example by steering his own ship

[1] Possibly this ' accident ' was also designed and part of Demosthenes' plan.

[2] For Brasidas see below, p. 168.

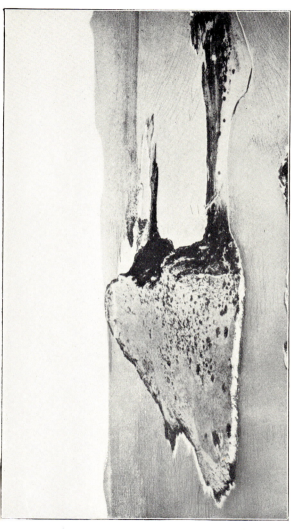

THE PENINSULA OF PYLOS,

as seen from the cliffs along the northern end of Sphacteria. In the foreground is the channel between Sphacteria and Pylos. At the top of the slope are remains of the Venetian castle. The line held by Demosthenes was (probably) a little way down beyond the top of the slope, the weak side strengthened by the Athenian defences being on the left. The rocky shore on which Brasidas made his attack is conspicuous at the S.W. corner. A line of wall had been built some little way above it. The sand-bar seen on the right did not then exist, and the lagoon beyond was the harbour where the Athenian ships anchored in 425 B.C. before occupying Pylos.

From a photograph by R. C. Bosanquet in the *Journal of Hellenic Studies* for 1898.

straight for the shore with a view to making good a
landing at any cost. But he was struck down as he stood
on the gangway and lost consciousness. His men
managed to carry him off, but his shield fell into the
water and the Athenians made prize of it. The attack
was a complete failure. Thucydides notices the odd turn
of fortune by which it came about that the Lacedaemonians were attacking from shipboard and trying to
force a landing in their own country, while the Athenians
were resisting them on land and that land part of Laconia.[1]
The attacks were repeated next day with no better
success. On the third day the ships of the Athenian
fleet, fifty in number, sailed in from Zacynthus, hot for
an immediate engagement. They found themselves
baffled by the dispositions made by the Lacedaemonian
commanders. The Peloponnesian fleet was in the
harbour and showed no willingness to come out and
fight, while the shore of the bay was held by troops.
There were troops also, a strong body of Lacedaemonian
hoplites, lining the rocks along the northern end of the
island of Sphacteria. For, like Xerxes at Salamis, the
Spartans had landed men to give their side support in
the event of a sea-fight ; and, like Xerxes also, they forgot
to take into account the contingency of a reverse. But
for the moment the Athenian admirals saw no means of
attacking ; and with the whole Bay of Navarino and its
shores occupied by the enemy in force, there was no place
at all where they could find anchorage. They therefore
withdrew, and sailing northwards along the coast of the
mainland, put in for the night at an island named Protê.
Next day they returned ; and this time, since the Peloponnesian fleet did not come out, they sailed straight
into the Bay of Navarino through both entrances, the
northern and the southern, engaged the enemy's ships,
captured five, and drove the rest ashore. This victory,
so easily obtained, at once effected a dramatic change
in the situation. For now, since the Athenians were
masters of the bay and of the channels leading into it,

[1] Thucydides, iv. 12. 3.

the Spartans posted on Sphacteria were cut off. This consequence, though it might have been foreseen as possible, filled with consternation both the Spartan troops on the spot and the authorities at Lacedaemon. Some of the men-at-arms now cut off in Sphacteria were scions of the noblest Spartiate families. We have seen before (ch. iii. p. 67), in what followed the battle of Coronea, the sacrifices a Greek city-state would make in order to ransom its citizens when prisoners of war. Now that the calamity had happened at Pylos, the Spartans were quick to grasp its extreme seriousness ; for since they had lost the command of the channels and the bay, there was no means at all of succouring the men on Sphacteria, and there was nothing before them but a choice of starvation or surrender. For this reason they at once proposed a truce while envoys should go to Athens to treat for peace. Pending the return of the envoys, it was agreed that daily rations should be conveyed across to the garrison in Sphacteria, on condition that the Spartans handed over to the Athenians not only the whole of the Peloponnesian fleet in the Bay of Navarino but all other war-ships in Laconia as well. When the truce was over the ships were to be restored. These terms were agreed to ; the Peloponnesian fleet was surrendered ; Spartan envoys were conveyed to Athens on board an Athenian trireme. It was now that Athens had her great opportunity. The Spartan envoys appeared before the Ecclesia in very chastened mood and made offers to the Athenian people which would have secured to them all that they were fighting for. "The Lacedaemonians," they said, "invite you to accept terms and bring the war to an end, offering you peace and alliance, and apart from this the maintenance of hearty friendship and intimacy one with the other ; asking on their side merely the return of the men on the island." [1] It was a magnificent opportunity. If it had been accepted by the Athenian people in the spirit in which (apparently) it was offered, the whole course of Greek history might have

[1] Thucydides, iv. 19 ; Loeb, p. 243.

been altered, with far-reaching results for the history of the world. For as the Spartan envoys said : " if you and we agree be assured that the rest of the Hellenic world, since it will be inferior to us in power, will pay us the greatest deference." [1] But unfortunately this amazing turn of good fortune which had come to them disturbed the judgment of the Athenians, and it was no longer Pericles who had their ear, but Cleon, the son of Cleaenetus, mover of the decree against Mytilene. Cleon advised the Ecclesia to demand that, as a preliminary to any peace negotiations whatever, the Lacedaemonians in Sphacteria should deliver up their arms, surrender themselves prisoners of war and be brought to Athens ; that when the prisoners had arrived in Athens, the Lacedaemonians should put the Athenians in possession of Nisaea, Pegae, Troezen and Achaia, of all in fact that Athens had given up twenty years earlier : [2] that then and only then, peace should be made for a term of years. The envoys met this demand with a request for the appointment of commissioners who might discuss with themselves the points at issue and try and reach an agreement mutually acceptable. This gave Cleon the opening to denounce the envoys for attempting to overreach the Athenian people, and seeking to obtain by underhand means concessions they did not venture to ask for openly. If the purposes of the envoys were honest, they could speak out then and there before the people. Upon this the envoys withdrew and returned to Sparta with nothing accomplished ; for if they had publicly offered concessions, and yet after all had failed to bring about peace, Sparta would have lost credit with her allies for nothing.[3]

On the return of the envoys to Sparta the truce was at an end and according to the compact made the ships held as surety by the Athenians must be given back. But the temptation to keep the enemy's ships now they had

[1] Thucydides, iv. 20. 4 ; Loeb, p. 245.
[2] Thucydides, i. 115 ; and see above, ch. iii. p. 68.
[3] Thucydides, iv. 22.

them was too much for the Athenians. They refused
to restore them, giving as a pretext certain alleged
breaches of the truce. The Spartans protested, but there
was no remedy : merely hostilities were resumed. The
Athenians kept patrol ships circling round Sphacteria by
day, and at night the whole fleet, now raised by reinforcement to seventy vessels, lay close anchored about
Sphacteria, except that, if the wind rose, they had to
leave the windward side of the island unguarded.[1] The
Spartans on their side renewed their attacks on Pylos
and at the same time strained every nerve to get food
across to their men on Sphacteria ; for the island itself
was utterly barren and uninhabited. They did this,
however, with such success that the Athenian blockade
proved quite ineffective. It was impossible for triremes
to be moored on the seaward side of Sphacteria when the
wind was blowing on shore, and on such nights daring
blockade-runners, mostly Helots spurred by the promise
of their liberty, would start from some point on the
Messenian coast, and, with the wind behind them, run
their boats on to the rocky coast of Sphacteria at the
most suitable points, where they were sure to find some
of the hoplites on the look-out to receive them. So the
days passed and the Athenians were no nearer getting
the men on Sphacteria into their hands than they were
when the blockade began. Meantime the summer was
passing and the men of the Athenian fleet were enduring
great discomfort and privation. Supplies were difficult,
they had no proper anchorage, and, worst of all, no
means of drawing water except from a single well
in the acropolis of Pylos. Dissatisfaction at Athens at
this want of progress was growing acute and the people
began to repent of having listened to Cleon's advice.
Upon this Cleon, after a vain attempt to discredit the truth
of the reports, threw the blame on the generals of the
year : it would be quite easy, he declared, if the generals
were any good, with a suitable force to sail to Sphacteria
and capture the Spartans : that is what he would himself

[1] Thucydides, iv. 23.

have done had he been in command.   And then a strange
thing happened.   When there was a mocking outcry
at this boastful statement of Cleon's, Nicias rose and in
the name of the generals invited Cleon to take what force
he would and make the attempt.   Cleon, not thinking
this seriously meant, at first professed himself ready to
go ; but when he found Nicias was in earnest, he tried to
back out of it.   But this the multitude, finding amusement in Cleon's discomfiture, would not allow.   The more
he drew back, the more they clamoured that he should go.
In the end this wild proposal was carried through.   It
seemed a mad freak ; for Cleon had no experience of
command either military or naval.   Cleon not only agreed
to go, but declared that he would not take a single man
from Athens, but only a body of Lemnian and Imbrian
allies then in the city, a band of targemen and four
hundred archers.   If these forces were entrusted to him
in addition to the troops already at Pylos, he undertook
within twenty days either to bring the Lacedaemonians
to Athens alive or to kill them there.[1]

It is a strange story, and the strangest part of it is that
Cleon after all made good his rash words.   He sailed with
his bowmen and peltasts and within twenty days he
brought to Athens as prisoners of war all that remained
alive of the Lacedaemonians who had been cut off in Sphacteria.   This result was achieved partly by good luck,
partly through Cleon's shrewdness in choosing Demosthenes for his colleague in the undertaking.   Demosthenes
had a plan for landing in Sphacteria and capturing the
Spartans all ready to put into practice before Cleon
arrived.   Sphacteria, we have already noted, was a
barren uninhabited islet, and when the Lacedaemonians
landed there, it was also for the most part thickly covered
with bush—as it is again to-day.   This growth of bush
had been a great obstacle to the success of a landing ;
for it obstructed the view and put the attacking party
at a great disadvantage.   But a little before this there
had been a fire—accidentally caused by one of a party

[1] Thucydides, iv. 27 and 28.

of Athenian soldiers who had landed to cook their food—
and much of the bush had been burnt. Here Demosthenes
saw his opportunity ; and, as a matter of fact, when Cleon
arrived, all Demosthenes' dispositions for an attack
had been already made. Demosthenes meant to leave
nothing to chance : he planned to use all the forces at his
disposal and land troops in numbers so overwhelming
as to make successful resistance impossible. The Lacedaemonians were in all 420 hoplites with, perhaps, the
same number of light-armed Helots in attendance.[1]
The main camp was on comparatively level ground about
the middle of the island, near a well. There was an
outpost of thirty men near the southern end. The highest
ground on the island at the north-east corner, opposite
Pylos, was held by another small detachment as a stronghold on which to retreat in case of necessity.[2]

One day a little before dawn Demosthenes landed his
hoplites, eight hundred in number, simultaneously on
both sides of the island. With these forces he rushed
the advance post and overwhelmed it : the defenders
were killed before they were well awake. At dawn the
rest of his troops disembarked, 800 archers, as many
more targemen, and large part of the crews of all his
seventy ships. These last must have amounted to some
eight thousand men, so that the total force landed to
deal with 420 Lacedaemonian hoplites and their attendant
Helots must have been well over 10,000. The dispositions
made by Demosthenes were certainly a superb compliment to the fighting value of Spartan training. These
troops were divided up by Demosthenes into bands of
about two hundred men ; and every point of vantage
round the Spartan encampment was occupied by one
or other of these bands, so that the Lacedaemonians
could be assailed from all sides and exposed to a shower
of missiles in whatever direction they turned.[3] The

[1] No account is taken by Thucydides in his description of the fighting
of light-armed on the Spartan side, but in giving the numbers of the
detachment cut off in Sphacteria (iv. 8. 9) he says " numbering four
hundred and twenty, besides the Helots who accompanied them. . . ."

[2] Thucydides, iv. 31.   [3] Thucydides, iv. 32.

little compact band of Spartans, nothing daunted, formed up and advanced upon the Athenian heavy-armed men. At once they were assailed by a swarm of light-armed on both flanks : for the Athenian hoplites made no advance, but stood where they were. If the Spartans turned against the light-armed on either side, they easily retreated out of reach ; for it was vain to press the pursuit over the rough ground. And all the time, too, the enemy hung upon their rear and harassed them. This skirmishing went on for a long time, till the Lacedae-monians began to tire and their resistance weakened. Encouraged by their immunity from punishment at the hands of foes they had thought so formidable, the Athenian light troops pressed on more boldly : " With a shout they came on all together, showering upon their foemen stones, arrows, and javelins, using severally the missiles that came to hand. The noise added to the terror of the charge and daunted troops unused to such fighting ; the ash from the recently fired woods rose into the air in clouds, and it was difficult for the men to see what was in front of them as the stones and arrows came hurtling through the ash-laden air. So the day now began to go hard with the Lacedaemonians. Their felt jerkins would not keep off the arrows, and the points of the javelins broke off short in those who were hit. Thus with their view ahead cut off, and the orders of their officers drowned by the deafening shouts of their assailants, with their position threatened in every direction and with no hope of beating off these attacks, they did not know what to do with themselves." [1] Then the surviv-ing Spartans closed their ranks and fought their way in slow retreat back upon their rocky citadel, followed by the swarms of enemies who pressed on after them more fiercely than ever. Some were overtaken and killed ; but the greater number reached the summit and were told off to hold their defences at all the assailable points. The Athenians came on with no less ardour than before, but now the Lacedaemonians were in a fortified posi-

[1] Thucydides, iv. 34, 1-3 (L. J.).

tion, no longer open to attack from all sides. The attack, therefore, this time made no progress, and the struggle went on through the long hot day without result. At last the commander of the Messenian troops, with Demosthenes' consent, took a party of javelin men and archers, and they crept along under the great east cliff till they found a place below the crest of the hill where, out of view of the garrison, it was possible to climb, and reach a part of the summit which on account of its natural strength was undefended. In this way he and his men suddenly emerged in view of both friend and foe on the rocks above the Spartan position ; for the rough fort the Spartans held was on the top of the hill but not the actual peak. The position had been turned : it was Thermopylae over again on a smaller scale.[1] Resistance was now hopeless and the end had come : the defenders were weak from want of food and physical exhaustion, and now they could again be attacked from every side. In a short while they must all have been overwhelmed and killed. But this was not what Cleon and Demosthenes wanted. They wanted something far more valuable than three hundred dead bodies. They wanted living Spartan prisoners to use as a lever in negotiations with the Spartan government. So at the critical moment, while there was still time, the Athenian commanders sent forward a herald who made proclamation in the hearing of the Spartans, inviting them to surrender at discretion. The rank and file were exhausted in will as well as in bodily power, and when they heard these words most of them "lowered their shields and waved their hands, indicating that they accepted the terms proposed."[2] So the fight was stayed and in conference with the Spartan commander it was arranged that a message should be conveyed to the Spartans on the mainland asking what they on the island should do. Messengers passed backwards and forwards more than once : the final answer sent was : " The Lacedaemonians bid you consult your own safety, but do nothing dis-

[1] The comparison is Thucydides', iv. 36. 3.

[2] Thucydides, iv. 38. 1.

graceful." [1] This was understood by the men on Sphacteria as equivalent to an injunction to make the best
terms they could for their lives : accordingly they gave
up their arms and became prisoners of war. It was an
event which struck all Greece with amazement. For it
was at this time an article of faith in Hellas that Spartans
died but never surrendered. Sphacteria brought disillusionment to the allies and was a shrewd blow to
Spartan prestige. The Athenians were proportionately
elated, and sailed away home with their prisoners on
shipboard.

And now a second time Athens held in her hands the
means of ending the war victoriously and of inaugurating
a new era of peace for Hellas. For Sparta was tamed in
spirit as never before. So great was the public anxiety
to recover her men that the Spartan government was
prepared to make great concessions. But the people of
Athens were lifted above themselves by their unlooked-for
success and their demands were extravagant. Spartan
ambassadors came again and again, but every time
they went away unsuccessful : the ' men of Sphacteria '
remained as prisoners in Athens and the war went on.

The Longing for Peace.—But although the influence
of Cleon and the ' war party ' frustrated the hopes of a
good peace in 425, there were many in Athens who were
thoroughly weary of the war, and who longed only for a
return to the calm delights of peace. Especially was this
true of the multitudes of honest farmers and country
gentlemen who were living pent up within the city walls,
cut off from their country homes. The feelings of such
sufferers have been vividly portrayed by Aristophanes
in the *Acharnians*, a comedy produced at Athens in this
very year 425. In this play the demesman of Colleidês,
Dicaeopolis,[2] insists on making a private peace for himself,
in defiance of the furious indignation of the Acharnians,
who cannot forgive the Lacedaemonians for cutting down
their vines. Aristophanes depicts Dicaeopolis " gazing
out into the country in a passion of desire for peace,

[1] Thucydides, iv. 38. 3.   [2] Aristophanes, *Acharnians*, l. 406.

hating the city and yearning for my own countryside."[1]
He even has the courage to hint that perhaps all the guilt
for the war was *not* Sparta's.[2] The play has been well
described as " an ardent declaration in favour of peace."[3]
It needed four more years of war to bring a majority in
the Ecclesia to this frame of mind. But after Athens had
suffered the severe defeat of Delium in 424 and had lost
Amphipolis and other of the ' Thraceward ' towns through
Brasidas' brilliant campaign, both sides were sufficiently
inclined to peace to conclude an armistice for one year.
When the year was up, hostilities were indeed renewed
(422) ; but in an action before Amphipolis, which Cleon
had gone to recover for Athens, Cleon was killed outright
and Brasidas mortally wounded. This removed on the
Spartan side, as well as on the Athenian, the personal
influence most inimical to peace ; and in 421 a peace for
fifty years was negotiated between Sparta and Athens
and their respective allies on the basis that each side should
renounce its conquests. It was an uneasy peace, because
there was no hearty reconcilement ; points remained in
dispute from the very first and were never settled. But
nominal peace between Sparta and Athens, between
Athens and the Peloponnesian League, continued for eight
years, from 421 to 413, and then there was again a general
embroilment, league against league, as it had been in the
Ten Years' War (431-421).

Before we leave this first period of conflict between
Athens and Sparta, sometimes called the *Ten Years' War*,
we may with advantage consider briefly two episodes of
the last four years of it—the affair of Delium and the
Thracian campaign of Brasidas.

Delium.—If the capture of Sphacteria did not secure
for the Athenians peace from Sparta on their own terms,
at all events it brought them sovereign relief in one
respect : it freed them from yearly invasion. For they
had their 292 Spartans and Lacedaemonians in Athens,

---

[1] Lines 32 and 33.   [2] Lines 509-514.

[3] Croiset, *Aristophanes and the Political Parties at Athens,* translated
by James Loeb, p. 52.

· and they let it be understood that if a Peloponnesian
army entered Attica these 292 men (including the 120
of noblest Spartiate blood) would die. The run of luck
meantime for Athens continued. In the year 424 the
Athenians conquered Cythera (Cerigo, the island south of
Cape Malea), not ten miles from the coast of Laconia. That
was another humiliation and hurt to the pride of Sparta,
hardly less serious than Sphacteria and Pylos. A little
later they captured and destroyed Thyrea, the city on that
border district so long in dispute between Sparta and
Argos, which the Spartans had given to the Aeginetans
when expelled from their island home by the Athenians.
The inhabitants of Cythera they put to tribute, but left
for the most part in possession of their island : all the
Aeginetans captured they put to death. Then fortune took
another turn. A promising intrigue with the democratic
party in Megara proved abortive, ending in the ruin of the
Megarian democrats. A larger enterprise, planned between that embodiment of restless energy, Demosthenes,
and the democratic parties in the Boeotian cities, ended in
sheer disaster. The plan was for an Athenian force to
seize a temple enclosure sacred to Apollo, called Delium,
on the Boeotian coast opposite Euboea, and turn it into
a fortress from which to foment revolution in the country.
In order to distract the Boeotians and give the Athenians
time to secure the position, Demosthenes with the fleet
from Naupactus was to make a landing on the opposite
side of Boeotia, where conspirators were prepared to put
the town of Siphae into his hands. The scheme miscarried owing to a wrong reckoning of days. Demosthenes arrived too soon and the Boeotians were able to
gather in great force to oppose him. In consequence of
this the partisans of Athens and democracy inside the town
made no movement and Demosthenes withdrew baffled.
But meantime Demosthenes' colleague, Hippocrates, had
made his *coup* and seized Delium. He came round the
shoulder of Mount Parnes with the full military strength of
Athens, citizens and ' metics ' alike. His troops dug a
trench all about the temple and made a rampart of

the earth extracted, and surmounted the rampart with a palisade. They spent four days and a half in advancing these fortifications ; then set off home, camping that night about two miles from Delium on the Attic side of the border. In the meantime the Boeotian levies had come together under the Boeotarchs to the number of some 18,000,—hoplites, cavalry and light-armed. The Athenians were without their light-armed troops, as these had already marched off home : of hoplites and cavalry they had about the same number as the Boeotians. In the battle which followed the Athenians on the left were pushed back by the Thebans (who were massed twenty-five deep) ; on the right they were at first victorious, but when some Boeotian cavalry suddenly appeared over a low ridge, they were seized with panic and turned in headlong flight. In the end the Athenian army was routed with a loss of nearly one thousand dead. The loss of the Boeotians was rather less than five hundred. The Athenian general, Hippocrates, was among the slain. A curious dispute, illustrative of Greek customs, arose over the dead. The Athenians sent, as was usual for the defeated side, a herald to ask permission to recover the bodies of those who had fallen. The Boeotians refused to give them up, unless the Athenians at once evacuated Delium. For they declared the occupation of Delium to be sacrilege. The Athenians denied the sacrilege and declined to do this ; on their part they reproached the Boeotians with violating the most sacred of Hellenic obligations. The dispute only came to an end when, seventeen days later, the Boeotians retook Delium.[1] They then restored the Athenian dead without further question.

Brasidas in Chalcidicê.—The defeat at Delium was one severe blow to the overweening self-confidence of the Athenians after Sphacteria. Another followed that same year through the achievements of Brasidas. Brasidas,

[1] It is interesting that for the capture of Delium the Boeotians used a rough form of flame-thrower. Thucydides' account of this is too long to quote and may be found, Bk. iv. 100. 2-4.

son of Tellis, is, with possibly one exception,[1] the most human and attractive figure Sparta ever produced. He is the one Spartan in the fifth century who may be called the peer of the great Athenians—of Themistocles and Aristides, of Cimon and Pericles. Brasidas was a leader in war as brilliant and resourceful as Phormio or Demosthenes, and he had that personal quality shown by all great commanders of rousing devotion in his soldiers. He has been called the most interesting of all the Hellenes of his time ; and indeed he had that touch of genius which enables a leader to do wonders with slender resources, to create the very material with which he achieves victory. Brasidas' first feat was to save the fortress in Laconia called Methonê at the time of the earliest Athenian raids round the Peloponnese (431 B.C.). With a hundred men he dashed through the Athenian forces besieging the place and by his presence prevented its capture. It was Brasidas who in the fourth year of the war projected a daring raid on Piraeus—and nearly succeeded. Among Brasidas' other services to Sparta was his fearless attempt to land on the rocks of Pylos, in which he was severely wounded.[2] It was Brasidas who had saved Megara.[3] After the saving of Megara and about the same time as the Athenian seizure of Delium, Brasidas set off for the Chalcidian peninsula with a force of 1700 hoplites. Of these 700 were Helots specially armed by the Spartans for the purpose ; the rest were volunteers from the Peloponnese serving for pay. His plan was to march north through Thessaly to Chalcidicê and by his presence extend the revolt which had already begun among the Chalcidian cities. It was a bold plan ; for the sympathies of the Thessalians were much in doubt and the body of the people at all events were with Athens. Brasidas carried his march through successfully by the speed with which he moved. At one point he was challenged by a body

[1] Agis IV., the reforming king of the third century B.C. (reigned 244-240). See Plutarch.

[2] See p. 156. [3] See p. 167.

of men belonging to the opposite party. By the exercise of tact he put them off, and then hastened on before opposition could gather in greater force. Perdiccas of Macedonia was his ally, so there was no difficulty in traversing the part of Macedonia between Thessaly and Chalcidicê. Chalcidicê is the broad upper portion of the peninsula which ends in the three promontories, Pallenê, Sithonia and Actê, the last-named being the easternmost through which Xerxes cut his canal.[1] Once arrived in Chalcidicê, Brasidas acted with swift decision. He found the people of Acanthus, the city just outside Actê [2] northwards, in two minds about welcoming him, and gave them the choice of making common cause with him or seeing their lands ravaged. After listening to his arguments (and for a Lacedaemonian he was not a bad speaker, says Thucydides),[3] they agreed to receive him within their city. In the winter he made a sudden march and won Amphipolis. This was a severe blow to Athens, for they had founded Amphipolis at a great cost, and set great store by its possession.

Amphipolis commanded an important trade route into the interior. Aristagoras of Miletus had tried to build a city in the neighbourhood and had failed.[2] Athens had promoted the establishment of a colony there and had failed : the whole settlement was wiped out by the Thracians.[4] Then in 436 a colony was successfully founded with Hagnon, son of Nicias, as founder. The city was protected on three sides by a curve of the river Strymon, and on the fourth by a wall across the bend. Eion, three miles below, was the port of Amphipolis, and above Eion was a bridge over which passed the highway between Thrace and Macedonia. The time of year was winter and Brasidas' march was unexpected. He easily overcame the guard at the bridge and crossed the Strymon. There was much property of the Amphipolitans in the open country between the bridge and the city walls. All this property fell into Brasidas' hands. The town

---

[1] See vol. i. pp. 301 and 302.   [2] Thucydides, iv. 84.
[3] See vol. i. p. 276.   [4] See above, ch. ii. p. 38.

was thrown into great commotion, but did not at once surrender, and might have been saved, as a majority of the townspeople were for Athens.   But Brasidas had proclamation made promising security of property to any citizens, whether Athenians or not, if they stayed after a surrender ; or if they preferred it, leave to depart freely. This moderation had its effect, and when a vote was taken, a majority were for surrender.   Thucydides explains that only a minority of the citizens were actually Athenian. The sequel has vivid interest for the reader of Thucydides. " Late the same day Thucydides and his ships sailed into Eion.   Brasidas was then just in possession of Amphipolis ; Eion he missed taking only by a night.   Had the fleet not come to its rescue with all speed, it would have been in his hands by morning." [1]

The Fifty Years' Peace.—It was after Athens had suffered this further reverse that the truce for one year (above, p. 166) was concluded between the Lacedaemonians and Athenians on terms of keeping what they held. But two days later than the conclusion of this armistice, Scionê, an Achaean city on the peninsula of Pallenê, joined Brasidas.   The Athenians demanded the exclusion of Scionê from the truce : Brasidas refused to hand it back.   The Athenians were very angry, and on Cleon's proposal passed a resolution " to destroy the city of the men of Scionê and put them to the sword."   In consequence of this and other causes of disagreement, when the year of truce came to an end hostilities were resumed, and the chief scene of action was Chalcidicê.   The Athenians sent fresh forces there with Cleon in command, thirty warships, 1200 Athenian footmen and 300 cavalry.   Cleon began with a notable success : he took Toronê.   Then he went to the mouth of the Strymon to deal with Amphipolis.   But there, unknown to him, a redoubtable foe

[1] Thucydides, iv. 106 (L. J.)   " But who would guess," comments Livingstone (*The Legacy of Greece*, p. 273), " that the Athenian general Thucydides was the historian Thucydides who wrote these words, and that the episode which he here describes with such detachment and neutrality earned him perpetual exile under pain of death, from the country which he passionately loved ? "

awaited him to his undoing. For Brasidas heard of his coming and entered Amphipolis. Cleon was expecting reinforcements and not intending as yet to assault the city, but his men (who were the fine flower of Athenian manhood) murmured at the delay and spoke contemptuously of their leader's military competence. And Cleon hearing of this led out his forces, not for attack but reconnaissance. Anticipating this purpose Brasidas massed his best troops near the gates of Amphipolis and made dispositions for a sudden sally before Cleon should have time to withdraw. The plan succeeded perfectly. As the Athenian troops wheeled to march away, Brasidas' men charged out upon them and quickly threw them into disorder, because they were unprepared for fighting and even in act to retreat. Cleon, who ran away, was overtaken and killed. The total Athenian loss was 600 ; and of the victors 7. But among the seven was Brasidas, who fell mortally wounded in the first onset. He was carried out of the fight and lived long enough to die, like General Wolfe, in the consciousness of victory. But his death turned gain into loss. The soldiers followed his funeral in military array, and the people of Amphipolis made him their hero and the second founder of their city. So died these two men on one day, the one of too coarse fibre for an Athenian, the other in his personal attractiveness unlike the typical Spartan. And with their passing, as we have already seen (above, p. 166), the way was smoothed to the Peace of Nicias.

A Greek Play of B.C. 421.—Of the thirteen surviving comedies of Aristophanes five belong to the years 425 to 421—from the year of Sphacteria to the year of the Peace of Nicias. The " Old Comedy " of Attica is as much a mirror of contemporary history as *Punch* is with us ; and these five comedies (*Acharnians*, *Knights*, *Clouds*, *Wasps*, *Peace*) reflect the thoughts and feelings of the people of Athens during these eventful years in a manner most intimate. Of none is this more true than of the last of the series, Aristophanes' *Peace*, which was performed before the Athenian people, massed tier above tier on seats under the south-east cliff of the Acropolis, about eight months after the deaths of Cleon and Brasidas at Amphipolis, and a few days before the signature of the Peace of Nicias. It comes down to us white-hot with the emotions of the time, and gives expression to the intense longing for peace which possessed many at Athens, and many also in the other warring states. " O most revered queen and goddess, our Lady Peace," cries Trygaeus, the hero of the play, the honest vine-dresser and cultivator, who stands for all the country and people of Attica, " mistress of the dance, mistress of wedlock, receive this our sacrifice." [1] And again : " Nay, rather in God's name, show thyself fully in thy noble graciousness to us who love thee—to us who have suffered sore tribulation these dozen long years past. Stay strifes and tumults, that we may call thee ' Strife-stayer.' End for us the fine-drawn suspicions, which keep us bickering one against another. Give once more, to us that are Hellenes, a taste of the good brew of ancient kindliness, infuse into our souls more of the spirit of forgiveness." [2] This was the spirit of Aristophanes in 421, when the Peace of Nicias was being made ; and there must have been some in Athens, and some in other parts of Greece who sympathized. Had there been more, the subsequent history of Greece would have been different.

PYLOS AND SPHACTERIA.

The topography of Sphacteria and Pylos is a fascinating subject. It was not convenient to introduce disputed points into the text and the full discussion of them is beyond the modest aim of this chapter. Happily the main questions have been completely settled. Two highly competent English archæologists, Dr. G. B. Grundy and Dr. Ronald Burrows, visited Pylos and Sphacteria in the same year 1895, and within a fortnight of each other, but quite independently. Papers embodying their conclusions were published simultaneously in the *Journal of Hellenic Studies* for 1896.

The main result was the complete clearing up of the most important points ; namely,

(1) that Sphagia is indisputably Sphacteria ;
(2) that Palaio-Kastro is indisputably Pylos ;

[1] Lines 974-977.   [2] Lines 987-998.

(3) that the Lagoon of Osmyn Aga is in process of being filled up and in the 5th century B.C. was deeper than now, and navigable, forming the most sheltered part of the Bay of Navarino, and therefore the harbour of Pylos.

The result is also to confirm in general, and illustrate, the accuracy of Thucydides' narrative both of the occupation of Pylos and the blockade of Sphacteria. One serious discrepancy, however, remains, the discrepancy which is responsible for there being a topographical problem. This is found inexplicable on any hypothesis but the simple admission that Thucydides made a mistake. The crucial passage (Book IV., ch. 8. 6 and 7) runs : " The island called Sphacteria extends lengthwise in front of the harbour and lies close to it, thus making the harbour safe and the entrances to it narrow ; on the one side, over against Pylos and the Athenian fortifications, allowing the passage of two ships abreast; on the other, towards the mainland, of eight or nine. Being quite uninhabited, the whole island was covered with brushwood and without path of any sort : its length was approximately a mile and three quarters. Now it was the intention of the Lacedaemonians to close the entrances completely with ships moored lengthwise down the channels, and because they were afraid the enemy might use the island as a base for prosecuting hostilities, they conveyed over into it a number of hoplites, and posted others along the mainland."

There are here plainly two mistakes :

    1. The length of Sphacteria is given as under two miles, whereas the true length is nearly three.

This is not a very serious mistake and more than one explanation is possible. Grundy suggests that the length given is the distance from the point where the Athenians landed to the cliffs of the north coast. On the other hand there is the possibility of an accidental textual error, ΔΠ represents 15. If we suppose that a Δ has dropped out, ΔΔΠ represents 25, approximately the correct distance. Or κε′ (25) may have been changed into ιε′ (15).[1]

    2. The channels into the Bay of Navarino at either end of Sphacteria are both described as narrow, and an estimate is given of their width in terms of the number of triremes that could sail in abreast. The northern channel (next to Pylos) is said to admit two triremes abreast, the southern to admit *eight or nine*. The width now by measurement is for the northern channel 220 yards, for the southern 1400. The southern channel is wide, and is very inappropriately described as admitting eight of the nine triremes abreast. It would admit thirty. Much greater is the difficulty of

[1] R. M. Burrows in *J. H. S.* vol. xvi. p. 76

supposing such a channel blocked by "ships moored length-wise down the channels." There is no ground for supposing that this opening has appreciably narrowed since the fifth century B.C. Yet it is quite plain from the wording of the passage that the channels intended are the openings at either end of Sphacteria, north and south. There is there-fore no escape from the conclusion that Thucydides has made a mistake in his estimate of the breadth of the southern channel.

How he came to make it is another question, an interesting question, but in itself, perhaps, not very important. Dr. Burrows made the acute suggestion that Thucydides based his estimates on statements made to him by ships' captains who had served at Pylos with Demosthenes, and that what they told him was that the Athenian fleet entered the Bay of Navarino through the two channels simultaneously, two ships abreast in the one, and eight or nine in the other. That is perfectly possible, though it cannot be *proved*. If we adopt this conjecture, we have to reject the whole story of the blocking of the channels by the Spartans, and suppose it an invention to account for the landing of Spartan hoplites on Sphacteria. Dr. Grundy, however, holds that there must have been some actual blocking of channels to account for the story, but conjectures that Thucydides was mistaken in describing the opening south of Sphacteria as one of them. He maintains that the sand-bar existed in the 5th century B.C. in the same position as now, though it shut in the harbour of Pylos less completely. He supposes that there was a channel close in under the S.E. cliffs of Pylos leading from the outer into the inner harbour, and that this was the other of the two channels which the Spartans intended to block. He supports those views by physiographical arguments which have great force. Several other interesting controversies have arisen out of the double visit to Pylos in 1895 and the papers in the *Journal of Hellenic Studies*. They concern the defences built up by the Athenians in Pylos, and the precise manner in which the light-armed Messenians gained the cliff top overlooking the position in which the Spartans were making their last stand. These will be found in four articles in the *Classical Review*, and four papers (one by Mr. R. C. Bosanquet, who visited Pylos in 1896 and took photo-graphs) in the *Journal of Hellenic Studies* for 1898. The photo-graphs, one of which is reproduced in this chapter, are specially note-worthy. There are also two interesting French prints at the end of Dr. Burrows' paper of 1896. The final Court of Appeal, even when his theories are called in question, is Dr. Grundy's careful survey, which has enduring value independently of all controversies. See Plate III. *Pylos and Its Environs* at the end of Dr. Grundy's article, *J. H. S.* vol. xvi. (1896).

The complete references are :—

Journal of Hellenic Studies, vol. xvi. (1896).

> *An Investigation of the Topography of the Region of Sphakteria and Pylos.*   G. B. Grundy, pp. 1-54.
> *Pylos and Sphacteria.*   R. M. Burrows, pp. 55-76.

Classical Review.

> G. B. Grundy (*Pylos and Sphacteria*), Nov. 1896, pp. 371-4.
> R. M. Burrows   ,,   ,,   Feb. 1897, pp. 1-10.
> G. B. Grundy   ,,   ,,   April 1897, pp. 155-9.
> G. B. Grundy (*Note on the Topography of Pylos*), Dec. 1897, p. 448.

Journal of Hellenic Studies, vol. xviii. (1898).

> *Pylos and Sphacteria.*   R. M. Burrows, pp. 147-155.
> *Notes by R. C. Bosanquet*, pp. 155-9.

Battles Ancient and Modern, G. B. Grundy, pp. 232-8.

See also pp. 228-230 in Dr. Grundy's articles, immediately preceding, on *A Suggested Characteristic in Thukydides' Work* ; and Dr. Burrows' reply to Dr. Grundy's two articles, pp. 345-350. Bury's *History of Greece* contains a full and vivid re-shaping of the whole story in the light of these personal studies of the locality. A comprehensive summary of results is included in the Supplementary Notes in Volume V. of Frazer's *Pausanias*, pp. 608-613.

CHAPTER VII

THE GAMBLE IN SICILY

" He told them that if they kept quiet and looked well after their fleet, and refrained from attempting new conquests during the war and from taking grave risks, they would come through safely."

Thucydides, ii. 65. 7.

" Adventures, so attractive to the romantic reader, are not for a great commonwealth."

Times Literary Supplement for June the 8th, 1922.

In 421 Athens had won her war. The aims of the Peloponnesian League had been to break the naval strength of Athens and end her control of the Confederacy of Delos. After ten years of conflict the navy of Athens was as strong as ever, she was still undisputed mistress of the seas ; her empire was intact except for the loss of Amphipolis, and as a set-off to the loss of Amphipolis she held Pylos and Cythera.

An Uneasy Peace.—Scarcely, however, was the Peace of Nicias ratified, when fresh matter of contention showed itself. The treaty had stipulated that the conquests each side had made should be restored. Amphipolis was naturally the first place noted for restoration to Athens. But the people of Amphipolis had not been consulted, and when Spartan commissioners appeared before the place and Clearidas (who had succeeded Brasidas in command of the Peloponnesian forces in Chalcidicê) received orders to hand the town over to the Athenians, he found the Chalcidians resolutely opposed

177

to the transfer and was unable, or said he was unable, to compel the surrender of Amphipolis against the will of its inhabitants. Of course this explanation did not satisfy the Athenians. They complained that the treaty had not been carried out and refused to give up Pylos. Each side considered itself aggrieved.

Alcibiades and Argos.—The chapters of Thucydides which follow [1] present us with a curious tangle of intrigue among the states interested in the settlement with Athens. Corinth, Boeotia, Elis, Megara refused to sign the peace at all. When Sparta tried to use pressure, they threatened revolt. Sparta, whose main concern now was to get back Pylos, thereupon made a separate treaty with Athens. The Corinthians retorted by forming a league with Argos, the traditional rival of Sparta ; and with Mantinea, which, like all Arcadian cities, had reason to dread interference from her powerful neighbour. These allies tried to get Boeotia to join them ; but the Boeotians had too lively a sense of old dangers from Athens, and stood firm for Sparta ; and Sparta soon after concluded a separate pact with them. Argos, fearing the strength of this combination, herself began to seek an understanding with Sparta. Meantime the Athenians took umbrage at the pact between Sparta and Boeotia, as being inconsistent with the treaty the Spartans had recently made with themselves,[2] and this opened to Argos the much desired opportunity of alliance with Athens. The Spartans, genuinely alarmed at the prospect of a combination of Argos and Athens, sent a pacific embassy to Athens with instructions to make all possible concessions. So Athens now became the focus of intrigue. In the end the Athenians were induced to draw away from Sparta and to ally themselves with Argos through a trick of the rising young statesman, Alcibiades.

[1] Thucydides, v. 22-48.

[2] Thucydides (v. 39. 3) evidently considers that there was an actual breach of the treaty which Sparta had made with Athens ; but there is no clause in that treaty as given v. 23, which expressly forbids either party to enter into new alliances without the consent of the other.

Alcibiades, at this time about thirty years of age, was kinsman and ward of Pericles. By birth and inheritance he had every advantage which could contribute to personal and public distinction. He had powerful family connections, great inherited wealth, and talents which must have brought him to the front even without these favouring circumstances. He had everything to make him successful for himself and useful to his country,— save and except a regard for what men call ' virtue.' He was the most ' brilliant ' of all the statesmen that Athens ever produced. He had by gift of nature all the qualities which most easily win popular applause. As boy and youth his cleverness and his beauty of face and form brought him general admiration. His success as an owner of race-horses, and winner of the four-horse chariot-race at Olympia, his foppery, his drinking-feasts, his very prodigalities, won the favour of the populace. The ultra-aristocrat Alcibiades became the hero of the Athenian demos. He was the spoilt child of Athens and of fortune. But he grew up—perhaps because of these profuse gifts of fortune—without scruple or sense of honour, with no principles to guide his life but self-glorification ; a patriot so long as it served the ambitions of Alcibiades ; afterwards the deadliest enemy Athens ever had. The leading statesman of the day was Nicias, who made the peace with Sparta—a man of great wealth, moderate talents, and of a very scrupulous and cautious temperament. It was Nicias who had conquered Cythera, and Nicias after whom the peace was called. Alcibiades, as was inevitable, was jealous of Nicias, all the more because each of the two was in his own way a Philo-Laconian. Nicias was of the school of Cimon, an admirer of Spartan morale, and one who desired friendship with Sparta. Alcibiades was hereditary ' proxenos ' or ' Consul-General ' for the Spartans, and he was piqued because in 421 the Spartan peace envoys had overlooked his claims and used the good offices of Nicias to bring about the peace. He saw his way now to avenging the slight, or, at any rate, to increasing his own importance at

Athens by breaking the 'entente' with Sparta and bringing about a close alliance between Athens and Argos. When the Spartan envoys came to Athens with full powers to settle outstanding disputes between Athens and Lacedaemon, and gave this out publicly, Alcibiades, with an outward show of friendliness, promised to get back Pylos for them and effect all else they wanted, if when they were before the Ecclesia they would deny that they had full powers. They did as he advised ; and then Alcibiades turned upon them, denounced them for double-dealing, and easily brought the Athenians into a mind to throw Sparta over and enter into definite alliance with Argos and Mantinea. This made a breach with Sparta, but did not at once lead to war, not indeed for another six years.

Melos.—In these years Athens was strong, and in the year 416 she used her strength in a way which showed her the 'tyrant' city, such as her enemies called her. Melos is a small island in the Aegean, lying on the western rim of the Cyclades about fifty miles from the Laconian coast.[1] Among all the islands of the Aegean its political position was unique, for it was neither allied with nor subject to Athens.[2] "The Melians," Thucydides says, "were colonists of the Lacedaemonians" ; [3] but they were not subjects of Sparta, nor were they members of the Peloponnesian League. In the war they had been strictly neutral, till the Athenians came and wantonly ravaged their lands. And now the democracy of Athens had decreed against them a greater wrong. They had no other wars on hand in 416 and it pleased them to give an exhibition of the strength of Athens by

[1] Melos is 52 square miles in area and has in it a mountain (Mount Elias) over 2500 feet high. Melos has considerable interest for the archaeologist. Excavations were carried out there by the British School from 1896 to 1899. See *Excavations at Phylakopi in Melos*, published by the Society for the Promotion of Hellenic Studies in 1904.

[2] It is an unsolved puzzle that we find the Melians included in the Tribute list of the year 425 B.C., and assessed at the rate of 15 talents (as much as the Naxians and Andrians).

[3] Thucydides, v. 84. 2.

enforcing the submission of the little independent island state. They sent to Melos a fleet of thirty-eight ships (six of these being Chian and two Lesbian) with an army of 3000 men, half of whom were troops of their allies. Thucydides felt the iniquity of what was done as sharply as any one could to-day, and he brings this out in dramatic form in his history by means of a dialogue between envoys from the Athenian commanders and the chiefs of the Melian state.[1] The Athenians make their appeal to the doctrine of force in its nakedness, advising the Melians to submit on grounds of expediency, with open cynicism dismissing all pleas of justice as irrelevant and in the eyes of men of the world ridiculous. The Melians admit the *de facto* cogency of the argument, yet decide to take their stand on considerations of honour and justice. The demands of the envoys are refused, and war follows. After a gallant resistance, and not before the Athenians had twice suffered a reverse and been obliged to send out reinforcements, Melos is forced to surrender : all the men are put to the sword, and the women and children sold into slavery. The Athenian envoys seemed to have been right, when they said : " As for the divine favour we think not that we shall miss our share of it. . . . Of men we know full well that by a law of their nature they enforce their will on those who are too weak to resist them." [2] A year later, in reliance on the same principles of action, they were fitting out an army and fleet for a larger enterprise, their expedition to Sicily.

The Lure of the West.—There were practical reasons for the Athenians' interest in Sicily. There was a great trade with Italy and Sicily, and with Sicily especially a corn trade. The Athenians drew their own supplies from the Black Sea ; but corn came to the Peloponnesus from Sicily and there were close bonds of union between towns in Sicily and certain Dorian cities. In especial, Corinth, now the settled enemy of Athens, was bound by intimate ties with Syracuse, her colony, the most powerful

---

[1] Thucydides, v. 85-112.   [2] Thucydides, v. 105.

of all the Sicilian states. Again, Athens herself was associated by old friendship and alliance with certain Sicilian communities, especially with Leontini,[1] which had suffered severely in a conflict with her too powerful neighbour and looked to Athens for protection. The race difference of Ionian and Dorian divided the cities of Sicily and Magna Graecia, just as it did the states of central Hellas, and the Sicilian cities tended to be grouped in alliances in accordance with racial affinities. The Euboean colonies, Naxos, Leontini, Catana, Himera and Rhegium were inclined to friendship with Athens. The Dorian colonies, Tarentum, Megara Hyblaea, Selinus, Gela, Agrigentum, and above all, Syracuse, sympathized with Sparta and the Peloponnesians. At the beginning of the war the Peloponnesian League looked to getting not only corn from Sicily, but ships. "The Lacedaemonians," wrote Thucydides, "gave orders to those in Italy and Sicily who had chosen their side to build, in proportion to the size of their cities, other ships, in addition to those which were already in Peloponnesian ports, their hope being that their fleet would reach a grand total of five hundred ships."[2] It is true these ships were never built and the Sicilians took no part whatever in the Ten Years' War. Yet there was, we see, a justification when in 427 Athens sent a squadron of twenty ships to Sicily to help the Leontines in their struggle with Syracuse.[3] In 424 they had despatched a larger fleet of just double that number : and it was out of the despatch of this fleet and the accident that Demosthenes sailed with it, that the whole affair of Pylos had come about.[4] But in 425 there was a general pacification in Sicily after a conference at which Hermocrates of Syracuse was the principal speaker and the guiding spirit : and after that there was nothing for the Athenian admirals

---

[1] Leontini, unlike most of the Greek cities of Sicily, is not on the sea coast, but eight miles inland, a little north of Megara and halfway to Catana.

[2] Thucydides, ii. 7. 2 ; Loeb, i. p. 271.   [3] Thucydides, iii. 86. 4.

[4] Thucydides, iv. 2.

to do but to come away.[1]   After that date the Athenians
for eight years took no part in the affairs of Sicily except
that in 422 they sent an officer named Phaeax to make
enquiries as to the possibility of forming alliances in
Sicily to check the rising power of Syracuse and help the
Leontines who were again in trouble.[2]   After this there
is no mention of Sicily again in Thucydides' pages till
the year 416, when an appeal for help came to the
Athenian people from the city of Segesta.

By this time there were people at Athens who were
looking to larger enterprises in Sicily.   Even in 424, when
the generals came back with their report of the pacification of Sicily, the people of Athens were angry.   The
generals were called to account, and on a charge of bribery
two of them were sent into banishment and the third
was fined.[3]   The incident is instructive.   It shows how
already the popular ear was open to the wild talk of
ambitious schemers.   The tide of Athenian good fortune
was just then in flood.   Pylos had been occupied, Sphacteria captured, the Spartan prisoners were safe at Athens
and it seemed as if Athenian ambition might ask anything of fortune.   There were men who talked of bringing
all Sicily under Athenian sway, of conquests beyond
Sicily—Italy, Tuscany, Carthage.   What bounds need
be set to the destiny of Athens ?   Segesta was not a Greek
colony, but a city of the Elymi.   There was a tradition
that the Elymi were fugitives from the sack of Troy, who
settled in Sicily and changed their name.   But in language
and customs, as far as can be judged from coins and
architectural remains, the Segestans were not very
different from Greeks.   The Segestans had an old quarrel
with their neighbours of Selinus, and in 416 Selinus had
the powerful support of Syracuse, so that Segesta was in
a desperate plight.   In their distress they turned to
Athens, with whom they had earlier entered into alliance :
they made a strong appeal for assistance, undertaking
for their part to defray the cost of any armament sent.
This appeal was far from unwelcome to the forward party

[1] Thucydides, iv. 58-65.   [2] Thucydides, v. 4.   [3] Thucydides, iv. 65. 3.

at Athens. It was the opportunity they were waiting for, a pretext for interference in Sicily. The decision for the time being was to send envoys to test the statement of the Segestan ambassadors that Segesta would defray the cost of the war.

Sicily.—Segesta and Selinus were only two out of the dozen or so city-states of Sicily, most of which were independent of one another—Hellenic city-states [1] on the pattern of those of the mother country. But in so far as public men or the populace at Athens found the proposition attractive as likely to lead on to a conquest of Sicily and limitless possibilities beyond, it is plain that, as Thucydides says, such dreams were in great part the offspring of ignorance. Sicily is a large island, rivalling Sardinia in the claim to be the biggest island in the Mediterranean. Its greatest extent is 185 miles from east to west, from north to south 130. Its area is very nearly ten thousand square miles, more than ten times that of Attica. It is one of the most richly productive countries in Europe ; in climate Sicily rivals the Riviera. It is true it was divided up among independent communities, often at war with each other. But the greatest of them, Syracuse, which was by implication marked out as the principal object of attack, if an Athenian expedition sailed for Sicily, was singly no mean antagonist of Athens herself. She had a harbour, the Great Harbour of Syracuse, as commodious, if not as famous, as the Piraeus : her population, the circuit of her walls, can have been little less than those of Athens. And if Athens had behind her her maritime empire, Syracuse had the sympathy and might expect the armed support of other Dorian cities, with the not improbable chance of obtaining ultimately the help of the whole Peloponnesian confederacy. It was a ' proposition ' to give any sober statesman pause. It was utterly contrary to the advice of Pericles inscribed at the head of this chapter.

[1] Segesta, it is true, was not by race Hellenic, but as Freeman writes (vol. i. p. 203), " Had we not been distinctly told that Segesta was not a Greek city, we should hardly have found it out from the facts of her history."

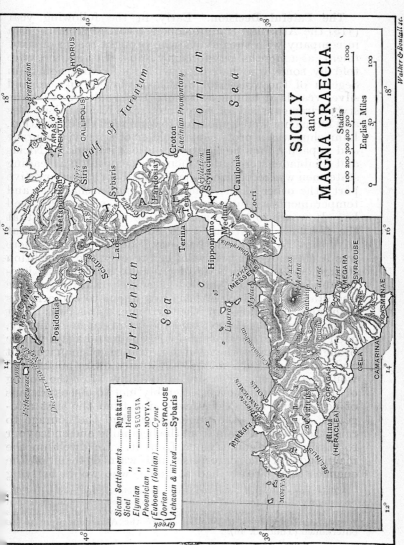

SICILY
and
MAGNA GRAECIA.

Stadia
0 100 200 300 400 500   1000

English Miles
0   50   100

Walker & Boutall sc.

Sican Settlements...... Η̄ηκκᾱτᾱ
Sicel   ,, ...Henna
Elymian   ,, ...SEGESTA
Phoenician   ,, ...MOTYA
Greek { (Euboean (Ionian)......Cyme
{ Dorian......................SYRACUSE
{ Achaean & mixed......Sybaris

The Fateful Decision.—Early in the following year (415) the Athenian commissioners returned from Segesta in company with the envoys who brought a sum of sixty talents as a months' pay for sixty ships. Stories, too, were told by some who had been with the commissioners in Segesta of the wonderful wealth displayed [1] in gold and silver vessels at banquets there. The result was that the sixty triremes asked for were voted, and Nicias, Alcibiades and Lamachus were appointed to command the expedition. Lamachus was a professional soldier of approved courage and capacity, but he had no political influence. Nicias and Alcibiades were public men, whose position as leading statesmen was recognized, the one head of the conservative party the other of the democratic, and in character and temperament as opposed as any two men could well be. It was into the hands of these two opponents that the fortunes of Athens were committed in the great adventure to which she had now bound herself. There was a clash of the two wills before ever the expedition started, indeed before the decision to send it was irrevocably fixed. For Nicias was acutely aware that the undertaking on which Athens was about to embark was rash and hazardous in the extreme. This was what Thucydides thought too ; and the judgment holds finally, even though, as the story unfolds, again and again we are brought to confess that but for strange mismanagement and gross, avoidable mistakes, the adventure might, and would have been, successful. Five days after the voting of the expedition another assembly met to discuss details of equipment, and Nicias, who was from the first altogether opposed to the undertaking, had the courage to raise the question again from the beginning and endeavour to dissuade his countrymen from it. He dwelt on the magnitude of the enterprise and warned them of the enemies they already had at home, who would be lying

[1] This impression of great wealth was produced by trickery. The Segestans gathered together all the gold and silver vessels in their own town and borrowed more from neighbouring towns, and sent all this round from one house to another where the Athenians were to be entertained (Thuc. vi. 46).

in wait for the opportunity which a reverse to the Athenian arms might give them.   But it was all to no purpose ; the notion of splendid achievements in Sicily had caught the imagination of young and old : most of the speakers who followed were in favour of it, and Alcibiades, who had all along been the prime mover and fomenter of the active policy in Sicily, undertook a refutation of Nicias' objections point by point.   Seeing there was no hope of dissuading the Athenians from their purpose by an appeal to reason, Nicias endeavoured to bring them to more sober views by insisting on the greatness of the provision that would be required.   But in this also he was defeated.   The only result was that he was pressed to state in definite terms what provision he considered necessary.   And when he gave figures, so far from being deterred from the enterprise, the Ecclesia passed a vote giving authority to the generals to make arrangements such in all respects as the public interest required.

Preparations.—The die was cast ; and forthwith preparations for the Sicilian expedition began amid the greatest enthusiasm.   Without doubt the imagination of the Athenians, young and old, had been caught by the dream of unlimited conquest.   Plutarch in his life of Nicias describes the effect of Alcibiades' successful propaganda before the expedition was voted : " the youth in their training schools and the old men in their workshops and lounging-places would sit in clusters drawing maps of Sicily, charts of the sea about it, and plans of the harbours and districts of the island which look towards Libya." [1] Aristophanes in the *Acharnians* draws a lively picture of what happened in the docks and shipyards when the people in their assembly had voted for war :

> " all the City had at once been full
> Of shouting troops, of fuss with trierarchs,
> Of paying wages, gilding Pallases,
> Of rations measured, roaring colonnades,
> Of wineskins, oarloops, bargaining for casks,
> Of nets of onions, olives, garlic-heads,
> Of chaplets, pilchards, flute-girls, and *black eyes.*

[1] Plutarch, *Nicias,* 12 ; Loeb, iii. p. 251.

> And all the Arsenal had rung with noise
> Of oar-spars planed, pegs hammered, oarloops fitted,
> Of boatswains' calls, and flutes, and trills and whistles." [1]

This bustle and business must have been intensified more than ever in the early summer of 415. For never had Athens undertaken an overseas expedition on so large a scale. The city was caught up in a wave of popular excitement. Every one connected with the expedition exerted himself in a spirit of emulation. Every trierarch was eager that his ship should be the best equipped and his crew the most perfectly trained. They willingly lavished money on additional fittings for the ships and extra pay for skilled rowers. It was the most splendid armament Athens had ever sent forth.

A " rag " in Ancient Athens.—These preparations were at their height and all seemed going well, when one morning all Athens was startled by the discovery that the *Hermae*, or square pillars supporting the bust of the god Hermes,[2] set up in front of public and private buildings all over the city, had been disfigured in the night and left all chipped and battered. The Athenians were a religious people, in some respects even superstitious, and they were horrified at the sacrilege. The affair was very mysterious : no one knew who had perpetrated the outrage, nor what the motive could be. There was intense excitement and a general sense of suspicion and uneasiness. Some thought this ' mutilation of the Hermae,' merely an outrageous prank of the Athenian ' bloods,' what we should call a ' drunken rag '; others suspected a political plot, more or less widespread. But there were no clues. In any case it was of ill augury for the enterprise they had in hand. A special commission was appointed with wide powers. Investigations were prosecuted with feverish energy and soon produced a crop of ' informations,' on the strength of which a number of men of good position, some, perhaps all, entirely innocent,

[1] Aristophanes, *Acharnians*, ll. 545-554 translated by Rogers.

[2] See vol. i. p. 47, *n* 4

were prosecuted, condemned, and, if they did not save themselves by flight, put to death.[1] One unfortunate consequence for the Sicilian expedition was that Alcibiades, the most notorious of the city's golden youth, early came under suspicion ; not indeed of participation in the actual mutilation of the Hermae, but of sacrilegious doings of a kindred nature, all supposed to be mixed up with a widespread conspiracy for the overthrow of democracy. Alcibiades protested his innocence and demanded an immediate trial. But this did not suit his enemies ; for they feared that if put on his trial now at the height of his popularity as author of the great expedition to Sicily, he would be acquitted. With malevolent cunning they opposed Alcibiades' reasonable plea, contending that it was not fitting to put one of the commanders of the expedition on trial when the country needed his services. Let him sail with the expedition to Sicily now. He could answer the charge on his return. In this way they would keep the charge hanging over him for future use and be more free to mature their schemes against him in his absence. The upshot was that Alcibiades was kept in his command and sailed with the expedition, but without being cleared of the accusation.

The Sailing of the Fleet.—May passed into June and it was high time to start for Sicily, if that year's campaigning season was not to be lost. The fleet was on a vast scale ; for the Athenians had not only to provide war-ships and a land army, but corn-ships, and merchantmen of all kinds carrying stores and tools and materials for siege operations, were to sail with the war-fleet. Corcyra was appointed the general rendezvous. And when at last the day of departure came, the Athenian war-ships and transports made a spectacular start from the Piraeus. All Athens came down to the harbour to see—" the whole multitude of the city, native Athenians and strangers alike : the Athenians to give their men a send-off—friends, kinsfolk,

---

[1] It was something like the reign of terror, infamous in English history, through the ' discovery ' of the ' Popish Plot ' by Titus Oates and Thomas Bedloe (1678).

sons—accompanying them half in tears and half hopefully, full of visions of conquests, yet, when they thought to what a distance from their own country these loved ones were going, wondering whether they should ever see them again."   " It was the most costly and the best appointed armament," says Thucydides, " that had ever up to that time started from any single Hellenic city." [1]

" And when the men were aboard their ships and the baggage and cargo all stowed, a trumpet-blast gave the signal for silence, and the prayers customary at departure for sea were recited, not ship by ship separately, but for all collectively by the herald's voice : bowls of wine were mixed and the officers and marines stepped forward and from vessels of gold and of silver poured libations in view of all the host.   The multitude crowding the shore joined in the prayer, not citizens only, but other well-wishers of Athens also who were there.   When the paean had been sung and the libations finished, they put to sea, sailing out in single file ; then when clear of the harbour, the triremes raced to Aegina." [2]

Syracuse.—That is how Thucydides describes the sailing of Athens' great armada.   He was not there to see (being still a banished man) ; but he received accounts from many eye-witnesses.   Meantime what of Syracuse ?

Syracuse, we have just said, was a city little less in size and population than Athens, and only a little less favourably equipped for defence.   There are no statistics for accurate comparison, but roughly what Plutarch says of Syracuse—' a city as large as Athens '—may be taken to be true.   The original settlement had been on the small island called Ortygia, which lies just off the coast between the Great and the Little Harbours : as the population increased suburbs were built on the mainland over the broad plateau of Epipolae, which rises from the coast and slopes back towards the west ; and these suburbs, Achradina, Tychê, Temenitês, now formed part of the city.   Syracuse, too, as well as Athens had had her

[1] Thucydides, vi. 30. 2 and 31. 1.   [2] Thucydides, vi. 32.

heroic conflict and her day of deliverance, when in 481
Gelon had defeated at Himera the vast army (said to have
numbered 300,000) with which Hamilcar had attempted
to subject Greek civilisation in Sicily to Carthage. And
in 480 this same Gelon is said to have offered an army of
20,000 hoplites—without counting archers, slingers and
cavalry—and a fleet of 200 ships, to help Hellas, his
mother-land, against Xerxes, provided he might hold the
chief command of the Pan-Hellenes either on land or on the
sea. Yet, though in a material aspect Syracuse may have
been the equal of Athens, in the things that belong to the
spirit,—in art and letters, in patriotism, in sober love of
liberty, she was greatly below.[1] Syracuse, the proud
Syracuse of history, is the city of Gelon and Hiero, of
Dionysius and Agathoclês—her despots—some of them
monsters who incarnated all that gave to the Greek word
' tyrant ' its evil connotation ; not of a free people democratically governed. In the year 415 Syracuse, freed
from tyrants and for the time being a democracy like
Athens, was considerably less powerful than Gelon's
Syracuse. Still Syracuse in 415 was a great and populous
city.

Wasted Opportunities.—The war-ships of Athens sailed
on to Corcyra, where the allied squadron, mostly ships
from Chios, the corn-ships and the merchant fleet, were
waiting for them. The total war-fleet was 134 triremes,
of which 100 were Athenian : there were besides 100
cargo-boats and 30 corn-ships. These were the fleets
in the state service. There was in addition to these a
swarm of vessels of various sizes and kinds which sailed
after the fleets for private trading. From Corcyra the
fleets struck across the mouth of the Adriatic and made
for the nearest point in Italy : then coasted along and
round the foot of Italy from the heel to the toe.[2]

[1] In one branch of art, however, Syracuse was supreme, and left
Athens far behind, as she left all other Greek cities,—the engraving of
coins. The coins of Sicily excel those of other Greek states ; and the
coins of Syracuse excel those of the rest of Sicily.

[2] Thucydides, vi. 44.

Strange as it may seem, the Athenian commanders when they left Corcyra had no plan. We find them a little later anchored at Rhegium (Reggio) on the Italian side of the Straits of Messina, and holding a conference to debate what plan to adopt. There can be little doubt, whether we look at the problem as presented to the generals in conference, or in the light of the subsequent course of events, that the best plan from a military point of view was to sail straight to Syracuse and attack the city by land and sea with the least possible delay, while their own strength was fresh. This was the opinion of Lamachus, the professional soldier, and had it been followed, it seems that Syracuse must have fallen in a few weeks. For at that time the Syracusans were little prepared for resistance and badly organized. But Lamachus' plan found favour neither with Alcibiades nor with Nicias. Nicias, as we know, was averse to the whole policy of interference in Sicily ; it was little in accordance with his inclination that he had obeyed the people's mandate which gave him a share in the command. So now his one thought was to get through with the business quickly and without loss of credit ; to bring, if he might, that costly armament safe back to Athens. The professed object of the expedition was to help Segesta against Selinus. His proposal accordingly was to sail to Selinus and force the Selinuntians to make terms with Segesta. This course had the advantage of being strictly consistent with the Athenian government's disinterested professions and was also in accordance with Nicias' cautious and scrupulous character. We might have expected Alcibiades to favour the plan of Lamachus, or to propose one equally bold. But there was another side to Alcibiades' nature : he was a past-master of intrigue. And Sicily at the time when the Athenian fleet entered Sicilian waters appeared a most promising field for the exercise of these gifts. In this Alcibiades saw himself once more in the leading rôle. So the plan he advocated was negotiation with the Sicilian states (Selinus and Syracuse, of course, excepted) ; with a view to getting as many of them as possible to side against Syracuse. When they had strengthened their position in Sicily by these alliances, it would be easy, he contended, to deal with Syracuse and Selinus ; unless, as did not seem probable, they would yield to the demands made on behalf of Leontini and Segesta. This last, Alcibiades' plan, was the plan adopted. For Lamachus, when his own proposal failed to get the support of his colleagues, gave his voice for that of Alcibiades.[1]

In accordance with this decision a strong squadron proceeded to cruise along the east coast of Sicily, visiting in succession Naxos, Catana and Camarina and making proposals of alliance. They also, in passing, reconnoitred Syracuse and its harbour at their leisure and made proclamation of what their intentions were in coming to Sicily ; but when the Syracusan fleet did not come out, they sailed away without beginning hostilities. The first results were disappointing ; but before the plan had been carried very far a dramatic change came over the position through the arrival of the state-trireme, the *Salaminia*,[2] to summon Alcibiades and certain others back to Athens to be tried for sacrilege. The paradoxical result followed that while Alcibiades' plan was adopted in this first year of the war in Sicily, Alcibiades himself was not there to carry it out. Nicias and Lamachus made a progress along the northern shores of Sicily, and having failed to win over Himera, attacked Hykkara, a coast town inhabited by Sicani with whom Segesta was at war, took it and sold the inhabitants into slavery. When later part of the Athenian forces made a similar attack on Hybla they suffered a repulse. With this repulse the active operations of the summer of 415 B.C. came to an end. No wonder the Syracusans now ceased to take the Athenian invasion seriously and were as contemptuous as before, when first the Athenians came, they had been

[1] Thucydides, vi. 46-50.

[2] The Athenians had two state despatch vessels, called from the districts where their crews were recruited, the *Paralus* and the *Salaminia*.

II   N

alarmed. Syracusan horsemen, who were free to scour
the country since the Athenians had no cavalry, rode
up to the Athenian lines near Catana and asked in mockery
whether the Athenians had come to Sicily to make a
settlement there. But as winter was beginning, Nicias
did bestir himself and prepared a surprise for the people
of Syracuse. He contrived by means of misleading
information to get the bulk of the Syracusan militia
away from Syracuse. Then with all his forces he sailed
to the Great Harbour and landed on the inner shore
somewhere near the point called Dascon, and encamped
on ground which it was easy to secure against cavalry
attack by improvised fortifications. The Syracusans
returned in haste in a day or two, marched out and
bivouacked in the plain under conditions which gave the
Athenians opportunity of bringing on a battle when they
chose. This they did next day. The Syracusans fought
bravely, but they had much to learn before they were a
match for the better disciplined Athenians, and they
were defeated. This victory did something to restore
Athenian prestige, but otherwise fulfilled no purpose.
For within a couple of days the Athenians re-embarked
and withdrew to Naxos and Catana for the winter. One
result of importance, however, the Athenians had effected
this year ; they had established a friendly understanding
with the Sicel tribes of the interior who were from of old
at feud with Syracuse. Nicias' land forces after the
capture of Hykkara had carried out a march right across
Sicily to Catana,[1] a distance of about a hundred miles,
and this was from any point of view a remarkable feat.
But on the whole the results of the first year's campaign
were in ludicrous contrast with the magnitude of the
expedition and the expectations raised by its arrival.
One lesson of importance also the year's experiences had
taught, the indispensable need of cavalry. For the
Athenians had brought only thirty horsemen ; and the
Syracusan cavalry, who numbered more than a thousand
were undisputed masters of the open country and could

[1] Thucydides, vi. 62. 3.

anywhere confine the Athenians to the ground they occupied. The generals, therefore, along with their report, sent home an urgent request for cavalry. An attempt was also made in the winter to gain over Messana, for its great importance as commanding the approach to Sicily was fully realized. But here they failed. For Alcibiades, as he left Sicily on the summons to return to Athens, already in his bitterness a dangerous enemy of his country, had been beforehand with them and warned the opposing faction in Messana, who had thereupon conspired together and gained the upper hand in the town.

Epipolae.—The Syracusans had been greatly alarmed at the first coming of the Athenians ; but this alarm had gradually worn off, when it was found that the great armada did nothing but make demonstrations along the coast of Sicily and indulge in petty operations against small towns, most of which met with no success ; it had even at one time changed into derision. In the course of the winter, on the advice of Hermocrates, the son of Hermon, their ablest and most patriotic citizen, they took three measures of very great importance. They reformed their army system ; they sent ambassadors to Corinth and Lacedaemon to ask for help ; and they built a new wall which considerably enlarged the fortified area of Syracuse, westward over Epipolae. Any plan of Syracuse which indicates the physical features of the site will show the critical importance of the plateau of Epipolae to the security of the city, when it was extended beyond the Island (Ortygia) along the broad headland to the north which forms the southern margin of the Bay of Thapsus. In fact ancient Syracuse, apart from the Island, may be regarded as built on a headland between two indentations of the coast, the Bay of Thapsus to the north, the Great Harbour to the south ; while the Island when artificially joined to the mainland became a peninsula, helping to shut in the Great Harbour. Epipolae is a triangular plateau of calcareous rock, which slopes gently upward from a three mile base along the

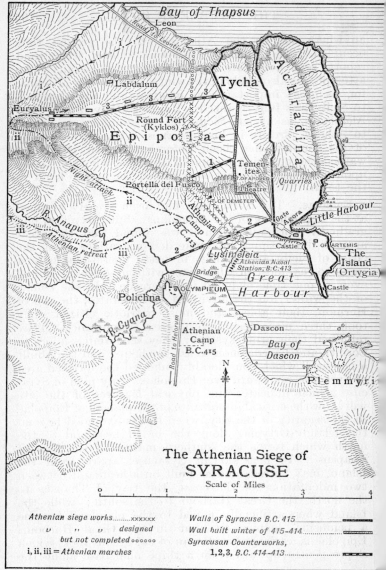

Bay of Thapsus

Leon

Labdalum

Euryalus

Epipolae

Round Fort
(Kyklos)

Tycha

Achradina

Temenites
T. OF APOLLO
Theatre

Portella del Fusco

Night attack

R. Anapus

Athenian retreat

Athenian
Camp
B.C. 413

T. OF DEMETER

Quarries

Gate
Agora

Little Harbour

Castle   T. OF ARTEMIS

Lysimeleia

Athenian Naval
Station, B.C. 413

Bridge

Great

Harbour

The Island
(Ortygia)

Castle

R. Cyana

Polichna

OLYMPIEUM

Road to Helorum

Athenian
Camp
B.C. 415

Dascon

Bay of
Dascon

N

Plemmyri

The Athenian Siege of
SYRACUSE

Scale of Miles

0   1   2   3   4

Athenian siege works.........xxxxxx
    "   "   "   designed
        but not completed ooooooo
i, ii, iii = Athenian marches

Walls of Syracuse B.C. 415...............
Wall built winter of 415-414.............
Syracusan Counterworks,
    1, 2, 3, B.C. 414-413.....................

Emery Walker l

coast (running south and north), with its apex and highest elevation due west, four miles inland. Syracuse at its furthest extent a dozen years later, when fortified anew by the tyrant Dionysius (in 402) included the whole of this plateau. But in 415, when the Athenians came to Sicily, the fortifications extended only over the easternmost strip of Epipolae, called Achradina, with an open suburb beyond the walls on the south-west, above the theatre. It was this suburb, Temenitês (afterwards called Neapolis), which Hermocrates now included within the fortifications, and further linked with the fortified suburb Tychê on the northern side towards the Bay of Thapsus by a wall across Epipolae in advance of Achradina. Outside this new wall the rough stony surface of Epipolae sloped gradually —very gradually [1]—upward, and contracted in width, till near its westward extremity, where it narrows to a point and was anciently called Euryalus, it attains a height of nearly 500 feet. The edges of this sloping plateau of Epipolae are bounded by cliffs, quite low about Achradina and higher towards Euryalus—cliffs not generally difficult of ascent, but mostly defensible. It is obvious that from a military as well as a physical stand-point the Heights of Epipolae [2] dominate Syracuse. For one thing, much of the water for the city came from the slope of the plateau and that supply could be cut off by an enemy occupying the heights. It was a per-ception, doubtless, of these facts, based partly on the experience of the Syracusans in the years we are describ-ing, which led Dionysius to enclose the whole western extent of Epipolae within his walls—a gigantic task—and to build a mighty fortress at Euryalus near the apex, the remains of which are one of the sights of modern Syracuse. When the Athenian commanders first realized

---

[1] " In walking westward from Achradina to Euryalos, there is not —except in particular places—any marked feeling of going uphill ; but if you look round at any point, you see that you have gone up a good way " (Freeman's *Sicily*, iii. p. 673).

[2] The name *Epipolae* means ' Heights.'

that Epipolae held the key of their problem we do not know, but at all events they did realize it early in the spring of 414, when a decision to undertake forthwith the siege of Syracuse had been reached. The truth seems also to have dawned on the Syracusans about the same time (the new commanders had just entered upon their office), but they expected the Athenian attack to come from the south side, from the shore of the Great Harbour, where Nicias had made his landing in the winter. They accordingly marched out in full force to the low ground between the river Anapus and the city, and after a review of all their heavy-armed, encamped there for the night. They also chose out 600 men to form a picked corps for the defence of Epipolae and to act in a sudden emergency. It does not seem to have occurred to them that the attack might come, not from the harbour side, but from the north, by way of the Bay of Thapsus. But to surprise the Heights from the north side was just Nicias' plan.[1] The fleet set out overnight from Catana and reached the Bay of Thapsus early in the morning. The troops were landed ; the fleet occupied the small peninsula of Thapsus and built a palisade across the isthmus to make the position more secure. The troops meantime made a forced march to Epipolae and climbed the ridge by the ascent which reaches the summit near the extreme western point called Euryalus. By good luck their arrival was not discovered till they were already in occupation of the ' Heights.' As soon as the news of this was brought the whole force of the Syracusans, including the Six Hundred, made an attempt to recover Epipolae by a hurried ascent from the south, but as the Athenians were already in possession of the higher ground, they suffered a severe defeat with a loss of three hundred dead, among them Diomilus, commander of the Six Hundred. Next day the Athenians advanced eastward down the slope of Epipolae towards Syracuse and offered battle under the walls of the city. When the Syracusans

[1] Perhaps it is rather Lamachus' plan, the plan he would have tried the year before, had he been allowed.

declined any further encounter, they marched back to the
Heights and built a fort on the edge of the northern cliff,
looking over the Bay of Thapsus where they had landed,
at a spot which Thucydides calls Labdalum.   This fort
was to serve as a depository for stores while the main
force began its siege operations.   After this events moved
fast.   Three hundred horse came from Segesta ; another
hundred from Naxos and the Siceli ; so that now with
two hundred and fifty Athenian ' knights,' for whom
horses had been found in Sicily, they had a body of 650
horsemen.   From Labdalum (in which a garrison was
left) they next marched forward in the direction of the
city, and at a convenient distance from the new wall
built by Hermocrates they constructed a circular fort,
which was to be the base from which they would build
lines across Epipolae to cut Syracuse off from the
rest of the world ; for these lines when completed were
to reach from sea to sea.   The men of Syracuse saw with
consternation a well-built fortress spring rapidly out of
the stony surface of the plateau.   They marched out in
order of battle, but when their commanders noticed
great unsteadiness in the ranks of the infantry, they
ordered their retirement.   Part of the cavalry remained
to harass the Athenian working parties and cut off
stragglers.   Presently, however, the Athenian cavalry
attacked in turn and with the support of a detachment of
hoplites drove the Syracusan cavalry off the hill.   The
Syracusans now abandoned further ideas of interrupting
the Athenian building work.   Instead they concentrated
their efforts on building a wall out from their own defences
which should ultimately cross the Athenian lines between
the Round Fort and the southern edge of Epipolae,
and so prevent the completion of the investment.   There
was plenty of time for this ; for as yet the Athenians were
working northwards from the Round Fort with the design
of carrying their wall first to the Bay of Thapsus, where
their fleet lay.   The Syracusans completed their cross-
wall to their satisfaction and manned the ramparts with
a garrison, while their main forces returned to the city.

The Athenians watched their opportunity and when the defenders of the cross-wall were somewhat off their guard, sent a picked force, including a special corps of Three Hundred, to attack it, while strong bodies of troops marched in the direction of the city to repulse any attempted sortie. This attack met with complete success ; the defenders of the cross-wall fled and the victors pulled down the Syracusan counter-work at their leisure.

Next day the Athenians made a new start : they left their northern wall unfinished, and began building southward from the Round Fort towards the edge of Epipolae and thence to the Great Harbour.[1] This (though Thucydides does not expressly say so) indicates a change of plan, or at all events a fresh phase in the general scheme of operations. For it implies a naval base in the Great Harbour instead of the Bay of Thapsus. And accordingly, not long after Thapsus was abandoned and the fleet brought round to the south. The Syracusans on their part began, in answer to this new menace, to build across the plain below Epipolae, through the marshy ground which there fringes the shores of the Great Harbour, a palisade and trench. The object of this second work was to prevent the Athenian wall reaching the sea on the Great Harbour side. When the Athenians had carried their wall to the edge of Epipolae, Nicias and Lamachus made preparations to attack and capture the Syracusan palisade, at the same time ordering the fleet to sail round from the Bay of Thapsus into the Great Harbour. The attack was made in the early morning and, so far as its immediate object was concerned, was completely successful. The assailants crossed the marsh where it was firmest by means of planks and stormed the palisade. They also defeated the Syracusan troops in the open ground beyond ; but the victory was spoilt by a

[1] Thucydides' words (vi. 101. 1) imply that the Athenians after destroying the Syracusan cross-wall first seized and fortified a point on the southern edge of Epipolae, in the line between the Round Fort and the sea. It may be inferred with great probability that this point on the edge of the cliff was the ravine now called *Portella del Fusco*.

mischance which cost the Athenians dear. Part of the
defeated force was making for the bridge over the river
Anapus, doubtless with the intention of finding shelter
in the fort called Polichna ; [1] which the Syracusans
held on this side the valley, and the Three Hundred
dashed forward to cut them off. In face of this danger
the Syracusan cavalry swept down upon the Three
Hundred and not only put them to flight, but threw
the whole right wing of the Athenians into disorder.
Thereupon Lamachus hurried up to stop the panic,
was isolated with a few men, and killed. At this piece
of good fortune the Syracusans' spirit revived ; they
poured out of the city again and renewed the fight.
At the same time a detachment was sent to attempt a
surprise attack on the Round Fort left weakly held on
Epipolae. This attempt very nearly succeeded. The
outworks were taken, but the Fort itself was saved by
the presence of mind of Nicias. Nicias was in the Fort,
for he was ill and unable to take part in the attack on the
Syracusan palisade. When he saw how critical the
position was, he took the drastic step of firing all the
woodwork used in constructing his siege-engines and so
kept the enemy at bay till succour came. It was at this
moment that the Athenian fleet appeared sailing into the
Great Harbour. The Syracusans thereupon abandoned
the struggle and withdrew once more into the city. The
death of Lamachus was a severe loss to the Athenians :
how much greater than we know, we can but surmise ;
for we cannot tell how much of the energy and enterprise
put into the Athenian operations before Syracuse was due
solely to Lamachus. But except for this loss all was now
going well : the fortunes of Athens in Sicily had reached
their highest point. Indeed all the signs now promised
success, if the Athenians persevered. They were already
at work on a double wall which was to extend from
Epipolae to the Great Harbour, and so in a fair way to

[1] Polichna was an outlying fort dating from early times. The name
being a diminutive of Polis = Little City, or Little-ton. Within its
defences was the **Syracusan** Temple of Zeus, the Olympieum.

complete their investing lines. Provisions were coming
in freely ; allies were rallying to them. The Sicels of
the interior showed zeal in a winning cause ; the Tuscans
sent three fifty-oared long-boats. On the other hand the
Syracusans were now thoroughly disheartened : they had
ceased to hope for the arrival of help from the Peloponnesus. They were short of water, because the Athenians
had discovered the aqueducts on Epipolae from which the
city drew water, and had diverted them. There was free
talk of surrender : overtures regarding terms had even
been made to Nicias.

The Shadow from Afar.—Alcibiades had slipped away
from the *Salaminia* at Thurii [1] in Italy and so escaped
the nets of his enemies. When this became known at
Athens he was condemned to death as a traitor, and so
for a time disappears from the scene. But Alcibiades
was very much alive, all the strength of his exuberant
nature turned into vehement desire to do hurt to the
country of his birth. His boundless dreams of ambition,
whether for himself or Athens, were dissipated, and now,
like another Achilles, he nursed the bitter resolve to make
his countrymen repent that they had forced Alcibiades to
be their enemy. One ill turn which he had done them
appeared when their plans to win over Messana miscarried (above, p. 195). They were now to suffer far more
fatal hurt. Alcibiades and his friends in misfortune,
in their flight, found their way from Thurii to Lacedaemon
and were there when the ambassadors from Syracuse
arrived to ask for help. It was at Alcibiades' urgent
persuasion that the Spartans undertook to help the
Syracusans, which implied a renewal of the Peloponnesian
war ; and at his suggestion that they sent a Spartan
to take command there, Gylippus, son of Cleandridas, a
commander of proved ability. Gylippus was now voyaging towards Syracuse : the reports he received on the
way were so discouraging that he had practically given
up hope of being in time to help Syracuse and thought
only of saving Italy. He was caught in a storm and

[1] In Southern Italy, founded on the site of Sybaris.

almost wrecked, but managed with difficulty to make the
harbour of Tarentum. Nicias heard of the voyage, and
took small account of it, so confident was he of the
position at Syracuse. Nevertheless he sent out four
triremes—but only four—to look for this new enemy. But
at Locri in Bruttium Gylippus got accurate information
of the position at Syracuse : he learnt that the Athenian
lines across Epipolae were *not*, as he had been told, completed. To a nature such as his, that was enough.
Rapidly balancing chances—this new possibility of getting
into Syracuse overland from some point on the north
coast through the gap in the Athenian lines, and the chance
of slipping into Syracuse from the sea by eluding the
Athenian blockade—he decided for the attempt overland.
In this way he avoided the four war-ships sent by Nicias ;
for they had not got so far as the Straits of Messina and
were waiting for him on the eastern coast of Sicily.
Gylippus landed at Himera and gathered there a force of
3000 men, heavy-armed and light-armed together, and
100 horse. With these he marched across Sicily to
Syracuse, as Nicias had marched to Catana. By this
time word of the approach of succour from the Peloponnese had been brought to Syracuse by a daring Corinthian ship's captain who ran the blockade and brought
his vessel safely up to the quay of the Little Harbour.
This happened on the very day which the Syracusans
had fixed for the consideration in their Ecclesia of definite
proposals for a capitulation. The proposed debate never
took place, or was utterly changed in character. Gongylus, the captain of the ship from Corinth, announced that
Gylippus was on his way and the Syracusans took fresh
heart. In a little time after messages came through from
Gylippus himself, to say that he was already nearing the
city with his 3000 men. The Syracusans marched out
in force over Epipolae to meet him. Gylippus soon
appeared on the Heights, having ascended by the same
path the Athenians had climbed on their first arrival
from the Bay of Thapsus. Why Nicias, why the Athenians, made no move to hinder either Gylippus, or the

Syracusans from the city, we shall never know. All we know is that the Syracusans marched out and Gylippus marched over Epipolae to meet them, just as if no beleaguering army had lain before Syracuse at all. The united forces of Gylippus and the Syracusans then approached the Athenian fortified positions. The Athenians drew up in order of battle, but did not come out to fight. Whereupon Gylippus sent forward a herald and made proclamation, offering the invaders an armistice, if they would agree to evacuate Sicily within five days. To this message the Athenians sent no reply. What reply could they send ? But the message itself shows how significantly the conditions were already altered through the mere presence of Gylippus.

CHAPTER VIII

DISASTER

"So much one man can do,
That does both act and know."
ANDREW MARVELL, *Horatian Ode.*

"Vanquished completely at all points, after suffering every extremity, they came, as the phrase goes, to utter destruction—landsmen and fleet, to the last ship and the last man : and few indeed of the many who went forth reached home again."

Thucydides, vii. 87. 6.

Gylippus.—By the next evening Gylippus had captured Labdalum, the Athenian fort on the northern edge of Epipolae, and put the garrison to the sword. Then began a new contest of wall-building. The Syracusans, by the orders of Gylippus, set to work upon a *third* counter-work, with still the same purpose in view,—to carry their cross-wall beyond the Athenian lines and so make investment impossible. This third attempt was made *north* of the Round Fort ; for the southern wall of the Athenians had now been completed to the sea, and it only remained to finish the northern wall—which was the earlier begun. Much material for completion of this wall had been collected and was lying on the rocky ground ready to be used. The Syracusans worked at their cross-wall with feverish energy, often appropriating the stone and wood which the Athenians had placed in position for *their* wall. The Athenians continued building too ; but not with the same concentration as before, since their energies were partly expended on other activities.

205

For Nicias had once more changed the station of his fleet and brought his ships across from the beach in front of the Athenian camp and double wall to Plemmyrium, the broad headland at the mouth of the Great Harbour opposite Ortygia. He made this headland now his naval base, and built three forts to strengthen it. Plemmyrium had the advantage of being more convenient for the maintenance of supplies, since it commanded the entrance to the Great Harbour. But— besides the dissipation of strength involved in this further scattering of the Athenian forces—it had one serious disadvantage. The new station was ill supplied with water; the seamen were obliged to fetch it from a distance; and as the open country between Plemmyrium and the Athenian camp was at the mercy of the Syracusan cavalry, who were now posted in considerable strength at Polichna, many were from time to time cut off and killed. The wastage from this cause, Thucydides tells us, did much to impair the efficiency of the Athenian fleet. At length, when he judged the moment opportune, Gylippus offered battle and was defeated. This fight took place over ground encumbered by building operations where no cavalry action was possible. Gylippus acknowledged his mistake to his men and a few days later fought again, choosing his ground more carefully, so that his horsemen were able to deliver a charge which threw one wing of the Athenians into disorder. This time it was a Syracusan victory : the whole Athenian army was driven in rout within their fortified camp. As a consequence the Syracusan cross-wall was next night triumphantly carried past the unfinished end of the Athenian lines, so that the hope of establishing a complete blockade of Syracuse by land and sea was all at once gone ; and therefore, in truth, all hope of ever taking Syracuse. Gylippus confirmed his hold on the Heights by carrying his counter work along the whole extent of Epipolae roughly parallel with its northern edge, right up to its extreme western point, Euryalus. At Euryalus he built a fort, and for the defence of his cross-wall established three fortified camps at intervals along the line of the cross-wall towards the city.[1]

Nicias' Despatch.—The summer was now coming to an end and active operations for a time ceased. Both sides took breath, but were not idle ; they were preparing for a renewal of the struggle in the spring. Gylippus set out on a tour through Sicily to collect troops, stir the half-hearted to greater zeal and bring in waverers. Very significant is it that a squadron of ships from the Peloponnese, the twelve companion ships of Gongylus, now reached Syracuse without being intercepted by the Athenian blockading fleet, and that the Syracusans once more manned their own fleet and commenced practising, with the obvious intention of challenging before long Athenian superiority at sea.

Nicias on his part sent home to Athens a letter which gave a faithful picture of the evil state to which the expedition was reduced and made urgent appeal, either for the despatch of reinforcements, or the immediate recall of the whole armament. The words of this despatch, as reproduced by Thucydides, exhibit in a most vivid manner the low ebb to which the fortunes of the Athenians in Sicily had sunk. The picture is in painful contrast with the fair prospects with which that year had opened. Nicias says : "After we had defeated the Syracusans in several engagements and built the fortifications we now occupy, Gylippus came with forces from the Peloponnese and from certain cities in Sicily. We beat him in one engagement, but the next day we were overborne by the multitude of his horsemen and javelin-men and withdrew within our fortifications. So now we have stopped our investment of the city owing to the number of our opponents, and remain inactive. . . . They have built a single cross-wall past our lines, so that we are no longer able to carry out our investment, unless we attack this cross-wall in superior force, and take it. We are supposed to be besieging them, but it has come about that we are rather ourselves the besieged—at least on land ; since by reason

[1] Thucydides, vii. **7**. 1 and 43. **4**.

of the enemy's cavalry we cannot venture more than a little way into the country." [1] He goes on to describe how the Syracusans are soliciting reinforcements from the Peloponnese and from Sicily and that he may look before long to be assailed by land and by sea. He goes on : " And do not take it ill that I say ' by sea.' Our fleet, as the enemy too very well know, was on its arrival, in a high state of efficiency, the hulls sound and dry, the crews at full strength. But now the ships' planks are sodden through being too long in the water, and the crews are depleted. It has been impracticable to draw up our ships and dry them, because the enemy's ships are as many as ours and even more in number, and so are able to keep us in constant expectation of attack." [2] After further explanation of the extreme gravity of the position he puts before the Athenians the alternative of withdrawal from Syracuse, or the despatch of a second armament on the same scale as the original expedition. The enemy's strength, he points out, is likely to increase and he can himself look for no succour in Sicily. He asks further for his own recall, since a wasting malady to which he is a prey makes it impossible for him to remain. " I claim this much indulgence," he says in conclusion, " since so long as I kept my health, I did you good service in several commands. And whatever you purpose, let it be done immediately on the return of spring : make no delay. The enemy will get their accession of strength from Sicily in a short while : the reinforcements from Peloponnese may take longer in coming, but unless you take good heed, they will get here without your knowing, as they did before, or before they can be stopped." [3]

The Tables Turned.—What the despatch of Nicias said about the position of the Athenians at Syracuse was no more than the truth. The Athenians were now the besieged rather than the besiegers. Early in the spring of 413 Gylippus returned to Syracuse bringing with him considerable reinforcements. Then by a well-planned

[1] Thucydides, vii. 11. 2-4.   [2] Thucydides, vii. 12. 3.
[3] Thucydides, vii. 15. 2.

coup he captured the three forts of the Athenians on Plemmyrium. This was a combined military and naval operation. For the most ominous sign of change in the relative strength of the contending parties was that the Syracusans were now thinking of disputing the Athenian command of the sea. For two whole years since the first arrival of the great Athenian fleet the Syracusans had not once ventured to try conclusions with the Athenians at sea. But now Gylippus encouraged them to try a sea-fight : it was taking a great risk, but the prize in the event of victory was worth it. Hermocrates urged that their most hopeful course was a bold initiative ; the Athenians, he argued, did not get their sea-craft by hereditary right, nor was their superiority inalienable ; there was a time when Athens had been as little a sea-power as Syracuse was now. Accordingly the Syracusans manned their ships and practised, and were eager to fight at sea : the attack on Plemmyrium was made under cover of a naval engagement. Simultaneously from the two sides of the ' Island ' the Syracusan galleys streamed out —a sight the Athenians had not seen since their first coming—five and thirty from the Great Harbour, forty-five from the Lesser. The Athenians had only sixty ships now to oppose to these eighty : with twenty-five they met the attack from the Great Harbour ; the residue sailed out against the squadron from the Little Harbour. The troops in Plemmyrium crowded down to the beach to watch the sea-fight, and while their attention was so engaged, Gylippus, who had moved forces from Syracuse the night before for the purpose, suddenly attacked and took first the largest fort on Plemmyrium, and then the other two. As for the sea-fight, at first it seemed going in favour of the Syracusans ; but the ships fighting their way into the Great Harbour lost their formation and fell into disorder, with the result that in the end the Syracusans were defeated with the loss of eleven ships. So at the end of the day the Athenians retained, though not so indisputably as heretofore, their supremacy at sea. But they had lost Plemmyrium. Now the loss of

Plemmyrium was most serious. The loss of material was in itself calamitous—provisions, stores, money, sails for forty triremes, three ships of the line hauled up on shore. But worse than the loss of material was the change for the worse in the whole position. Plemmyrium commanded the entrance to the harbour; with the loss of Plemmyrium the provisioning of the Athenian forces became much more difficult. The Syracusans now had a naval post there, and the Athenian supply-ships might at any time have to fight their way in.

The Spectre of Defeat.—The interest of the struggle is now concentrated about the Great Harbour, where the fight for Plemmyrium and the naval battle had taken place. The Great Harbour of Syracuse—a sheltered bay rather than a mere haven—is still potentially one of the finest in Europe. From the northern shore, where of old the Syracusans had their docks, there is a two-mile stretch of water; from the entrance to the point of Dascon is nearly a mile and a half: the area is fully three square miles, and there is a good depth of water everywhere—except along the northern shore and about the mouth of the Anapus. If we look at the plan, we see how straitened and uncomfortable the position of the Athenians now was. They occupied one strip of coast only on the western shore opposite the harbour mouth, roughly from their double wall to the Anapus. All the rest of the circuit of the harbour was in hostile occupation, and on the west of the Athenian position the Syracusans also had, as we have seen, an outlying fort, Polichna. Worst of all, the enemy was established on both sides of the entrance to the harbour; on the north was Ortygia, the original Syracuse; and since the capture of Plemmyrium the south side was Syracusan too. In the recent sea-fight the Athenians had held their own, and a little more. But it must have been obvious to all that the margin of superiority was dangerously slight. Already the shadow of calamity hung over the Athenians, clouding their spirits. The Syracusans were proportionately elated. It is a sign of the changed times that a squadron of twelve

THE GREAT HARBOUR OF SYRACUSE.

This view is taken from Achradina in the neighbourhood of the Theatre and looking S.E. Across the harbour is Plemmyrium; on the extreme left modern Syracuse (Ortygia) just comes into the picture. The mouth of the Great Harbour opens between Ortygia and Plemmyrium.

Adapted from Mauceri's *Siracusa*, p. 44 (fot. Crupi).

ships sailed from Syracuse, and, after detaching one ship to cross to Greece, waylaid a fleet of supply-ships bringing stores to the Athenians and destroyed most of them ; and then made a landing on the Bruttian coast and burnt a quantity of timber for shipbuilding which had been destined for the use of the Athenians ; and that all but one of these ships got safely back, eluding the twenty ships the Athenians sent after them.[1] There was daily skirmishing in the harbour, but for some time the Syracusans made no further attempt to challenge the Athenian mastery of the sea. Presently news came of the approach of a large Athenian fleet with reinforcements. The Syracusans thereupon hastened to try their fortune in a fresh fight before these reinforcements arrived. They were learning from defeat, and, with a view to counteracting the superior skill of the Athenian seamen, they altered the build of their ships in a way which they hoped would bring them victory. Athenian superiority, as we saw in Phormio's sea-fights (Ch. vi. p. 140), depended on rapidity of movement and skill in ramming ; but in the Great Harbour, large as it was for a harbour, there was not enough space for hostile fleets to manoeuvre freely, and this would tell against the Athenians. The Syracusans proposed further to counter the Athenian mode of attack by charging prow to prow, and with this in view they strengthened the bows of their triremes with extra beams. Their expectation was that when a charge took place the bows of the lighter Athenian ship would be stove in, while their own ships, specially strengthened for such encounters, would take no harm. So one day the Syracusans began an attack on the Athenian camp from two sides, from the city and from the fort Polichna, while the fleet sailed out in battle array, eighty ships in all. The Athenians put to sea to meet them with seventy-five. The whole day passed in manoeuvring and skirmishing, but things did not come to a general engagement. Next day there was no renewal of the fight at all. On the third day the Syracusans again attacked in full

1 Thucydides, vii. 25.

force by land and sea. And this time, at the suggestion of the Corinthian, Ariston, they tried a *ruse*. The morning passed as before in skirmishing without any close engagement and about mid-day the signal was given for the Syracusans to retire on their stations. The Athenians, supposing the fighting was over for the day, likewise withdrew to land and left their ships. But the Syracusans by arrangement snatched a hasty meal at the quay-side and went on board again. Suddenly they were seen to be bearing down upon the Athenian shore. The Athenian seamen, who were partly dispersed, hastily hurried back to their ships and re-embarked, most of them without having broken their fast. When the Syracusans still delayed their attack, the Athenians took the initiative and brought on a general engagement. The fight fell out as the Syracusans had planned. Whenever they got the chance, they charged prow to prow, and then the heavy bows of the Syracusan ship crashed through the bows of the lighter-built Athenian and disabled her. The Athenians on their ships suffered also from the missiles of javelin-men with whom the Syracusans had crowded their decks ; and still more from small craft, which in this fight daringly rowed about among the triremes and getting under an enemy's oars hurled their weapons into the waist of the ship at the seamen as they pulled.[1] In the end the Athenians gave way and fled to the protection of their palisade with the loss of seven ships. The Syracusans had won a victory at sea. It was the beginning of the end. The victors were overjoyed, and full of new confidence, prepared to renew the attack next day.

Demosthenes to the Rescue.—And then, to the consternation of the Syracusans and the immeasurable relief of Nicias and his army, Demosthenes and Eurymedon sailed into the Great Harbour with 73 fresh ships, 5000 heavy-armed footmen and large bodies of archers, slingers and javelin-men.[2]

When Nicias' letter came to Athens and was read in the Ecclesia, the Athenians without hesitation and with-

[1] Thucydides, vii. 40. 5.   [2] Thucydides, vii. 42.

out recrimination had voted new expeditionary forces very little inferior in numbers and equipment to the first. And now at the very moment of despair these lavish reinforcements had arrived. To the Athenians at Syracuse it was " like the return of health to one long sick." Above all, these new forces had with them a commander who was a born leader of men with a quick eye for a situation and resolution to carry through a plan once formed. Demosthenes could not fail to grasp the vital fact, that for any further prosecution of the siege of Syracuse the capture of Gylippus' cross-wall was essential : Nicias himself had seen that.[1] But Demosthenes saw even more clearly that, failing the recovery of the command of Epipolae by the capture of the cross-wall, the only course left was withdrawal from Syracuse : for the position of the Athenian forces there had become untenable. He urged that the struggle should be brought at once to a decisive issue by an attack on the cross-wall. If it succeeded, ultimate victory was assured. If it failed, they must sail away.

The Night Attack on Epipolae.—The obvious way to capture the cross-wall was by direct assault from the Athenian lines. For though the Athenians were prevented by the cross-wall from completing their plan for the investment of Syracuse, they still kept possession of a large part of Epipolae south of the Syracusan counter-work. The Round Fort remained in their hands and the stretch of wall southward from the Round Fort to the edge of the cliff. Demosthenes tried first a regular assault from this side with the help of military engines. Every attack was beaten back and his engines burnt. It seemed vain to make further attempts on the cross-wall from this side. But Demosthenes had in reserve another and bolder plan : to march round once more to the western extremity of Epipolae and get up, as Nicias and Gylippus had already done, by the paths leading over Euryalus. The assailants would then be, as we see from

[1] Above, p. 207.

the plan, *behind* the Syracusan defence works. The cross-wall would be turned, and it was then a matter of defeating the Syracusans in a straight-forward fight on equal terms. The difficulty was how to get up on to Epipolae without being seen by the enemy. For if the Syracusans were aware that such an attempt was about to be made, they could easily repel it by occupying Euryalus in force. They already had a fort and a garrison there. The only hope of success lay in a surprise, and Demosthenes' plan was for a night-attack. There was hazard involved, as there is in all night-attacks; but the risk was worth taking, Demosthenes argued, and Nicias and Eurymedon gave their consent. Demosthenes laid his plans with the utmost care. The troops were to take five days' rations and march about midnight along under the southern side of Epipolae to the western end, and then climb up. Workmen and masons and stores of all kinds were to go with the troops with the object of setting to work at once on the unfinished wall, should they succeed in driving the enemy off Epipolae and securing their own position. Then in no long time the northern section of the investing lines might be completed and Syracuse would at last be really shut in. It was a promising plan—if all went well.

It was a bright moonlight night, and when in tense excitement the Athenian columns started, this at first stood them in good stead. They marched for some time over the level of the valley parallel with the table-land of Epipolae, then wound into the more hilly ground till they came under Euryalus itself and began to ascend more steeply. It was a long way round, but so far all was going well: they reached the top undiscovered, and surprised and captured the Syracusan fort. Many of the defenders, however, got away, and like wild-fire the alarm spread along the ridge. The special corps of Six Hundred, now commanded by Hermocrates,[1] were the first to meet the attack. They were overborne and scattered. One detachment of the Athenians turned to

[1] Diodorus, xiii. 11. 4.

the demolition of the Syracusan wall; the main body
pushed straight on. The defenders came swarming out
of their camps headed by Gylippus, but they were at a
disadvantage through the suddenness of the alarm and
at the first shock gave ground. Demosthenes' men,
in their eagerness to follow up these first successes,
pressed on too impetuously and failed to keep their
formation. Their foremost men now came up against
a solid body of Boeotian hoplites,[1] who checked their
onset: then charged and put them to flight. At this
point the fortunes of the fight completely changed. In
their flight these routed men collided with their comrades
still hurrying up to the attack and threw them in turn
into disorder. The moonlight, which had been a help
to the Athenians at first, now played them false. They
could see men coming on, but could not distinguish
friends from foes. Men shouted at the advancing figures
demanding the pass-word: the air grew thick with
confused outcries, incessant challenge and answer;
words of command became indistinguishable. Soon the
enemy got to know the Athenian watch-word and used
it either to lure small parties to destruction or to save
themselves when outnumbered. The accident that some
on the Athenian side were Dorian—Argives, Corcyreans
and Messenians—completed the confusion. For hearing
the Dorian battle-cry on the lips of their allies the
Athenians were smitten with fresh dismay. Soon the slope
of Epipolae was a scene of wild disorder, in which men
hardly knew what happened, and among the Athenians
all cohesion and sense of direction were lost. Many
threw away their shields and leapt over the edge of the
cliff, often losing their lives in this way. Many reached
the level plain only to find themselves bewildered and
lost, more especially those newly arrived with Demosthenes; and these next day were rounded up and slain

---

[1] They were probably men of Thespiae. For the only Boeotians we
hear of as arrived by this time were a body of Thespian hoplites, who,
while the Syracusan squadron was on its cruise (above p. 211), had been
transhipped from a merchantman and brought on to Syracuse.

by the Syracusan horsemen. The night attack had ended in disastrous failure.[1]

Dangerous Delays.—Demosthenes was in no manner of doubt what ought now to be done. The one safe and reasonable course was to get away out of the harbour of Syracuse with the least delay possible. Demosthenes had deliberately staked all on the chance of re-capturing Epipolae. The judgment of the sword had gone against him ; he accepted the verdict and urged the necessity of immediate withdrawal from Syracuse. Eurymedon supported him. But Nicias would not agree to it. By some strange fatality, or paralysis of will, he clung to this scene of his long martyrdom. The Syracusans, he argued, were in even worse case than the Athenians, bankrupt and exhausted, and would surrender if only pressure were maintained a little longer. He was relying on secret intelligence from Syracuse, where there had all along been a party favourable to Athens and ready to betray the city. At any rate it was impossible to leave Sicily without express orders from Athens. Perhaps the truth was there, Nicias dared not face his countrymen. Life had no value for him unless he could return to Athens once more a victor.[2] But if that was his motive, terrible is his responsibility. A little later when fresh reinforcements reached the Syracusans, and they were observed to be preparing a fresh attack by land and sea, Nicias gave way. Yes, they must go. Preparations for evacuation were expedited ; but as secretly as possible, to avoid interference from the enemy. All was ready ; and orders were even sent to Catana countermanding supplies. Then on August the 27th, 413, there was an eclipse of the moon. Great part of the army looked on this as a sign and a portent directed against the enterprise they had in hand ; and unfortunately among these victims of super-

[1] Thucydides, vii. 43-45. Plutarch (*Nicias*, 21) gives the number of the Athenian dead as 2000 ; Diodorus (xiii. 11. 5) as 2500.

[2] It had been Nicias' pride, before he went to Sicily, that in every expedition in which he had commanded he had been successful. See Plutarch, *Nicias*, 2.

stition was Nicias, the commander-in-chief. Nicias pronounced that there must not be a word more of departure
till thrice three times three days had passed. Just a
lunar month ! There were sane men in that armament
who must have cursed the folly of this decision ; but the
reasoning were overborne by the unreasonable. This,
however, it was which finally brought Nicias, Demosthenes,
and every soldier and sailor in that great armada of
Athens to destruction.

Defeat of the Athenian Fleets.—The Syracusans were
kept informed of what was passing in the Athenian camp.
They were elated at what they heard, as it confirmed their
own feeling of having got the better of their adversaries
and they were more than ever resolved that the hated
foe should not escape. They practised sea tactics for
some days ; then made an attack by land on the Athenian
walls and cut off a party of Athenians who attempted a
sortie. Next day there was a simultaneous attack by
land and sea. In the sea-fight this time the Athenians
had the advantage of numbers, 86 ships to 76. But they
were beaten. Eurymedon in attempting to outflank
the Syracusans on the right weakened the Athenian centre
which the Syracusans were then able to defeat ; got
driven into the S.W. corner of the harbour (the Bay of
Dascon) and was there cut off and destroyed with all his
squadron. The rest of the Athenian fleet were chased to
land, taking refuge behind the improvised defences which
Nicias had made for them. It was but a small set-off
to this shameful overthrow that the Syracusans met
with a reverse on land in attempting to get possession of
the Athenians' hulls which had run ashore between the
Athenian lines and Syracuse. The number of Athenian
ships captured that day was eighteen.

The Closing of the Harbour Gates.—And now the plight
of the Athenians was bad indeed ; for the Syracusans had
beaten in fair fight, not the water-sodden ships of Nicias'
fleet only, but these together with the fresh fleet brought
recently by Demosthenes. Their aim was no longer to

save Syracuse, but to destroy the proud enemy who had
sailed to Sicily to conquer her. If they pressed their
advantage now, not a ship, not a man should escape.
Already they were able to move freely once more about
their great harbour without fear of molestation, and they
now entertained the design of closing the entrance with a
boom, so that the Athenian forces could no longer escape
by sea. The way they did this was by mooring boats of
all sorts lengthwise across the entrance from Ortygia to
Plemmyrium and making them fast by chains. The
distance is over half a mile, so it was no light undertaking ; but the work proceeded rapidly.

The Agony in the Great Harbour.—The significance of
this last move of the enemy was not lost upon the Athenian commanders. They saw they must fight to prevent
the closing of the harbour if that were still possible, or,
if necessary, break through and force a passage out.
As a preliminary to departure they now also entirely
abandoned Epipolae, bringing what was left of their
stores and material down to the camp by the Great
Harbour. Then they made ready for battle, recognising
that their fate depended on the issue of the next sea-fight.
They were able to man 110 ships. They crowded the
decks with archers and javelin-men, because they were
now resting their hopes on clearing the enemy's decks
with missiles in close fighting, not on superior skill in
manoeuvring. At the same time, to countervail the
advantage which the Syracusans had had in the last two
fights from the artificial strengthening of the bows
of their triremes, they fitted their ships with grappling
irons which were to be let fall on the enemy's decks and
hold the ships fast locked while the fighting men on
board fought it out. When everything that could be
thought of had been done to secure victory, Nicias
harangued the crews in words which, as Thucydides
reports them, reveal the tense emotion of the moment.
After making all customary appeals, addressed alike to
those who were citizens of Athens and those who were
their allies—to patriotic pride, to memories of past

victory, to the hope of seeing their homes again, he touched one last chord of loftier patriotism, reminding the Athenians that Athens had no more ships in her docks like these that were now going into battle, no more soldiers in the prime of life. If their valour failed now, there was no prospect, for themselves or Athens, but servitude. "Therefore, since in this one last battle you contend both for yourselves and them, fight as never before, and keep in mind, man by man and all together, that on shipboard with you will be all the land forces of Athens, and all her fleet—yea the entire remainder of the commonwealth too, and the great name of Athens." [1]

Gylippus and the Syracusan commanders were no less forward to encourage their men, appealing to the glory of what they had achieved already and to the fierce hope of glutting their vengeance to the full on the enemies who had wronged them. At the same time means were taken to neutralize the new device by which the Athenians sought to restore the chances of the fight. They covered the bows and great part of the decks of their ships with hides, so that the grapnels when dropped might fail to get a hold. Then both sides went aboard. Nicias in the extremity of his anxiety and fearing to leave anything unsaid that might avail, called his ships' captains round him again and conjured them by every tie they held sacred to quit them like men ; and it was then that as a climax he reminded them of all that liberty meant at Athens, how each might live his own life there, free of interference.[2]

This time the disparity in number of ships was greater, for, whereas the Athenians had 110 ships, the Syracusans had about the same number as in the last battle, 75 ; but against this advantage must be set the deterioration in the crews now manning the Athenian ships. For when trained men fell short the generals completed the crews by pressing into the service any who were strong enough and of suitable age.[3]

[1] Thucydides, vii. 64. 2. [2] Thucydides, vii. 69. 2. See also ch. iv. p. 108.
[3] Thucydides, vii. 60. 3.

The Athenians, led by Demosthenes, Menander and
Euthydemus, charged straight at the boom : at the
first onset they overpowered the ships stationed on guard
before it and began to cut the fastenings. But at once
the rest of the Syracusan ships swept down from all
sides and the engagement became general. The whole
harbour was filled with the turmoil of the struggle, for
little less than two hundred ships in all were engaged.
The desperate nature of the stake nerved both sides to
supreme efforts : for the last hopes of the Athenians
depended on it. And what gave this struggle its most
moving aspect was that it took place—like a mock sea-
fight in an amphitheatre—before the straining eyes of
two bodies of spectators whose lives and fortunes depended
on the issue. The harbour has a circumference of nearly
six miles, and about half that circuit was lined with
crowds of spectators. The sea-front and quays of the
Island, old Syracuse—and the docks and esplanades to
the westward and the terraces of Achradina above
—were filled with the people of Syracuse, men, women
and children, eager to see the destruction of the hated
enemy. Along the shore to the south, beyond the double
wall, came the Athenian camp, and on either side of it
were extended by Nicias' directions all the Athenian
troops not fighting on shipboard, so as to occupy as much
of the shore as possible and give their own men any
support they could. There was little manoeuvring in
this fight and not much skilled ramming. For the most
part the hostile crews just lay their ships one alongside
the other and fought a ding-dong battle from the decks.
It was more like a battle on land than a sea-fight. " It
happened oftentimes," says Thucydides, " through the
want of room that one ship rammed another on one side
and was itself rammed on the other : two ships would
be engaged with one, and sometimes several would
unavoidably become entangled together, and the pilots
must needs look to attack and defence not with relation to
a single adversary, but to several together and from all
sides : the din of the clashing ships was itself terrifying

and made it impossible to hear the words of command." [1]
Especially vivid is Thucydides' description of the spectators' emotions and the changes of feeling varying with
the swiftly changing fortunes of the fight. "They were
too close for a general view, and were not all looking on
the same part of the scene. When they saw their own
side winning, they would take heart again and fall into a
passion of appeals to heaven not to rob them of this
deliverance ; while others, seeing the fight going against
them, poured out cries and lamentations, and from the
mere sight of the action were more overwhelmed than
the actual combatants. Others again, who had before
their eyes a struggle evenly contested, in an agony of
suspense swayed their bodies to and fro in accord with
the agitation which the long-drawn crisis induced, and
were in a state of acute distress ; each moment seemed
to bring them within an ace of escape or destruction." [2]
At last after an obstinate struggle and much loss on both
sides, the Syracusans fairly routed the Athenians, and,
pressing upon them with triumphant outcry, chased them
to land.

Despair.—There was a scene of frenzied activity for a
time along the beach in front of the Athenian encampment and on either side of it, while the soldiers who had
been agonized spectators of the defeat gave what help
they could to their comrades struggling to shore from
disabled or abandoned triremes ; or hurried to man the
defences of the camp, lest the Syracusans should follow
up their victory in the Great Harbour by an attempt to
storm them. Then despair settled down upon that
mixed multitude of soldiers, seamen, artizans, traders
and camp-followers. No means of escape seemed left to
them, or only by one way most perilous ; and they had
none of them any mercy to expect if they fell into the
hands of the Syracusans. But there were brave men
there who never lost hope, foremost among them Nicias
himself, whose character shines brightest in this last dark
page of his story, and who in spite of bodily infirmity

[1] Thucydides, vii. 70. 6.   [2] Thucydides, vii. 71. 3 (L. J.).

seemed to gather strength and dignity as the abyss of
disaster closed over him and his doomed army. Demosthenes did even better. He came to Nicias and proposed
that early next morning they should man their ships and
make one more effort to fight their way out. For even
now they had more ships than the enemy.[1] Nicias
agreed ; but the seamen had utterly lost heart and would
not go on board. There was but one thought in all that
host—instant retreat by land to some friendly city.
The stranded ships, their unburied dead, everything
else was forgotten. And even now the destinies had
kept one chance of escape open for them. The Syracusans
in the exultation of victory and deliverance were that
night so given over to feasting and riotous rejoicing,
that their commanders could do nothing with them.
If the Athenians had but retreated then and there without
a moment's delay, they would have found the roads open
and would probably have got away safely. There would
have been no one to oppose their march. But again,
and for the last time, there was delay. Hermocrates,
like another Themistocles, tricked the Athenians into
staying by a false message. When he could not succeed
in persuading the other Syracusan commanders to take
troops and beset with barriers and ambuscades all the
routes by which the Athenians might attempt to retreat,
he sent horsemen after dark to the Athenians' lines to
warn Nicias from his friends in Syracuse not to march
that night, since all the roads were blocked ; but to wait
for daylight. It seems a simple trick. But the Athenian
leaders were deceived, and waited. They waited not
only that night, but the next day too—in order to sort
and pack their baggage better ! When they did start on
the second [2] day after the last battle in the Great Harbour
it was too late, Hermocrates and the Syracusans had had
time by then to make the preparations which finally sealed
the doom of the Athenian expedition against Syracuse.

[1] They had sixty ships, whereas the Syracusans could scarcely
muster fifty.

[2] The third by the Greek mode of reckoning, Thucydides, vii. 75. 1.

Retreat.—Thucydides' account of the departure of the Athenians from their encampment is the most pathetic part of all the moving story told in his History with such incomparable skill : " After this, when Nicias and Demosthenes judged everything to be ready, the force was actually set in motion. This was the morrow of the day following the sea-fight. It was a terrible situation, not from any one particular—the withdrawal with the loss of their whole fleet, the shattering of their hopes, the peril to themselves and their country ; the evacuation itself, meant to each man everything that was most painful for eye to see or mind to dwell on. The dead lay unburied, and as men caught sight of the bodies of their friends they were stricken with grief and terror ; the sick and wounded now being abandoned to their fate alive were far more distressing than the dead to their living comrades, far more pitiable than those whose troubles were ended. In blank despair they broke out into entreaty and lamentation, crying aloud to any friend or comrade they caught sight of and begging him to take them with him ; clinging to their departing shipmates and following to the limit of their powers ; and when their bodily strength gave out dropping behind, with here and there a ' God help me ! ' or a groan. Tears were in every soldier's eyes : there was no help for it but to go, but it was hard to break away, though it was from enemy soil, though they had already met with sufferings too deep for tears and feared still worse in the dread unknown. A sort of self-contempt too and self-reproach hung heavy over them ; they were for all the world just like a city that could hold out no longer seeking some escape—a great city too, for in all no less than two score thousand were starting on this march." [1]

The contrast of this scene of misery and humiliation with the splendour and pride of that day on which the Athenian war-fleet sailed out of Piraeus was most poignant of all. " They had come intending the enslavement of others, they were leaving in fear of suffering this fate

[1] Thucydides, vii. 75. 1-5 (L. J.).

themselves ; they had put to sea amid prayers and songs of victory, the sounds amid which they were starting back were of very different import ; instead of voyaging on ship-board, they were marching on foot, their hopes dependent on infantry prowess, no longer on naval skill." [1]

Nicias.—In this hour of supremest anguish Nicias himself displayed a fortitude, and more than a fortitude— a spirit of heroic cheerfulness and self-forgetfulness, which redeems his memory, and goes far to lift the heavy burden of reproach which his faults of character and errors of judgment deserve. He went about from rank to rank, exhorting, encouraging, raising his voice to the utmost of his power, that more might hear him, refusing to give up hope and by his bearing inspiring others with hopefulness : "Men of Athens, and allies," he cried, " even in this plight you must keep up hope—men have ere now come safe out of dangers even greater than yours. Nor must you blame yourselves too much either for your disasters or for the undeserved distresses you now suffer. See ! I myself am neither better off than any of you for bodily strength—indeed, you see for yourselves how I am prostrated by my complaint— nor have I been second to any in the happiness of my private fortune or in any other respect, who now am tossing on the same deep and perilous flood as the humblest of you. Yet my life has been much spent in obedience to God's laws ; much too in just and blameless dealing with my fellow men. And this gives me, in spite of all, sure confidence in what is to come, and calamities do not daunt me in proportion to their terrors." [2]

Ruin.—The plan of the generals was to march inland as directly as possible to the territory of the friendly Sicels.[3] The most direct way to reach it was to strike up into the hills to the west beyond Euryalus. It would

[1] Thucydides, vii. 75. 7.

[2] Thucydides, vii. 77. 1-3 (L. J.). The ' speech ' ends with a phrase which has become immortal : " It is *men* who make a city, and not walls or ships with no men in them."

[3] The ultimate goal of the retreat was Catana.

have been quite an easy undertaking had the march been unopposed. Nor was the Sicel country altogether strange and unknown, since Nicias during the first summer had ordered a march right across Sicily from

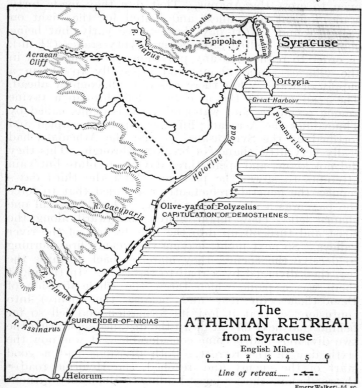

ADAPTED FROM E. A. FREEMAN.

Himera (above, ch. vii. p. 194). They marched in two divisions, one under the command of Nicias, the other of Demosthenes in hollow square formation, with the baggage and non-combatants inside. The division of Nicias led. Progress was very slow; for every one, officers as well as men, must carry everything for himself, rations, water, cooking vessels. The Syracusan cavalry and light-armed were swarming over the plain to impede and harass the retreat ; the Athenian columns had to fight even to cross the Anapus. That day they made forty stades (about five miles) and halted for the night on rising ground. Next day they started early, but being short of food, halted after going twenty stades ($2\frac{1}{2}$ m.), in order to requisition any provisions they could find in the villages round about, and especially to obtain a supply of water. For there was difficult country ahead. The road up into the mountains led through a ravine among precipices and water-falls. This defile, called by Thucydides the Acraean Cliff, was already occupied and fortified by the Syracusans, so that the Athenians had really very little chance of breaking through. This they did not know, and spent three days in resolute but vain attempts to storm the passage. After the third day's repulse the generals reluctantly concluded that to force the pass was a sheer impossibility. There was still one chance left. They might march southward along the coast and turn off up into the hills by one of the river valleys. So next night, leaving their camp fires burning to deceive the enemy, they marched back towards the sea, then diverged by a road to the right. In the night there was a panic which threw the whole division of Demosthenes (in rear and nearest the enemy) into confusion, so that it lost its formation and fell so far behind that next day at dawn the distance separating the two divisions had become considerable. It was now the sixth day of the retreat. Both divisions had a good start of the enemy and reached the Helorine road— the road along the sea-coast leading to Helorum—without molestation ; and not long after the leading division under Nicias reached the river Cacyparis, where they expected to be met by Sicel guides. But, instead, they found the river held by the Syracusans in force, and the way up the valley barred by artificial defences. All they could do was to effect the passage of the river after

a fight, and march on by the coast. In the evening of
the same day they came to another river, the Erineus.
This also Nicias crossed; and halted his men for the
night on rising ground near it. Demosthenes' division
meantime had fared very differently. They never recovered from the panic of the night before and were
overtaken by the pursuing Syracusans towards evening.
The country here being comparatively level, the Syracusan horse got in front, and soon the whole division was
in difficulties with the enemy all round. Nicias and the
leading division were too far ahead now to lend any
succour. Demosthenes' task had been the more difficult
all along; his division being in rear, it had to bear the
brunt of the fighting, his men had to think all the time of
repelling attacks as much as of getting away. And now
by an unfortunate blunder they had entered a large
walled enclosure,[1] exit from which was difficult. At once
the enemy closed in upon them, and from all sides poured
in missiles which struck down many. The tactics of the
Syracusans were to avoid coming to close quarters, and
to wear the fugitives down by persistent assaults from a
distance. They could afford now to be sparing of their
own lives and began to think of capturing instead of
killing their adversaries. The method proved quite
effective. Demosthenes' men bore up under this punishment for the rest of the day, till they were utterly worn out.
Then Gylippus sent a herald with an offer of terms:
surrender on condition that all lives should be spared:
no one was to be put to death either by the sword or by
ill-treatment. On these terms Demosthenes and the
survivors of his division gave up their arms and to the
number of 6000 men surrendered.[2]

Next day, the seventh of the retreat, news of this
surrender was carried to Nicias by the Syracusans along
with the demand that he should surrender in like manner.
At first Nicias refused to believe the report: he was

[1] Plutarch (*Nicias*, 27) has preserved the exact name of this spot—
the Olive-yard of Polyzelus.

[2] Thucydides, vii. 82.

allowed to send a horseman to enquire, and his messenger brought back confirmation of the worst. Nicias, still unbroken in spirit, proposed his own terms : he would undertake that Athens would repay to Syracuse the whole cost of the war, if he and his men might go free. This proposal Gylippus and the Syracusans rejected and attacks began again. The distress of Nicias' men was now extreme, yet they bore up to the end of that day. At dead of night they attempted to steal a march on their pursuers ; but the movement was discovered and had to be given up.[1]

Next morning, the eighth day of the retreat, Nicias once more led on his exhausted soldiery. The enemy pressed after them ; arrows and javelins rained upon them from every side. The Athenians struggled on, till famished, exhausted, and wild with thirst, they reached the next river along the coast, the Assinarus. Then came the end. Hard pressed as they were by the enemy's attacks, there yet seemed hope of escape if they could but reach and cross the river ; and raging thirst drove them on. By a common impulse the foremost ranks made a headlong rush for the river. It was but to end their march in a scene of unresisting bloodshed. "On reaching the river they threw themselves in ; all order was abandoned, each man eager to be first over ; and this, and the enemy on the bank above, increased the difficulty of the crossing. Crowded inevitably in mass, they kept knocking down and trampling on each other ; in the confusion some were spiked on the javelins, others tripped up on pieces of their kit and fell. Meanwhile the Syracusans, from the cliff-like farther bank which they lined, were firing down on the Athenians, who were most of them greedily drinking all jumbled together in the river bed. It was the Peloponnesians mainly who went down and made a shambles in the stream. The water was immediately fouled, but was none the less eagerly drunk— in most cases, indeed, fought over—all muddy and blood-stained as it was. At last, when the dead lay in heaps

[1] Thucydides, vii. 83. 4 and 5.

one upon another in the bed of the stream and the whole
force had come to ruin, any survivors from the slaughter
in the river being ridden down by the enemy's horse,
Nicias surrendered to Gylippus, whom he trusted more
than he did the Syracusans : for himself, Gylippus and
the Lacedaemonians might do with him as they pleased
if they would but stop the slaughter of his men.   Then
Gylippus gave the order to take the men alive." [1]

There were not many ' official ' prisoners, since there
had been no formal capitulation as of Demosthenes'
division :   but   a   great   number   were   surreptitiously
carried off by private persons, so that—as Thucydides
says—" all Sicily was filled with them." [2]   A certain
number, however, managed to hide and were not captured
at all ; these, together with any who escaped later from
captivity, found a refuge at Catana.

The Quarries.—Yet one more scene and the tragedy of
the Athenians in Sicily has an end.

If to-day you cross from Siracusa (modern Syracuse),
between the Great and the Little Harbours, by the bridges
connecting the Island with the mainland, and follow the
carriage-road round the coast above the Little Harbour
for rather over a mile, you come to the Convent of the
Capuchins on your left.   Within a stone's-throw is the
place where the prisoners captured with Demosthenes
and Nicias were confined after their surrender—a place
so remarkable that it might be counted among the wonders
of the world.   It is a series of excavations of vast extent,
cut down into the limestone rock, with perpendicular
sides some sixty feet deep.   It is not one single pit, but a
succession of chambers opening one out of the other, and
forming an underground labyrinth.   The whole of this
deep-sunk area has been turned into gardens by the
labours of the former owners of the Convent, the Capuchin monks, and now forms a scene of exquisite beauty.
" It is a solemn and romantic labyrinth, where no wind
blows rudely, and where orange-trees shoot upward

---

[1] Thucydides, vii. 84. 3-85. 2 (L. J.).   [2] Thucydides, vii. 85. 3.

luxuriantly to meet the light. The wild fig bursts from the living rock, mixed with lentisk shrubs and pendant caper-plants. Old olives split the masses of fallen cliff with their tough, snake-like, slowly-corded and compacted roots. Thin flames of pomegranate flowers gleam amid foliage of lustrous green ; and lemons drop unheeded from fragile branches. There too the ivy hangs in long festoons, waving like tapestry to the breath of stealthy breezes ; while under foot is a tangle of acanthus, thick curling leaves of glossiest green, surmounted by spikes of dull lilac blossoms. Wedges and columns and sharp teeth of the native rock rear themselves here and there in the midst of the open spaces to the sky, worn fantastically into notches and saws by the action of scirocco. A light yellow, calcined by the sun to white, is the prevailing colour of the quarries. But in shady places the limestone takes a curious pink tone of great beauty, like the interior of some sea-shells. The reflected lights too, and half-shadows in the scooped out chambers, make a wonderful natural chiaroscuro." [1]

Such, described by one great English master of words, is the modern aspect of the strange prison in which the captives of the Syracusans were confined after the destruction of the Athenian expedition to Sicily. " The prisoners they had taken, Athenians and allies of the Athenians alike, they put down in the stone-quarries, as the securest place in which to keep them : Nicias and Demosthenes, in spite of the opposition of Gylippus, they put to death." [2]

" The place was deep down in the ground, and the space too small for numbers so great. It was open to the sky, so the sun's rays, and the stifling heat which came later, caused cruel suffering. Conversely, the nights— since it was late autumn and they were chill—brought on illnesses through the violent contrast. The prisoners were crowded together and everything must be done

[1] J. A. Symonds, *Sketches and Studies in Italy and Greece*, third series, pp. 328-9.

[2] Thucydides, vii. 86. 2.

just where they were. Men died, some from wounds, some from the various ill-effects of this confinement, and their bodies lay heaped one upon another : the stench was intolerable. Hunger and thirst together tormented the prisoners ; for their allowance was half a pint of water a day, and a pint of corn. They were spared no form of suffering that might be expected to afflict men cast into such a prison." [1]

For seventy days all the prisoners, 7000 in number, were confined under these conditions. Then those of them who were not Athenians, or Sicilian or Italian Greeks, were—as an act of mercy—sold into slavery. The Athenians were kept in torment six months longer before they were brought out—such as survived—to work for the rest of their days in penal servitude.

It was disaster, as Thucydides says, surpassing in scale and completeness anything that had happened up to that time in Greek history : indeed, it is not easily paralleled in all history. But for us its peculiar interest and pathos is that it was Athens that suffered this hideous overthrow, that the men who died in the gorge of the Assinarus and in the charnel-house of the Latomia were the countrymen of Sophocles, of Pericles, of Plato.

Thucydides, vii. 87. 1 and 2.

CHAPTER IX

THE PASSING OF THE SPLENDOUR

" Nevertheless, desperate as things were, they resolved not to give in."
                                        Thucydides, viii. 1. 3.

" The Lacedaemonians refused to sell into slavery an Hellenic city which had done great service to Hellas in time of utmost peril."
                                        Xenophon, *Hellenica*, ii. 2. 20.

" Yet though those glories endured only for a brief space of time, their significance is one which outweighs the history of centuries."
                                        Curtius, *History of Greece*, iii. p. 553.

No messenger brought to Athens swift tidings of the destruction which had befallen her great Sicilian expedition. For no ship of hers had escaped from that ruin, and it was long indeed before the scattered fugitives of the retreat dribbled back to Athens by devious ways. And that was after the stupor of the first awakening to the reality had passed.

Bad News at Athens.—If Plutarch may be believed,[1] the first whisper of the calamity reached the Athenians in a curiously fortuitous manner. No news from Sicily had been received for some weeks. Yet there was no special alarm, though the failure of the night attack on Epipolae and Demosthenes' proposals to abandon the siege were known. Then one day a man sitting in a barber's shop, a visitor to Athens, just come ashore, spoke of the complete destruction of the expedition as

[1] Plutarch, *Nicias*, 30.

of a thing well known. The barber rushed off to the magistrates with his startling news, and the magistrates forthwith called a meeting of the Ecclesia. The barber was brought before the assembly and told his tale. The people would not believe it and treated him as an impostor. When presently full confirmation came, alarm and distress overwhelmed the people of Athens. " They were heavily afflicted, by personal bereavements individually, and all by the public loss—knights and men-at-arms in such number, the flower of their manhood, the like of which they looked for in vain among those who were left ; and further, when they saw that they had not ships enough left in their sheds, nor money in the public treasury, nor seamen to man the ships, all hope to be saved seemed gone. They quite expected that their enemies in Sicily, after a victory so decisive, would sail straight for the Piraeus ; and that their enemies at home, now redoubling their preparations, would assail them in force by land and sea, aided by their own allies, who would revolt from them." [1] It seemed indeed to all Hellas, friends and foes alike, and to the Athenians themselves that Athens had received a hurt to which she must rapidly succumb. In this extremity the real greatness of the Athenian people was once more displayed. As soon as they had time to recover from the first bewildering effects of the blow, they set to work to build and equip a new fleet (in spite of the difficulty of finding timber or money) ; and with the ships they built they gained notable victories —at Cynossema, at Cyzicus, at Arginusae ; and once more restored something like the old Athenian superiority at sea. This they did, moreover, in the face of revolt abroad (for in 412 revolt broke out as expected in the islands and in Ionia) and of revolution at home, the temporary reign of the oligarchy of Four Hundred. It was only through the inexcusable remissness, or treachery, of the Athenian commanders which preceded the one overwhelming Peloponnesian victory at Aegospotami, that Athens was at last beaten to her knees. The Athenian

[1] Thucydides, viii. 1. 2.

democracy had made many mistakes, and was guilty of more than one crime in those eight years from the autumn of 413 B.C. to the late summer of 405; but Athens made a gallant fight, and as we watch her splendid effort at recovery, and her last grim resistance when all hope was gone, we are compelled again to admiration, and confess that Athens, supreme in arts and literature, was for a time unsurpassed in the field of action.

The Shame of Sparta.—The moment Athenian power was shaken to its base in 413 by the ruin of the Sicilian expedition, Persia's claim to the tribute of the Asiatic Greeks revived. Thucydides relates [1] how in the winter of 413 there came to Lacedaemon (in company of envoys from Chios seeking to revolt) an ambassador from Tissaphernes, satrap of the coast districts, promising liberal money support if the Spartans would prosecute the war against Athens on the Asiatic side of the Aegean. Tissaphernes had been incited to this course by demands recently pressed from Susa for payment of the arrears of tribute which had been accumulating since Ionia had been ' liberated ' by Athens. We could scarcely ask for a more convincing vindication of the policy which had guided Athens in her control of the anti-Persian confederacy. While the Athenian empire was strong, not a whisper of the tribute due to Persian overlords : as soon as disaster to Athens weakened the strength of the confederacy, instantaneous revival of the claim. And to the eternal shame of Sparta she yielded readily to the temptation.[2] In the following year a treaty was concluded between Sparta and the Persian king, the first clause of which ran : " Whatever country or cities the king has, or the king's ancestors had, shall be the king's." [3] If that clause was to be literally interpreted, not only Ionia, the Thracian Chersonese, Chalcidicê and

---

[1] Thucydides, viii. 5. 4 and 5.

[2] Is it more defensible, one might ask, in the twentieth century A.D., to hand back Greek cities that have been freed to other barbarian overlords ?

[3] Thucydides, viii. 18. 1.

Macedonia were Persian territory, and most of the islands of the Aegean, but Thessaly, Phocis and Boeotia—even the sacred soil of Delphi itself. There were Spartans who saw the turpitude and the ignominy of this treaty, and it was twice revised, each time in the direction of limiting this betrayal of Greeks by Greeks. But even the third and last form of the treaty did not wholly remove the stigma of handing back under the yoke of Persia Greek cities which had once been free, and which had been freed anew by the warfare following the creation of the Delian Confederacy. The clause then ran : [1] " The country of the king in Asia shall be the king's, and the king shall treat his own country as he pleases." This did indeed remove part of the reproach that one sturdy Spartan had urged against the treaty in its earlier forms, " that it was monstrous that the king should at this date pretend to the possession of all the country formerly ruled by himself or by his ancestors—a pretension which implicitly put back under the yoke all the islands, Thessaly, Locris, and everything as far as Boeotia . . ." ; [2] but it still left out of this exception the Greeks of Asia and virtually consigned the Ionians and others who had been fain to throw off allegiance to the Athenian confederacy, to absorption in a Persian satrapy : it still made the Lacedaemonians " give to the Hellenes instead of liberty a Median master." [3]

The Falling away of the Allies.—For under the false lure of freedom held out by the enemies of Athens a great number of the subject states were in the spring of 412 scheming to break away from her. Already in the winter of 413 envoys from several places sent to Agis at Decelea [4]

[1] Thucydides, viii. 58. 2.   [2] Thucydides, viii. 43. 3.
[3] Thucydides, viii. 43. 3.

[4] Decelea (now Tatoi, where the king of the Hellenes has a country estate and a villa), 15 miles from Athens, a position commanding the route from Boeotia by Oropus, had—at the malevolent suggestion of Alcibiades—been occupied and fortified by the Spartans in the spring of 413, and was thenceforth to the end of the war held permanently by a Peloponnesian garrison commanded by the Spartan king Agis, thereby causing new and acuter distresses to the people of Athens. Thucydides, vii. 19. 1 and 2 ; cf. vii. 27 and 28.

and to the Spartan government at Lacedaemon in eager competition for Peloponnesian aid in their revolt. Chios revolted first, the one surviving independent member of the Delian Confederacy ; then Erythrae, then Miletus ; and after that Lesbos and Clazomenae. The Athenians, spurred by the imminence of the danger —for the whole fabric of their empire was crumbling— rescinded the penalties which overhung any one who proposed to touch the special reserve of a thousand talents which had been set aside by Pericles' advice at the beginning of the war, and safeguarded by law against the occurrence of some extreme need. With the help of these funds they fitted out a fleet to check the spread of revolt. They were able to stop the revolt in Lesbos and to recover Clazomenae. But the disaffection spread to Byzantium and other cities of the Hellespont, to Rhodes, and even to Euboea.

Samos.—A remarkable exception was Samos, which had revolted and been reduced thirty years earlier. In 412 at Samos—where, since the struggle of 440-439 no less than before, the government had been oligarchical —there was revolution, violent and bloody, not from democracy to oligarchy, but from oligarchy to democracy. We are not told the circumstances very fully ; it was " a rising of the commons against the upper classes,"[1] and the crews of three Athenian warships, which happened to be at Samos, took part in it. For the unfortunate ' upper classes ' at Samos it was a terrible calamity— two hundred were put to death, four hundred were banished ; the property of all (they appear to have been an exclusive landed class) was confiscated and re-divided among the people. But the result, as far as Athens was concerned, was a close union and understanding which lasted to the end of the war. The Samians were released from their condition of dependence and restored to the status of free allies : and this seems to show that all the severities attributed to the Athenian democracy in the regulation of the confederacy of which they were the

[1] Thucydides, viii. 21.

chosen head arose from considerations of domestic politics and the impossibility of reposing any settled trust in governments of oligarchical constitution and, consequently, Peloponnesian sympathies. It resulted also, that in the political crisis through which Athens herself was about to pass, Samos became the very centre and rallying point of the democracy of Athens. For naturally as soon as the loyalty of Samos was assured beyond doubt by the democratic revolution, Samos became the base for the operations of the Athenian navy and army in the struggle to reduce her revolted dependencies, and most of all Miletus

Revolution at Athens.—For the traditional government of Athens this turned out to be a saving circumstance. The disastrous ending of the Sicilian adventure had at the same time discredited the dearly loved Athenian polity. The censurers of the democracy had now such license of criticism as never before. The most loyal adherents of the democratic faith were staggered and reduced to silence. The men of wealth and family—not all of them, but those whose profession of the democratic creed was lip-service, who, like the satirist of the Xenophontic *Politeia*, thought scorn of the artisans and sailor-men who made up the majority of the voters in the Ecclesia and the judges in the dicastery-courts and valued themselves as ' the noblemen and gentlemen ' of Athens, could not fail to see their opportunity. Always they had been well organized for party purposes with their political clubs and brotherhoods (*hetairiae*). Already, when the full extent of the disaster had come to be recognized, a special board of ' elder statesmen ' had been appointed with exceptional advisory powers ; and at once on the restriction of full democratic sovereignty implied in the appointment of these *Probouli* the clubs became more active. It was easy to make it appear a duty of sound patriotism to take the control of affairs out of the hands of the blind and ignorant masses, whose mismanagement had brought Athens to the brink of destruction, and establish in its place the government of a moderate democracy, in which only men of birth and education with a stake in the country should share political power. In name the plan was for a reformed democracy ; in reality the leaders who pulled the strings and their active partisans were high-handed aristocrats with a craving for oligarchical power.

Alcibiades.—The oligarchical intrigue as it developed was complicated by another for the recall of Alcibiades. That colossal and incurable egotist, having inspired all the measures of the enemy that had done Athens the most fatal hurt, had through his profligate self-seeking now brought himself into disfavour with his patrons, the enemies of Athens. The Spartan government had ceased to trust him ; King Agis for good reasons was his personal enemy. Alcibiades was looking round for an opportunity of again changing sides. For after all the social and political atmosphere of Athens and the tone and temper of Athenian society suited his mercurial temperament better than anything the Spartan alliance had to offer. Alcibiades was versatile enough to be able to affect Spartan manners and endure to live at Sparta and in the company of Spartans, but he could never be at ease under such conditions. Already he had been paying court to Tissaphernes, the Persian satrap of the coast, and had no more difficulty in ingratiating himself with an oriental magnate than some clever western adventurer in India in the eighteenth century. Tissaphernes listened with complacency to the suggestion that it was most to the advantage of Persia to allow neither Sparta nor Athens to gain a decided ascendency in the war, but to keep the balance nicely in suspense so that each might weaken the other by continual conflict. But this playing with Tissaphernes was to Alcibiades only a means to an end. Alcibiades' passionate desire was to win his recall to Athens. By this he could at once most effectively triumph over the enemies who had sent him into exile, and attain what was really his own heart's desire, a return to Athens. For, next to himself, Alcibiades loved Athens, and in so far as he was capable of a

genuine attachment, it was for this city of his birth.
For all his brilliant qualities on their better side were
characteristically Athenian. He managed the intrigue
with such extraordinary dexterity, that while it was he
who set going the movement for a revolution in the
direction of oligarchy, he ultimately returned to Athens
as the champion of democracy.

Army Intrigue at Samos.—The conspiracy began at
Samos, not in Athens. It was given out by agents of
the chief conspirators that Alcibiades had great influence
with Tissaphernes, and was able to bring him and his
pay-chest over from the Peloponnesian to the Athenian
side, if in place of democracy there were a government
Tissaphernes could trust. The anger of the rank and file,
which ordinarily would have blazed out at any meddling
with the constitution, was checked by this talk of pay
from Persia, and the conspirators were emboldened to go
forward. They sent an influential deputation to Athens
to arrange a change in the constitution and the recall of
Alcibiades.[1]

Revolution at Athens.—At Athens the conspirators
proceeded with the same mixture of boldness and caution.
Their proposals for a modification of the constitution were
openly made, but they were grounded upon the desperate
state of the city's resources and the relief which the help
of Persia offered. " The safety of the state," they
argued, " not the form of its government, is for the
moment the most pressing question, as we can always
change afterwards whatever we do not like." [2] This
argument disarmed opposition. Next an atmosphere
of uneasiness and suspicion, even of terror, was created
in the general body of the citizens, partly by the ostentatious display of the numbers of the revolutionary
faction, partly by the secret putting away of any loyal
citizen who made himself conspicuous in opposition.
There was no certainty who was, and who was not, in the
conspiracy, and ordinary people knew not whom to trust.

[1] Thucydides, viii. 49.   [2] Thucydides, viii. 53 3.

In the end there was something like a *coup d'état*. An assembly was held, not in the Pnyx but at Colonus, a good mile outside the city. A resolution was passed suspending the law against unconstitutional proposals [1] and enacting heavy penalties against any one who should attempt to put the statute into force. Then a bill was brought in to abolish all the existing machinery of government—council, dicasteries, ecclesia and all—and elect five commissioners, with power to nominate a hundred councillors, each of whom was to choose three colleagues. The Four Hundred, so appointed, were to take the place of the Council of Five Hundred and govern with full powers. Behind them was to be an Ecclesia, limited in number to five thousand and convened at the pleasure of the Four Hundred. These proposals were unanimously accepted and the meeting was dissolved. So far constitutional forms had been outwardly observed. Then the newly appointed Four Hundred, secretly armed with daggers and escorted by a band of hired bravos in their employ, proceeded to the Council Chamber and ordered the members present to receive their pay and begone. Each councillor had the rest of his year's allowance paid to him in full as he went out ; and the revolution was accomplished. The Four Hundred were now the government of Athens : and that was a very long way from democracy. For they had no intention whatever of calling into reality the Five Thousand. Though constitutional forms had been observed, the new oligarchy really ruled by force. The Four Hundred imprisoned political opponents at their pleasure, and put to death some few : yet on the whole acted with moderation. The principal thing they did was to try and make peace with Sparta ; and this failed. [2]

Democratic Reaction at Samos.—But while the revolution was thus easily effected at Athens, the affair had meantime taken an altogether different turn at Samos. Though, as we have seen (p. 239), the first motion for a change of government came from Samos, when attempt

---

[1] See above, p. 92.   [2] Thucydides, viii. 71. 3.

was made to carry through the revolutionary movement there, the army and fleet declared unequivocally for democracy. Not only so, but when news of the *coup d'état* of the Four Hundred was brought to Samos and was followed by exaggerated accounts of the violent doings of the oligarchs, the men of the army and fleet bound each other by solemn oaths to maintain democracy at Athens, to carry on the war with energy, and to make no terms with the Four Hundred.

There now arose a struggle " between the army trying to force a democracy upon the city, and the Four Hundred an oligarchy upon the camp." [1] Samos had become, for the time being, the true, the better Athens : the greater part of her military and naval strength was there, and the army and navy at Samos were better able to carry on the war and to shift for themselves than the non-combatants, the old and infirm, and the disaffected oligarchs, enclosed within the walls of Athens. And this was what the sworn confederates of the Army at Samos themselves thought. Under the leadership of Thrasybulus, son of Lycus, staunchest of patriots, and Thrasyllus, they purged the army command of disaffection to democracy, in a formal assembly deposing any generals and ships' captains who were suspected of oligarchical leanings. Next at the instance of Thrasybulus they took steps for the recall of Alcibiades.

Alcibiades at Samos.—In this wise it came about that Alcibiades, who had been the first instigator of the oligarchical conspiracy, was actually brought back as the saviour of the democracy he had plotted to subvert. Undoubtedly what weighed most alike with the original oligarchical conspirators, the democratic war-leaders, and the ordinary citizens serving in army and navy, was the belief that Alcibiades, and Alcibiades alone, could ward off the destruction which manifestly overhung the Athenian cause, if Tissaphernes, in accordance with his promise to the Spartan chiefs, brought up the Phoenician fleet. Since the disaster in Sicily the Athenians had only

[1] Thucydides viii. 76. 1 (Crawley).

been just able to hold their own at sea without being able to gain any decisive advantage. The Phoenician fleet numbered close on 150 ships, fully manned and fresh.[1] If the strength of the Phoenician fleet were added to the strength of the Peloponnesian fleet, the odds must be overwhelmingly against Athens. She would not have a chance ; she must at once be irretrievably defeated ; Athens would be lost. The Spartans knew this ; Tissaphernes knew this ; and the Athenians all knew this. Hence the intensely critical character of the intrigue now centring in the question whether Tissaphernes would bring up the Phoenician fleet or not. The Phoenician fleet was a little shadowy, but it served the purposes of intrigue none the worse for that. It served Tissaphernes as a bait to keep the Peloponnesians to the zealous prosecution of the war at sea : it served Alcibiades for the double game of playing off the Athenians against Tissaphernes, and Tissaphernes against the Athenians. Accordingly when Alcibiades was brought by Thrasybulus to Samos and introduced to a formal assembly of the Athenian forces, he was not only well received, but actually elected Strategos. Soon after a deputation sent by the Four Hundred in Athens to explain the meaning and purpose of the change of government to the fighting forces at Samos and reconcile them to it, arrived and attempted to carry out their mission. They had a very stormy reception : they were greeted with outcries demanding that they should be put to death, and it was with difficulty they got any hearing at all. Their plea that the change of government had been made to save Athens, not to injure her, was ill received ; and so was the contention that the change was after all slight, because the Five Thousand would exercise the wonted powers of the Ecclesia. Angry clamour arose, and from all sides came the demand that the fleet should sail forthwith to the Piraeus. Then it was that for once in his life Alcibiades did his country a genuine service. He calmed down the excited soldiers and induced them to realize

[1] Thucydides, viii. 87. 3.

the madness of what they asked.   For, if once the Athenian
fleet left its station at Samos, not only was Ionia lost,
but the Hellespont too, and the Black Sea route : the
Athenian empire would be at an end.   This is Thucydides'
testimony ; and he adds : " There was no one else at
the time who could have restrained them ; but Alcibiades
put a stop to all thought of sailing against Piraeus, and
by his vehement speech silenced those who were moved
by personal animosity to the envoys." [1]   He further took
upon himself to give the deputation their answer ; he
approved the abolition of payment for civil offices, offered
no objection to the limitation of political rights to the
Five Thousand, but insisted that the arbitrary rule of the
Four Hundred must cease and the Council of Five
Hundred be restored.

Fall of the Four Hundred.—In the end the oligarchical
revolution at Athens collapsed without any direct intervention from Samos.   The immediate effect of Alcibiades'
message was to create a division in the ranks of the Four
Hundred.   A large number of them were already uneasy
at the course events had taken and anxious to return to
constitutional government.   These now under the leadership of Theramenes, son of Hagnon, and others, formed a
Moderate party within the oligarchy ; the policy they
advocated was to give immediate reality to the Five
Thousand.   The extremer oligarchs under the original
chiefs of the oligarchical conspiracy, Pisander, Antiphon
and Phrynichus, made a desperate effort to get peace
made with Sparta on any terms barely tolerable.   At
the same time they began to turn the rocky spit of land
which protects the entrance to Piraeus on the north-west
into a fortress by adding a wall on the side towards the
harbour.[2]   The alleged purpose was to strengthen the

---

[1] Thucydides, viii. 86. 5.

[2] " Eetionea is a mole of Piraeus, close alongside of the entrance of
the harbour, and was now fortified in connexion with the wall already
existing on the land side, so that a few men placed in it might be able to
command the entrance ; the old wall on the land side and the new one
now being built within on the side of the sea, both ending in one of the
two towers standing at the narrow mouth of the harbour."   Thucydides,
viii. 90. 4 (Crawley).

defences against a possible attack on Piraeus from Samos. Theramenes, however, declared that the real purpose of the work was to give the Oligarchs command of the entrance to Piraeus, so that, when it suited them, they could admit the Spartans. This suspicion appeared to receive confirmation when a fleet was reported to be gathering off the coast of Laconia; its destination was said to be Euboea, but obviously it could just as readily sail against the Piraeus. Thucydides is of opinion that the more fanatical oligarchs did really cherish the project of calling in the enemy, in the event of their first plans miscarrying. The work at Eetionea, at all events, was being pushed on with feverish energy and the excitement in the city grew. It is a sign of the rising tide of popular passion that at this conjuncture Phrynichus was assassinated openly in the Agora. News of a raid by the enemy's fleet on Aegina brought matters to a head. The two parties confronted each other in the streets, and it was only with the greatest difficulty, through the good offices of those who saw how fatal civil strife must be with the enemy at their gates, that a conflict was avoided. In the end the hoplites employed on the oligarchs' work in the Piraeus took matters into their own hands and, with Theramenes' approval, themselves demolished the offending fortifications.

Next day there was a renewal of the tumult. A large body of hoplites marched from the Piraeus into the city and demanded the immediate publication of the roll of the Five Thousand. They were calmed with a promise of compliance, and with a view to the restoration of civic harmony, a day was fixed for holding an Ecclesia in the Theatre of Dionysus. The day, when it came proved one of unexpected excitement. Just at the time when the assembly was to meet news came that the Peloponnesian fleet (which had moved on to Megara was off the coast of Salamis. It seemed as if Theramenes warning was about to come true, and that in the absence of the effective fleet of Athens on the other side of the Aegean, the Piraeus was at last to experience direc

attack by the enemy. The citizens *en masse* rushed to
the harbour town : " some went on board the ships
already afloat, while others launched fresh vessels, or
ran to defend the walls and the mouth of the harbour." [1]
But the forty-two enemy ships passed on down the
coast, and rounding Sunium sailed along the eastern side
of Attica and made for the town of Oropus. It then
appeared that their destination was, as had been given
out, Euboea. But this menace was scarcely less alarming
than an attack on the Piraeus itself. For in Euboea
were the flocks and herds which had been removed from
Attica : " Euboea was everything to them now that they
were shut out from Attica." [2] Every ship that could
be manned was sent out in haste to fight for Euboea.
A fleet of thirty-six ships (against the Peloponnesian
forty-two) was assembled at Eretria ; but the crews were
untrained men. They were forced to engage almost
immediately on arrival there ; and unfortunately they
were not ready. The Eretrians played traitor and made
it impossible for the crews of the Athenian fleet to obtain
food near the shore. Just when the men were scattered
about the outskirts of the town over their marketing, the
Peloponnesian fleet was descried sailing to the attack.
Oropus is only seven miles off across the Euboean channel
and the traitors in Eretria raised a signal to notify the Peloponnesians of the moment to attack. So the Athenian
ships put to sea in a hurry and before the crews had taken
any food, with the natural result that they were disastrously defeated with the loss of twenty-two ships out
of thirty-six. Immediately after all Euboea revolted—
with the exception of Oreus (formerly Histiaea, above,
p. 68), which was now an Athenian settlement.

[1] Thucydides, viii. 94. 3 (Crawley).

[2] Thucydides, viii. 95. 2.   They were shut out from Attica because of
the fortified post established by the enemy at Decelea, which intensified
acutely the distresses suffered by the Athenians in this second war,
sometimes on this account called the Decelean War. Thucydides
draws a lurid picture of these distresses in chs. 27 and 28 of Book vii.
It was much worse than the annual invasions of the first period of the
war.

Thucydides asserts that the alarm, which ensued at Athens when the news became known, was greater even than that which followed the knowledge of the disaster in Sicily. Though the loss in Sicily was far greater, this blow struck nearer home. " The camp at Samos was in revolt ; they had no more ships or men to man them ; they were at discord among themselves and might at any moment come to blows ; and a disaster of this magnitude coming on the top of all, by which they lost their fleet, and worst of all Euboea, which was of more value to them than Attica, could not occur without throwing them into the deepest despondency." [1] It might well seem that the Peloponnesians had but to follow up their victory by sailing into the Saronic Gulf and threatening Piraeus, and Athens was done. For either the city must fall straightway ; or, if the army and fleet at Samos should leave the seat of war in Asia and come to the rescue, there was an end of the Athenian empire. Indeed, Thucydides is at a loss to understand how these consequences did not follow, and can only account for it by Spartan incapacity to rise to the occasion. " But here, as on so many other occasions, the Lacedaemonians proved the most convenient people in the world for the Athenians to be at war with. The wide difference between the two characters, the slowness and want of energy of the Lacedaemonians as contrasted with the dash and enterprise of their opponents, proved of the greatest service, especially to a maritime empire like Athens. Indeed this was shown by the Syracusans, who were most like the Athenians in character, and also most successful in combating them." [2]

The Rally of the Democracy.—This was the lowest point the fortunes of Athens reached in the disastrous years 413 to 411. Wonderful as it may seem, there was now for the last six years of the war a recovery which for a time even gave promise of final victory to Athens. While the enemy at Oropus delayed to strike their blow

[1] Thucydides, viii. 96. 2 (Crawley).

[2] Thucydides, viii. 96. 5 (Crawley).

at Piraeus, the Athenians, again showing their greatness in adversity, rallied their forces to meet the crisis. For the defence of Athens they manned yet another twenty ships and soberly proceeded to set their house in order. The people returned to its time-honoured meeting-place, the Pnyx, and in session there passed a series of resolutions for the restoration of constitutional government. The Four Hundred were formally deposed and a new citizen-body was constituted under the name of the Five Thousand, but consisting of all citizens able to provide for themselves a shield and a suit of body armour. The abolition of payment for state service of all kinds was formally confirmed : in other respects the familiar polity was revived. This was, it will be seen, a compromise in the shape of moderate democracy, and it earned the un-qualified approval of the historian to whom we owe these details. "It was during the first period of this constitution that the Athenians appear to have enjoyed the best government that they ever did, at least in my time. For the fusion of the high and the low was effected with judgment, and this was what first enabled the state to raise up her head after her manifold disasters." [1] Another measure now determined was the recall of Alcibiades and other exiles. A report of these trans-actions was sent to the naval base at Samos together with encouragement to press the war with new vigour.

The Victories of Athens by Sea.—Prospects at the seat of war were already since the reception of Alcibiades at Samos taking a turn for the better. Tissaphernes and the Peloponnesian leaders were completely at odds. There was no sign of the appearance of the Phoenician fleet, nor did Tissaphernes himself return from Aspendus. The Spartan commanders in disgust now took into consideration the invitation of another Persian satrap, Pharnabazus, who wished them to come to the Hellespont which was in his satrapy, and bring about the defection of the cities confederate with Athens there. Mindarus, the Spartan admiral recently appointed in succession to

[1] Thucydides, viii. 97. 2 (Crawley).

Astyochus, listened to these persuasions, abandoned
active operations off the Ionian coast, and sailed for the
Hellespont with the design of effecting the revolt of all

THE HELLESPONT AND PROPONTIS.

the cities of the Athenian empire from the Hellespont to
the Bosphorus. He tried to evade the Athenian fleet
altogether, but was discovered and pursued. Ultimately

there was a general engagement of the fleets off Abydos
—eighty-six ships on the Peloponnesian side ; on the
Athenian seventy-six ; and in spite of some ill success at
first the Athenians were completely victorious: twenty-one
ships of the Peloponnesians were captured with a loss of
fifteen ships by the victors. This was a new turning-
point in the war. News of the victory was received at
Athens with a joy proportionate to the alarms and
distresses through which the whole people had recently
passed : it " gave them fresh courage, and caused them
to believe that if they put their shoulders to the wheel
their cause might yet prevail." [1]

This battle of Abydos, or of Cynos-sema as it is also
called, from the promontory on which the victors set up
their trophy, was the first of a series of brilliant victories
which shed a departing glory on the last years of the
Athenian empire. Towards the end of this year 411
they were victorious a second time off Abydos, this time
capturing thirty ships of the enemy. Early in 410 they
won a much more signal victory off Cyzicus. In this
battle the Athenians had the advantage of numbers,
for they had eighty-six ships and the Peloponnesians only
sixty ; but not one of these sixty ships escaped. Most
of the empty hulls became prizes ; but the men of the
Syracusan squadron (for the Syracusans had by this time
sent a contingent to help in the overthrow of Athens)
burnt their ships rather than that they should fall into
the hands of the enemy. As a result of this victory the
Athenians regained undisputed control of the Black
Sea route, and they established a new port at Chrysopolis,
on the Asiatic side of the entrance to the Bosphorus, to
enforce the payment of the customs duty of ten per cent.
on all goods passing through the Straits. At Cyzicus
the Spartan admiral Mindarus was among the slain, and
it was after this battle that the famous despatch of his
second-in-command was intercepted and brought to
Athens. The despatch is a good example of Spartan
brevity. It ran : " The ships are gone. Mindarus is

[1] Thucydides, viii. 106. 5 (Crawley).

dead. The men are starving. We know not what to do." [1] For the moment the Peloponnesians were without a fleet in Asiatic waters. It is characteristic of the comparative ease with which a navy could be replaced, provided wood were obtainable, that Pharnabazus bade the Peloponnesians not to be discouraged, since, so long as the men were safe, timber did not matter, for there was plenty of that in the king's land. And he was as good as his word, and had a new fleet built for the Peloponnesians at Antandros from wood cut on Mount Ida.

Arginusae.—It was not till 406 that another general action was fought, and then the Athenians won the great victory at Arginusae, notorious in history for the outrageous treatment of the admirals who won it. But in the intervening years important things had happened which bore upon the ultimate result ; and in particular, Alcibiades had been a second time banished. For a time after his arrival in camp at Samos everything he touched had prospered. It was he who, coming up at the critical moment with a fresh squadron of eighteen ships at Abydos,[2] had decided the battle in favour of the Athenians. Cyzicus was definitely his victory. He caught Mindarus out at sea manoeuvring, cut him off from the harbour and, as we saw, destroyed his whole fleet. In contrast with this brilliant success was a defeat of other Athenian forces under Thrasyllus at Ephesus : the attempt on Ephesus met with even less success than the Ionian attack on Sardis in the Ionian Revolt.[3] In 409 again Alcibiades defeated Pharnabazus at Abydos and he recovered Chalcedon and Byzantium which had revolted in 410. So great was his reputation and popularity at this time that in 407 he was invited back to Athens and landed at the Piraeus. This was the great day of Alcibiades' life. A vast crowd had gathered to see the famous Alcibiades, and he was escorted in triumph by a band of friends to a meeting of the Ecclesia and there was chosen

---

[1] Xenophon, *Hellenica*, I. i. 23 ; Loeb. p. 11.
[2] Xenophon, *Hellenica*, I. i. 5.   [3] Vol. i. p. 272.

general-in-chief with absolute authority.   But his triumph was short-lived ; a little later his star deserted him ; he was unsuccessful in an attack on Andros, and then during his absence on state business the officer left in charge of the fleet, against his express orders, offered battle to the Peloponnesians, was defeated, and lost fifteen ships. " And it would seem," writes Plutarch,[1] " that if ever a man was ruined by his own exalted reputation, that man was Alcibiades.   His continuous successes gave him such repute for unbounded daring and sagacity, that when he failed in anything, men suspected his inclination ; they would not believe in his inability."   This was the nemesis at once of his brilliancy and of the instability of his character.   The people chose other commanders in his place, and Alcibiades once more left his countrymen and betook himself to a stronghold he had built in the Chersonese, and "there assembling mercenary troops made war on his own account against the Thracians, who acknowledge no king." [2]   To whatever causes this new breach between Athens and her brilliant but erratic son was due, it was soon to prove fatal both to him and to Athens.   But first came the victory of Athens at Arginusae.

In 407 Lysander had come from Sparta as admiral, and it was he who defeated Alcibiades' lieutenant, Antinous, at Notium.   Lysander was both cautious and capable, and he had the good fortune to win the friendship of Cyrus, prince of the royal house of the Achaemenidae, who here makes his first appearance in Greek history.[3] Lysander was succeeded by Callicratidas, a leader of true Spartan courage, but without the qualities which made success easy for Lysander ; and he suffered from the handicap that Lysander, and Lysander's friends, were intriguing against him.   Callicratidas acted with vigour, captured Methymna, and blockaded an Athenian squadron under Conon in the harbour of Mytilene.   The

---

[1] Plutarch, *Alcibiades*, 35 ; Loeb. iv. p. 103.

[2] Plutarch, *Alcibiades*, 36 ; Loeb. iv. p. 107.

[3] He is the Cyrus of Xenophon's *Anabasis*.

Athenians made a special effort to rescue Conon and his
squadron ; " they voted to go to the rescue with 110 ships."
In the end they gathered together a fleet of 150 ships,
Callicratidas went to meet them with only 120, and in a
hard-fought action was defeated and himself lost his life.
It was the biggest naval action of the war, for nearly 300
triremes were engaged. There should have been boundless
rejoicing at Athens and honours for the victorious admirals,
eight in number. But the public joy was clouded by one
unfortunate circumstance. A storm had come on after
the battle, and the crews of the Athenian war-ships disabled in the fight had not been rescued, though orders
for their rescue had been given. There were twenty-five
Athenian ships lost, so the death roll was considerable,
some 5000 men. Even this great loss would have been
not irremediable had it been met in a proper spirit ;
but through the machinations of certain interested persons
the populace were, quite unjustifiably, stirred to indignation
against the generals, and through the accident that the
festival called the Apaturia (when families were united
for worship as at Christmas with us) occurred at the time,
this indignation got completely out of hand. Demands
were made that the admirals should be tried for their
lives, and tried, not separately man by man, as Athenian
law required, but collectively in a batch. The madness
of the hour prevailed, and—though the people afterwards
repented of it—this was done. The Ecclesia voted instantly upon the illegal resolution, and the vote was for
death. All the admirals but two, who had previously
effected their escape, were put to death. Among the six
put to death was a son of Pericles and Aspasia. The
whole story is told at length by Xenophon ; [1] it is a strange
story, barely credible, were not the truth of history so
often stranger than fiction.

The people of Athens are said to have repented of this
injustice to their victorious generals, but little place was
left for repentance. The hour was at hand, when through
the incredible carelessness and folly of other commanders

---

[1] Xenophon, *Hellenica*, I. vii.

her whole fleet was to be betrayed into the hands of the enemy, and Athens left with nothing between her and surrender through starvation. Whether this betrayal was due to deliberate treachery or only to criminal negligence and ineptitude cannot be known.

Aegospotami.—In the year 405, the year after Arginusae, Lysander came back to command the Peloponnesian fleet at the urgent request of the allies, and with a view of striking at the Athenian corn supply he sailed for the Hellespont. The Athenians followed with their whole fleet, now raised to 180 ships. Lysander attacked and took Lampsacus. The Athenians were then at Elaeus, and on receiving news of this loss they sailed up the Hellespont, and as all the Asiatic shore was now hostile territory, took up their station at a place called ' Goat's-rivers '—*Aegos-potami*—on the European shore opposite Lampsacus. The position was a bad one—an open shore, and no market near ; the seamen of these two hundred ships were obliged to seek their food at Sestos, quite a long distance away. Alcibiades, who could see the Athenian fleet from his fort, advised the commanders not to stay there. He was repulsed with insult, and no precautions were taken to guard against surprise, though Lampsacus, where the Peloponnesians had supplies close at hand, was little over two miles away. Lysander laid his plans accordingly. When on the day after his arrival the Athenians put out to sea, rowed across and offered battle outside the harbour of Lampsacus, Lysander had his ships all manned and ready, but would not allow them to move out and fight. When late in the day the Athenians, seeing that the enemy declined battle, rowed back to Aegospotami, he sent swift-sailing ships after them to note exactly what they did, and till the return of these scouts he kept his fleet ready manned and afloat. The scouts reported that as soon as the Athenian ships reached the shore at Aegospotami, the crews disembarked and scattered along the coast in search for food. Next day and for three days more after that this procedure was repeated, and each day the Athenians grew more careless. On the fifth day Lysander changed his orders. As soon as his scouts saw that the Athenian crews had disembarked and scattered they were to hoist a shield as a signal. When the signal appeared, Lysander with his fleet behind him dashed straight across the Hellespont, and bore down upon the Athenian fleet. Conon, one of the admirals, made strenuous efforts to call the seamen back and get the ships manned. But there was not time. The Athenian warships were caught, some half manned, some hardly manned at all, some quite empty. Of all that fleet nine ships only escaped—eight ships of Conon's squadron, and the Paralus. All the rest fell into Lysander's hands. Some of the crews escaped to forts held for Athens ; but most of them were made prisoners. This was ruin final and irretrievable. For all Athens' naval strength, the fleet that kept the seas open for the corn-ships and guarded Piraeus, was there at *Aegospotami*. These were all captured without one blow struck in defence : and there were no others.

The Cup of Humiliation.—Thucydides is no longer our main authority, but Xenophon in his *Hellenica* ; and for once at least Xenophon's account of the reception of the fatal news at Athens is Thucydidean in its force and brevity. " It was at night that the Paralus arrived at Athens with tidings of the disaster, and a sound of wailing ran from Piraeus through the Long Walls to the city, one man passing on the news to another ; and during that night no one slept, all mourning, not for the lost only, but also, and far more, for their own selves, thinking that they would suffer such treatment as they had visited upon the Melians, and upon the Histiaeans, and Scionaeans, and Toronaeans, and Aeginetans, and many other Greek peoples." [1] Yet even in this extremity the old spirit nerved the remnant of her fighting people left in Athens. " On the following day they convened an Assembly, at which it was resolved to block up all the

---

[1] Xenophon, *Hellenica*, II. ii. 3 ; Loeb, pp. 103 and 105. Thucydides' *History* breaks off unfinished in the autumn of the year 411.

harbours except one, to repair the walls, to station guards, and in all other respects to get the city ready for a siege." [1]

Lysander came on leisurely; there was no need to hurry. Time was his most effective weapon, and he knew it. Famine would do his work for him more surely than siege engines or storming parties. So wherever he found an Athenian garrison, and whenever he fell in with Athenians anywhere he sent them with a safe conduct to Athens that they might augment the number of mouths to be fed there. At length, after laying Salamis waste, Lysander anchored with a fleet of 150 ships in front of the Piraeus, and closed the harbour against all entrance, while a large Peloponnesian army under the Spartan king Pausanias lay encamped in the district called the Academy, close under the city walls. And now "the Athenians, being thus besieged by land and by sea, knew not what to do, since they had neither ships nor allies nor provisions; and they thought that there was no way out, save only to suffer the pains which they had themselves inflicted, not in retaliation, but in wantonness and unjustly upon the people of small states, for no other single reason than because they were in alliance with the Lacedaemonians." [2]

Resistance was hopeless from the first, but the Athenians held out indomitably notwithstanding. People were dying daily of starvation, and at last supplies were all but exhausted. An attempt was made to negotiate terms of peace, but the Athenian spirit was as yet unbroken, and they asked simply to be admitted to alliance with Sparta, keeping their walls and harbours intact. To this the Spartan government would not listen. Then Theramenes offered to go to Lysander and find out what terms really were obtainable; and as the best means of bringing his countrymen to a frame of mind which might incline them to submit to the inevitable, he stayed three months with Lysander

[1] Xenophon, *Hellenica*, II. ii. 4 ; Loeb, p. 105.
[2] Xenophon, *Hellenica*, II. ii. 10 ; Loeb, p. 107.

before he returned. Matters were then quite desperate, and in this extremity the people of Athens sent Theramenes and nine other envoys with full powers to make what terms they could. The Ephors, seeing that the Athenian envoys were now in earnest, brought them to Lacedaemon. "When they arrived, the Ephors called an assembly, at which the Corinthians and Thebans in particular, though many other Greeks agreed with them, opposed making a treaty with the Athenians and favoured destroying their city. The Lacedaemonians, however, said they would not enslave a Greek city which had done great service amid the greatest perils that had befallen Greece, and they offered to make peace on these conditions : that the Athenians should destroy the long walls and the walls of Piraeus, surrender all their ships except twelve, allow their exiles to return, count the same people friends and enemies as the Lacedaemonians did, and follow the Lacedaemonians both by land and sea wherever they should lead the way. So Theramenes and his fellow-ambassadors brought back this word to Athens. And as they were entering the city, a great crowd gathered around them, fearful that they had returned unsuccessful ; for it was no longer possible to delay, on account of the number who were dying of the famine. On the next day the ambassadors reported to the Assembly the terms on which the Lacedaemonians offered to make peace ; Theramenes acted as spokesman for the embassy, and urged that it was best to obey the Lacedaemonians and tear down the walls. And while some spoke in opposition to him, a far greater number supported him, and it was voted to accept the peace. After this Lysander sailed into Piraeus, the exiles returned, and the Peloponnesians with great enthusiasm began to level the walls to the music of flute-girls, thinking that that day was the beginning of freedom for Greece." [1]

Epilogue.—This was the end of Athens as an imperial city ruling over subject states and of the dream of an

---

[1] Xenophon, *Hellenica*, II. ii. 19-23 ; Loeb, 111 and 113.

united Hellas confederated under her leadership. She had fought a losing fight gallantly. But the odds were too heavy against her. The democracy of Athens had made foolish mistakes, and in their pride of power had committed crimes at variance with the mild and generous spirit of her best days ; but the sheer exhaustion of material and moral forces in the wearing struggle of those twenty-seven and a half years is explanation enough of the deterioration of which we are spectators, and of her ultimate defeat. Yet the story does not close in unrelieved gloom. There is an epilogue which is prelude to a long and strangely varied history leading on through the centuries to the Athens we may visit to-day. There was a revival of Athens as a political power, even of Athens as head of an Hellenic confederacy, a second Athenian empire, though it was not the Athens of Pericles and Cimon and Themistocles.[1] This revival, too, came within a dozen years of Aegos-potami.

The Reign of Terror.—But before this revival the Athenians passed through evil days. After the surrender of the city and the destruction of the Long Walls, while all real power was in the hands of Lysander, thirty citizens of high rank had been chosen to form a special commission for the framing of a constitution in accordance with the ancient laws ; and that meant a constitution somewhat on the pattern of the democracy as it was left after the reforms of Clisthenes. These thirty came ultimately to be known as the Thirty Tyrants, and their memory was accursed. The Thirty set up a Council and appointed magistrates, but delayed to proceed further with the framing of a constitution ; and as the Council and magistrates were entirely subordinate to them, their rule was irresponsible and arbitrary. To make their

[1] For all this the measure of what had happened to Athens, and through Athens to Hellas, is only taken, when we see how, not quite a hundred years later, in the Athens of Cimon and Pericles, two Macedonians, Demetrius the Besieger and his father Antigonus, were not only hailed as saviours with extravagant flattery, but actually worshipped as gods. This is the true measure of the tragedy of Aegospotami.

arbitrary power secure they asked and obtained from
Lacedaemon, with Lysander's aid, a Spartan force to
garrison Athens. In reliance on the support of this
garrison they introduced a reign of violence and injustice.
A great number of people were put to death by their
orders. First it was politicians on the popular side, who
under the democratic régime had made a profession of
watching over the public interests, calling officials to
account and instituting prosecutions of the rich, not infrequently on insufficient grounds. They were commonly called
'informers' (*sycophant*[1] was the Greek word for them)
and held in detestation by the well-to-do classes. Public
feeling on the whole approved the judgment with which
they were now visited. But the Thirty went on from
this to proscribe political opponents and even doom to
death citizens whose sole crime was that they were not of
a rank or character to submit quietly to the total deprivation of political rights. Finally the Thirty killed
their fellow-citizens merely to obtain possession of their
property. It became a veritable reign of terror. This
wickedness was too much for one of their number, Theramenes, whose name appears in the history of his times
in curiously contrasted lights, good and evil. He was of
very distinguished birth, son of Hagnon, founder of
Amphipolis, and we have seen the part he played in
setting up and pulling down the Four Hundred.[2] He was
a man who shrank from extremes, and whether justly or
unjustly, had earned the nickname of '*the Buskin*'—a
buskin being a boot which fits either foot. It is arguable
that this nickname does no more than illustrate the penalty
the moderate man has to pay in trying to mediate between
violent extremes. A more sinister doubt, however,
attaches to Theramenes' conduct at the time of the trial
of the admirals after Arginusae.[3] Theramenes appears
among their accusers ; and it was to Theramenes as a
trierarch, along with others, that the task of rescuing the

---

[1] Literally 'fig-shower' ; but how from this it came to mean 'in
former' is not known.

[2] Above, p. 243.   [3] Above, p. 252.

men on the disabled ships had been committed by the admirals. But whatever the final judgment on his character, Theramenes at all events played a worthy part now. He boldly opposed Critias, the most high-handed of the Thirty and instigator of the worst atrocities, a man without scruple and without pity, but of undaunted will and great intellectual force.[1] Save these two, Critias and Theramenes, the rest of that Thirty are to us mere names. A duel now went on for a time between Theramenes and Critias in the counsels of the Thirty. Theramenes urged the necessity of widening the government by extending political privileges, as originally proposed when the Thirty received their commission. Critias gave way and the Thirty enrolled a body of Three Thousand, who were to fill the same rôle in the new Oligarchy as the Five Thousand under the government of the Four Hundred. Then by a trick, the rest of the citizens who had the status of hoplites were deprived of their arms. "And now, when this had been accomplished, thinking that they were at length free to do whatever they pleased, they put many people to death out of personal enmity, and many also for the sake of securing their property. One measure that they resolved upon, in order to get money to pay their guardsmen, was that each of their number should seize one of the aliens residing in the city, and that they should put these men to death and confiscate their property."[2] This Theramenes would not do, and Critias made up his mind to be rid of him. He denounced him in the Senate as a turncoat and traitor ; and when the senators showed signs of sympathy with Theramenes' defence, overawed them by means of the Spartan guards and a band of his own partisans armed with daggers ;[3] and by the simple expedient of striking Theramenes' name out of the roll of the Three

---

[1] A famous dialogue of Plato is named after him.

[2] Xenophon, *Hellenica*, II. iii. 21 ; Loeb, p. 123.

[3] The dagger at Athens, we see, plays the same part as the revolver in modern Europe : it is the weapon of extremists, revolutionary or reactionary.

Thousand, dispensed altogether with any legal forms, merely ordering Theramenes off to execution ; for it had previously been enacted that the Thirty were to have absolute power of life and death over all citizens outside the roll of the Three Thousand. The scene in the Senate House is vividly portrayed by Xenophon.[1] After this murder proscriptions and confiscations went on apace. The number of victims done to death by the Thirty is estimated at 1500.[2] These were the slain. A great number were banished or fled the country. The exiles found a refuge wherever they could, and especially at Megara and Thebes.

Thrasybulus.—Among the exiles was Thrasybulus, son of Lycus, the soldier statesman who had taken a leading part in thwarting the oligarchical conspiracy at Samos in 411, and in the subsequent recall of Alcibiades. He had been Strategos in 411. Thrasybulus was at Thebes ; and one day with a band of 70 fugitives of a like resolute spirit he climbed the defile of Mount Parnes and took possession of Phyle, one of the Athenian border fortresses, in a position singularly bold and dominant above the mule-track which is the shortest route between Athens and Thebes. The position is so strong that only part of the summit needs the defence of walls ; for nearly half the circuit the precipitous cliff is defence enough ; the walls that protect the rest are of the finest Hellenic masonry, course above course of squared blocks regularly laid. And to one who looks southward from the summit the Acropolis of Athens is visible at a distance of some thirteen miles, and beyond the Acropolis the sea. Hither Thrasybulus came and gazed and waited ; and his band of patriots grew gradually from 70 to 700. But it was not long before the Thirty, fully alive to the danger, marched out against Thrasybulus with all their cavalry and the

[1] Xenophon, *Hellenica*, II. iii. 50-55.

[2] " And some of them actually joined the Thirty, who killed more than fifteen hundred of the citizens without trial, before they had even heard the charges on which they were to be put to death . . ." (Aeschines, *Speech against Ctesiphon*, 235 ; Loeb, p. 493).

ANGLE OF THE FORTRESS OF PHYLÊ,
which looks down the Pass, towards Athens.
From a photograph by Lionel James.

Three Thousand.   A direct assault failed ignominiously, and the plan of investing the stronghold and cutting off supplies was frustrated by an exceedingly heavy snowstorm which came on in the night and compelled a retreat. When a little later the main body of the Spartan garrison and a portion of the cavalry were sent to patrol the country around Phyle and prevent plundering, their camp was surprised by Thrasybulus at early dawn, and they were chased away with considerable loss.   When his numbers had grown to a thousand, Thrasybulus took the initiative and marched by night to Piraeus.   Next day he occupied a strong defensive position on the hill Munychia, and though the partisans of the Thirty from the city attacked him with greatly superior numbers, they were defeated and Critias himself was slain.   It was some time yet before the civil conflict ceased and the democracy was restored ;   and before this was achieved the Spartans once more intervened.   The ultimate deliverance from arbitrary rule was only accomplished with the friendly consent of Sparta, who through all this time, it must in fairness be acknowledged, played on the whole a generous part towards her great antagonist.   But the end finally reached was the triumph of Thrasybulus and the restoration of democracy :   " and the men from Piraeus went up to the Acropolis under arms and offered sacrifice to Athena." [1]

The restored democracy, in spite of the bitter things done, set an example of moderation in victory, so that Xenophon could write :   " pledged as they were under oath, that in very truth they would not remember past grievances, the two parties even to this day live together as fellow-citizens and the commons abide by their oaths." [2]   There could be no better tribute to Athenian democracy

Phyle.—A peculiarly romantic interest attaches to Phyle, the inspiration of which Byron felt ; and saw his

[1] Xenophon, *Hellenica*, II. iv. 39 ; Loeb, p. 169.

[2] Xenophon, *Hellenica*, II. iv. 43 ; Loeb, p. 171.

vision of freedom and by it helped in some measure to
forward the deliverance of a later Athens from tyranny
more grievous even than that of the Thirty. The place
has ennobling associations and the scene is strikingly characteristic of Greece. Perhaps I may be pardoned if I
conclude with a description written after a visit made
many years ago, but remembered as well as yesterday.

" Finer situation for a fortress could hardly be. It
stands out defiantly on the top of its rounded, pine-
clothed hill, amid scenery which is on all sides wild and
impressive. It is the very place for a robber stronghold
or the last sanctuary of free men who disdain submission
at the price of liberty. Deep ravines run past it on all
four sides—more open and even cultivated in front of
the pass, grimly abysmal behind. On one side only is the
hill accessible, that by which we have come through
the thick screen of pines ; a steep slope, but not abrupt
as on the other sides. Looking forth from the ramparts
in any direction, we face lofty ridges of grey rock, intermittently wooded, while on the lower steeps the patches
of corn between the pines make a fine contrast of colour.
The rock on the ridge and where it crops out through the
green below is mostly grey, but up the great ravine west
the russet red prevails. The outlook back south-east
over Chasia is (in the immediate foreground) exceedingly
stern and rocky ; but beyond the rugged edge of rock
Athens and the sea are, we know, somewhere in the haze,
just visible on a clear day over the great wall that shuts
out most of the plain."

To Thrasybulus, doubtless, that glimpse of Athens
through the haze brought vision of restored democracy and hope of a revival of the material splendour
which Athens had lost. To us it may rather suggest thoughts of the more enduring empire of the
mind which, even in defeat, Athens had won. This she
will never lose as long as western civilization continues ;
and we have our part in it. For in this spiritual realm
Athens was destined to effect what she had failed to
effect in the political sphere—a union of all Hellas under

her hegemony. Greek literature and art culminate in fifth-century Athens, and in the ages which follow the unity of Greek art and literature is the unity which Athens gave to them. This achievement in its leading aspects will be the subject of the fourth and concluding division of this book.

OUTLINE OF DATES

Note.—It is to be understood that many dates are approximate only. Dates in Greek history are difficult to fix with exactitude and are often matter of controversy. In this outline the Table in Bury's *History of Greece* has generally been followed. It is well also to remember that the Athenian year began nominally with the Summer solstice (now June the 21st) and that allowance has to be made for this, just as in earlier English history for the beginning of the year with March instead of January. Thucydides reckons the years of the Peloponnesian war by campaigning seasons.

Dates in Literature or Art are indented, and the event is in Italics.

B.C. 480. Battle of Salamis.
     479. Battles of Plataea and Mycalê.
         Capture of Sestos by Xanthippus and the Athenians.
     478. Pausanias commands the Greek fleet and takes Byzantium.
         Rebuilding of the walls of Athens.
         Misconduct and recall of Pausanias.
         Confederacy of Delos formed.
     477. Spartans withdraw from the contest with Persia.
         Fortification of Piraeus begun.
     476. Eion on Strymon captured by Cimon.
     473. Reduction of Scyros by the Athenians.
     472. Carystus compelled to join the Confederacy of Delos.
              472. *The Persians of Aeschylus.*
     471. Themistocles banished by ostracism.
     469. Secession and reduction of Naxos.
     468. Battle of the Eurymedon.
     465. Secession of Thasos.
         Athenian disaster in Thrace (at Drabescus).
     464. Earthquake at Sparta followed by Helot revolt.
     463. Surrender of Thasos.
     462. Mycenae reduced and depopulated by the Argives.
         Democratic assault on the Areopagus led by Ephialtes.
         Pericles enters upon public life.
         Remuneration introduced for dicastery-service.

B.C. 461. Ostracism of Cimon.
460. Athens breaks with Sparta and allies with Argos.
459. Athens acquires Naupactus and settles Messenians there.
Megara invites alliance with Athens.   Long walls from
Megara to Nisaea built by the Athenians.
Athens at war with Corinth and Epidaurus.   Battles
at Halieis and Cecryphalea.
Athenian expedition to Egypt.   Capture of Memphis.
458. War with Aegina.   Defeat of the Aeginetans at sea.
Two victories of Myronides over the Corinthians.
Building of the Long Walls of Athens begun.
458. *The Oresteia of Aeschylus.*
457. Athenian defeat at Tanagra.
Athenian victory at Oenophyta.   Athens in control of
Boeotia.
456. Surrender of Aegina.
Tolmides sails round the Peloponnese and burns
Gythium.
454. Destruction of the Athenian forces in Egypt.
The series of Temple Tribute lists begins.
453. Achaia allied with Athens.
452. Truce for five years between Athens and the Peloponnesians.
450. Cimon's last campaign and death in Cyprus.
449. Double victory by land and sea at Cyprian Salamis.
448. Suspension of hostilities with Persia.   So-called ' Peace
of Callias.'
Pericles' unsuccessful effort to bring about a Pan-
Hellenic Conference at Athens.
447. Athenian defeat at Coronea.   Athens loses control of
Boeotia.
447. *Parthenon begun.*
446. Revolt of Euboea.
Treachery of Megara.
Reduction of Euboea by Pericles.
445. Thirty Years' Peace.   Athens relinquishes Nisaea,
Pegae, Troezen, and Achaia.
443. Foundation of Thurii on the site of Sybaris.
Five ' regions ' distinguished in the Tribute lists.
442. Ostracism of Thucydides, son of Melesias.
440. Secession of Samos and Byzantium.
439. Reduction of Samos.   Submission of Byzantium.
438. *Dedication of the Parthenon.*
437. *Propylaea begun.*
436. Amphipolis founded.
435. Quarrel of Corinth and Corcyra over Epidamnus.
Naval victory of the Corcyreans.
435,4. Vigorous preparations at Corinth for revenge on Corcyra.

B.C. 433. Defensive alliance between Corcyra and Athens.
          Naval victory of the Corinthians off Sybota.
          Megarian decree passed at Athens.
     432. Revolt of Potidaea and beginning of the siege.
          Debates on peace or war at Sparta.
     431. First year of the Peloponnesian war.
          Theban surprise attack on Plataea.
          Invasion of Attica by the Peloponnesians.
          Expulsion of the Aeginetans from Aegina.
     430. Second invasion of Attica.
          Plague at Athens.
     429. Victories of Phormio in the Gulf of Corinth.
          Siege of Plataea begun.
          Death of Pericles.
     428. Third invasion of Attica.
          Revolt of Lesbos.
     427. Fourth invasion of Attica.
          Surrender of Mytilene. Decree against the whole
             population passed at Athens, but next day rescinded.
          Surrender of Plataea and judicial murder of the garrison.
     426. Athenian disaster in Aetolia.
          Purification of Delos.
     425. Fifth invasion of Attica.
          Seizure of Pylos by Demosthenes.
          Blockade and capture of Sphacteria.
          Athenian fleet in Sicilian waters.
          Pacification of Sicily.   Athenians withdraw.
               425. Acharnians of Aristophanes.
     424. Capture of Cythera by Nicias.
          Capture of Nisaea and the Long Walls of Megara.
          Athenian defeat at Delium.
          Brasidas in Thrace wins over Acanthus and Amphipolis.
          Eion saved by Thucydides, the historian.
          Thucydides banished for failing to save Amphipolis.
               424. Aristophanes' Knights.
     423. Truce for one year between Athens and the Pelopon-
             nesians.
          Revolt of Scionê.
          Leontini seized by the Syracusans.
               423. The Clouds of Aristophanes.
     422. Deaths of Cleon and Brasidas at Amphipolis.
               422. The Wasps of Aristophanes.
     421. Peace of Nicias.   End of the Ten Years' War.
               421. Aristophanes' Peace.
                     Euripides' Suppliants.
          Scionê taken and destroyed by the Athenians.
          Separate treaty between Athens and Sparta.
     420. Alliance of Athens with Argos : breach with Sparta.

B.C. **418.** Battle of Mantinea. Spartans victorious over Argos and her allies.

417. Ostracism of Hyperbolus.

416. Athenian conquest of Melos.

Embassy from Segesta to the Athenians.

    415. *Euripides' Trojan Women.*

415. The Sicilian Expedition sails from Athens.

Mutilation of the Hermae.

Arrest of Alcibiades in Sicily, and escape to Sparta.

Victory of the Athenians before Syracuse and subsequent withdrawal into winter quarters.

414. Landing of the Athenians in Thapsus Bay and seizure of Epipolae.

Siege of Syracuse. Destruction in succession of two Syracusan counter-works. Death of Lamachus.

Nicias left in sole command.

Arrival of Gylippus from Sparta.

    414. *The Birds of Aristophanes.*

413. Peloponnesian war renewed and Decelea occupied.

Demosthenes with Athenian reinforcements arrives at Syracuse.

Failure of night attack on Epipolae.

Battles in the Great Harbour.

Attempted retreat of the Athenians.

Total destruction of the Sicilian Expedition.

Persian claim to tribute revived.

412. Chios, Erythrae, Miletus, Lesbos, Clazomenae revolt.

Treaty between Sparta and the Persians.

Alcibiades breaks with the Spartans and intrigues with Tissaphernes.

411. Oligarchical conspiracy in Samos and at Athens.

Revolution at Athens. Rule of the Four Hundred established, and after three months overthrown.

Alcibiades recalled to the army at Samos.

Athenian defeat off Eretria.

Revolt of Euboea.

Athenian victory at Cynossema in the Hellespont.

Victory of the Athenians at Abydos.

410. Athenian victory at Cyzicus.

Democracy fully restored at Athens.

409. Pylos recaptured by the Spartans.

408. Athens recovers Byzantium and Chalcedon.

407. Alcibiades lands at Piraeus and is received with acclamation.

Lysander comes from Sparta as admiral and wins the friendship and support of Cyrus.

Athenian defeat at Notium.

Alcibiades once more in exile.

B.C. 406. Great Athenian victory at Arginusae. The victorious
admirals condemned and six of them put to death.

405. Lysander again in command.
The whole Athenian fleet surprised and captured at
Aegospotami.
Blockade of Athens.

404. Surrender of Athens. Long Walls pulled down.
Rule of the Thirty Tyrants.

403. Thrasybulus at Phylê.
March of Thrasybulus on Piraeus and victory of the
exiles in the battle of Munychia.
Restoration of democracy at Athens.

NOTE ON BOOKS

Two books, in particular, are of inestimable value to the student of Athens and her empire. The one is Zimmern's *Greek Commonwealth* [1] —which with an inspired sureness of touch portrays stroke by stroke the ideal city-state, as actualized for some brief moments of history in the commonwealth of Athens : the other is Hill's indispensable *Sources*. [2]

For the light which the recovery of inscriptions has thrown on historical problems the student may most conveniently consult Hicks and Hill, *Greek Historical Inscriptions* (Oxford University Press, 1901) ; or, as an alternative, Roberts and Gardner's *Introduction to Greek Epigraphy*, Part II. (Cambridge University Press, 1905). All topographical points which come within the limits of Pausanias' Itinerary are explained and discussed with astonishing insight and completeness in the four volumes of Sir James Frazer's Commentary (Macmillan 1898) and are readily traceable by means of the full Index to Notes in Vol. VI. The maps and plans, too, are excellent. For formal study of the topography and archaeology of Athens we naturally go first to Professor Ernest Gardner's *Ancient Athens* (Macmillan, 1902), and may supplement with Weller (C. H.) *Athens and its Monuments* (The Macmillan Company, 1913) or D'Ooge's *The Acropolis* (Macmillan, 1908). Other books which incidentally reveal aspects of the charm of Athens are : Mahaffy, *Rambles and Studies in Greece* (Macmillan 1876) ; Mrs. Bosanquet's *Days in Attica* (Methuen, 1914) ; and, in another way, Casson (Stanley), *Catalogue of the Acropolis Museum*, Vol. II. (Cambridge University Press, 1921). For a sympathetic understanding of the Athenian democracy ample help will be found in Greenidge (A. H. J.), *Handbook of Greek Constitutional History* (Macmillan, 1902), especially the section on the Athenian Empire, Chapter VI., 5, pp. 189-204, and there is a brilliantly suggestive chapter in W. Scott Ferguson's *Greek Imperialism* (Constable, 1913). For social and domestic life there is Tucker's *Life in Ancient Athens* (Macmillan, 1907), and for the deeper meanings of this study Dickinson's *The Greek View of Life* (Methuen, 1896) and Livingstone's *The Greek Genius* (Oxford University Press, 1912 and 1915). Whibley's *Companion to Greek Studies* (Cambridge University Press, 1916) will be found useful under a variety of heads.

The standard *Greek History* for the purpose of this note is Bury's (Macmillan, 1900 and 1913). It does for the twentieth century what Grote's *Greece* did for the second half of the nineteenth. It co-ordinates

---

[1] Zimmern (A. E.). *The Greek Commonwealth*, Clarendon Press, 2nd edition, 1915.

[2] Hill (G. F.). *Sources for Greek History* 478-431 B.C., Oxford University Press, 1907.

in a narrative of sustained interest and charm the results of contemporary archaeology, epigraphy, travel and criticism. The story of Athenian ambition in Sicily and its ruinous ending has been told by Freeman with all the master's eloquence and thoroughness of research in the first four hundred pages of the Third Volume of his *History of Sicily* (Oxford University Press, 1892).

But the ultimate satisfaction comes only from a recourse to the original sources, even if the reading must be done in translations. For the whole period 478-403 Thucydides' *History* is, of course, the capital authority, till in 411 it breaks off abruptly and Xenophon takes up the tale in the first two books of his *Hellenica*. Translations of Thucydides and Xenophon are, therefore, of first necessity to the student who cannot read the original Greek. There are happily several good translations of Thucydides in English. The most recent, Foster Smith's in the *Loeb Classical Library*, is completed only to the end of Book VI. It has the great merit of being presented, page by page, alongside the Greek original : as a translation it is sometimes better than, sometimes not so good as, other current translations. Jowett's (Clarendon Press, 2nd Edition, 1900) has, on the whole, the highest claim as literature ; but Crawley's revised by R. Feetham for the Temple Classics (Dent) in 1903, is very good and for terseness and vigour often holds the palm. Thomas Hobbes' seventeenth century translation is racy, if by modern standards sometimes inaccurate, and still very readable. Xenophon has a delightful translator in H. G. Dakyns, whose work in four volumes includes all Xenophon's varied writings. The Hellenica are also translated by C. L. Brownson in the Loeb series (Heinemann).

Thucydides relates at full length only the story of the first twenty years of the Peloponnesian War, B.C. 431-411 : yet he is our chief authority also for the fifty years from 478-431, which he merely summarizes. Thucydides died without completing his history Xenophon takes up the story roughly where Thucydides drops it in the autumn of 411, and he takes us to the end, the restoration of the democracy in 403. Diodorus the Sicilian, who composed a *Universal History* in the time of Augustus, covers the whole ground in his 11th, 12th and 13th books, but adds comparatively little to our knowledge. A good deal more may be gathered from seven of Plutarch's *Lives*—Themistocles, Aristides, Cimon, Pericles, Nicias, Alcibiades, Lysander. For constitutional history Aristotle's *Constitution of Athens* [1] has, since its recovery from an Egyptian tomb, been our chief authority. Aristophanes' comedies [2]— *Acharnians, Knights, Wasps, Peace*—are in an especial degree illuminating ; and occasionally a ray of light comes from one or other of the great tragedies.

---

[1] Translated by Sir F. G. Kenyon, its first editor (Oxford University Press, 1890).

[2] Rogers' translations of Aristophanes come nearest to completeness. Hookham Frere made spirited translations of four including the *Acharnians* and the *Knights,* and of parts of the *Peace*; and earlier than Frere as a translator is Mitchell.

PART IV.

THE ABIDING SPLENDOUR

"We have not done with the Hellenes yet . . . we have not entered into full possession of the inheritance bequeathed to us."
EVELYN ABBOTT, Preface to *Hellenica.*

"Each successive generation must learn from ancient Greece that which can be taught by her alone; and to assist, however little, in the transmission of her message is the best reward of a student."
R. C. JEBB, *Growth and Influence of Classical Greek Poetry*, p. 285.

CHAPTER X

THE GREAT TEACHERS

1. SOCRATES

" Great is the stake, yea great beyond men's deeming, whether we be good or bad."

PLATO, Republic, 608 B.

" But if ye suffer for righteousness' sake, happy are ye."

In 399 B.C. all Athens—the Athens that had heard the news of Aegospotami and endured long agonies of siege and revolution—was stirred by the trial and condemnation to death of an old man named Socrates. " Served the old rascal right " (or the equivalent of this in classical Attic), said the man in the street, " the fellow was an enemy of the people and a public nuisance." But a circle of friends, mostly young men of good family, who of their own accord had sought Socrates' company and listened with delight to the words that fell from his lips, were stricken with sorrow. And this is how one of them describes the death-scene, when the time came for Socrates to die in accordance with the sentence of the Athenian people.[1] The passage is from one of Plato's dialogues.[2]

---

[1] There was for certain special reasons an interval of thirty days before the sentence could be carried out. During that time Socrates was kept a prisoner, but his friends had free access to the place where he was confined, and he spent the time in conversing with them. The subject of the last day's discussions had been the immortality of the soul.

The form of capital punishment usual at Athens was the drinking of a cup of hemlock, a drug which acted swiftly and painlessly, as described in the text.

[2] *Phaedo*, 116 B to end.

Phaedo of Elis, after whom the dialogue is called, relates for the benefit of Echecrates of Phlius, the story of Socrates' last hours and death.

The Death of Socrates.—" It was by this time close on sunset, for Socrates had been away quite a long while. He now came back to us from the bath and sat down ; and there was not much conversation after this before the officer of the Eleven came and stood by him, and said : ' Socrates, I shall not have to reproach you, as I do other prisoners, for being angry and railing at me, when I tell them to drink the hemlock, as I am bound to do by my orders. Nay I have found you during the whole time you have been here noble, gentle, and good, above all who ever before came hither ; and now also I know full well you are not angry with me—you see it is not my fault—but with those who are really to blame. You know my errand, I am sure. Ah ! fare you well ; and try to bear easily what needs must be.' And tears filled his eyes as he turned to go. Then Socrates looked up and said to him : ' May you, too, fare well, I will do as you say ' : and added to us : ' What a good fellow it is ! He has been visiting me the whole time ; we have had many a talk, and he has been the best of men to me. And now what a generous spirit he shows in shedding tears for me. Come then, Crito, let us do as he bids : go some one and fetch the draught, if it is ready pounded ; if not, ask the man to pound it.'

" Then said Crito : ' Oh no, Socrates, I am sure the sun is still upon the mountains ; it has not yet set. I know that others have taken the draught quite late, long after word was brought to them : they have dined and drunk deep, and have held converse, some of them, with those whose company they desired. Pray do not be in a hurry ; there is time enough yet.'

" Socrates thereupon said : ' Those you speak of, Crito, doubtless had their reasons for so doing—they expected some gain from acting as you say, and I, with good reason also, will *not* do as they. I do not think I should gain anything by postponing the draught for a little, only incur my own derision for clinging to life and being sparing of what is already gone and done with. But do you do exactly as I bade.'

" On this Crito made a sign to the servant who was standing near ; and he went out, and after some time came back with the man whose business it was to administer the poison ; and he brought it ready pounded in a cup. On seeing the man, Socrates said to him : ' That is well. And now my excellent friend—you understand these matters ; tell me what to do.'   ' Just drink it,' said he, ' and walk about until your legs feel heavy. Then lie down ; if you do this, it will act of itself.' At the same time he held out the cup to Socrates.

" And he took it in all graciousness, Echecrates, without a tremor, without loss of colour or change of countenance, but glancing upward at the man with that keen look of his, said : ' Now tell me—about a libation from this cup —may I make one, or not ? '   ' We mix just so much, Socrates, as we think sufficient.'   ' I understand,' said he ; ' but at all events a man may, and must, pray the gods that his journey from this to the other world may be fortunate. This then is my prayer ; and may it so come to pass.' As he spoke these words he put the cup to his lips and very quietly and calmly drank off the potion. And most of us till then were fairly able to restrain our tears ; but when we saw him drinking, and the cup drained, we could refrain no longer ; and, for my part, in spite of myself, my tears were rising fast, so that I covered my face and gave way to my grief—not that I mourned for Socrates, but for my own misfortune in losing the companionship of such a friend. Crito, too, even before I broke down, when he could not restrain his tears, had got up and gone out. As for Apollodorus, who had been weeping all the time and never stopped, he now burst into a storm of sobs and by his lamentations and distress upset the self-control of every one present except Socrates.

" ' What strange behaviour is this, my friend," said the master. ' Why it was in great part for this reason that

I sent the women away, that they might not offend in this manner. For I have heard it said that in a man's death-hour there should be a holy stillness. So bear up and keep quiet.'

"On hearing these words we were ashamed and checked our weeping. Socrates walked about for a while; and when, as he told us, his legs felt heavy, he lay down on his back: for such were the officer's instructions. And this man who had given him the draught now took him in hand; and a little later tested his feet and legs; then pressed his foot hard and asked him if he felt the pressure; and he replied 'No.' After this he next pressed the calf of the leg, and proceeding upward in this way showed that his limbs were growing cold and stiffening. Then once more he applied the test and told us that when the cold reached his heart he would be gone. And now when the chill had spread almost to the waist, Socrates uncovered his face (for he had meantime drawn his garment over his head) and said—and these were his last words: 'Crito, we owe a cock to Asclepius, do not fail to pay the debt.'

" 'It shall be done,' said Crito, 'is there anything else ? ' To this question, however, there was no reply: and a little later a tremor passed over his body, the attendant uncovered his face and we saw that his eyes were fixed: and thereupon Crito closed his mouth and his eyes.

"Such, Echecrates, was the end of our friend—a man who was, in our esteem, the best of all whom we had ever known; yea, and the wisest and the most righteous."

Why was Socrates condemned ?—How, we may ask, had it come about that a man whose last hours are thus described, was condemned to death as a criminal by an Athenian dicastery-court ? We have, it happens, abundant material for judgment. For among the young Athenians who loved Socrates and regarded him as a great teacher were two of the supreme masters of Attic prose, Xenophon and Plato, and through their writings Socrates has become one of the best-known characters of all time.

Socrates' Times.—Socrates was seventy years old at his death, so his life had extended over most of the period during which the power of Athens had risen to its height and declined. He had been born in 469, just ten years after the great deliverance of Plataea and Mycalê. He was an infant when (in 468) Cimon won the battle of the Eurymedon. He was ten years old when the Long Walls were being built ; he was passing from boyhood into manhood through the years in which Athens' short-lived land-empire was won and lost (457-447). He was just over thirty when the Parthenon was finished and the Propylaea begun (438). He had seen that stately approach to the Acropolis rise in magnificent proportions year by year, and hastily finished off without being completed, when the peril of war grew imminent. He was thirty-eight years of age when the Peloponnesian war broke out. In his forty-fifth year he had seen the Spartan prisoners from Sphacteria brought in chains to Athens ; next year he fought in person at the battle of Delium (424). Then nine years later, when already well over fifty, he had witnessed the sailing of the great armada for Sicily (415), had lived through the alternate hopes and fears of the next two years ; had watched, calm himself but not indifferent, the popular elation over the earlier successes, and the stupefaction that followed, when the incredible news of total disaster came. He had had his part in the anxious years which followed, had seen the slow breaking up of Athens' sea-empire, the gleams of reviving hope brought by Cyzicus and Arginusae, the sudden closing in of despair after Aegospotami. He had lived, too, through the agony which ensued, had gone hungry in the siege of Athens, and seen the strong walls, the building of which in his boyhood he could remember, broken down stone by stone to the insolent flutings of his country's enemies. He had lived, now an old man, through the terror of the Thirty and witnessed the restoration of democracy by Thrasybulus. No man who in the years from 460 to 400 B.C. had lived in the full tide of Athenian life can be said to have had an uneventful life. And

Socrates did live in the full tide of that life, and, though
taking no part in its public activities (except that he
served as a hoplite at the siege of Potidaea and fought
in the battle of Delium), he was observing all that happened with an acutely critical intelligence. In social
position he was just a citizen of free birth, not an Eupatrid
like Solon or Pericles. By profession he was a stone-
mason or sculptor (the Greek word used means literally
a worker in stone), like his father before him.   Five
hundred years after his death the traveller Pausanias [1]
saw on the Acropolis a Hermes and a group of draped
statuary representing the three Graces, which were said
to be Socrates' work. But it was not for long that
Socrates followed his father's calling. In early manhood
he had passed through a mental crisis in which he had
come to a resolve to cease practising the craft by which
he earned his living, in order that he might have leisure
to give himself wholly to what he took to be a divinely
appointed mission. This was, strangely enough, neither
more nor less than to talk ; to talk with every one he
met, who was willing to enter into conversation. To talk ;
but not to talk at random. Socrates always talked with
a purpose, a purpose which those he talked with were
apt to find exceedingly disconcerting. This purpose was
to discover if they had any true understanding of the
things they supposed themselves to know, whether this
was education or government, poetry or politics, military
science or the art of public speaking, or just some ordinary
handicraft like pottery and carpentering. The reason
doubtless was that he felt within himself an irrepressible
desire to penetrate to a true understanding of all matters
of deep human concern,—matters such as conduct, public
and private, the meaning of justice, beauty, knowledge ;
and he was deeply impressed with most men's ignorance
and apathy regarding these things of great moment, an
ignorance which went along with an egregious conceit of
knowledge and a stupid self-complacency. Men talked
glibly of just and unjust, beautiful and ugly, of courage

[1] Pausanias i. 22. 8 and ix. 35. 7 ; Frazer, vol. 1, pp. 32 and 488.

and wisdom and holiness, without any true discernment of what they meant by the words they were using. So he conceived it to be his mission to apply to every one who would converse with him the test of a rigorous cross-examination, the result of which invariably was that his interlocutor became involved in contradiction and was shown up as hopelessly ignorant of the very subject he professed to know most about. For Socrates had a quite terrible subtlety and power as a conversationalist. No one was ever known to get the better of him in argument ; most men, even foreign visitors to Athens, famed in other lands for their eloquence and efficiency as teachers, were as wax when once fairly entangled in conversation with Socrates. These discussions were generally held in public and the onlookers found it vastly amusing, especially when some showy and pretentious citizen was made to look ridiculous. For the victim, the man caught in the toils of Socrates' close questioning, it was another matter ; such a one was apt to be vexed when put out of countenance. A piquancy was added to Socrates' invincible skill in this kind of discussion by his protestation of his own ignorance and desire to learn ; it came to be called Socrates' *irony*.[1]

Socrates' way of life and personal appearance.—This was an odd way of living and soon made Socrates a marked man in Athens. " Socrates," says Xenophon, " ever lived in the public eye ; at early morning he was to be seen betaking himself to one of the promenades, or wrestling-grounds ; at noon he would appear with the gathering crowds in the market-place ; and as day declined, wherever the largest throng might be encountered, there was he to be found, talking for the most part, while anyone who chose might stop and listen." [2] There were other peculiarities about Socrates. As he earned no money, his means were very scanty. He seems to have possessed property

[1] Socrates' own account of these matters, and of the part therein attributed to the Delphic Oracle, will be found in the *Apology*, 20 c to 24 a.

[2] Xenophon, *Recollections of Socrates*, i. 1. 10 ; Dakyns, vol. iii. Part I. pp. 3 and 4.

enough to afford to his family and himself the bare
necessaries of life. But this was only possible by a stern
economy bordering on indigence. He usually went about
barefoot, and wore only a shabby old cloak (without any
under-garment), which became a standing joke among
those who knew him. All luxuries he dispensed with, yet
professed himself well off and content because (like the
' new poor ' in England) he had learnt to limit his wants.
One way and another he was an oddity, and not the least
odd circumstance about him was his personal appearance.
He had a bulging forehead, prominent eyes, a snub nose,
and thick lips—a combination of features which justified
his friends in likening him to old Silenus or a Satyr.
Small wonder that he was a marked man and one of the
best-known figures in Athens. No wonder there were
many who laughed at Socrates, and some who scowled.
Such characteristics, while they may intensify the devotion of friends, feed the dislike of enemies.

The Clouds of Aristophanes.   Misconceptions of Socrates' character and teaching current in his own life-time
at Athens have been perpetuated in an amusing form
by the genius of Aristophanes in his comedy *The Clouds*.
In *The Clouds* Socrates is brought upon the stage as
founder and director of a Thinking School or Contempla-
torium—a Phrontisterion in the Greek—where along with
his disciples he indulges in all sorts of ridiculous speculations, and openly professes, for a fee, to equip those who
come to him with such acuteness of wits as would enable
them to get the better of an antagonist in any argument,
independently of the merits of the case. In the play,
Strepsiades, an Athenian father who has been brought to
the verge of bankruptcy by his son Pheidippides' passion
for horses, resorts in desperation to the ' Phrontisterion,'
and begs Socrates to impart to him the marvellous secret
by which the worse cause can be made to appear the
better, so that he need not pay his debts.[1]   Socrates con-

---

[1] " Teach me, I beg, that argument of yours,
    The one that pays no debts. By Heaven, I swear
    I'll plank down any fee you like to ask."
        Aristophanes, *Clouds*, ll. 244-6. See also ll. 112-118.

sents, and when Strepsiades is found too old and stupid to learn, Pheidippides takes his place, with the disastrous result that the first use he makes of his new powers is to give his father a thrashing, and then prove him wrong when he objects. The whole comedy turns on this professed power to make the worse cause appear the better. The worse and the better cause personified as the Just and Unjust Argument are actually brought upon the stage to wrestle in debate for the soul of Pheidippides ; and the Unjust Argument is made to win.[1] Finally Strepsiades, in a fury at the evil way in which his resort to Socrates is turning out, climbs on to the roof of the Phrontisterion with a lighted torch and burns it down.

The Clouds was brought out in 423, when Socrates was in his forty-seventh year ; [2] it belongs to a much earlier period of his life, therefore, than that of his trial and condemnation. Yet it is curious that the play anticipates in set terms the indictment on which in 399 Socrates was condemned and put to death. In that indictment there were two counts : (1) Socrates is guilty of rejecting the gods in whom the State believes and of introducing strange gods in their place ; (2) he is guilty also of corrupting the minds of the young. These counts are both clearly anticipated in the play.

> " Oh what a fool I've been ! What utter madness
> To disenthrone the gods for Socrates ! " [3]

cries Strepsiades in repentance at the end of the play. At the first encounter with Strepsiades Socrates is made to declare that the gods are abolished, and that the Clouds, Ether and King Whirlwind reign in their stead. " Zeus did you say ? " cries Socrates. " Don't talk such nonsense ! Why there is no Zeus ! " [4] And Strepsiades indoctrinates in turn his son Pheidippides :

> " Whirlwind is king now ; Zeus has been deposed." [5]

[1] Aristophanes, *Clouds*, ll. 889-1104.

[2] The text we have is not, however, that of the play as originally performed, but of a revision made subsequently by the poet.

[3] Aristophanes, *Clouds*, ll. 1476-7.   [4] Line 367.   [5] Line 828.

Chaos, Air, Respiration, are the deities that Socrates swears by in the play, not Zeus and Apollo.[1] The play takes its name, *The Clouds,* from a band of these new divinities, who come sweeping up over Parnes at Socrates' prayer and act as Chorus :

> " Ever we float and we fleet !
> Clouds compact all of shimmering dewdrops, lo we are
>   rising
> Forth from our father, Ocean deep-murmuring,
> Upward, up, to the lofty mountain summits
>   Clad thick with forest trees !
> There will we scan all the far-seen pinnacles ;
> Watch Earth, the holy, whose fruitage we water,
> And the sacred rivers singing as they flow,
> And the seas chanting in deep-toned accordance.
> Come, for the eye of Heaven is flashing his full splendour
>   In beams of glittering light.
>   Come, let us shake off the mist of tiny rain-drops
>   Veiling our immortal forms ; let us view the earth
>   With gaze far flung the landscape over." [2]

Such is the song we hear as they approach.

The whole action regarding Pheidippides, and in particular the contest between the Worse and Better Reason illustrates the second charge, that of misguiding and perverting the young. The contest, in effect, is a debate between the good old-fashioned type of education which bred up the victors of Marathon, and the new-fangled ideas introduced by the subtle-minded teachers of the day. The final act of the drama is the burning down of the house of Socrates. As he breathes out imprecations and threats against the false teacher, Strepsiades even suggests the alternative of attacking him by course of law. " And pray be my adviser," he whispers to the image of Hermes standing in the street, " shall I bring a suit at law against them . . .? " [3]

The concluding words of the dialogue, as Socrates' Thinking School is burning, are :

> " Have at them, smite and strike, for many reasons,
> But chiefly for their sin against the gods." [4]

[1] Aristophanes, *Clouds,* line 627.   [2] Lines 275-290.
[3] Lines 1481-2.   [4] Lines 1508-9.

It may reasonably be concluded that while it is improbable that there can be any direct connection between Aristophanes' burlesque production in 423 B.C. and the trial and condemnation of Socrates twenty-four years afterwards, the prosecution and death of Socrates grew out of the same popular misconception of his life and teaching as Aristophanes' comedy, that is (1) the belief that Socrates, like certain Ionian thinkers, engaged in physical speculations which explained away the gods, as did Heraclitus and Anaxagoras for instance ; (2) the confusion of Socrates with the professional teachers known as ' Sophists.'

Socrates and Physical Science.—Strange as it may seem, each of these beliefs was exactly contrary to the facts. We have the witness of both Plato and Xenophon that Socrates took little interest in the physical speculations which in his day occupied some of the chief Ionian thinkers. His interest was wholly centred in practical life, in human conduct. " And to speak generally," writes Xenophon, " in regard of things celestial he set his face against attempts to excogitate the machinery by which the divine power performs its several operations. Not only were these matters beyond man's faculties to discover, as he believed, but the attempt to search out what the gods had not chosen to reveal could hardly (he supposed) be well pleasing in their sight." [1] " *Up to the limit set by utility*, he was ready to join in any investigation, and to follow out an argument with those who were with him ; but there he stopped." [2] From this last quotation it would appear, therefore, that Socrates was even something of a ' Philistine ' in respect of *pure* science, and would not have accepted Bacon's *dictum* regarding ' light-giving ' experiments.[3]

Socrates and the Sophists.—That the Greeks came to attach a reproachful meaning to the name ' sophist ' is

---

[1] *Recollections of Socrates*, iv. 7. 6 ; Dakyns, vol. iii. Part I. p. 177.

[2] IV. 7. 8 ; Dakyns, p. 178.

[3] Bacon, *Novum Organum*, Aphorism 70.

illustrated by the modern use of the word ' sophistical.'
But it had not been so always. In its origin ' sophist '
simply meant a ' seeker after wisdom,' a meaning closely
akin to ' philosopher,' which signifies a ' lover of wisdom.'
But in Socrates' time and somewhat earlier there had
appeared in Hellas a class of professed teachers calling
themselves ' sophists,' about whose teaching and influence
there has been much disagreement.   These professional
sophists went about from city to city offering to impart
their skill for a fixed fee.   Gorgias, Protagoras, Prodicus,
Thrasymachus, were famous sophists.[1]   Socrates was unlike the sophists in two important respects : (1) he never
took payment for any service he might do to those with
whom he conversed ; (2) he never professed to teach, on
the contrary he always made profession of his own ignorance and sought to learn from others, and this peculiarity
of his was the Socratic ' irony.'   At the same time it
must be acknowledged that popular instinct was so far right
that there was a certain broad resemblance between the
influence of Socrates at Athens and that of the professed
sophists in other cities, only with a difference that wholly
changed the moral character of that influence.   For all
Socrates' powers were concentrated on fighting the battle
of the Just against the Unjust Argument, and all his
influence, both by precept and example, and especially
by his method of discussing, or ' dialectic '—was directed
to making those with whom he talked, and most of all the
young, more thoughtful, more temperate, more self-
controlled and better disciplined.   The whole bent of his
teaching was towards the regulation of life in accordance
with principles.

[1] As there was no organized system of advanced teaching in fifth
century Greece, the instruction proffered by the sophists to the men of
their generation has been aptly designated ' higher education.'   See
this point very lucidly developed in *The Pageant of Greece* (R. W.
Livingstone), pp. 252 and 255.   It is hardly fair, perhaps, to call their
teaching immoral, but they certainly challenged established beliefs and
standards of conduct, and their teaching was so far subversive.   So also
was Socrates'.   Both were symptomatic of a stirring of thought in
the fifth century B.C., another aspect of which is seen in Euripides'
dramas.

Nevertheless, there can be little doubt that a confusion of Socrates with the professional sophists did him harm in the minds of many of the dicasts who sat in the court which tried him in 399 B.C., as well as with Aristophanes and the Athenian public in 423. Aristophanes, indeed, may possibly have been well aware that his representation of Socrates was gross caricature. Aristophanes and Socrates appear from the witness of Plato's *Banquet* [1] to have been good friends in spite of the buffooneries of the *Clouds* ; but Socrates' face and figure were too apt for the comic poet's dramatic purpose, and he could not resist the temptation to use them, when he set out to denounce the new teaching in Athens, which he regarded as destructive of good morals. The injury to Socrates, however, remained, and a long time after bore evil fruit.

Xenophon's ' Recollections.'—We have not one, but two full accounts of Socrates from disciples who had loved his society and who reverenced his memory. The two accounts are different, but not inconsistent with one another. Each pupil saw a different side of the beloved master, and that is the side which his testimony brings out. Xenophon's portraiture has not the delicate subtlety of Plato's, nor the same exquisite charm ; it is simple and straightforward, some call it common-place. But, there is virtue in its simplicity and directness. Xenophon illustrates aptly and amply Socrates' personal piety and uprightness, the soundness of his advice to his friends, the wise benevolence of his life and conversation. His own personal impressions of Socrates' character he sums up as follows :

" To me, personally, he was what I have myself endeavoured to describe : so pious and devoutly religious that he would take no step apart from the will of heaven ; so just and upright that he never did even a trifling injury to any living soul ; so self-controlled, so temperate, that he never at any time chose the sweeter in place of the better ; so sensible, and wise, and prudent that in distinguishing the better from the worse he never erred ;

[1] Especially *Banquet*, 223 c.

nor had he need of any helper, but for the knowledge of these matters, his judgment was at once infallible and self-sufficing. Capable of reasonably setting forth and defining moral questions, he was also able to test others, and where they erred, to cross-examine and convict them, and so impel and guide them in the path of virtue and noble manhood. With those characteristics, he seemed to be the very impersonation of human perfection and happiness." [1]

Of Socrates' favourite manner of procedure in conversation he says : " His own,—that is the Socratic— method of conducting a rational discussion was to proceed step by step from one point of general agreement to another : Herein lay the real security for reasoning, he would say, and for this reason he was more successful in winning the common consent of his hearers than any one I ever knew." [2] Xenophon adds " at the same time . . . he was no less eager to cultivate a spirit of independence in others. . . ." Such, according to Xenophon, was his life ; and his death was in keeping with it : " he bore the sentence of condemnation with infinite gentleness and manliness." " No one within the memory of man ever bowed his head to death more nobly." [3] And of his memory : " But amongst those who knew Socrates and recognised what manner of man he was, all who make virtue and perfection their pursuit still to this day cease not to lament his loss with bitterest regret, as for one who helped them in the pursuit of truth as none else could." [4]

Socrates in Plato's Dialogues.—Xenophon's portraiture of Socrates has been undeservedly slighted, because Plato's is better. There is a fineness of touch in the delineation of Socrates in the dialogues of Plato which is beyond Xenophon's skill. The Socrates of the Platonic dialogues is one of the most perfect artistic creations of all time. It is a work of genius. Plato's *Socrates* lives

[1] *Recollections*, iv. 8. 11 ; Dakyns, p. 182.
[2] iv. 6. 15 ; Dakyns, p. 175.
[3] iv. 8. 1 and 2 ; Dakyns, p. 179.
[4] iv. 8. 11 ; Dakyns, pp. 181 and 182.

like the most vivid characters in plays and novels—like
Hamlet or Shylock, Sam Weller or Colonel Newcome.
How nearly the Socrates of the dialogues exactly corresponds to the Socrates of real life, how much Plato puts
into it through the intuitions of his own genius is beyond
any critic's sagacity to say. Without doubt it is an
idealized Socrates, but the idealized likeness sometimes
gets closer to the real object than the duller but more
accurate likeness—just as the painting of a great artist
is truer than a photograph. It is Plato's dialogues at all
events which have supplied that image of Socrates which
has dominated the imaginations of men for two thousand
years, and will so long as the dialogues are read.

Socrates' contribution to the history of thought.—It is
the dialogues which give Socrates his chief importance
in the history of philosophy. Socrates himself left no
writings. It is possible, however, through careful comparison of what others have written about him to estimate
his contributions to the history of thought in the narrow
sense. Aristotle definitely says [1] that the actual services
of Socrates to philosophy were (1) the making of definitions ; (2) the use of induction ; and he seems to be
right in ascribing to Socrates' procedure and influence
these two significant advances. In the dialogues of Plato
we find Socrates continually endeavouring to arrive at
the common element in things beautiful, or just, or good,
or honourable : again and again in discussion he presses
for a definition of knowledge, of courage, of holiness, of
prudence. He saw how loosely men are apt to make use
of these terms without any consistency or clear conception
of what they mean.[2] It was necessary to render the use

---

[1] *Metaphysics*, xii. 9. 3.

[2] It is not very different in our own time. Take politics. How the
words *self-determination, nationality, liberalism, equality, reform, retro-
grade,* are bandied about ; and how little clear meaning do most readers,
and a good many writers, attach to them ! How many of us are prepared to define the terms we use, and give guarantees for their consistent
use. Take literature and the arts. The use by critics of terms such as
purity of style, distinction, realism, symbolism, impressionist, is frequently
vague, loose, and arbitrary. We think we know, but often we do not know.

of such conceptions more exact before there could be any
clear and accurate reasoning at all. Socrates' insistence
on definition was therefore a most valuable preliminary
to the working out of a system of thought. Systematic
thinking, moreover, requires general principles. Socrates
was constantly endeavouring to advance from the particular to the general, from just acts or beautiful objects to
conceptions of justice and beauty ; and this advance from
the particular to the general is *induction*.

The real Socrates.—As we have noted already, Socrates
was not a writer. So far as we know, he left no scrap
of writing.[1] Neither was he a leader in the active public
life of his day.[2] He had no career in the ordinary sense :
he was neither soldier, statesman, nor man of letters.
And yet he was one of the world's greatest men, one of
the few who have impressed their influence deeply on
humanity. His greatness is shown not by any outward
achievements, but through his influence on other men.

Even in the world of school we use words and phrases like *good form,
patriotism, sporting spirit,* without stopping to think what exactly we
mean by them. It seems so simple and obvious, but is not. A modern
Socrates would find as much scope in cross-examining modern politicians, schoolmasters, journalists, Trades Union leaders, and schoolboys,
and could get as much fun out of it, as ever did Socrates, the son of
Sophroniscus, in fifth-century Athens. It is not suggested that terms
like the above have no definite and useful meaning, but that it takes
trouble—the sort of trouble Socrates took—to guard against error in
using them.

[1] There is one trifling qualification to be made. In the opening of
the *Phaedo* Socrates is described as employing himself while in prison
with the composition of a Hymn to Apollo, and in turning some of
Aesop's Fables into verse. For this and the reasons given by Socrates
in explanation, see *Phaedo,* 60 and 61.

[2] Once, and once only, Socrates held public office in Athens. He was
one of the Council of Five Hundred in the year 406 B.C., and it happened
that at the time of the impeachment of the admirals (above p. 252) his
tribe was in office. Both Xenophon and Plato relate that Socrates,
alone of the Prytaneis, or acting councillors, refused to bow to the
will of the populace in putting forward the illegal proposal to try the
admirals together, and so brought himself into imminent danger of
sharing their fate. For this, and other examples of Socrates' moral
courage and steady refusal to do wrong for any fear of man, see *Recollections of Socrates,* iv. 4. 1-3 ; Dakyns, pp. 153-4 ; and Plato, *Apology,*
32 B-D.

His great gift was character. He affected those with whom he came in contact by some wonderful charm of personality, combined with an astonishing acuteness of intellect, and a genius for conversation,—the sort of talk which the Athenians of his day called " dialectic." We have a measure of his greatness in the number of the schools of thought which owed their origin to his stimulus—Cynic and Cyrenaic, Stoic and Epicurean, and above all Plato's *Academy*. Their variety attests his manysidedness.

We thus know Socrates through the influence of his mind and discourse on other men, since he left nothing else of his own. The real Socrates is made known to us in the effects of his force of character on men so unlike as Antisthenes, Aristippus, and Alcibiades ; on Xenophon and Plato. And surely we get nearest to the real Socrates through the man who felt the inspiration of his character most deeply and reacted upon it most powerfully—Plato. The figure of Socrates, as worked out indirectly and subtly, but most completely, in the thirty or so dialogues of Plato, is so full and definite and self-consistent as almost to compel acceptance of its reality. It is not inconsistent with the more direct and matter-of-fact portrait drawing of Xenophon, which makes of Socrates an incarnation of glorified good sense,—only finer, subtler, more individual, more complete ; and therefore, truer. And what are the leading traits in this character ? In Socrates, as limned by Plato in the dialogues, we discern, firstly, a charming inoffensiveness and urbanity, qualities which move one student of Plato to call Socrates the most perfect gentleman found in literature, excepting only the Christ of the Gospels. Along with this urbanity goes a delicate and penetrating humour. There is his untiring persistence in the search for the true understanding of the things that interest him, and his intolerance of shams. Above all there is his passion for righteousness, his invincible belief in goodness, his firm conviction that the soul's integrity in thought and action is the one thing that matters.

II   T

Conclusion of the 'Gorgias.'—This highest aspect of Socrates' character and teaching is, perhaps, presented with more fulness and force in the concluding paragraphs of the Gorgias than anywhere else in Plato. There, after relating a beautiful myth of the judgment of the dead, Socrates is made to say :

" I for my part, Callicles, am fully convinced by these stories and I study how I shall present my soul for judgment whole and clean to the utmost possible. I put aside the honours that most men value and, with a single eye to truth, I try steadfastly as I may both to live in the practice of all virtue and, when my time comes, therein to die. And I call other men to this life to the extent of my power ; and you, in particular, I answer with a call thereto, and to that contest which I declare to be a contest of more importance than all our contests in the city ; and I make it a reproach to you that you will not be able to help yourself when the trial and the judgment of which I speak are appointed for you ; when you are haled to court and stand before the judge, the son of Aegina,[1] you will gasp and turn giddy, as you say I might before a court in Athens here . . ."

" It may be that all this seems to you an old wife's tale, and you reject it with scorn ; and in fact it would be reasonable enough to scorn it, if by diligent seeking we could find a better and truer tale to put in its place. But now, see how you, and Polus, and Gorgias, three of the wisest of the Hellenes, are unable to prove that we ought to live any other life than this which appears to be to our interest in that unseen world also. In all our long argument, while every other contention has been refuted, this alone stands firm, that we should be more careful not to do wrong than not to suffer wrong ; that every man should above all else practise not to seem to be good but to be good, both in public life and in private ; that if on occasion a man fall into vice, he should suffer chastisement, and that the next best thing to being just is this to become just and pay the penalty of injustice by being

[1] Rhadamanthus, one of the judges of the dead.

chastised ; that one should avoid every form of flattering deceit whether it regard oneself or others, the few or the many ; that one should employ the art of rhetoric, and every other form of action, for just ends always."

"So heed my words, and follow the path which, as our discussion signifies, leads to happiness, both while you live, and after life is ended. Suffer who will to scorn you for a fool and to heap upon you insults, if he wishes—nay have courage even to endure the dishonouring blow : 'twill be nothing worthy of account, if by the practice of virtue you are in very truth "a man of honour and a gentleman." And later on, when together we put these principles into practice, it will be time, if it seems right, to set our hands to public affairs, or to follow any other plan that may seem good, with the assurance that we are then better able to take counsel than we are now. It is surely disgraceful, being as we now are, to carry things with a high hand as though we were of some account, though we are never twice of the same mind even concerning matters of the highest moment : to such a length does our lack of proper education go. So then let us take our present conclusions for guides ; they tell us that this fashion of life is best, and bid us live and die in the practice of justice and every virtue." [1]

[1] *Gorgias*, 526 D to end.

CHAPTER XI

THE GREAT TEACHERS

2. PLATO

" If this had been what was said by all of you from the first, and such your admonitions to us from our youth up, we should not have been on the watch to prevent each other from doing wrong, but each one would have kept strict watch over himself, afraid lest by wrong doing he should live in fellowship with the greatest evil."

PLATO, *Republic*, 367 A.

SOCRATES is known solely through the impression which his words and character made on the minds of other men. Plato, the second supremely great name in Greek philosophy, is known almost wholly from his writings, the writings which have made his master, Socrates, the most familiar figure of all antiquity. But while Plato's dialogues reveal Socrates, they keep himself concealed.

Plato's Life.—Born of one of the most aristocratic families in Athens, an Eupatrid, connected on both sides with the house of Codrus, Plato approached philosophy as one of the gilded youths who cultivated Socrates' society to sharpen their wits, but to very different purpose from most of them. He not only listened to Socrates, but was attached to him by an intense personal devotion. The death of Socrates, which happened when he was between twenty-five and thirty years of age, was the decisive turning point in his life. Tradition says that immediately after the carrying out of the sentence in the manner described in the *Phaedo*, Plato left Athens. All his views

292

of public life and of his own career were changed. He
turned from the honourable ambition which earlier had
occupied his mind, and bent his whole power of thought
to working out various aspects of the questions he had
heard discussed in the society of Socrates. This purpose
he carried out not in systematic treatises, but in a succession of studies in dialogue form. Mostly the dialogues
purport to be conversations between Socrates and some
personage, or personages, well known in the Athenian
society of Plato's day. Plato's own name occurs three
times only in the whole series[1] and then only by way of
casual allusion. But his two brothers, Glaucon and
Adeimantus, are chief interlocutors in the *Republic*,
most famous of all the dialogues. To read the dialogues
of Plato is an education in philosophy and the humanities.
For they cover a wide field of speculative reasoning, and
they are written in the most charming Greek prose existing. And though much is inevitably lost in a translation, there is literary charm in the *Banquet* [2] as translated
by Shelley, or in the *Republic* or *Phaedo* in Jowett's
English. A single dialogue well chosen from a list of those
in which the literary form is most studied—and these are
the more dramatic dialogues—will give an attentive reader
a vivid impression at once of Plato's genius and of the
characteristics of the Platonic Socrates.

The Dialogues.—There are in all thirty-five dialogues
with some claim to be accounted genuine, and of these
twenty-four may reasonably be accepted as genuine
beyond question.[3] The subjects are very varied. The
easiest to read are the *Apology*—not properly a dialogue,
but a study of the speeches made by Socrates to the
Athenian dicasts, when tried for his life,—the *Crito*,

---

[1] Twice in the *Apology* (34 A and 38 B); and once at the beginning of
the *Phaedo* (59 B).

[2] *Convivium* in Latin; in Greek *Symposium*.

[3] Thrasyllus, in the first century A.D. established a *canon* of the
writings of Plato which contains in all thirty-six works; thirty-five
dialogues and a volume of Epistles. The probabilities are against the
genuineness of the epistles.

the *Gorgias*, and the first four books of the *Republic*. No writing of Plato's is quite easy reading, but the more metaphysical dialogues like the *Parmenides*, the *Sophist*, the *Statesman*, the *Philebus*, and parts of the *Republic*, require a natural taste for abstract thinking. If one dialogue is to be singled out, no better choice could be made than the *Gorgias*, which enshrines the sublimest moral doctrines that Plato anywhere teaches and at the same time affords apt illustration of the characteristic method of discussion attributed to Socrates. A course consisting of the *Gorgias*, the *Apology*, *Crito* and *Phaedo*, the *Republic*, the *Phaedrus* and the *Banquet*, would familiarize the reader with the most generally interesting and least technical of Plato's writings. There is special charm also in the *Lysis*, the *Laches*, the *Charmides*, the *Theaetetus*; while in the *Timaeus* and the *Critias* will be found the immortal myth of the island Atlantis.

The setting of the Dialogues.—Part of the charm of the more literary dialogues is found in their setting. They are full of touches which illustrate social life at Athens in a life-like way. For instance in the opening of the *Protagoras* Socrates describes how he was awakened early one morning by his friend Hippocrates, son of Apollodorus, and carried off to see the famous foreign teacher, Protagoras, in the house of Callias. The friends have a difficulty in obtaining admission through the surliness of the hall porter, who has no love for sophists, and takes Socrates and Hippocrates for two of them. Then the scene within is vividly brought before us ; the crowd of admirers following Protagoras up and down the covered court as he talks ; Hippias of Elis seated in another court answering enquiries on physics and astronomy, while Prodicus of Ceos is in bed holding forth to a select few. One of the most dramatic openings is that of the *Theaetetus*. Euclides of Megara (the philosopher not the geometrician) meets his friend Terpsion and relates how he has just seen Theaetetus, a young Athenian of noble family and splendid promise, being carried home to Athens at the point of death. Theaetetus had been wounded in the fighting at Corinth,[1] then attacked by dysentery. This recalls a notable conversation between Theaetetus and Socrates some years before, of which Euclid possesses an account in writing, and this account is the dialogue. Most often the scene is some palaestra or wrestling-ground at Athens as in the *Charmides* and the *Lysis*. In the *Phaedrus* it is a shady spot by the Ilissus. To this place Socrates has been brought by Phaedrus whom he meets near the city-wall and who carries him off to listen to a discourse on love composed by Lysias, son of Cephalus, the roll of which Phaedrus had with him. The scene of two dialogues, the *Crito* and the *Phaedo*, is the Town Jail, in which Socrates was kept after his trial and condemnation. In the former Crito is represented as coming very early to the prison with the news that the sacred ship from Delos has returned, and consequently the day when Socrates must die is very near. And he tries to persuade Socrates to escape while there is time. But Socrates will not listen. He holds that to do so would be to be false to his own principles of loyalty to his country's laws and would stultify his whole life and teaching.

The Myths of Plato.—Plato is poet and prophet no less than philosopher and at certain points in the dialogues, where dialectic argument fails, he leaves the dialogue form of exposition and seeks expression for the truth he wishes to convey through imaginative stories. These stories from their resemblance to the stories of traditional mythology,[2] are conveniently known as ' myths.' The myths of Plato are not usually allegories, though some of his stories are allegories, or in part allegories.[3] Two of the most famous are in the *Republic*, the allegory of the Cave and the myth of Er the Pamphylian. The myth of Er is a vision of the Judgment of the Dead and of the fortunes of the soul after death. The allegory of the Cave explains by elaborate symbolism the disadvantage at which the philosopher finds himself in the transactions of ordinary life. He

[1] In 394, five years after Socrates' death.
[2] Vol. i. p. 59.
[3] Stewart (J. A.), *The Myths of Plato*, p. 20 ; 230 ; and 243-4.

who has dwelt for a time in the full light of reality is
dazed and half-blinded when he comes back to the twilight of ignorance in which most men live. In the *Phaedrus* is another myth of the soul's history and destiny
which includes the allegory of the Charioteer and Horses,
a figure of the struggle in man's soul between his higher
and lower nature, between passion and conscience. In
the *Protagoras* is the myth of Prometheus and Epimetheus which illustrates man's need of the social virtues as
well as the arts, to overcome his natural defencelessness in
the animal world. We have already referred to the myth
of Atlantis in the *Critias*, one of the most interesting
because of its hint of a great continent beyond the Atlantic.[1]
The whole of the *Timaeus*, most puzzling of the Dialogues
for modern readers, but best known and most closely
studied in the Middle Ages, is one vast Myth of Creation.
A story from the *Phaedrus*, less well-known, but piquant
from its sharp criticism of literacy, is as follows :

" Well, the story is that at Naucratis in Egypt was one
of the ancient Egyptian gods—the god to whom belongs
the sacred bird they call the Ibis ; and the god's name is
Theuth. This is the god who first discovered arithmetic
and numbers ; draughts and dice also, and what most
concerns my story—the art of writing. The king of all
Egypt at that time was Thamuz, whose seat was the great
city of upper Egypt, which the Hellenes call Egyptian
Thebes : and the god they call Ammon. To him came
Theuth to show off his inventions, declaring that they
ought to be communicated to the rest of the Egyptians.
Thamuz enquired the use of each, and as Theuth went
over them assigned praise or blame, according as he was
satisfied, or not, with the account given. According to the
story there was much that Thamuz said to Theuth in
praise and blame of the various arts, which it would take
too long to recount ; but when they came to the art of
writing, Theuth said, " This invention, O king, will make

---

[1] See Stewart, p. 466 : " I do not think it is necessary to suppose, or
that it is even likely, that Plato had any sailors' stories of a great land
beyond the Western Ocean on which to found his Myth."

the Egyptians wise and will improve their memories ; my discovery is an elixir of memory and wisdom." But Thamuz replied : " O most inventive Theuth, of a truth one man has skill to conceive and bring forth inventions, and another to judge of the good and harm they are like to bring to those who use them. Now you who are father of the art of writing, through partiality ascribe to it an efficacy the very reverse of that which it possesses. It will induce forgetfulness in the souls of those who learn it through disuse of their own memories, seeing they will rely for remembrance on an external thing, writing, by means of characters which are no part of themselves, not on a power within them ; it is an elixir of prompting the memory you have discovered, not of memory. You are furnishing your disciples with the appearance of wisdom not with anything true. They will by your means become loaded with information without teaching and they will deem themselves well-instructed, though they will for the most part be ignorant and difficult to deal with, inasmuch as they have become seeming-wise but not wise." [1]

Plato's Humour.—All the dialogues have a serious purpose ; those which are associated with the prosecution and death of Socrates contain masterly touches of pathos. Some are lightened by the play of a delicate humour peculiarly Platonic. The more subtle forms of this humour are widely distributed. Here and there we come across a studied elaboration of comic effects. One example is Aristophanes' description in the *Banquet* of the primitive round-bodied race of men : they had four arms and four legs, and two faces, though only one head on a round neck. They walked as men do now, but if they wished to go fast, they used all eight limbs, four arms and four legs, to whirl themselves round wheel-wise. They were strong and insolent and, like the giants, tried to conquer Heaven. And Zeus, to bring down their pride, slit them in two, thus producing the present race of men with two arms and two legs. Aristophanes adds a warning. There is reason to fear that if mankind are guilty of any additional impiety

[1] *Phaedrus*, 274 C-275 B.

towards the gods, " we may be cut in two again, and may go about like those figures painted on columns, divided through the middle of our nostrils, as thin as split dice." Or there is the description in the *Republic* of the blustering Thrasymachus when forced by Socrates to contradict himself : " Now these admissions were not made by Thrasymachus in this easy way, but they had to be dragged from him against his will, and—the day being hot —the exertion made him stream with perspiration : and then I saw a sight I had never seen before—Thrasymachus blushing." Or again in the *Laches* the delightful picture of Stesilaus and his scythe-spear. " This fellow Stesilaus," Laches is made to say, " whom you and I together saw in so large a company making a display and talking big about himself in the way he did, I saw to better advantage elsewhere, in real truth making an exhibition of himself without meaning to. The ship on which he was marine had engaged a merchantman. He was fighting with a scythe-spear—a remarkable weapon, just as he was a remarkable man. The rest of his adventures are not worth relating ; but only the result of this invention of a scythe on the end of a spear. As he fought it got entangled somehow in the ship's rigging and stuck fast. So Stesilaus kept tugging away at it trying to disentangle it, but could not. Meanwhile the ships were crossing. For a time he ran along by the gunwale, clinging on to the spear ; but when the other ship was passing his and was dragging him on holding on to the spear, he let the spear slip through his hands till he clung to the end of the butt. The crew of the merchantman laughed and cheered at his get-up, and when someone threw a stone at his feet on the deck and he let go the spear, his companions on the trireme could no longer contain their laughter, when they saw that wonderful scythe-spear swinging in the air from the rigging of the merchantman."[1]

Plato's Ideas.—Attempts have been made to construct out of the dialogues with their penetrating sifting of opinion, their provisional conclusions, and their flashing

[1] *Laches*, 183 C-184 A, translated by Lionel James.

side-lights on truth, a complete and self-consistent system of thought. It may be doubted whether such an achievement is possible ; and, at any rate, the attempt is far beyond the scope of this chapter. But something ought, perhaps, to be said of the conception which is the centre and pivot of Plato's doctrine of reality—the Doctrine of Ideas.

Our word ' idea,' though taken from the Greek, does not help to our understanding of the Platonic doctrine of reality, but rather hinders. The word has passed through many changes of meaning, and the popular use of ' idea ' is now very loose and vague, as in the phrase, ' I have no *idea* what you mean '; ' He has no lack of *ideas* '; ' It had become a fixed *idea* with him.' The most frequent, and on the whole most proper, meaning of the word in English now is what is technically called a 're-presentation,' that is, any mental image of an impression of sense. The sound of a motor horn is an impression of sense, or ' presentation ' ; the revival of that sound in memory is a ' representation.' Similarly, a scene before the eyes and the recollection of the scene afterwards are ' presentation ' and ' re-presentation.' But what Plato meant by an ' Idea ' was the universal and eternal form of any class of things which has a number of particular objects included within it. We perceive through our senses individual men, and particular objects like tables and chairs. Plato seeking, after the example of Socrates, to reach the unity which lies behind the use of general names, suggests that there must be an ideal man, chair, table, of which the tables and chairs and men of ordinary experience are imperfect copies. And equally there must be an idea of beds, books, roses, insects, and of all the multitudinous classes of things that make up the material universe. It may take a good deal of time before those unused to reflection see any meaning at all in this use of Idea ; but it requires no great effort of thought from anyone who has once reflected on the puzzle of general names. What is it that the individual things which we call by general names have in common ? It is not easy to say when we get away from the obvious classes which every one recognizes, and ask this question about such things, for instance, as *stone, metal, hat, shrub, vegetable* ; and still more of such difficult terms as *freedom, right, labour, capital, value.* We see at once, also, how this question is bound up with the problem of definition, at which Socrates was working. Sometimes it seems as if Plato meant literally that ideal forms, or archetypes, of all classes of material things, changeless and always the same, exist in a *world of intelligence* apart from the senses, and have more reality than the things of sense (which shift and change in countless ways as we look at or handle them)—are indeed the only reality. But more probably he is only serious about qualities and abstractions — *beauty, justice, health, courage, knowledge.*[1] What was the underlying reality of each of these ? Men's everyday notions seemed so various and so confused. It was for the sake of these truths, so vital to know, that Plato formulated, sometimes playfully, sometimes in earnest, his doctrine of Ideas.[2] For the better understanding of these the theory was illuminating. The reality of Justice and Beauty and Knowledge is something beyond and above things just and beautiful and known. From these 'ideas' Plato was led on to the conception of an Idea of Good, and so to the Idea of the Good, the supreme reality, only verbally distinguishable from the infinite perfection of the Godhead.

Justice.—But the doctrine of Ideas is metaphysical ; and while some find in it the culmination of all philosophy and the secret of reality, to others it is merely incomprehensible, not mystic but mystifying. There is another side to Plato's idealism which is of the nature of a moral revelation, and which even a child may understand. It

---

[1] This precise issue is raised by Plato himself at the beginning of the *Parmenides*, 130 B.

[2] A good way to reach out towards Plato's meaning is to think of mathematical conceptions, *line, circle, diameter, equality*—illustrations used by Plato himself in the *Phaedo*. The lines and circles the mathematician treats of are not those of sense, for these all deviate from his definitions. We never reach absolute equality through the senses, but we have the idea of it.

is the conviction that righteousness, justice, all that we mean by virtue as opposed to injustice, wickedness and vice, is the true good for men, inestimably desirable in itself independently of any gain or loss that goes with it ; that in very truth virtue is its own reward, because virtue is the health and well-being of the soul. In the *Republic* Socrates sets out to ask what is justice ; and he easily refutes the overbearing sophist, Thrasymachus, who maintains (as many maintain to this day) that Justice is the interest of the stronger. And then Socrates is assailed by Glaucon and Adeimantus, Plato's brothers, who put to him certain deeper difficulties concerning the nature of justice and injustice. Glaucon and Adeimantus object that justice is cried up and valued not in itself as good but for the sake of its rewards, the reputation and prosperity it brings in this life, and the favour of Heaven in the life to come ; and yet more because of the pains and penalties of injustice, not least to the evil-doer himself, when he is found out. How are we to be satisfied that justice is not after all merely a more cunning sort of prudence ? For were the just man free to do wrong without fear of discovery and punishment, he would be found no better than the unjust. The only convincing test of the contrary—that is, that the just man chooses justice for its own sake—would be to eliminate all the rewards that wait upon virtue and the penalties that follow vice. We must compare the perfectly just man and the perfectly unjust. The perfectly unjust man must be so accomplished a scoundrel that by his cunning and strength combined he can escape all the ill consequences of injustice and even win a reputation for virtue, " for it is the very consummation of wickedness to seem just without being just." Then with such a consummate scoundrel we must compare "some man of noble simplicity, who resolves, in the words of Aeschylus,[1] not to seem but to be good. And we must take from him the seeming. For if he shall be reputed just, he will possess all the honours and rewards which come to one so reputed ; and then it will

[1] *Seven against Thebes*, 592.

be uncertain whether he is just for the sake of justice itself, or for the sake of honours and rewards. So we must strip him of everything but his righteousness, and make his fortune precisely the reverse of the other's ; without ever doing wrong he must have the reputation of being extremely wicked, in order that his righteousness may be thoroughly tested by taking no taint from evil repute and its consequences. And so he must continue without relief, until his death, being esteemed wicked all his life-time, though he is righteous. In this way if the two are brought to an extreme, the one of righteousness, the other of wickedness, it may be judged which of the two is more happy." There can be no doubt, Glaucon maintains, what—in common opinion—the result must be. The one who is consummately wicked will prosper throughout life in every respect, and, may be, even win the favour of heaven, because he has ample means of paying his dues in prayer and sacrifice. The other, the perfectly righteous man, who in popular judgment is esteemed wicked, " will be scourged, tormented, thrown into bondage ; he will have his eyes burnt out, and after enduring every extremity of suffering will end by being impaled."

The whole of the rest of the *Republic* is an elaborate argument to refute this position and prove the paradox that even were such an extreme case possible (which, of course, it is not),[1] the righteous man in his unmerited suffering is better off and happier than the unrighteous in his undeserved prosperity. For unrighteousness, vice, injustice are the sickness and ruin of man's soul, while righteousness, virtue, justice are its health and welfare.

The reasonings of the *Republic* are worth weighing, and they are metaphysically and logically sound. The conclusion for most men must be a matter of faith even more than of reasoning. It is a saving faith, and the enunciation of this moral and religious truth—that goodness is to be sought and loved for its intrinsic quality, not for its external results ; that virtue *in itself* is better than vice,

---

[1] Before the end of the *Republic* the admissions made at the outset are expressly taken back ; see Book X. 612 and 613.

love than hate, justice than injustice—is the inspired culmination of Plato's teaching and the supreme gift to mankind of Hellenic thought, the pearl of great price for which a man may well sell all else that he has.

3. ARISTOTLE.

" . . . a guide to the book of Nature, a revealer of the Spirit, a prophet of the works of God."

D'ARCY THOMPSON in *The Legacy of Greece*, p. 160.

There is one other Greek teacher whose place in the history of European thought is not less important than Socrates' and Plato's, namely Aristotle. He was not an Athenian like Socrates and Plato, but a Greek of Chalcidicê, from Stagira, a small city state on the coast of Macedonia half way between the peninsula ending in Mount Athos and Amphipolis ; his father's family came from Andros, his mother's from Chalcis in Euboea. But though not an Athenian by birth, Aristotle spent quite half his life at Athens. Of less dominating character than Socrates, and far below Plato as a master of literary style, he yet surpassed them both in the extent and thoroughness of his scientific attainments. His philosophy is the culmination of the efforts to think out the meaning of the universe which began in Ionia with Thales of Miletus. He summed up all the knowledge of his time, and not only gave it scientific form, but divided and co-ordinated its parts on systematic principles. His is, in fact, the first philosophical *system* at once scientific and complete. His thought, as we have it, is expressed not in conversations like Socrates', nor in dialogues like Plato's, but in formal treatises. Aristotle's writings embrace Logic, Physics, Metaphysics, Psychology, Natural History, Physiology, Meteorology, Political Philosophy, Ethics, Rhetoric, and Criticism. This is an astonishing range of achievement. " How a single man could have done all that he did in so many departments, is almost inconceivable."[1] For in every branch of knowledge Aristotle either sums up all that was known to previous

[1] Davidson, *Aristotle* (in Great Educator Series), p. 158.

thinkers and makes a notable advance beyond them, or breaks entirely new ground and lays out the framework of a science which has ever since been recognized as having a distinct subject-matter. His writings, as we possess them, do not pretend to the literary charm of Plato's : their most striking characteristic is their pregnant terseness. Sometimes they are so like lecture notes that they have been taken to be veritably such.[1] Yet scattered through them, and especially in the ethical books, are passages of lofty eloquence.

His Life.—A few personal details about Aristotle have been handed down by his biographers ; but the earliest biography extant now is that of Diogenes Laertius, and he lived some five hundred years after Aristotle's death, so that no very great confidence can be felt in his accuracy. If his description may be accepted, Aristotle in the flesh was of slender build, very careful of his personal appearance, and even something of a dandy. Perhaps the most remarkable event in his personal history was his association with Alexander the Great as tutor. This came about naturally through hereditary connection with the Macedonian royal family ; for Nicomachus, his father, was court physician to Amyntas II., king of Macedon, and his personal friend.[2] We have already noticed that great part of Aristotle's life was spent at Athens. For twenty years he was Plato's disciple, the most admired of the students of the Academy : for twelve years, from 335 to 323, he was head of a rival school, which he established in the Lyceum, a gymnasium on the opposite side of Athens, just outside the walls ; and because he was wont to pace up and down the walks there (*peripatoe*) as he lectured, his philosophy has come to be called 'Peripatetic.'

[1] What exactly the writings which have come down to us as Aristotle's really are is a puzzle never likely to be solved. The manuscripts from which we get our texts have a very curious history : it may be read in Strabo the Geographer's 13th book, chapter 56. Or see Sir Alexander Grant's *Aristotle* (in *Ancient Classics for English Readers*), pp. 33-35.

[2] The family was a branch of a clan which traced its descent from the god Asclepius (Aesculapius) ; they were all hereditary physicians from father to son.

He died in 322, being then only 62 years of age.[1] It is curious that this was also the year of the death of Demosthenes, the statesman and orator. They were almost exact contemporaries ; but the circumstances of their lives drew them to opposite sides in the national conflict. Demosthenes was sworn enemy of the house of Philip, while Aristotle was born into friendly association with it.

The Aristotelian Tradition.—It is difficult to say which of the two great masters, Plato and Aristotle, has had most influence on European thought. In spite of their relation as teacher and disciple the two men represent opposite tendencies of the human mind. It was Coleridge who said that every one " is born either a Platonist or an Aristotelian," [2] a Platonist if the tendency of his mind is to soar away from the things of sense and find rest among abstractions ; an Aristotelian if he is drawn rather to the concrete and real. The Aristotelian attitude of mind favours more naturally the progress of natural science. The Alexandrian schools of experimental science are a continuation of the influence of Aristotle. When in the ninth century A.D. the Abbasid khalifs established their government at Baghdad and began to encourage learning, Aristotle's writings were translated into Arabic. Hence it came about that the writings of Aristotle were preserved in Arabic versions when the originals were lost to Western Europe. When by means of the Crusades European and Arabian thought were brought into close contact, mediaeval scholars translated the works of Arabian doctors into French and Latin, and Aristotle became known again in Western Europe as the great thinker and

---

[1] His will, the text of which is given by Diogenes Laertius, is illuminating of the character of the man. His second wife, Herpylis, who survives him, is to be helped to marry again, ' because she has behaved so well towards me.' But for the wife of his youth, who predeceased him, his affection is different : her bones are to be taken up and buried with him ' as she herself charged.' Nicanor, his friend and executor, is to marry his daughter. There is careful remembrance of faithful servants and provision is made for their enfranchisement. " Every clause," it has been said, " breathes the philosopher's humanity."

[2] See *Table Talk*, under date July the 2nd, 1830.

II U

teacher. And then by a strange irony of circumstances, for a time Aristotle became actually a stumbling-block in the way of the advance of knowledge. For Aristotle, imperfectly understood through translations, was taken under the patronage of the Church, and then every supposed doctrine of Aristotle was invested with full ecclesiastical authority. The state of knowledge resulting from this alliance between the mediaeval Church and Aristotle is known as Scholasticism, St. Thomas Aquinas and Albertus Magnus being the chief schoolmen ; and to break the bonds of scholasticism was the achievement of Francis Bacon and the thinkers of the later Renascence. Science knows neither Pope nor Bible ; but the text of Aristotle, or rather the confused and perverted doctrine of Aristotle—was used to thwart the spirit of Aristotle, which was the spirit of free scientific investigation. To free the spirit of man for the tasks of modern science, the unquestioned authority of Aristotle's precepts had to be shattered. But it was shattered only by a fresh application of the spirit of independent research by which Aristotle himself had been guided.

Aristotle's Works.—We have no key to the order in which Aristotle's works were composed. It cannot be known certainly whether he advanced, like Herbert Spencer, in accordance with an orderly plan, or wrote his several treatises[1] without set order, as this or that branch of universal knowledge occupied his attention. It is perplexing that a detailed and extensive list given by Diogenes corresponds very imperfectly with the titles and contents of Aristotle's works as we possess them. In our brief review here we may follow the ordinary classification from the more abstract to the more concrete—from Logic

[1] Perhaps ' treatises ' is not the proper term to apply to Aristotle's surviving writings, at least not in the sense of formal and finished treatises. The account of them which agrees best with appearances is that of a body of detached writings which a teacher keeps by him for lecture purposes, and alters and amplifies as occasion arises. Other works of his there were, dialogues and poems, which are almost entirely lost. Cicero knew the dialogues and quotes them as examples of eloquent style.

and Metaphysics through Physical treatises of all kinds to Natural History and the more human studies, Ethics, Politics, Rhetoric, Criticism. The branches of science and art are now carefully differentiated and the distinctions are familiar. But this clear differentiation is in large part the work of Aristotle. Before him Physics and Metaphysics, Ethics and Politics were imperfectly distinguished ; Logic and Psychology had no separate existence. Socrates was the first to struggle to arrive at clearer definition, and Plato continued the process of discrimination. But thinkers before Aristotle had only got so far as a broad distinction of enquiry into physical, practical, and poetical.

Logic.—India divides with Greece the honour of the invention of Logic. Greece has not an exclusive claim to the devising of a norm or standard, by which the conclusiveness of reasoning might be tested, but the Greek forms of *syllogism* may claim to be the simpler, and easier to apply. And these, as he expressly affirms,[1] are the discovery of Aristotle. Logic is the science which discusses the means of testing the correctness of human reasoning and examines the processes connected with reasoning. It distinguishes between true reasoning and false, and shows how the one may be known from the other. Aristotle did not himself give the name of Logic to this science, but among his works is a number of tracts under various names, *Categories, Interpretation, Analytic*.[2] In these he treats of terms and propositions and predicables, of induction and deduction, of syllogisms and fallacies. All the details of the modern handbook of Logic are found in these treatises and are taken from them.

Metaphysics.—We now mean by metaphysics the investigation of ultimate first principles, the presuppositions required to make knowledge and existence intelligible. We get the name from Aristotle's editors ; and

[1] In the last chapter of his work on fallacies (De Sophisticis Elenchis).

[2] The logical treatises were at one time known as the *Organum*, or ' Instrument,' with the implication that Logic is the instrument by means of which other sciences reach their conclusions.

it only means the books which follow or *come after*
Physics. In his metaphysical books Aristotle discusses Plato's *ideas* and gives his own theory of the
ultimate nature of Being or Substance, of Matter, and of
Cause.[1] These are the most abstract of all conceptions
and consequently the most difficult. It is most difficult
of all to find words to express what we mean ultimately
by reality and being. In the last resort explanation is
impossible : what is possible is analysis. Plato as the
outcome of analysis found ' Ideas,' the eternal, changeless, types of existing things. Aristotle's contribution to
the solution is the distinction of *form* and *matter*, and the
distinction has permanent value. In every existing thing we
can discern these two aspects ; there is the crude formless
matter of the thing, and there is the form which makes
it what it is. In a statue we can obviously distinguish
the marble, as matter, from the form. But again in the
marble itself also the distinction into matter and form
may be repeated.

Psychology.—Aristotle's psychological writings are intensely interesting to psychologists, but are not very
helpful to a beginner. There is an initial difficulty about
the words to be used. For although our word psychology
is derived from the Greek *psychê*, and psychology for us is
the science of mind, Aristotle's psychê is not exactly our
' mind ' ; for plants to Aristotle have psychê (though
they have not any form of sensation), and ' growth ' or
nutrition which is seen in plants as well as animals is the
elementary form of psychê. And yet psychê is not *life*.
Greek has another word for " life," zôe, which appears in
Zoology. There is in nature an ascending manifestation
of ' psychê ' or ' soul ': (1) nutrition and growth, common
to plants and animals; (2) movement and sense-perception,
common to all animals; (3) reason, the peculiar endowment
of mankind. Again, Aristotle's definition of psychê is
metaphysical, and unintelligible without a preliminary
study of his metaphysics. And yet Aristotle was the first

[1] The distinction of causes as *material, efficient, formal, and final*, is
Aristotle's.

thinker to treat mind scientifically in its proper relation to body, and has a claim to be considered the founder of Psychology hardly less than of Logic. Much of his treatment of the subject has only an historic interest, much of it is misleading now ; but his services to the new science are great. In his opening sentence he makes a striking claim for the importance of Psychology. His treatment of memory and imagination anticipates much that finds place in modern books. His conception of the relation of mind and body shows an insight extraordinary in his day. We must " no more ask whether the soul and the body are one, than ask whether the wax and the figure impressed upon it are one . . ." [1] " And yet," he says elsewhere, "nothing prevents " a possible separation from the body of some higher form of soul ; perhaps *that* soul is in the body " like a sailor in a boat." [2]

Physics.—In Physics, which for Aristotle means (as the name implies) in a wide sense Science of *Nature*, he is following up speculations that go back to the beginnings of Greek philosophy. While he says much that is ingenious about movement, time, and space, he is a long way from modern Physics with its familiar division into Sound, Heat, Light, Electricity. His scientific writings include treatises on the movements of the heavenly bodies, on meteorology, and nearly twenty books on Natural History, that is on Zoology and Physiology.

Natural History.—Perhaps the most amazing achievement of Aristotle's scientific industry is these twenty or so books on Natural History. In the nine books of his Enquiry concerning Animals (*Historia Animalium*) he passes in review the whole animal creation, and though he nowhere outlines a formal classification, he shows incidentally that he recognizes the main distinctions which now form the framework of scientific Zoology. More surprising than the comprehensiveness of this survey is the keenness of his interest in all living creatures and the accuracy of his observation. In no qualified sense he

[1] De Anima, ii. 1. 7 ; Wallace, p. 61. [2] De Anima, ii. 1. 13.

was (three hundred years before Christ) a great biologist ; "biology was in his hands," D'Arcy Thompson says in the *Herbert Spencer Lecture* of 1913, " a true and comprehensive science." "When he treats of Natural History, his language is our language, and his methods and his problems are well nigh identical with ours. He had familiar knowledge of a thousand varied forms of life, of bird and beast and plant and creeping thing. He was careful to note their least details of outward structure, and curious to probe by dissection into their parts within." He is particularly full and precise in his description of marine animals, and the reason seems to be that his study of natural history took place mainly during a two-years residence on the shores of the island of Lesbos, when he was about forty years of age.[1] The frequency with which he mentions places in Lesbos in illustrating his statements makes this probable.

Even more interesting are his four books *On the Parts of Animals* (*De Partibus Animalium*), together with his short work on *Respiration* ; for these contain his physiological observations and theories. Aristotle was working under great disadvantages, and it is not surprising that he is more often wrong in his conclusions than right. What else indeed was possible in so difficult a field before the necessity of experiment as a supplement to direct observation was understood.[2] The importance of accurate observation Aristotle understands fully, but he is far from realizing that observation alone is not enough. His most successful achievement in physiology is to have described the structure of the lungs with a very fair degree of accuracy. On the other hand his theory of respiration, though ingenious, appears now merely fantastic. It is only trained students of science who can

[1] This fact which Prof. D'Arcy Thompson's brilliant elucidation makes very probable is of great importance in the full understanding of Aristotle's philosophy as a whole. For it follows that it was as a trained biologist that he approached the ultimate problems of philosophy.

[2] That Aristotle practised dissection with his own hand is practically certain, but to what extent cannot be known. Several times in the *History of Animals* he refers to a book of anatomical diagrams, which has unfortunately been lost.

judge properly of the difficulties under which Aristotle worked and measure the greatness of his success. " By insisting on the absolute necessity of anatomical observation," says Dr. William Ogle, " he carried biology at one step from the world of dreams into the world of realities ; he set the science on a substantial basis, and may indeed be said to have been its founder, for the vain imaginings of his predecessors can hardly be dignified with the name of science." [1] Of his nine books of the *History of Animals* it has been said that " probably no work on Natural History of equal merit and completeness was written before Cuvier." [2] His greatest merit of all is the spirit in which he worked. In a memorable passage in Book I. of the *Parts of Animals* Aristotle vindicates biological study from the reproach that it has to do with things trivial and ignoble : " We therefore must not recoil with childish aversion from the examination of the humbler animals. Every realm of nature is marvellous : and as Heraclitus, when the strangers who came to visit him found him warming himself at the furnace in the kitchen, is reported to have bidden them not to be afraid to enter, as even in that kitchen divinities were present, so we should venture on the study of every kind of animal without distaste ; for each and all will reveal to us something natural and something beautiful." [3] All this makes Aristotle's claim to be numbered among the very greatest of the world's creative thinkers very high. Yet even this is scarcely his greatest claim of all.

[1] Introduction to Aristotle *On Life and Death and on Respiration*, p. 29.

[2] D'Arcy Thompson, Introduction to Aristotle's *Historia Animalium*, p. vii.

[3] Aristotle *On the Parts of Animals*, i. 5, Dr. Ogle's translation, p. 17. In what immediately precedes he says : " Having already treated of the celestial world, as far as our conjectures could reach, we proceed to treat of animals, without omitting, to the best of our ability, any member of the kingdom, however ignoble. For if some have no graces to charm the sense, yet even these, by disclosing to intellectual perception the artistic spirit that designed them, give immense pleasure to all who can trace links of causation, and are inclined to philosophy." " He was the first of Greek philosophers and gentlemen," writes D'Arcy Thompson in *The Legacy of Greece* (p. 144), " to see that all these things were good to know and worthy to be told. This was his great discovery."

Humane Studies.—However remarkable Aristotle's work in biology and natural history may be in relation to his time, the advance of knowledge in these sciences has inevitably made most of it obsolete. The natural sciences are ever moving on to new discoveries which correct the explanations accepted earlier. Consequently the greater part of Aristotle's results in this field are now out of date. They were, it is true, not out of date as recently as three hundred years ago, though nearly twenty centuries had passed since his death. But in the 17th century of the Christian era science in Europe made a new forward movement, which advanced with accelerated energy through the 18th and 19th, till the science of the 20th century has become something altogether different from the science of the 4th century B.C.[1] Aristotle's work in physiology and physics is now wholly superseded. But there are other spheres in which his teaching has not been superseded and never will be, because in dealing with this subject-matter he was not, as in Physics and Physiology, at a disadvantage compared with modern times. Man and society have not altered in essentials, though many relevant circumstances have greatly changed. In dealing with these subjects Aristotle has even an advantage over students of our own day. His problems were offered in a less complex form and could be treated with a freshness and clearness unattainable now. Hence the peculiar value of Aristotle's conclusions in Ethics and Political Philosophy. He analyses problems like our own in a simpler and more manageable shape.

Aristotle's Politics.—Aristotle's limitations as a political thinker are that his generalizations are all based on a study of the one hundred and fifty-eight city-states included in his great work on constitutions (all of which is lost to us except for a portion of the *Polity of the Athenians*),[2] supplemented by rather superficial reflections

[1] See vol. i. p. 14.

[2] See above pp. 88 and 89 and vol. i. pp. 243 and 244. This incomplete but invaluable *Constitution of Athens* was recovered late in the nineteenth century ; it was first edited for the Trustees of the British Museum by Sir Frederick Kenyon in 1890.

on different forms of monarchical rule. A constitutional national state like England in the 14th century, or republican France, or even the modern kingdom of the Hellenes, is altogether outside his range of vision. Could one such have been described to him, it is probable that he would have summarily repudiated the notion ; he would have said it was no ' polis,' no constitutional state at all.[1] He would have objected that it was vastly too large ; for, says Aristotle, " a great state is not the same thing as a populous."[2] " We see clearly," he says, " the best limit of population ; it is that the number of citizens should be the largest possible in order to ensure independence of life, but not so large that it cannot be comprehended in a single view."[3] And what he means by this last is curiously illustrated by an earlier remark on the over-populous state : " Who could be town-crier," he asks, " for such a state, unless he had the voice of a Stentor ? " Always he has in mind the city-state with from five to twenty, or at the utmost, thirty thousand able-bodied citizens. And we must add that to the city-state as he conceived it slavery was an economic necessity. Yet, if we consider attentively, we shall see that Aristotle is in the line of thought which leads directly to the League of Nations. For he conceives of the state from first to last as a moral institution. It exists as a means to noble living. The end for states and for individuals is the same.[4] Justice between states is as necessary as justice between individual men living in community ; and " as in his condition of complete development, that is in the state, man is the noblest of all animals, so apart from law and justice he is the vilest of all."[5] Militarism is wrong, and is proved to be wrong by the teachings of history.[6] Valour and endurance are, indeed, indispensable virtues in states since " a people incapable

---

[1] He does, however, in one place (iv. 7), say of the Hellenes, that " if they were united in a single polity they would be capable of universal empire " (Welldon, p. 181).

[2] *Politics*, iv. 4 ; Welldon, p. 174.   [3] iv. 4 ; Welldon, p. 176.

[4] iv. 14 and 15 ; Welldon, pp. 207-8.

[5] i. 2 ; Welldon, p. 7.   [6] iv. 14 ; Welldon, p. 206.

of facing dangers valorously are the slaves of every assailant."[1]   But more than this is required in the state where noble living is the end.   We are brought at last to the positions, that education is a main concern of the state, and that the noble employment of leisure is the true end of education.   " For if the right conduct of business and the noble employment of leisure are both requisite, and at the same time leisure is preferable to business and is the end of human existence, we are bound to investigate the right manner of employing leisure." [2]   And we are made to see that in this lies the importance of the artistic side of education.   For this reason training in music and in the art of design are parts of a liberal education,—in the art of design that the young may come to be " scientific observers of physical beauty [3] ; " in music, because it is valuable for the noble employment of leisure.   " We see clearly," writes Aristotle, " that there is a certain education which our sons should receive not as being practically useful, nor as indispensable, but as liberal and noble."[4] He has something also to say in this connection of the cult of athletics. Gymnastic training has its indispensable place in his scheme of education, or it would not be Hellenic at all ; but " to give up our children overmuch to bodily exercises and leave them uninstructed in the true essentials of education, is in effect to degrade them to the level of mechanics by rendering them useless in a statesman's hands for any purpose except one and, as our argument shows, not so useful as other people even for this."[5]   These are, perhaps, the most valuable aspects of Aristotle's teaching in the *Politics*.   But scattered about the eight books of this treatise is a wealth of political wisdom and practical good sense.   It is hardly too much to say that in spite of the vast difference of scale between the modern nation and the little republics that Aristotle has in view these books have lost little of their value

---

[1] *Politics*, iv. 15 ; Welldon, p. 208.   [2] v. 3 ; Welldon, p. 226.

[3] v. 4 ; Welldon, p. 229.   On the whole subject of artistic education among the Greeks see Freeman, *Schools of Hellas*, pp. 117 and 257-258.

[4] v. 4 ; Welldon, p. 228.   [5] v. 4 ; Welldon, p. 231.

with the passage of time, and in some respects have even gained.

The Nicomachean Ethics.—But of all his works that which has the greatest positive value to-day is the " Ethics." In Aristotle's view Ethics and Politics are interrelated, and his ' Politics,' therefore, are best appreciated in close association with his ethical theory. The work in which Aristotle's theory of conduct is most fully and effectively expounded is that known as the *Nicomachean Ethics* in ten books. It is not too much to say that no work on Ethics of equal extent is of so great a value—for lucidity, for stimulus, for good sense and sound reasoning. " Notwithstanding some rather serious defects of form and arrangement," writes Marshall in the preface to his book on *Aristotle's Theory of Conduct*, " it is still the best introduction to moral philosophy, the earliest and, take it for all in all, the most interesting book on the subject."[1] " Aristotle's Ethics is one of the books which will never be forgotten or superseded. It is the first attempt in any European language to formulate a comprehensive theory of conduct." [2] No modern treatise on conduct can do for us what Aristotle's Ethics can do ; for no modern treatise can approach the subject with the same naïveté. Moral problems to-day are obscured by faint reminiscences of old controversies, which overspread them like a sort of mildew—controversies regarding free-will and necessity, or the paradox of the selfishness of self-sacrifice. The very terms in which we speak of them have become sophisticated : it is almost impossible to think of them simply. In Aristotle's presentment we get the problems in their simplicity, free from these accretions. In following his thought we are better able to reach the problem in its essence : for we reach it at a simpler stage of human experience. Nothing more is possible here than to indicate some excellent points in Aristotle's handling of the subject.

He begins by asking what is the end and aim of life. He takes it as self-evident that all human activities, like the arts, have an aim or end ; and that mediate and

[1] *Aristotle's Theory of Conduct*, p. 6.   [2] P. 16.

partial ends lead on to some end beyond themselves, as the making of bit and bridle is subordinate to horsemanship, horsemanship to the art of war, the art of war to victory. From this he goes on to infer that there must be some supreme end for life as a whole, to which *all* particular aims are subordinate. This supreme end is called ' happiness,' and happiness Aristotle defines as conscious activity guided by virtue.[1] Happiness is an end pursued for its own sake only, and it is the end for which all lesser aims whatever are pursued. It is all-sufficing, in need of nothing beyond itself : it is of all things best and noblest, and is accompanied by the greatest pleasure. Happiness requires, indeed, as conditions of its realization, certain favouring circumstances—a measure of wealth, and health, of fortune and friends. Yet it does not consist in material things ; in its essential nature it is this active exercise of virtue, in which alone is found the proper function of man's being. This position is reached in the first eight chapters of the first book, which contain the pith of Aristotle's ethical doctrine ; the rest of the treatise is mainly a development of this conception of a life of activity in accordance with virtue. For human nature is diverse : there are virtues of man's intellectual powers and virtues of his moral nature. The intellectual virtues are five—*art, science, prudence, wisdom, reason* : they are " the modes in which the soul reaches truth in affirmation and negation."[2] The moral virtues, which are what we ordinarily mean in English when we talk of virtue, are courage, self-control, liberality, munificence, magnanimity, courtesy, truthfulness, geniality, friendliness. Aristotle explains these moral virtues as forming each a golden mean between extremes of excess

[1] *Nicomachean Ethics*, i. 7. 15 ; *literally* " activity of soul (psychê) in accordance with virtue." Of course Aristotle is well aware that happiness is variously conceived by different persons, and even by the same person at different times—as *pleasure, riches, health, virtue* and so on. His definition claims to rise to a philosophical conception of happiness having universal validity.

[2] *Nic. Eth.* vi. 3. i. The Greek words cannot be adequately rendered in English. They can be understood only through Aristotle's account of them.

and defect (these extremes being contrasted vices) ; as courage is a mean between recklessness and timidity, liberality a mean between extravagance and parsimony. Aristotle has striking things to say about each of these. Most remarkable of all [1] is what he says about magnanimity ; for the "man of a great spirit" seems to embody his own personal ideal : he does, in fact, say that the man of a great spirit must possess all the other virtues.

For our practical purpose here the most important point is that Aristotle (herein following Plato and Socrates) lays down that the supreme good of man, or happiness, is unattainable without moral virtue. He is not committed to the stoic paradox that the good man is happy even if afflicted with every misfortune, or falsely accused and put to torture. In fact he deliberately repudiates this paradox.[2] But he does say that the happiness that comes from virtuous living is the most steadfast and abiding happiness. " All his life with little exception he will be engaged in virtuous action and virtuous contemplation ; he will bear nobly all turns of fortune and at all times and in all ways behave conformably, at least if he is our truly good man, our man of perfect mould." [3] And again, " never could one who was truly happy become wretched, since he will never do what is mean and hateful.

---

[1] ' Remarkable,' but not at all points admirable, still less lovable. Embodied in the flesh this ' man of a great soul ' would be insupportable. He is free of the meaner vices and of large stature, morally and intellectually, but a colossal egotist. The best that can be said for him is what Henry V. says of himself :

> " But if it be a sin to covet *honour*,
> I am the most offending soul alive."

Aristotle's whole treatment of the moral virtues is open to criticism. He is best on *Courage* and on *Friendship*. To Friendship he devotes two whole books (viii. and ix.), and these make one of the most interesting disquisitions on the subject in all literature. A sentence from his opening chapter gives his standpoint. "Indeed without friends," he says, "no one would choose to go on living, though possessed of every other advantage."

[2] i. 5. 6. " Or again he might fall into the utmost misfortune and affliction ; and one who lived thus no one would call happy, unless it were for the sake of argument."

[3] i. 10. 11.

We conceive indeed that he who is truly good and wise will bear every fortune becomingly and turn the circumstances of his lot ever to fairest account, even as a good commander uses the forces under his orders in the manner best for the purposes of war, and a leather-cutter will make the best shoe he can out of the leather put into his hands." [1]   He recognizes that his happy man may meet with sore affliction and admits that afflictions mar happiness ; but he adds : "Nevertheless even in these afflictions nobility shines conspicuous, when a man bears many heavy misfortunes without impatience, not through want of feeling, but because he is noble-natured, and of a great spirit." [2]

Rhetoric and Criticism.—There is a deal of human nature in Aristotle's *Rhetoric* and much acute psychological observation, but the treatise as a whole is unattractive. Its range is comprehensive : it begins with a book on *Proofs*, and ends with one on *Style*, an intermediate book dealing with the influence of feelings and character. Aristotle defends the formal study of the means of persuasion on the ground that if it is concerned with a kind of skill which may be abused, the same may be said "of all good things except virtue." And yet in places his argument bears a curiously painful resemblance to the art of making the worse appear the better reason. For he shows how every argument is double-edged, and urges "We must take whichever view may serve." [3]

It is otherwise with the few chapters on Poetry, which is all we have left of Aristotle's critical writings, their every authentic [4] sentence is golden. The *Poetics* has invaluable, though scanty, notes on the origin of tragedy and comedy and a full and interesting discussion of tragedy. Its most famous and most valuable chapter is the sixth, which includes Aristotle's definition of tragedy and its function. His definition runs : "Tragedy is the representation of an

---

[1] *Nic. Eth.* i. 10. 13.   [2] i. 10. 12.

[3] Aristotle, *Rhetoric,* ii. 23. 15 ; Jebb, p. 127.

[4] The text is in an unusually bad state even for a work of Aristotle. Not only is the text faulty, but there are obvious interpolations and omissions.

action serious and complete, and of a certain magnitude, in language made attractive in each kind in its different parts; shown in the doing, not narrated; by pity and fear effecting the purging of emotions of these kinds."[1] To consider this theory of purgation, or any other of the interesting problems raised in the *Poetics*, would carry us too far.   But no student of poetry or the drama can afford to neglect the *Poetics*.

Hellenic unity in the sphere of thought.—Plato and Socrates were Athenians; Aristotle was a man of Andrian descent from Chalcidicê.   Yet Aristotle was the pupil of Plato and hands on the spiritual mantle received from Socrates.   Athens was the home of the Peripatetic School no less than of Plato's Academy.   Greek speculation and Greek science pass on from them in a single stream; philosophical writings were in Plato's Attic tongue.   The earlier thinkers and teachers who preceded Socrates had been of many races and cities.   Greek speculation begins at Miletus with Thales and the Ionian School to which Anaximenes and Anaximander also belong.   Pythagoras was born in Samos; Empedocles at Agrigentum; Democritus at Abdera; Anaxagoras at Clazomenae. We may notice that the friends of Socrates are, many of them, not Athenians; Phaedo himself was an Elean, Echecrates was of Phlius, Simmias and Cebes, leading speakers in the *Phaedo*, were Thebans, and Euclides was of Megara.   Though the exposition of Plato's doctrine in the *Laws* is put into the mouth of an Athenian, his interlocutors are a Spartan and a Cretan.   The Sophists, Socrates' rivals, came from various Hellenic cities; Gorgias from Leontini, Protagoras from Abdera, Hippias from Elis, Prodicus from Ceos.   Onward from Plato's day there is a difference.   In spite of the strife and bloodshed of the Peloponnesian war Greek thought is Panhellenic; in spite of Aegospotami and the dissolution of the Athenian empire, Athens has won the unchallenged hegemony of Hellenic philosophy.

---

[1] Aristotle, *Poetics*, vi. 2 (L. J.).

CHAPTER XII

HISTORY AND THE GREEK HISTORIANS

" They were not the first to chronicle human events, but they were the first to apply criticism. And that means they originated history." BURY, Harvard Lectures, 1909.

The Standpoint of the Great Historians.—Philosophical speculation, then, while Athens was its chosen home, tended to become Panhellenic, the common possession of all men of Hellenic race. It is the same with the writing of history, though the way in which history acquires a Panhellenic character is different. Thucydides and Xenophon were Athenians : Herodotus was a Dorian of Halicarnassus, not an Athenian, nor even an Ionian, though at one time of his life he came under strong Athenian influences. All three wrote history from a broad national standpoint, not a narrow. Herodotus, the earliest in time, has actually the broadest outlook of the three ; for he writes with a remarkable appreciation of oriental civilizations, does justice alike to the valour and loyalty of the Persian enemy, and holds the balance even between Greeks and Barbarians. Thucydides shows in unmistakable ways his love for Athens and his admiration of her greatness ; yet he writes with entire dispassionateness of the growth of the Athenian *archê*, of the grounds of quarrel between the Peloponnesian and the Athenian leagues ; of class strife at Corcyra or Samos ; of Sparta's jealous fears and pretensions. Thucydides writes history without any Athenian bias ; at times, he seems to deal more severely with Athenian policy than with

Peloponnesian ; and what he most clearly sees in the Peloponnesian war, and makes us see, is the havoc worked by Greeks upon Greeks, and the general demoralization caused by this fratricidal strife. Xenophon, though characteristically Athenian in temperament and by education, is even more aloof from narrow Athenian sympathies. He rests indeed under the imputation of a decided partiality for Sparta.

Meaning of History.—The word history by derivation contains no implication of the sequence of events in time. It belongs to a group of words connected with knowledge, and means ' enquiry.' A history, as originally named, is simply an enquiry. The present meaning of the word, as a narrative of past events in their formal and causal sequences, is secondary. The recorded history of Greece has a range of over two thousand years, from the seventh century B.C. to the fall of Constantinople, so that the fifth century B.C., to which our survey has mainly been confined, is a very small fraction of the whole. But that small fraction of the whole is, as was claimed at the outset, for our purpose of greater value than all the rest, and not least because the writers who have preserved the history of this century have set the pattern of all history to the western world. If the Greeks did not *invent* history in its present sense, they certainly gave it a character different from any earlier history ; and, we may add, from any later history written independently of Greek influence. This we may test, if we will, by comparing the historical books of the Bible, Kalhana's *History of the Kings of Cashmir*, the brick tablets of Babylonia and Assyria, or the Anglo-Saxon Chronicle, with Herodotus. At bottom the difference is that implied by the original meaning of history. To the Greek history was a process of investigation, as it never has been to oriental writers. The enquiring frame of mind readily turns to the critical, and in Thucydides passes into the deliberate sifting of evidence.

1. HERODOTUS

His Great Enquiry.—There were Greek writers in the domain of history before Herodotus, but we know very little about them. In particular there was Hecataeus of Miletus ; but even of Hecataeus our knowledge is almost wholly confined to Herodotus' disparaging references. What led Herodotus to his great and comprehensive conception of history we do not know ; but we have his own words, the opening words of his ' Enquiry,' defining the exact scope of his design : " There is here set forth the Enquiry of Herodotus of Halicarnassus, which he took in hand in order that the events of the past might not be lost to remembrance, and that the great and wonderful doings of Greeks and Barbarians might not miss their meed of renown : incidentally, too, he designed to set forth the reasons why they warred one with the other." To the immense gain of succeeding ages he took a remarkably ample view of his subject. It is an integral part of his scheme to unfold the antecedents of all the principal nations that come into his story, and even of many comparatively unimportant tribes. His work has consequently been found a mine of anthropological, ethnological and antiquarian lore, as well as being our prime authority for the great Persian War. Fully half of his work consists of digressions : he frankly says in one place : " indeed the addition of digressions came within the scope of my work from the beginning " : [1] and some might say that the digressions, which comprise a large part of what we know at first hand of the ancient Egyptians, Babylonians, Persians, Lydians, Scythians, and the wild tribes of Africa in his time, are the most valuable part of his work. His method, which may be called a method of involution, is an interesting study in the art of construction. Herodotus wrote his whole history as a continuous narrative without division into ' books.' Our division into nine books is the work of an early Alexandrian

[1] Herodotus, iv. 30. 1.

editor ; but it has been well done, corresponding to divisions into which Herodotus' treatment naturally falls.[1]

Scheme of the Nine Books.—Herodotus, as we have said, takes a large view of his theme. He has a vision of that age-long interaction of Europe and Asia, the flux and reflux of invasion, of which the latest episode was the onsweep of the Turks across Asia Minor in September 1922, only stopped at the Bosphorus by the firm action of the British government of the day. He begins with mythical stories like the Rape of Io and the Trojan War, and dismissing these continues : " I for my part am not going to say whether these things happened in accordance with one story or the other, but I will indicate who first to my knowledge began to inflict wrongs on the Hellenes and so go forward with my story, bringing in alike cities great and small ; for the cities that were great aforetime have most of them become small, and those that are great in my day were formerly small." [2] This brings him to the Lydians, who were the first foreign power to attack the Greek settlements in Asia Minor. The Lydians lead on to the Persians, by whom the Lydian empire was overthrown. Croesus, king of the Lydians, was advised by the Delphic oracle to ally himself with the strongest of the Hellenic states ; this gives opportunity for a description of Athens under Pisistratus and of Sparta in the sixth century B.C. The conquest of the Asiatic Greeks by the generals of Cyrus is described, and then the history to the end of Book I. follows the expansion of the Persian Empire; the conquest of Caria and Lycia, the taking of Babylon, the conflict with the Massagetae in which Cyrus himself lost his life. Cyrus' son and successor, Cambyses, was the conqueror of Egypt : this leads to a long disquisition on Egypt and the Nile, on the manners and customs, the monuments and the history of the Egyptians, which takes up the whole of Book II. Book III. narrates the actual

---

[1] Bury remarks (*Harvard Lectures*, p. 38) that " this distribution perfectly exhibits the construction of the book and could not be improved by any change."

[2] Herodotus, i. 5. 3.

conquest of Egypt and the wild doings attributed to Cambyses after it : and then we find we are being told of the ' wonders ' of the island of Samos, and its tyrant (the friend of Amasis of Egypt) Polycrates, who after a career of amazing good fortune came to a horrible end : and through Polycrates we are led on to stories of Periander son of Cypselus, tyrant of Corinth. The history of Persia through the reign of the usurper who personated Cambyses' murdered brother, Smerdis, the slaying of the false Smerdis, the accession of Darius and his organization of the Persian Empire, follow to the end of Book III. And then we are among the mighty rivers and vast steppes of Southern Russia, through the greater part of Book IV. For did not Darius undertake the famous Scythian expedition in which his forces barely escaped destruction after penetrating (if Herodotus' account can be believed) to the Volga ? These first four Books, which in bulk make up half the ' History,' are all preliminary to the main narrative, the conflict between Greeks and Persians which began with the Ionian Revolt in Book V. It is argued with great probability that the last three books, the story of Xerxes' invasion and its repulse, were the first written,[1] the account of Egypt in Book II. last of all : but, however that may be, the whole has been worked up with great skill into an artistic unity.[2]

Herodotus of Halicarnassus.—The history of Herodotus is one of those books in which the author draws his own portrait at full length, and the portrait of Herodotus which appears in the history is very human and amiable— not without engaging foibles. His large humanity and open intelligence are, perhaps, the two qualities that shine out most conspicuously. Prolix our author certainly is,

[1] See Introduction to Macan's *Herodotus*, iv-vi. pp. xcii-xciv.

[2] Bury, in agreement with Macan concludes (*Harvard Lectures*, p. 39) : " Thus the unity of the whole composition sharply displays itself in three parts, of which each again is threefold. The simplicity with which this architectural symmetry has been managed, without any apparent violence, constraint or formality, was an achievement of consummate craft." There is, however, also something to be said for a main division into *two* parts, (1) Books I. to IV ; (2) Books V. to IX.

and perhaps a little vain, somewhat given to superstition, and decidedly avid of the marvellous. But these faults, if faults they are, are completely overweighed by his virtues ; his eager desire for knowledge (inquisitiveness in the old uncorrupted sense), his love of truth, his genuine piety, his moral reverence, his good sense, his fair-mindedness, his shrewd sagacity. Of his personal history not very much is known. He was a native of Halicarnassus, a Dorian colony in Asia Minor ; Troezen, the city that gave generous shelter to Athenian fugitives before Salamis,[1] had a large part in its foundation. He was born in 484, six years after Marathon, four earlier than Salamis. After 454 Halicarnassus was a member of the Delian Confederacy, but till near that time was under the rule of a native dynasty owning allegiance to the king of Persia. Halicarnassus was ' freed ' from its tyrants and from Persia while Herodotus was in his prime ; and he is said to have taken active part in this emancipation, and his near kinsman, Panyasis, fell a martyr to the cause of liberty. But for some reason Herodotus did not care to remain a citizen of the city he had helped to free. He withdrew first to Samos : later he lived for a time at Athens. When the Athenians established a colony on the site of Sybaris, and called it Thurii, Herodotus joined this community, and is therefore sometimes spoken of as Herodotus the Thurian. But the most interesting and important side of Herodotus' life must have been his travels. The extent of these travels is difficult to determine exactly, but it must have been wide ; we have his own word for them in certain cases.

His Travels.—Herodotus had certainly been in Egypt and made long stay there. Words of his that prove it are : " There is much besides that I learnt at Memphis from conversations with the priests : moreover I went on to Thebes and Heliopolis expressly to test whether what they said would agree with what I heard at Memphis." [2] He had voyaged up the Nile as far as the first Cataract (Syenê, now Assuan). Tyre, again, he had certainly

[1] Vol. I. p. 340.   [2] Herodotus, ii. 3. 1.

visited : " desiring to know something certain of these matters so far as might be, I made a voyage to Tyre of Phoenicia." [1] What he says in one place in his account of Babylon clearly implies that he had been there : for in describing the ascent to the great eight-storeyed tower of Bel he says : " about half-way up in this ascent there is a resting-place and seats ; and here persons who make the ascent are wont to sit and rest." [2] A man would not write in this way, unless he had undertaken the long climb and rested on the seats. From these and other similar allusions it is conjectured with probability that Herodotus had journeyed into the interior of the Persian empire, and voyaged round the coasts of the Black Sea, as well as visited most parts of Greece, the islands, and Magna Graecia in Italy.

The Charm of Herodotus.—Readers for not far short of two thousand years, from Lucian and Plutarch to the present day, have testified to the charm of Herodotus. One chief secret of his charm is without doubt that he is a prince of story-tellers. "It is something," says Dr. Macan, "to have written the best story-book in Greek literature, perhaps in European literature." [3] His stories delight partly because he so evidently takes pleasure in telling them ; he tells a story for the story's sake, just because it is a good story. In his less fanciful stories, several of which found place in Vol. I, he shows a fine sense of literary form and dramatic point. Not all his stories have a moral tendency, but his own outlook on life is deeply ethical and many of his stories, like the stories of Glaucus, of Cleobis and Biton, of Xerxes' talks with Demaratus, have fine moral implications. Others of his stories are not moral at all, and remind one of the Arabian Nights or Geoffrey of Monmouth. Such are the stories of Gyges, of Polycrates of Samos, of Democedes of Crotona, of Ramsinitus king of Egypt, of the Babylonian queen Nitocris, of the Conspiracy of the Seven. His manifest

---

[1] Herodotus, ii. 44. 1.   [2] Herodotus, i. 181. 5.

[3] Macan, *Herodotus*, iv-vi. p. lxxiii.

pleasure in relating things strange and marvellous is another source of interest. That strange people the Egyptians were a perpetual joy to Herodotus. He loved to note how everything they did was done in the reverse way to other men : the Egyptians wrote from right to left, instead of from left to right ; they wove by pushing the woof upwards instead of downwards like other men ; other sea-faring races fasten ropes and stays outside their boats, the Egyptians inside ; the Egyptian women go out and do the marketing instead of the men ; the Egyptians let their hair grow long in token of mourning instead of cutting it short ; and so on and so on : and in illustrating this hasty generalization, he is as often wrong as right. He loves to make mention of ants, big as foxes and swifter than dromedaries, of gold-guarding griffins and one-eyed Arimaspians, of headless men with eyes in their breasts, and cattle that graze backwards ; [1] but this is a different thing from saying that he believes in the existence of these marvels. With all his simplicity (and simplicity is part of his charm) Herodotus is shrewd. He is often sceptical of things told to him, sometimes when we are able to see that the things of which he doubted were true. He may be credited also with a sense of humour ; some of his ' tall ' stories are evidently narrated with a twinkle in his eye.

His Critical Sagacity.—In all his narrative and in all his description of marvels Herodotus holds his mind free ; he questions, judges, selects. He is fully alive to the difference between hearsay evidence and the testimony of his own eyes and more than once emphasizes it. He by no means swallows all he is told on his travels (though he seems to swallow a good deal which we easily condemn as absurd) : he just genially passes on what he was told for the entertainment of his audience. He is garrulous, if you like, but it is a happy garrulity for which we have cause to be thankful. Not infrequently he plainly expresses his own disbelief in a story or a marvel ; or he gives

[1] Because, if, as they grazed, they moved forward, their horns would stick in the ground.

more versions than one and leaves his readers to use their judgment. This generous amplitude of method has had useful results for later enquirers, not in history only, but in allied sciences also. It has preserved much material which anthropologists, ethnologists, archaeologists, and other learned persons now turn to account. This material is not least valuable where Herodotus' own opinion has proved to be wrong. Thus in discussing the cause of the yearly overflowing of the Nile he definitely rejects the theory that the rising of the river is due to the melting of snow ; and for this rejection he gives grounds which were quite reasonable at the time. But it has now been ascertained that this explanation is exactly true for one of the two great branches of the river, the White Nile which comes from the region of the great lakes.[1]   He disbelieves in the Tin Islands, which did exist if we understand the name to be a misnomer for Cornwall.[2] The most interesting instance of his scepticism about a statement which we see to have been true has to do with the circumnavigation of Africa by Phoenician seamen in the days of Pharaoh-Necho, king of Egypt. The explorers started from a port in the Red Sea and proceeded southward along the African coast. " When autumn came on," the narrative continues, " they landed wherever they happened to be on the coast, sowed a crop and waited till it was ripe for cutting. Then they reaped it and set sail again, and two whole years passed in this way. In the third year they turned through the Pillars of Hercules and reached Egypt again. And they told a story,—*which I for my part do not believe*, though perhaps others may— that as they were sailing round Africa they had the sun on the right." [3] This detail which Herodotus found incredible, proves to us that the voyage really took place as described ; for, of course, when the ships rounded the Cape of Good Hope and began sailing west and northwest, the mariners would have seen the sun on their right at times when previously it had been on the left. It is

[1] Herodotus, iii. 20 and 22.   [2] Herodotus, iii. 115.
[3] Herodotus, iv. 42.

tempting to illustrate further Herodotus' habit of dis-
cursiveness and its interesting results. Two examples
must suffice. One shall be his account of how another
Egyptian king sought to ascertain which branch of the
human race was the oldest. " The Egyptians," he says,
" before the reign of Psammetichus believed that they
themselves were the oldest race of men. But after
Psammetichus became king and resolved to ascertain who
really were oldest, they believed that the Phrygians were
older and they themselves came next. The device which
Psammetichus adopted, when he found himself baffled
in the enquiry, was as follows. He took two newly-born
infants of the common people and gave them to a shepherd
to rear along with his flock on the following plan ; he
enjoined on him to let no one utter a word of speech in
their presence, but to keep them by themselves in a lonely
steading, bringing goats to them at stated times to supply
them with milk, and making proper provision in other
respects. The object of what Psammetichus did and the
orders he gave was that he might learn what word the
children would first utter apart from inarticulate cries.
Two years went by in this way, when one day, as the
shepherd opened the door and went in, both children
stretched out their hands to him and said ' bekkos.' The
shepherd took no notice when he first heard this, but
when as he came again and again to attend to them, they
kept repeating the word, he informed the king and by his
command brought the children into his presence. And
when Psammetichus himself heard it, he enquired what
people have in their language a word ' bekkos,' and he
learnt that the Phrygians have a word ' bekkos ' meaning
' bread.' Accordingly, on the ground of this test, the
Egyptians agreed that the Phrygians were more ancient
than themselves." [1] Such is Herodotus' story : a more
common-sense explanation is that the children, having
learnt to associate feeding-time with the bleating of goats,
had taken to imitating those sounds when they felt
hungry.

[1] Herodotus, ii. 2.

The other story concerns the source of the Nile. Herodotus says that no one, Egyptian or Libyan or Greek, of whom he inquired pretended to know anything about it with certainty except a clerk of the Sacred Treasury at Saïs. He goes on : " I did not, however, take the man seriously when he pretended to know exactly. But what he said was that there are two mountains with sharp-pointed peaks rising between the city of Syenê in the Thebaid and Elephantinê, and that the name of the one is Crô-phi, of the other Mô-phi. And he said that the springs of the Nile flow from between these two mountains and are of unfathomable depth ; and that half of the water flows towards Egypt and the North, the other half towards Ethiopia and the South."[1] At first this story seems merely grotesque ; but the modern Egyptologist recognizes real Egyptian words in Crôphi and Môphi. The Egyptian name of the Nile-god is Hâpi ; Crôphi is probably a corruption of Qer-Hâpi, meaning ' Cavern of the Nile-god,' Môphi of Mu-Hâpi, ' Water of the Nile-god.' [2]

2. THUCYDIDES

Thucydides, son of Olorus, was a contemporary of Herodotus, though considerably younger ; that is to say he was born when Herodotus was a boy of twelve. It hardly admits of doubt that he profited greatly by having Herodotus as a predecessor. His style and method are very different, and so is his theme ; but he received from Herodotus a spacious conception of what history might be, and also, in a wide sense, the principle of research—that evidence must be sought for and diligently sifted. But he was writing of the events of his own day, and was therefore in a far better critical position than Herodotus. He had himself taken a part in the history he relates and had abundant opportunities of conversing with and questioning eyewitnesses.

[1] Herodotus, ii. 28.

[2] See How and Wells, *Commentary on Herodotus*, vol. i. p. 172.

His Critical Standpoint.—He has himself given the reasons which led him to his history and outlined the principles by which he was guided in writing it. "Thucydides, the Athenian, has put together the history of the war between the Peloponnesians and Athenians. He began to write as soon as the war broke out, in the expectation that it would be a great struggle and more memorable than any previous war." [1] These are his opening words. A few pages further on he explains his principles. "The events of the war I did not think good to describe on the authority of any chance information, nor according to my own estimate of the probabilities ; what I relate, I was either present at myself, or, in accepting the witness of others for it, I tested every detail with exactitude to the utmost of my ability. This proved a laborious method of procedure, because the eyewitnesses of events did not agree in their accounts, but varied them according to their partiality for one side or the other and the accident of what they happened to remember. It may well be that this absence of an element of fable will make my history less attractive, but if those who wish to gain a clear view of past events, and of the future in so far as in all human probability events shall recur or be similar, judge my work profitable, that will be enough for me. My history is written to be a possession for all time, not like a prize composition for the immediate pleasure of the ear." [2] Later on when his narrative has been carried down to the Peace of Nicias and he is about to proceed to the story of the uneasy peace and the ultimate renewal of hostilities, he gives a fresh and somewhat expanded statement of his procedure. "This history also Thucydides the Athenian wrote in orderly succession, summer by summer and winter by winter, as things happened, to the time when the Lacedaemonians and their allies put an end to the dominion of the Athenians and captured the Long Walls and the Piraeus. And the years of war to this point were in all seven and twenty. . . . I lived through the whole time myself, at a ripe age for under-

[1] Thucydides, i. 1.   [2] Thucydides, i. 22. 2-4.

standing, and I paid close attention to the course of events in order that I might be accurately informed. It happened, moreover, that I was an exile from my own country for twenty years after my employment in command at Amphipolis, and since I had access to information on both sides, and, in particular, about Peloponnesian affairs because of my banishment, was all the better able to watch events quietly." [1] These passages suffice to show how at a leap Thucydides had arrived at a mature conception of the leading principles of sound work in history—the collection and testing of first-hand evidence. He does not specifically mention documentary evidence in the way a modern scientific historian would, and in his work he makes comparatively slight use of official records or state papers.[2] He may have had larger access to such sources than actually appears, but at any rate he does not refer to these sources of evidence as a modern writer would. Except for this difference he is as alive to the paramount importance of first-hand evidence and the comparative method as the most convinced historian of the documentary school.

Contrast with Herodotus.—In these respects there is obviously a strong contrast between Thucydides' method of writing history and Herodotus'. In spite of his honesty of purpose and love of truth Herodotus has a far less steady hold on the principle that the truth of history depends on a comparison of first-hand evidence than has Thucydides. He forgets it in the sheer pleasure of story-telling. His history has quite rightly been called an epic or saga, a work of the poet's art as much as the historian's. But if his history gains in picturesque and romantic quality, it is less accurate history. In Thucydides the picturesque and dramatic aspects of history—though when the truth of history requires it he can soar to a pitch beyond Herodotus' reach—are strictly subordinated to

[1] Thucydides, v. 26. 1 and 5.

[2] Notable exceptions are the treaties quoted *verbatim* in Book V. chapters 18, 23, 47, 77, 79 ; and an inscription on an altar dedicated at Delphi by the grandson of Pisistratus, quoted vi. 54. 7.

accuracy. Again the mental attitude of the two men towards the connection of events is markedly different. Herodotus seems hardly able to conceive large public motives and wide national impulses. He tends to envisage the links between great events through petty personal emotions and passions, which are indeed present and at work, but as the occasions of great events rather than the causes. Thus he can believe that the first impulse to the vast movement of forces which threatened to overwhelm Hellas in 481-479, was given through the reckless longing of a Greek physician, kept in gilded captivity at the Great King's court, to get back to his native city ; [1] and Histiaeus is made to stir up the Ionian revolt from analogous motives.[2] Thucydides with surer comprehension pays no attention whatever to the gossip about Pericles and Megara which we find in Aristophanes and in Plutarch. He does indeed give due weight to what happened at Epidamnus and Potidaea, but points to the real cause of the Peloponnesian war as lying deeper ; " the truest reason of all, though it has not often been plainly stated, was the growth of Athenian power and the alarm this inspired in the Lacedaemonians." [3] In a word Thucydides has risen to a philosophical conception of history, based on a scientific knowledge of human nature and a just estimate of forces and motives. Herodotus has not got beyond the feeling for history as story, sometimes even as fairy story.

Philosophical History.—This it is which makes Thucydides so admirable an introduction to the serious study of history. He is not only the supreme historian of the ancient world, he is a model for all time. It is well worth while to illustrate this side of his great work a little more freely. This philosophic temper is nowhere more effectively shown than in his treatment of the moral aspect of political transactions. Herodotus is preoccupied with his belief in moral causation of the naïve sort which sees in history a succession of special judgments. His mind

[1] Herodotus, iii. 129-138.   [2] Herodotus, v. 35.
[3] Thucydides, i. 23. 6.

is deeply tinged with these characteristically Hellenic conceptions—which also dominate Greek tragedy—of the divine jealousy—*Phthonos*—which will not tolerate for long great and unbroken human prosperity, and of the retribution—*Nemesis*—which sooner or later falls, when man's heart is lifted up with pride of power (*Hubris*), and he forgets the law of righteousness. There is nothing of this in Thucydides. He has been charged with a cynical indifference to the distinction of right and wrong in the conduct of states and public men ; with treating all public actions merely as questions of conflicting interests and relative power. Certainly he shows pointedly how large a part interest plays in determining international politics, how little powerful states are swayed by consideration of justice, and even of honour and good faith. The actual treatment of the Plataeans by Sparta and of the people of Melos by Athens are glaring examples. Thucydides certainly is not, as Herodotus is, obsessed by the idea of divine retribution and for ever pointing morals. He never points a moral. And yet, like Shakespeare, he is a more powerful teacher of morality than consciously didactic writers. Silently, inexorably, he makes manifest the majesty of the moral law by the mere juxtaposition of events in their actual connection. We see the Spartans paying the penalty of their selfishness and stupidity in the humiliations of Pylos and Sphacteria. We see the evil harvest of unbridled class passions in the horrors of Corcyra. We see the arrogance of imperial Athens rising with success and throwing away opportunity after opportunity. The moral climax is reached in the simple narration of the crime of Melos,[1] followed immediately by the inception of the Sicilian madness. Men and nations work out their destinies in accordance with character and the right or wrong use of the opportunities which circumstances bring. It is true of the Greeks collectively in the fifth century B.C., and equally true of the Greeks and other peoples in the century in which we live. Nothing is more characteristic of Thucydides' method in this sphere of moral

[1] Thucydides, v. 116 and vi. 1.

causation than his management of the episode known as
the Melian Controversy.[1] The Melians plead, weakly as
it seems, the old-fashioned ethical distinctions only to be
scornfully argued out of countenance by the shameless
avowal in the mouths of the Athenian envoys of the sole
validity of self-interest and force. So it may appear on
the surface ; but all the time to the intelligent reader the
falsehood of the brilliant Athenian sophistry is patent,
and the real invincibility of the more generous principles
of action is demonstrated with greater force. Right and
wrong are felt not to depend upon argument, but on
something deeper and more secure. And at the end of
the argument comes the Sicilian ruin.[2]

The Speeches.—The use made by Thucydides of the
speeches, which at certain important turning points in his
narration are put into the mouths of leading actors, is one
of the more effective resources of his art.   These ' speeches '
are no mere ornamental excrescences any more than the
choruses in the Aeschylean drama. They are a powerful
means of representing graphically contending forces and
principles, and in particular of bringing out national
character. The contrast of Athenians and Spartans is
effectively displayed by what is said in dramatic form in
the speeches ; and not alone in the formal contrast put
into the mouth of Corinthian speakers, Cleon and
Diodotus in the Mytilenaean debate, throw side-lights on
Athenian psychology, which make more intelligible the
mistakes of the Peloponnesian war, and not that only but
the difficulties with which the patriot Demosthenes had
to contend in the next century.   " Your way is to look on
at speeches like spectators at a show, and to provide an
audience for things done ; you form your judgment of
proposals from the fine words of speakers who argue them
feasible, while as for things done, you put no more trust
in the accomplished fact that you have seen with your eyes,

[1] Thucydides, v. 85-113.   And see above pp. 180-1.

[2] Thucydides shows also very clearly—when war was renewed in
413 after the abortive Peace of Nicias—how great was the moral effect
on the Spartans of the conviction that *now* they were in the right.
(See Book vii. ch. 8).

than in what you are told, if the speaker has a fine turn for caustic rhetoric. You are clever at being deceived by the novelty of an argument, and at refusing to follow advice when it is founded on recognized principles ; for you are at the mercy of every paradox and think scorn of the beaten track. Each of you wishes most of all to shine in debate himself ; failing that to outrival those who do by not seeming behind them in quickness of wit, since he catches the point of a smart saying before the words are out of the speaker's mouth. In a word you are slaves to the pleasures of the ear and are more like spectators at an exhibition of sophists than men who take part in the deliberations of a state." [1] And those are the Athenians of whom Pericles had said : " we have compelled every sea and every land to give access to our daring ! " The words quoted are put into the mouth of Cleon, but the thought is Thucydides' ; and the full significance is not seen till we follow the fortunes of Athens through the next century.

Spartan character and policy are similarly better understood for the defence against the strictures of the Corinthians spoken by Archidamus : " And as for this slowness and deliberation with which they reproach us so much, do not you be ashamed of it. Haste at the outset may make delay in coming to an end, if you enter upon war insufficiently prepared ; and the city which is ours to dwell in has ever been free and of highest renown. This quality in us may well be held to be wise self-control : at any rate by reason of it we alone among the nations do not wax arrogant through good fortune, and in ill fortune we give ground less than others. . . . It is even by reason of our orderly spirit that we excel in war and counsel : in war, because sense of honour is largely made up of self-control, and courage is largely made up of sense of honour ; in counsel because our training is too plain to allow us to despise the laws, our discipline too hard to permit us to disobey them. . . ." [2] We understand the better for this study of Spartan character, why the Spartans were

[1] Thucydides, iii. 38, 4-7.   [2] Thucydides, i. 84. 1-3.

lenient to defeated Athens, and why, when Sparta was humbled in her turn, the Spartans went down fighting. It was numbers that failed her men, not the spirit of their discipline.

Thucydides' political opinions.—There is nothing greater in Thucydides than the completeness with which he keeps his personal grievance out of his history. He records the saving of Eion, the loss of Amphipolis, and his twenty years of exile, but his only further reference to his banishment is to point it out as a circumstance which favoured the writing of his history. Whatever more he felt he kept to himself. There is no trace of vindictive feeling against Athens, only a just appraisement of her great glory, of her people's errors, and the causes of her defeat. As for Athenian politics, if he had any political bias, he keeps it sedulously within bounds. We may reasonably infer that his own position was that of steady loyalty to Athenian democracy with a leaning towards some limitation of democratic license ; for he expresses the opinion that the qualified democracy established after the overthrow of the Four Hundred was the best government Athens had in his time.[1] He clearly disapproves of the popular leaders who came to the front during the Peloponnesian war, yet he appears to have loyally accepted the democracy as completed by Pericles, and his admiration for Pericles himself was whole-hearted. Some think he is unfair to Cleon. That he disliked Cleon is plain enough, and dislike doubtless colours his portrait of the demagogue ; but his portrait, true or untrue, agrees with that painted by Aristophanes. His account of the revolution of 411 is quite dispassionate and betrays no sign of sympathy with the oligarchical conspirators. In the class war which led to massacres at Samos and Megara, and the horrors at Corcyra which he describes so vividly, he doubtless sympathized with the victims ; but the judgment tacitly expressed is condemnation of civil discord and of the violent passions which had effects so hideous.

[1] Thucydides, viii. 97. 5.

Descriptive power.—Some of the best descriptive
passages in Thucydides have already been cited in the
first part of this volume ; the Theban attack on Plataea,
the sea-fights in the Gulf of Corinth, the race to save the
Mytilenaeans, the defence of Pylos, the capture of Sphacteria, the death of Cleon, the sailing of the fleet for Sicily ;
the night attack on Epipolae ; the last fight in the harbour
of Syracuse ; and, above all, the retreat of the Athenians.
These passages, and others like them, show Thucydides,
in spite of his restraint and refusal of meretricious arts, a
greater master of narrative than even Herodotus.   There
is nothing greater in all prose literature than the best
descriptive passages in Thucydides.   Nor is his sense of
dramatic action and situation less powerful.   Individual
character in action he is less successful in drawing, but he
has left us two character sketches, perfect in their kind,
the ' characters ' of Themistocles and Pericles.   His
best character shown in action is Nicias ; after that come
Brasidas and Alcibiades.   But such portraiture is not
Thucydides' characteristic excellence.   He excels rather
in generalization and reflection.   A good instance of his
extraordinary power in this is his description of the
demoralization among the people of Athens caused by
plague.[1]   Even more impressive are his comments following a recital of the atrocious deeds done at Corcyra, on the
savagery which affected all Hellas as the disastrous war,
with its combination of racial, social, and political antago-
nisms, ran its course ; " To such extremes of cruelty did
the revolution go ; and this seemed to be the worst of
revolutions, because it was the first.   For not long
afterwards the whole Hellenic world was in commotion ;
in every city the chiefs of the democracy and of the
oligarchy were struggling, the one to bring in the Athenians,
the other the Lacedaemonians.   Now in time of peace,
men would have had no excuse for introducing either, and
no desire to do so, but when they were at war and both
sides could easily obtain allies to the hurt of their enemies
and the advantage of themselves, the dissatisfied party

[1] Thucydides, ii. 53.

were only too ready to invoke foreign aid. And revolution brought upon the cities of Hellas many terrible calamities, such as have been and always will be while human nature remains the same, but which are more or less aggravated and differ in character with every new combination of circumstances. In peace and prosperity both states and individuals are actuated by higher motives, because they do not fall under the dominion of imperious necessities ; but war, which takes away the comfortable provision of daily life, is a hard master, and tends to assimilate men's characters to their conditions." [1] There is much more, but the whole is too long to quote. It serves to illustrate, as much else in Thucydides does, the truth of Dr. Arnold's words in concluding the preface to the last three books of his edition : " the history of Greece and Rome is not an idle enquiry about remote ages and forgotten institutions, but a living picture of things present, fitted not so much for the curiosity of scholars, as for the instruction of the statesman and the citizen."

3. XENOPHON

Xenophon, son of Gryllus, is by no means the peer of Thucydides and Herodotus in the writing of history, but his versatility as a man of letters gives him importance of another kind, and personally he is more interesting than either : at all events we know more about him. Besides being a man of letters and a thinker, he was a sportsman and a country gentleman (Xenophon would have been happy as an English squire in a fox-hunting county), and he had proved himself in circumstances of peculiar difficulty a capable leader of men. He was born about the time of the outbreak of the Peloponnesian war, in 431 or a little earlier ; his mature life was varied and adventurous. In his youth he came under the personal influence of Socrates : how deep and lasting the impression was his *Memorabilia* show. What part Xenophon took in the public life of Athens during the last years of the war and

[1] Thucydides, iii. 82 ; Jowett, i. pp. 221-2. See also chs. 83 and 84.

the period of acute civil strife which followed is not known ;
but after the overthrow of the Thirty and a little before
the trial and death of Socrates he left Athens on the great
adventure of his life.   At the invitation of his friend Prox-
enus, a Bœotian soldier of fortune in the service of Cyrus,
the younger brother of the Persian king, he went out to
Sardis, and as a guest and personal friend of the Prince,
not a paid soldier, he accompanied the march into the
interior of the Persian empire, which ended in the death of
Cyrus and the retreat of the Ten Thousand Greeks.   In
399 he was back among the Greek cities of Asia Minor
after two years of crowded experience.   He had made the
march through Asia Minor and from Syria to the Euphrates (in part now the air route from Irak), he had been
present at Cunaxa (on the Euphrates, but not far distant
from Baghdad).   Then when the Greek commanders were
treacherously seized at a friendly conference and put to
death, and the Greek troops, the Hellenes as Xenophon
always calls them, were sunk in despondency, the young
Athenian came forward and by his sensible suggestions
roused their drooping spirits to fresh confidence.   The
Retreat of the Ten Thousand Greeks from the neighbourhood of Baghdad on the Tigris, through Mesopotamia and
Kurdistan and Armenia to Trapezus (Trebizond) on the
Black Sea, is one of the great military feats of history.
It had momentous consequences, for it was this which
made fully manifest to the Greeks the weakness of the
Persian empire, and so led directly to the conquests of
Alexander the Great.   There is no reason to doubt that
Xenophon played a foremost part in leading the retreat.
Called in this unexpected way to responsible command he
displayed surprising capacity, and it was largely owing
to his cheerfulness and tact, his military resourcefulness
and presence of mind, that the Ten Thousand held
together and won through.   Isolated as they were in
the middle of Mesopotamia, in the midst of a teeming
population, with the King's armies all round them
and great rivers and mountain chains barring their
retreat, it seemed impossible to fight their way to safety,

until the thing was done.   Xenophon himself wrote the
story in the book called the *Anabasis*, which is one of the
great realistic and personal adventure books, like Robinson
Crusoe and Scott's Antarctic Expedition.   Xenophon
came out of the adventure with a name famous throughout
all Hellas ; but this reputation cost him dear, inasmuch
as his banishment from Athens was decreed because of it.
That he had been a friend to Cyrus, the friend of Lysander
and the Spartans, was crime enough.   For some years
more he remained in Asia Minor, following the campaigns
of successive Spartan commanders, and especially the
campaigns of King Agesilaus with whom he formed a close
friendship.   His two sons, Gryllus and Diodorus, must
have been born in these years.   For some years after this
(399-387) he lived at Sparta and his sons were educated in
the Spartan discipline.   In 387 he was settled by the
Spartan government in an estate at Scillus in Elis, not far
from Olympia.   He describes this in the *Anabasis* [1] and
how, with a portion of his prize-money from Asia, he bought
a plot of ground there and built a shrine and an altar to
Artemis, his patron deity.   " The place lies on the direct
road from Lacedaemon to Olympia," he writes, " about
twenty furlongs from the temple of Zeus, and within the
sacred enclosure there is meadow-land and wood-covered
hills, suited to the breeding of pigs and goats and cattle
and horses, so that even the pack animals of the pilgrims
passing to the feast fare sumptuously.   The shrine is
girdled by a grove of cultivated trees, yielding dessert
fruits in their season." [2]   Every year Xenophon paid
tithe of the produce of the land to the goddess and celebrated a festival in which " all the citizens and neighbours,
men and women, shared."   " The goddess," he adds,
" herself provided for the banqueters meat and loaves and
wine and sweetmeats, with portions of the victims sacrified
from the sacred pasture, as also of those which were slain
in the chase ; for Xenophon's own lads, with the lads of the
other citizens, always made a hunting excursion against

[1] Xenophon, *Anabasis*, v. 3. 7-13 ; Dakyns, i. p. 218-220.
[2] *Anabasis*, v. 3. 11-12 ; Dakyns, p. 219.

the festival day, in which any grown men who liked might join." [1] Here he lived happily for sixteen years in the enjoyment of everything his heart desired—dogs and horses and country pursuits and the means of showing hospitality to his friends ; above all, with leisure to think and write amid beautiful scenery. There he farmed and reared stock and kept a pack of harriers ; and a great part of his literary work was done. But in 371 came the defeat of the Spartans at Leuctra and after it the Spartan strength no longer availed to overawe the Eleans. Armed force broke in upon Xenophon's peace, and he and his had to flee. For the rest of his life Xenophon lived at Corinth ; there he completed his *Hellenica* and there he worked on with his pen till he died. But soon after Leuctra Athens, in the whirligig of Greek politics, made alliance with Sparta (for now Thebes was the more formidable). Xenophon's sentence of banishment was revoked, and he and his sons once more became citizens of Athens. His sons, who inherited their father's good looks and manly tastes and love of horsemanship, served, as became their knightly rank, in the Athenian cavalry. In 362 they fought in this capacity at the battle of Mantinea, and the elder, Gryllus, was among those who fell. Diogenes Laertius has passed on to us the story that, when the grievous news was brought to Xenophon, he was engaged in offering sacrifice and wearing a sacred wreath, or chaplet. " Your son has fallen " said the messenger, and the father's hand removed the festal wreath. But when the messenger added " nobly," Xenophon replaced the wreath upon his head.

Xenophon on Horsemanship and Hunting.—We have had occasion already to make use of some of Xenophon's writings, those which were inspired by his admiration for Socrates. His other literary works are many and varied, including subjects as widely removed as a long oriental romance and a discourse on the Athenian ' budget '; it would serve no useful purpose to run through the whole list. But peculiar interest attaches to two treatises, the

[1] *Anabasis*, v. 3. 9-10 ; Dakyns, p. 219.

one about field sports and the other about riding, which
have come down bearing his name and bring him very
near us. They bring him near, because what he says
shows more fellowship between the ideas on these subjects
of an Athenian of the fourth century B.C. and those of our
day than, perhaps, we quite realized.

As an account of field sports among the Greeks, this
treatise of Xenophon's on hunting is fairly comprehensive;
it treats of beagling, of deer-hunting, of boar-hunting, of
the pursuit of big game ; it treats of nets and net-keepers,
and the sportsman's equipment generally. Above all it
contains the whole art and mystery of chasing the hare.
This, it is evident, is Xenophon's own favourite recreation,
pursuing the hare with harriers. " So winsome a creature
is it, that to note the whole of the proceedings from the
start—the quest by scent, the find, the pack in pursuit
full cry and the final capture—a man might well forget
all other loves." [1] There are sections on the points of the
harrier, on the keeping of a pack, on the naming of hounds,
on breeding and training, and an especially long and
loving section on the hare and her ways. Xenophon
writes like a nature lover and a lover of animals. Young
leverets are on no account to be chased. " Of course a good
sportsman will let these very young things alone." [2] This
sport of catching hares takes up the largest space in
Xenophon's manual, but as already implied there are
chapters also on hunting deer, on boar-hunting, and a
short one on the pursuit of big game—lions, leopards,
panthers and bears ; but for these last the sportsman
must go outside Greece. Boar-hunting has the excitement of danger added. Xenophon testifies to the strength
and fierceness of the wild pig, especially in defence of its
offspring. Facing the boar on foot, boar-spear in hand, was
a riskier game even than pig-sticking in India. Our
author gives careful directions to the hunter how to bear
himself in such a close encounter : he is to grasp his spear

---

[1] *Cynegeticus*, v. 33 ; Dakyns, iii. 2. p. 93.

[2] *Cynegeticus*, v. 14. It is disappointing after this to find Xenophon
has no similar scruples about molesting the young of the deer.

firmly " with the left hand forward and with the right
behind ; the left is to steady it, and the right to give it
impulse ; and so the feet, the left advanced in correspondence with the left arm, and right with right. As he
advances, he will make a lunge forward with the boar-
spear, planting his legs apart not much wider than in
wrestling, and keeping his left side turned towards his left
hand ; and then, with his eye fixed steadily on the beast's
eye, he will note every turn and movement of the creature's
head. As he brings down the boar-spear to the thrust,
he must take good heed the animal does not knock it out
of his hands by a side movement of the head ; for if so he
will follow up the impulse of that rude knock. If this
misfortune happens, the huntsman must throw himself
upon his face and clutch tight hold of the brushwood
under him, since if the wild boar should attack him in that
posture, owing to the upward curve of its tusks, it cannot
get under him ; whereas if caught erect, he must be
wounded. What will happen then is, that the beast will try
to raise him, and failing that will stand upon and trample
him." [1]   And then the only chance for him is the opportune
intervention of another hunter, who may draw off the
boar's attack. In Xenophon's code of sportsmanship
there is a larger use of nets and pits and calthrops than is
permitted now. On the other hand there are many
considerate and judicious precepts about the care and
training of dogs ; for instance that the owner should
make a point of always feeding the hounds with his own
hand, and of not taking a hound out when it has refused
its food.

Xenophon's treatise on the horse and horsemanship
will delight the horse-lover even more for its sympathetic
and practical understanding of horse nature ; it is not easy
to find a literary parallel in these respects. Xenophon
bases all his hints and precepts about the treatment of
horses on the principle of association : whatever you want
a horse to do for you, study to connect the doing with
some gratification or relief, and his cardinal maxim is

[1] *Cynegeticus*, x. 11-13 ; Dakyns, pp. 113-4.

" Never approach a horse in anger." [1]   He gives elaborate
hints for guidance in buying a horse.   Before everything
else he insists on the importance of sound hoofs ; and
remembering that the Greeks did not shoe their horses,
we acknowledge he is right.   For the same reason he urges
special precautions against a damp stable-floor and
recommends a stable-yard flagged with cobble-stones.
The stable itself should be near the house so as to be
under the master's eye and he may be sure his horse is
really getting its corn.   There are useful hints for acquir-
ing a good seat and about the training of horses for
cavalry work, which must include " leaping ditches,
scrambling over walls, scaling up and springing off high
banks." [2]   But Xenophon looks on the horse not only as
a useful servant and valuable ally in war, but also as a
beautiful natural object, and his treatise includes precepts
for enhancing the natural grace of the horse and bringing
out his fire and spirit for ceremonial purposes.   His
principle is still the same, kindliness, the understanding
of the horse's psychology ; and always his golden rule :
" and so throughout, as we never cease repeating, at every
response to your wishes, whenever and wherever the
animal performs his service well, reward and humour him.
Thus when the rider perceives that the horse takes
pleasure in the high arching and supple play of his neck,
let him seize the instant, not to impose severe exertion on
him like a taskmaster, but rather to caress and coax him,
as if anxious to give him a rest." [3]   " What we need is
that the horse should of his own accord exhibit his finest

---

[1] Vi. 13 ; Dakyns, p. 52.   Particularly excellent are his remarks on
what may be done before the process of ' breaking in ' is begun to
make a colt ' gentle, tractable and affectionate.'   "That is a condition
of things which for the most part may be brought about at home
by the groom—if he knows how to let the animal connect hunger and
thirst and the annoyance of flies with solitude, whilst associating food
and drink and escape from sources of irritation with the presence of
man.   As the result of this treatment the young horse will acquire—
not fondness merely—but an absolute craving for human beings."   *On
Horsemanship*, ii. 3 ; Dakyns, p. 43.

[2] *On Horsemanship*, iii. 7 and viii. 1 ; Dakyns, pp. 45 and 56.

[3] *On Horsemanship*, ix.; Dakyns, p. 59.

airs and paces at set signals. Supposing, when he is in the riding-field, you push him to a gallop, until he is bathed in sweat, and when he begins to prance and show his airs to fine effect, you promptly dismount and take off the bit, you may rely upon it he will of his own accord another time break into the same prancing action. Such are the horses on which gods and heroes ride, as represented by the artist. The majesty of men themselves is best discovered in the graceful handling of such animals. A horse so prancing is indeed a thing of beauty, a wonder and a marvel, riveting the gaze of all who see him, young alike and greybeards." [1] We think of the Parthenon frieze, and a new aspect of the secret of Pheidian art is revealed to us.

Xenophon's Hellenic History.—But it is after all with Xenophon as a writer of history that we have to do here, and it cannot be claimed that the *Hellenica* have anything like the same interest and importance as Herodotus' history of the great Persian War, or Thucydides' history of the Peloponnesian war. To begin with Xenophon is less fortunate in his subject. There is a splendid artistic unity in the story of Xerxes' invasion and its repulse and there is unity in the story of the struggle for mastery between Athens and Sparta. Xenophon's Hellenic history covers a range of fifty years within his own life-time, but there is no connecting unity other than continuity in time. Two books of the *Hellenica* are the completion of the design which Thucydides left unfinished, comprising the last seven years of the Peloponnesian War, from the battle of Cynossema in 411 B.C. to the capitulation of Athens in 404 ; the other five are a medley of disjointed episodes and personal experiences. There is no central interest in the *Hellenica* ; it is not in a true sense a single work, though from Lysander's triumphant entry into Piraeus and the pulling down of the Long Walls Xenophon goes straight on to the history of the Thirty Tyrants and thence to the doings of the Lacedaemonians in Asia Minor. In so far as there is no deliberate break

[1] Xi. 6-9 ; Dakyns, pp. 65-6.

and new beginning the work is continuous and one. But the conclusion of scholars who have carefully studied the internal evidence is that it really falls into three divisions written at wide intervals of time.[1] If we consider how the history of a man's own times must ordinarily be written, this conclusion is seen to be what might have been expected beforehand. The whole length of time is considerable, just half a century : the treatment varies greatly in scale ; it is full and detailed of affairs which came under Xenophon's own observation, brief and defective about other events not less important. Some matters of great interest are omitted altogether : for instance there is no account whatever of the formation of the second Athenian confederacy, and, stranger still, not a word of the foundation of Messenê and Megalopolis.[2] The nearest approach we have to unity of subject in the *Hellenica* is the struggle between Sparta and Thebes. Thebes wronged by Sparta gathered strength and under the inspiration of two great leaders, Pelopidas and Epaminondas, overthrew the Spartan power at Leuctra (in 371) and again at Mantinea (in 362). Here Xenophon had a great opportunity of which he fails to take full advantage. His strong Laconian sympathies blind him to the heroism which Thebes, whose part in the Persian wars had been an ignoble one, rose to at this time. If we had only the *Hellenica*, we should know nothing of the chivalrous spirit of Pelopidas and have but a poor measure of the real greatness of Epaminondas. Taken as a whole, however, the history of Hellas after 404 is insignificant history ; that is to say, it deals with events which affect after history very little, except in so far as the frittering away of the strength of the city states by incessant divisions and conflicts—Argos against Sparta, Thebes against Athens, Athens against Sparta, Sparta

---

[1] See Dakyns, vol. i. p. lx. ; or Loeb *Hellenica*, p. viii.

[2] The return of the Messenians to the Peloponnesus after 300 years of exile is one of the most curious of Time's revenges in all history, only to be paralleled, perhaps, by the restoration of dismembered Poland in our own time.

and Athens against Thebes, old border feuds of Thebans, Phocians and Locrians, of Arcadians and Lacedaemonians —paved the way to the rise of Macedonia.

Xenophon's reflections on Mantinea,—almost the concluding words of the *Hellenica*—are a telling commentary on the futility of it all : " The result of these events turned out the very opposite of what all men had expected. When nearly the whole of Hellas had gathered together and set in array against each other, there was no one who did not believe, that if there were a battle, the conquerors would rule, and the conquered would be their subjects. But God so brought it to pass that while both sides set up a trophy as having been victorious, and neither tried to hinder the other in doing this, and while both gave back the enemy's dead under a truce as though they were victorious, yet both received back their dead under a truce as if defeated. While both claimed the victory, neither was found to have any advantage either in territory or state or sway other than they had before the battle was fought ; but there was more confusion and disorder in Greece after the battle than before."

Qualities of Xenophon as an Historian.—Xenophon has little of Herodotus' gift for story-telling or the tense descriptive power of Thucydides. The difference is seen if we compare Xenophon's account of Arginusae with Phormio's sea-fights ; or Aegospotami with the last fight in the harbour of Syracuse. Xenophon's narrative rises in these places to a moderate vividness, but it has nothing of the thrill which Thucydides at his best communicates. Xenophon's merits are that he has a good clear style, not lacking in vigour, and transparent honesty of purpose ; and that he is accurate according to his lights. He lets fall sensible observations at times, but he has not Thucydides' breadth of philosophical vision. His history without being great literature is eminently readable, and to have written a clear first-hand account of these fifty years is a valuable service to Calliopê. Nor are there wanting passages which derive a special interest, and even beauty, from the engaging personal qualities of the writer.

Xenophon's affection for Sparta gives him a pathetic eloquence when he has to tell of the evil days that came to her after Leuctra. In the year after that fatal reverse to the Spartan arms a great army under Epaminondas, said to have numbered 70,000 men, Boeotians, Phocians, Thessalians, Euboeans, Locrians, Acarnanians, marched into the Peloponnese and invaded Laconia. Down from the slopes of Parnon they marched through the district of Sellasia till they came to the Eurotas, ravaging as they went. There was a bridge, to cross which was to be in Sparta ; but the invaders did not venture on the attempt : "for they caught sight of the heavy infantry in the temple of Alea ready to meet them." So formidable even in defeat was Spartan valour. And then comes Xenophon's unforgettable picture. " So keeping the Eurotas on their right, they tramped along, burning and pillaging homesteads stocked with numerous stores. The feelings of the citizens may be well imagined. The women who had never set eyes upon a foe could scarcely contain themselves as they beheld the cloud of smoke. The Spartan warriors, inhabiting a city without fortifications, posted at intervals here one and there another, were in truth what they appeared to be, the veriest handful. And these kept watch and ward." [1] This description shows the strength of Xenophon's feelings ; admiration and gratitude make Sparta's humiliation a personal calamity : and who shall blame him ? To this chivalrous sensibility is due another of the gems of the *Hellenica*, perhaps the purest gem of all—his tribute to Phlius. Phlius was but a little city, an Achaean city, neighbour to Sicyon and Corinth, and faithful ally of Sparta. This little city Xenophon singles out for a special tribute of praise (had not Gryllus and Diodorus charged with the horsemen of Phlius ?) for gallant bravery and the staunch loyalty of its citizens, a tribute which extends over several pages of Book VII. And the reason he gives for so doing is a pleasing one : he says " It is the way of historians, I know, to record only the noble achievements of the great cities, but to me it seems

[1] Xen. *Hell*. vi. 5. 27 and 28 ; Dakyns, ii. p. 178.

a still more worthy task to bring to light the great exploits of even a little state found faithful in the performance of fair deeds." [1] We may acquiesce in the judgment and lay to heart the lesson. The civilization of Hellas, the customs and laws and institutions ; the mental endowment of the Hellenes, the accomplishments and artistic gifts, were not a monopoly of the bigger states, of Athens and Argos, Sparta and Thebes, but were shared in greater or less degree by every city, great and small, which had a right to the Hellenic name. The small states had, everyone of them, their particular constitutions (did not Aristotle describe 158?), their military systems, their games, their temples, their art treasures. It is these scores of little autonomous states which collectively are Hellas : and Hellas is greater than Sparta or Thebes, greater than Athens herself. The Hellenes were learning this lesson slowly and painfully in the fifth and fourth centuries, too late and too imperfectly for their national salvation, not too late for the completion of the great inheritance they were to hand on to Rome and to the modern world.

[1] Xenophon, *Hellenica*, vii. 2. 1.

CHAPTER XIII

ATHENIAN ORATORY AND DEMOSTHENES

"Defeated undoubtedly the Athenians were, but they had become themselves once more, if only for a moment."
PICKARD-CAMBRIDGE, *Demosthenes*, pp. 389-90.

"For every one of them felt that he had come into being, not for his father and his mother alone, but also for his country. And wherein lies the difference ? He who thinks he was born for his parents alone awaits the death which destiny assigns him in the course of nature : but he who was born for his country also will be willing to die, that he may not see her in bondage, and will look upon the outrages and the indignities that he must needs bear in a city that is in bondage as more to be dreaded than death."
DEMOSTHENES, *On the Crown*, 205.

Speeches as Literature.—Of all forms of literature oratory is the least truly literary. A speech, as such, is addressed to the ears of listening men. Drama, also, is speech and action before it is literature ; but drama, being imaginative creation, readily becomes an affair of the study, the product of leisure and meditation. A speech in its very nature has to do with realities and fits a particular occasion : it may be premeditated, but it must be spoken. Oratory, however, has come to be accepted as a form of literature ; great speeches have been written down and preserved ; some of the most famous ' speeches ' were never spoken at all, like Cicero's Verrine orations [1] and Demosthenes' indictment of Meidias. There are extant literary speeches which were never even intended to be spoken ; and these cease in any true sense to be

[1] Except the first.

speeches ; they become a kind of drama. The Greeks were the first people who deliberately made speaking a fine art, and called it *rhetoric*. Rhetoric played a great part, we might say too great a part, in the history of Athens during the fourth century B.C.

Rhetoric.—Oratory, as studied compositions intended to be written down and preserved, does not come into Athenian history till the great days of Athens are over. Thucydides does indeed illuminate his history with speeches which bring out the content of a situation at critical moments ; and greatest among these are three attributed to Pericles ; but all are so Thucydidean in form that it is impossible to estimate with any probability how much of the speaker's actual words they preserve for us. The historian's own account of them is that they convey the substance of what was said. Public speaking was, however, in a sense, an art among the Hellenes from the earliest times. The Boulê and the Agora were primitive institutions among them : there are speeches, eloquent and effective speeches, made in Council and Assembly both in the *Iliad* and the *Odyssey*.[1] Naturally in democracies the part played by public speaking was greater than under kingly or oligarchical government. At Athens, the complete democracy, there were two forms of public speaking which assume a growing importance through the period best known to history— political speeches in the Ecclesia, forensic speeches in the Dicastery Courts. No man could aspire to a political career at Athens without possessing a capacity for speaking in public. Any citizen might at some time find himself summoned before one of these courts ; and then his fortune, perhaps even his life, depended on his ability to plead in his own cause. For at Athens, in spite of the prominence of the democratic law-courts, there were no professional advocates. There was a prejudice against the very notion of them. Every citizen must plead in his

[1] " With the Greeks oratory was instinctive ; in the earliest semi-historical records that we possess, eloquence is found to be a gift prized not less highly than valour in battle." Dobson, *The Greek Orators*, p. 1.

own case, whether as complainant or defendant.[1] It therefore became a matter of great practical importance that everyone born to a good social position should be able to marshal an argument and speak in public without timidity or confusion. The same happened in other democracies. It is not wonderful if a class of persons appeared who claimed to be able to train others to speak. The sophists put this forward among their pretensions. It was at other places than Athens, that such teachers first attained fame. Protagoras was, we have seen, of Abdera ; Prodicus was of Ceos ; Gorgias, most famous of them all, of Leontini. Later than the sophists came the ' speakers,' from whose Greek name, *rhetor*, we get our words *rhetoric* and *rhetorical*. Rhetoric, more especially the art of persuasion in the law courts, was cultivated at Athens with remarkable elaboration and subtlety.[2] The ' speakers,' known distinctively by this title, appear in a later age than that of Cimon and Pericles : the first who were so called, Antiphon and Andocides, belong to the time of the Peloponnesian war. Ultimately ten chief masters of Attic oratory came to be distinguished, but the list is not quite authoritative.[3] The greatest of the ten all belong to the fourth century, which for Athens may be called the age of the rhetoricians. It is significant of the decline of Athenian public life after Aegospotami. No one thought of calling Cimon or Pericles, Themistocles or Aristides, a *rhetor*. The statesmen of Demosthenes' time are called as a matter of course rhetors, public speakers : public

[1] The statement that no professional advocacy was permitted in Athenian law-courts needs qualification in two ways. By the fourth century, and possibly a good deal earlier, it was a recognized custom that parties to a suit in an Athenian court should have speeches written for them and should deliver these as their own ; and in this way a class of speech-*writers* grew up which by Demosthenes' time may be regarded as a profession. In the fourth century, also, personal friends were allowed to appear in court and plead for either of the parties (a non-professional form of advocacy), and it was in this capacity that Demosthenes composed and spoke the most famous of all his speeches, the speech *On the Crown*.

[2] See Plato, *Phaedrus*, 266 D-267 D.

[3] Antiphon, Andocides, Lysias, Isaeus, Isocrates, Aeschines, Demosthenes, Hypereides, Lycurgus and Dinarchus.

speaker has come to mean statesman. With some truth
rhetoric may be called the vice of the age. We shall see
presently how rhetoric infected the drama. Rhetoric
acquired, and still retains, a slightly sinister meaning.[1]
We praise a speaker for his eloquence, his earnestness, his
honesty, but not for his ' rhetoric.' Rhetoric came to
connote the bad side of speech-making, the meretricious
and dishonest. The reason is that in the Athenian
dicastery-courts, with their hundreds of judges, and in the
Ecclesia also, the qualities and accomplishments which
brought success were not the best. A barrister in modern
England, similarly, aims at winning his case, not at
considering first and last the attainment of justice ; and in
Parliament and at public meetings politicians are usually
more concerned with justifying their party or themselves
than with impartial reasoning and true conclusions. At
Athens both in the Ecclesia and the law-courts, the conditions were such as to favour the lower rather than the
higher arts of speech. The judges in the law-courts were
a mixed crowd of from 200 to 2000 ordinary citizens, of
intelligence probably rather below than above the average.
Appeal to their pride, to their prejudices, to their liking
to be amused and to be flattered, was the readiest way to
success with them. In the Ecclesia, numbers were greater
still ; it was a mass meeting of citizens ; and there, too,
argument to be successful must suit the mercurial temperament of the Athenians.[2] Rhetoric, the tricky art
of the clever speaker, got a bad name and has kept it
since. Nevertheless, in spite of these baser tendencies,
public speaking attained a noble excellence at Athens,
and the greatest of the Attic orators deserve the fame that
attaches to their names. Athenian prose writing in the
hands of these ' orators ' comes near to rivalling the prose
of Plato. There are critics who place the masterpieces

---

[1] No one has ever exposed the weak side of *rhetoric* more effectively
than Plato in the *Gorgias* and the *Phaedrus*. In the *Gorgias* (463 A
and B) Socrates is made to describe rhetoric as one of four branches
of an art of flattery.

[2] See Cleon's description in Thucydides, iii. 38.

of Lysias, Isocrates and Demosthenes even higher. We have materials for judgment since a considerable body of oratorical writing has come down to us, though this is only a small part of the whole literature of Greek oratory which once existed.[1]

Value for History.—But higher even than the value of the Greek orators for literature is their value for the vividness with which they light up the last phase of ancient Hellenic liberty, the years during which the Hellenic city-states were offering, without common plan or foresight, hesitating and fitful resistance to the rapidly growing military power of the kings of Macedonia. Here once again in the history of Greece we have a drama of absorbing human interest. It was not only the impact of a strong and coherent military monarchy upon the several disunited Hellenic city-states, never more than partially confederated for temporary ends, and intermittently at war among themselves, but it was also a clash of ideals. Athens and the cities which resisted Philip of Macedon, stood for the ideas of political and personal freedom, which had inspired the Hellenes throughout their previous history, and especially in their struggle with Persia. Philip and Alexander, and their supporters in the several Greek states, stood also for an idea, the ideal of a Hellas welded together for the purpose of overthrowing their hereditary enemy, the Persian Empire. The complete expression of that ideal was the life-work of one of our orators, Isocrates. The protagonist on the other side, the inflexible champion of that vivid political freedom which had inspired and sustained the Hellenes in all their achievements, spiritual and material, was Demosthenes, the greatest orator of them all.

Fourth Century Hellas.—Fourth century Hellas, the Greek world in which Isocrates thought and Demosthenes strove, triumphed, and suffered defeat, was very different from fifth century Hellas. At the beginning of the century Athens was stripped of empire, and the Spartans

[1] Some 600 speeches in all, out of which, in round numbers, 150 survive.

were everywhere dominant. But it was not long before the Spartans had demonstrated their own unfitness for 'empire.' As liberators of the Hellenes, they had lowered the pride of Athens. It was now proved that the *harmosts*, that is, the governors set in authority by Lysander and the Spartans, were harsher and more arbitrary in their methods than ever Athens had been.[1] This produced so much discontent that, ten years after the surrender of Athens, the Athenians, in alliance with their once bitter enemies the Corinthians, were fighting against the Spartans in Corinthian territory. In the same year, 394, Conon, the one Athenian admiral who carried his ships safely out of the ruin of Aegospotami, defeated a Spartan fleet off Cnidus, in command of Persian naval forces. In 378 a second Delian Confederacy came into existence with Athens at its head. But, meantime, the power of Thebes had grown, and it is Thebes, not Athens, which challenges Spartan supremacy. In 371 the battle of Leuctra definitely transferred the leadership in Hellas from Sparta to Thebes. This decision was confirmed in B.C. 362 by the battle of Mantinea, in which the Spartans were defeated, though Epaminondas, the Theban, who won Thebes her victories, fell. Sparta never recovered her old position, but more and more declined. The hegemony of Thebes also ended with the death of Epaminondas : and then there was no leadership in Greece at all, but only confused rivalry and purposeless conflict.[2] In 359, Philip, brother of Perdiccas III., became king of Macedonia and a new factor of quite different character came into the sphere of Hellenic politics, which was to revolutionize Europe and great part of Asia.

Philip of Macedon.—Macedonia has once or twice come into Hellenic history as we have followed the main

[1] No better defence of the Athenian ' archê ' has ever been made than Isocrates', when he claims (*Panegyric*, 106), that during the seventy years it lasted the subject states lived " safe from tyranny, free from molestation by the barbarians, untroubled by faction in their own land, and at peace with all mankind."

[2] See Xenophon, *Hellenica*, vii. 5. 26.

course of events through the fifth century B.C. One
Macedonian king made submission to Darius' generals
on the first advance of the Persians into Europe [1] ;
another claimed credit for bringing a friendly message
to Pausanias before the battle of Plataea.[2] At the beginning of the Peloponnesian war, the reigning king, Perdiccas,
appears as the enemy of Athens before the revolt of
Potidaea ; and later as the ally of Brasidas (above, pp. 125
and 170). Up to 359, however, the Macedonians had
been only of quite secondary importance, whether as
friends or enemies.[3] But Philip was a man of uncommon
energy of will and intelligence, as well as of great bodily
activity ; and he saw clearly what the conditions were of
a powerful and wealthy Macedonia ; saw also the opportunities which the incurable divisions and weaknesses of
the Hellenic cities offered to his ambition. The royal
house of Macedonia, to which Alexander, Perdiccas, and
Philip belonged, claimed pure Hellenic descent, and this
claim had been formally admitted at Olympia.[4] The
Macedonian people were not regarded as Hellenes at all,
yet they were undoubtedly of kindred stock, speaking a
language distinct from, yet related to, Greek. Greeks who
admired Philip, called him a Heraclid, but it was always
open to anyone who disliked him to reproach him with the
name barbarian.[5] And not only was Philip descended

---

[1] See vol. i. pp. 270 and 300.   [2] See vol. i. pp. 371-2.

[3] The ancestral kingdom to which Philip succeeded was much less
extensive than the Macedonia of the modern Balkan Question. Hogarth
writes (*Philip and Alexander of Macedon*, p. 13) : " the original holding
of the Macedonians was just that semi-circular expanse of low land
which lies west and north of the Gulf of Salonica. Whoever has sailed
up that sea and ridden three days north to Vodhena, and three days
east to Cavalla, has seen the whole cradle of Macedonian power." The
mountains beyond were held by warlike tribes, Thracians, Paeonians,
Lyncestians, whose hereditary princes usually acknowledged the
suzerainty of the kings of Macedonia, but often were in rebellion.
Further west were the wild Illyrians, the hereditary enemies of Macedonia. Perdiccas, Philip's brother, died in battle against them.

[4] See Herodotus, v. 22.

[5] Demosthenes (*Third Philippic*, 40) goes so far as to brand Philip
as " not even a barbarian from a country one can speak of with respect ! "

from Macedonian kings, who claimed to be Hellenes ;
he had been trained in Hellenic ways during three of the
most plastic years of his life in a Greek city-state. The
city was Thebes, but Thebes when she had won the
primacy of Hellas.   He was one of many hostages brought
to Thebes by Epaminondas after his expedition to
Macedonia in 368, and fourteen years of age at the time.
He learnt two things there which were invaluable to him
in his after career.   The one was a knowledge of the new
tactics invented by the Thebans.[1]   The other was an
inside view of the weakness of the Greek political system.
He came to the throne unexpectedly on the death in
battle of his brother Perdiccas, whose son was an infant
and, therefore, set aside by the Macedonians.   Philip
began by organizing a national army, which he inured to
war by a series of campaigns against the turbulent tribes
on the borders of Macedonia, who had hitherto owed
but a doubtful allegiance to their Macedonian overlords.
He next turned his attention to the Greek cities planted
along the Macedonian seaboard, and especially to the
peninsula of Chalcidicê with its three promontories,
Actê, Sithonia and Pallenê.   If Macedonia was to
grow in wealth and power, harbours were indispensable.
Earlier Macedonian kings [2] had sought to conquer the
coast towns, but they had not been strong enough.
Philip began in a position as little advantageous as his
predecessors.   Macedonia was poor and struggling, in
spite of its nominal extent of territory.   The Greek cities
were wealthy and many in number ;   especially powerful
was Olynthus, which, since the dissolution of the Athenian
Empire, had become head of a considerable confederacy of
Chalcidian towns.   Athens herself, too, still had interests
along this coast, where once all the towns had been
included in her confederacy ;   and, in particular, she had a

---

[1] This was to hurl a massed column, many spears deeper than customary, at one point of the enemy's front, while holding all the rest with
a comparatively weak line, and so break through.   This was how
Leuctra and Mantinea were won.   A beginning of similar tactics is
discernible at Delium as early as 424.

[2] The ablest of them was Archelaus.   See Thucydides, ii. 100. 2.

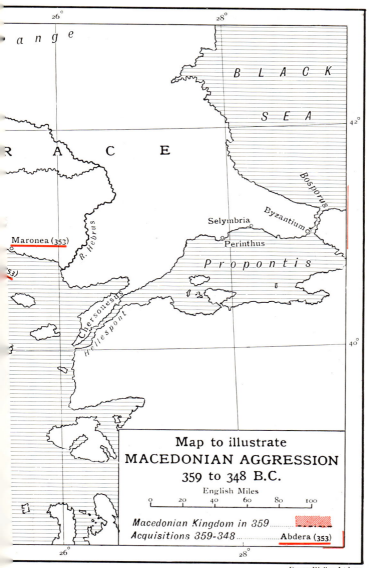

Map to illustrate
MACEDONIAN AGGRESSION
359 to 348 B.C.

English Miles

0   20   40   60   80   100

Macedonian Kingdom in 359
Acquisitions 359-348 Abdera (353)

Emery Walker Ltd. sc.

claim which her people could not forget to the possession of Amphipolis.[1] There were her Thraceward interests, also, to be considered—Thasos and the gold mines of the mainland, and most important of all, the Thracian Chersonese, commanding the Hellespont and the corn-ships from the Black Sea, which had been closely connected with Athens since the days of Miltiades. The seaward ambitions of the Macedonian kings necessarily brought them into antagonism with Athens and with Olynthus. Philip's method of dealing with this situation was characteristic. He made the Athenians believe he was favourable to their claim to Amphipolis. A little later when he had obtained possession of the place with their consent, he kept it and thus gained a footing in the gold region of Mount Pangaeus. He then made alliance with Olynthus and helped the Olynthians to take Potidaea from Athens. He thus played each of his adversaries off against the other ; keeping his own ends firmly in view and taking advantage of his rivals' mistakes, he pushed on step by step eastward into Thrace and southward towards Thessaly. In twelve years' time, from 359 to 348, he had gained possession of the whole coast from Maronea and Abdera in Thrace to Mount Olympus, and was master of a military and naval power already formidable to all Hellas. He was helped in all this, partly by the supineness and shortsightedness of the city-states, partly by the fortunate occurrence of two wars. One followed a breach between Athens and the strongest of her allies, which in effect put an end to the second naval confederacy. This war, inappropriately called the Social War, ended in 355 in the defeat of Athens, a defeat which left her again much weakened. In the same year, 355, a quarrel between Thebes and the Phocians led to what is known in Greek history as the Second Sacred War.[2]

[1] See above, pp. 170-1 and 177 ; also pp. 37 and 38.

[2] The first was that in which Solon the Athenian is said to have played a leading part ; it broke out early in the sixth century B.C., and resulted in the destruction of Cirrha, the port of Crissa, and the devotion to the god of plain lands adjacent to the harbour. See also below, pp. 372-3.

The Sacred War and the Peace of Philocrates.—This enmity between the Thebans and the Phocians was of ancient date and was aggravated by the sudden rise of Thebes to power through the overthrow of the Spartans at Leuctra. The Phocians refused to follow the Theban lead and retained their friendship with Sparta. To pay them out the Thebans laid a charge against them of cultivating lands consecrated to Apollo. For this a fine was imposed on the Phocians by the Council of the Amphictyonic League, which had been formed in very early times for the defence of the oracle and shrine of Apollo at Delphi.[1] There were twelve *tribes* confederated in the League, including the Phocians and Boeotians. Athens had a vote in the Council as representing the Ionians, Sparta as representing the Dorians. These ' tribes ' belonged to a state of society which had preceded the city-state and passed away ; and some of those represented in the Council of the League were now of very little account. Thebes exercised a vote for the Boeotians as Athens for the Ionians. The adverse vote against the Phocians had been doubtless ' worked ' by the Thebans and Thessalians out of their hereditary hatred, and the Phocians declined to pay. They cherished the memory of an early claim to the possession of Delphi, and now, goaded by Theban and Thessalian spite, they seized Delphi and the temple. Thereupon the Thebans and Thessalians persuaded the Council to proclaim a ' sacred war ' against them. The Phocians replied by seizing the temple treasure ; and before long their leaders were employing the wealth of the god to hire mercenaries. As long as the treasure lasted the Phocians more than held their own in the struggle. They had the sympathy, though not the armed support, of Sparta and Athens. In 347 the Thebans, tired of their ill-success, invited Philip to help them, blind to any ulterior consequences to themselves from such dangerous aid. About the same time the Athenians, exhausted by their own struggle with Philip, which had been going on since 354, were strongly

[1] See above, p. 83 *n.*

inclined to make peace. Philip wanted peace, too, and used his diplomatic skill, which was scarcely less than his mastery of war, to secure a peace which should leave him free to deal with the Phocians as he saw fit. Consequently before the year 346 was over Philip had marched unopposed through Thermopylae and awed or forced the Phocians to submission. The punishment meted out was that their cities were broken up into villages after the dismantling of their existing defences, and that for the repayment of the plundered treasure a huge indemnity was imposed, payable in a term of years. The place and vote of the Phocians in the Amphictyonic Council were declared forfeit, and conferred on Philip. When the Pythian Games were celebrated at Delphi in September, Philip acted as President.

Philip and the War with Persia.—The dominant feeling among the Athenians was that they had been cheated over the peace, deceived and betrayed by their own ambassadors acting in collusion with Philip. But many Hellenes, dazzled by Philip's personal brilliancy and successes, were willing to see in him the man of destiny and accept his leadership for Hellas. There were many in Athens who took this view. Nor was it altogether without reason. No one among the Greeks who observed and reflected could fail to be aware of the evils produced by the ceaseless conflicts of Greeks against Greeks (which were really civil war) and of the collective impotence which resulted from them. This almost continual state of civil war had ended in making the King of Persia, whose might had been broken in the glorious years from Salamis to the Eurymedon, arbiter of destiny to the Hellenic peoples. Throughout the last phase of the Peloponnesian war the king's fleet clearly held the balance between the contending confederacies. We have seen (p. 235) how Persian support had been bought by the Spartans at the price of the liberty of the Asiatic Greeks. After the victory of Sparta, desultory attempts were made by Agesilaus and other Spartan leaders to recover the seaboard where the Ionian and Dorian cities were planted.

But this new attempt to liberate the Asiatic Greeks was shortlived. In 387 the Great King, acting in concert with Sparta, imposed a peace on Hellas, the Peace of Antalcidas, which formally confirmed the King's dominion over all Asia Minor. Many Hellenes, however, felt the ignominy of such a peace and the scandal of the subjection of Hellenic cities to Persian satraps. There were those who talked and wrote of a new war with Persia, a war in which a united Hellas should retort upon the Persian Empire the invasion of 480 and many humiliations since. The old terror of the Persian name was long ago dead. The easy superiority of Greek men-at-arms to Asiatic troops had been demonstrated in many encounters. The campaigns of Agesilaus, though fruitless of permanent results, had revealed the weakness of the Persian Empire beneath an appearance of strength. Above all, the Greeks who had marched with Cyrus into the very heart of the Persian Empire and then, in defiance of the Great King's utmost efforts, fought their way back to the shore of the Black Sea, had shown that a compact body of Greek soldiers could do pretty much what they pleased, so long as they kept together with arms in their hands, however great the number of barbarian enemies who swarmed around them. To those who meditated these things it seemed preposterous that any Hellenes should be ruled by Persian satraps, when the superiority in arms of Greeks to barbarians was really so great.

Isocrates.—It was the lifelong mission of Isocrates to preach to all Hellenes the wisdom and the duty of laying aside the petty jealousies and enmities which had so long kept Hellas divided, and of uniting in a war of liberation and of conquest against the Persian Empire, now palpably too enfeebled to resist a resolute attack. At first he had hoped for union under the joint leadership of Sparta and Athens. This is the tenor of his most finished and perfect discourse, the Panegyric,[1] which

---

[1] Pan-egyric is an adjective formed from *pan-egyris*, which means a general gathering, *i.e.* a gathering of all Hellas ; and *a panegyric* is a speech delivered before such a national assemblage.

purports to be addressed to all the Hellenes assembled at Olympia for the festival of 380 B.C. The idea was far from novel—who that pondered the state of Hellas for the half century backward to 430, but must have seen the folly of the strife of Greeks against Greeks and have welcomed as an escape from it the project of a national war against Persia ? Lysias had advocated this in an Olympic address in 388, and Gorgias considerably earlier. But thirty years later, in the year of the Peace of Philocrates (346), Isocrates had come to despair of ever winning Thebes, Athens, Sparta, Argos, and the lesser city-states, to any voluntary union, and had turned instead to the hope of some personal sovereign, some prince of Hellenic stock, who might effectively take the lead and compel the Hellenes to follow him as their general-in-chief—to Jason of Pherae, Dionysius of Syracuse, and now, finally, with better promise to Philip. Accordingly, in 346 (the year of the Peace of Philocrates), when Isocrates was already ninety years of age, he addressed to Philip a sort of open letter, inviting, persuading, him in plain terms to take up this task of leading the whole confederate strength of Hellas against the Persian Empire. " It is my purpose," he says, expressly, early in this pamphlet, " to urge you to take the lead in promoting unity among the Hellenes and in conducting an expedition against the barbarians." [1] The objects of such an expedition he states quite frankly : " if possible to conquer the whole of the king's dominions, or, failing this, to detach large part of it, I mean all Asia west of a line drawn from Cilicia to Sinopê." [2]   He presses this undertaking on Philip as a duty, a mission to which he is called as a prince and a Heraclid, born ruler of a country beyond the bounds of Hellas, and so aloof from and above the traditional enmities and rivalries of the city-states. " You who by your birth are free of particular ties, it behoves," he writes, " to consider all Hellas as your fatherland . . . and to face danger on its behalf no less than on behalf of those who are your special concern." [3]   These are remarkable views for one who had

[1] *Philippus*, 16.   [2] *Philippus*, 120.   [3] *Philippus*, 127.

lived a retired life as thinker and student for three-quarters of a century, and who had no motive whatever to flatter Philip or mislead his fellow-countrymen. They are the views, too, of the man who had elaborated the art of writing persuasive speech (Isocrates never spoke in public) to a finish never approached before or since.[1]

National Party at Athens.—This was one possible view of Philip and his rise to power. In every Greek state there were men who were friendly to Philip's schemes ; some, like Isocrates, from honest conviction of the needs of the times ; some because they had met Philip and been attracted by his liberality, his manly frankness and his *bonhomie* ; others, again, because Philip made bribery as effective a means of accomplishing his purposes as weapons of war. But it was, to say the least of it, a difficult view for a patriotic Athenian, who had been brought up to regard her championship of Hellenic liberty as the peculiar glory of Athens, and her democratic institutions as the consummated expression of that liberty. There was, therefore, a strong national party at Athens opposed to the pretensions of Philip in the conviction that, not the Great King, but Philip, was now the enemy. Foremost among these was the statesman-orator Demosthenes, whose speeches are the most splendid monument of Attic oratory. It is Demosthenes' heroic struggle to nerve his countrymen to energetic action in face of the Macedonian danger, and his proud choice for Athens of resistance rather than tame submission out of keeping with her glorious past, which makes a chapter on Greek oratory worth while.

Demosthenes.—Demosthenes, the son of Demosthenes, of Paeania, was born in 384, three years after the Peace of Antalcidas. He was not, any more than Themistocles, of absolutely pure Athenian descent ; he had a grand-

[1] Isocrates is said to have devoted ten years to the composition of his *Panegyric*, a work filling some fifty ordinary octavo pages of modern print. He exercised extraordinary care in the avoidance of *hiatus*, that is, the juxtaposition of vowel sounds, one at the end of a word, the other at the beginning of the next. He also elaborated many subtle rules for the structure of the prose *period*.

mother who was a ' Scythian ' of the Tauric Chersonese.
This furnished his enemy, Aeschines, with a cheap taunt,
but does not appear otherwise to have affected his position
and influence. His father belonged to the commercial
class and possessed considerable wealth ; but died when
Demosthenes was seven years old, leaving to his two
children an ample fortune. Demosthenes, when he
reached manhood, should have been wealthy ; but his
guardians, two being cousins and the third his father's
dear friend, were unfaithful to their trust and cheated him.
With difficulty, and after wearisome litigation, Demosthenes recovered part of his patrimony ; but much was
wasted in the process. It was the necessity of fighting
for his rights in the law-courts which first led Demosthenes
to study the art of public speaking ; the need of supple-
menting narrow means which induced him afterwards to
adopt the writing of speeches for litigants as a profession.
Then something fired him with ambition ; he resolved to
become a public speaker in the Ecclesia. He had serious
difficulties to overcome, and curious stories are told of the
determined perseverance by which he overcame them.[1]
He was shy, awkward, and with a defect in his speech.
No aspirant to the honours of public speaking can well
have started with more against him. Of his shyness,
or rather nervousness, in later life a notable instance has
been recorded by Aeschines.[2] But something more than
ambition must have carried Demosthenes to the course
of action on which his fame mainly rests. He had a
profound belief in the greatness of Athens as the guardian
of Hellenic ideas and Hellenic freedom, and was imbued
with admiration for the part she had played during and
after the Persian War. These convictions he had drunk
in through his study of Greek history, more particularly
of Thucydides, the influence of whose ' speeches ' can be
traced in his own style.

[1] See Plutarch, *Demosthenes*, 6-8.

[2] Aeschines in his speech *On the Embassy*, describes Demosthenes as
breaking down completely when his turn (as one of ten ambassadors)
came to speak in presence of Philip.

Public Life and Speeches to 346 B.C.—It was in 354, when he was thirty years of age, that he first took part in a debate on public affairs : the object of his speech was to remedy existing abuses in the system of boards called ' symmories,' which at this time provided the state service, formerly discharged by the trierarchs. His first speech of general historic interest is the speech, delivered in 351, known as the First Philippic.[1] Philip was pushing his advance along the coast both eastward and to the south : he had taken Methonê in 354, Abdera and Maronea in 353. The war had been dragging on since 355 and only once had Philip been effectually checked. This was in 352 when he was marching on Thermopylae. At this threat of danger to the northern gates of Hellas, the Athenians for once acted with promptitude and vigour. They sent ample forces to reinforce the defence, and Philip withdrew baffled. In the year of Demosthenes' speech the Athenian Assembly was discussing the position of affairs and Demosthenes took the opportunity to press the necessity of measures to put the military and naval forces of Athens into better order. His scheme, which is carefully thought out in all details, is itself eloquent of the contrast between fifth and fourth century Athens. Demosthenes advocates the maintenance on a permanent war-footing of an expeditionary force of 2000 infantry and 200 cavalry, and, over and above a fleet of fifty ordinary warships, ten fast-sailing triremes for the safe convoy of the expeditionary force. He proposes, further, to make provision for the regular payment of the troops and of the ships' crews.[2] These points are so elementary that one can but marvel that such reforms should have been necessary. It is a measure of the decline of Athens in warlike spirit. Most of all eloquent is his insistence on the imperative need of personal service. Not less than 500 of the infantry and fifty of the

---

[1] It is the first of three speeches in which Demosthenes puts forth his utmost power to bring home to the Athenians what manner of enemy they have in Philip, and the measures necessary to meet the danger.

[2] *First Philippic,* 16-29.

horsemen must be native-born Athenians. *This* to the descendants in the second or third generation of the men who had hurried to man the fleet at every crisis in the Peloponnesian War. But now in 351, though Athens was wealthier than before, and not less populous, her citizens shirked personal service and preferred to get mercenaries to do their fighting. Only the generals in command were Athenians. The Athenian people did not even as a rule pay their mercenaries, but let them live on the war and, if that failed, from ' benevolences,' that is, forced contributions from their allies, justifying Demosthenes' taunt that Athenian armies had become a greater terror to her friends than to her enemies. Demosthenes contrasts Philip's energy and courage with Athenian remissness ; at the same time he assures them that if they will but rouse themselves, and resolve each man to do his part, they may even yet retrieve their fortunes : " God willing, you will get back what is your own, you will recover what has been lost by neglect and you will punish Philip." [1] After all Philip is but human and may be beaten : " There are those who hate him and fear him and envy him." [2] The Athenians show efficiency in the management of their state festivals, the Pana-thenaea, the Great Dionysia, why not, pleads Demos-thenes, in the conduct of a campaign. They must learn to plan beforehand and anticipate Philip's strokes. He compares Athenian methods of warfare to the movements of an inexpert boxer : " Hit him in one place, his arms move in the direction of the blow ; hit him in another and there go his hands. He neither can nor will parry in time or look his antagonist in the face." [3] His description shows the Athenians of the fourth century changed indeed from the Athenians who excited the fear and envy of the Corinthians in B.C. 431 [4] :—" Just in the same way, if you get intelligence that Philip is in the Chersonese, you vote an expedition to go there ; or if you hear of him as at Thermopylae, or in any other place, you run hither and

---

[1] *First Philippic*, 10.
[2] *First Philippic*, 11.
[3] *First Philippic*, 46.
[4] See Thucydides, **i**. 70. 1-9.

thither after him and let yourselves be led. You have never yourselves formed any sound plan for the war ; you show no foresight whatever, but wait till you hear that something has happened or is happening." [1] Demosthenes is, in fact, urging upon the Athenians the importance of the initiative in war. But it is a bold orator who speaks thus to the sovereign demos, less capable of decision and action than the demos whom Aristophanes burlesques in comedy, but not less masterful in his own house, not less potent to kill and to leave alive. Never was there a statesman who pointed out more plainly to his countrymen the path of duty, or insisted more uncompromisingly on unpleasant truths. "Indeed it is not by reason of his own strength that he is grown so great but by reason of your negligence." [2] "But when, I pray you, gentlemen, shall we resolve to do our duty ? " [3] Most of all he reiterates the supreme necessity of personal service : "Shall we not go on board ? Shall we not serve in some part in our own persons—now if never before ? " [4]

Nothing that Demosthenes so vehemently urged was done, with the result that Philip went on in his career unchecked. In 349 he was threatening Olynthus ; in 348 Olynthus and all the towns of her confederacy were destroyed. On three occasions Demosthenes made passionate appeal to the men of Athens to go to the rescue of Olynthus, while there was time. "When you consider all this, men of Athens, I say you must be resolved, you must kindle your zeal to the utmost and give your minds to the war, now if never before ; you must contribute eagerly, you must serve in your own persons, there must be nothing left undone." [5] The Athenians sent troops to Chalcidicê ; but the force was not constituted as Demosthenes counselled, nor was it properly paid. A better organized force, despatched when Olynthus was in the throes of her death-struggle, arrived too late. And so one

[1] *First Philippic*, 47. [2] *First Philippic*, 14.
[3] *On the Chersonese*, 52. [4] *First Philippic*, 50.
[5] *First Olynthiac*, 6.

more barrier between Athens and Macedonian aggression
was down.

Demosthenes and Aeschines.—In 346, as we have seen,
both Athens and Philip were tired of war and inclined to
peace. A peace was made, known as the Peace of Philocrates, but so badly managed for Athens that Philip
secured all the advantages, Athens nothing but the bare
cessation of hostilities. The Phocians, who were virtually,
though not technically, in alliance with Athens, were
sacrificed, with the result that Philip now slipped through
the barrier of Thermopylae and appeared with an army in
territories separated from Athens only by the breadth of
Boeotia, territories at the time unfriendly to Athens.
Demosthenes had been in favour of peace, and had been
one of an embassy of ten who negotiated it, but for the
disastrous character of the peace actually made, he blamed
two of his colleagues on the embassy—Philocrates, after
whom the peace was named, and Aeschines, who lives in
history as Demosthenes' antagonist in two famous trials.
Philocrates went into exile rather than face a trial on a
charge of betraying the interests of his country, and was
condemned to death in his absence : Aeschines was
prosecuted by Demosthenes on a similar charge. The
business of the embassies is far too tangled to be entered
upon here ; we must be content only to note that in 343
the case against Aeschines was tried and that he escaped
condemnation by a small majority. The speeches of the
two eloquent rivals, Demosthenes and Aeschines (for
Aeschines too was no mean orator), remain for us to read
to-day and make one of the most interesting state trials
on record. The other and still more interesting trial came
on thirteen years later, and then the rôles were reversed.
Aeschines was now the accuser and Demosthenes on his
defence, though, technically, the defendant was Ctesiphon.
The charge was a graphê paranomôn, based on alleged
illegalities in Ctesiphon's proposal (B.C. 336) that a crown
of honour should be conferred on Demosthenes for his
services to his country ; but really it was the whole
policy and career of Demosthenes which was on trial, and

all Athens knew it. It was a duel between two public men, one of whom had taken sides with Philip and the other opposed him steadily. It is a state trial comparable in interest and significance with the trial of John Hampden before the Star Chamber, or of Warren Hastings in Westminster Hall, when principles were arraigned and judged rather than men. For six years Aeschines did not venture to follow up his indictment of Ctesiphon ; but in 330, when Alexander had begun his career of conquest in Asia and Macedonian power was dominant throughout Greece, he thought his opportunity had come. The verdict of the Athenian judges was clear and decisive. Aeschines failed to obtain the fifth part of the votes and thereby became liable to heavy penalties for bringing a frivolous charge, and rather than pay the fine he went into exile for the rest of his days.

Yet the policy which the Athenians thus deliberately ratified with their approval many years after the event had brought on Greece the disaster of Chaeronea. The cause in which Demosthenes spent the strength of his eloquence, the maintenance of the independent life of the Hellenic city-state in face of the expanding power of the Macedonian kingdom, had ended in defeat and humiliation : he himself in the end was to pay the last price of resistance.[1] It might seem that there was nothing but a tragic futility in the story of the most famous of Athenian orators. For long years Demosthenes appears to be engaged in the heart-breaking task of repeating convincing arguments in the ears of men perfectly able to appreciate them intellectually, but too comfortably sunk in the refined ease of fourth century Athens, or too wanting in will-power to turn conviction into action. His effort seems to exhaust itself in words. Yet there was one short period of two years, from a little after the delivery of the Third Philippic (341 B.C.), during which Demosthenes wielded a commanding influence at Athens and

[1] This was not till the year after Alexander's death, and was by command of Antipater, Alexander's viceroy in Europe. See Plutarch's *Life of Demosthenes.*

was a leader of men worthy of the days of Athenian greatness.

Demosthenes and Philip.—Philip's aggrandisement did not cease with the Peace of Philocrates, but rather received a new impetus. Demosthenes in his speeches reiterates the conviction that hostilities were really renewed by Philip "from the very day on which he annihilated the Phocians." Steadily his army continued to advance along the coast of Thrace, threatening the Thracian Chersonese and the Bosphorus. When news came that Philip was attacking Perinthus and Selymbria, Greek cities on the Propontis within a short distance of Byzantium, the Athenians became suddenly alive to the nearness of the peril that again hung over them. If Philip gained command of the Bosphorus, Athens was at his mercy ; for, as we have so often noticed, that way came her corn. So the Ecclesia was roused at last and listened to Demosthenes. It was by his advice that an expedition, under Phocion, was sent to Euboea to checkmate Mace donian influence there. Demosthenes himself went on a mission to Byzantium and brought the jealous rival city into close alliance with Athens. Then came open war, and a Macedonian attack on Byzantium : but Philip in 340 was completely foiled ; after prodigious effort and the use of every device known to his engineers he had to abandon the sieges of both Perinthus and Byzantium. Golden crowns were voted to Athens in token of gratitude by these two cities and by the cities of the Chersonese. Demosthenes was the hero of the hour. In 339, again, the event of war went against Philip. This time he led his army with daring and success northward as far as to the Danube, reducing one warlike tribe after another, but was attacked in the Balkans on the way back by the Triballi and badly wounded. Meantime, at Athens, Demosthenes at last carried the reform in the working of the trierarchic system, which he had proposed vainly in 354. Its object was to ensure that the wealthy shouldered a fair share of the burden by contributing in proportion to their wealth.

The measure, therefore, had to be carried in face of the opposition of powerful vested interests. The effect was marked improvement in efficiency. Demosthenes was able afterwards to claim that during the two years, from 340 to Chaeronea, not a single ship was lost at sea, or kept from sailing through defective equipment. How long this success might have continued, and how far it would have gone to change the current of history, who shall venture to say ? The more hopeful prospect for Athens was ruined by an incident, trifling in its origin, but momentous in its consequences, which took place at Delphi in the autumn of 339.

Aeschines at Delphi.—The story is more like romance than sober history. It happened that at the spring meeting of the Delphic Amphictyony the Locrians of Amphissa, to gratify their friends the Thebans, charged the Athenians with an offence against religion,[1] and sought to get a heavy fine imposed as punishment. When Aeschines, who was one of four officers [2] representing Athens on the Council, attempted to reply, he was interrupted by a speaker from Amphissa, who roundly denounced the people of Athens as unfit to be represented on the Council of the Amphictyons at all. Aeschines himself provides the account of what followed. He describes himself as extremely angry : " I was never so incensed in my life," he says.[3] From where he stood he could look down over the valley of the Pleistus and see the plain of Cirrha (the port of Crissa) and the harbour itself beyond.[4] We may see the same view from the steeps of Delphi to-day. And he remembered the curse pronounced on this stretch of land after the early sacred war of Solon's time, on those who should ever cultivate the land again, or rebuild the harbour ; on those also who

---

[1] They were charged with replacing the shields dedicated as spoils of war after Plataea, before the temple itself had been reconsecrated on its restoration. The restoration had been necessary in consequence of damage done by fire in 373 B.C.

[2] A Hieromnemon and three Pylagori : Aeschines was one of the Pylagori.

[3] Aeschines, against Ctesiphon, 118.   [4] See I. p. 214 n.

THE VALLEY OF THE PLEISTUS.

As seen from Delphi.

From a photograph by the English Photographic Company, Athens,

failed to punish the authors of any such sacrilege. He pointed all this out to the Amphictyons ; he read to them the words of the oracle spoken from Delphi, of the oath of the Council, and of the curse. Aeschines was master of a readier eloquence than Demosthenes, and he was angry. He spoke with such passion that the Amphictyons —men unused, as Demosthenes says, to oratory of a finished kind—were swept off their feet. Soon there was excitement and uproar in all Delphi, and next morning, in obedience to a proclamation made overnight, the whole male population of full age, slaves and free men alike, marched down in a tumultuous body into the plain below Delphi, armed with picks and shovels, and there proceeded to demolish the little harbour of Cirrha and burn down the houses about it. This work of destruction accomplished in the name of religion, the Delphians set off homeward. On the way back they were attacked by the men of Amphissa, who sallied out under arms when they heard what was afoot, overtook the aggressors, and chased them back to Delphi. This act of the Amphissaeans was naturally represented by their enemies as an aggravation of their guilt and the result was the proclamation of a ' sacred war.' Nothing more was heard of the supposed offence of the Athenians. Aeschines might naturally enough plume himself on the efficacy of his counter-stroke for Athens.

Elatea and the Judgment of the Sword.—But there were other effects he had not thought of. Demosthenes himself believed that Aeschines was deliberately playing into Philip's hands. At any rate, his action opened to Philip the way to a new interposition in Hellenic affairs, which once and for all ended Greek political independence. For the Amphictyonic Council, when they found the execution of judgment on the Amphissaeans by force of arms too difficult for them, adopted the convenient expedient of calling in Philip to fight for them. Philip responded with alacrity ; it was again the very opportunity he had been waiting for. On receiving this invitation from the League, he at once set his troops in motion and marched from Lamia into Phocis. Thence, instead of going straight on through what is now the Pass of Gravia to Amphissa, his supposed objective, he turned aside and occupied Elatea, one of the strong places of Phocis before its fortifications were destroyed and its people scattered in 346. What his intentions were cannot be known with certainty, but this action excited the greatest alarm at Athens, which at the time, it must be remembered, was at war with him. Elatea did not lead to Amphissa ; but it was on the direct route into Attica through Boeotia. Demosthenes in his speech ' On the Crown ' gives a vivid description of the panic at Athens when Philip's presence at Elatea became known. " It was evening, you remember, when the news came to the Prytanes that Elatea had been occupied. They were at supper, but rose at once, some to turn the shopmen out of their booths in the market-place and make a bon-fire of the wicker materials ; some to send word to the generals and summon the trumpeter. The whole city was in commotion. Next morning at daylight the Prytanes summoned the Council to the Council Chamber, while you took your way to the Assembly : the whole people was seated on the slope of the hill before the Council had finished its business and passed a draft resolution. And after this when the Council came and reported the news that had been received, and had brought the messenger in, and when he had made his statement, the herald proceeded to put the question, ' Who wishes to speak ? ' [1] No one, however, came forward ; and though the officer put the question several times, there was still no response." Demosthenes goes on to relate how he alone that day showed the qualities of a statesman, and took upon himself the responsibility of directing affairs at this crisis. It was at his suggestion and through his influence, that overtures were made to Thebes and an alliance, offensive and defensive, eventually concluded, in spite of the ancient enmity between the two peoples ; that this alliance was strengthened by the adhesion to it of the Euboeans,

[1] Demosthenes, *On the Crown,* 169.

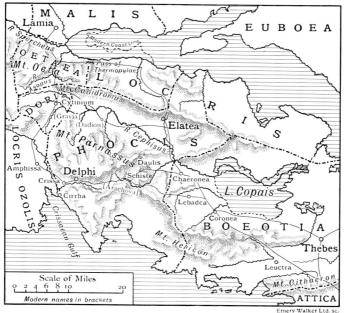

Emery Walker Ltd. sc.

Map to illustrate PHILIP'S MARCH TO ELATEA IN 339 B.C.,

showing alternative routes (1) by Thermopylae ; (2) through Cytinium
and Dadion (line of the modern road).

Acarnanians, Achaeans, of Corcyra, Leucas and Megara ; that Philip's advance was checked in the winter of 339, and that in the spring of 338 a powerful Hellenic army confronted Philip at Chaeronea. The citizen forces of Thebes and Athens fought bravely, but they were scarcely a match for Philip's veteran army ; and they had no leader of even moderate ability, whereas Philip was master of the art of war and had with him in command of one wing the son who was to be famous as a conqueror through Europe and Asia. A charge of horsemen, led by Alexander in person, broke the stubborn defence of the Thebans ; the Athenians were drawn on by a feigned retreat, then counter-attacked and routed. Demosthenes' policy had ended in disaster.

Chaeronea—The price in immediate physical suffering, indeed, was paid by Thebes, not Athens. The Theban prisoners were sold into slavery, the Theban patriots were punished with confiscation, exile and death. A Macedonian garrison occupied the Cadmeia. Athens was admitted to terms and the terms granted by Philip were generous. Her 2000 prisoners were restored without ransom ; the bones of her slain were brought back to the city with military honours. The Chersonese was at last lost to her and her confederacy was finally dissolved, but even so she was allowed to keep possession of Delos, Lemnos, Imbros, Scyros and Samos. Her great name had saved her from destruction in 404 ; and now in 338 (and again three years later on a fresh appeal to arms after Philip's death) her primacy in arts and literature protected her and her degenerate people from the consequences of defeat. Thebes in 335 was so utterly blotted out that Aeschines in his speech *On the Crown* shrinks from even speaking her name, saying only, " I pray that misfortune like to hers may not come upon any city of the Hellenes " ; Athens was spared by Alexander, as she was spared by Philip, his father. It was policy, no doubt, in part : Athens was the intellectual capital of Hellas, and Philip's aspiration, and Alexander's after him, was to be not only master of Hellenic military strength, but also the enlightened propagator of Hellenic culture. Yet in the verdict of posterity, over against Demosthenes' denunciation of the Macedonian ' barbarians,' must be set this gentleness and generosity towards ' the mother of arts and eloquence.'

There is no need to refuse admiration to Philip's great qualities because we sympathize (if we do) with Demosthenes. Yet it is with good reason that Chaeronea has been graven on the tablets of history as the death-blow of Hellenic liberty. For after Chaeronea there was no more political liberty in Hellas as we and the fifth-century Hellenes understand it. If we look into the matter a little deeply, we see that in essence the issue between Demosthenes and Philip, Athens and Macedonia, was again the conflict between free institutions and autocracy.[1] The Greek city-states, it is true, through their narrow self-concentration and their inability to find any principle of free, but stable, union ; and through the bitter feuds by which their strength was exhausted, had by this time proved the insufficiency of the ideal of a nation of autonomous city-states. In Athens the Athenians of Demosthenes' day had so fallen away from their earlier standard of courage, energy, and devotion, as to seem hardly worth the saving ; the Macedonian monarch professed to adopt Hellenic culture, and carried this culture with him, when he set out on a career of conquest in Asia.[2] Yet in essence the issue fought out at Chaeronea was the issue of Marathon and Salamis—autocracy versus free institutions—and this time autocracy won. The empire which Alexander conquered in twelve astonishing years with the weapons made ready by his father Philip, was almost as much a despotism as the Persian. The real issue was scarcely revealed while Alexander lived, but only in the dynasties which fought over and broke up the

[1] Compare vol. i. pp. 390-93.

[2] Professor Jebb writes (*Attic Orators*, vol. ii. p. 439): " Philip, Alexander and their Successors were indeed the apostles of Greek language, Greek art, Greek social civilisation : but between Hellas and Hellenism there was a spiritual separation which no force of the individual mind could do away."

dominion his genius created. What the victory of Macedonia meant for Athens is not seen in 338, or even in 335 : it is seen rather when, in 307, Demetrius Poliorcetes entered Athens to be worshipped there as a god, and to pollute the temple of Athena Polias with his debaucheries. Milton judged rightly when he called Chaeronea ' that dishonest victory.'

Even looking to the larger world-issues it is by no means clear that the Athenians were wrong to resist Philip rather than accept with complacency his proffered favours and lend their good-will and the great name of Athens to the support of his designs. The history of Syria under the Seleucids, of Egypt under the Ptolemies, of Macedonia under the House of Antigonus, is for the most part sorry reading. But on the narrower ground of what was due to their own self-respect as inheritors of the traditions of Athenian statesmanship, without doubt the Athenians were right when they listened to Demosthenes and made a last great effort to maintain the real freedom of their institutions. That Demosthenes had the will and the ability so to persuade them was, notwithstanding the adverse verdict of Chaeronea, a noble achievement worthy the Athens of Themistocles and Pericles. Demosthenes' own words get nearest to the ultimate truth : " Even if the issue had been manifest to all beforehand, if all the world had known what it must be . . . even then I say our city should not have turned from the course she followed—not if she was to take account of her fame, of our forefathers, and of future ages." [1] " But it is not possible, it is not possible that you were wrong, men of Athens, when you chose to risk everything for the freedom and safety of all." [2]

[1] Demosthenes, *On the Crown*, 199.

[2] Demosthenes, *On the Crown*, 208.

CHAPTER XIV

GREEK DRAMA

1. A TRAGIC TRILOGY IN FIFTH CENTURY ATHENS

"Not so I deem, though sole I stand : it is the impious deed
That sin on sin begetteth, like children of ill breed."

AESCHYLUS, *Agamemnon*, ll. 757-60.

"The soul that sinneth, *it* shall die."

Ezekiel, 18, 20.

GREEK drama is almost wholly Attic, the peculiar glory of
Athens ; yet it ultimately became a possession in which
all Hellenes took pride and delight. A thousand years
later in the world's history, through imitation and inspiration, it gave impulse to the unfolding of the modern drama
in all its forms. Our part in it is twofold. One part
is independent of our own volition. Whether we are
interested or not, the drama of our own times derives from
the Greek.[1] The other depends on ourselves. If we take a
little trouble, the forty-four surviving dramas of the
Greek theatre may be to us a source of high and noble
pleasure.

Unlikeness of Greek to Modern Plays.—People reading
a Greek play for the first time in an English translation
are apt to be repelled by a certain high-strung artificiality
in the language, and what seems a crude simplicity of
plot and action. And certainly, if, uncritically, we
apply modern standards of judgment, the verdict is likely
to be unfavourable. In important respects a Greek play
is very unlike a modern play, in spite of the historic

[1] See vol. i. pp. 10 and 11.

continuity which can be traced between them. Before we are in a position to appreciate a Greek play justly, we must take account of the differences. The greatest difference of all is that the performance of a Greek play was not primarily a means of amusement, or even a form of artistic expression. It was first and foremost an act of religion.

Dramatic Contests at Athens.—It was at Athens that tragedies and comedies were developed into literary drama, and at Athens new plays, both tragedies and comedies were written for dramatic competitions which were incidental to the festivals of Dionysus. Both were produced at one or other of two great festivals, and especially at the Great Dionysia held at Athens in the early spring.[1] In the Great Dionysia there were contests of rival choirs, choirs of men and choirs of boys ; and there were contests between poets who wrote tragedies and poets who wrote comedies. It was not, however, open to any citizen who thought himself competent to write plays to enter for these great public competitions. Every year a preliminary trial was held by the archons, and three poets, and three only, were chosen to compete for the prize in tragedy ; and three in comedy. This at least was the practice in the fifth century.[2] And in tragedy the demand on the poet's genius was peculiarly exacting. Each of the three competitors was required to produce not one play, but four—three tragedies and a burlesque after-piece called a satyric drama. These sets of three tragedies and a satyric drama came to be known in certain cases as tetralogies ; and the three tragedies as a trilogy or set of three. The subjects of the four plays

---

[1] The other Dionysiac festival at which dramas (especially comedies) were produced was the *Lenaea*. This came two months earlier in the year (as we reckon it), in January. The *Lenaea*, the winter festival, was the vintage thanksgiving and a time of jollity and license. The *Great Dionysia* was the spring festival, the festival of the renewing of life. And these festivals at Athens were but special examples of vintage feasts celebrated in the villages of Attica (*Rural Dionysia*), and throughout all Greece.

[2] Later, in the fourth century, there were *five* comedies.

might be connected, but were not necessarily so. The
four plays might be, and were more often, if we may
judge from the information that has come down to us,
independent in subject. But when three tragedies were
connected, dealing with successive episodes in the history
of one of the great legendary families, the House of
Labdacus, or the House of Atreus, we manifestly reach a
highly complex and massive form of art. And this was
a *trilogy*. If the satyric drama also bore upon the
same general subject the four connected plays were a
tetralogy.

Aeschylus' Oresteia.—It happens that among the thirty-
three Greek tragedies that survive, we possess three
which make a trilogy, Aeschylus' *Agamemnon*, *Choephoroe* [1]
and *Eumenides*, together forming an Oresteia, or story of
Orestes. This is the one surviving example of such an
associated group of plays, the tragic trilogy, in which
Greek drama culminates, and has, therefore, peculiar
interest. We know, too, the year, and the circumstances
in which these plays were produced, and perhaps no
better way is open to us of reaching some apprehension of
what Greek drama at its height was, and was not, than
to outline briefly the action of this Aeschylean trilogy.
Such accordingly will be the method of this chapter.

The Great Dionysia, 458 B.C.—It was the year 458 B.C.,
the year following what we have called (p. 39 above) ' the
annus mirabilis ' of Athenian imperial expansion when in
distant Egypt Memphis became the prize of Athenian
arms ; and at home the Peloponnesians were defeated in
the Saronic Gulf, Naupactus was garrisoned for Athens
by the exiles from Ithomê, and Megara became an Athenian stronghold commanding the Isthmus. In 458 the
war with Aegina was going on : the Aeginetans were
defeated at sea, while on land Myronides gained his two
famous victories with his army of middle-aged men and
youths, and the *Long Walls* of Athens had been begun.
These years were the climax of the external fortunes of
Athens, when the consciousness of her imperial mission

---

[1] Choe-phoroe means ' Libation-bearers.'

was at its height. It was shortly after the great crisis in her internal history, as a result of which the Council of the Areopagus was shorn of its ancient power and of much of its remaining prestige. Cimon had been ostracized in 461 ; and the long period of Pericles' predominance had begun. In 460 Athens had entered into close alliance with Argos. All these events have significance in relation to the Oresteia.

The Great, or City, Dionysia took place from the 11th to the 15th Elaphebolion, that is approximately the last days of March and the first days of April, when the Athenian year is at its best. On the first day there was a procession through the streets of Athens in which many of the citizens and their wives and daughters took part. This procession partook somewhat of the nature of a carnival and the crowd was in sportive mood : many wore the disguise of Satyrs and Sileni.[1] On three of the other days the people crowded to the Theatre of Dionysus to see the plays exhibited in the dramatic contests. The theatre, though not in important particulars the theatre of which we visit the remains to-day, was in the same position under the south-east cliff of the Acropolis ; and some, if not all, of the rows of stone seats still to be seen there, were there in 458 B.C., not, however, either the marble chairs of the magistrates nor the throne of the Priest of Dionysus. The crowd came early ; for the four plays had to be got through with daylight enough left for a comedy in the late afternoon. The crowd that filled the spacious auditorium was mostly men, and the men were, in the main, full-grown citizens of Athens ; but there were a few women—in a block specially reserved for them—many resident aliens (metics), and a good number of foreign visitors ; even slaves were admitted by special favour. The whole number of persons present

[1] *Sileni* were the attendants of Dionysus in Ionian mythology, *Satyrs* in Dorian. Sileni had horses' ears and hoofs and tails ; Satyrs were like goats. But in the course of the fifth century B.C. the Attic conception of Dionysus' attendants came under Dorian influences and the result was some confusion and compromise. See Flickinger, *The Greek Theater and its Drama*, p. 16.

did not fall far short of 20,000.[1] They were close-packed, without any division between seat and seat ; the seats rose, tier above tier, up to where once was the Choregic Monument of Thrasyllus, and where the Chapel of our Lady of the Cavern now is. The noise, as the crowd surged to their places, was like the roar of the distant sea. The auditorium of the Theatre of Dionysus at Athens is in shape two-thirds of a great circle. On the ground level was the *orchestra*, the dancing-ground of the original singers of the goat-song,[2] from which the literary drama took its origin. Beyond a passage (called the *parodos*) which cut one segment from the full circle of which the seats took up two-thirds, was a wooden building extending nearly the whole length of the chord : and the front of this building was hung with painted canvas representing scenery. On this day of the Feast of Dionysus in 458 B.C. the scene represents the façade of a stately building soon to be recognized as the Palace of Agamemnon. This was not designed, as it would be now, with any eye to archaeological accuracy. The Athenians were too much occupied in building up their empire and in making new experiments of the possibilities of human achievement in drama and in architecture and the plastic arts, to trouble about the proper construction of a Mycenaean fortress-palace. The building facing the audience was more like a temple of the fifth century than a palace at Tiryns or Mycenae. There were Doric columns supporting an architrave and pediment ; in the front of the building were three doors ; a wide and lofty central door (after the fashion of the great double doors afterwards built for the Propylaea and the Erechtheum), and a smaller door on either side, right and left. In front of the central door was a small altar ; in the spaces between the doors

---

[1] The number of spectators in the Theatre is more than once referred to as 30,000 ; careful calculation in modern times makes the seating capacity of the auditorium 17,000.

[2] *Tragos* is a he-goat, and the word tragedy is formed by the combination of 'tragos' with 'ôdê,' song or ode. If we can find out what the goat-song in Attica was, or who were the goat-singers, we are obviously on the way to discover the origin of Greek tragedy.

stood images of Zeus, Apollo, Hermes, and other gods. Three steps lead up to the palace : for the rest the " stage " is on the level of the orchestra.

The Agamemnon in outline.—Presently a trumpet-blast sounds and a herald comes forward and proclaims : " A play of Aeschylus, the Agamemnon."

A figure is seen on the parapet which runs as a narrow ledge along the top of the palace-front, the figure of a man in the dress and armour of an Homeric warrior. He paces up and down the parapet ; then comes to a stand and begins to speak. He tells of the tediousness of a night-watch he has now kept for a twelve-month at the bidding of the queen-regent, looking south-eastward across the plain of Argolis for a beacon-light which should flare on the great mountains, and signal to him the fall of Troy. He complains, as he resumes his slow patrol, that his life has been no better than a dog's ; then he stops again, and after gazing fixedly to the left, breaks suddenly into a shout :

> " Oh welcome, welcome light ! Thou blaze that bringest
> A day-dawn in deep night. How many a dance
> In Argos shall be ordered for thy sake ! "

He calls on the queen to welcome the glad tidings ; and soon an answering shout comes from within the palace, the women's exultant outcry.[1] But even in the midst of his own rejoicings at the new hope of the homecoming of his lord, the watchman hints darkly that all is not well in Argos itself : there is something of which he dare not openly speak. The audience know well what it is. For the queen is Clytaemnestra, wife of Agamemnon, king of men ; and she has betrayed her husband in his absence

---

[1] Mr. J. T. Sheppard develops very skilfully the dramatic significance of this triumphant cry—the Greek word is ' ololugmos ' (see also ll. 587, 1236 and 1394). In the *Choephoroe* and in the *Eumenides* analogous use is made of a cry ; in the one case the queen's cry of terror in the night, in the other the priestess's cry of alarm from within the temple. See Mr. Sheppard's study, " The Prelude of the Agamemnon " in the *Classical Review* for February-March, 1922, a miracle of keen-eyed and illuminating criticism.

and taken for her lover his kinsman and sworn enemy, Aegisthus. This she has done, not from lightmindedness, as Helen, her sister, betrayed Menelaus, but because of the deep hatred she has cherished in her heart on account of the sacrifice of her beloved daughter, Iphigeneia.[1] By a trick Iphigeneia was lured from her side and ruthlessly put to death for the sake of her father's ambition ; and in league with Aegisthus, who had his own discontents to avenge, she has vowed to lie in wait for her husband whenever he shall return from Ilium, and slay him without pity, as without pity Iphigeneia was slain at Aulis.

The Watchman withdraws into the palace. Signs of movement at once begin to appear ; lights are shown ; attendants come hurriedly out by twos and threes ; they hang garlands on the doors and pillars and images, and are busied in various ways which the Athenians would recognize as the preliminaries of sacrifice. A chant of men's voices is heard and a band of old men, Argive Councillors, who form the *Chorus* of this play, come marching in. Their chant is of the flight of Helen and the weary ten years' war ; of the weakness of age which has kept them useless at Argos while the fighting-men are all away at Troy. As they sing, Clytaemnestra the queen glides in and is seen taking part in the preparations. The old men question her of the meaning of what is going on, but she takes no notice, and passes out as silently as she came in. The choral ode then takes a more impassioned tone (we must here call in the analogy of opera ; for great part of a Greek play, all the parts which, like this, are choral odes, are sung to a musical accompaniment).[2]   It is now of the fateful augury of Calchas when the fleet was assembled at Aulis ; of the anger of Artemis and the terrible means of relief announced by the prophet. The father's awful conflict of mind, when faced with the dread alternative of the ruin of his warlike plans and the

[1] See vol. i. p. 78.

[2] Professor Blackie plainly contends (*The Lyrical Dramas of Aeschylus*, p. xlvi.) that the proper designation of the dramas of Aeschylus is " Sacred Opera, and not Tragedy." All would admit the analogy.

sacrifice of his daughter, is feelingly depicted : " Sore is
the doom, if I obey not ; yet sore, if I shall slay my child,
the light of my home, sore if the father's hand must be
stained with the maiden's life-blood ! Yet how can I
wrong the chieftains, my allies, by keeping the fleet at
stay. Needs must be that of right they vehemently crave
this sacrifice, if the shedding of the maiden's blood will
free the winds. 'Twere better *so*." [1] The whole bitter
story—the ruthlessness of the chiefs, the girl's pitiful
pleadings for life, the dreadful scene at the altar—is told
to the point when the knife is about to fall : " what
happened after that I saw not, and I will not tell," they
cry. But these old counsellors make it clear that in their
judgment (as in ours) the sacrifice of Iphigeneia was a
sinful act, which may yet bring retribution on the per-
petrator. At this point Clytaemnestra enters again and
makes known the meaning of the preparations which
have excited the wonder of the Council. Troy has fallen !
When, half incredulous, the old men ask for proof, the
queen describes with vivid imagery how the news has been
flashed from Mount Ida to Lemnos, from Lemnos to the
summit of Athos, from Athos to Mount Macistus in
Euboea, from Euboea to Cithaeron, from Cithaeron to the
Arachnaean heights which overlook the plain of Argos.
It was the blaze on Mount Arachnê which the watchman
had seen. All this had happened on the night which has
just ended.

Clytaemnestra withdraws again ; and the Chorus
break into reflections on the justice of the doom which has
fallen on Troy in expiation of the sin of Paris. [2] This leads
them to thoughts of the losses suffered by the Argive
host through the long years of warfare, and of the discontent which has smouldered among the people, who feel

---

[1] *Agamemnon*, ll. 206-216.

[2] In this Chorus there is a singularly beautiful passage describing
Menelaus and Menelaus' empty halls after Helen had fled and left
them desolate, lines 410 to 426 (I quote R. C. Trevelyan's translation) :

" Ah home of woe ! Home and woeful princes, wail !
Ah woeful bed, printed yet with love's embrace !
Behold the spouse ! Bowed with shame, there he sits apart

that their cruel bereavements have been incurred ' for another man's wife.'

A new turn is given to the scene when the Chorus descry the approach of a man dressed in herald's garb and carrying branches of olive in his hand. As he draws near, his war-worn aspect shows that he is from the absent Achaean host. He is seen to throw himself on his knees in ecstasy of joy at once more reaching his native city. He venerates in turn the images of Zeus, Apollo and Hermes, which stand before the palace. Lastly he salutes the palace itself and its altars ; then proclaims to his countrymen the victorious homecoming of Agamemnon. Troy has fallen ; the rape of Helen has been avenged in bloodshed and ruin. He describes the hardships suffered by the Achaean soldiery on shipboard and camped in the open near the enemy walls, exposed to burning heat in summer, to cold blasts from Mount Ida in the winter. Clytaemnestra now reappears to glory in this confirmation of her own belief in the beacon message, and protest the rectitude of her conduct as wife and queen during Agamemnon's absence. An enquiry about the safety of Menelaus draws from the herald the further news that disaster has overtaken the returning Greeks ; Menelaus and his squadron have completely disappeared ; the fleet of Agamemnon has suffered shipwreck except only the one ship in which the king and his companions have reached the Argive land. On hearing these disastrous tidings the Chorus return to the theme of Helen and

> In silent unreviling grief.
> For her beyond seas he yearns :
> Pined with dreams sits he, a sceptred phantom.
>
> > Hateful now to his mood seems
> > The grace of loveliest statues.
> > Lost the light of her eyes, and lost
> > Now that love they enkindled.
>
> Anon there come dream-revealed semblances,
> Beguiling shapes.   Brief the joy, vain the sweet delusion.
> For vainly, when he seems to view the phantom bliss,
> Between his arms, lo ! the vision is flown
> And vanishes away beyond recall
> On shadowy wings down the paths of slumber."

the curse she has proved to Greeks and Trojans alike. They see here proof of the moral governance of the world : it is not, as the ancients thought, divine jealousy which brings calamity on the prosperous, but sin : " 'tis the impious deed which breeds increase of evil, producing ever its like." [1]

All at once in the midst of this moralizing the Chorus change their song to a chant of loyal welcome, as they see the king's slender company approaching, a poor remnant of warriors from the storm-tossed fleet. [2] They hail Agamemnon conqueror, and at the same time warn him that all in Argos are not faithful. Agamemnon speaks in reply from the chariot in which he is riding, first with words of gratitude to his country's gods for victory and safe return : he sees in the destruction of Troy the manifest hand of heaven. It shall be his task now, in concert with his Council, to take measures for the remedying of what is amiss at home. While he is speaking Clytaemnestra comes in followed by a train of her women, with concealed dread and sullen anger in her eyes and words of fulsome welcome on her lips. She stands by the chariot and boldly protests her wifely fidelity ; she makes a long story of the unhappy plight of the faithful wife racked with agonies of apprehension through the false reports that come one after another from abroad, haunted by lurking fear of disaffection at home. It is because of

[1] Lines 750-771.

[2] Of course, if the beacon-light signalling the fall of Troy was seen by the Watchman only the night before, it is physically impossible for Agamemnon and his ship's company to be arriving at the palace *now*, which is next morning. An interval of several days is required for the sacking of Troy, the division of the booty, the embarkation, and the voyage across the Aegean. Yet probably, in their absorption in the action of the play, the spectators were not conscious of any incongruity. Accordingly neither Dr. Verrall's attractively ingenious suggestion that the beacon-watch was a trick, a means devised by Clytaemnestra and Aegisthus for getting early warning of the king's approach, nor Dr. Headlam's supposition (accepted by Professor Gilbert Murray) of a break at l. 487, a little before the arrival of the Herald, is necessary. Similar inconsistencies are found in Shakespeare's plays—for instance in the *Merchant of Venice*—and are explained by the theory of " double time," a real time, and a dramatic. Anyone interested in this problem should see also E. S. Hoernle's *Problem of the Agamemnon*, Blackwell, 1921.

the fear of domestic sedition that her young son, Orestes, is not with her, but away in Phocis, in the care of his kinsman, Strophius. She invites Agamemnon to enter the palace and with mock flattery declares that his conquering foot must not touch the base earth. At the same time she bids her women spread purple robes on the ground before the palace. Agamemnon accepts the queen's protestations with a cold sarcasm which shows he does not trust her. From her proposal to strew royal purple under his feet he recoils as from an insolent tempting of Providence. Such honours are for the gods alone. He is not an Asiatic despot. Clytaemnestra combats his reluctance with a cunning mixture of persuasion and simulated scorn ; and Agamemnon in spite of his suspicions and scruples suffers himself to be persuaded. Yet, to deprecate the nemesis that waits on arrogance, he first orders his sandals to be removed. Then commending to Clytaemnestra's care his prize of war, the captive princess Cassandra, he descends from his chariot and passes over the purple carpet to his doom.

We here notice that a second chariot follows Agamemnon's and in it Cassandra is standing dressed in the robe and fillet which mark her priestess of Apollo.

The choral ode which follows expresses the uneasy feelings of the Councillors, who dread they know not what. Cassandra meanwhile remains in the chariot still and silent. Now Clytaemnestra comes out, and with insulting tone and gesture orders Cassandra in. When the captive prophetess takes no notice, and does not even seem to hear, she loses patience and withdraws in anger. The leader of the Chorus gently lays a pitying hand upon the stricken woman to waken her from her trance. All at once Cassandra's lips move, and at the sounds that come from them a shiver of horror runs over the theatre : most of all because of what the audience know. For Cassandra is that unhappy daughter of Priam loved by Apollo to her undoing : to win her love the god gave her the gift of prophecy, and angered at her denial of the love promised, he laid on her the doom never to be believed.

Now through her prophetic insight she sees with terrible distinctness the murders being prepared within the palace. With sharp cries and bodily shudderings, little by little, she makes known to the frightened Councillors her own vision—first as a vague horror, then more and more distinctly. She proves to them her credibility by her uncanny knowledge of dark horrors transacted within that house a generation earlier.[1] At length in plain terms she describes the murder of Agamemnon by Clytaemnestra, ' the lioness couched with the wolf,' and foretells with shuddering clearness her own bloody death. Then, with a final prophecy of the vengeance which shall hereafter fall on Clytaemnestra and Aegisthus, she goes in, leaving the vast auditorium tense with horrified expectation.

Scarcely have the chorus begun their pious comments, which at this crisis in the action cannot but seem to us inept, when a cry of mortal agony is heard from within, followed almost immediately by a second. The Chorus recognize their king's voice and know that the murder foretold is in the doing. In helpless agitation and distress they ask each other what is to be done ; and while they are still hesitating, the central doors swing open and a square platform is thrust out on which may be seen, like a moving tableau, the tall figure of Clytaemnestra, splashed with blood, and in her hands the axe with which she has killed Agamemnon : at her feet, half hidden in a bath-like vessel, is the body of the king entangled in a mesh of heavy material,[2] with the dead Cassandra on the ground beside him.

Clytaemnestra speaks : there is no remorse, or shame, or fear, in her utterance, only exultation. She boldly

---

[1] Atreus and Thyestes were sons of Pelops. Thyestes seduced his brother's wife. Atreus, after a pretended reconciliation invited Thyestes to a banquet and served up to him the flesh of two of his sons, which the unhappy father ate without knowing. Aegisthus was a third son of Thyestes, brother of the murdered boys.

[2] Mr. Sheppard holds that this was a sleeveless bath robe, wrapped in which, when once it was over his head, Agamemnon was powerless to move. Aeschylus very definitely compares the contrivance used to a fisherman's *net*, but the comparison may be figurative only.

avows deep and irreconcilable hatred of her husband, and glories in the cunning plot by which she has compassed his death. She enacts the murder before the shocked eyes of the Chorus and a new tremor of horror runs through the theatre at her words :

> I struck him twice : two cries escaped his lips,
> And all his limbs were loosed. As he lay prone
> I gave him a third blow, service of grace
> To Hades, the safe-keeper of the dead.[1]

The old men at first almost speechless with horror, at length find voice to denounce the crime and threaten the murderess with punishment. Unmoved Clytaemnestra justifies herself. The man she has slain was the murderer of his own daughter, the child of her love and pain ; the insolent flaunting of his captive Cassandra was an insult not to be forgiven. In a wild chant the Chorus cry out upon the curse which pursues the House of Atreus. Clytaemnestra takes this word from them ; she accepts for herself the rôle of the Avenger, but prays with sudden vehemence that with the vengeance now by her accomplished the curse may pass away. At this point Aegisthus arrives, an armed band of partisans with him. He gloats over the death of Agamemnon, professing to see in it a just requital of the shocking crime of Atreus against Thyestes. The Chorus rebuke him, call him coward and threaten him with death by stoning. Aegisthus stung to fury orders his bodyguard to use their weapons ; the old Councillors carry arms too, and it seems for a moment that more bloodshed must ensue. But Clytaemnestra interposes with counsels of moderation. There has been bloodshed enough. She and Aegisthus have all the power now, the old men's reproaches and taunts do not matter.

Nay, these idle yelpings hold thou lightly, let them howl their fill,
Thou and I together now may rule the kingdom as we will.

With these words the first drama of the tetralogy comes to an end. There is no curtain to fall or rise ;

[1] *Agam.* ll. 1384-87.

merely the actors withdraw and the Chorus moves off in solemn procession as it had entered.

The Interval.—A great sigh of relief passes over the auditorium, and the pent-up feelings of the audience find expression. Not that an Athenian audience is particularly self-restrained. On the contrary it is accustomed to express its feelings with lively vigour. Sentiments which appeal to it are vigorously applauded, sometimes ' encored ' ; and unpopular actors are known to have been hissed off the stage. But to-day something impressive in the subject and treatment has kept them unusually quiet, and now that tension is relaxed, tongues wag and cramped limbs are stretched. There is a great munching of sweetmeats and cracking of nuts : for an Athenian audience is very human (even grossly so) and the scene in essentials is not unlike the gallery of a London theatre on Boxing-Day. But the interval does not last long, and all are back in their places when the trumpet rings out a second time and Aeschylus' second play, the Libation-bearers, is announced.

The Choephoroe.—The scene is again before the Palace at Argos,[1] but on the right there now rises a mound crowned with a tall slab of stone, which represents the tomb of Agamemnon. Two young men enter, one a youth on the verge of manhood, the other a little older. The younger man approaches the tomb, kneels and lays beneath the tombstone one of two long tresses of curling hair which he is carrying. His words make known that he is Orestes, and that his purpose in coming is to avenge his father's murder. (Enough time, then, must have elapsed since Agamemnon's death to allow his son, who was at that time but a boy, to grow to manhood.) While he is still kneeling, the sound of women's singing is heard. Orestes notes that the singers are dressed in mourning colours and wonders what this may signify. Can they be coming to make expiatory offerings at the dead man's

[1] Argos is put for Mycenae in these plays by a convention. Mycenae itself had been sacked and left desolate by the Argives four years before the date of the trilogy (see vol. i. p. 117).

tomb ? It would be strange if it were so, considering
who now reigns in Argos ; but he thinks he discerns
among these women his sister Electra, though it is many
years since he was sent away from Argos a mere boy.
He calls to his companion, Pylades, to stand aside, and
watch what happens.

The singers (who form the Chorus of the play) are
handmaids of the palace, once free women of Troy but
brought to Argos as captives by Agamemnon. Years
have passed, and now, out of hatred for Clytaemnestra
and Aegisthus, they are personally devoted to Electra, and
to Orestes the rightful heir to the kingdom. From this
wild and mournful song the audience gather that Clytaemnestra, in spite of her stern spirit and obstinate impeni-
tence, has been terrified by a dream which seems to her to
signify some brooding menace from the angry ghost of
her murdered husband. For this reason she has sent
Electra with these women to make placatory offerings [1]
at the tomb of Agamemnon ; for this is a rite which with
all her boldness she dare not herself perform. Orestes
then has guessed rightly ; Electra is with the women,
and words she addresses to them show him that she is in
doubt how to discharge the strange duty laid upon her.
As she stands by the tomb, she starts and cries out.
She has seen with bewilderment the long lock of hair
which Orestes has placed there. Whose can it be ?
Only some member of the family of Atreus could make
such an offering. It cannot be Aegisthus or Clytaemnestra. *Can it be Orestes ?* She notes the colour and
texture of the hair, and is agonized with hope and uncertainty. Then she notices footprints made in the sand.
Whoever made the offering has but recently left the tomb.
Can it be Orestes? Is he even now somewhere near at
hand, braced for his mission of vengeance ? At this
moment Orestes himself comes forward and declares
himself. Electra is at first incredulous. Slowly conviction comes to her as Orestes persists in his story and

[1] It is from these offerings, or libations, that the drama takes its
name.

shows to her in further proof a piece of needlework which Electra recognizes as her own, a gift of long ago to her brother. For some moments brother and sister give way to wild joy : then are recalled to a sense of reality and their present danger. They must contrive with swift boldness and cunning so that their plot may succeed, and the murderers be slain even as they slew. But first they proceed to the performance of the expiatory rites for which Electra and her women have come. It is a weird scene which follows steeped in superstitions which still survived among the Athenians of the fifth century. For it is all very real and significant to them. Orestes and Electra call on the spirit of their dead father with vehement insistence, protesting their orphaned state, recalling the foul treachery by which Agamemnon died, the ignominy of his fate. It is a long-drawn and passionate scene. At last the rites are fully accomplished, though to very different purport from that intended by Clytaemnestra. For all its meaning is concentrated into a savage cry for the safe execution of Orestes' purpose of vengeance. This done, Orestes and Electra discuss more quietly their plans. Orestes and Pylades will gain entrance into the palace disguised as travellers from Phocis, and if but for a moment Orestes finds himself face to face with his enemy, Aegisthus is as good as dead. Electra and her women will help by their silence and by timely speech, as occasion may require. Orestes and Pylades leave the scene, and the Chorus sing another ode.

As the song ends Orestes and Pylades reappear in their disguise as Phocian strangers, and Orestes boldly knocks at the palace gates. A slave challenges from within ; Orestes answers that he brings news and is in haste to tell it to someone in authority. Clytaemnestra herself then comes out and proffers hospitality to the strangers. The pretended visitor from Phocis tells her that Orestes is dead : he has been charged by Strophius the Phocian to deliver this message. The queen, who has no suspicion who the Phocian stranger is, dissembles her sense of relief at this release from a dread that has been heavy

upon her since her dream—the dread of her son's return
as his father's avenger. She pretends to be overwhelmed
with sorrow. But as this is no fault of the messenger, she
promises him all the customary hospitality of the palace
and orders her servants to conduct both strangers to the
men's apartments. She herself follows them in. After
a very short interval an old woman comes out. This is
Kilissa, once Orestes' nurse and devoted to him. She is
charged with a message to Aegisthus. The Chorus
question her of its purport, and hearing that her errand is
to summon him to the palace together with his bodyguard, they adjure her to contrive that Aegisthus comes
unattended and alone. The old woman gives her promise
and hastens on her way. The Chorus pour out impassioned
prayers for Orestes' success. As they conclude, Aegisthus
enters. After a few words which veil his jubilant feelings
at the news from Phocis, he goes in. Immediately after,
his death cry is heard : for Orestes wastes no time but
cuts him down as soon as they meet. A slave rushes
out, calling for help. Now we reach the climax of the play.
Clytaemnestra returns to learn the reason of this outcry,
and guessing the meaning of the danger calls for the axe,
the fatal weapon with which she had slain Agamemnon.
But before it is brought Orestes appears, the dripping
sword in his hand ; and mother and son are face to face.
" You also am I seeking : *he* is well sped," cries Orestes.
Disguise no longer hides from Clytaemnestra the dreadful
reality. Her son is come indeed as the avenger of blood
to slay his mother for the murder of his father. For all
her bravery Clytaemnestra pleads for mercy, appealing
to the soft ties of nature which bind mother and child.
For a moment Orestes hesitates. Then, and then only,
Pylades speaks. His words are few but decisive :

> What then of thy sworn oath and the command
> Spoken by Loxias from Pytho's shrine ?
> Oh ! make mankind thine enemy, not the gods ! [1]

The audience has heard already from Orestes' lips the
fearful duty laid upon him by the Delphic oracle on pain

[1] *Choephoroe*, 900-902.

of outlawry during life and damnation after death. They know that thus reminded he dare not shrink ; and again a thrill of awe runs through the theatre as Orestes, sword in hand, leads his mother away.

The slaying of Clytaemnestra is done out of sight of the audience, but as in the Agamemnon the bodies of the king and Cassandra were shown lying in death, so now by the same device we see the bodies of Aegisthus and Clytaemnestra, and Orestes standing by them, his sword still reeking with his mother's blood. The Chorus exult in the accomplishment of a divinely appointed retribution and the deliverance of Argos from the tyranny of the ursurpers. But Orestes is human. He has killed his own mother. He was driven to it by what seemed the express mandate of heaven. But the struggle of conflicting impulses has been agonizing, and now at the moment of accomplishment he realizes the appalling nature of his act. His reason begins to give way : already he seems to see the shadowy forms of the grim divinities, avengers of slain kinsfolk, whom the Athenians euphemistically call the Eumenides, the Gracious, or Kindly, Ones, fearing to utter their true name, Erinyes. The women of the Chorus try to reassure him, praise his daring deed, call him the most faithful son father ever had. But Orestes finds no comfort in their assurances. They do not see what he sees —the spectral shapes of the Avenging Furies. He dare not stay. He must seek escape by flight, his one hope to find purification and protection at the shrine of Apollo, by whose express command the unnatural deed of blood was done. The Chorus pray for his safe-keeping and deliverance, as he hurries away : then they march out to a solemn chant recounting the successive woes of the House of Atreus; the banquet of Thyestes, the murder of Agamemnon, and now this great act of retributive justice the end of which is veiled from them as yet.

The Third Play of the Trilogy.—There has been much speculation in Athens about the third and concluding drama of the trilogy. It is known to take its name from the terrible supernatural beings whose presence was just

hinted in the last scene of the *Choephoroe*. A good deal
more is known among Aeschylus' friends and in literary
circles ; and rumour has it that the poet's treatment of
the subject is novel and powerful. It is said that the
Areopagus is brought into it; and that is felt to be a
delicate subject. For in recent years a fierce political
struggle has centred in the Council of the Areopagus.[1]
The extremer democratic party—of which, since the
assassination of Ephialtes, Pericles is head—was for its
total abolition. A conservative minority had fought
hard for the maintenance of all its privileges, bound up as
these were with much that was venerable and glorious
in their city's past. The outcome of the strife had been a
compromise. The Areopagus had been deprived of its
political influence and of a large part of its judicial powers ;
it had kept its jurisdiction in cases of homicide : a result
with which the defeated conservative party were little
content. Expectation about this third drama of Aeschylus'
trilogy was accordingly general and keen.

The Eumenides.—When the interval was over and the
Eumenides announced as before by herald, the scene was
no longer Argos, but the Temple of Apollo at Delphi. The
Pythia, Apollo's priestess, is standing on the stylobate
of the temple, and before entering to her appointed
duties, invokes in succession the deities believed to have
possessed sanctuaries on the site before Apollo,[2] then
Apollo himself, Pallas Athena, Dionysus, the nymphs of
the Corycian Cave, the streams of Pleistus, Poseidon, and
Zeus, praying for a blessing on her ministry. She then
enters the temple ; but immediately on her entry we hear
a startled cry and at once she comes out again in great
perturbation. While she is describing what she has seen
the central doors once more open and to our surprise
reveal the radiant form of Apollo.[3] With him is Hermes,
his brother, easily known by the wand he carries and the
symbolic wings attached to his sandals. In the back-

[1] Vol. i. p. 239.

[2] These were Gaia (Earth), Themis and Phoebê.

[3] This point also I owe to Mr. Sheppard.

ground we can discern clinging to the altar that stands in the inmost shrine the figure of a man (and we see at once it is Orestes), with a suppliant's wreath of olive round his brows, and in his hands, which drip with blood, a drawn sword. Around him outstretched in sleep lie dim grisly shapes like women, yet hideously unlike women. Apollo speaks, promising protection to Orestes and deliverance at the last ; but bidding him now flee, while the Erinyes, put to sleep for a time, are powerless to harm him. He is to seek fresh sanctuary in the temple of Athena at Athens : His cause shall there be tried by fit judges. At this Orestes leaves the altar and departs accompanied by Hermes, to whose guiding care he is committed by Apollo. Apollo withdraws also.

As soon as all these are gone the phantom form of Clytaemnestra appears and seeks to rouse the Furies from their sleep. This is no easy matter, since the sleep into which they have been thrown by Apollo is deep. At first they respond only with blood-curdling muttering and moaning. The cries they utter in their sleep show that, like hunting-dogs, they are dreaming of the chase. One by one they awake, and finding their victim escaped raise furious outcry, which takes shape as a wild ode ; for in this play the Erinyes themselves are the Chorus. They assail Apollo with reproaches for baulking them of their prey and denounce the usurpation of the ' younger gods.' Upon this Apollo reappears and with opprobrious words drives them out of his temple. The Erinyes do not venture to resist Apollo in his own temple, but they boldly affirm against him their right to wreak their will on the slayer of his mother. They vow never to give up the pursuit till they have hounded Orestes down.

The scene now changes to Athens. A few simple arrangements convert the Temple of Apollo at Delphi into the Temple of Athena on the Acropolis : in the centre the audience recognize the familiar image of Athena,[1] and this Orestes is seen to be clasping. He has just reached

---

[1] Not of course a Pheidian Athena, but some ruder and more ancient image.

sanctuary in time, with the Furies hot upon his track. The first words spoken are Orestes' appeal to Athena for protection. He comes to her at the bidding of Apollo ; he claims that through his wanderings and sufferings he has already in part made atonement. He is no longer the bloodstained outlaw from human society, but by ritual purification has now been admitted back into fellowship with mankind. He has come to Athena's temple to abide judgment of his guilt or innocence. As he is speaking the Erinyes enter in their most terrifying aspect, serpents hissing in their hair, their wild blood-lust unappeased. At first they do not see Orestes, but snuffle around seeking him like questing hounds. Presently one of the monsters sees him and with terrifying yells the whole troop gather round, pointing at him, claiming him as their victim and gloating over the agonies he must soon suffer. Undismayed Orestes answers that the blood that stained his hands is now washed away by the cleansing rites performed over him at Delphi. He cries to Athena for succour and protection, and the words he uses thrill every Athenian and Argive in the theatre ; for he vows that in days to come the Argive land and people shall be the faithful allies of Athens (glancing skilfully at the league of amity which now unites the Athenian and Argive peoples). The Erinyes, stung to fiercer rage at this defiance, circle round Orestes in fantastic dance, shrieking out threats, calling on Night, their mother, to bear witness to the dishonour done to them by Apollo, chanting the inexorable law of the penalty of blood-guiltiness with a weird refrain which falls on the ear with piercing iteration :

> " Over the victim doomed
> Sing we our chant, driving men mad,
> Driving to frenzy, searing the heart ;
> This is the hymn that we sing,
> Blasting the hearts of men,
> Tuneless, yet strong to bind." [1]

Their task may be abhorred by gods and men : yet they hold it of indefeasible right by a law of the universe.

[1] *Eumenides*, 328-33 and (repeated) 341-6.

The ordinance by which they exercise their dread office is god-given and none may take from them the reverence due.

Athena now appears and enquires the reason of these cries which have summoned her from the Trojan land, where the victorious Achaeans have assigned to her and her people, the Athenians, a goodly portion of the conquered land. [1] The Furies point to Orestes as one doomed to punishment for the murder of his mother. Athena refuses to condemn him without hearing his defence. The Furies offer to submit their claim to her judgment as arbitrator. Athena cannot (she explains) give judgment on this dispute herself, but she undertakes to choose judges from among her Athenian people and constitute a court, which shall thenceforward be established for all time. A choral ode follows which rises gradually into majestic affirmation of the law of righteousness. [2]

The scene shifts a second time : we are no longer on the Acropolis, but on the Areopagus. [3] Athena ushers in twelve citizens of Athens who are to act as judges, and

---

[1] The audience would recognize with pleasure this covert allusion to the Athenian claim to the Thracian Chersonese (Gallipoli), where in one form or another Athens had been in possession since before the Persian wars, when the family of Miltiades had ruled a small principality there.

[2] *Eumenides*, ll. 538-543 and 550-557.

> " Never then forget thou this :
> Reverence the throne of Right.
> Let not gain
> Tempt thee to spurn and abase it with impious foot ;
> Else punishment follows,
> Biding till its time be rife."

> . . . .

> " Whoso is just willingly without constraint,
> Shall not fail to prosper,
> Nor ever sink, whelmed in utter ruin.
> But he who dares, bold in sin, to carry freight
> Of wealth unjustly swept together from all sides,
> In due time perforce shall haul his sail down,
> When on the labouring boat the storm
> Bursts, and the yard is breaking."
>   (R. C. Trevelyan's translation, p. 137).

[3] The Areopagus (Mars' Hill) is the low hill (375 ft.) N.W. of the Acropolis, just across the dip below the Propylaea.

declares that the Court of the Areopagus, thus instituted, shall continue for ever. The Furies are there as accusers ; Orestes is the accused ; Apollo is present as witness for the defence. Athena presides and invites the Erinyes to open the case. They charge Orestes with matricide. Orestes admits the fact, but pleads justification. He did indeed slay his mother, Clytaemnestra, but it was as the divinely authorized avenger of blood, because she had murdered Agamemnon, her husband, Orestes' father ; and he appeals to Apollo in confirmation of his plea. Thus appealed to, Apollo vindicates the authority of his oracle, declaring that no response is ever delivered from his prophetic shrine, which is not ordained by Zeus, father and king of the Olympians. It was the heinous character of Clytaemnestra's crime, the guileful and treacherous trapping and doing to a shameful death of the war-leader who should have been protected by the veneration due to his office, that makes Orestes' act, not only justifiable, but necessary. The Furies press on their side the enormity of the presence in a righteous community of one stained with his own mother's blood. Apollo retorts with fresh arguments and then the newly-created Areopagites are called upon to pronounce judgment according to their oath. Athena once more proclaims that the Court now about to pronounce judgment shall remain an Athenian institution under the title of the Council of the Areopagus. If the Athenians preserve and reverence it, she promises they shall find it a bulwark and glory of their land, such as no other race of men possesses,

" Pure from corruption, reverend, quick to wrath,
.   .   .   .   .   .
A vigilant guardian of the land's repose." [1]

This said, she charges the judges to record their votes, adding that should the votes prove equal, the accused is to be held acquitted. The Areopagites come up, one by one, and throw the tablet inscribed with their votes into

[1] *Eumenides,* 704-6 (Trevelyan).

an urn. A count shows that the votes are equally balanced, six against six : therefore Orestes is acquitted. Orestes offers fervent thanks to Athena ; but the Erinyes are vehement in their outcry against the verdict. Athena endeavours to soothe them, promising that a shrine in their honour shall be consecrated by the Athenians under the Acropolis. For a long while the Furies only repeat their laments and denunciations, refusing to be appeased. But at length they give way before Athena's calm and patient insistence and allow themselves to be persuaded. In the end they accept with manifest satisfaction the honours in perpetuity offered to them at Athens. Henceforth they will dwell in a cavern beneath the Areopagus, to be worshipped there with peculiar honour as the Holy Goddesses. They promise on their part to protect the crops and fruit-trees in Attica from storm and blight, and to bless the flocks with increase. Better than that, they will safeguard the children of the land from untimely death and from the curse of civic strife. Their angry upbraidings change to friendly greetings, which are answered with glad friendliness by Athena on behalf of the City. A procession is formed to conduct the goddesses to their new abode under the Areopagus and a solemn chant is raised :

" Come to your home, Great ones high in honour,
   Daughters of Night, our loving train attends you.
      Speak good words and guarded, people of this land !
   Lo, 'neath the earth in your primaeval grotto
   Sacrifice and worship shall be yours for ever.
      Speak good words and guarded, people one and all !
   Gracious to our land and righteous-minded
   Come, Holy Maidens, deign to be well-pleased
   While the flashing torches light your way.
      Let the exultant triumph-song ring out."

To the strains of this processional hymn all move away ; and so with reconciliation and rejoicing Aeschylus' great trilogy ends.

The ' satyric drama ' which followed was called the *Proteus*. We may guess with some probability that it dealt with the wanderings of Menelaus (as described in

Book IV. of the *Odyssey*), since an adventure with Proteus is one of the episodes ; [1] but this is all we can know, and that it necessarily dealt with the story in a burlesque manner : for that was the fashion of the satyric drama. [2]

Moral Purport of the Oresteia.—We have enough, I think, in common with fifth century Athens to make us follow these three plays with interest, though there is much in them to which we cannot respond with the same intensity of feeling as the Athenians themselves. But while it is possible to tell the story in English, it is not at all possible to tell it with the splendour of Aeschylus' language. To appreciate this splendour is not even for everyone who can read Greek : on the contrary a chorus of Aeschylus requires for its mere understanding a high degree of scholarship. [3] As an appreciation of Milton has been said to be " the last reward of consummated scholarship," [4] so it might be said of an appreciation of Aeschylus' Greek. The grandeur of the thought is, however, to be reached in English ; and there are several more than adequate translations. [5] As we read we see unfolded before us a sublime spectacle of human passion and crime, the moral significance of which is forcibly impressed upon us. Manifestly this trilogy of dramas deals with the problem of evil ; of sin and the punishment of sin. The whole might be deemed an illustration in action of the eastern saying, " because evil produces evil, therefore it is to be shunned more than fire." Thyestes sins, and his sin provokes the vengeance of Atreus. The crime of Atreus is repeated in the sin of Agamemnon, and that sin entails the vengeance of Clytaemnestra. Clytaemnestra's sin

[1] See vol. i. pp. 141-2. Two lines of the *Proteus* survive as a fragment of Aeschylus' (210), but give us no clue to the mode of treatment.

[2] We have only one complete surviving satyric drama to judge by, Euripides' *Cyclops*, revived for performance at Cambridge in the summer of 1923.

[3] " How many 'varsity dons," asks Mr. E. S. Hoernle, " who do not happen to have studied Aeschylus, could read him ' unseen ' " ?

[4] Mark Pattison, *Milton*, p. 215.

[5] See *Note on Books*, below p. 1.

leads on to the matricide of Orestes and that makes him
the victim of the avenging Erinyes. But here we come
up against a new principle, Orestes is saved and healed by
the mediation of Apollo and Athena, two of the most
ethically conceived deities of the Hellenic Pantheon.
This new principle is the inner purpose of Aeschylus'
drama. We have in it a conflict of moralities, an old and a
new. The ancient traditional morality of Athens is just
the *lex talionis*, ' reprisals,'—an eye for an eye, blood for
blood. It is this ancient law, conceived almost as a law
of the universe, which the Erinyes represent, the law that
killing inexorably and implacably entails the punishment
of death. Aeschylus has had vision of a higher law, a
law which admits of bloodless expiation, of reconcilement,
even of mercy. The Erinyes argue that if their iron law
is relaxed, if the slayer can ever be held justified, there
is an end of all moral sanctions. Murder will riot in its
most abhorrent forms ; fathers and mothers, done to
death by their own children, will learn too late how
dangerous it is to tamper with the primordial sanctions.
Apollo and Athena stand for a more enlightened dis-
pensation which discriminates between crime and crime,
and admits the possibility of justification. Orestes is
purified from the blood-guilt which made him an outlaw
from human society, pursued by demons ; and the curse
comes to an end.

That certain families are pursued by an hereditary
curse, which the Greeks called Atê (Mischief), is a doctrine
which meets us more than once amongst the legends on
which the tragic poets drew. Aeschylus exhibits in these
plays how this ' curse ' is no arbitrary fatalistic ' Mischief '
from which there is no escape, but error, preventable
human error, repeated from generation to generation,
through individual acts of wickedness for which the doer
is morally responsible. The disposition, indeed, which
leads to misjudgment through faults of character may be
hereditary—headstrong self-will, ungoverned wrath, lust
of conquest or of pleasure. The very same tendency,
amounting to an hereditary curse, is traceable—in less

violent forms—in family histories still, and is explicable by the same causes. Families are ruined by errors of character, slight perhaps in themselves, yet cumulative in their effects, which repeat themselves in one generation after another. To our own age as to fifth-century Athens the lesson is the same : *Sophrosunê*, sane-mindedness, moderation, balanced self-control, is best ; and to observe the commonly accepted laws of righteousness. These dramas of Aeschylus have in them that which impressively drives home these truths.

2. A COMEDY OF 421 B.C.

" His Comedy is the old Comedy, his poet is Aristophanes."
W. P. KER, *The Art of Poetry*, p. 134.

It is a curious change from drama of this solemn character to Aristophanic comedy. But the afternoons were, as we have said, given to the performance of comedy ; and when the four plays of the tragic tetralogy were played out, there would be one of the year's competing comedies on the same stage and before the same audience. We have no comedy of the year 458 B.C. The only complete comedies that have come down to us are Aristophanes', and the earliest of these surviving comedies of Aristophanes is *The Acharnians*, performed in B.C. 425. We may, however, complete our representation of a day in the Theatre of Dionysus by exhibiting one of Aristophanes' comedies much as we have exhibited the *Oresteia*, and we will take for this purpose Aristophanes' *Peace*, the comedy performed in the year 421, partly because we have quoted from it already (p. 173), partly because still in this year 1924 the subject has shrewd interest for us.

The Circumstances at Athens.—In the year 421 both the Athenians and most of the Peloponnesians were thoroughly tired of the war, which had then been going on for ten years. The Athenians were in possession of Pylos and of Cythera ; but on the other hand, they had met with humiliating defeat at Delium. Moreover, their treasury was depleted. Cleon, the leader of the war party at Athens, and Brasidas, the most enterprising leader the war had produced on the Peloponnesian side, were both dead (above, p. 172). Early in 421 the Peace of Nicias was being negotiated, and while success was still in the balance, the Dionysia were celebrated at Athens and Aristophanes competed with *The Peace*. We shall find an Athenian comedy, except for its spirit of rollicking drollery, which is independent of time limits and makes the whole world kin, even less like any form of drama of our own day than were Aeschylus' tragedies.[1]

Outline of Aristophanes' "Peace."—The play opens with a dialogue between two slaves of a farmer named Trygaeus, who in his longing for peace has formed the desperate resolve to get to heaven and expostulate with Zeus for allowing such a ruinous war to go on. To effect this purpose he has been feeding up a huge beetle on whose back he means to fly up into the air and make his way to Heaven. The beetle is an ordinary dung beetle of vast size ; and much unsavoury fun is made of the unsavoury food which it is the slaves' task to supply to the beast. The feeding over, one of these servants peeps through the doors of the court-yard and sees his master already mounted and preparing to start. At this point the doors of the court-yard are thrown open and Trygaeus is disclosed, astride on his beetle beginning to rise into the air. The poor man is plainly nervous and is trying to quiet his steed with soothing words, " Softly, softly, my beastie ! " [2] The servants try to stop him ; his little daughters run out and beseech him not to leave them, but all in vain. Trygaeus refuses to listen, although his language shows him to be divided between the desire to soar heavenward and fear of coming a cropper. Suddenly the scene changes and Trygaeus is seen to be alighting in

[1] And yet the kinship with *The Beggar's Opera* and modern musical comedy generally is fairly obvious. In artistic aim and efficacy the musical comedies of Gilbert and Sullivan offer the nearest parallel. See also ch. xv. p. 439 below.

[2] Aristophanes, *Peace*, l. 82 and foll.

Heaven.   The mechanical means by which this is effected
is sufficiently simple.   A broad platform is thrust out
from the back scene just under the beetle and Trygaeus
as they hang in the air, and on this steed and rider come to
rest.   New scenery at the back of the platform represents
the palace of Zeus ; in front of it is a pile of great stones,
which we are later to learn covers the mouth of a cavern.

Trygaeus knocks boldly at the palace door, and this
brings out Hermes, who is employed as Hall-porter.   In
this capacity Hermes shows himself, like any pampered
house-porter of the day,[1] truculent and abusive, till
bribed by a present, when he becomes quite friendly.
But it appears that Trygaeus' desire to see Zeus cannot
be gratified ; for all the gods, except only Hermes, have
gone away to the top of Heaven's dome (Hermes being
left as care-taker) in disgust at the endless bickerings of
the Hellenes, and War has occupied the palace in their
place.   When Trygaeus enquires of the reason for all this
Hermes replies :

> " Because you *would* have war, when oftentimes
> They were for peace.   If the Laconian folk
> Had just a bit the better, they would say :
> " Yea, by the Twin Gods !   Now shall Athens smart ! "
> While if victorious Athens had th' advantage
> And the Laconians came to ask for peace,
> You always said at once : ' We are being cheated !
> Don't, don't for Heaven's sake give way to them.
> They'll come again, if only we keep Pylos ! ' " [2]

And Trygaeus is obliged to admit :   " Yes that's the very
way we used to talk."   He is further admonished that
the Hellenes are never likely to see the face of Peace
again :   for she has now been imprisoned by War in a
deep pit.   " Where ? " asks Trygaeus.   " Right below us
here," answers Hermes.

> " And don't you see
> The big stones he has piled about the mouth
> To stop your rescuing her. . . . " [3]

How dire is this peril for all Hellas is soon shown by the
appearance of War himself carrying a gigantic mortar,

---

[1] See above, ch. xi. p. 294.   [2] Lines 211-20.   [3] Lines 224-6.

in which he intends to pound up the Greek city-states.
War is seen throwing into his mortar leeks, garlic, cheese,
and honey (these ingredients representing Prasiae in
Laconia, Megara, Sicily, and Attica). By good luck he
has not at the moment a pestle handy—since he only
' moved in ' yesterday ; but he sends his boy *Havoc* to
fetch one. Havoc has no success. For the Athenian
pestle, ' the leather-seller who embroiled all Hellas,' [1] is lost
and the Lacedaemonian is not to be had either. For that
was lent to people in the Thraceward regions and there
lost.[2] So War must put off his pounding, till he has had
time to make himself one. He goes indoors to do this.
Trygaeus at once sees his chance : he catches at this
delay in the hope of saving Hellas. He cries out

> " Now have we, men of Hellas, a fair chance
> To free ourselves of war and tribulation
> By drawing Peace out—Peace so dear to us all—
> Before we're hindered by another pestle.
> Come farmers, merchants, craftsmen and artisans ;
> Come settlers from abroad ; come foreigners ;
> Come men of the Islands—oh come one and all !
> Bring levers, shovels, ropes, and hither speed.
> Now is our chance to snatch the better luck we need ! " [3]

This appeal brings on the Chorus (for Comedy requires a
chorus no less than Tragedy), Athenian farmers of the
deme Athmon, but treated as representing all the Hellenes
suffering from the miseries of war. They hurry in, eager
to haul Peace up to the light of day ' with cranes and
levers,' Peace " the greatest of all the gods and goddesses
and the most vineyard-loving." They are so excited at
the prospect of recovering Peace and make such a noise
that Trygaeus fears they will wake War up. They begin
to move the stones, Trygaeus taking the lead. This
provokes vigorous remonstrances from Hermes ; he tells
them that Zeus has denounced death upon anyone found
digging Peace out. With some difficulty, by prayers,
promises, cajoleries and the gift of a gold cup, he is

---

[1] Line 270 ; meaning Cleon, killed at Amphipolis ; see p. 172 above.
[2] Brasidas : lines 283 and 4.   [3] Lines 292-300.

prevailed upon to assist instead of opposing. The stones are rolled away, ropes are adjusted and the word is given to pull ; there is a shouting and a straining as all haul on the ropes. Long they pull away without making any progress. Hermes incites the Chorus to effort, like ' a coach ' handling a tug-of-war team. " Pull," he cries, " now, now." But still no progress is made. Some of the Hellenes are pulling half-heartedly, or not pulling at all. The Boeotians are merely pretending : the Argives not pretending even. The Laconians are pulling like men ; they want their prisoners back from Pylos. The Megarians, starved and ravenous as they are, are pulling askew. Presently Hermes bursts out :

" You men of Megara, confound you all !
Hateful you are to Peace, when she remembers
How you were first to drive her into strife.
And you Athenians, I bid you cease
Pulling awry as you are doing now.
Why you do nothing else but go to law !
But if you really mean to draw Peace out,
Shift your ground somewhat nearer to the sea."

Chorus.
" Come, you who are on the land, let's take the job and do it."
Hermes.
" Yes, now that's better far, stick to it, now you're gaining."
Chorus.
" He says we're doing better now, cheer up and pull together."
Trygaeus.
" My word !   It's those who till the ground, and no one else who's
     doing it ! "

Chorus.
" Heave and haul, one and all,
Pull all of you together now !
Don't get slack, but put your back
Well into it ! Now you'll do it !
Now, boys, now : see here she comes !
     Heave and haul, one and all !
Heave, heave, heave, heave, heave, heave,!
With a yeo-heave-ho, together oh ! " [1]

At last the head and shoulders of a colossal Peace appear out of the aperture representing the opening into

[1] Lines 500-519.

the cavern and from beside her step out on to the orchestra two comely maidens, her attendants, whom the poet calls Opôra and Theôria. "Good morning, Opôra," cries Trygaeus, "good morning, Theôria "

"O what a charming face you have, Theôria ! "[1]

and he kisses her. He now indulges in happy visions of all the joys which Peace is bringing back with her :

"Ivy, the wine-vat, little bleating lambs,
Full-bosomed matrons trotting off to the fields,
The merry maid, the jar turned upside down,
And heaps of other blessings. . . . "[2]

The Chorus join in this welcome to Peace and to the prospect she brings of a happy return to the vineyards and fruit-trees they have so long been parted from :

"Hail blest day so long desired by true-hearted husbandmen,
In my gladness I would hasten to behold my vines again ;
And the fig-trees that I planted, when I still was but a boy,
After long, long years of absence I would fain salute with joy."[3]

Trygaeus revels in thoughts of an early return to his farm and as we listen to his raptures we realize more clearly what it had been to the peasants of Attica to leave their homesteads and huddle into the City :

"Oh to think of it, my comrades,
That old happy way of living
Which Peace once bestowed upon us !
All the delicate confections—
Figs and myrtles, and the sweetness
Of dried grapes ; and beds of violets
Clustered all about the well !
Come, let's welcome her who brings
All these dear, desired things !
Best belovèd and most longed for, all that's best to thee we owe,
We who soothly all life long
Live and work the fields among,
Thee, dear lady, thee alone
Our best benefactress own."[4]

How was it that Peace had so long hidden her face from the Hellenes ? Why was she so angered with the

[1] Line 524.   [2] Lines 535-8.   [3] Lines 556-9.   [4] Lines 571-591.

Athenians ?   Hermes tells us.   Peace herself is too deeply
offended with the Athenians even to speak to them, but
she whispers to Hermes, and he reports what she says : [1]

> " This then is why she holds you all to blame :
> When she came, after that affair of Pylos,
> With a whole sheaf of treaties with her, *you*
> Voted against her thrice in the Assembly." [2]

Peace, on her part, asks for news of city matters, and
Aristophanes works in ridicule of the coward Cleonymus,
and of Hyperbolus the lampseller, popular favourite
since Cleon's death ; of Cratinus, the bibulous comic poet
—even of Sophocles !   And now Hermes gives Opôra in
marriage to Trygaeus and destines Theôria to be the bride
of the Council.   Trygaeus, enraptured, proposes to go
home at once and looks about for his redoubtable beetle.
The beetle, however, has disappeared.   Hermes explains :

> " Harnessed in Zeus' car he carries lightnings." [3]

a line quoted in derision from Euripides.   The problem of
how to get back to earth is nevertheless soon solved by
Hermes' pointing out an easy passage down through the
cavern.

At this point there is a pause in the action ; the
Chorus come forward and deliver what is known as
the *Para-basis*.   This so-called parabasis, which means
expressly the 'coming-forward,' forms a recognized
part of Athenian comedy in the fifth century.   It
was by old-established custom the poet's opportunity
to address the audience in his own person, and in
this parabasis we hear Aristophanes claiming that he has
done much to raise the character of Athenian comedy,
putting true wit in the place of vulgar buffoonery.   While
this is going on the scene changes back to Athens
and the house of Trygaeus.   Trygaeus himself has just
got back to the surprise and delight of his servants, who

---

[1] The real reason why Peace does not herself speak is that she is
represented by a colossal head only, and there is no actor taking a part
for her.   The number of actors permissible is limited in Comedy as well
as in Tragedy.

[2] Lines 664-7.   [3] Line 722.

listen eagerly to the story of his adventures. Opôra is
introduced as his bride-elect and is led into the house to be
dressed for the wedding. The rest of the performance is
mainly taken up with the details of a sacrificial offering to
be made on the inauguration of peace. What shall the
offering be ? A simple pot of vegetables is too mean.
A stall-fed ox, a great fat pig ? Neither is a suitable
offering to Peace. It must be a ' baa-lamb,' because that
should conduce to a lamb-like frame of mind in the
sacrificer. At last all is ready, the basket, the wreath, the
sacrificial knife and the pan of sacred fire. We are now
to be witnesses of a solemn sacrifice in fifth-century
Athens, and may note the preliminaries. First Xanthias,
one of Trygaeus' servants, paces round the altar from
left to right, carrying the basket and lustral water to
sanctify it. Next Trygaeus snatches a blazing torch
from the altar-fire and dips it in the water. This is to
sanctify the water. Then water from the dripping torch
is sprinkled over the victim's head : the object is to make
the victim shake its head and so seem to assent to its
own death. Barley is brought in a basin : the slave
washes his hands, then scatters the barley over the
audience. It is at this point that the prayer to Peace
quoted on p. 173 comes in. The knife is presented to
Trygaeus, but at the last moment he has a scruple. No
blood-sacrifice at all may be made to Peace. So the
victim is spared. Jokes of all kinds are interposed
throughout all this, and now comes a farcical interlude
provided in the person of Hierocles, an ' oracle-monger '
from Oreus, and an arch-humbug. He is anxious to get
a share of the sacrificial meat, but his ' oracles ' only provoke ridicule and he is driven off with mockery. When he
is gone the Chorus express once more their delight at their
escape from the distress and discomfort of war and draw
an idyllic picture of country pleasures in time of peace :

" For there is no greater pleasure than when all your sowing's
    sped,
When the skies are dripping, dripping, and you hear a neigh-
    bour's tread :

' On a day like this Comarchides,' says he, ' what should we do ' ?
' For this great blessing a carouse, say I ; and what say you ?
So, wife, just roast three bushels of your kidney-beans, and mind
To mix with them good wheaten flour, and figs of choicest kind.
Let Syra summon Manes from the farm without delay.—
'Tis no good to think of picking leaves from off the vines to-day,
Nor yet to delve the roots about, for the ground is soaked with
    rain.
Send someone to my house for a fine thrush, and finches twain.
There should be beestings, too, indoors, and four good bits of
    hare—
There's three to bring for supper here ; and one's for father's
    share :
—That is unless a weasel came and stole them in the night ;
I heard a scuffling certainly and it gave me quite a fright.
Get myrtles from Aeschinades, the ones with berries, please.
And as you pass just give a shout to bid Charinades
          Come and pass the wine-cup with us,
          In Heaven's bounteousness rejoicing—
          God's good promise of increase." [1]

Yet another comic interlude follows. A sickle-maker
and a caskmaker come to offer profuse thanks to Trygaeus
for restoring their trades ; they beg him to take as many
casks and sickles as he pleases, and accept a gift of money
besides as a wedding present. The helmet-crest maker and
the breastplate maker, on the other hand, and the man
whose trade is to burnish spears, come to complain of the
ruin of their industries. They offer spears, breastplates
and helmet-crests for anything they will fetch ; and go
away disconsolate when—after various ludicrous suggestions of the uses to which they might be put in peace
time—no demand whatever is found for their goods.
There is a good deal of incidental fooling. A trumpet-
maker and a helmet-maker fare no better. Trygaeus
suggests that trumpets, set on end and filled with lead,
would make a serviceable stand for a pair of scales.
Helmets might be sold in Egypt to hold the huge draughts
of physic, which report says Egyptians are dosed with
three times a month. The spear-burnisher is disgusted
at an offer to take his spear-shafts (sawn in two) as vine
props at ten a penny.

[1] Lines 1140-1158.

And now the wedding-guests have all arrived, eager for the marriage-feast, and the bride is brought in, carried high on the shoulders of one half of the Chorus. The other half-Chorus lift Trygaeus high in air, and our comedy concludes with a regular marriage-song to the refrain " Hymen, Hymenaeus O ! "

> " You who ready stand to play
> Your appointed part to-day,
> Lift the happy bridegroom high !
> Hymen, Hymenaee, cry,
> Hymen, Hymenaeus oh ! "

CHAPTER XV

GREEK DRAMA

3. ORIGIN AND HISTORY

" From improvised beginnings. . . . tragedy advanced little by
little. . . . passing through change after change, until it had
attained suitable form."

ARISTOTLE, *Poetics*, 4, 12.

" . . . . no one is capable of feeling that Sophocles is supreme
who does not feel that Euripides is admirable."
" Euripides is human, but Sophocles is more human. . . ."
" Sophocles is the purest type of the Greek intellect at its best."

JEBB, *Attic Orators*, pp. xcvii. and xcviii.

Peculiarities of Greek Drama.—We have endeavoured
so far to let Greek tragedy and comedy at Athens speak
for themselves. This is what they were like at their best.
But there is much certainly that is strange to us and
not a little difficult to reconcile with our instinctive and
acquired notions of drama. Leaving comedy aside for
the time being, we may recall what in the Aeschylean
trilogy was most opposed to our preconceived ideas of
drama, and enquire if there is any explanation. The
most startling peculiarity of Greek tragedy is the presence
of the Chorus (this applies indeed to Comedy also, but
in a less degree). In each of the three dramas of our
trilogy a band of singers came upon the scene early in the
course of the action, and remained upon it till the close of
the play. In the *Agamemnon* it is a body of Argive
Councillors, members of the Boulê or Senate ; in the
Choephoroe it is a number of women of the royal household,
slaves brought from Troy after its destruction ; in the

THE THEATRE AT EPIDAURUS,

showing the position of the orchestra in a Greek theatre. The view is taken from outside the remains of the stage buildings and looks across the orchestra to the auditorium. This theatre is considered the most beautiful of surviving Greek theatres and is more regular and symmetrical than the theatre of Dionysus at Athens. The diameter of its orchestra is 66 feet.

From a photograph in the collection of the Society for the Promotion of Hellenic Studies.

Eumenides the Chorus is formed of the supernatural beings who give their name to the play itself. The Chorus are not ' on the stage ' in the same sense as the actors, though they take part in the action of the play. Their station, the station to which they march when they come, and where their odes are sung and their movements performed throughout, is the circular area between the front of the scene where we have our stage and the auditorium. The Greeks, as we have already had occasion to note (above, p. 382), called this area the orchêstra, or dancing-floor. This in the Theatre of Dionysus in fifth-century Athens was a circle about 80 feet in diameter.[1]

The Chorus.—The main function of the Chorus is to drone out long chants in a sort of recitative varied by livelier measures, to the accompaniment of music and stately dancing movements. The chants are called *odes*, and they bear closely on the action of the play, though they are not always essential to it. Now all this is very odd to us, and so alien to the purpose of the drama as we understand it, that we naturally wonder how such a convention established itself.[2] For the Chorus is a necessary part of a tragedy as fifth-century Athens conceived of it ; the dramatist had no choice in the matter. It was a rule to which he had to conform. Every play must have its chorus, and a chorus of the kind described above. To accept a play for production (which was done by the archons) was, in the phrase of the day, to ' give a chorus ' to the poet. The manager, who put the plays on the stage and found the expenses, was the chorus-trainer, or choragus. The hampering effect, from our point of view, of such a convention is at once perceived, if we suppose it applied to the modern, or to the Elizabethan, stage. Suppose it necessary to reconstruct *Hamlet*, so as to afford place for a Chorus of Danish councillors, or *King Lear*

---

[1] The later orchestra, which is what we see on the site to-day, has a diameter of 65 feet only.

[2] The Chorus in modern opera and musical comedy is like, and yet very unlike, the Chorus of the Greek drama ; broadly like as musical embellishment, unlike in that its dramatic connection with the action is at most very slender.

with a Chorus of British maidens, attendants on Cordelia, or Galsworthy's *Strife* with a Chorus of elderly Trades Unionists. The continued presence of the Chorus, however, and the name of their dancing-floor, orchêstra, really afford the key to a right understanding of Greek drama. Orchêstra *means* ' dancing-floor,' neither more nor less, the place set apart for the trained band of Choreutae, where they may sing and perform their evolutions. The *orchestra*, so understood, existed before either theatre or stage-buildings, and it becomes clear that the Chorus itself was not an accessory of the drama, added to produce certain effects, but part of the original rite out of which drama grew. The Chorus in fact is primary : drama derivative.

Evolution of Tragedy.—Aristotle here, as in so many matters, puts us in the way of reaching the true explanation. He remarks that tragedy was developed out of dithyrambic poetry ;[1] and a dithyramb is just a choral ode. It is a highly wrought and emotional song in honour of Dionysus : the name comes seemingly from Asia Minor ;[2] and so possibly (by way of Thrace) did the cult of Dionysus.[3] The problem now is to see how out of the choral chant sung by a band of fifty trained Choreutae the acted drama was evolved. Aristotle does not tell us ; but we can see that if the dithyrambic ode itself tended to take on a dramatic character (and this it certainly did through the very nature of the worship of Dionysus) ;[4] and that if some outside person was introduced talking with the Chorus or its leader ; and if further that person were made to assume some ' character ' with which the ode had to do, we have the germ of the Aeschylean drama. This is what tradition says actually happened in the townships of rural Attica, when Thespis of Icaria travelled

[1] Aristotle, *Poetics*, 4. 12. What exactly Aristotle says is that Tragedy arose " from the *leaders* of the dithyramb " ; and what this means appears from the account given above.

[2] " The Dithyramb—an Anatolian Dirge " is the title of a paper in the *Classical Review* for February-March, 1922.

[3] See vol. i. p. 55.   [4] See vol. i. p. 56.

about with his waggon-load of chorus-singers. Their faces were smeared with wine-lees, and one of the members of his 'company' was dressed up to represent various characters, and so they enacted rudimentary dramas. It is the Roman poet Horace who has handed on this account of Thespis and his waggon ; [1] but from other sources we get the names of plays attributed to him and the statement that he 'discovered one actor.' [2] Here again philology reinforces our argument. For the Greek word for an actor means literally 'answerer' : that is to say, the first actor was the person who 'answered' the Chorus leader, and so began dramatic dialogue. We have it on Aristotle's authority that Aeschylus introduced a second actor, and Sophocles a third. *There were never more than three* in the fifth century ; so that we have to bear in mind this other limitation restricting the freedom of Greek tragic drama, that the play must be so constructed that all the parts can be distributed between three actors. This holds of each of the dramas of the Aeschylean trilogy and (with a few doubtful exceptions which seem to require a fourth actor) of all the Greek tragedies that have come down to us. The actors were named first, second, and third actor, *prot*-agonist, *deuter*-agonist, *trit*-agonist ; and it is from this contrast that our word *protagonist* gets its special meaning.

Aeschylus.—But Aeschylus did very much more than add a second actor. Far more than anyone else he *made* the Greek drama as we know it. He gave it elevation, and perfection of form and dramatic quality. Not that Aeschylus was the first Athenian writer of tragedy worthy to be called a dramatic poet. There was an interval of more than a full generation between the probable date of Thespis' wanderings with his touring company, and the date at which Aeschylus began to

[1] Horace, *Ars Poetica*, ll. 275-7.

[2] In Diogenes Laertius. Hence the importance of Thespis (who has given us the adjective Thespian). For as Professor Norwood writes : " If this was done by Thespis, he was the founder of European drama." (*Greek Tragedy*, p. 5).

exhibit plays (Thespis 535, Aeschylus 500). We have
the names of three celebrated dramatists earlier than
Aeschylus, and we know of at least one of those, Phrynichus, that he was a true poet and a skilful playwright.
One famous drama of his, the *Fall of Miletus*, we had
occasion to mention in Vol. I.[1]

His Seven Surviving Tragedies.—Aeschylus was a native
of Eleusis born in 525, and so thirty-five years old when,
as we have seen, he fought at Marathon ; he was forty-
five at the time of the battle of Salamis. All his life from
the age of twenty-five he was exhibiting tragedies. His
first tragic victory (that is *first* prize) was in 485 ; his last,
with the *Oresteia*, in 458. He died in Sicily soon after
458 ; one story said, in enforced exile. His lofty mind
and character are witnessed by his surviving dramas.
There are only seven of these, though the names of many
more are known and the whole number is said to have been
about ninety. The four other surviving plays besides the
linked plays of the trilogy—are *The Suppliant Maidens,
The Persians, The Seven against Thebes*, and the *Prometheus*.
There is very marked development between the earliest
of these and the Orestean trilogy.[3] Two of them, the
Persians and the *Prometheus*, are of very special interest.
We have already had occasion to speak of each ; of the
Persians in connection with the battle of Salamis, for in
the play we have the description of an eye-witness;[4] of the
Prometheus in the chapter on Gods and Heroes.[5]

His Prometheus.—The *Prometheus Bound* must be placed
among the grandest achievements of human genius.
Like Dante's *Divine Comedy* and Milton's *Paradise Lost*
it is cosmic in reach. It takes in the whole destiny of man
from brute savagery (before the use of fire was known)
to the civilization of fifth-century Athens, and it goes
back further into the past beyond mankind to the war of
rival dynasties in Heaven. Its inner and spiritual mean-

---

[1] Vol. I. p. 276.   [2] Vol. I. p. 296.

[3] More than half of the *Suppliant Maidens* is Choral chant ; only *one*
actor is employed and there is no scenery.

[4] See Vol. I. p. 350-55.   [5] See Vol. I. p. 72.

ing transcends time altogether : it is a drama of the
invincibility of spirit by material force : it is a conflict
of power and goodness. Prometheus out of a divine pity
has intervened to save the human race from annihilation.
Zeus, monarch of the Younger Gods,[1] in dissatisfaction
at the weakness and ineptitude of mankind, has decreed
to do away with them altogether. Prometheus by the
gift of fire to man enables him to overcome his original
feebleness [2] and enter upon the path of progress, which
leads from savagery to civilization. But in order to
endow mankind with fire, Prometheus must steal it out
of heaven. And this brings him into conflict with the
will of the new monarch of the universe, Zeus, who is
now omnipotent, and who is implacably angered. The
giants, Force and Violence (*Kratos* and *Bia*), are his
servants and instruments. By his command they fasten
the great-souled Titan to a rock amid wild and desolate
scenery, there to expiate his offence against *the power that
is* in everlasting torment. The action of the play consists
in the inflexible endurance of Prometheus in spite of all
attempts to shake his firmness. Hephaestus, out of his
own compassion, tries to work upon him, even while he
helps to execute the cruel will of Zeus. Oceanus urges
trite prudential reasons for submission, since it is useless to
resist omnipotence. Prometheus, for man's sake, holds
firmly to his resolve in spite of every persuasion, every
menace, every pang—eternal type of those who defy
power for honour's sake and their own sense of right.
The Titan's sufferings and indomitable spirit are presented
in poetry in which Aeschylus' majestic diction is mellowed
into tenderness and beauty, with a force of poetic imagination which transcends the bounds of space and time.
The height of sublimity which Aeschylus attains in this
masterpiece has never been more adequately expressed
than recently in Professor Norwood's words : "Above

[1] Compare *Eumenides*, l. 162.

[2] Hobbes' famous description of man's life in the ' state of war ' seems
here in point : "And the life of man, solitary, poore, nasty, brutish, and
short." *Leviathan*, i. 13.

all, the maturity of Aeschylus' poetic strength is to be
seen in the terrific perspectives which he brings before us—
perspectives of time, as the voice of the tortured prophet
carries us down through a vista of centuries through the
whole history of Io's race [1] to the man of destiny ; perspectives of scenery, as the eye of the Ocean-Nymphs from the
summit of earth gazes down upon the tribes of men, horde
behind horde fading into the distance, all raising lament
for the sorrows of their saviour ; perspectives of thought,
as the exultant history of civilization leaps from the lips
of him who dies hourly through untold years to found and
uphold it, telling how that creeping victim of his own
helplessness and the disdain of Heaven goes from weakness
to strength and from strength to triumph." [2]

Sophocles and Euripides.—Aeschylus was the first great
master of Greek tragedy, and there are two others,
Sophocles and Euripides.   One was thirty years younger
than Aeschylus, the other forty-five.   Sophocles was the
elder of the two born in 496 or 497 ; but he outlived
his younger contemporary though only by a few months.
Both died in 406 B.C., the year of Arginusae.   Sophocles
had first wrested the prize from Aeschylus in 468 ;
Euripides' first victory was in 428.   Regarding Sophocles
the judgment of his own day and the judgment of future
ages has been practically unanimous.   He was accepted
in his own time as the peer of Aeschylus, and by many
judges was held even to surpass him.   These are the only
two opinions of his place and merit now.   Sophocles
produced dramatic masterpieces throughout his long life,
more than a hundred plays altogether.   The first prize
was adjudged to him no less than eighteen times, and he
was never placed lower than second.   The last of his
plays, the *Oedipus at Colonus*, written when he was in his
ninetieth year, contains some of his most beautiful poetry.
His life was in other respects uniformly successful and

---

[1] Io, one of the ' dramatis personae ' in the *Prometheus*, was ancestress
of Heracles who, according to the received legend, ultimately delivers
Prometheus.

[2] *Greek Tragedy*, p. 96.

happy. He was popular for his amiable disposition and social geniality. More than once he was chosen to fill the highest official positions at Athens.[1] " Blessed was Sophocles," wrote one of his contemporaries,[2] "who passed so many years before his death, a happy man and brilliant, who wrote many beautiful tragedies and made a fair end of life which knew no misfortune." Euripides' life was far less equable and fortunate and the history of his literary reputation has been quite different. There were violent disputes about his merits and demerits in his lifetime, and critical controversy has been busy about him in our own day. He is still the most debated of the great Greek poets. And the reason was that Euripides reflected new tendencies and expressed a new spirit. Aeschylus, though not untroubled by the deeper questions which lay beneath the popular mythology and accepted ethics, expressed the spirit of conservative Athens, the spirit which Aristophanes looked back to admiringly of the men who fought at Marathon. It is a spirit of reverence, of faith in national ideals, of conflict in their defence, and victory. Sophocles expresses the same spirit calmed and perfected in the great years which followed the repulse of the Mede ; it is the spirit which we see wrought out in the Parthenon and the Propylaea, and in the Parthenon sculptures. Euripides was of the new age, the age which came in with Anaxagoras and the Sophists and Socrates. His was a spirit of doubt and questioning and unrest ; of dissatisfaction with current beliefs and standards of conduct, of a quest for truer criteria. His acutely critical intellect was combined with a passionate appreciation of beauty, whether in literary expression or the portrayal of character, not a whit inferior to Aeschylus' or Sophocles'. There results consequently a sharp conflict of tendencies in the poet and in his work. His tragedies have neither the spiritual exaltation of

---

[1] He was ' strategos ' or general in 440 B.C. ; and his name is found in the Tribute List (see above, p. 20) of 436 as one of the Helleno-tamiae.

[2] Phrynichus, the *Comic poet*. The translation is Norwood's (*Greek Tragedy*, p. 14).

Aeschylus' nor the serene loveliness of Sophocles'. But they are vividly human ; and on this account their appeal to some minds is even more compelling. In his own day, what was new in his outlook and method excited fervent admiration in some few ; others it roused to alarm, opposition and mockery.

Conflicting opinions about Euripides.—Aristophanes was one of the latter. Nearly all his earlier comedies, from the *Acharnians* to the *Thesmophoriazousae*, contain some gibe at Euripides, whether it takes the form of personal ridicule, or of the parodying of lines from his tragedies. In the *Frogs*, in particular, Aristophanes makes merciless fun of Euripides, his prologues, his subjects, his metrical novelties, his argumentativeness, his verbal cleverness.[1] And in doing this he is appealing to popular judgment. It is clear that in Euripides' own time there were critics at Athens who regarded his innovations in tragic method and style as a deplorable falling away from Aeschylus and Sophocles, and the tendencies of thought induced by his poetry as highly pernicious. After he had been for some time dead there was a complete reversal of this judgment. Euripides became, not all at once, but gradually, the most admired of the great three. Aeschylus and Sophocles, more especially the former, fell into neglect. Possibly our possession of nineteen of his dramas as against seven of Sophocles' and seven of Aeschylus' is a reflection of this greater vogue.[2] His popularity continued through the Middle Ages, and down to comparatively modern times. About a century and a half ago there was a reaction ; there was something like an agreement among scholars to disparage Euripides. Still more recently Euripides has found powerful champions.[3] The truth seems to be that judgment of Euripides

---

[1] See Aristophanes, *Frogs*, from l. 830 to the end.

[2] The plain reason, however, for the preservation of the surviving plays of Sophocles and Aeschylus, and of nine out of the nineteen of Euripides, is that the plays were in ancient times selected for school use.

[3] Especially Dr. Verrall in *Four Plays of Euripides* and *Euripides the Rationalist* ; but Haigh, Dr. Gilbert Murray, and Professor Norwood, all in various ways, also, pay homage to Euripides' genius.

is partly matter of temperament, and partly a matter of changing standards. Judged by the canons of Greek tragedy he represents decline ; but in relation to drama universally considered he represents advance. Greek drama as perfected by Sophocles could not outlast the special political and social conditions of fifth-century Greece. If there was to be drama as a common possession for mankind, there must be a movement away from the peculiar limiting conditions of the Attic drama. The process has begun when already in the lifetime of Aeschylus the Chorus takes less space in the play and dialogue more. It is continued in a progressive weakening of choruses and strengthening of the drama proper in Sophocles. But in Sophocles the chorus is still an integral part of the drama and essential to it. The first decisive step in emancipation was to disconnect the chorus altogether from the action of the play and make it simply a musical interlude between acts. Now though this step, as Aristotle writes,[1] was only taken finally by Agathon, it was anticipated by Euripides in certain of his plays. A not less important advance in the direction of universal drama was the elaboration of problems of character on the plane of ordinary human nature instead of on the plane of antique heroic character. Euripides treats Agamemnon, Orestes, Theseus, Jason, Admetus, Alcestis, Helen, Creusa, as men and women of his own day, to the scandal of his conservative-minded contemporaries, but the great gain of drama as an universal form of art.

Surviving Dramas of Euripides.—But it should be possible to put aside all these accidents of literary history, and form for ourselves an estimate of Euripides' quality as poet and dramatist from his nineteen surviving plays. The *Alcestis* is probably the best known of these. And it may be read with much advantage in Browning's ' transcript ' under the title *Balaustion's Adventure*. But it is far from being the greatest of his works ; indeed, strictly speaking, it is not a tragedy at all, but a satyric drama, modified to a form little distinguishable from the

[1] Aristotle, *Poetics*, 18. 7

other plays of a tetralogy.   Euripides has the good fortune
(for the English reader who has no Greek) that seven
of his plays (*Alcestis*, *Hippolytus*, *Bacchae*, *Trojan Women*,
Electra, *Medea*, and *Iphigenia in Aulis*) and the *Rhesus*
which is usually included in his works, may be read as
English *poetry* in Gilbert Murray's translations.   Any one
of these (especially, perhaps, the *Hippolytus*, *The Trojan
Women*, or the *Medea*) will give the reader a good measure
of the tragic power and the ' modernity ' of Euripides.
Most of them have been acted in these versions.   In particular Londoners had recently several opportunities of
seeing the *Trojan Women* (and also the *Medea*).   The
Trojan Women must have been a revelation to many who
saw it.   Doubtless experience of war from 1914 to 1918
had prepared the minds of these audiences to follow this
war-drama of another day with an understanding and
insight impossible before.   Euripides' tragedy is one
of the most powerful anti-war pamphlets ever written.
The subject is the sufferings of women in war portrayed in
the fate of the women of Troy after the capture and sack
of that city by the Achaeans.   The poet's extraordinary
genius is shown most of all by the art with which the
anguish of the whole calamity is concentrated in Hecuba,
wife of Priam and mother of Hector.   Pitiable as is the
fate of Polyxena, of Cassandra, of Andromachê, it is
tolerable in contrast with the measureless burden of
sorrow borne by this aged queen and mother whose whole
existence is bound up in Ilium and the royal House of
Priam.   Even when the mangled body of Astyanax
(Andromachê's little son) is brought in (he has been thrown
from the battlements of Troy by order of the victors), we
feel as we hear the old woman crooning her agonized love
and bereavement over this tender nurseling, that it is *her*
anguish, which is sorest, not Andromachê's.   It seems
impossible, but it is so.   Perhaps part of this effect is due
to the acting of Miss Sybil Thorndike, whose Hecuba is
unforgettable.

On the other hand there are bad plays of Euripides,
which are thoroughly disagreeable in the reading, and the

acting of which could bring no pleasure—the *Helen*, the *Orestes* and, strangely enough, the *Hecuba*. And there are plays which, while their power and insight are beyond question and compel admiration, leave mixed impressions of pleasure and pain—the *Medea*, the *Hippolytus*, the *Bacchae*. The last, which was produced in 405, the year after Euripides' death, marvellous as a *tour de force*, is yet revolting. The catastrophe is merely horrible, and none of the horror is veiled. The *Iphigeneia in Aulis*, written and produced, it is believed, in the same year, is finely imagined as well as cleverly constructed.

Such are the strange contrasts of Euripides' genius.

Probably no reader of to-day will fail to recognize its brilliant qualities, the power of realizing character, the resourcefulness in dramatic construction, the mastery of language. Few probably will deny that the very fulness of the last of these gifts was a snare to him. Some of the plays certainly suffer from those rhetorical tendencies [1] which became so strong in Hellas in the fourth century B.C. (as we noted in Chapter XIII.), and which had already set in with the teaching of the sophists in the latter half of the fifth century. Even in the *Trojan Women*, which we selected for special admiration, there is a bad example of this in the debate over Helen's guiltiness to which Menelaus is made to listen. We find it in the *Hecuba*, in the *Orestes*, even in the *Alcestis*. This *rhetoric* is a real blemish spoiling the poetry and offending our sense of dramatic fitness. But while this fault detracts from our enjoyment of much of Euripides, it does not affect the splendour of his greatest work.

Sophocles.—No one who reads the *Troades*, the *Hippolytus* or the *Bacchae* in Professor Murray's English can doubt, I think, that Euripides was a very great poet and dramatist. He comes indeed much nearer to the modern conception of drama than either Aeschylus or Sophocles. With him the play has come to be the thing, not the choral odes, or even the poetry. He sets out to realize

[1] Aristotle remarks (*Poetics*, 6. 16): "Now the older poets gave their dialogue a truly civic cast, the poets of to-day make it rhetorical."

character and situation imaginatively and develops the action out of these. But for the perfection of that unique combination of religious and dramatic motives which is Greek tragedy we must look to Sophocles. For in him by the consensus of all critics ancient and modern, as well as in the judgment of his contemporaries, Greek drama reached its perfect accomplishment. When one turns to the seven surviving plays in the hope of making intelligible to those who cannot read Sophocles the noble excellence of beauty attained by Greek drama in his hands, one is met by the difficulty of deciding which play of his to select for illustration. Shall it be *Oedipus King* for its tragic completeness and the exactitude with which it answers to Aristotle's canons ? Shall it be the *Electra* for convenience of comparison with Euripides' and Aeschylus' treatment of the same subject ? Shall it be the *Ajax* for the sake of its Salaminian seamen, and the scent of the sea which breathes through its lyrics, and of the magnificent death-scene of the hero ? Or the *Philoctetes* for the island scenery and the touches which disprove the charge that Greek poetry lacks appreciation of wild natural beauty, for the warmth of human feeling in Philoctetes and Neoptolemus ? Or the *Oedipus at Colonus* for a certain other-worldly quality in its last scenes and for the match-less choral ode which (according to a story in itself little probable) convinced an Athenian law court of the master's perfect sanity ? All these I put aside, and take the *Antigonê*, from a conviction that in all the marvellous riches of Greek drama there is nothing greater than this play. Here, as in Aeschylus' *Oresteia*, the centre of interest is a spiritual conflict ; not the problem of the recurring blood-feud and escape from it, but that deeper and ever-latent conflict of the higher and lower moral law, the man-made and the god-given. Temporal power in the person of Creon publishes abroad a certain edict : Antigonê through instinctive recoil from something in that edict which violates the sanctions of a higher duty, disobeys and is condemned to a cruel death. This and its further tragical consequences is the subject of the *Antigonê*.

The Story of the House of Oedipus.—But to follow the *Antigonê* we need the previous story as told in two other plays of Sophocles, which deal with the terrible calamities of the house of Labdacus. These plays do not, as one might expect, form a trilogy with the *Antigonê*. The existing evidence shows that the three plays, *Oedipus King*, *Oedipus at Colonus*, and *Antigonê*, were produced at widely different dates. Sophocles, we are told independently, departed from Aeschylus' practice of shaping his three plays into the higher unity of a trilogy. Each of his tragedies is self-contained, and the four dramas of his sets are unconnected in subject. Nevertheless these three plays so far form a connected story that the events of the two *Oedipus* plays are presupposed in the *Antigonê*.

Sophocles' *Oedipus King* is regarded by Aristotle as the perfect example of the characteristic excellences of Greek tragic drama. The play is a marvel of skilful construction and there would be special pleasure in exhibiting the art by which it is put together. The subject is almost too painful for dramatic representation, but so great is the intensity of the poet's tragic power that this is forgotten when the play is actually seen. By contrast, the *Oedipus at Colonus*, the latest composed of Sophocles' plays, is also the most serenely beautiful ; and the scene is Colonus, Sophocles' own native place, a village about a mile northwest of Athens, where there was in Sophocles' day a wooded enclosure consecrated to the Eumenides. But it would take too long to follow the dramatic action of these two plays at length : it must suffice to sketch as much of the story as is necessary for the understanding of the *Antigonê*.

Oedipus was son of Laius and Jocasta, king and queen of Thebes. It had been prophesied of him before his birth that he was fated to kill his father and marry his mother ; and the story was that in spite of the parents' agreement to make fulfilment impossible by destroying the babe as soon as born, through the secret workings of destiny the horror was in the end brought to pass. The *Oedipus King* turns on the discovery of the terrible truth

when (long after the death of Laius) Oedipus and Jocasta
are living in seemingly secure prosperity, parents of
four children, two sons Polynices and Eteocles, and two
daughters Antigonê and Ismenê.   When the full horror is
made plain, Jocasta takes her own life and Oedipus stabs
his eyes to blindness with the pin of a brooch snatched
from her dress.   The play ends with the spectacle of
Oedipus, sightless and bleeding, lamenting in appalling
words the extremity of his misfortune.   The action of the
Oedipus at Colonus takes place some years later.   Oedipus
driven forth from Thebes as a pollution, has been wandering from city to city, a homeless outcast, sustained in his
blindness and affliction by the loving care of Antigonê,
the elder of his two daughters, who refuses to leave him.
At the last Oedipus, like Orestes, finds deliverance.
Without any stain of moral guilt—for all he did and
suffered was in ignorance—he has borne the utmost
malice of destiny, and has become, as it were, sanctified by
suffering.   He now finds refuge at Colonus, in the grove of
the Eumenides, and is protected by Theseus, king of
Athens, from further outrage which threatened from
Thebes.   The ' passing of Oedipus ' is described towards
the close of Sophocles' play in a passage [1] which " in
breathless loveliness, pathos, and religious profundity is
beyond telling flawless and without peer." [2]

. The *Antigonê*, though a drama of much earlier date,
carries the sorrowful history of the House of Labdacus one
stage further.   Antigonê and Ismenê have returned to
Thebes, but their coming does not avert a struggle which
had long been threatening between their two brothers, who,
on reaching man's estate had been appointed joint sove-
reigns in their father's room.   Eteocles, the younger, has
dispossessed the elder Polynices, and, with the support of
Creon, his mother Jocasta's brother, refuses to receive
him back to a share in the sovereignty.   The cause of the
exiled Polynices is taken up by Adrastus, king of Argos,
who has given him one of his daughters in marriage,

---

[1] *Oedipus at Colonus*, ll. 1587 to end.
[2] Norwood, *Greek Tragedy*, p. 171.

and vows to restore him in his right by force of arms. Polynices and the Argive host enter Boeotia and appear before the walls of Thebes. The invaders are marshalled in seven divisions under seven chieftains,[1] one against each of the seven gates of Thebes. At each of the seven gates the assailants are defeated : Adrastus, the Argive king, escapes by flight ; before the other six gates the leaders of the attack lie dead. At one of them the brothers Eteocles and Polynices have met in single combat and fallen, each by the other's hand. It is at this point that the action of the *Antigonê* opens.

The "Antigonê" in Outline.—It is the morning after the repulse of the attack on Thebes. The dead bodies of Polynices and Eteocles lie in front of the gate called Uppermost. The Argive army is in flight. Antigonê and Ismenê meet outside the palace, once Oedipus', now, since Eteocles' death, Creon's. Antigonê has called her sister out to speak with her in secret. Creon has issued a proclamation that Eteocles shall be buried with royal honours, but Polynices, as a traitor who plotted to destroy his native city with fire and sell her children into slavery, is to be left where he lies, a prey to dogs and vultures. Antigonê tells of this decree with a shudder, for it violates the deepest seated of Hellenic pieties, the duty of giving rest to the dead. She makes known her resolution to bury Polynices secretly in defiance of the proclamation, and invites Ismenê to aid her in this pious deed. Ismenê, nurseling of a palace, shrinks from this daring proposal in natural terror, and the sisters part in anger. The Chorus, a band of Theban elders, now march in, singing a splendid ode of triumph over the Argive foe, to greet the rays of the sun, which, slanting over the streams of Dircê, usher in the most glorious of days for seven-gated Thebes, since the Argives with their white shields have all fled in headlong rout. As they conclude their song, Creon enters full of his proclamation, and its righteousness in distinguishing between the hero who had died fighting for his country and the traitor who came to destroy it. The Chorus show

[1] Hence the title of Aeschylus' play *The Seven against Thebes.*

signs of uneasiness at this purposed outrage on the dead, but outwardly profess acquiescence. At this point one of the soldiers set by Creon to watch over the dead body of Polynices, and prevent any attempt to give it burial, approaches in evident agitation. With comical reluctance he makes known the errand on which he has come. It is to inform Creon that in spite of his edict the corpse has been tampered with. Some unknown hand has thrown over it a little loose earth. The old men are inclined to see in this the hand of Heaven. This adds fuel to the flames of Creon's anger at the breach of his edict; he threatens death with torture to all the guards, if they fail to discover who it is that has dared thus to cross his will. The soldier withdraws disconsolate. The choral chant which follows descants on the daring of man, how he crosses stormy seas, tames earth to the plough, and compels birds, beasts, and fishes to minister to his needs. Before they have well finished, they see to their amazement, the guard returning along with the rest of the picket, and in the midst of them Antigonê, a prisoner. The guard relates how at noontide a blinding dust-storm came on, and when the air began to clear again, he and his companions caught sight of Antigonê wailing over her brother's corpse, which by Creon's order had been once more bared of earth. They had then and there arrested her and have brought her with them. Creon in cold rage turns on Antigonê, demanding if she avows the deed. She makes no denial. He asks her whether she knew the proclamation; and when she says 'yes,' how she dared break the law by him enacted. Calm and unterrified Antigonê makes her confession of faith:

> " It was not God who made this proclamation,
>   Nor Right that harbours with the gods below.
>   Nor did I deem thine edict had such strength
>   That a mere mortal might transgress the sure,
>   Unwritten, ordinances of the gods.
>   Not of to-day, or yesterday, are these ;
>   But everlasting since time first began.
>   Never would I, for fear of any wrath
>   Of man, incur the judgment of the gods.

> I knew that I shall die, e'en though thy word
> Had not proclaimed it. If before my time
> 'Tis fated that I die, I count it gain.
> For whoso in a sea of miseries
> Lives, as I live, in dying has great gain.
> Therefore I grieve not, though to meet this doom
> Is now my destiny. But had I borne
> To leave my mother's son in death unburied,
> That had been grief : I am not grieving now.
> And if, perchance, to thee my deeds seem folly,
> Maybe 'tis but a fool that judges so." [1]

At this high self-vindication, which he reckons mere insolence, Creon is more than ever enraged, and knowing the close affection between the two sisters he is at first for involving Ismenê in Antigonê's doom. In a verbal duel which follows Antigonê makes one profession which throws a revealing light on her character. Creon is reproaching her for showing regard for Polynices, her country's enemy, and cries : " An enemy dead is never the more a friend." Antigonê answers : " To share in love, not hatred, was I born."

Ismenê in her distraction is eager now to be doomed to die with Antigonê ; but Antigonê will not allow it ; and her seeming hardness in repulsing Ismenê's proffered sacrifice is the only harsh trait in an otherwise exquisitely tender character. In the end Creon clears Ismenê and orders Antigonê alone to death. The Chorus lament this new addition to the sorrows of the house of Labdacus. The drama now takes a fresh pathetic turn with the appearance of Haemon, Creon's son, who is betrothed to Antigonê and figures as the chivalrous lover of romance born out of time. Creon bids him choose between his affianced bride and his father. Haemon professes a dutiful readiness to submit his wishes to his father's will, but is bold to plead with his father for his father's sake. The people do not really, he says, approve Creon's proclamation, though fear keeps them from showing open disapproval. In their hearts they abhor the treatment of Polynices and honour Antigonê. But Creon only hardens.

[1] *Antigonê*, 450-470.

He is haunted by a miserable fear of being worsted by a
woman, and taunts Haemon with weakness. When
Haemon protests that he is pleading in his father's interest,
the only reply is that Antigonê must die. Haemon hints
darkly that he will not survive Antigonê; his father
mistaking the words for a threat against himself, declares
that Antigonê shall be put to death before her lover's very
eyes. "That shall never be," Haemon answers; and goes
out telling his father that he shall look upon his face no
more. When he is gone the Chorus hymn the matchless
power of love "couching in the soft cheek of a maid";
it is a short ode of a delicate beauty unique among choral
odes in tragedy.[1] Their ode changes its tone to sorrow as
Antigonê is led in by her guards. A forlorn figure she now
makes on her way to death. The high courage which
sustained her while her daring deed was still in the doing
has fallen from her. She feels her isolation already, the
clumsy sympathy of the Chorus seems to her mere
mockery. She is not so strong as she seemed. Her
strength is in loving. Has she not said, "To share in love
not hatred was I born?" All her protective mother-love
had gone out to the erring, but unfortunate, brother,
doomed to the everlasting restlessness of the unburied.
She had dared the utmost to save him from that, and this
was her reward; for her act of piety an impious death.
And for compassion the old men tell her: "Your own
self-will has undone you." She feels abandoned by god
and man:

> "Unwept, unwedded, friendless, lo! I tread
> The path of death.   Never may I behold again
> The sacred light of day.
> There's not a friend who mourns my fate with tears." [2]

Creon's baleful ire pursues her. Her doom is to be
immured in a tomb with a little food, and there left to die.
Now her courage rises again; she addresses the tomb as her
bridal-chamber and consoles herself with the hope that in
the world of the dead her father, mother, brother, will greet

---

[1] *Antigonê*, ll. 781-90.   [2] *Antigonê*, 876-881.

her with a loving welcome. She gains confidence as the
end draws near. She is sure her deed was right and will
be acceptable to heaven.

A short choral ode follows, and then comes Teiresias,
the same blind seer who revealed the awful truth to
Oedipus. A boy leads him by the hand. He has come to
warn Creon of certain deadly portents ; ill auguries from
birds in noisy conflict ; fire refusing to burn the sacrifice.
He knows the reason to be that the altars of the gods have
been polluted by dogs and vultures with the rotting flesh
of Polynices. He adjures Creon to consider well, and, if
he has fallen into error, to retrieve his steps before it is too
late. Mere obstinacy is stupid. Creon finds it hard to
give way and at first answers the seer with reproaches.
But when Teiresias in plain terms denounces the sacrilege
of keeping above earth the unburied body of a kinsman,
and warns him of the just vengeance of the Furies, Creon is
terrified. The prophet has departed after uttering dreadful prophecies, and the Chorus testify that they have
never known his predictions falsified. Soon Creon, now
thoroughly alarmed, is hastening to pay tardy death-rites
to the body of Polynices and to release Antigonê.

After a short interval we learn that retribution has fallen
on Creon almost as overwhelming as the doom of Oedipus.
Haemon is dead. Creon reached the tomb too late, only
to find Antigonê hanging by the neck, dead, and Haemon,
distraught with grief, clinging to her body. When
Haemon saw his father, he drew his sword as if to
slay him ; then turned it on himself. Eurydicê, wife
of Creon, and mother of Haemon, enters in time to
listen to this story, and at its close departs without
a word. And now we hear the voice of Creon raised in
agonized lamentation, blaming himself as cause of his son's
violent death. Even as he speaks, a messenger comes
forth from the house to tell him that another blow has
fallen. Eurydicê is dead, slain by her own hand. Creon's
pride is utterly broken. Like Oedipus when many years
before doom came upon him, he prays to be cast forth
from Thebes as a man accursed. The Chorus in a few

words point the moral. Happiness depends on good
sense : men must beware of the sin of impiety. We who
see the play, realize that it is the tragedy, not of Antigonê,
but of Creon.

Other Greek Dramatists.—Any one of these dramas
handed down from ancient Athens is in itself alone a
possession beyond price for the human spirit. Together—
and there are over thirty of them—they form a not
inconsiderable part of what we inherit from Hellas.
Any one who goes through life without ever reading a
Greek play, even in translation, has lost one of the great
possibilities of experience.

Aeschylus, Sophocles, and Euripides so far surpassed
other tragic dramatists that for posterity they have come
to mean practically the Greek tragic drama. Yet in their
life-time they had many competitors and not infrequently
the prize went to some other than one of the great three.
As a matter of fact Greek tragedy continued as a living art
for several centuries, and was vigorous enough in the
second century B.C. to impel Latin poetry to imitation.
But its full inspiration was short-lived : already by
the end of the fifth century the powerful originality
by which Aeschylus, Sophocles, and Euripides towered
above their contemporaries was failing, and the centuries
which follow are, so far as the Attic drama is concerned,
centuries of long-drawn decline. We have the *names*
of over 150 tragic poets, though all but very few are
mere names.

Later History of the Greek Drama.—The splendour of
Greek drama belongs to Athens, and Athens only ; but
among tragic poets admitted to compete at the great
Athenian festivals were some who were not native-born
Athenians. Ion was one of these, and there were others,
both in the fifth century B.C. and later. Ion was a
Chian by birth, and was a versatile man of letters, who
wrote comedies as well as tragedies, and dithyrambic and
lyrical poetry, and a book of ' Memoirs.' Almost the only
other tragic poet who has attained to lasting remembrance
is the Athenian Agathon ; and he lives chiefly because he

is the host in Plato's immortal *Banquet*.[1] Aristotle records two facts about him. Agathon was the first to compose choral odes for his tragedies which had no bearing on the story (above, p. 423). He wrote a play called *The Flower*, the characters of which were wholly imaginary. This was an innovation, which, if it had been followed up, might have deeply affected the subsequent history of Greek drama. But it was not : on the contrary (as Aristotle tells us incidentally) the subjects taken for tragedy were more and more confined to the traditional legend cycle, like the stories of Orestes and Oedipus. Consequently the changes were rung on a narrowly limited stock of subjects, until all prospect of originality of treatment was exhausted. This in the end was one of the causes of the extinction of Greek drama. Yet in the fourth century, at all events, there was no falling off of productivity ; new tragedies were written in prodigious numbers. And in another way there was an enormous expansion of Greek drama and its influence. Theatres were built and plays performed in other cities besides Athens. This diffusion of Attic drama was vastly extended through the conquests of Alexander the Great. Greek cities were founded all over the East, and wherever a Greek city was founded a theatre was built and Greek plays were performed. For a time one city, Alexandria, even outshone Athens as the home of tragedy. The Attic tragedy, as Haigh puts it,[2] was transformed "into a cosmopolitan institution." But along with this wider diffusion productive vigour waned, till at last no new plays at all were produced. The custom of reproducing regularly at the Dionysiac festivals one or more of the masterpieces of the past had begun as early as the fourth century B.C. ; and as the records show, the representation of ' old ' and ' new ' tragedies for a long time went on together. As originality failed, ' new ' plays were produced less and less, till finally only ' old ' plays remained. From the first

---

[1] The occasion of the feast was Agathon's victory in the tragic contest in the year 416 ; and the banquet was held at Agathon's house.

[2] *The Tragic Drama of the Greeks*, p. 434

almost the ' old ' plays were restricted to the great three, Aeschylus, Sophocles, and Euripides.[1] In process of time Aeschylus almost wholly dropped out ; then to a great extent Sophocles, so that Euripides was at last left in almost sole possession of the Greek theatre. It must be noted, however, that this brief review takes in a long stretch of time. The total cessation of fresh dramatic production did not come till the second century A.D. Greek drama in the land of its origin came to an end in the fifth century A.D. At the last.it was suppressed through the moral reprobation of the theatre and all its works, which followed the victory of Christianity over paganism. But by that time there was very little left of tragedy to suppress. Through political and social decay and the accompanying depravation of popular taste tragedy had ceased to please. Performances took place in the theatres, but they were of debased forms of drama—mimes and pantomimes, neither tragedy nor comedy, and, perhaps, not very unlike modern ' revues.' Greek and Latin classical drama disappeared from Europe till interest in it revived at the Renaissance through the re-discovery of Greek. Yet even so the Greek dramatic tradition had not wholly been lost ; it lingered on among the few scholars who still studied the classics—especially in monasteries ; and so influenced to some slight extent the revival of drama, hundreds of years later, in the form of Miracle Play and Mystery.[2]

Connection with Modern Drama.—With the revival of classical studies Greek tragedy influenced the rise of the modern drama more directly. But the links between modern and ancient drama are clearer in comedy than in tragedy. The *origins* of Greek Comedy are too vexed a question to occupy us here. As with Tragedy they are traced back to the primitive worship of Dionysus ; [3] but Attic comedy took on literary form at Athens later than tragedy, and Aristotle declares that less was known about its history.[4] The most acute and the most copious

---

[1] *The Tragic Drama of the Greeks*, p. 447.
[2] See Vol. I. p. 10.   [3] Vol. I. p. 56.   [4] *Poetics*, ch. v.

treatment of the subject in English is Cornford's in *The Origin of Attic Comedy*. For our purpose nothing is better than Jebb's suggestive summary : " At the Dionysia, when people were assembled to worship the god and to see tragedy, the merry procession called a *comus* had become a recognized feature of the festival. It was at first a voluntary and unofficial affair. One or more troops of men dressed themselves up in mummers' costume, and marched into the sacred precinct to the music of the flute. They then sang a song in honour of Dionysus ; and one of their number addressed the audience in a humorous speech, turning on civic interests and on the topics of the day. The festal procession then withdrew again. The name Comedy, Komoedia, originally denoted this ' Song of the Comus,' and was doubtless coined at Athens, on the analogy of *tragoedia*. About B.C. 465 the *comus* was adopted into the official programme of the festival : instead of being the voluntary work of private persons, it was now organized with aid from the State. The steps by which a dramatic performance was built up around the comus-song and speech can no longer be traced. But some five-and-thirty years later, at the beginning of the Peloponnesian War, Attic Comedy, as we know it, was mature." [1]   No complete Attic comedies have come down to us except Aristophanes' eleven, of which the *Clouds* and the *Peace* are two. Most of these belong to what is called the ' Old Comedy,' the original full and vigorous form of entertainment developed at Athens, in which the wit of the poet is under no legal restriction, public affairs are subject to free comment, and evil-doers (or those whom the poet regards as such) come under the lash *by name*. Through the stress of war and domestic strife this freedom of personal allusion was curtailed by penalties, and we have the Middle Comedy, exemplified by the *Plutus* of Aristophanes. Later again the freedom of Middle Comedy was further restricted, and the New Comedy came into being. The New Attic Comedy is

[1] Jebb, *The Growth and Influence of Classical Greek Poetry*, pp. 227-8.

purely a comedy of manners, such as modern times are familiar with, and Menander is its traditionally greatest name.   Not a single play of the New Comedy has come down to us complete,[1] but we have fortunately very fair means of appreciating its qualities in the six extant comedies of Terence, which, except for the Latin in which they are written, are domestic dramas of the New Comedy. The scene is Athens, the types of character are Athenian, the domestic life is the life of Athens in the fourth and third centuries B.C.   From the *Andria* the *Hecyra*, the *Hauton-timoroumenos*, the *Eunuchus*, the *Phormio*, the *Adelphi*, we may know exactly what the New Comedy at Athens was like.[2]   The last of these titles means 'The Brothers,' the third is Greek for ' The Man who punished himself,' the Hecyra means ' The Mother-in-Law.'   The same is true, but to a much less extent, of the comedies of Plautus, which in their dialogue are racy of Italian soil. Their titles, too, are Latin, yet in subject and setting they are all, like the *Captivi* and the *Rudens*, Greek. The New Comedy from the point of view of dramatic evolution connects rather with Euripides than with Aristophanes.   From the surviving fragments of Menander, as also of Eubulus and Diphilus, it can be seen how much the poets of the New Comedy were under the spell of Euripides.

The Acting of Greek Plays in Modern Times.—Scarcely less important than the literary influences of the study was the revival for stage representation of Latin comedy at the universities and grammar schools.   In Queen Elizabeth's time Plautus and Terence, and plays written on the same model, were frequently performed at each of the universities and in schools.   The 'Westminster Play,' that is the annual performance of one of a

[1] Portions of three comedies of Menander have recently been recovered from papyri, enough to give some taste of the limpid beauty of Menander's Greek and the delicacy of his wit.

[2] Professor Gilbert Norwood's new book (published towards the end of last year by Blackwell) shows rare and admirably just appreciation of *The Art of Terence*.

select cycle of Latin comedies by the King's (or Queen's) Scholars of St. Peter's College, Westminster, was instituted by the express desire of Queen Elizabeth, and continues to this day. The Latin ' Epilogue,' composed every year for performance as a topical afterpiece, gives perhaps a better idea of the spirit of the Old Comedy than anything on the modern stage. It offers some analogy also to Satyric drama. Opportunities of seeing Greek plays, both in the original and in English versions, have become more and more frequent since the last quarter of the 19th century. In England this revival under latter-day conditions began with the representation of the *Agamemnon* at Oxford and in St. George's Hall, London, in 1880. A notable new departure was the institution in 1892 by the Warden of Bradfield College, the Rev. H. B. Gray,[1] of the Bradfield plays in a theatre shaped on the ancient Greek model out of the side of a Berkshire hill.[2] The Radley plays in emulation of Westminster but with a wider choice, including Greek as well as Latin comedy, go back to 1881.[3] Not the least remarkable achievement in this revival—which is very much wider than can be indicated here [4]—has been the series of Greek plays acted in a Sussex village,[5] under the energetic and scholarly direction of Mrs. Godwin King of Stonelands. The performances of Greek tragedy at the ' Old Vic ' in 1919-20 have been already referred to.

[1] Before he went to Bradfield as Warden, Dr. Gray had been for a time an Assistant Master at Westminster.

[2] The first Bradfield Play was the *Alcestis* in 1881. The first play to be performed in the Greek theatre (the cutting of which had begun in 1888) was the *Antigonê* in 1890. Since 1892 plays have been triennial. The play of that year was the *Agamemnon*, and the three plays named now form the Bradfield cycle.

[3] The play of that year was the *Phormio*. Notable productions since have been Aristophanes' *Frogs* (1900) and *Wasps* (1905) ; Plautus' *Aulularia* (1897), *Captivi* (1898), and *Rudens* (1904).

[4] For example looking only to schools, there have been series of Latin plays at the Oratory School, Birmingham, and at Bath College under Dr. Dunn.

[5] West Hoathly.

CHAPTER XVI

ARCHITECTURE AND SCULPTURE. I.

Greek architecture stands alone in being accepted as beyond criticism, and therefore the standard by which all periods of architecture may be tested.

BANISTER FLETCHER, *History of Architecture*, p. 68.

Not only is Greek architecture the purest ever conceived, but it was enriched with the finest sculpture the world has ever seen.

SIMPSON, *History of Architectural Development*, Vol. I. p. 92.

Among the arts of all lands and of all ages Greek sculpture sits enthroned.

JOHN WARRACK, *Greek Sculpture*, p. ix.

Hellenic and Gothic.—If we look at a Greek temple, or at a photograph or picture of the finer examples surviving (the Parthenon, the Theseum, the Temple of Apollo at Bassae, the Temple of Poseidon at Paestum), and ask ourselves how it compares and contrasts with the sacred architecture best known to us, our own churches and cathedrals, the most obvious point of contrast is the presence or absence of the arch. Gothic architecture depends primarily for its effects on the arch, and endless variation in the form, decoration, and grouping of arches. There are no arches in a Greek Temple ; there are no curves even, except for decorative purposes.[1] All the constructional lines are straight lines—vertical, horizontal, or slanting. This is not the result of accident ; neither does it appear to be due to ignorance of the principles of the arch.[2] Greek architects must have avoided the use of

[1] This statement must be qualified by what is said later.

[2] " They " (the Greeks and Egyptians) " were perfectly acquainted with the use of the arch and its properties, but they knew that its

the arch deliberately, because it did not accord with their conception of what was appropriate and pleasing in temple architecture. The reason may be in part also climatic. It has been well said : " The methods of building followed by the Greeks were largely due to the fact that the climate permitted an out-of-doors existence, and of open-air ceremonials, which in more northern climates are impossible. The effect aimed at was therefore an external one." [1] The plan of a Greek temple, even of a fifth century temple, if we look at it, is seen to be of an extraordinary simplicity. It consists, primarily, of a rectangular chamber or shrine, the *cella*, sometimes divided in two by a party-wall, to which a fore-chamber and a back-chamber may be added : columns are frequently ranged on all four sides of this enclosed building, sometimes on two sides only, back and front : there is hardly any complexity of structure beyond this. And yet it will probably be acknowledged, that in the best examples this form of temple is wonderfully beautiful.

The main purpose of this chapter is to trace out the secret of this beauty. And for that purpose it seems of most advantage to make a detailed study of one temple as typical. By common consent there is no Greek temple more beautiful than the Parthenon, of which we have already made some study in Chapter III. [2] This chapter will, accordingly, be taken up largely with a more careful study of the Parthenon. He who understands the Parthenon holds the key of all Greek architecture ; perhaps one might say, of all architecture.

Construction and Measurements of the Parthenon.—The columns of the Parthenon rise from a stylo-bate (pillar-base) or platform, 228 feet in length from west to east, 102 feet in breadth from north to south, which is lifted above the surface of the Acropolis rock on two sets of steps.

employment would introduce complexity and confusion into their designs, and therefore they wisely rejected it." Fergusson, *History of Architecture*, vol. i. p. 22.

[1] Simpson, *History of Architectural Development*, vol. i. p. 57.

[2] Especially pp. 56-57 and 60-61.

The upper set of three steps is of marble, each 1 foot 8 inches high,[1] 2 feet 4 inches deep. These three steps form the immediate substructure of the Parthenon. But below them again are two more steps, originally built as the substructure of the temple planned earlier ; and these are of local Piraic stone. The main temple building was an oblong roughly 150 feet by 70 ; and this length was divided into two unequal parts by a crosswall. The eastern chamber, 100 Attic feet in length and hence called Hecatompedos,[2] contained the image of the goddess, the gold and ivory statue of Athena carved by Pheidias, and is therefore the main shrine or *cella*. The western chamber, not quite 50 feet long, was the *Parthenon*, the shrine of the Maiden goddess, from which the whole building takes its name. At either end, East and West, was a shallow porch some 18 feet across ; the eastern called the *Pro-naos* or Fore-temple, the western the *Opistho-domos* or Back-chamber ; each with a row of six columns in front of it. These columns are of exactly the same type as the columns of the great colonnade or peristyle surrounding the whole temple, but slightly smaller. The columns of the peristyle are 34 feet 2 inches in height with a diameter of 6 feet 3 inches at the base : the columns of the inner porticoes are 33 feet in height, with a diameter of 5 feet 6 inches. All these columns are of the Doric style and have twenty grooves or flutings. There are 46 external pillars, eight at each end and 17 on each side (the four corner pillars being reckoned twice), making with the twelve similar pillars of the porches 58 in all. All these pillars taper upwards : thus the pillars of the peristyle, 6 feet 3 inches in diameter at the base, measure 4 feet 7 inches only at the top. Shrine and porches together make a total length of 193 feet 6 inches, so that the full dimensions of the temple building enclosed by

[1] Curiously, one of the steps, the topmost, is one inch and a quarter higher than either of the other two.

[2] Ninety-eight English feet equal almost exactly one hundred feet by the old Attic standard, this Attic foot being slightly shorter than the English.

the peristyle are 193 feet 6 inches by 71 feet. The breadth of the colonnade itself is 15 feet at the two ends, East and West, and one foot less at the sides.

Over the whole of this building was a sloping roof forming at either end (East and West) a gable, or *pediment*. The supports of the roof form the *entablature*. First, immediately above the squared capitals of the pillars, were the massive lengths of the *architrave*, three blocks side by side, stretching from pillar to pillar. Above the architrave came the *triglyphs* and *metopes*, forming a broad decorative band on all four sides. The *cornice* with its border called *cymatium* was the topmost member of the entablature, down to which the roof sloped along the sides. The gables formed at each end (East and West), by the slope of the roof, were filled with the sculptured groups which were the supreme glory of the Parthenon. The apex of the pediment was one foot less than 60 feet above the pavement of the stylobate, and this was further set off by a sculptured floral ornament called the *anthemium*.

The roofing and lighting of a Greek temple are disputable subjects because, from the nature of the case, no roof or ceiling has survived. The Parthenon is believed to have been completely covered in, not *hypaethral*, or partially open to the sky, as some temples were. The roof was seemingly formed by slabs, or tiles, of Parian marble, and these marble tiles were carried by wooden beams and rafters. The Parian marble was relatively transparent, and this is the most probable solution of the problem of lighting. Under the bright sunshine of Greece enough light for practical purposes usually came through the marble tiles. The *wooden* framework is sufficient explanation of the disappearance of the roof. The wood perished and the roof fell in. Below the sloping roof was a horizontal ceiling formed of square slabs or panels let into a framework of marble beams. No piece of the ceiling is left, but a ceiling of the kind has been in part preserved in the Theseum and from this we may infer what the ceiling of the Parthenon was like.

Decoration.—The columns of the peristyle, and those of the two porches in front and in rear, are of the Doric order, the plainest and most dignified of the three recognized styles, Doric, Ionic, Corinthian. This implies that they spring directly from the floor or stylobate without any other base, and that they are crowned with a capital consisting of two parts, the rounded *echinus* (sea-urchin) and the square slab above it called the *abacus* ; and every column, as already said, is grooved with twenty flutings.

All four sides of the Parthenon, but especially the eastern and western ends, were adorned with sculptures. The Frieze was, as we saw in Ch. III. (p. 60), *inside* the peristyle (that is the corridor between the columns and the walls of the temple), above the columns of the two porticoes and along the sides of the temple itself. Its slabs are three feet four inches high and of various lengths, the total length being (as we have seen), nearly 525 feet. Above the colonnade *outside*, on all four sides, in panels between the architrave and the cornice, were the *metopes*. These do not form a continuous band, but alternate with the triglyphs, square blocks of stone with deep vertical grooves lining the outer face. The name *metope* means originally ‘ opening ’ (or ‘ window ’), and the original metopes were open spaces between the ends of beams. When these spaces were used for decorative sculpture and filled with light slabs of marble, the name ‘ windows ’ or openings was retained. There were 32 of these metopes on each side of the Parthenon, and 14 at each end, East and West, making 92 in all. But the noblest of its adornments, both in scale and character, were the pediment sculptures. The triangular spaces forming the ends of a Greek temple obviously offered the most ample field for sculptural decoration.[1] How and when the gable ends of temples were first so used archaeology cannot say. The older temple of Athens, the temple

---

[1] “ One important lesson,” writes Simpson (vol. i. p. 94), “ to be learnt from Greek architecture, especially of the Doric order, is that sculpture on a building is most suitable and effective when framed in.”

destroyed by the Persians, was, it has been discovered, so adorned : the monstrous figures from its pediments may be seen in the Acropolis Museum.[1] There were notable pediment groups on the temple of Zeus at Olympia, and on the temple of Apollo at Delphi. The pediment sculptures of the Parthenon excelled anything that had previously been achieved in Hellas. We shall return to these pediment groups and the other sculptures of the Parthenon in our next chapter.

The Temple Shrine.—All this concerns the outside of the temple. The shrine was inside the walls enclosed by the peristyle, and consisted, as already noted, of two chambers, each with a portico in front of it—the Hecatompedon and the Parthenon. The Parthenon, despite the name which was after a time extended to the whole building, was the smaller and less important. It was entered from the Opistho-domos through great bronze folding-doors, 33 feet high and 16 wide ; and it was used as the main temple treasury. Both Pronaos and Opisthodomos were also used for the safe-keeping and display of temple treasures, and for that reason each was protected by tall metal gratings, extended from column to column of the porch. The Shrine of Athena herself, the cella, was on the East, entered from the Pronaos. Down its length extended two rows of columns, ten on each side, dividing the interior space into a nave and aisles, and the endmost pillars on the further side were linked by three more pillars of the same kind. These were Doric pillars, 3 feet 8 inches in diameter with 16 flutings : the height is unknown since all have perished. This was where the gold-and-ivory Athena stood ; the mark can be seen on the pavement to-day.

Scale of the Parthenon.—There is a certain interest in comparing the Parthenon, as now described, with some of the great churches of Christendom. The area of the Parthenon is approximately 23,000 feet ; Westminster Abbey is 46,000 feet ; St. Paul's Cathedral 84,000 ; Notre

[1] They are fully described in Part I. of the *Catalogue of the Acropolis Museum* by Guy Dickins, pp. 79-85.

Dame de Paris 64,000 ; Cologne Cathedral 91,500 ; St Peter's, Rome, 227,000.[1] If we compare heights, the apex of the gable of the Parthenon is not quite 60 feet. In Westminster Abbey the height of the Nave is 102 feet ; the dome of St. Paul's is 225 : while the abbey towers are 225 feet high and the top of the cross on the dome of St. Paul's Cathedral is 365 feet above the pavement of the street below. We see, then, that in point of size the Parthenon cannot compete with the great cathedrals of Europe. But if in the Elgin Room of the British Museum we look at the Doric capital from one of its pillars, we see that the Parthenon was on a scale grand enough to be impressive. Yet it is certainly not its size which most excites admiration. There were many larger Greek temples.[2] There are very many much larger buildings in the world.[3]

Workmanship.—The shattering of the Parthenon by Morosini's bomb in 1687 was undoubtedly a calamity for the art of Europe. Yet curiously there are for us compensating advantages in its present ruined state for a study of the art which went to its perfecting. " The workmanship of all parts of the Parthenon, whether visible or concealed, is of an extraordinary excellence." [4] Nothing about the Parthenon is more astonishing than the skill with which parts made up of detached blocks (like the drums of columns) are fitted together and made one. The pillars are in no case monoliths ; they are built up of *drums* or sections (generally 12 to a pillar) : but the drums are so deftly fitted one upon another that the pillar appears to be a monolith. How is it done ? We are able to say, because the method can be learnt from study of the drums that have fallen to the ground. It appears on

[1] Fergusson, *History of Architecture*, vol. i. p. 24.

[2] The Temple of Hera in Samos had an area of 65,740 feet ; the Artemisium at Ephesus of 57,072 feet, the Temple of Zeus at Athens of 47,790 feet (Fergusson, i. p. 258).

[3] The Hall of a Hundred Columns at Persepolis was 230 feet square, which gives an area of 52,900 feet ; the Great Hall at Karnak has an area of 57,800 feet. The Taj Mahal at Agra has an area of about 30,000 feet.

[4] Weller, *Athens and its Monuments*, p. 281.

examination that very special means were taken to ensure the perfect adjustment of the two surfaces. It was difficult, or impossible, to do this, that is bring the two surfaces to an absolutely even smoothness, over the whole of a circle whose diameter was more than six feet. So what the Athenian masons did was to bring to this high degree of smoothness an outer rim some ten inches broad. The rest of the surface, with the exception of a circle round the centre about the same measurement in diameter, was slightly depressed and left in the rough, so that the only parts of the two drums actually in contact were the circles of the prepared rims and the centre. We can further see from examination of the fallen drums that in the middle of each drum a square hole was cut and into this a wooden plug was fitted. In the centre of the plug there was a round hole, in which a small peg was fixed, and there was a corresponding hole in the centre of the drum to be superimposed. This peg was not designed as a fastening to hold the drums together, but as a help merely to the exact adjustment of the two surfaces. Some think it was intended as a pivot on which the upper drum might move backwards and forwards, while the two surfaces were brought to an exact smoothness by rubbing one against the other. Rough projections were left on the drums to serve as handles by which the upper drum might be moved. An equally fine diligence was bestowed on the fitting together of the blocks which form steps and architrave (or any horizontal member of the building): " To say that a knife-blade could not be inserted between the blocks," says Gardner, " is a very rough and inadequate way of expressing the fact ; the joint shows often so fine a line as scarcely to be perceptible to the eye." [1] Penrose notes of these joints that they " are made invariably to fit so closely that, unless where the stones have been separated by the violence of earthquakes or other concussions, it is frequently difficult to perceive them ; and when discovered it is almost impossible to imagine a finer line than they show." And he adds his conviction :

[1] Gardner, *Ancient Athens*, p. 274-5.

"This can hardly have been produced by other means than by the stones having been rubbed upon one another ; no third surface used as a plane could have given such a degree of fineness." [1]

Subtle Use of Curves.—But the most surprising revelation of the fineness of Athenian craftsmanship has come through the gradual discovery, since the study of Greek architecture was resumed a century and a half ago, of a number of devices for correcting optical distortions and softening the rigidity of straight lines.   The first discovery of this sort was made by Stuart, joint author of *The Antiquities of Athens* (above, p. 81).   He pointed out that the Doric columns of the peristyle do not merely taper from base to capital, but in doing this they at the same time expand in a gentle curve.   This swelling of the shaft in a single harmonious curve is technically known as the *entasis*.   Stuart's discovery of the entasis was in 1755, and it is recognized that the reason for its use is a trick of our normal eyesight which makes a pillar, the lines of which are exactly straight, appear concave.   Most remarkable of all is a discovery made nearly a hundred years later that all lines bounding the length of the Parthenon—along the edges of the platform or stylobate and of the steps below and the entablature above—which at first sight appear perfectly straight, are in reality very delicately curved. The curve is extremely slight, a rise of four inches only in the full length of the stylobate from East to West, that is 4 inches in 228 feet, but all the same it is perceptible by the eye, if the observer stoops to the level of the step and looks along it.   Now it happens that this peculiarity is actually noticed by Vitruvius, our chief ancient authority on Greek architecture, who wrote in the time of Augustus, as a fundamental principle of Hellenic architecture ; but the passage had been overlooked, or misunderstood, so that when Mr. John Pennefather detected and pointed out the peculiarity in the Parthenon in 1837, it came as a discovery. Penrose, whose book published in 1851—the most interest-

---

[1] Penrose, *Principles of Athenian Architecture*, p. 24 (p. 22 in the original edition of 1851).

ing classic of Hellenic architecture—had these curves as its main subject, remarks : " Now, however strange it may seem that no one had attempted to collate on the spot these passages of Vitruvius . . . with the architecture of the Parthenon, it is by no means so unaccountable that the curves were not sooner discovered from an inspection of the building itself ; for the amount of the curvature is so exquisitely managed that it is not perceptible to a spectator standing opposite to the front ; at least not until the eye has been educated by considerable study founded on knowledge of the fact. It may indeed easily be remarked by anyone who places his eye in such a position as to look along the lines of the step or entablature, from end to end . . ." [1]

The reason why delicate curves are in these positions substituted for straight lines is that long lines when perfectly straight appear to sag, or drop in the middle, and this appearance is accentuated, when upright lines are drawn from this straight line, as by pillars on a stylobate. There are other ingenious contrivances beside for counteracting optical distortions and softening the harsh effects of straight lines. These are summed up by Simpson : " Some minor refinements which exist in the Parthenon and in a few other buildings are not actually apparent, although they make their influence felt when one is conscious of their existence. Angle columns are an inch or two wider than the others, as they stand out against the sky, and consequently appear rather less in diameter than they really are. All the columns incline inwards a trifle, and the faces of the architrave, frieze, tympanum of pediment, and stylobate all have a similar inward inclination. This helps to give that pyramidal appearance to the Parthenon, which is one of its most charming characteristics." [2] There can be no doubt that the peculiar graciousness of the form and outline of the Parthenon is largely due to the use of these subtle devices which correct imperfections in our own way of seeing things. They depend for

---

[1] *Principles of Athenian Architecture*, p. 23 (original edition, p. 20).
[2] *History of Architectural Development*, p. 92.

their efficacy on a singularly acute observation of optical effects and of the laws of beauty.

These subtleties of construction are not confined to the Parthenon, though not found in all Greek temples. The presence or absence of some of them appears to depend not on knowledge, but on the character of the stone of which the temple is built. The inward inclination of walls is found in the Theseum and Erechtheum and in the Propylaea. The curvature of long horizontal lines is found in the Theseum and the Propylaea : it is not found in the temple of Apollo at Bassae or in the temple of Aphaea in Aegina ; and the reason is probably the difference of the stone used. The Theseum and the Propylaea, like the Parthenon, are built of Pentelic marble; the temple in Aegina and the temple at Bassae are of limestone, and neither the yellow limestone of Aegina nor the grey limestone of Bassae is a suitable material for such delicate workmanship as the graduated curves require.

The Three Orders of Hellenic Architecture.—The Parthenon is described as a *Doric* temple. The distinction of three orders, or styles, of Greek architecture is primarily a distinction of columns. It is usual to speak of the three orders as wholly distinct and to praise the Greeks for refusing to contaminate one order with another. Greek standards of taste did not tolerate a mixture of styles. This statement, however, needs qualification. The Parthenon is wholly Doric ; the Erectheum and the Temple of Victory are Ionic. But in the Propylaea, the columns of the porticoes, front and back, are Doric ; the flanking pillars on either side of the central road of ascent are Ionic. The Temple of Apollo the Helper at Bassae again shows a combination of Doric and Ionic ; the external pillars were Doric, the internal Ionic. Strangely, also, in this temple there was found a single column of the Corinthian order : it stood at one end of the cella, towards the South.[1] It is not, therefore,

---

[1] Alone among Hellenic temples the temple at Bassae faces North and South instead of East and West. For the ultimate fate of this Corinthian column, see below p. 502.

DORIC.   IONIC.   CORINTHIAN.

ORDERS OF GREEK ARCHITECTURE.

Reproduced from Statham's *Short Critical History of Architecture*, by kind
permission of the publishers, B. T. Batsford, Ltd.

true that the Doric and Ionic styles are always kept rigidly separate. In the Propylaea and at Bassae the contrast of the Doric and Ionic pillars must have been one element of beauty. It is, however, quite true that the three types are clearly distinguished and that the distinguishing characters of the styles are never mixed in the same column, or system of columns.

The characteristic features of the Doric column are three :

1. The pillars spring from the stylobate without other base.

2. They are relatively solid and taper from below upward.

3. They are surmounted by a simple form of capital, consisting of the rounded *echinus* crowned by the square *abacus*.

The contrasting characters of Ionic are :

1. The pillars have bases more or less ornate.

2. They are more slender than Doric and do not taper.

3. The capitals are *voluted*, that is are folded over in the form of a double scroll with other incidental ornamentation.

Doric and Ionic both attain their perfect development in the fifth century : the third order, the Corinthian, is later, appearing only in the fourth century.

Its developed characteristics are :

1. Elaboration of the base.

2. Increase in height of column.

3. Use of the acanthus leaf pattern to decorate the capital.

The last is the readiest distinguishing mark of the Corinthian style, as the volute is of Ionic and the square abacus of Doric.

The best Athenian example of a temple in the Corinthian style was the Temple of Olympian Zeus as completed in the second century A.D. The Corinthian style was in fact more Roman than Greek. Earlier examples of Corinthian, or of innovations leading to the Corinthian style, are seen in the Choregic Monument of Lysicrates (above, p. 98) and the Tower of the Winds. The earliest known example of a Corinthian column is the pillar at Bassae already mentioned. Corinthian may with some justice be considered as merely a development of Ionic. The contrast is mainly between Ionic and Doric. We see pure and unmixed Doric in the temple of Apollo at Corinth—of which only seven columns are now standing— and in the temple of Poseidon at Paestum. The most complete and splendid example of a purely Ionic temple was the temple of ' Diana of the Ephesians,' the Artemisium at Ephesus—fourth century successor to the Artemisium, of which Xenophon's little shrine at Scillus was a diminutive copy.[1]

There are differences also in the arrangement of the entablature in Doric and Ionic temples, which are readily seen in the diagram facing p. 451.

Origin of the Orders.—The origin of these two contrasted styles and of the Greek temple generally is a speculation of great interest, but it is not easy to reach sure conclusions. On the one hand there is the supposition that the Greek temple was derived by conscious adoption and imitation from Asia and from Egypt (some features from the former, others from the latter), successively through Minoan and Mycenaean tradition. And beyond doubt we have in the discoveries of Schliemann at Mycenae and of Sir Arthur Evans and other archaeologists in Crete, strong evidence of intercourse between Egypt and Crete, and between Egypt, the Isles and the Peloponnese. This is the newer hypothesis, strengthened, as naturally it has been, by the great achievements of archaeology in the last fifty years. On the other hand there is the older theory that the Greek temple in its characteristic features was developed on the mainland of Greece by the peoples ultimately known as Hellenes. It is necessary in any consideration of the subject to bear in mind the purpose of a Greek temple and how this differs from the purpose of a Christian church. The Greek temple was thought of literally as the god's abode, the place where the image of

[1] See above, ch. xii. p. 341.

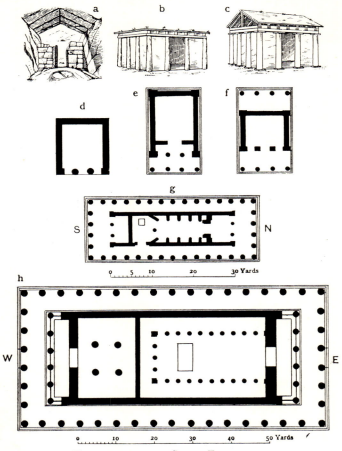

EVOLUTION OF THE GREEK TEMPLE.

a. Grotto in Delos. *b.* and *c.* Conjectural early temples with wooden pillars. *d.* Distyle temple. *e.* Prostyle temple. *f.* Amphiprostyle temple. *g.* Temple of Apollo at Bassae. *h.* The Parthenon.

[*a. After Bell, b. c. g. Fletcher, and d. e. f. Simpson.*

the god was sheltered and preserved in honour. The ancient Greeks never assembled inside a temple for congregational worship as we go to church. The temple began then as a simple shelter, or hut, for the reception of the carved image of the divinity, such as may often be seen in an Indian village—four walls with the idol dimly glimpsed within. There is one such primitive shelter surviving in the island of Delos, a grotto formed by roofing in the sides of a rocky gully with slabs of stone and adding a doorway at one end.[1] From simple structures such as this temples like the Parthenon and the Artemisium were gradually evolved, as men's desire to do honour to the gods and lavish adornment on their dwellings found scope through advances in wealth and artistic skill. First a couple of pillars were planted on either side of the door-way ; then a row of four. This is a *pro-style* temple, a temple ' with pillars in front.' Next similar pillars are added in rear, and it becomes *amphi-prostyle*, a temple ' with pillars at both ends.' What first suggested the colonnade of pillars on all four sides we cannot say : colonnades are a feature of Minoan architecture, and traces of a colonnade on three sides of a courtyard are found at Tiryns. When the colonnade is added, the temple becomes *peri-pteral*, or ' winged-about.' The Parthenon is both amphiprostyle and peripteral. The temple is the walled building within the colonnade and is technically spoken of as the *cella*. In the Parthenon the cella, as we have seen, is double : the eastern and larger chamber is the shrine for the image of the goddess and therefore in a more special sense the *cella* ; the western chamber is a store-house for the temple treasure. At either end, as we have seen, is a portico ; the *pronaos*, or foretemple, at the eastern end, the *opisthodomos*, or back-chamber, at the western. There may even be a double surrounding colonnade as in the Artemisium at Ephesus and the Temple of Olympian Zeus at Athens. But to the end the Greek temple remains in essence a glorified hut, the func-tion of which is to receive and shelter the image of the god.

[1] See Bell, *Hellenic Architecture*, p. 59.

Another interesting speculation, which again can hardly be settled decisively, is whether the shapely rounded pillars of the Greek temple were arrived at by gradually cutting away the corners of squared blocks of stone set on end (like a child's building ' bricks '), or by imitating in stone the trunks of trees, which are themselves natural pillars.   A good deal may be said for either view.

Certain peculiarities in the pillars of the Heraeum at Olympia (accepted as the oldest Greek temple of which remains survive), suggesting the probability of an original wooden system,[1] taken with Pausanias' own statement that one of two pillars in the back-chamber was a wooden pillar in his time, are striking evidence pointing to the derivation of Greek temple columns from tree-trunks. *Against* this derivation is the fact that the pillars of Doric temples of earlier date—at Corinth, for instance, and Paestum—are shorter and thicker than those of later date, instead of being relatively slender, as we should expect if they were imitated from tree trunks.   There can at all events be no doubt that certain other features of Greek temples are *made intelligible*, if we suppose that the stone-work imitates and replaces wood-work.   The triglyphs, for instance, gain significance, if regarded as representations in stone of the ends of wooden beams, carved with grooves as a simple form of decoration.   The architrave, as the very name implies, represents in stone the main beams which support a roof.   What are called *guttae*, that is ' drops,' which in stone seem meaningless, are explained, if they are recognized as imitations in stone of wooden pegs which originally served to fasten the roof-timbers in position.   There is no need to settle these questions dogmatically ; probably neither view can be fully proved. On the whole the evidence supports the view that the Greek temple was in the main developed independently by the Hellenes, but owed some features to Egyptian and

[1] See below p. 493 (ch. xviii.).   The *variation* there noted is explained, if we suppose that all the pillars were wooden originally and that stone pillars were substituted at different dates, as one by one the wooden pillars rotted and had to be replaced.

Asiatic influences ; and that in the construction of the Greek temple the use of wood preceded the use of stone.

The Doric temple was evolved on the mainland of Greece, the Ionic on the coast of Asia Minor, so the history of the two orders is not identical. The slender form of the Ionic pillar and the character of its flutings (deep and narrow with a band between, in contrast with the sharp edges of the Doric flutings) agree better with derivation from wooden models. But its most characteristic feature, the volute of the capital, can be clearly traced to Asian sources.

The Secret of the Greek Temple.—The foregoing analysis and exposition do something, it may be hoped, to answer the question with which this chapter started—what is the secret of the beauty of the Parthenon ? The analysis of the constituent elements in the structure of the Parthenon and the examination of the relation of the parts to each other, and most of all the exhibition of the subtler devices by which those who built it softened and corrected the impressions of the senses, do surely enable us to understand why architects and artists, and other competent judges, find this wonderful beauty in the Parthenon and praise it in unqualified terms of admiration.[1] Perhaps more still might be revealed, if we could understand all that Vitruvius meant when he said that the Greek temple depended for its beauty on the observance of subtle laws of proportion reduced to a science by Greek architects. Modern students have devoted great pains to the search for these laws of proportion, have invented formulas and written treatises to expound them.[2] The result is not

[1] Sir James Fergusson writes of the Parthenon : " for intellectual beauty, for perfection of proportion, for beauty of detail, and for the exquisite perception of the highest and most recondite principles of art ever applied to architecture, it stands utterly and entirely alone—the glory of Greece and a reproach to the rest of the world " (Vol. I. p. 253). Similarly Gardner (*Ancient Athens*, p. 271) speaks of " the exquisite combination of strength, simplicity and grace, which distinguishes it beyond all buildings preserved to us from antiquity."

[2] See, for instance, the report of Mr. Jay Hambidge's lectures in the *Journal of the Hellenic Society* for 1920 (p. xxxvii) and 1921 (p. xix).

very convincing. When mathematical ingenuity has done its utmost, there seems something in symmetry and beauty which eludes the most recondite mathematical investigation.

One other element in the effect produced by Greek temple architecture is simpler and more readily intelligible. The sensuous effect of the Greek temple depends in part on the physical facts of climate and scenery. It has been well observed that the most beautiful of the Greek temples would not produce the same effect, if taken out of their setting and planted down in a modern park or city. This is a circumstance which was overlooked by the enthusiasts of the Renascence, who initiated the movement for what is known as Renascence architecture, that is, the reproduction of the detail of classical architecture in Christian churches and in public buildings. The readiest means of testing the result is to compare St. Paul's Cathedral with Westminster Abbey on the one hand, and with the Parthenon on the other. St. Paul's in London (and St. Peter's in Rome still more), are impressive from their vastness. It is open to doubt whether either strictly attains to beauty. It may safely be asserted that many Renascence buildings in London offend by their incongruity with their surroundings.

So, for the peculiar delight which Hellenic architecture can convey at its highest, you must travel to Greece, and see the wreck of the Parthenon against the brilliant light of morning (or, if you are very fortunate, framed in a double rainbow above the Acropolis) ; you must climb the rough mountain track from Andritsena till, over the last rise, you catch a glimpse of the " Stelous " under the open sky.

CHAPTER XVII

ARCHITECTURE AND SCULPTURE. II

" The Greeks alone have been unique in sculpture : what survives of Pheidias and Praxiteles, of Polycleitus and Scopas, and of their schools, transcends in beauty and in power, in freedom of handling and in purity of form, the very highest work of Donatello, Della Quercia, and Michael Angelo."

JOHN ADDINGTON SYMONDS.

" . . . beauty, as discovered and felt by the Greeks, has an immortal virtue, a flame-like efficacy for the spirit, which cold erudition cannot supply."

WARRACK, *Greek Sculpture*, p. xxxi.

"My quiet, great-kneed, deep-breasted, well-draped ladies of necessity, I give my heart to you ! "

R. L. STEVENSON, *Letters*, Vol. I. p. 91.

ART, like literature and theology, is a subject on which every human being claims the right to an opinion. And yet on no subject is there more need for instruction, if one cares about holding right opinions. Without question there is such a thing as natural good taste, and some people naturally form right opinions in literature and art. But even such fortunate people really need study that they may know the reasonable ground of their opinions, and have something firmer to stand upon than an instinctive judgment that they are right. It is true also that conventions play a great part in aesthetic judgment, sometimes rightly, but often irrationally. Now no one should be asked to admire the Elgin Marbles, or the Parthenon, merely because a succession of ·competent judges has pronounced them to be works of art of a splendour unsurpassable ; or because the painter Haydon, or the sculptor Canova, or the great art critic and man of letters John Ruskin, has used about them the language of exalted admiration. If a young student, boy or man, can go into the Elgin Room and at first see nothing but chipped and defaced fragments of sculptured stone, he is not to be blamed. But if he is wholly without curiosity and indifferent, when he is told what great artists and men of action have felt and thought and written about these fragments, he is certainly open to blame. And if, shunning this blame, he returns and gives more careful attention to the fragments in the Elgin Room, and to what besides he can readily learn of Greek sculpture and architecture, there is a strong probability that his mind will begin to work as the minds of other well-endowed human beings have worked before him, and a new world of wonder and beauty will gradually be unfolded to him.

So it is worth while in this chapter to return to the Elgin Marbles and give a little time to their more careful examination. For they are affirmed to be the most splendid relics of Greek sculpture left to us, and they illustrate the doctrine that sculpture in its first and most appropriate use is associated with architecture and almost a branch of the larger craft. There were two clearly distinct uses of sculpture among the Greeks : the one was the beautifying of their temples ; the other was embodying in some lasting material ideal representations of the human form ; divine beings in human shape first, and then mortal men of a god-like beauty or fame. The total wealth created by the Greeks in these two kinds of sculpture, temple decoration and statuary, was once very great—great beyond computation. This we know from Pausanias and Pliny and Lucian and other literary sources. Between the fifth century B.C. and the second century A.D., eastern Europe and Italy and western Asia became, from generation to generation, more and more filled with masterpieces, and copies of masterpieces, of Greek sculpture, and of metal work, especially bronzes, like sculpture. Of this vast wealth little indeed compared with its former richness and abundance remains to us ; but that little is of inestimable value, and is sufficient in amount to form no inconsiderable part of the heritage of art to which we are born. Its value is so great, whether measured in terms of sheer enjoyment, or viewed as material for the training of aesthetic judgment, that it is worth some effort to attain an understanding and appreciation of Greek sculpture.

The Appreciation of Greek Sculpture.—There is but one way to reach a full appreciation of this wonder ; and that is to see the actual handiwork of the masters of the great age. Books and illustrations, photographs, engravings, will do a great deal, and casts will do more ; but however good and however beautiful photographs and casts may be (and some are very beautiful), photographs and casts are but a poor substitute for marble statues and reliefs. For the Hermes of Praxiteles you must go to Olympia ; for the Bronze Charioteer to Delphi ; for the Victories of the Nikê balustrade to the Acropolis Museum ; for the Dying Gaul and the Laocoon to Rome ; the Aphroditê of Melos (Venus of Milo) and the Victory of Samothrace are in the Louvre. But for all this—in the rooms of Greek sculpture in the British Museum, in the very heart of England, there are opportunities for a first-hand study of Greek sculpture so ample and complete that it is difficult to speak of them in moderate terms.

Greek Sculpture in the British Museum.—If you turn left on entering the Museum and traverse the length of the galleries beginning with the Gallery of Roman portrait sculpture (Roman Gallery) till you come to a descending flight of stairs, there is one gallery of sculpture in which are crowded *casts* of *all* the most noteworthy classical statues from archaic Heras and Apollos, dating from 800 B.C., to the finest work of imperial Roman times, a thousand years later. *All* the best-known masterpieces are there : *Harmodius and Aristogeiton*, Polycleitus' *Doryphoros* (Spear-Bearer), Myron's *Discobolos* (Quoit-thrower) and *Marsyas* ; the *Victory of Paeonius* and the *Victory of Samothrace* ; the *Hermes* of Praxiteles ; the Cnidian and the Melian *Aphroditê* ; the *Dying Gaul* ; the *Niobê* group ; the *Laocoon* group ; the *Apollo Belvedere*. All these are *casts* not marbles ; and that makes an immense difference : no one could guess the winning qualities of the Hermes at Olympia from the cast in the British Museum. An even more pertinent consideration is that few of the statues from which these casts are taken are the original masterpieces ; they are mostly skilful copies of famous masterpieces made to gratify the connoisseurship of rich Roman collectors long after the sculptor's own day. So it is on the whole with disappointment that we come away from these reproductions of famous statuary. Not one of them possesses the mysterious quality by which genius in a masterpiece impresses itself upon us, as the Hermes at Olympia does, as do the horses of the Pheidian frieze and the Victories of the Nikê balustrade. The treasure of the British Museum is not here, in the Gallery of Casts.

But in the rooms of architectural sculpture it is very different ; the Room of the Nereids, the Phigalean Room, the Mausoleum Room, and most of all, and out of all comparison, the Elgin Room. In the Elgin Room you can see more great original Hellenic sculpture than anywhere else in the world, Athens alone, perhaps, excepted. For among sculptured Greek temples the Parthenon had the grandest pediment groups, and metopes which are not only more numerous than those of any other known temple, but also of finer workmanship. The Parthenon frieze is by far the most elaborate, the most perfect in design, the most skilfully executed. And, as we saw in Ch. III., large part of the frieze, the best preserved of the metopes, and nearly all that remains of the pediment groups are in the Elgin Room. We will take these three kinds of decoration in order, beginning with the frieze.

The Parthenon Frieze.—The Panathenaic frieze, as we have seen,[1] is inside the colonnade which surrounds the Parthenon, but outside the temple : it forms a border along the top of the cella wall and passes on above the inner columns of the eastern and western porticoes ; it could only be seen from within the colonnade itself. What distinguishes this frieze from all other temple friezes is, firstly, the large unity of design ; the subject is one and continuous, not broken into sections

[1] Vol. I. p. 60.

as in most friezes. It was a happy thought of the artist, whether Pheidias or another, who hit upon the design of the Panathenaic procession : it was a large enough subject to fill the space (though its length is not far short of 200 yards), and yet was charmingly diversified ; and it was exactly appropriate to the shrine of Athena. Secondly, there is the matchless perfection of workmanship ; and, thirdly, the rich variety of the details. It represents— not with matter-of-fact exactitude, but with the freedom demanded by a work of art—the whole Panathenaic procession, from the assembling in the Outer Ceramicus to the delivery of the peplos at the shrine of Athena Polias. For a right understanding of the detail of the frieze reference to the actual ceremony is necessary, though it would be a mistake to cite the frieze as conclusive evidence on a point of archaeological nicety. All classes joined in the procession, priests, magistrates, knights, maidens and youths, citizens and foreign residents. All these we see in the frieze taking appropriate part in the procession ; and besides these there are four-horse chariots—a great number of them—and oxen and sheep for sacrifice. Finally at the east end is the conclave of the gods, seated in curiously easy and detached attitudes, a study in repose.

The whole frieze, with the exception of the fifty feet altogether lost, is to be seen in the Elgin Room arranged in order along the walls, though the arrangement does not conform to the actual shape of the Parthenon. Where the original slabs remain on the walls of the Parthenon itself, or have been taken to some other place than England, the gap is supplied by casts ; but close on half of the original frieze is actually in the British Museum. It has always to be borne in mind that the slabs were not sculptured to be seen as we see them in London, but as they were seen on the Parthenon itself, that is at a height of 40 feet from the ground. The method used took careful account of this consideration : this is why very shallow relief is used, never more than two inches deep : had the relief been deeper, since all the light came from below, shadows would have been thrown from the lower portions upon the upper.

For the same reason the whole surface is tilted forward slightly in its upper part.

A tour of the room begins best at the western end of the frieze. There you see the young horsemen, the knights, flower of the noble youth of Attica—some preparing to mount, some just mounted and holding in their steeds ; and in front of these, for half the length of the northern side, the stream of gallant youths riding off in loose order to form ranks and join in the procession, at once the most spirited and the most skilfully diversified part of the frieze. The prancing horses—one hundred and twenty-five have been counted—each of them individual and different from all the rest, are in most effective contrast with the processional calm of the figures further on. Chariots come next, with their teams of four horses and their two occupants, the fighting man with spear and shield trained to leap down from the car and back again while the chariot is in motion, and the long-robed charioteer. Next in front of these you see a group of Athenian citizens in easy conversation, and beyond these you overtake in succession musicians with lyres, musicians with pipes (four of each) ; youths carrying wine-jars, one of whom is resting (a specially graceful group) ; men carrying trays of cakes. Then come the animals for sacrifice, oxen and sheep ; and this brings us to the corner where the north side meets the east. Here we come upon the procession of maidens accompanying the peplos. Most of them carry vessels and other sacred objects ; the two foremost are empty-handed ; it is pleasant to think of them as weavers of the peplos. This procession of maidens is received by two officials, and beyond again is another group of citizens, who possibly represent high officers of state. We are now close to the scene in which the theme of the frieze culminates : we are in presence of the gods (though they must be supposed invisible), six of whom, Aphroditê, Artemis, Apollo, Poseidon, Hephaestus, and Athena herself, face the procession from the north side ; six, Zeus, Hera, Ares, Demeter, Dionysus, Hermes, that from the south. Eros stands at his mother Aphroditê's knee, and behind Hera and Ares is a female figure, which is probably Iris.[1] Between the two groups of deities stands a priest receiving a great mantle from the hands of a boy-attendant. This must be the peplos. It has been brought to Athena's temple, and is now to be hung upon her image. The procession coming from the south side is very similar to that now described, but there are differences of detail. The more noticeable are in the sacrificial animals and in the grouping of the cavalry. On the north side the victims for sacrifice are oxen and sheep ; on the south cattle only. And in the southern frieze the cavalry are represented in somewhat more regular formation. In contrast with the varied scene of preparation and the mounted men riding off in a continuous stream, you have the massed effect of cavalry advancing rank behind rank in orderly array. There is vigour and variety and a splendid vitality in what is left of these horsemen of the south frieze ; but it is the horsemen of the north frieze that are the crowning achieve- ment of Pheidias' great design. They are truly " without rival or parallel in the world's art." [2] The very poetry of movement has in them received living expression per- petually renewed. The eye passes again and again over the changing throng of curvetting horses and gracefully balanced riders. It is as when we watch water flowing over a weir, or the Atlantic ground-swell breaking upon Cornish rocks : fascinated we gaze on, and never weary of delight.

The Metopes.—Not much can be usefully said here of the metopes. Of the original 92 only about half survive at all, and some of these are disfigured beyond recognition. There are 15 original panels and 5 casts in the Elgin Room. All but two of these come from the south side of the Parthenon and represent Centaurs fighting Lapithae and carrying off Lapith women. From the existing evidence it appears that the Marriage of Peirithous and the Fight with the Centaurs formed the subject of the

[1] The identifications are those of the *Short Guide to the Sculptures of the Parthenon*, pp. 30-32. Only six of them, Hermes, Zeus, Hera, Athena, Hephaestus, Ares, can be regarded as practically certain ; the rest are disputable.

[2] *Short Guide*, p. 35.

metopes on both long sides of the Parthenon (north and
south), duplicated with differences much as the procession is in the frieze ; that the subject on the east front
was a Battle of Gods and Giants, on the west a Battle
of Greeks and Amazons.   All three may be regarded as
variations of one theme, the struggle between a higher
civilization and a lower, between Hellas and Barbarism.[1]
The metopes of the Parthenon have not the grandeur of
the pediment sculptures, nor the beauty of the frieze,
but the best of them are fine bold work.   In contrast
with the frieze they are in high relief.   The metope form
greatly restricts the artist's opportunities, as there is not
space for more than two figures in each panel, and treatment cannot be continuous.   The sculptor's skill consists
in diversifying the incidents within these limiting conditions.   The subject is, of course, one of the common-
places of Greek sculpture and it is interesting to contrast
the metopes with other examples.   There are three such
in the British Museum, two friezes and a pediment group.
The readiest comparison is with the frieze of the temple of
Apollo at Bassae, which is in the Phigalean Room.
Reproductions of the other frieze, the frieze of the
Theseum, and of the west pediment of the Temple of Zeus
at Olympia, will be found in the gallery of Casts.

The Pediment Groups.—When all considerations are
duly weighed the frieze of the Parthenon is the most
valuable work of sculpture that has come down to us from
antiquity : for the greater part of it actually survives in
fair preservation and nearly the whole can be reconstructed
with the help of drawings made by Carrey in 1674 (before
the Venetian bomb had done its evil work) and by Stuart
in 1751 ; while the best preserved slabs are nearly perfect
and of surpassing beauty.   There can be little doubt,
however, that originally the most splendid work of all was

[1] See Murray, *The Sculptures of the Parthenon*, Chapters IV. and V.,
for full discussion.   Indeed to a right understanding of the Parthenon
sculptures Murray is indispensable ; and see especially his opening
pages (pp. 1-7) for the relations to each other of frieze, metopes, and
pediments, and for the unifying purpose of the scheme of sculptural
decoration as a whole.

FIGURES K, L, M, FROM THE EAST PEDIMENT OF THE PARTHENON.

From a photograph in the collection of the Society for the Promotion of Hellenic Studies.

that of the pediment groups. It may be difficult to recognize this now on a first introduction to the fragments of sculpture, disposed as far as possible in their true relations of position and distance along the two sides of the length of the Elgin Room. Unfortunately there is no full description of the groups extant dating from early times. Pausanias barely mentions the existence of the sculptures and supplies the names of the subjects : the *Birth of Athena* for the eastern group ; the *Contest of Athena and Poseidon* for the western. We have the further help of the drawings made by Carrey in 1674. At that time there was more of the west pediment group left than of the east, and so Carrey's drawings are specially helpful in the reconstruction of the western group. But it was the western group which suffered most at Morosini's hands and now more is left of the eastern group. It is, also, the more interesting. It is from the figures brought to the British Museum from the two ends of this pediment that the modern estimate of the beauty and majesty of the pediment sculptures of the Parthenon is mainly drawn. For all the central figures of the eastern pediment have absolutely perished and what is left of the western pediment is little more than wreckage.

The Eastern group.—Of the group in the eastern pediment, besides the horses' heads already spoken of (above, p. 79), there are in all seven figures, four on the left, three on the right. All but one are headless, and the one remaining head, the head of the 'Theseus,' is badly damaged. There is an astonishing effect of ease and dignity about the two seated figures on the left, Demeter and Persephonê.[1] The grace of the reclining male figure next them on the same side,[2] the suggestion of vigour in repose, is unsurpassable. And yet the charm of the three draped female figures,[3] which occupy the corresponding positions on the right, is more overpowering still. The gracious beauty of

[1] E and F in fig. 11 on p. 14 of the *Short Guide.*

[2] D in fig. 11.

[3] K L M in fig. 13, p. 16. See illustration on the opposite page and the quotation from R. L. Stevenson at the head of the chapter.

these figures combined with an irresistible impression of more than human dignity is what most of all compels wonder and admiration. These mutilated figures of a broken group, even by themselves, without the mighty central figures which gave the key to their meaning, make an incomparable masterpiece of composition. And yet the central figures, being the most important of all, were probably the most splendidly executed. They are missing from Carrey's drawing, and Pausanias fails to supply the hints which would have given us some ground of certainty. Nevertheless it is possible by sympathetic imagination to reconstruct this part of the group with some plausibility. Zeus must have been there in the centre ; for it was from his cleft forehead that the goddess leapt forth fully armed, as Hesiod sang.[1] Hephaestus must have been there ; for it was his axe which cleft open the head of Zeus and freed the goddess to her birth. Athena herself must have been there, and in such form and place as to impress beholders with the splendour of her divinity ; for the Parthenon is her temple and its sculptures were dedicated to her glory. It is therefore probable that she stood next to Zeus on the right, armed in full panoply.

The Western Group.—Though less of it is actually left to us now, the *Contest of Athena and Poseidon* can be restored with greater confidence. This is chiefly because of Jacques Carrey's drawings. Without Jacques Carrey's sketch the detached fragments now to be seen in the British Museum would give no idea whatever of the subject; but the drawing gives a clear and vivid impression of the grouping, and with its help the fragments, formless as some of them are, readily fall into their places. The story illustrated is the dispute between Poseidon and Athena for the first place in the affections of the Athenian people and the prior right to be regarded as the tutelary deity of Athens. The moment seized by the sculptor is that immediately after the creation of the olive, the miracle by which Athena made good her claim. Athens was to be adjudged to whichever of the two bestowed on the land

[1] Vol. I. pp. 41 and 42.

the greater benefit. Poseidon with a stroke of his trident created the salt spring, symbol of Athenian sea-power, and took one step forward, preparing to seize his prize. Then Athena smote the ground in turn and created the olive, significant of the ancient wealth and power of Athens before her sea-power grew great : and Poseidon starts back discomfited. The other figures in the group are mostly matter of uncertain conjecture ; doubtless they were all persons of local and mythological significance. For four or five of them names are suggested with much probability. The youth whose recumbent form fills the left-hand corner [1] may well be the river Cephisus, balanced by Ilissus and the fountain Callirhoê, the figures in the opposite angle.[2] Next to Cephisus come a pair of figures, the only figures in this pediment which have survived : how gladly would we know if they are, as has been suggested, Cecrops and one of his daughters.[3] Near the centre was the chariot of Athena with the splendid horses which Morosini coveted for Venice, and destroyed in the attempt to remove. Behind these horses was a male figure, possibly Hermes. Beyond Poseidon on the right-hand side, we may infer with certainty there was another chariot and horses, Poseidon's, though even in Carrey's drawing these are missing. Poseidon's charioteer is in all probability Amphitritê, his queen : a dolphin may be seen under her feet, as she sits.[4] The running figure beyond Amphitritê, balancing Hermes on the left, may be Iris. The intermediate groups on each side are obscure. Demeter, Persephonê, and the boy Iacchos is a title suggested for the group of three in Carrey's drawing on the left.[5] There was evidently more vigour and more variety in this western group, but it has not the majestic loveliness of the eastern.

Other Pediment Groups.—There are two chief criteria of the merits of architectural sculptures such as these : (1)

[1] A in fig. 16 on p. 19 of the *Short Guide.*

[2] V and W in fig. 19, p. 21.   [3] B and C on p. 19.

[4] O in fig. 18, p. 21.   [5] D E F in fig. 15, p. 18.

the beauty of the several figures individually ; (2) the grouping of the figures as a whole. By both of these standards the pediment sculptures of the Parthenon must be put in a class by themselves. There are no ancient sculptures of equal harmony and beauty : it is difficult to think of any modern sculpture to compare with them. Their higher excellence is strikingly brought out by a comparison with other surviving pediment groups, of which enough is left for the purpose. The groups that readily come to mind are two only, the Aeginetan Marbles and the pediment sculptures of the Temple of Zeus at Olympia.

The Aeginetan Marbles, casts of which [1] have been set up in the Archaic Room at the British Museum in correct pediment form, are the groups from the temple of Aphaea in Aegina.[2] Each represents a fight between Greeks and Trojans. There is a sturdy energy in the figures individually, but a glance shows that compared with the Parthenon sculptures these groups are formal and stiff. There is but one figure which touches the feelings, the bearded warrior in the eastern group wounded to the death : all the rest leave us cold.

The probabilities point to a date not long after 480 B.C. for these Aeginetan sculptures. The pediment groups from the temple of Zeus at Olympia, which are believed to be not many years later in date, show considerable advance in technical skill, but these also are stiff and ineffective compared with the freedom and grace of the Parthenon figures. Reduced models of these pediments may be seen in the Gallery of Casts. The inartistic formality of the arrangement of the Oenomaus group in the east pediment hardly needs pointing out : the figures on either side of Zeus and the two four-horse chariots balance each other too exactly. There is more life in the west pediment group, which is another example of the Centaur-Lapith story, with Theseus and Peirithous in

[1] The originals are at Munich.

[2] Aphaea is a little-known goddess, worshipped in Aegina. She appears to have been associated with Artemis.

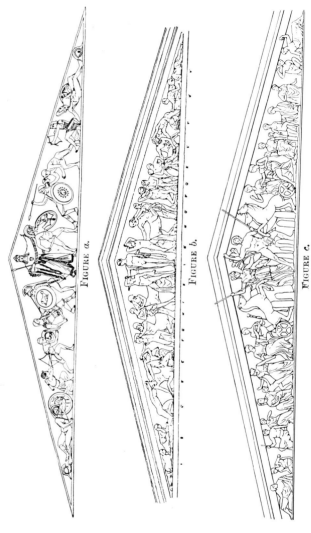

FIGURE a.

FIGURE b.

FIGURE c.

RESTORED PEDIMENT GROUPS.

For comparison.

a. East Pediment of the Temple of Aphaea, Aegina.
b. West Pediment of the Temple of Zeus at Olympia.
c. West Pediment of the Parthenon.

a and b are from Professor Gardner's *Handbook of Greek Sculpture*, c is from a photograph in the collection of the Society for the Promotion of Hellenic Studies.

the leading rôles. Here we find more variety and more vigour. One incident, in particular, catches the attention from its sheer savagery : a young Lapith has thrown his arm round the neck of one of the Centaurs ; the Centaur has fixed his teeth in his assailant's forearm and holds it with his hands so that it cannot be withdrawn. But neither of the principal figures gives any great impression of beauty or power, while the Apollo who stands in the centre as arbiter of the fight is merely conventional. These Olympian sculptures, like the Aeginetan, do but bring into relief the higher art and more moving beauty of the Athenian.

Metopes and Friezes.—The superiority of the Parthenon metopes is not so decided. The metopes from the temple of Zeus at Olympia, badly as they have suffered, show livelier imagination, though not, perhaps, equal technical skill. Their subject is the *Labours of Heracles.* All are characterized by a refreshing boldness of treatment ; in one or two there is a subtle suggestion of humorous intention. What else is the quiet mockery of Atlas' holding out apples to Heracles, when with Atlas' load on his head he is unable to move a hand ? Or the edifying vigour with which the divine hero wields a broom at his task of cleansing the Augean stables ? Twelve slabs depicting twelve labours have been found, but some are very badly mutilated. The best are in the Louvre ; the rest in the Museum at Olympia. Only three, that is to say, casts of three, are in the British Museum ; but one of these is the delightful Heracles and Atlas.

For comparison with the Parthenon frieze we have in the British Museum three contemporary, or nearly contemporary friezes : the frieze of the Nikê temple, the frieze of Phigalean Bassae, the frieze of the Theseum. The whole of the frieze from Bassae is in the Phigalean Room ; a portion of the Nikê frieze—4 slabs out of 14—is in the Elgin Room ; casts of the Theseum frieze are found, one part (the eastern frieze) in the Elgin Room, the other (the western) in the Gallery of Casts. None of these friezes approaches the scale of the Parthenon. The largest of the three, the frieze from Bassae, is a little over 2 feet high and just 102 feet in length. The Parthenon frieze was over 520 feet long, 3 feet 4 inches high. The beauty of the Nikê frieze places it high for workmanship, but its scale is insignificant—just 18 inches high. There is abundant vigour in the execution of the Phigalean frieze, and as it ran along the top of the side walls of the cella and the cella was hypaethral or open to the sky, its bold and deep relief must have shown up well in the sunlight ; but it is curiously rude, and even in places clumsy, work compared with the Parthenon frieze. The battle of Centaurs and Lapithae takes up not quite half of it, the rest is a conflict of Greeks and Amazons.[1] The frieze of the Theseum is closely comparable in style with the Parthenon metopes, but does not approach the beauty of the Parthenon frieze. The friezes which most nearly rival the perfection of the Parthenon frieze—so far as may be judged from the fragments left of them—are not contemporary but of later date, the friezes of the Mausoleum. The Mausoleum was the monument built in the fourth century B.C. for Mausolus, her husband, by Artemisia of Halicarnassus, a later Artemisia than the Artemisia whom Xerxes honoured.[2] The remains of this monument, which has given the word mausoleum to the English language, fill most of the space in the Mausoleum Room. There are two friezes. Of the one the subject is a battle of Greeks and Amazons : how fiery is the vigour and how tender the pathos of the best of these [3] can be seen in the Mausoleum Room. They express, as no other representation of the Amazon legend does, the horror of merciless physical combat between men and women. Whether these splendid young Amazons are dealing lusty blows with sword or battle-axe at their male opponents, or with steadfast eyes and face uplifted wait undaunted their

[1] For an account of the finding and recovery of this frieze see chapter xviii. pp. 500-502.

[2] See Herodotus, viii. 69 and 88.

[3] See especially 1014, 1022 and 1006 (slabs 9, 17 and 1) in the Mausoleum Room.

conqueror's death-stroke, the sculptor seems to compel our sympathies to side with them even against the national Hellenic cause. The other frieze illustrated a chariot race. There is one figure from this, unfortunately badly mutilated, which bears comparison with the loveliest of the Elgin Marbles—the Mausoleum Charioteer. Style and spirit are different, showing the character of another age than that of Pheidias : the figure is beautiful with a difference, but not less beautiful.

The History of Greek Sculpture.—To trace in detail the history of Greek sculpture is quite beyond our purpose here, but the main outline is simple and it is possible to indicate briefly the points of chief interest. Sculpture distinctively Greek is generally dated from the sixth century B.C. It then appears sporadically at many centres on the mainland, on the coast of Asia Minor, and in the islands of the Aegean. Several of the islands—in particular, Chios, Samos, Naxos, Paros, Thasos, Crete—came early into note as centres of artistic activity. The antecedents of this Hellenic art go back into a distant past during which influences from beyond Greece, and especially from Egypt and Asia Minor, undoubtedly made themselves felt. Twice the artistic impulse had risen to a high point, first in the far distant past called Minoan ; secondly in the age of which the Homeric poems give, or purport to give, a picture. But how crude were the beginnings of Greek art in sculpture, before and during the sixth century, may be seen in the early sculptures found at Selinus in Sicily, in the Pre-Persian pediment sculptures dug out of crevices in the Acropolis rock, and in the archaic statues of all kinds in museums. It was far below the level attained in very early times by the Egyptians, and markedly inferior to the best Assyrian reliefs. During the sixth century these scattered endeavours became focussed in two contrasted styles or schools, which (once more) follow the race distinction of Ionian and Dorian. The Ionic school shows, as we should expect, the characteristic Ionian tendency to softness and richness of decoration. It centred first in Ionia and later at Athens, where its softness was corrected through the influence of the more virile Doric School. The Doric or Peloponnesian School, which with its greater strength and firmness showed a certain hardness and want of charm, came to a climax in the Argive School. The Argive School concentrates its efforts on portraying in bronze or marble the manly athletic form. The fifth century, the great century in architecture and sculpture as well as in literature and in national life, begins with this contrast of Athenian and Argive Schools. But the two schools mutually influence each other, and out of this reciprocal influence came the art of the great Hellenic sculptors. This interaction of the schools can be illustrated by great names. Ageladas of Argos was the foremost master of the Peloponnesian style towards the close of the sixth century, and Ageladas was the teacher of Polycleitus and Myron and Pheidias. Polycleitus perfected the Argive style ; it was transmuted by Pheidias into a higher beauty. Myron gave his own individuality to the Argive type without attaining to the high ideality of Pheidias. The rapidity with which Greek sculpture advanced from the stiffness and hardness of the Aeginetan and Olympian pediments to the perfection of the Parthenon sculptures is itself great part of the marvel. And the impetus which gave fifth century sculpture its grandeur did not cease with the century. Hellenic sculpture of the fourth century, if we may draw conclusions from the scanty data we have for judgment, was scarcely a less glorious achievement than that of the fifth. It had less ideal grandeur, but a gracious beauty which was more divine than human. Praxiteles was its greatest master, no mean rival of Pheidias. Scopas, a slightly older contemporary of Praxiteles, gave to marble a life-like intensity which was alien to fifth century canons, but brought new power to sculpture. Lysippus of Sicyon continued, though he could not excel, the more limited achievement of Polycleitus. Hellenistic sculpture follows. It goes beyond Hellenic in the range of emotion to which it appeals, and in its delineation of human suffering. It rises to a height at Pergamos and Rhodes

The one school gives us the *Dying Gaul* ; the other the *Laocoon* group. The sculptor of the Laocoon was Agesander of Rhodes ; we get the name from Pliny : the sculptor of the Dying Gaul is not known. The Hellenistic period, as distinct from the Hellenic, is reckoned as lasting down to about 100 B.C. from approximately 320. It has no names to equal Polycleitus, Pheidias, Scopas, and Praxiteles. Graeco-Roman sculpture continues the Hellenistic tradition without any fresh breath of life [1] down to the first half of the fourth century A.D., when Constantine transferred the capital of the Roman empire to Constantinople and made Christianity the state religion. And then, with the dissolution of the religious beliefs in which it was grounded, Greek sculpture died a natural death. There was no supremely great name again in sculpture till Michael Angelo, over a thousand years later.

Masterpieces of Greek Sculpture.—The whole period during which Hellenic sculpture flourished and was held in high estimation throughout the western world, both popularly and by the most cultivated portion of mankind, was something like eight hundred years (B.C. 450 to 350 A.D.), though it was for little more than two hundred years (from 450 to 250 B.C.) that the original work on which the claim of Greece to supremacy in sculpture is founded was being produced. Indeed the greatest works of all, the masterpieces whose almost superhuman excellence was famed throughout the Graeco-Roman world, are all included within a period of not much over a hundred years, from 450 to 330 B.C. The great masters of highest rank are six only : three in the fifth century B.C., Polycleitus, Myron, Pheidias ; three in the fourth, Scopas, Praxiteles, Lysippus. After these come a host of lesser sculptors, some like Alcamenes and Paeonius, whose work is known to us ; others who are merely names and reputations. There must be a vastly greater number whose names are not recorded at all. Pausanias gives us

---

[1] The vivid individual portrait sculpture which Roman taste introduced does, however, constitute a new departure ; it was unknown to Hellenic art.

some idea how full Greece was of glorious sculpture in the second century A.D. At each city to which he comes in his travels—in Phocis, in Boeotia, in Attica, and throughout the Peloponnese — he describes one by one the temples and enumerates with descriptive touches and mythological elucidations the works of art. All Greece on his showing was, as Gardner puts it, 'a vast museum.' It must have been much the same throughout the flourishing Greek cities of Asia Minor and Syria, and in the Greek cities of Italy and Sicily, though outside Greece proper there would be more works of inferior masters and more ' copies.' At Rome, as late as the middle of the fourth century A.D., there were counted " four thousand bronze statues, apart from marble statues too numerous to be counted, and over 150 statues of more costly material, gilt and chryselephantine images of gods and 22 large equestrian statues." Pliny, in the last five books of his *Natural History*, in dealing with metal and stone, takes in hand to enumerate and sometimes describe the most remarkable works of art in bronze and marble existing in his time, and so becomes a mine of information to us about Greek sculpture and sculptors. From Pausanias and Pliny combined we get an overpowering impression of the large amount of notable sculpture existing when they lived, and of the marvellous perfection of the most celebrated masterpieces. And if now, approaching our subject from this new standpoint, we ask how much of what Pausanias saw and Pliny describes has come down to our day, the answer is surprising.

Of original works of great masters, apart from temple sculptures, that is to say single statues and groups of statuary, very few indeed are left. You may count them on your fingers. In fact there are only *two* works of which we can say with complete confidence that in them we look upon the authentic work of one of the great masters ; the Hermes of Praxiteles and the Victory of Paeonius. And Paeonius is a master of second rank. There are, it is true, a good many other statues which may fairly be called ' originals,' though the names of the sculptors who made them are not known, or not known with certainty. The *Victory of Samothrace* is one such ; so is the *Dying Gaul*, and the statue found at Subiaco and called the *Kneeling Boy* ; possibly also the Niobê group. Nor can any sharp line be drawn between statues and architectural sculptures. The Mausoleum was a building and its sculptures may therefore all be described as architectural ; but the figures of Mausolus and Artemisia are clearly statues. Yet when all this has been taken into account, and account has also been taken of the ' copies ' which are of a quality to give some just impression of the genius of the masters whose work they reproduce, the sum of all surviving Greek sculpture is very little compared with the wonderful wealth which Pliny and Pausanias describe. How was this wide and almost universal destruction brought about ?

Dispersal, Destruction, and Recovery of Greek Master-pieces.—The destruction was a long-drawn process still going on when, early in the nineteenth century, Lord Elgin learnt from his Turkish householder on the Acropolis that some of the Parthenon sculptures had recently been pounded up to make mortar. The Romans began it, when Mummius set his soldiers to lay hands on precious works of art at Corinth and stipulated with the contractors commissioned to convey them to Rome, that any article destroyed was *to be replaced by another of equal value.* Oppressive governors like Verres, and art-loving emperors like Caligula and Nero, plundered Greece of her artistic treasure to beautify their palaces in Italy ; and for centuries many of the most famous Greek masterpieces of sculpture were to be found in Rome. But as these works of art were only removed from one place to another, not injured or destroyed, such depredations did not diminish the sum total of excellent sculpture in the Graeco-Roman world. Nor was it otherwise when in the fourth century A.D. Constantinople took the place of Rome, and a large portion of the artistic riches of Rome was removed thither. This was still dispersal, not destruction ; but in-directly it led to destruction, through the great conflagra-tions which occurred both at Rome and Constantinople ;

several masterpieces are known to have perished in this
way by fire. The age of the Antonines is probably the
time when the world was fullest of noble Hellenic sculpture, of masterpieces and copies of masterpieces. This
continued with little alteration up to the middle of the
fourth century A.D., when the note of the bronzes and
statues in Rome quoted above was made. A little more
than half a century later Rome itself had been sacked by
Alaric's Goths (A.D. 410); with successive barbarian
invasions and the frequent pillage of the towns, the
destruction of works of art had begun and proceeded
apace. But in the long run a far more widespread and
searching influence tending to banish from the earth the
glory of Greek sculpture was that decay of the old religion
which had already set in when Euripides was writing his
plays. When a new and eagerly militant faith took the
place of uneasy scepticism, the moral confusion at the
heart of paganism soon led to its utter rejection as a
system of belief. For the time being Christianity was
necessarily inimical to Greek art. The old religion was
first neglected, then persecuted ; and the art of sculpture,
intimately bound up as it was with the old religion, came
under the ban. Interest in art as one of the glories and
joys of life became less and less. Men and women ceased
to care for material beauty as something good and delightful in itself, lifting the mind above sordid and petty things.
Simultaneously wars, invasions, devastation, the immigra-
tion of horde upon horde of alien races at a ruder stage of
culture, all contributed to a lowering of life and the
disintegration of the old order. Floods, earthquakes,
epidemic fevers, played their part in what was nothing
less than the ruin of civilization. In an utterly changed
world art at last counted for little or nothing. "Works
of art gradually lost their value as creations of the mind ;
and their destruction commenced whenever the material
of which they were composed was of great value, or
happened to be wanted for some other purpose more
useful in the opinion of the possessor." [1] To take but one

[1] Finlay, *History of Greece*, i. 191.

example, in the reign of Anastasius I. a number of very fine bronze statues were melted down to make a statue of the emperor. Of the last stage Professor Gardner writes : " When bronze and marble had become more precious in themselves than the art which had found in them the means of perpetuating its noblest ideals, the fate of sculpture was sealed. Bronze, not to speak of more precious metals, was ruthlessly melted down, and even marble was burnt to produce mortar—the lime kilns upon every classical site record the fate of the statues that once peopled it." [1] For a thousand years and more Greek sculpture almost dropped out of men's recollection.

Human interest in Greek sculpture begins again in the fifteenth century. It was then that, in new-found enthusiasm for classical literature, great ecclesiastics and noblemen in Italy began to make collections of antiques. The Capitoline collection was begun by one Pope in 1471, the Vatican by another in 1506. The marbles recovered for these collections were sometimes found by accident, sometimes by eager search on the sites of palaces and villas ; one at Tivoli, another at Antium ; many at Rome —on the Esquiline or Palatine hill, or in the bed of the Tiber. The Niobê group was found in a vineyard near the Vatican. The fashion of collecting spread from Italy to France and England. The first English collection was the Arundel Marbles (now mostly at Oxford), made in the reign of Charles I. by the nobleman of that name. But up to the beginning of the nineteenth century these collections contained hardly anything of first-rate value. With scarcely a single exception the marbles were " not originals but Roman copies of Greek works of the most different periods. The major part was the work of artisans, in which it is hard to discern the character and charm of the originals. Even the famous Apollo Belvedere is only distinguished from others by the comparative excellence of the reproduction." [2] The true recovery of Greek

[1] Gardner, *Handbook of Greek Sculpture*, p. 6.

[2] Michaelis, *A Century of Archaeological Discovery* (translation by Miss Kahnweiler), p. 8.

sculpture begins with the Elgin Marbles. It was completed, so far as completion was possible, by the more and more systematic exploration and excavation on Hellenic soil which has gone on since Hellas became again a free country. It is going on actively now, though with diminishing probability of finds to equal in value the Hermes of Praxiteles, the Victory of Paeonius, or the Charioteer of Delphi. Luck naturally has played a part little less decisive than the industry and sagacity of archaeologists. A fox's ' earth ' led to the discovery of the Phigalean frieze.[1] A peasant in the island of Melos chanced upon broken fragments of a marble statue out of which the Aphroditê of Melos was pieced together. Another Aphroditê, now in the British Museum, came from the ruins of sea-baths at Ostia.[2] The Cerigotto bronze, a male athletic statue which rivals the work of Polycleitus and Lysippus, was recovered by sponge-fishers out of thirty fathoms of water near the little island from which the statue takes its name, out of a wreck which had lain there for full two thousand years. There is many a romantic chapter in the story of this recovery of the spirit of Hellas expressed in its marble statuary.

Hellenic Pre-eminence in Sculpture.—The more carefully judgment is weighed, the stronger probably will be the conclusion that the energies expended, whether with spade or pen, in winning back for mankind these relics of a splendid skill which has passed away, are well worth while. The Hermes of Praxiteles seems to have been restored to us to give us some measure of the greatness of our loss. For the Hermes, though it appears to those who have seen it a miracle of perfect workmanship, was by no means in ancient times regarded as Praxiteles' greatest work, nor did he himself so esteem it. Modern judges see in it the very embodiment of divine excellence in human shape. But from report we know that in the great days, when Greek sculpture was most a living art, there were other embodiments of the divine which produced a far more overpowering impression on men's minds : the

[1] See below, p. 501.   [2] Numbered 1574 in the Ephesus Room.

Zeus and the Athena of Pheidias, the Hera of Polycleitus. Pausanias, to whom we owe it that we are able to identify the Hermes as Praxiteles' work, makes nothing special of it ; he merely describes it briefly and passes on. One of the very finest modern critics of Greek sculpture points out how " among all the sculptures which have outlived the ravages of time and the destructive fury of man there is perhaps not one that was admitted in Greece as of the highest rank." [1] This appears on reflection to be true in the main ; and yet we have the Elgin Marbles, the Victories of the temple of Athena Nikê, and the Hermes ! And that these sculptures are of transcendent merit seems to be admitted beyond question. We can ourselves see that they are. What then must have been the full perfection of Greek sculpture at its best ! There can have been nothing like it on earth before or since ; for even " the haphazard residue of fragments " which we now possess excels all other sculptured works of ancient or modern times. One may in the British Museum get a forcible impression of the amazing difference between Greek and other ancient sculpture if one approaches the Elgin Room, not through the Roman portraits, but through the great Egyptian hall. From among weird monstrous shapes of Assyrian man-lions, and colossal Egyptian kings with heavy features seated in rigid posture, you look across the room of the Nereids and see through the opening beyond—like a vision from another world—the long lithe shape of the ' Theseus.'

Why the Greeks among all the nations of the earth attained—almost at a bound—to this unapproachable primacy in sculpture must to the end of time appear partly mysterious. But it can to some extent be made intelligible by consideration of the general and special conditions under which the marvellous advance between the Persian and the Peloponnesian wars was made. The general conditions are the same as those which help to explain Hellenic greatness in other spheres, architecture, drama, state-craft, history : the intensified national

[1] Warrack, *Greek Sculpture*, p. xix.

consciousness after the repulse of the Persians, the elation of victory over a powerful enemy and of deliverance from a great danger.   Athens felt this most of all ; hers had been the greatest peril and the most heroic effort.   This exalted national consciousness gave the grandeur of outlook and the inspiration to high artistic achievement. But there were more special causes which helped the peculiar development given to Hellenic art in general and to sculpture in particular.   Without doubt the supreme achievement of Hellenic sculpture is the delineation in stone of the perfect human form, of the athletic human frame primarily ; and then of beauty of bodily form generally.   The Greeks above all other men, we might almost say, alone among the races of men, had an eye for the beauty of the natural body and a delight in contemplating that beauty.   The perception of this beauty is part of their gift to the human race, no mean part of *our* Hellenic heritage.   The Greek put soul higher than body, but he had an inspired vision of the beauty of the human body, both male and female.   He did not *say* man's body is the temple of the Living God, but his attitude towards it might reasonably be expressed in these words.   With proper safeguards and restraints this respect for, admiration of, delight in, the well-shaped and well-proportioned human body is not evil but good ; not demoralizing but in a high degree moralizing.   Edmund Spenser expresses the truth exactly :

" Of all God's workes, which doe this world adorne,
     There is no one more faire and excellent
     Than is man's body, both for power and forme,
     Whiles it is kept in sober government." [1]

Now at the Olympic Games in the fifth century B.C. the Greek competitor, contrary to our own customs and the customs of every other race, barbarous or civilized, entered for their athletic contests without a stitch of clothing on. Thucydides expressly says, that this custom had come in shortly before his own time, and that

[1] *Faerie Queene*, II. ix. 1. 1-4.

previously competitors in the Games had contended girt
with a loin-cloth. Similarly all exercising in the gymnasium
and the wrestling-ground in Greek cities was done stark
naked. We are not concerned here with the expediency
or inexpediency of this custom ; but manifestly it was of
extraordinary advantage to Greek artists, and above all to
sculptors. The Greek sculptor as a citizen of Athens or
Argos could be present daily in the palaestra and
gymnasium and had opportunity of observing the athletic
body in every imaginable posture and movement. The
Greek sculptor, as has been pointed out, did not need
models to pose to him in an Art School. The models
were daily, almost hourly, before his eyes in the civic
exercising-grounds of his native city. The advantage for
the sculptor of this familiarity with the naked human
body in energetic action and in repose can scarcely be
exaggerated. Along with this interest in and admiration
of the human bodily form, and these opportunities for
observation and study, went the Greek belief in bodily
exercise as a chief source of health and his balanced ideal
of a healthy body. These conditions coming together
produced the unique greatness of Hellenic sculpture. It
is, perhaps, sufficient reason why no later sculpture,
especially of the nude figure, has ever yet quite equalled
the Hellenic, that these conditions have never been
exactly repeated.

CHAPTER XVIII

TRAVEL AND DISCOVERY

"Few men there are who having once visited Greece do not contrive to visit it again."

MAHAFFY, *Rambles and Studies in Greece* (5th edn.), p. 1.

OUR consideration of Greek architecture and sculpture has brought us back to the charm of travel in Grecian lands. A final chapter given expressly to this subject will not be outside the purpose of this book. For familiarity with the actual land of Greece, its mountains and the seas that wash its coasts—either by travelling ourselves or by reading the travels of others—is part of the full enjoyment of our Hellenic heritage. These experiences are ours if we will. Especially interesting are the experiences of the early travellers from the West, who made journeys to Greece, when Greece was still a land to be discovered, and who put on record accounts of their adventures and successes.

The Separation from Western Europe.—Athens, and through Athens Greece, remained the intellectual centre of Europe down to the time (330 A.D.) when Constantine removed the imperial court to Byzantium, which he renamed Constantinople and made the capital of the Roman empire. From that day a divergence began which ended in the complete separation of western Europe from direct Hellenic influences. The young western nations looked to Italy and the Papacy for light and leading, till in the fourth Crusade (1204 A.D.) Constantinople appeared to the soldiers of the West a foreign city with an alien faith. In 1453, when Constantinople was captured by the

Turks, the Greek lands became part and parcel of the Turkish empire, and were more than ever cut off socially and economically from the rest of Europe ; but with this other consequence, which was to have momentous results for western Europe and the world, that a new knowledge of Greek literature was communicated to Italy by Greek men of letters who came to the western peninsula as fugitives from the Turk.   Italy passed on the new learning to France ;   France to Spain, Germany and England. With the acquisition of this knowledge of Greek and the revelation of the splendours of Greek literature, the men of the West began to desire to see the Greek lands.

The Earliest English Travellers.—After the painstaking itinerary of Pausanias in the second century A.D. the literary record of travellers in Greece is for a long time very meagre.   For many hundred years, we might without exaggeration say for 1500 years, even literary allusions— outside the pages of Byzantine historians—are few and scanty.   Among the writers who speak of Greece are a few travellers from the West ; for instance Kiriacus of Ancona in 1447, Louis des Hayes in 1632, and the Jesuit Père Babin, 1672.   The first Englishman whom we know to have eagerly desired to see Athens was John Milton. He has himself related how in the year 1639 his purpose of visiting Greece was frustrated : "When I was desirous to cross into Sicily and Greece the sad news of Civil War in England called me back ; for I considered it base that, while my fellow-countrymen were fighting at home for liberty, I should be travelling abroad at ease for intellectual culture."   Thirty years later another young Englishman, born just two years before Milton's visit to Italy, educated at Westminster School and Christ Church, Oxford, Francis Vernon by name, started ("out of an insatiable desire of seeing," as he himself puts it) on a journey to eastern lands which ended in his death by violence near Ispahan in Persia.   A little before his untimely death this Francis Vernon had written a letter to a friend at the Royal Society (of which Vernon was a Fellow), from which it appears, that besides making a two months' stay in

Athens, he had visited Corcyra, Zante, Thebes, Corinth, Argos, Sparta and Delphi. At Athens, though the ignorant suspicions of the Turks made investigation difficult, he nevertheless succeeded in making a study of the Parthenon and took some measurements. His letter, dated January the 10th, 1676, merely gives the outline of these travels, but refers also to the journals which he had kept. These are in the possession of the Royal Society and have never been published. At the time of Francis Vernon's death, Sir George Wheler, whose *Journey into Greece*, published in 1682, is the first book of Greek travel in English, was on his travels along with the Frenchman, Spon. Wheler, at the time a young graduate of Lincoln College, Oxford, had spent two years in travelling on the Continent, then in 1675 started from Venice with Dr. Spon, whose acquaintance he had made on his earlier journeys. Spon and Wheler went first to Constantinople ; then travelled for a year in Asia Minor, visiting among other places the sites of the ' Seven Churches,' including Smyrna and Ephesus. They then crossed the Aegean to Athens, and afterwards spent a year travelling in Greece. Wheler's later fortunes were very different from Vernon's. He returned safely to England towards the end of 1676, and lived to be a Canon of Durham and the father of eighteen children. He died in 1723.

Eighteenth Century Travellers.—After Wheler there is a long interval before the eighteenth century travellers begin. The first is a nobleman, Lord Charlemont, who in 1749 voyaged among the isles of Greece, made some stay at Athens and visited the Peloponnesus. Two years later Stuart and Revett went out to Athens with the help and encouragement of the Society of Dilettanti. They were at work there for four years, and the results of their work may be seen in the *Antiquities of Athens*, the first volume of which appeared in 1762.[1] The next book of travels was Chandler's, published in 1776. Chandler was

[1] There are five volumes of the *Antiquities* in all, but only the first and second were published in Stuart's life-time. The fifth volume appeared as late as 1830.

a young Oxford scholar who had made his mark as a student of antiquity and was sent out along with Revett, the companion of ' Athenian ' Stuart, and a young painter named Pars, by the Society of Dilettanti—to travel in Asia Minor and Greece and study antiquities. Chandler and his companions left England in June 1764 and first travelled for a year in Asia Minor, visiting the Troad, Smyrna, Miletus, Ephesus, Mt. Mycalê, Mt. Tmolus and Mt. Sipylus. They went on to Greece in August 1765 and travelled widely both in Northern Greece and over the Peloponnese, returning to England in September 1766.[1]

Early Nineteenth Century.—There were other eighteenth-century travellers, but it was not till the opening years of the nineteenth century that the impulse to systematic exploration reached its height. Then within a dozen years, between 1800 and 1811, Lord Elgin, Colonel Leake, Dodwell, Sir William Gell, Byron and his friend John Cam Hobhouse,[2] and the famous architect, Charles Cockerell, were all in Greece, travelling and exploring, each with a special purpose of his own, but with a common enthusiasm. What Lord Elgin did has been already considered (pp. 79 to 81), and the results form one of the great attractions of London to-day. Dodwell wrote a book in two volumes folio, which is more lively reading than either Chandler or Wheler, but is nevertheless rather heavy going. Gell's *Journey in the Morea* is a vigorous narrative, which aims chiefly at giving a picture of the country under the Turks before the rising of 1821. Leake's is by far the most solid work. He was a born topographer, and on every route which he followed in the Peloponnese or in Northern Greece he surveys and discusses every step of the way. The result is that his books, four volumes on Northern Greece, four on the Peloponnese, and two on Athens, are a mine in which

[1] The results of their labours appeared in the first two volumes of *Antiquities of Ionia* issued by the Society of Dilettanti.

[2] Afterwards Lord Broughton.

later travellers may dig ; but they do not, except to
enthusiasts and serious students, afford very exhilarating
reading.

Byron and Hobhouse.—The most interesting of these
travellers are certainly Byron and Hobhouse. Probably
more of the spirit of Greek travel is distilled into certain
stanzas of *Childe Harold* [1] than can be found in any prose
narrative. No English poet, no English writer, except
Sir Rennell Rodd in our own day, has caught the atmosphere of modern Greece, the combination of moving
historical associations with enchanting physical beauty,
as Byron has. Byron himself in a letter written in 1810 [2]
puts the enduring splendour of natural scenery higher ;
and perhaps Byron is right. But for the inheritors of
Hellas the charm of classical associations is necessarily
very great ; and Byron felt it acutely, even while refusing
to express enthusiasm over ' antiquities ' and affecting a
certain disdain of the raptures of professed students.
Certainly Byron saw Greece under romantically fortunate
conditions, as an English nobleman of high lineage, and
at the same time a young man of genius about whose
satirical poem *English Bards and Scotch Reviewers* all
London was talking when he left England. Ambassadors,
British consuls, and captains of British men-of-war,
made things pleasant for Lord Byron wherever he went.
He began by traversing the wilds of Albania and paid a
visit to Ali Pasha of Yanina at his country residence,
Tepelene, where he was received with the utmost distinction by that formidable Albanian chieftain. He and
Hobhouse visited Delphi, but they did not follow the
ordinary route from Corinth or from Thebes. They set
out from Vostizza [3] in a boat manned by fourteen Greek
seamen, sailed diagonally across the Gulf of Corinth to a
point on the opposite shore, where their sailors, like the
crew of an ancient trireme, anchored to cook their dinner.

[1] *Childe Harold*, ii. 85-93.

[2] Letter 136 in vol. i. of Prothero's edition of the *Letters and Journals*,
p. 265.

[3] Aegium.

The rest of the voyage was performed with oars, not indeed the trireme's hundred and seventy-six, but just ten , and after the manner of ancient navigation they followed the turns and windings of the coast, till they reached the Scala, or port, of Salona (now called Itea) very late and by moonlight. If Byron sought romance, what could be more romantic ! Of their inspection of Delphi next day the account is given by Hobhouse, not Byron (Byron disdained the ' scribbling ' of travel notes), and he only writes : " On the whole anyone would, I think, be disappointed with the situation of this place, which is hidden in a nook, or a sort of natural amphitheatre, so as to afford a prospect neither of the depth of the precipice below, nor of the height of the rocks above." [1] Neither he nor Byron had any vision of the wonderful transformation that was to be brought about in another hundred years (see pp. 494-6 below). From Delphi the travellers returned to Chryso and next day started for Livadhia, resting the next night at the flourishing village, Aráchova, four miles beyond Delphi under Parnassus. They journeyed on through Phocis and Boeotia to Attica and the Muse of romance again favoured them. For they had their first glimpse of Athens from the top of the Pass of Phylê, and entered the city itself at half-past eight on the evening of Christmas Day, 1809. Byron wrote afterwards of Athens—" a place which, I think, I prefer, upon the whole, to any I have seen." This was during a second stay in 1810-11, when he was by himself and made the Capuchin Convent his headquarters, while he toured from time to time in the Peloponnese. This first Christmas he and Hobhouse stayed ten weeks, making themselves very much at home in Athens and riding out almost every day into the country, till all Attica became familiar. In the spring of 1810 they went on in a war-ship to Constantinople, and it was on this voyage, while waiting till the Etesian winds would allow them to pass the Dardanelles, that Byron, to test the story of Leander, himself swam the Hellespont. It was

[1] Hobhouse, *Travels in Albania*, vol. i. p. 205.

not quite literally from Sestos to Abydos, but across the Narrows between Kilid-ul-Bahr and Chanak-Kalessi, the Castle of Romelia and the Castle of Natolia. The difficulty of the feat does not lie in the distance, which is not much over a mile, but in the swiftness of the current running from the Sea of Marmora to the Aegean. Byron made a first attempt on April the 16th (Hobhouse is precise in his dates) : "Having crossed from the castle Chanak-Kalessi in a boat manned by four Turks. . . . we landed at 5 o'clock in the evening half a mile above the castle of Chelit-Bawri, and my friend, together with an officer of the frigate, depositing their clothes in the boat, began their passage. We kept near them, and the boatmen gave them instructions from time to time as appeared necessary for them in taking advantage of the current. For the first half hour they swam obliquely upwards, rather towards Nagara Point than the Dardanelles, and notwithstanding all their skill and efforts, made but little progress. Finding it useless to struggle with the current, they then went rather with the stream, but still attempting to cross. We lay upon our oars, and in a few minutes were between the castles. The swimmers were close to us. We were not then half over the passage, and were every moment falling into a wider part of the channel, but notwithstanding the exclamations of the Turks the effort was still continued, and it was not until the swimmers had been an hour in the water and found themselves in the middle of the strait, about a mile and a half below the castles, that they consented to be taken into the boat." The successful attempt was made on May the 3rd. Profiting by the lessons of the first attempt, Byron and Lieutenant Ekenhead started from a point a mile further up the passage beyond Chelit-Bawri : "They swam upwards as before, but not for so long a time, and in less than half an hour were floating down the current close to the ship. They then swam strongly to get within the bay behind the castle, and, soon succeeding, reached the still water, and landed about a mile and a half below our anchorage. Lord Byron was one hour and ten minutes in the water ; his companion, Mr. Ekenhead, five minutes less." [1]

Conditions of Travel before 1830.—Of Athens in 1810 Hobhouse writes : " Were there no other vestiges of the ancient world than those to be seen at this day at Athens, there would still be sufficient cause left to justify the common admiration felt for the genius of the Greeks." He makes light of the difficulties of travelling in Greece and says : " Until within a few years, a journey to Athens was reckoned a considerable undertaking fraught with difficulties and dangers . . . only a few desperate scholars and artists ventured to trust themselves among the barbarians, to contemplate the ruins of Greece. But these terrors, which a person who has been on the spot cannot conceive could ever have been well founded, seem at last to be dispelled : Attica at present swarms with travellers. . . . " [2] For all this it would appear that the earlier travellers even down to Hobhouse's time had a good deal of discomfort to put up with and found Greek travel something of an adventure. Wheler and Dr. Spon began with a voyage in a ship the captain of which had recently been a pirate, and still kept up the habit of carrying off women who took his fancy ; they started for home two years later under a lively apprehension of being followed by shot from the Turkish forts guarding the mouth of the Gulf of Corinth. Francis Vernon was actually at one time made prisoner by corsairs, sold as a slave, and, as he writes, " endured great misery " in that condition. Dodwell had a real adventure with real brigands, a band of Klephts over a hundred in number, and only escaped with his life owing to the lucky arrival in the nick of time of a troop of Turkish horsemen. On the other hand, the first comers had all the excitement of exploring undiscovered country. They had to identify ancient sites by the exercise of their wits with the help of the classical writers, not merely confirm, or combat, the identifications of those who went before them. Sometimes, too, it was their fortune to light upon some temple

[1] Hobhouse, vol. ii. pp. 194-5.   [2] Hobhouse, i. p. 252-3.

or work of art not yet known to scholars. This could happen as near to Athens as Aegina, where the Aeginetan marbles were 'discovered' by a party of four travellers, two German and two English, one of the latter being the architect, Charles Cockerell.

Exploration and Excavation after 1830.—Systematic topographical research begins with Leake, and he and others advocated excavation as the best means of arriving at sure results. The era of excavation, however, comes only after the Greek war of independence. The travellers whom we have been considering so far came in Turkish times. The Turks were ignorant, quite indifferent to archaeology and all its works, though not always unfriendly or obstructive to classical students. But it was not till the country was free of Turkish rule that archaeological research could go forward under favourable conditions. The dividing-line is the decade 1820-1830. The Greeks (as we have seen) rose in insurrection April 6, 1821 (ten years after Byron's visit). The desperate struggle of the next nine years falls into three stages : (1) the first successes of the Greeks, sullied by cruel, and sometimes treacherous, massacres of Turkish prisoners-of-war ; (2) the gradual reconquest and devastation of the Morea by the army of Ibrahim Pasha, brought over from Egypt for the purpose ; (3) the ultimate intervention of France, Russia and England, leading to the recognition in 1830 of the independence of Greece. After a distracted interval of four years, Otho of Bavaria was accepted as first King of the Hellenes. One of the earliest cares of the national government was to create a department of Antiquities. Ludvig Ross (p. 59), under the title of Ephor-General, was the second chief of this department ; and the Acropolis, which in 1834 ceased to be a fortress, was gradually cleared of all buildings later than classical. In 1837 a Greek Archaeological Society was founded. A good deal was discovered from time to time, but the great discoveries, some of which we have had occasion to notice, were the outcome of the systematic excavation of the whole sur-face of the Acropolis undertaken in 1882. By that date memorable excavations had been carried out in other parts of Greece. The French Expedition de Morée had worked at Olympia and other places in 1829-30. The discoveries of Schliemann at Mycenae had been made in 1876 (Troy was in 1871-5), and there were important finds in other parts of Greece. The work of the Greek Archaeological Society had been supplemented by archaeological institutes established at Athens by foreign Hellenists. The French School at Athens was the first of these institutions, founded in 1846 ; and next came the German founded in 1874. The British School did not follow till 1885 ; the American was three years earlier. Valuable work in exploration and excavation has been done by each of these. The greatest achievements—less only in their importance than the epoch-making work of Schliemann at Troy and Mycenae and Sir Arthur Evans at Knossos—have been the excavation of Olympia between 1875 and 1881 by the Germans, and excavation of Delphi between 1890 and 1900 by the French.

Olympia.—" At Olympia," wrote Leake after his visit in 1805, " as in many other celebrated places in Greece, the scenery and topography are at present much more interesting than the ancient remains." Clark, whose travels were fifty years later, writes : " Of all the monuments with which this famous spot was once crowded—so numerous that Pausanias devotes about one-eighth of his whole work to their enumeration—not a trace remains with the single exception of the ruins of the temple of Zeus. But for them it might have been doubted whether this were Olympia or not." [1] Just what was to be looked for at Olympia we do know, as Clark says, from Pausanias' detailed description occupying Books V. and VI. of his *Tour of Greece*. The greater part of those two books is indeed taken up with a history of the Olympic Games and an enumeration of statues ; but Chapter X. of Book V. tells of the sacred enclosure, or Altis, and of the temple of Zeus ; Chapter XI. of the gold-and-ivory image of Zeus ; Chapters XVI. to XIX. of the Temple of Hera. The French

[1] Clark (W. G.), *Peloponnesus*, p. 266.

in 1829, as their manner is, sent a scientific mission to the
Morea, which spent six weeks on the site of the Temple
of Zeus. "They cleared a great part of the stylobate,
obtained an exact measurement of it, discovered the
lowest portions of 13 columns in their places, and would
probably have found more if they had completed their
excavation : they brought to light, also, some remains of
the metopes, of the pronaos and posticum, and had the
satisfaction of observing that they are in exact conformity
with the description of Pausanias." [1] Leake adds : " no
remains of the sacred inclosure are now to be observed ;
though possibly its foundations may hereafter be found
beneath the present surface." [2] But Leake also noticed
a difference of level in the ground below the hill of Cronos
and between the Cladeus and Alpheus ; in particular, a
" cliff or bank " traceable right across the valley and in
one place as much as " 25 feet high, and perpendicular."
From this and other signs he conjectures " that in the
course of the last fifteen centuries all the south-eastern
extremity of the Altis has been destroyed by the river,
and consequently that all the remains of buildings and
monuments in that part of the Sacred Grove have been
buried beneath the new alluvial plain, or carried into the
river." This amounts to a belief that under " the fine turf
carpeting the valley of Olympia," as he saw it in 1805, was
lying—how deep could only be found by digging—the stone
foundations of all the buildings which Pausanias visited
in the second century A.D., and possibly remains of
statues and temple sculptures, none could tell how much.
This was the faith much earlier of Johann Joachim
Wincklemann, author (among other works) of the *History
of Ancient Art*, whose enthusiasm for Greek art marks an
epoch in European speculation. Nothing was done during
Wincklemann's life-time, nor for a century after his death ;
but in 1875, largely through the enlightened encouragement of Frederick, Crown Prince of Prussia, afterwards for
a few months the Emperor Frederick, a comprehensive

[1] Leake, *Peloponnesiaca*, pp. 12 and 13.
[2] Leake, *Peloponnesiaca*, p. 14.

scheme of excavation was taken in hand by German archaeologists, with the consent of the Hellenic Government. The work went on till 1881 ; nearly £40,000 was spent on it ; and the result was to restore the ground plan of Olympia as it may be seen to-day, " a grey chaos of scattered stones and pillar-stumps in a rich setting of green fields and sylvan scenery." But under Pausanias' guidance this chaos has gradually been reduced to order, and all the chief buildings have been traced out exactly as he describes them. From the platform of the Temple of Zeus the great drums of the temple pillars may be seen lying in rows, detached but retaining the columnar form, just as the earthquake of the 6th century A.D. shook them down.[1] The platform of the Heraeum can be made out close under Cronos hill, and enough of the pillars is left to enable us to verify the statement that no two pillars of the peristyle are exactly alike. They differ in size, in the number of flutings, in their ornamentation, even in their mode of construction ; for, while most were built up of drums, one was a monolith. And so through all the series of buildings which Pausanias describes. It was on the platform of the Heraeum that the Hermes of Praxiteles, the one nearly perfect surviving masterpiece of Hellenic sculpture, was found. We owe its preservation to the fact that the upper part of the walls of the cella was built of unburnt bricks. The bricks, being merely sun-dried, in process of time crumbled and turned back into clay. It was in this clay that the Hermes was found imbedded, and it is because of the softness of this bed and its protective nature that the Hermes has suffered so little injury. The Hermes and the Victory of Paeonius alone make the pilgrimage to Olympia in these days worth while, but there is much other sculpture in the Museum there of great interest, and the physical beauty of the whole scene counts for much.

The Excavations at Delphi.—Olympia, as seen to-day, is one great recovery which the spade of the archaeologist has effected. The transformation at Delphi is even more

[1] See also Vol. I. p. 38.

wonderful. Wheler and Spon in 1676 had to assure themselves that Salona (or Amphissa) was not Delphi ; and when they got to Castri, it was the situation and scenery which convinced them that the temple of the Pythian Apollo had been there, not remains of buildings visible on the site, though it is true that they found the name Delphi in one inscription. Dodwell, writing of the year 1805, actually remarks, " the remains of this celebrated edifice have vanished like a dream, leaving not a trace behind." [1]   But he adds : " It appears that the far-famed temple of Apollo must be sought for under the humble cottages of Kastri, as the whole village probably stands within its ancient peribolos." This is how things still were when I first saw Delphi in 1888. I came from Thebes and Livadhia, and so approached Delphi along the mountain path through Arachova, and entering by the gorge of Castalia and the precipitous cliffs which tower above the valley of the Pleistus on that side. Nothing could be more impressive. But the site of the Delphic sanctuary and oracle was occupied by a ramshackle mountain village, very like one of the hill villages one sees in the Himalayas. When I came a second time in 1899, it was as though a magician's wand had been waved over the scene. The village of Castri had been shifted half a mile further west towards Chryso, and where Castri had been there lay extended beneath the Phaedriades the whole ground-plan of Pausanias' Delphi wrought in massive stone. It is a marvellous transformation to eyes that once saw Castri perched in picturesque disorder above the ground where this great archaeological treasure-house has been disinterred. The French have done their work skilfully and thoroughly. The whole area has been cleared of the superimposed litter and each site that has been identified is marked by a neat wooden placard, inscribed in plain letters. There are more than a score of these at different levels over the steep incline of the rock.

A day on the site of Delphi is now a stimulating if exhausting experience. The whole of the ground above

[1] Dodwell, *Tour Through Greece*, vol. i. p. 174.

the carriage-road has been cleared by the French archaeologists. What has been revealed is nothing less than the
complete framework of ancient Delphi, a skeleton indeed,
but a nearly perfect skeleton. You ascend towards the
temple of Apollo by the Sacred Way, a broad paved road
of stone which starts not far from the basin of Castalia
and runs across and back along the face of the rock
towards the west. It is still in very tolerable repair.
First you have on either hand the bases of statues of
early kings of Argos, and of the Epigoni, offerings once
dedicated by the Argives. You pass on your left the
treasuries of Sicyon and Cnidos [1] from which came the
most interesting sculptures now in the Museum ; then the
Theban treasury, and after a sharp turn to the north-east
the treasury of the Athenians.[2] Some little way higher
up is the Stoa of the Athenians ; and behind that you see
a long stretch of polygonal wall pieced together with
extraordinary nicety. The edges of the stones fit so
closely as to make a seemingly continuous surface marked
with a quaintly variegated pattern, though the stones are
irregular in shape. This polygonal work surpasses in
finish any masonry of the kind at Mycenae or Tiryns.
The eastern end of this wall was used as a sort of public
record office and is covered with inscriptions ; it happened
also that this space of wall was opened to view while most
of the rest of Delphi was still concealed by the houses of
Castri. Since the excavation it has been seen to form the
outer face of the substructure supporting the platform of
the temple of Apollo. The road sweeps past the end of this
polygonal wall, then turns again and ascends to the
temple platform. The platform and its substructure are
all that now survives of Apollo's temple, but these serve
to indicate how large and splendid the temple itself must
have been.

Another striking feature is the Delphic stadium, an open
race-course with seats on three sides in a state almost as
perfect as if the Pythian Games had been recently held

---

[1] The second of these two treasuries has also been assigned to Siphnos.
[2] See **Vol. I.** p. 293.

there.   The enclosure is a long oval, 220 yards in length
and about 60 broad.   The course is smooth and level ;
the rows of seats rise symmetrically one above another ;
on the upper, or northern, side twelve rows ;   on the
lower six ;   and six rows at the western end.   There are
seats too beyond the eastern end of the course, but these
are not continuous with the rest and are not very well
defined.   Between the eastern rows of seats (which are
cut in the rock) and the goal-line are four bases surmounted by niches, which probably held sculpture ; and
there is space for one more.   The highest row of seats
all the way round has a back of solid stone skilfully
accommodated to the spectator's body : for the ancient
Greeks, as may be personally tested here and elsewhere,
understood how to make chair-backs comfortable better
than some moderns.

There were many other sites discovered in this restoration of Delphi ; among them, a theatre, a Council-house,
and the hall where Polygnotus' famous pictures were
displayed.   But the Sacred Way, the temple-platform,
and the Stadium are the most interesting.   The sculptures found during the process of excavation have for
better preservation been removed to a museum building.
Nothing so exquisite has been found here as the Hermes
of Praxiteles ; but there is much archaic sculpture of
curious interest, especially the friezes from some of the
treasuries ; and competent judges put a high value on the
bronze Charioteer.

The Gleaming Rocks.—There is one sight at Delphi,
not the least remarkable, which owes nothing to archaeology.   The cliffs which form the background of Delphi
were in ancient times called the Phaedriades, or the Gleaming Rocks ; and it is natural to ask why.   You need to go
to Delphi and watch the sun rise to be sure of the answer.
But if you take your stand on the temple platform a little
before sunrise, this is what you will see.   As you watch,
the sky gradually grows luminous above the cliff, and
presently the edge of the rock seems to glitter along all
its length, and a faint coruscation streams from it, which

slowly brightens and takes on gorgeous rainbow colours. Then, when the sun's glowing disc shoots its first direct rays over the top, the illusion vanishes. It is doubtless this peculiar coruscation of the edge of Hyampeia at sunrise which gave the rocks their ancient name.

Bassae.—The pleasures of travel in Greece—at least to him whom the Greeks called *Euzonos*, the ' well-girt man ' —are inexhaustible in their combination of glorious scenery and stirring associations. And no journey combines these two sources of delight in fuller measure than an expedition to the ' Stelous,' as the Greeks call the place—that is ' the Columns '—at Bassae on the borders of Elis and Arcadia. Pausanias speaks of a temple of Apollo built by the men of Phigalea on Mount Cotilium, which he esteems the finest in Peloponnesus, second only to the Temple of Athena Alea at Tegea. The Arcadian shepherds knew it always,[1] but scholars, even those who read Pausanias, had forgotten it till in 1765 Joachim Bocher, the French architect, came upon it accidentally, when on a journey from Pyrgo to Karytena.[2] It is not the easiest of places to visit, but the reward to those who undertake the fatigues of getting there is great. Andritsena is, on the whole, the most convenient taking-off place. The march from Andritsena takes about three hours. What follows is the description of a visit made towards the end of March 1899 :

" After a hot climb our path turns abruptly to the left and we skirt an immense ravine, the sides of which are great open slopes where multitudinous goats are feeding, both above and below. The scenery which has hitherto been rough and stern is softer here, and the bells tinkle melodiously. The watch-dogs bay deep and fierce as we go by. On the further side we find a welcome spring of cool water. After this we climb again by an even steeper

[1] Mr. E. F. Benson has made effective use both of the ' Stelous ' and the Arcadian shepherds in his novel *The Vintage*, which no one interested in modern Greece, land or people, should fail to read. See especially the frontispiece.

[2] Chandler, *Travels in Asia Minor and Greece*, p. 96.

and more rugged path. We twist deeper into the mountains which now begin to hem us in. We seem to be making for a dip in a long ridge that lies right ahead of us. Somewhat to the right is a big grey summit. We climb the ridge-wall, go over it, and, descending a little, come suddenly in view of ranged columns : the temple is before us.

"The Temple of Apollo at Bassae is, of course, a ruin. It stands gaunt and open to the winds, its roof, and all that stood above the architrave—friezes, pediments, triglyphs and metopes—are gone : gone, too, its shrine, the inner walls and divisions and all that they contained, all that made it distinctively a place of worship—except for the broken fragments that strew the pavement, and some scanty remains of the walls of the cella. But for a ruin it is remarkably complete. Of the thirty-eight pillars originally surrounding it thirty-five still stand, and the blocks of stone that formed the architrave, stretching two-and-two from pillar to pillar, have suffered most at the southern end, which is exposed, the northern end being sheltered by the slope of the hill. Two of the pillars are somewhat clumsily strengthened with clamps and boards, and one on the west side is propped up in an unsightly manner with scaffolding. With these deductions the tale of pillars is complete. And here on the open hill side, in the solitude of great mountains, with a bold sweeping landscape on three sides, and no other company than the lizards and the tinkling sheep-bells far down on the lower steeps, you may enjoy moments that outlive whole years of humdrum experience.

"What a view it is that is offered to eye and mind from this place ! Looking out upon it from a vantage point a little higher on the ridge, the temple of Apollo is forgotten and we are merged in the prospect of mountain, sea, and sky ; majestically sweeping lime-stone ridges, line upon line, with glimpses of snowy summits through the gaps ; and far away to the south and to the west the effulgent blue of the waters that lap the coasts of Greece. We are ourselves on the back of an open ridge,

The Temple of Apollo at Bassae from the North-East.
Mount Ithomē and the Gulf of Coronē are seen in the distance.
From an engraving in the Supplementary Volume to Stuart and Revett's *The Antiquities of Athens.*

and mountain ridges hem us in all round. Behind to the north and west, the wall over which we have climbed, dominated by the grey summit of Mount Cotilium, closes up and shuts out any further view. More to the east and north, the heights of central Arcadia rise massively ; through a small dip in the far distance a bit of snow-white Chelmos peeps up. Eastward we look over long ranges of rocky hills, which separate us from the valley of the Alpheus and the plain of Megalopolis. Westward there is a rapid descent, and through the gap we see a beautiful little stretch of coast with the sea a very deep blue beyond. But it is the view to the southward, opening before us as we came over the ridge, that first riveted our eyes and that draws them back. Straight in front, through a big dip in the hills, lies a long stretch of comparatively flat country, reaching to the curve of the Gulf of Coronê on the very margin of sight. On either side of the gulf the hills rise again and stretch further than our eyes can follow ; on the right the hills of the Pylian land right down to Cape Gallo ; on the left past Kalamata the high-lands of Maina dimly out towards Taenarum. South-east but nearer, there is a big mass with four distinct peaks, called Tetrasi in modern Greek (hiding somewhere Eira, the stronghold of Aristomenes) ; and through the breaks in Tetrasi can be seen the long snowy stretch of Taÿgetus. In the very centre of this magnificent landscape, due South and in the middle distance, one object particularly arrests attention, a bold, square-shouldered, flat-topped hill, standing up steep and conspicuous above the Messenian plain. This is Ithomê, long held stubbornly by the Messenians in the war in which they first lost their freedom, and again seized by the revolted Helots in 464 B.C. and kept for nine years in defiance of all the efforts of Sparta."

That so much more of this temple survives than of more famous buildings is doubtless due to the reasons which Leake suggests—the loneliness of the situation, the difficulty of transport in such a country, and consequently the absence of temptation to turn the ruin into a quarry.

Such damage as has been done is probably due to earth-quakes, which have occurred at one time or another all over Greece. The identification of the ' Stelous ' as the temple of Apollo the Helper we owe entirely to Pausanias, who wrote : " Kotilium is about forty stades distant from the city " (that is from Phigalea) : " therein is a place called Bassae and the temple of Apollo the Helper, both the temple and its roof of stone." " Without those few words," remarks Leake, " the existence of such a magnificent building in such a wilderness must ever have remained a subject for doubt and discussion." Even as it is there is room for wonder at the beauty of the temple and its strange situation. Leake himself says : " That which forms on reflection the most striking circumstance of all is the nature of the surrounding country, capable of producing little else than pasture for cattle and offering no conveniences for the display of commercial industry either by sea or land. If it excites our astonishment that the inhabitants of such a district should have had the refinement to delight in works of this kind, it is still more wonderful that they should have had the means to execute them. This can only be accounted for by what Horace says of the early Romans :

> ' Privatus illis census erat brevis
> Commune magnum. . . .'

This is the true secret of national power, which cannot be equally effective in an age of selfish luxury." [1]

Recovery of the Phigalean Marbles.—The frieze from the cella of this lonely mountain temple is now, as we saw (above, p. 469) in the British Museum, the chief treasure of the Phigalean Marbles. The story of the recovery of this frieze is a good example of the romance of excavation. We have seen how M. Bocher first made known the existence of the temple in its remote solitude ; but it was reserved for the Englishman Charles Cockerell, in company of four friends with whom he was making the tour of the Morea, to discover the frieze in 1811, three

[1] *Travels in the Morea,* vol. ii. p. 9.

months after the discovery of the pediment sculptures in Aegina (p. 490). The party started from Zante (at that time in British occupation as one of the Ionian Islands), landed at Pyrgo and thence rode to Olympia. They approached the Stelous from Andritsena by the route already described. Cockerell's own account of the discovery, or rather his son's, is worth giving in full : " The interior of the temple—that is to say the space inside the columns—was a mass of fallen blocks of some depth. While Haller and Cockerell with the labourers were scrambling about among the ruins to get their measurements, a fox that had made its home deep among the stones, disturbed by the unusual noise, got up and ran away. It is not quite a pleasant task to crawl down among such insecure and ponderous masses of stone with the possibility of finding another fox at the bottom ; but Cockerell ventured on, and on scraping away the accumulations where the fox had his lair, he saw by the light which came down a crack among the stones, a bas relief. I have heard this story also from his own lips. Stackelberg further says that the particular relief was that numbered 530 in the Phigalean Marbles at the British Museum, and naïvely adds, ' indeed one may still trace on the marble the injuries done by the fox's claws.' Cockerell managed to make a rough sketch of the slab and carefully covered it over again. From the position in which it lay it was inferable that the whole frieze would probably be found under the dilapidations." [1]

Local superstition and the desertion of the shepherds engaged to do the digging brought operations to a premature close that year. The party had to return to Andritsena and afterwards continued their tour. Cockerell gives a piquant account of the stay at Bassae. " We spent altogether ten days there living on sheep and butter, the only good butter I have tasted since leaving England, sold to us by the Albanian shepherds who lived near.

[1] *Travels in Southern Europe and the Levant*, 1810-1817. *The Journal of C. R. Cockerell, R.A.*, edited by his son, Samuel Pepys Cockerell (1903), pp. 75-76.

Of an evening we used to sit and smoke by a fire, talking to the shepherds till we were ready for sleep, when we turned into our tent, which though not exactly comfortable, protected us from weather and from wolves. For there were wolves—one of them one night tore a sheep to pieces close to us." [1] The restoration of the whole frieze to the light of day was not effected till next year, and then Cockerell himself was away in Sicily. His son writes : " The party of excavators established themselves there for nearly three months, building huts of boughs all round the temple, making almost a city, which they christened Francopolis. They had frequently from fifty to eighty men at work at a time, and in the evening after work, while the lamb was roasting on a wooden spit, they danced." The opposition of the local authorities was overcome by the powers obtained from Constantinople, but even so at the last the plan for the rescue of the frieze was almost brought to naught through a change of Governors. Veli Pasha had made terms satisfactory to himself, but the new Governor who had no share in the profit sent troops to stop the embarkation of the marbles. It was this which caused the loss of the capital of the one Corinthian column at Bassae (above, p. 450) : " Everything had been loaded except the capital in question, which was more ponderous than the rest, and was still standing half in and half out of the water when the troops came up. The boat had to put off without it, and the travellers had the mortification of seeing it hacked to pieces by the Turks in their fury at having been foiled." [2]

These earlier triumphs of archaeology were only achieved at a great cost of endurance and not a little personal danger. Cockerell himself was ill of malarial fever in Athens and lay for weeks at the point of death. His Danish friend Bronstedt was robbed by brigands. Baron Stackelberg was carried off by pirates and barely escaped with his life. Cockerell writes also in one place : [3] " For three weeks I had slept with my clothes on and with only one blanket to wrap myself in." His name deserves to be remembered

      [1] P. 74.   [2] P. 220   [3] P. 101.

among the other heroes of the archaeological renascence in Hellenic lands — Schliemann, Leake, Wheler, Chandler, Sir Arthur Evans and many another. The pioneers won their victories in face of danger and physical hardships of all kinds. The work of archaeology, let us remember, still goes on and needs support. In our time excavation has been raised to a fine art and the archaeological schools at Athens send out their bands of well trained explorers— Greek, French, American, German, British. All that is needed more is money : willing apprentices will not be wanting, if funds are forthcoming. Successes as great as the greatest of the past can hardly, perhaps, be expected, though the wonder of Sir Arthur Evans and Crete shows how boundless are the prospects of the unexpected. We cannot all take part in the fascinating work of fresh discovery, but reasonable support of the British School at Athens and of the Society for the Promotion of Hellenic Studies is open to all. Homer has a beautiful word *threptra*, ' requital for nurture ' ; all and any who become conscious of what they owe to Hellenic life and thought may claim this one privilege more, to pay back according to their means their portion in the great debt.

OUTLINE OF DATES

Dates in Literature or Art are indented, and the event is in Italics.

B.C. 404. Fall of Athens.
The Terror under the Thirty.
403. Democracy restored.
403-2. Archonship of Euclides.
401. Battle of Cunaxa. Retreat of the *Ten Thousand.*
400. The Ten Thousand reach the Black Sea.
   399. *Death of Socrates.*
397. Revolutionary plot at Sparta (Conspiracy of Cinaedon)
396. Agesilaus in Asia Minor.
   395. *Plato returns to Athens.*
394. Corinthian War. Battle at Corinth.
Victory of Conon over the Spartan fleet at Cnidus.
393. Long Walls of Athens rebuilt by Conon.
    392. *Aristophanes' Ecclesiazousae.*
    389. *Aeschines born.*
    388. *Lysias' Olympic Speech.*
     Aristophanes' Plutus.
387. Peace of Antalcidas.
     386. *Plato's teaching in the Academy begins.*
     384. *Demosthenes born.*
     Aristotle born.
382. The Cadmeia of Thebes seized in time of peace by the Spartans.
     380. *Isocrates' Panegyric.*
379. Thebes liberated and the Spartans expelled from the Cadmeia.
378. Second Athenian Confederacy formed.
374. Jason of Pherae dominant in Thessaly.
373. Temple of Apollo at Delphi damaged by fire.
371. Battle of Leuctra.
370. March of Epaminondas through Laconia.
Foundation of Megalopolis and Messenê.
Jason of Pherae assassinated.
368. Philip as a boy of fourteen taken to Thebes.
     367. *Aristotle comes to Athens.*
364. Death of Pelopidas in Thessaly.
Timotheus recovers Methonê, Pydna, Potidaea and Toronê for Athens.

B.C. 362. Battle of Mantinea.   Death of Epaminondas.
      359. Death in battle of Perdiccas III. of Macedonia.
           Philip, his brother, succeeds.
      357. Social War—Chios, Cos, Rhodes and Byzantium against
           Athens.
           Philip takes Amphipolis and Pydna.
      356. Philip takes Potidaea and founds Philippi.
           Alexander, son of Philip, born.
           Philip victorious at Olympia.
      355. Athenians defeated in the Social War.
           The Phocians seize Delphi and the Sacred War begins.
      354. Philip captures Methonê.
               354. *Demosthenes' speech On the Symmories.*
                    Eubulus Finance Minister at Athens.
      353. Philip takes Abdera and Maronea.
      352. Philip baffled at Thermopylae.
               351. *Demosthenes' 1st Philippic.*
                    Death of Mausolus, Prince of Caria.
      349. Philip attacks Olynthus.
               349. *Demosthenes' 1st and 2nd Olynthian Speeches.*
               348. *Demosthenes' 3rd Olynthian Speech.*
      348. Philip takes Toronê.
           Philip destroys Olynthus and the cities of Chalcidicê.
               347. *Death of Plato.*
      347. Philip's intervention in the Sacred War invited by
           Thebes.
      346. Athenian embassies to Philip and Peace of Philocrates.
           Phocians crushed by Philip.
           Philip made a member of the Amphictyonic Council.
               346. *Demosthenes' speech On the Peace.*
                    Isocrates' Philippus.
               344. *Demosthenes' 2nd Philippic.*
      343. Philocrates goes into exile.
           Aeschines tried and acquitted.
               342. *Aristotle made tutor to Alexander.*
               341. *Demosthenes' On the Chersonese.*
                    Demosthenes' 3rd Philippic.
      341. Byzantium makes alliance with Athens.
      340. Philip fails in his sieges of Perinthus and Byzantium.
      339. Aeschines at Delphi.
           Sacred War against Amphissa.
           Philip wounded in the Balkans.
           Philip invited to help the Amphictyons in their war
           with Amphissa.
           Philip's march, and occupation of Elatea.
           Alarm at Athens.   Demosthenes' mission to Thebes.
           League of Thebes and Athens to resist Philip.

B.C. 339-8. Philip takes and destroys Amphissa, but is checked in two engagements.
338. Battle of Chaeronea.
Peace of Demades.
Hellenic League under Philip.
    338. *Death of Isocrates.*
    338-326. *Administration of Lycurgus.*
336. Ctesiphon's proposal in honour of Demosthenes.
War with Persia begun by Parmenion.
Philip assassinated.
Alexander's reign begins.
335. Thebes destroyed by Alexander after an attempted revolt. Athens pardoned.
334. Alexander crosses into Asia and wins the battle of the Granicus.
    334. *Aristotle's teaching at the Lyceum begins.*
333. Alexander routs the Persians at Issus.
332. Alexander besieges and captures Tyre and Gaza; occupies Egypt and founds Alexandria.
332. Alexander crosses the Euphrates and wins the battle of Arbela.
330. Unsuccessful rising of the Spartans.
King Darius murdered in Parthia by Bessus.
330. Trial and acquittal of Ctesiphon.
    330. *Demosthenes' speech On the Crown.*
329. Alexander crosses the Oxus.
327. Alexander crosses the Indus.
326. Battle of Taxila and defeat of Porus.
325. Alexander at the mouth of the Indus.
324. Demosthenes fined and imprisoned.
323. Death of Alexander the Great.
Lamian War. Successes of the Greeks.
322. Antipater's victory at Crannon.
Athens again submits. Demosthenes and Hypereides condemned to death.
    322. *Demosthenes takes poison at Calauria.*
    Aristotle dies at Chalcis.
321. Partitioning of Alexander's empire.

272. The House of Antigonus established as Kings of Macedonia.

197. Defeat of the Macedonians by the Romans at Cynoscephalae.

168. Battle of Pydna and end of Macedonian independence.

NOTE ON BOOKS

The best way to make Socrates' acquaintance more intimately is to study Plato's dialogues and supplement with the *Memorabilia*. Or you may reverse the order, beginning with the *Memorabilia* and following that up by readings from Plato. The first book of the *Republic* is the best short study, or else the *Apology*; but the Socrates of the dialogues can only be assimilated gradually, and by a course of reading like that suggested in the text (p. 294); and this is, perhaps, rather a study of Plato. The single work which in briefest compass gives a comprehensive view of the Platonic system of thought is the *Republic*; but there is no dialogue which does not contribute something distinctive. Jowett's five volumes contain all the dialogues, including the *Laws*, and Jowett communicates as much of the charm of Plato as is possible in a translation. Notable translations of particular dialogues are Shelley's of the *Banquet*, Davies and Vaughan's of the *Republic*, and F. J. Church's of the *Euthyphron, Apology, Crito* and *Phaedo* in *The Trial and Death of Socrates* (Golden Treasury Series). Of books about Plato and Socrates mention may usefully be made of Grote's *Plato*, Pater's *Plato and Platonism*, Godley's *Socrates and Athenian Society in his Day*, and *The Life and Death of Socrates* recently published by Dent. Anyone willing to pursue a study of Plato more deeply will find the utmost help and inspiration in Professor J. A. Stewart's *The Myths of Plato*.

Aristotle's *Ethics* may be read in Peters' or Welldon's translation. Marshall's *Aristotle's Theory of Conduct* is an excellent exposition of the content. For the *Politics* there is a choice of Welldon's and Jowett's translations; Welldon's the freer and more readable. Of the *Poetics*, that brief treatise on the theory of poetry which no one should miss, there are translations by Butcher and Bywater, each in its way a classic. The *Rhetoric* has been translated by Jebb. Aristotle's writings on physical science are only for the adventurous; and the same may be said of his logical works and his *Metaphysics*. All are included in Bohn's Series. The two chief works on Natural History have been attractively translated, his *History of Animals* by D'Arcy Thompson (1910), his *Parts of Animals* by Dr. William Ogle (1882). The minor biological treatises have also found their translator in Dr. Ogle. But since the publication of *The Legacy of Greece* the essays of Dr. Singer and Professor D'Arcy Thompson in that volume have made an understanding of what the Greeks, including Aristotle, achieved in natural science easy and delightful. For Aristotle's *Psychology* the standard English work is Dr. Edwin Wallace's. For a brief survey of Aristotle's system as a whole Sir Alexander Grant's *Aristotle* in the series "Ancient Classics for English Readers" (Blackwood) will be found most helpful; or (with some knowledge of Greek) Wallace's *Outlines of the Philosophy of Aristotle*. A fuller and more complete exposition of the content of Aristotle's works, very recently published, is W. D. Ross's *Aristotle* (Methuen, 1923). The relations of Plato and Aristotle to earlier and later thinkers can be studied in any standard history of Philosophy, Burnet's, or Schwegler's, or Ueberweg's. Davidson's *Aristotle* in the "Great Educator" series is valuable especially for Aristotle's views on education.

For the further study of the great historians the following may be recommended :

> Bury (J. B.), *Lectures on the Greek Historians.*
> The Introduction to Macan's *Herodotus, Books IV., V. and VI.*
> Jebb's essay on the Speeches of Thucydides in *Hellenica.*
> The chapter on Thucydides in J. A. K. Thomson's *The Greek Tradition.*
> Dakyns on Xenophon in *Hellenica* ; and the introductions to his translations of the historical works.

This, however, should supplement, not take the place of, attentive reading of the histories themselves. For English translations see Note on Books to Part III. above, p. 270.

The most recent work in English on the *Greek Orators* is Dobson's (Methuen, 1919), a useful study within convenient compass. For students prepared to go deeper there is Jebb's *Attic Orators* in two volumes, published by Macmillan (1893), a work of high scholarship and literary charm. For readers interested in the historical issues two fascinating books are Hogarth's *Philip and Alexander of Macedon* (Murray, 1897) and Pickard-Cambridge's *Demosthenes* (Putnam, 1914). Demosthenes' public speeches are all translated by Pickard-Cambridge (Oxford University Press, 2 vols.) ; *Aeschines* will be found in the Loeb Classics, translated by C. D. Adams ; of Isocrates' masterpieces there are full and admirable abstracts in Jebb's second volume, and all Isocrates is translated by J. H. Friese in Bohn.

Of the larger books on Greek tragedy the latest published in England is also the most inspiring. This is Professor Gilbert Norwood's *Greek Tragedy* (Methuen, 1920). Haigh's *Tragic Drama of the Greeks* (1896), together with his *Attic Theatre* (1889, both Clarendon Press), forms the most complete and thorough study in English. Roy C. Flickinger's *The Greek Theater and its Drama* (University Press, Chicago, 1918) presents the latest results of research with admirably sane judgment and literary skill. The illustrations and plans add greatly to the attractiveness of this book. Cornford's *Origin of Attic Comedy* (Arnold, 1914) is the most original and suggestive study extant of Athenian comedy. There are, however, two small handbooks, Sheppard's *Greek Tragedy* (Cambridge University Press, 1911) and Lionel Barnett's *Greek Drama* (Dent, 1900, 1901, 1903, and 1912), which, each with some individuality of treatment, give what is needed for the intelligent reading of Greek plays. For the Greek dramatists in English the following *complete* editions are recommended :

> *Aeschylus*, Morshead (Macmillan, 1901).
> *Sophocles*, Lewis Campbell (Murray, 1896).
> *Euripides*, A. S. Way (Loeb, and Macmillan, 3 vols., 1907).
> *Aristophanes*, Rogers (Bell, 1866 to 1913).

Taking plays singly, there are no translations of Greek drama into English with quite the charm of Gilbert Murray's : almost alone of translators Professor Murray transmutes the Greek into English poetry.[1]

---

[1] This is to be qualified by what is said afterwards of R. C. Trevelyan's translation of certain plays of Aeschylus.

Murray's translations comprise *eight* dramas of Euripides (*Alcestis, Bacchae, Electra, Hippolytus, Iphigenia in Aulis, Medea, Rhesus, Trojan Women*); the *Agamemnon* of Aeschylus and Sophocles' *Oedipus King*.

There are several good translations of the *Oresteia* besides Morshead's : into *verse* by R. C. Trevelyan (1922), Dr. Warr (George Allen, 1900), Miss Swanwick (Bell, 1899), Lewis Campbell (Kegan Paul, 1890), and John Stuart Blackie (Parker, 1850) ; into *prose* by Walter Headlam (Bell, 1909) and Lewis Campbell (Methuen, 1893). Campbell, Headlam, Miss Swanwick, and Blackie translate the whole of Aeschylus. Of the *Prometheus* there is an excellent translation by Edwyn Bevan (David Nutt, 1902), and another by the fourth Earl of Carnarvon. Browning has translated the *Agamemnon* ; and an impressive version by Dr. Thring of Uppingham was published (posthumously) in 1904. Mr. Platt's translation of the *Agamemnon* into Biblical prose (Grant Richards, 1911) is an interesting (though to me unconvincing) experiment. But of all translations of Aeschylus, prose or verse, Trevelyan's translations of the *Oresteia*, in my judgment, come nearest to the force and grandeur of the original. They aim at reproducing " for those who cannot read Greek, not only the meaning, but the form, phrasing and movement of the original " ; and succeed in this more than antecedently would seem possible.

Other translations of *Sophocles* are Plumptre's (1867) and J. S. Phillimore's (2 vols., Allen, 1902) ; Sir George Young (1888, 1917, and in Dent's " Every Man Series ") includes the fragments of lost plays. R. C. Trevelyan has translated the *Ajax* (Allen, 1919).

For translation of Aristophanes, see above, p. 270. The recovered portions of *Four Plays of Menander* have been edited by Edward Capps and published (1910) by Ginn : they well repay study.

For a first study of ancient Greek architecture Bell's *Hellenic Architecture* (Bell, 1920) is all that can be desired. At the same time there are excellent sections on Hellenic architecture in each of several standard histories :

> Fergusson (Sir James), *History of Architecture,* vol. i., 3rd edition, Murray, 1893.
>
> Simpson (F. M.), *History of Architectural Development,* vol. i., Longmans, 1905.
>
> Statham (H. H.), *Short Critical History of Architecture,* Batsford, 1912.
>
> Banister Fletcher, *History of Architecture on the Comparative Method,* 6th edition, Batsford, 1921.
>
> And there is Anderson and Spiers' *Architecture of Greece and Rome* (Batsford, 1902 and 1907).

For the architecture of the Parthenon, besides Gardner's *Ancient Athens* (Macmillan, 1902), there are accounts, also excellent, in Weller, *Athens and its Monuments* (Macmillan Company, 1913), and D'Ooge, *The Acropolis* (Macmillan, 1908). These more recent works give the results of the latest research, but do not displace the great classics of an earlier time, Penrose's *Principles of Athenian Architecture* and Stuart and Revett's *Antiquities of Athens* (vol. i. 1762 ; vol. ii. 1787 ; vol. iii. 1794 ; vol. iv. 1816 ; Supplementary Volume, 1830). Whoever can obtain access to any of these will be well repaid.

The standard English text-book of Greek sculpture is Professor E. A.

Gardner's *Handbook* (Macmillan, latest edition, 1915) : there is also an excellent *Introduction to Greek Sculpture* by L. E. Upcott (Clarendon Press, 1887). Murray's *History of Greek Sculpture*, in two volumes (Murray, 1890), is the standard history. The history of sculpture down to modern times is made an enchanting study in Short's *History of Sculpture* (Heinemann, 1907). Other books to be noted are Hill (G. F.), *One Hundred Masterpieces of Sculpture* (Methuen, 1909) ; Von Mach, *Greek Sculpture, Its Spirit and Principles* (Ginn, 1903) ; Guy Dickins, *Hellenistic Sculpture* (Clarendon Press, 1920 [1]). All these are helpful ; but for quickening insight into, and unfaltering interpretation of, the very spirit of Greek sculpture there is nothing equal to the short monograph, *Greek Sculpture* by John Warrack, published by Schulze at Edinburgh in 1913.

How beautiful the plates reproducing Greek sculpture can be, may be seen to great advantage in Murray, *The Sculptures of the Parthenon*. Excellent illustrations of sculpture—in addition to those in the books already mentioned—are to be found in Von Mach's *Handbook of Greek and Roman Sculpture* (Boston, 1905). For monumental reliefs, that exquisite branch of Greek art so fully illustrated at Athens,[2] there is Percy Gardner's *Sculptured Tombs of Hellas* (Macmillan, 1896).

The most interesting books of Greek travel from the sixteenth to the nineteenth century are, perhaps, sufficiently indicated in Chapter XVIII. Of more modern books of travel the following may be recommended :

>Mahaffy, *Rambles and Studies in Greece*, 5th edition, 1907 (Macmillan).

>Mrs. Bosanquet, *Days in Attica*, 1914 (Methuen).

A most useful and interesting book in this connection is Michaelis, *A Century of Archaeological Discovery*, translated by Miss Kahnweiler (Murray, 1908). Marshall (F. H.), *Discovery in Greek Lands* (Cambridge University Press, 1920), brings the story nearly down to the present time.

The publication of *The Legacy of Greece* in 1921 and of *The Pageant of Greece* in 1923 (both edited by Mr. Livingstone and published by the Clarendon Press) has richly enlarged for English readers the means of appreciating, in all departments, the debt of European civilization to the Greeks. For completeness on the literary side a literary history is indispensable ; for this in freshness, originality, and vivid interest, Professor Gilbert Murray's History of Ancient Greek Literature, published by Heinemann in 1897, holds its place.

[1] Published posthumously. Guy Dickins died of wounds in July, 1916.

[2] I regret very much that no appropriate place for describing some of these has been found in Chapter XVII.

INDEX

PRINTED IN GREAT BRITAIN BY ROBERT MACLEHOSE AND CO. LTD.
THE UNIVERSITY PRESS, GLASGOW.